The Editor

SHARON O'BRIEN is James Hope Caldwell Professor of American Cultures at Dickinson College. She is the author of *Willa Cather: The Emerging Voice*, *Willa Cather*, and *The Family Silver: A Memoir of Depression and Inheritance*. She is the editor of the Library of America *Willa Cather* (Volumes I–III) and *New Essays on* My Ántonia.

W. W. NORTON & COMPANY, INC.
Also Publishes

English Renaissance Drama: A Norton Anthology
edited by David Bevington et al.

The Norton Anthology of African American Literature
edited by Henry Louis Gates Jr. and Nellie Y. McKay et al.

The Norton Anthology of American Literature
edited by Nina Baym et al.

The Norton Anthology of Children's Literature
edited by Jack Zipes et al.

The Norton Anthology of English Literature
edited by M. H. Abrams and Stephen Greenblatt et al.

The Norton Anthology of Literature by Women
edited by Sandra M. Gilbert and Susan Gubar

The Norton Anthology of Modern and Contemporary Poetr
edited by Jahan Ramazani, Richard Ellmann, and Robert O'Clair

The Norton Anthology of Poetry
edited by Margaret Ferguson, Mary Jo Salter, and Jon Stallworthy

The Norton Anthology of Short Fiction
edited by R. V. Cassill and Richard Bausch

The Norton Anthology of Theory and Criticism
edited by Vincent B. Leitch et al.

The Norton Anthology of World Literature
edited by Sarah Lawall et al.

The Norton Facsimile of the First Folio of Shakespea
prepared by Charlton Hinman

The Norton Introduction to Literature
edited by Alison Booth, J. Paul Hunter, and Kelly J. Mays

The Norton Introduction to the Short Novel
edited by Jerome Beaty

The Norton Reader
edited by Linda H. Peterson and John C. Brereton

The Norton Sampler
edited by Thomas Cooley

The Norton Shakespeare, Based on the Oxford Ei
edited by Stephen Greenblatt et al.

For a complete list of Norton Critical Editions, visit
wwnorton.com/college/English/nce_home.htm

A NORTON CRITICAL EDITION

Willa Cather

O PIONEERS!

AUTHORITATIVE TEXT
CONTEXT AND BACKGROUNDS
CRITICISM

Edited by

SHARON O'BRIEN

DICKINSON COLLEGE

W. W. NORTON & COMPANY

New York • London

W. W. Norton & Company has been independent since its founding in 1923, when William Warder Norton and Mary D. Herter Norton first published lectures delivered at the People's Institute, the adult education division of New York City's Cooper Union. The Nortons soon expanded their program beyond the Institute, publishing books by celebrated academics from America and abroad. By mid-century, the two major pillars of Norton's publishing program—trade books and college texts—were firmly established. In the 1950s, the Norton family transferred control of the company to its employees, and today—with a staff of four hundred and a comparable number of trade, college, and professional titles published each year—W. W. Norton & Company stands as the largest and oldest publishing house owned wholly by its employees.

This title is printed on permanent paper containing
30 percent post-consumer waste recycled fiber.

Printed in the United States of America
First Edition

The text of this book is composed in Fairfield Medium
with the display set in Bernhard Modern.
Composition by PennSet, Inc.
Manufacturing by Maple Press.
Production manager: Benjamin Reynolds.

ISBN 978-0-393-92466-4

W. W. Norton & Company, Inc., 500 Fifth Avenue, New York, NY 10110-0017
www.wwnorton.com

W. W. Norton & Company Ltd.
15 Carlisle Street, London W1D 3BS

3 4 5 6 7 8 9

Contents

Criticism

Illustrations

Introduction

When Willa Cather inscribed a copy of *O Pioneers!* to her childhood friend Carrie Miner Sherwood, she wrote "This was the first time I walked off on my own feet—everything before was half real and half an imitation of writers whom I admired. In this one I hit the home pasture and found I was Yance Sorgeson [a Nebraska farmer] and not Henry James."[1] Written in 1912 and 1913 and published in 1913, *O Pioneers!* marked Cather's return to the Nebraska of her past and to the stories of the immigrant settlers she had known during her childhood and adolescence in Red Cloud, Nebraska, during the 1880s.

O Pioneers! was her second novel. Cather's first published novel, *Alexander's Bridge*, appeared in 1912, just as *O Pioneers!* was emerging. When Cather looked back at her literary beginnings in "My First Novels [There Were Two]," an essay published in 1931, she disparaged *Alexander's Bridge* as imitative of Henry James and Edith Wharton and praised *O Pioneers!* as expressing her authentic, original voice. Here she had left the constraints of Henry James's London drawing rooms for the wide expanse of the Nebraska prairies.

In the 1930s Cather continued to honor *O Pioneers!* when she arranged a special "Library Edition" of all her fiction, poetry, and essays. Ferris Greenslet, her editor at Houghton Mifflin, told her he assumed that Volume I would be *Alexander's Bridge*. But Cather decided to make *O Pioneers!* her point of origin and declared that this was her Volume I. She relegated *Alexander's Bridge* to Volume III, requiring it to follow *The Song of the Lark* (1915). The editorial decision reflects her shaping of her own myth of literary origins. "Every artist makes himself born," she wrote in *The Song of the Lark*, and she chose *O Pioneers!* to mark her literary birth.

The contrast between *Alexander's Bridge* and *O Pioneers!* is not as stark as she describes it. Although *Alexander's Bridge* has its share of London drawing rooms scenes and stilted, Jamesian dialogue (as in the section reprinted here), the hero is a rough-hewn

1. Mildred Bennett, *The World of Willa Cather* (Lincoln: University of Nebraska Press, rev. ed. 1963), p. 200.

American engineer and bridge builder whose work requires the taming of nature, as is the case for the pioneer farmers in *O Pioneers!* She had also written of Nebraska settlers and immigrants in early stories like "Peter," "Lou the Prophet," "The Sculptor's Funeral," and "A Wagner Matinee," but since these stories, written while she was still striving to escape her Nebraska origins, gave a bleak portrayal of the land and viewed the culture as hostile to art, she did not view them as inhabiting the "home pasture" she created in the more celebratory *O Pioneers!*

We associate Willa Cather with the sweeping, open expanses of the Nebraska prairies she evokes in novels such as *O Pioneers!* and *My Ántonia*, but she spent her childhood in a very different landscape: the enclosed green world of Virginia's Shenandoah Valley where her home was cradled by low-lying hills. Born in 1873, Cather lived in Back Creek, Virginia, until she was nine years old. In that year her father Charles Cather decided to join his parents and brother George in Webster County, Nebraska, located on the Divide—the plains between the Republican and Little Blue rivers. The Cather family lived on the Divide for several months, and then moved to the little prairie town of Red Cloud. The change in landscape—from a sheltered valley to an exposed prairie—was dramatic and at first disturbing for the young Willa. "I would not know," Cather would later tell an interviewer, "how much a child's life is bound up in the woods and hills and meadows around it, if I had not been jerked away from all these and thrown out into a country as bare as a piece of sheet iron."[2] Eventually she learned to love the prairies' openness. "When I strike the open plains, something happens. I'm home," she told an interviewer. "That love of great spaces, of rolling open country like the sea—it's the grand passion of my life."[3]

Cather was not only "home" in Nebraska—she could also travel to foreign lands, visiting immigrant communities from Bohemia, Scandinavia, France.

> Few of our neighbors were Americans—most of them were Danes, Swedes, Norwegians, and Bohemians. I grew fond of some of these immigrants—particularly the old women, who used to tell me of their home country. I used to think them underrated, and wanted to explain them to their neighbors. . . . This was, with me, the initial impulse [to write].[4]

2. *The Kingdom of Art: Willa Cather's First Principles and Critical Statements*, ed. Bernice Slote (Lincoln: University of Nebraska Press, 1966), p. 448.
3. *Lincoln State Journal*, November 2, 1921, p. 7.
4. Latrobe Carroll, *The Bookman*, 53 (May 1921), p. 213.

Nebraska's prairies may have been the "passion" of Cather's life, just as the stories of its immigrant settlers were one of her inspirations, but she would never write in Nebraska. She evoked the home pasture from a safe distance—in New York, where she resided with her partner Edith Lewis until her death, in 1947, or in one of her favorite literary retreats—the Shattuck Inn in Jaffrey, New Hampshire, and the simple cottage on Grand Manan island she built with her partner Lewis. Like many other American writers, she needed geographic and emotional distance to write about the past.

Cather's beginnings as a writer date back to her days as an undergraduate at the University of Nebraska in the early 1890s. Her first published short story, "Peter," concerned the suicide of an immigrant farmer who cannot adjust to the harsh life on the Divide. Homesick for Bohemia and his artistic life as a violinist, knowing he will never escape Nebraska, Peter breaks his violin across his knee and shoots himself. The young writer ends her story with an image of death that, unlike the closing paragraph of *O Pioneers!*, gives no hope of transcendence or rebirth.

> In the morning Antone found him stiff, frozen fast in a pool of blood. They could not straighten him out enough to fit a coffin, so they buried him in a pine box.[5]

Cather's most controversial early story would be "A Wagner Matinee," the story of an Eastern woman, a cultivated lover of music, who marries at Nebraska farmer and puts aside her piano for a grim and isolated life. Her years of exile on the prairies have made her "pathetic and grotesque" in the view of her nephew, the story's narrator. "She wore ill-fitting false teeth, and her skin was as yellow as a Mongolian's from constant exposure to a pitiless wind and to the alkaline water, which hardens the most transparent cuticle into a sort of flexible leather." She has been reduced from human to animal; her pianist's hands that once played concertos in Boston have been "stretched into mere tentacles to hold and lift and knead with." Her nephew brings her to a concert in Boston, the "Wagner matinee" of the title, and her desiccated spirit returns to life, for the moment. She does not want to return to Nebraska:

> For her, just outside the door of the concert hall, lay the black pond with the cattle-tracked bluffs; the tall, unpainted house, with weather-curled boards; naked as a tower, the crook-backed ash seedlings where the dish-cloths hung to dry; the gaunt, moulting turkeys picking up refuse from the kitchen door.[6]

5. *Willa Cather's Collected Short Fiction*, introduction by Mildred R. Bennett (Lincoln: University of Nebraska Press, 1965), p. 543.
6. *Collected Short Fiction*, pp. 235–42.

"A Wagner Matinee" did not go over well in Nebraska. Her family was insulted and disturbed by the story because they believed that the character of Aunt Georgianna was based on Cather's Aunt Franc, who had attended Mt. Holyoke Female Seminary in Massachusetts, studied music, married George Cather (Willa's uncle), and moved to Nebraska to live as a farmer's wife. "Cather wrote a friend that the whole affair had been the nearest she had ever come to personal disgrace." She also received a professional reprimand from her colleague Will Own Jones, editor of the Lincoln *Journal*: "If the writers of fiction who use western Nebraska as material would look up now and then and not keep their eyes and noses in the cattle yards, they might be more agreeable company."[7]

Cather's literary apprenticeship would be a long one: it would take her twenty years to move from her first story to her first novel. In part, this was because as a single woman she had to earn a living, first working as an editor and teacher in Pittsburgh, then ascending to a powerful position as the managing editor of *McClure's Magazine*. She found time to write poetry and short fiction, and published a book of poems (*April Twilights* [1903]) and a short story collection (*The Troll Garden* [1905]) that brought her modest attention. But her demanding job as editor of *McClure's* drained her time and energy, and she knew her gifts were not maturing; she was unable to deepen and lengthen her talent.

Like many beginning writers, Cather found it difficult to discover her own voice and subject matter. She had written of Nebraska in *The Troll Garden* (1905), but after that she increasingly fell under the spell of Henry James, then considered the foremost writer of American fiction. As Cather observed, James was the "mighty master of language" and the only person writing in English who was "sticking for perfection."[8] The expatriate James, who lived in England and chose international settings for his fiction, had little in common with the Nebraska-born Cather. Yet she strove to imitate his elegant, cerebral, controlled fiction, filling her stories with upper-middle-class characters, country estates, and stilted dialogue. Remembering those times, Cather observed that the "drawing room was considered the proper setting for a novel, and the only characters worth reading about were smart people or clever people."[9] When she imitated James in stories like "The Willing Muse," she was conforming to literary conventions preferred by the

7. Quotations are from James Woodress, *Willa Cather: A Literary Life* (Lincoln: University of Nebraska Press, 1987), pp. 177–78.
8. *The Kingdom of Art*, p. 301.
9. Willa Cather, "My First Novels [There Were Two]," *On Writing: Critical Studies in Writing As an Art*, with a foreword by Stephen Tennant (New York: Knopf, 1949), p. 93.

Eastern establishment of publishers and reviewers. Speaking in James's rhythms, using his elevated and abstract vocabulary, Cather was not yet creating what she would attribute to Sarah Orne Jewett: a fresh and vital language, a "quality of voice that is exclusively the writer's own, individual, unique."[1] As she later said of her Jamesian period, "I was trying to sing a song that did not lie in my voice."[2]

Writing a Woman's Life

Growing up in the late nineteenth century, Willa Cather confronted the expectations for female identity summarized by historian Barbara Welter as the "cult of true womanhood": purity, piety, submissiveness, and domesticity.[3] She scorned such restrictions as an adolescent, dressing in mannish clothes, cutting her hair to a boy's length, and preferring to be called "William" or "Billy." During her years at the University of Nebraska and her early years working in Pittsburgh and New York, she believed that "woman" and "artist" were contradictory identities. She admired women singers and actresses but felt that most women writers had limited themselves to romantic and domestic plots, making her impatient with their inability to transcend typical, and limited, female roles. "As a rule," she wrote in an 1897 review, "if I see the announcement of a new book by a woman, I—well, I take one by a man instead. . . . I have noticed that the great masters of letters are men, and I prefer to take no chances when I read."[4] Cather did acknowledge some exceptional women writers: she admired the "great Georges, George Eliot and George Sand, and they were anything but women." Even here, though, Cather suggests that literary greatness is still connected with masculinity. And her literary advice to young women writers also suggests her early association of "artist" with "male" and "inferior writer" with "female":

> Women are so horribly subjective and they have such a scorn for the healthy commonplace. When a woman writes a story of adventure, a stout sea tale, a manly battle yarn, anything without wine, women, and love, then I will begin to hope for something great from them, not before.[5]

1. Willa Cather, *Not under Forty* (New York: Knopf, 1936), pp. 78–79.
2. Elizabeth Sergeant, *Willa Cather: A Memoir* (Philadelphia: Lippincott, 1953), p. 86.
3. See Barbara Welter, "The Cult of True Womanhood: 1820–1860," *American Quarterly* 18 (Summer 1966): 151–174.
4. *The World and the Parish: Willa Cather's Articles and Reviews, 1893–1902*, ed. William M. Curtin (Lincoln: University of Nebraska Press, 1970), Vol. 1, p. 362.
5. *The Kingdom of Art*, p. 409.

Cather was not impressed by a novel that current critics find important to the female and American literary canon: Kate Chopin's story of a married woman's sexual awakening and rejection of the cult of true womanhood, *The Awakening* (1899). She thought that the heroine, Edna Pontellier, belonged to a common "feminine type"—the love-obsessed heroine who "demands more romance out of life than God put into it."[6] Chopin's novel was not the narrative without "wine, women, and love" that Cather hoped for.

Eventually Cather would find a woman writer and mentor whom she admired, the New England writer Sarah Orne Jewett, whose example aided her in integrating the once-opposed identities of "woman" and "artist." Cather met Jewett in Boston in 1908, and the older writer adopted the young Cather as a literary apprentice. Jewett's masterwork, *The Country of the Pointed Firs*, was one of the three American works of fiction (along with *The Scarlet Letter* and *Huckleberry Finn*) that Cather thought would endure as classics. The friendship she established with Jewett became a turning point in her life as an artist; the older woman believed in her and encouraged her talent and showed that a woman writer could create consummate art without having to produce "manly" narratives. Cather's dedication of *O Pioneers!* to Jewett ("in whose beautiful and delicate work is the perfection that endures") connects Jewett's influence to her own literary emergence.

I first became interested in Cather's fiction when I was a graduate student in English at Harvard University in the early 1970s. In those days there were no courses on women writers and no inclusion of women writers in the survey course in American literature (with the exception of Emily Dickinson, who was not viewed, in any way, as gendered). I had been reading nineteenth-century American literature and taking a seminar on Hawthorne and James. One day I complained to a fellow student, "Why do all the strong and interesting women in American literature end up punished or dead? Hester Prynne has to decide she's a sinner, Zenobia drowns, Edna Pontellier and Lily Bart kill themselves, Ellen Olenska gets banished, Isabel Archer has to go back and live in that sadist Gilbert Osmond's decorated prison. This is depressing!" "Read Willa Cather," he said, and so I picked up *O Pioneers!* and couldn't put it down. I felt I'd entered a new fictional world where women could be powerful and independent and not be required to wear scarlet A's for the rest of their lives or throw themselves into forest pools or stayed married to soul-destroying esthetes. *O Pioneers!* gave me hope: there could be other plots for women besides the "true

6. *The World and the Parish*, Vol. 2, p. 698.

womanhood" story for marriage-minded heroines and the death-punishment ending for transgressors.

Literary critic Rachel Blau DuPlessis would later have a term for Cather's achievement: "writing beyond the ending." In her book of the same name, she studies twentieth-century women writers who "replace the alternate endings in marriage and death that are their cultural legacy from nineteenth century life and letters" by offering different choices to their female characters, a narrative and social act of revision.[7] In *O Pioneers!* Cather gives the romance and death plot to Marie, but Alexandra's story will be a rewriting of the traditionally male story of independence and heroism: she is the "pioneer" of the title.

The Creative Process

In "[hitting] the home pasture," Cather experienced the creative process as many artists describe it. Painters, sculptors, and musicians, as well as writers, describe heightened states of inspiration in which their material seems to be expressing itself through them. Artistic activity is then an act of exploration and discovery rather than the recording of a vision or story that is already complete in the artist's mind. Whereas she said she had consciously shaped and fashioned *Alexander's Bridge*, *O Pioneers!* emerged organically, as if she were the channel through which the art work flowed. In her "Preface" to the second edition of *Alexander's Bridge* (1922) she describe her creative process as something intuitive, like "the thing by which our feet find the road home on a dark night, accounting of themselves for roots and stones which we had never noticed by day."[8] In her essay "My First Novels [There Were Two]," she referred to writing *O Pioneers!* as "taking a ride through a familiar country on a horse that knew the way, on a morning when you felt like riding."[9]

The sources of *O Pioneers!* were two Nebraska stories that Cather had written at different times. The first one was composed in 1911 while Cather was finishing *Alexander's Bridge* and writing "The Bohemian Girl." It was the story of a Swedish pioneer and farm woman; Cather titled it "Alexandra." According to Edith Lewis, Cather thought that the story was too personal, of no interest to readers.

7. Rachel Blau DuPlessis, *Writing beyond the Ending: Narrative Strategies of Twentieth-Century Women Writers* (Bloomington: University of Indiana Press, 1985), p. 4.
8. Willa Cather, "Preface" to *Alexander's Bridge* (Boston: Houghton Mifflin, 1922), p. ix.
9. Willa Cather, "My First Novels [There Were Two]," pp. 92–93.

> ["Alexandra"] ran about the same length as *The Bohemian Girl* but was very unlike *The Bohemian Girl* in theme and treatment. In fact, it was very unlike anything she had done hitherto; she doubted whether anyone but herself would find it interesting. She read it to me before she went West. It began with what is now the first chapter of *O Pioneers!* and continued, almost unchanged, according to my recollections, through Part I of that story—*The Wild Land*. It ended with a dream the girl Alexandra had—now told at the end of Part III.
>
> She had this story very much at heart; but she was dissatisfied with it. She made no attempt to publish it. I think she felt there was something there which she did not wish to waste by inadequate presentation.[1]

Cather left New York and "Alexandra" in the summer of 1912 for a trip to the Southwest and Red Cloud. Back in Nebraska, she visited with old friends and neighbors and saw the wheat harvest. A new story arose in her imagination, a story of love and death in the cornfields, and in the fall of 1912 she completed "The White Mulberry Tree." Then, somehow, she realized that the two stories belonged together. The intertwining of the stories in her imagination was "a sudden inner explosion and enlightenment," she told her friend Elizabeth Sergeant, and she interwove the two stories to shape *O Pioneers!*, linking them by making the two lovers people whom Alexandra loved—her brother Emil and her best friend Marie Shabata. She described her book to Sergeant as a "two-part pastoral."[2] At last satisfied, she brought the manuscript to editor Ferris Greenslet at Houghton Mifflin, who promptly offered her a contract.

Contemporary Reviews

There would be only one disgruntled reviewer of *O Pioneers!* Frederick Cooper, writing for *Bookman*, found the novel depressing and tedious. All the other reviews were positive, stressing the novel as a breakthrough in American literature. They agreed that Cather was telling a new story in placing a woman at the center of a heroic plot, a story they considered uniquely American. "It stirred me like a trumpet call," confided one reviewer.[3] Cultural and literary critics had long been calling for an American literature that was not sub-

1. Edith Lewis, *Willa Cather Living* (New York: Knopf, 1953), p. 83.
2. Elizabeth Shepley Sergeant, *Willa Cather: A Memoir* (Lincoln: University of Nebraska Press, 1963), pp. 86, 116. For a discussion of the unity of Cather's novel, see Sharon O'Brien, "The Unity of Willa Cather's 'Two-Part Pastoral': Passion in *O Pioneers!*," *Studies in American Fiction* 6 (1978): 157–71.
3. Celia Harris, *Lincoln Sunday State Journal*, August 3, 1913, p. A7.

servient to British and European influences, and Cather's novel—with its central characters Midwestern immigrants rather than East Coast elites—seemed to epitomize democracy and egalitarianism. Equally important, this was a novel set on the prairies that did not tell a story of rural tragedy. Reviewers had become impatient with stories by writers like Hamlin Garland who focused on the blighted, narrow lives of country folk, and they found Alexandra's strength and optimism a bracing rejection of such literary bleakness.

It was not just Cather's portrayal of hard-working immigrant farmers that seemed strikingly American, reflecting as it did the waves of immigrants entering the United States in the nineteenth century, seeking a better and more prosperous life. Even more important to the early reviewers was the story of Alexandra's triumph in taming the stubborn land. In their view, *O Pioneers!* was the story of America—and American expansion into western lands — and Alexandra a representative American heroine. As one reviewer observed, the novel gave readers "hope," and this notion of hope—a belief in the possibilites of progress, self-transformation, and upward mobility—was central to the myth of America as the land of opportunity. As Andrew Delbanco observes in *The Real American Dream*, "hope" and "nation" were synonymous with "free individual" in the nineteenth century. The very grounding of hope was "the idea that Americans were not fixed in their circumstances of birth, but were free to become whatever they could imagine."[4]

Looking back, we can see that the American dream of individual and national destiny was a myth, not a reality. Although many did realize the hope of advancement, many did not succeed in their new land; many had been brought to America as slaves; many had been displaced from tribal lands by white settlers. Cather's reviewers did not mention these disenfranchised groups. The reviewer for the *Lincoln Sunday State Journal* did wish that Cather had included "native Americans" among her immigrant characters, but she was not referring to Indians: she meant white people of Anglo-Saxon ancestry. These early reviewers unconsciously equated "American" with "white," as did Cather herself. In *O Pioneers!* Alexandra Bergson's skin is described as "white as snow," and the image evokes not only her Scandinavian fairness but also the cultural category of "whiteness" that was evolving in the late nineteenth and early twentieth century.[5]

4. Andrew Delbanco, *The Real American Dream: A Meditation on Hope* (Cambridge: Harvard University Press, 1999), p. 61.
5. For a discussion of the construction of whiteness as a cultural category in the late nineteenth and early twentieth centuries, see Matthew Frye Jacobson, *Whiteness of a Different Color: European Immigrants and the Alchemy of Race* (Cambridge: Harvard University Press), 1999.

Encouraged by the reception of *O Pioneers!*—which validated her use of Nebraska materials—Cather plunged into work on *The Song of the Lark* (1915), then moved quickly to *My Ántonia* (1918). She had tapped into a deep vein of creativity that would sustain her for the rest of her life.

Willa Cather and Her Critics

Willa Cather's literary reputation began its ascent with *O Pioneers!* In the following years, literary excellence kept pace with prolific literary production. After *The Song of the Lark* and *My Ántonia* would come the Pulitzer prize–winning *One of Ours* (1922), *My Mortal Enemy* (1923), *The Professor's House* (1925), *Death Comes for the Archbishop* (1928), *Shadows on the Rock* (1933), and *Sapphira and the Slave Girl* (1940), along with collections of short stories and essays. Cather became recognized as one of American's foremost novelists by the mid-1920s. During the 1930s, however, her literary reputation suffered as a result of attacks from left-wing critics who found her work escapist and romantic and the author unwilling to engage with the stern economic and social issues of the time.[6] But Cather's work continued to find a large readership, and all of her works remained in print. Beginning in the 1960s and 1970s, academic critics began to rediscover Willa Cather as an important American writer. Up until 1970, only a dozen books focusing on Cather's life and work had been published; since 1970, over fifty books concentrating either in whole or in part on Cather's life and work have appeared. The number of academic articles published since 1970 is over three hundred.

Since I have had the benefit, as a literary critic, of the insights offered by feminist criticism, deconstruction, and cultural studies, I look back at the range of Cather criticism, and criticism of *O Pioneers!*, with the awareness that the literary canon is not a neutral list of objectively "great" writers but a historically situated construction. Of course we can read *O Pioneers!* from multiple points of view and assess its literary merit according to different standards of value. But what is most interesting to me is the ways in which the literary criticism of *O Pioneers!* over the past four decades has been historically shaped. Certain questions and reading strategies simply weren't available, for example, to Cather's earliest biographer E. K. Brown, writing the authorized biography of Cather in the 1950s. He did not raise issues of gender or sexuality, but we

6. See Sharon O'Brien, "Becoming Noncanonical: The Case against Willa Cather," *American Quarterly* 40 (1988): 110–26.

should not chastise him for this: such concerns were not part of the literary and cultural conversation of the time.

The academic literary criticism of *O Pioneers!* included here reflects theoretical approaches and interpretive questions ranging from the 1970s to the early 2000s. As you will see, the selections don't simply embody different points of view: they draw on the questions and issues that were being raised at the time the article or book was being written.

The excerpt from David Stouck's book *Willa Cather's Imagination* (1975) shows the influence of the "new criticism" in his close reading of the text as well as the bourgeoning interest in intertexuality and literary influence. John Murphy's article (published in 1984) is both a thematic study exploring religious references in *O Pioneers!* and an analysis of Cather's connection to Walt Whitman. In the 1980s (and later), feminist criticism, inspired by the women's movement, reread Cather as a woman writer who was resisting patriarchal narratives and creating new stories for her pioneer heroines. The excerpt from my biography of Willa Cather (*Willa Cather: The Emerging Voice*, 1987) shows how Cather broke new fictional ground in creating Alexandra Bergson, a heroine who integrates conventionally "masculine" and "feminine" qualities without being male-identified. At the same time, Cather rewrites the masculine story of the conquering pioneer celebrated by Walt Whitman in "Pioneers! O Pioneers!" Although I had discussed Cather's lesbian identity in my biography, I did not focus on the interplay between her sexuality and her art. C. Susan Wiesenthal's article on "Female Sexuality in Willa Cather's *O Pioneers!*" views Cather as a lesbian writer and places her creative emergence in the context of the scientific debates defining lesbianism as "unnatural" in the late nineteenth and early twentieth centuries.

The development of new critical theories and approaches in the 1980s, 1990s, and early 2000s — critical race studies, queer studies, new historicism, and cultural studies—presented us with a politically complex and at times problematic novel and writer. All these critical approaches share the understanding that a writer may be challenging some conventional social assumptions (as Willa Cather challenged the patriarchal cult of true womanhood in her life and writing) while, at the same time, reinforcing and reflecting others, as Cather conveyed dominant assumptions about race and power. Such readings share the belief that no writer is an autonomous artist fully in control of a novel's implications or even consciously aware of its ideological assumptions and contradictions. As Toni Morrison observes in *Playing in the Dark*, commenting on Cather's novel of slavery and escape, *Sapphira and the Slave Girl* (1940), "But things go awry. As often happens, characters make claims, impose demands of imaginative accountability over and above the author's will to control them."[7]

Critic Marilee Lindemann, drawing on queer studies and cultural studies, finds *O Pioneers!* filled with contradictions. On the one hand, Cather destabilizes patriarchal structures, as when Alexandra becomes the managerial farmer who controls both the land and her doltish brothers. But it is still Alexandra's father who chooses his daughter to be the head of the family, and so in some ways her power is the gift of the patriarch. Yes, Alexandra defies her narrow-minded brothers, but she also embodies and enforces constricting social codes. In the selection from Lindemann's work included here, we see how limited the term "authorial intention" is in analyzing the complexity of any work of art. Cather did not consciously intend to tell a story of confinement, for example, or think of Alexandra as policing Ivar. And yet, like any writer, Cather reflects the political unconscious of her time and culture.

In the past decades, critics have learned to ask what may seem unusual questions of literature: What is *not* there? What stories are *not* told? What stories are silenced, camouflaged, or hovering on the margins? Writers have been asking such questions as well and finding new, unspoken stories to tell. Valerie Martin retells *Doctor Jekyll and Mr. Hyde* from the point of view of the Irish female servant; Derek Wolcott retells *The Tempest* as Caliban's story; Toni Morrison places African-American history in the center of the story of the American West in *Paradise*.

In terms of Willa Cather's fiction, critics have been asking questions like, What does it mean to say that she is telling an "American" story? Which Americans are we talking about? What vision or myth of America is being conveyed, and how might it connect to, or conceal, historical reality? Which troubling or contradictory stories might be silenced in order to portray America as a land of hope and optimism?

Mike Fischer raises such questions in exploring Cather's relationship to Native American history and experience. In "The Burden of Conquest" his main focus is on *My Ántonia*, but the issues he raises are relevant for *O Pioneers!* The history of Nebraska's settlement by native-born whites and immigrants from Europe was also the history of the massacre and displacement of Indians. Cather's prairie town, Red Cloud, was named for the chieftain who led the Lakota Sioux resistance against the U.S. government. And yet, in *O Pioneers!* we read passages that tell us that Nebraska's prairies were untouched, uninhabited, and unloved until gazed upon by white

7. Toni Morrison, *Playing in the Dark: Whiteness and the Literary Imagination* (Cambridge: Harvard University Press, 1992), p. 28.

settlers. In one famous passage, we see the author make Alexandra an Adamic figure who discovers an untouched Paradise:

> For the first time, perhaps, since that land emerged the from waters of geologic ages, a human face was set toward it with love and yearning, It seemed beautiful to her, rich and strong and glorious. Her eyes drank in the breadth of it, until her tears blinded her. Then the Genius of the Divide, the great, free spirit which breathes across it, must have bent lower than it ever bent to a human will before. The history of every country begins in the heart of a man or a woman.[8]

If we read this passage only from a feminist perspective, without thinking of race and without thinking historically, we may see only Cather's progressiveness in adding the phrase "or a woman," which expands Alexandra's story. But if we place this passage in a broader historical and cultural context, we can ask, Can it be that no one, male or female, loved this land between the time of geologic ages and the 1870s, when settlers like the Bergsons arrived? Is Cather speaking only about white settlers? What about the Indians? The fact that Cather was unable, historically, to ask questions does not mean that we should not ask them. Seeing this absence does not diminish her as an artist; it makes her novel more contradictory and complex.

Using words like "settler" or "pioneer" to represent the history of the West may be problematic, as Patricia Limerick suggests in her groundbreaking history of the West, *The Legacy of Conquest.*[9] What if we used the word "conquest" to describe westward expansion instead of "settlement"? Limerick chooses "conquest" for her title because she wants to stress that the West was not uninhabited territory but a place of struggle between Native Americans and the United States government. In her essay on *O Pioneers!* Melissa Ryan helps us to understand how *O Pioneers!* both erases and reveals a story of conquest and empire. Guy Reynolds takes an analysis of the contradictions in the novel in a different direction in the selection from his book *Willa Cather in Context: Progress, Race, Empire* (1996). Focusing on the myth of the pioneer, he reminds us that we should not romanticize the journey from "The Wild Land" to "Neighboring Fields." Alexandra does learn how to farm the land effectively, but she also deals shrewdly in land speculation, a practice that profited from farmers who went bankrupt.

Such analyses of the ways in which Cather both challenges and accepts dominant cultural assumptions in *O Pioneers!* does not

8. p. 34.
9. Patricia Limerick, *The Legacy of Conquest: The Unbroken Past of the American West* (New York: Norton, 1988).

detract from the importance of her novel. In fact, the political complexity of the novel does make it, in a way, a representative American text, although not in the way the early reviewers assumed. Imbued with the ideology of individualism, American novels, films, and popular culture frequently tell a story of individual triumph or upward mobility that conceals or reinforces structures of inequality. (Think of films like *Pretty Woman* or *Working Girl*—we see individuals rise from working class, and this optimistic narrative can deflect our attention from the fact that the gap between the rich and the poor has been widening in the United States, rather than narrowing.) Like these contemporary texts, *O Pioneers!* contains contradictions that have marked American society from the beginning—in particular the tension between ideals of democracy and egalitarianism and the conflicting realities of forms of oppression.

Let us return, in conclusion, to authorial intention and literary craft, important not to forget in our consideration of Cather's achievement as a writer in *O Pioneers!* Her transition from *Alexander's Bridge* to *O Pioneers!* changed her creative life. "Life began for me," she once said, "when I ceased to admire and began to remember."[1] In moving from admiration of Henry James to her memories of Nebraska, she found a voice and created a simple yet resonant style. Contrast these two passages—and see and hear Cather's emerging voice.

> Sir Harry Towne bowed and said that he had met Mr. Alexander and his wife in Toyko.
>
> Mainhall cut in impatiently.
>
> "I say, Sir Harry, the little girl's going famously to-night, isn't she?"
>
> Sir Harry wrinkled his brows judiciously. "Do you know, I thought the dance a bit conscious to-night, for the first time. The fact is, she's feeling rather seedy, poor child. . . ."
>
> He bowed as the warning bell rang, and Mainhall whispered: "You know, Lord Westmere, of course,—the stooped man with the long gray mustache, talking to Lady Dowle. Lady Westmere is very fond of Hilda."[2]

> One January day, thirty years ago, the little town of Hanover, anchored on a windy Nebraska tableland, was trying not to be blown away. A mist of fine snowflakes was curling and eddying about the cluster of low drab buildings huddled on the gray prairie, under a gray sky. The dwelling-houses were set about

1. Sergeant, p. 107.
2. Willa Cather, *Alexander's Bridge* (Boston: Houghton Mifflin, 1922), p. 35.

haphazard on the tough prairie sod; some of them looked as if they had been moved in overnight, and others as if they were straying off by themselves, headed straight for the open plain. None of them had any appearance of permanence, and the howling wind blew under them as well as over them. . . . About the station everything was quiet, for there would not be another train in until night.[3]

3. Willa Cather, *O Pioneers!* (New York: Literary Classics of the United States, 1987), p. 139. (Page 9 in this Norton Critical Edition.)

Acknowledgments

I thank the archivists at the Nebraska Historical Society and the Archives and Special Collections of the University of Nebraska Library for helping me find original documents and photographs. Guy Reynolds and Melissa Homestead of the University of Nebraska English Department made my stay in Lincoln enjoyable. Dickinson College gave me generous financial support for travel and research expenses, and my colleagues and friends cheered me on and up. My student assistant, Rebecca Thurber, excelled at gathering sources. My editors at Norton, Carol Bemis and Rivka Genesen, provided encouragement, guidance, and patience.

Note on the Text

O Pioneers! was published by Houghton Mifflin in June 1913 with an initial print run of 2,000 copies. It would have many printings during Cather's lifetime. For Volume I of the Library Edition in 1937, the type was reset. This second edition is identical to the first, except that "chince-bugs" has been corrected to "chinch-bugs." This edition uses the text of the first printing, with the one error corrected.

The Text of O PIONEERS!

O PIONEERS![1]

"Those fields, colored by various grain!"[2]
Mickiewicz

1. The title is taken from Walt Whitman's poem "Pioneers! O Pioneers!"
2. The epigraph is from the epic poem *Pan Tedeusz* (lines 20–21) by Polish Romantic poet Adam Mickiewicz (1798–1855).

TO THE MEMORY OF
SARAH ORNE JEWETT
IN WHOSE BEAUTIFUL AND DELICATE WORK
THERE IS THE PERFECTION
THAT ENDURES

Prairie Spring[3]

Evening and the flat land,
Rich and sombre and always silent;
The miles of fresh-plowed soil,
Heavy and black, full of strength and harshness;
The growing wheat, the growing weeds,
The toiling horses, the tired men;
The long empty roads,
Sullen fires of sunset, fading,
The eternal, unresponsive sky.
Against all this, Youth,
Flaming like the wild roses,
Singing like the larks over the plowed fields,
Flashing like a star out of the twilight;
Youth with its insupportable sweetness,
Its fierce necessity,
Its sharp desire,
Singing and singing,
Out of the lips of silence,
Out of the earthy dusk.

3. Cather's poem, published in *McClure's Magazine* (December 1912) and reprinted in her collection *April Twilights and Other Poems* (New York: Knopf, 1923).

Contents

Alexandra.

Part I. The Wild Land

I

One January day, thirty years ago, the little town of Hanover, anchored on a windy Nebraska tableland, was trying not to be blown away. A mist of fine snowflakes was curling and eddying about the cluster of low drab buildings huddled on the gray prairie, under a gray sky. The dwelling-houses were set about haphazard on the tough prairie sod; some of them looked as if they had been moved in overnight, and others as if they were straying off by themselves, headed straight for the open plain. None of them had any appearance of permanence, and the howling wind blew under them as well as over them. The main street was a deeply rutted road, now frozen hard, which ran from the squat red railway station and the grain "elevator" at the north end of the town to the lumber yard and the horse pond at the south end. On either side of this road straggled two uneven rows of wooden buildings; the general merchandise stores, the two banks, the drug store, the feed store, the saloon, the post-office. The board sidewalks were gray with trampled snow, but at two o'clock in the afternoon the shopkeepers, having come back from dinner, were keeping well behind their frosty windows. The children were all in school, and there was nobody abroad in the streets but a few rough-looking countrymen in coarse overcoats, with their long caps pulled down to their noses. Some of them had brought their wives to town, and now and then a red or a plaid shawl flashed out of one store into the shelter of another. At the hitch-bars along the street a few heavy work-horses, harnessed to farm wagons, shivered under their blankets. About the station everything was quiet, for there would not be another train in until night.

On the sidewalk in front of one of the stores sat a little Swede boy, crying bitterly. He was about five years old. His black cloth coat was much too big for him and made him look like a little old man. His shrunken brown flannel dress had been washed many times and left a long stretch of stocking between the hem of his skirt and the tops of his clumsy, copper-toed shoes. His cap was pulled down over his ears; his nose and his chubby cheeks were chapped and red with cold. He cried quietly, and the few people who hurried by did not notice him. He was afraid to stop any one, afraid to go into the store and ask for help, so he sat wringing his long sleeves and looking up a telegraph pole beside him, whimpering, "My kitten, oh, my kitten! Her will fweeze!" At the top of the pole crouched a shivering gray kitten, mewing faintly and clinging desperately to the wood with her claws. The boy had been left at the store while his sister went to the doctor's office, and in her absence a dog had chased his kitten up the pole. The little creature had never been so high before, and she was too frightened to move. Her master was sunk in despair. He was a little country boy, and this village was to him a very strange and perplexing place, where people wore fine clothes and had hard hearts. He always felt shy and awkward here, and wanted to hide behind things for fear some one might laugh at him. Just now, he was too unhappy to care who laughed. At last he seemed to see a ray of hope: his sister was coming, and he got up and ran toward her in his heavy shoes.

His sister was a tall, strong girl, and she walked rapidly and resolutely, as if she knew exactly where she was going and what she was going to do next. She wore a man's long ulster (not as if it were an affliction, but as if it were very comfortable and belonged to her; carried it like a young soldier), and a round plush cap, tied down with a thick veil. She had a serious, thoughtful face, and her clear, deep blue eyes were fixed intently on the distance, without seeming to see anything, as if she were in trouble. She did not notice the little boy until he pulled her by the coat. Then she stopped short and stooped down to wipe his wet face.

"Why, Emil! I told you to stay in the store and not to come out. What is the matter with you?"

"My kitten, sister, my kitten! A man put her out, and a dog chased her up there." His forefinger, projecting from the sleeve of his coat, pointed up to the wretched little creature on the pole.

"Oh, Emil! Didn't I tell you she'd get us into trouble of some kind, if you brought her? What made you tease me so? But there, I ought to have known better myself." She went to the foot of the pole and held out her arms, crying, "Kitty, kitty, kitty," but the kitten only mewed and faintly waved its tail. Alexandra turned away decidedly. "No, she won't come down. Somebody will have to go up after her. I saw the Linstrums' wagon in town. I'll go and see if I can find Carl. Maybe he can do something. Only you must stop crying, or I won't go a step. Where's your comforter? Did you leave it in the store? Never mind. Hold still, till I put this on you."

She unwound the brown veil from her head and tied it about his throat. A shabby little traveling man, who was just then coming out of the store on his way to the saloon, stopped and gazed stupidly at the shining mass of hair she bared when she took off her veil; two thick braids, pinned about her head in the German way, with a fringe of reddish-yellow curls blowing out from under her cap. He took his cigar out of his mouth and held the wet end between the fingers of his woolen glove. "My God, girl, what a head of hair!" he exclaimed, quite innocently and foolishly. She stabbed him with a glance of Amazonian fierceness and drew in her lower lip—most unnecessary severity. It gave the little clothing drummer such a start that he actually let his cigar fall to the sidewalk and went off weakly in the teeth of the wind to the saloon. His hand was still unsteady when he took his glass from the bartender. His feeble flirtatious instincts had been crushed before, but never so mercilessly. He felt cheap and ill-used, as if some one had taken advantage of him. When a drummer had been knocking about in little drab towns and crawling across the wintry country in dirty smoking-cars, was he to be blamed if, when he chanced upon a fine human creature, he suddenly wished himself more of a man?

While the little drummer was drinking to recover his nerve, Alexandra hurried to the drug store as the most likely place to find Carl Linstrum. There he was, turning over a portfolio of chromo "studies"[4] which the druggist sold to the Hanover women who did china-painting. Alexandra explained her predicament, and the boy followed her to the corner, where Emil still sat by the pole.

"I'll have to go up after her, Alexandra. I think at the depot they have some spikes I can strap on my feet. Wait a minute." Carl thrust his hands into his pockets, lowered his head, and darted up the street against the north wind. He was a tall boy of fifteen, slight and narrow-chested. When he came back with the spikes, Alexandra asked him what he had done with his overcoat.

"I left it in the drug store. I couldn't climb in it, anyhow. Catch me if I fall, Emil," he called back as he began his ascent. Alexandra watched him anxiously; the cold was bitter enough on the ground. The kitten would not budge an inch. Carl had to go to the very top of the pole, and then had some difficulty in tearing her from her hold. When he reached the ground, he handed the cat to her tearful little master. "Now go into the store with her, Emil, and get warm." He opened the door for the child. "Wait a minute, Alexandra. Why can't I drive for you as far as our place? It's getting colder every minute. Have you seen the doctor?"

"Yes. He is coming over to-morrow. But he says father can't get better; can't get well." The girl's lip trembled. She looked fixedly up the bleak street as if she were gathering her strength to face something, as if she were trying with all her might to grasp a situa-

4. Color lithographs.

tion which, no matter how painful, must be met and dealt with somehow. The wind flapped the skirts of her heavy coat about her.

Carl did not say anything, but she felt his sympathy. He, too, was lonely. He was a thin, frail boy, with brooding dark eyes, very quiet in all his movements. There was a delicate pallor in his thin face, and his mouth was too sensitive for a boy's. The lips had already a little curl of bitterness and skepticism. The two friends stood for a few moments on the windy street corner, not speaking a word, as two travelers, who have lost their way, sometimes stand and admit their perplexity in silence. When Carl turned away he said, "I'll see to your team." Alexandra went into the store to have her purchases packed in the egg-boxes, and to get warm before she set out on her long cold drive.

When she looked for Emil, she found him sitting on a step of the staircase that led up to the clothing and carpet department. He was playing with a little Bohemian[5] girl, Marie Tovesky, who was tying her handkerchief over the kitten's head for a bonnet. Marie was a stranger in the country, having come from Omaha with her mother to visit her uncle, Joe Tovesky. She was a dark child, with brown curly hair, like a brunette doll's, a coaxing little red mouth, and round, yellow-brown eyes. Every one noticed her eyes; the brown iris had golden glints that made them look like goldstone, or, in softer lights, like that Colorado mineral called tiger-eye.

The country children thereabouts wore their dresses to their shoe-tops, but this city child was dressed in what was then called the "Kate Greenaway" manner,[6] and her red cashmere frock, gathered full from the yoke, came almost to the floor. This, with her poke bonnet, gave her the look of a quaint little woman. She had a white fur tippet about her neck and made no fussy objections when Emil fingered it admiringly. Alexandra had not the heart to take him away from so pretty a playfellow, and she let them tease the kitten together until Joe Tovesky came in noisily and picked up his little niece, setting her on his shoulder for every one to see. His children were all boys, and he adored this little creature. His cronies formed a circle about him, admiring and teasing the little girl, who took their jokes with great good nature. They were all delighted with her, for they seldom saw so pretty and carefully nurtured a child. They told her that she must choose one of them for a sweetheart, and

5. Bohemia, an independent Slavic kingdom in central Europe, joined with Moravia and Slovakia to form the nation of Czechoslovakia in 1918. All Slavic immigrants from this region were known as "Bohemians" in Nebraska.

6. Kate Greenaway (1846–1901) was an English painter and widely imitated illustrator of children's books. Her depictions of little girls with frilly caps, flowery dresses, and aprons influenced fashion in both England and the United States.

each began pressing his suit and offering her bribes; candy, and little pigs, and spotted calves. She looked archly into the big, brown, mustached faces, smelling of spirits and tobacco, then she ran her tiny forefinger delicately over Joe's bristly chin and said, "Here is my sweetheart."

The Bohemians roared with laughter, and Marie's uncle hugged her until she cried, "Please don't, Uncle Joe! You hurt me." Each of Joe's friends gave her a bag of candy, and she kissed them all around, though she did not like country candy very well. Perhaps that was why she bethought herself of Emil. "Let me down, Uncle Joe," she said, "I want to give some of my candy to that nice little boy I found." She walked graciously over to Emil, followed by her lusty admirers, who formed a new circle and teased the little boy until he hid his face in his sister's skirts, and she had to scold him for being such a baby.

The farm people were making preparations to start for home. The women were checking over their groceries and pinning their big red shawls about their heads. The men were buying tobacco and candy with what money they had left, were showing each other new boots and gloves and blue flannel shirts. Three big Bohemians were drinking raw alcohol, tinctured with oil of cinnamon. This was said to fortify one effectually against the cold, and they smacked their lips after each pull at the flask. Their volubility drowned every other noise in the place, and the overheated store sounded of their spirited language as it reeked of pipe smoke, damp woolens, and kerosene.

Carl came in, wearing his overcoat and carrying a wooden box with a brass handle. "Come," he said, "I've fed and watered your team, and the wagon is ready." He carried Emil out and tucked him down in the straw in the wagon-box. The heat had made the little boy sleepy, but he still clung to his kitten.

"You were awful good to climb so high and get my kitten, Carl. When I get big I'll climb and get little boy's kittens for them," he murmured drowsily. Before the horses were over the first hill, Emil and his cat were both fast asleep.

Although it was only four o'clock, the winter day was fading. The road led southwest, toward the streak of pale, watery light that glimmered in the leaden sky. The light fell upon the two sad young faces that were turned mutely toward it: upon the eyes of the girl, who seemed to be looking with such anguished perplexity into the future; upon the sombre eyes of the boy, who seemed already to be looking into the past. The little town behind them had vanished as if it had never been, had fallen behind the swell of the prairie, and the stern frozen country received them into its bosom. The homesteads were few and far apart; here and there a windmill gaunt against the sky, a sod house[7] crouching in a hollow. But the great fact was the land itself, which seemed to overwhelm the little beginnings of human society that struggled in its sombre wastes. It was from facing this vast hardness that the boy's mouth had become so bitter; because he felt that men were too weak to make any mark here, that the land wanted to be let alone, to preserve its own fierce strength, its peculiar, savage kind of beauty, its uninterrupted mournfulness.

The wagon jolted along over the frozen road. The two friends had less to say to each other than usual, as if the cold had somehow penetrated to their hearts.

"Did Lou and Oscar go to the Blue[8] to cut wood to-day?" Carl asked.

"Yes. I'm almost sorry I let them go, it's turned so cold. But mother frets if the wood gets low." She stopped and put her hand to her forehead, brushing back her hair. "I don't know what is to become of us, Carl, if father has to die. I don't dare to think about it. I wish we could all go with him and let the grass grow back over everything."

Carl made no reply. Just ahead of them was the Norwegian graveyard, where the grass had, indeed, grown back over everything, shaggy and red, hiding even the wire fence. Carl realized that he was not a very helpful companion, but there was nothing he could say.

"Of course," Alexandra went on, steadying her voice a little, "the boys are strong and work hard, but we've always depended so on father that I don't see how we can go ahead. I almost feel as if there were nothing to go ahead for."

"Does your father know?"

"Yes, I think he does. He lies and counts on his fingers all day. I think he is trying to count up what he is leaving for us. It's a comfort to him that my chickens are laying right on through the cold weather and bringing in a little money. I wish we could keep his mind off such things, but I don't have much time to be with him now."

"I wonder if he'd like to have me bring my magic lantern[9] over some evening?"

Alexandra turned her face toward him. "Oh, Carl! Have you got it?"

"Yes. It's back there in the straw. Didn't you notice the box I was

7. Sod is the topmost layer of soil, dense and woven with roots; it made good building material for early settlers in treeless Nebraska.
8. The Little Blue River, which flows through south-central Nebraska.
9. The magic lantern—an early form of slide projector—provided a popular form of home entertainment in Victorian America.

carrying? I tried it all morning in the drug-store cellar, and it worked ever so well, makes fine big pictures."

"What are they about?"

"Oh, hunting pictures in Germany, and Robinson Crusoe and funny pictures about cannibals. I'm going to paint some slides for it on glass, out of the Hans Andersen book."

Alexandra seemed actually cheered. There is often a good deal of the child left in people who have had to grow up too soon. "Do bring it over, Carl. I can hardly wait to see it, and I'm sure it will please father. Are the pictures colored? Then I know he'll like them. He likes the calendars I get him in town. I wish I could get more. You must leave me here, must n't you? It's been nice to have company."

Carl stopped the horses and looked dubiously up at the black sky. "It's pretty dark. Of course the horses will take you home, but I think I'd better light your lantern, in case you should need it."

He gave her the reins and climbed back into the wagon-box, where he crouched down and made a tent of his overcoat. After a dozen trials he succeeded in lighting the lantern, which he placed in front of Alexandra, half covering it with a blanket so that the light would not shine in her eyes. "Now, wait until I find my box. Yes, here it is. Good-night, Alexandra. Try not to worry." Carl sprang to the ground and ran off across the fields toward the Linstrum homestead. "Hoo, hoo-o-o-o!" he called back as he disappeared over a ridge and dropped into a sand gully. The wind answered him like an echo, "Hoo, hoo-o-o-o-o-o!" Alexandra drove off alone. The rattle of her wagon was lost in the howling of the wind, but her lantern, held firmly between her feet, made a moving point of light along the highway, going deeper and deeper into the dark country.

II

On one of the ridges of that wintry waste stood the low log house[1] in which John Bergson was dying. The Bergson homestead was easier to find than many another, because it overlooked Norway Creek, a shallow, muddy stream that sometimes flowed, and sometimes stood still, at the bottom of a winding ravine with steep, shelving sides overgrown with brush and cottonwoods and dwarf ash. This creek gave a sort of identity to the farms that bordered upon it. Of all the bewildering things about a new country, the absence of human landmarks is one of the most depressing and disheartening.

1. Settlers would build log houses when timber was available. A log house would have been cleaner than a sod house (no dirt floor) and a sign of upward mobility. ("The Bergsons had a log house, for instance, only because Mrs. Bergson would not live in a sod house" [p. 19].)

The houses on the Divide[2] were small and were usually tucked away in low places; you did not see them until you came directly upon them. Most of them were built of the sod itself, and were only the unescapable ground in another form. The roads were but faint tracks in the grass, and the fields were scarcely noticeable. The record of the plow was insignificant, like the feeble scratches on stone left by prehistoric races, so indeterminate that they may, after all, be only the markings of glaciers, and not a record of human strivings.

In eleven long years John Bergson had made but little impression upon the wild land he had come to tame. It was still a wild thing that had its ugly moods; and no one knew when they were likely to come, or why. Mischance hung over it. Its Genius was unfriendly to man. The sick man was feeling this as he lay looking out of the window, after the doctor had left him, on the day following Alexandra's trip to town. There it lay outside his door, the same land; the same lead-colored miles. He knew every ridge and draw and gully between him and the horizon. To the south, his plowed fields; to the east, the sod stables, the cattle corral, the pond,—and then the grass.

Bergson went over in his mind the things that had held him back. One winter his cattle had perished in a blizzard. The next summer one of his plow horses broke its leg in a prairie-dog hole and had to be shot. Another summer he lost his hogs from cholera, and a valuable stallion died from a rattlesnake bite. Time and again his crops had failed. He had lost two children, boys, that came between Lou and Emil, and there had been the cost of sickness and death. Now, when he had at last struggled out of debt, he was going to die himself. He was only forty-six, and had, of course, counted upon more time.

Bergson had spent his first five years on the Divide getting into debt, and the last six getting out. He had paid off his mortgages and had ended pretty much where he began, with the land. He owned exactly six hundred and forty acres of what stretched outside his door; his own original homestead and timber claim, making three hundred and twenty acres, and the half-section adjoining,[3] the homestead of a younger brother who had given up the fight, gone back to Chicago to work in a fancy bakery and distinguish himself in a Swedish athletic club. So far John had not attempted to cultivate the second half-section, but used it for pasture land, and one of his sons rode herd there in open weather.

2. High plains in Nebraska between the Republican and Little Blue rivers.
3. Public lands in the Midwest were surveyed in townships six miles square, each containing 36 sections of 640 acres. Quarter sections (160 acres) and half sections (320 acres) were the most common subdivisions. The Homestead Act of 1862 offered a quarter section to anyone who would settle on and develop the land for five years.

John Bergson had the Old-World belief that land, in itself, is desirable. But this land was an enigma. It was like a horse that no one knows how to break to harness, that runs wild and kicks things to pieces. He had an idea that no one understood how to farm it properly, and this he often discussed with Alexandra. Their neighbors, certainly, knew even less about farming than he did. Many of them had never worked on a farm until they took up their homesteads. They had been *handwerkers* at home; tailors, locksmiths, joiners, cigar-makers, etc. Bergson himself had worked in a shipyard.

For weeks, John Bergson had been thinking about these things. His bed stood in the sitting-room, next to the kitchen. Through the day, while the baking and washing and ironing were going on, the father lay and looked up at the roof beams that he himself had hewn, or out at the cattle in the corral. He counted the cattle over and over. It diverted him to speculate as to how much weight each of the steers would probably put on by spring. He often called his daughter in to talk to her about this. Before Alexandra was twelve years old she had begun to be a help to him, and as she grew older he had come to depend more and more upon her resourcefulness and good judgment. His boys were willing enough to work, but when he talked with them they usually irritated him. It was Alexandra who read the papers and followed the markets, and who learned by the mistakes of their neighbors. It was Alexandra who could always tell about what it had cost to fatten each steer, and who could guess the weight of a hog before it went on the scales closer than John Bergson himself. Lou and Oscar were industrious, but he could never teach them to use their heads about their work.

Alexandra, her father often said to himself, was like her grandfather; which was his way of saying that she was intelligent. John Bergson's father had been a shipbuilder, a man of considerable force and of some fortune. Late in life he married a second time, a Stockholm woman of questionable character, much younger than he, who goaded him into every sort of extravagance. On the shipbuilder's part, this marriage was an infatuation, the despairing folly of a powerful man who cannot bear to grow old. In a few years his unprincipled wife warped the probity of a lifetime. He speculated, lost his own fortune and funds entrusted to him by poor seafaring men, and died disgraced, leaving his children nothing. But when all was said, he had come up from the sea himself, had built up a proud little business with no capital but his own skill and foresight, and had proved himself a man. In his daughter, John Bergson recognized the strength of will, and the simple direct way of thinking things out, that had characterized his father in his better days. He would much rather, of course, have seen this likeness in one of his sons, but it was not a question of choice. As he lay there day after day he had to accept the situation as it was, and to be thankful that there was one among his children to whom he could entrust the future of his family and the possibilities of his hard-won land.

The winter twilight was fading. The sick man heard his wife strike a match in the kitchen, and the light of a lamp glimmered through the cracks of the door. It seemed like a light shining far away. He turned painfully in his bed and looked at his white hands, with all the work gone out of them. He was ready to give up, he felt. He did not know how it had come about, but he was quite willing to go deep under his fields and rest, where the plow could not find him. He was tired of making mistakes. He was content to leave the tangle to other hands; he thought of his Alexandra's strong ones.

"*Dotter*," he called feebly, *"dotter!"* He heard her quick step and saw her tall figure appear in the doorway, with the light of the lamp behind her. He felt her youth and strength, how easily she moved and stooped and lifted. But he would not have had it again if he could, not he! He knew the end too well to wish to begin again. He knew where it all went to, what it all became.

His daughter came and lifted him up on his pillows. She called him by an old Swedish name that she used to call him when she was little and took his dinner to him in the shipyard.

"Tell the boys to come here, daughter. I want to speak to them."

"They are feeding the horses, father. They have just come back from the Blue. Shall I call them?"

He sighed. "No, no. Wait until they come in. Alexandra, you will have to do the best you can for your brothers. Everything will come on you."

"I will do all I can, father."

"Don't let them get discouraged and go off like Uncle Otto. I want them to keep the land."

"We will, father. We will never lose the land."

There was a sound of heavy feet in the kitchen. Alexandra went to the door and beckoned to her brothers, two strapping boys of seventeen and nineteen. They came in and stood at the foot of the bed. Their father looked at them searchingly, though it was too dark to see their faces; they were just the same boys; he told himself, he had not been mistaken in them. The square head and heavy shoulders belonged to Oscar, the elder. The younger boy was quicker, but vacillating.

"Boys," said the father wearily, "I want you to keep the land together and to be guided by your sister. I have talked to her since I have been sick, and she knows all my wishes. I want no quarrels among my children, and so long as there is one house there must be one head. Alexandra is the oldest, and she knows my wishes. She will do the best she can. If she makes mistakes, she will not make so many as I have made. When you marry, and want a house of your own, the land will be divided fairly, according to the courts. But for the next few years you will have it hard, and you must all keep together. Alexandra will manage the best she can."

Oscar, who was usually the last to speak, replied because he was the older, "Yes, father. It would be so anyway, without your speaking. We will all work the place together."

"And you will be guided by your sister, boys, and be good brothers to her, and good sons to your mother? That is good. And Alexandra must not work in the fields any more. There is no necessity now. Hire a man when you need help. She can make much more with her eggs and butter than the wages of a man. It was one of my mistakes that I did not find that out sooner. Try to break a little more land every year; sod corn is good for fodder. Keep turning the land, and always put up more hay than you need. Don't grudge your mother a little time for plowing her garden and setting out fruit trees, even if it comes in a busy season. She has been a good mother to you, and she has always missed the old country."

When they went back to the kitchen the boys sat down silently at the table. Throughout the meal they looked down at their plates and did not lift their red eyes. They did not eat much, although they had been working in the cold all day, and there was a rabbit stewed in gravy for supper, and prune pies.

John Bergson had married beneath him, but he had married a good housewife. Mrs. Bergson was a fair-skinned, corpulent woman, heavy and placid like her son, Oscar, but there was something comfortable about her; perhaps it was her own love of comfort. For eleven years she had worthily striven to maintain some semblance of household order amid conditions that made order very difficult. Habit was very strong with Mrs. Bergson, and her unremitting efforts to repeat the routine of her old life among new surroundings had done a great deal to keep the family from disintegrating morally and getting careless in their ways. The Bergsons had a log house, for instance, only because Mrs. Bergson would not live in a sod house. She missed the fish diet of her own country, and twice every summer she sent the boys to the river, twenty miles to the southward, to fish for channel cat. When the children were little she used to load them all into the wagon, the baby in its crib, and go fishing herself.

Alexandra often said that if her mother were cast upon a desert island, she would thank God for her deliverance, make a garden, and find something to preserve. Preserving was almost a mania with Mrs. Bergson. Stout as she was, she roamed the scrubby banks of Norway Creek looking for fox grapes and goose plums, like a wild creature in search of prey. She made a yellow jam of the insipid ground-cherries that grew on the prairie, flavoring it with lemon peel; and she made a sticky dark conserve of garden tomatoes. She had experimented even with the rank buffalo-pea, and she could not see a fine bronze cluster of them without shaking her head and murmuring, "What a pity!" When there was nothing more to preserve, she began to pickle. The amount of sugar she used in these processes was sometimes a serious drain upon the family resources. She was a good mother, but she was glad when her children were old enough not to be in her way in the kitchen. She had never quite forgiven John Bergson for bringing her to the end of the earth; but, now that she was there, she wanted to be let alone to reconstruct her old life in so far as that was possible. She could still take some comfort in the world if she had bacon in the cave, glass jars on the shelves, and sheets in the press. She disapproved of all her neighbors because of their slovenly housekeeping, and the women thought her very proud. Once when Mrs. Bergson, on her way to Norway Creek, stopped to see old Mrs. Lee, the old woman hid in the haymow "for fear Mis' Bergson would catch her barefoot."

III

One Sunday afternoon in July, six months after John Bergson's death, Carl was sitting in the doorway of the Linstrum kitchen, dreaming over an illustrated paper, when he heard the rattle of a wagon along the hill road. Looking up he recognized the Bergson's team, with two seats in the wagon, which meant they were off for a pleasure excursion. Oscar and Lou, on the front seat, wore their cloth hats and coats, never worn except on Sundays, and Emil, on the second seat with Alexandra, sat proudly in his new trousers, made from a pair of his father's, and a pink-striped shirt, with a wide ruffled collar. Oscar stopped the horses and waved to Carl, who caught up his hat and ran through the melon patch to join them.

"Want to go with us?" Lou called. "We're going to Crazy Ivar's to buy a hammock."

"Sure." Carl ran up panting, and clambering over the wheel sat down beside Emil. "I've always wanted to see Ivar's pond. They say it's the biggest in all the country. Are n't you afraid to go to Ivar's in that new shirt, Emil? He might want it and take it right off your back."

Emil grinned. "I'd be awful scared to go," he admitted, "if you big boys were n't along to take care of me. Did you ever hear him howl,

Carl? People say sometimes he runs about the country howling at night because he is afraid the Lord will destroy him. Mother thinks he must have done something awful wicked."

Lou looked back and winked at Carl. "What would you do, Emil, if you was out on the prairie by yourself and seen him coming?"

Emil stared. "Maybe I could hide in a badger-hole," he suggested doubtfully.

"But suppose there wasn't any badger-hole," Lou persisted. "Would you run?"

"No, I'd be too scared to run," Emil admitted mournfully, twisting his fingers. "I guess I'd sit right down on the ground and say my prayers."

The big boys laughed, and Oscar brandished his whip over the broad backs of the horses.

"He would n't hurt you, Emil," said Carl persuasively. "He came to doctor our mare when she ate green corn and swelled up most as big as the water-tank. He petted her just like you do your cats. I could n't understand much he said, for he don't talk any English, but he kept patting her and groaning as if he had the pain himself, and saying, 'There now, sister, that's easier, that's better!' "

Lou and Oscar laughed, and Emil giggled delightedly and looked up at his sister.

"I don't think he knows anything at all about doctoring," said Oscar scornfully. "They say when horses have distemper he takes the medicine himself, and then prays over the horses."

Alexandra spoke up. "That's what the Crows said, but he cured their horses, all the same. Some days his mind is cloudy, like. But if you can get him on a clear day, you can learn a great deal from him. He understands animals. Did n't I see him take the horn off the Berquists' cow when she had torn it loose and went crazy? She was tearing all over the place, knocking herself against things. And at last she ran out on the roof of the old dugout[4] and her legs went through and there she stuck, bellowing. Ivar came running with his white bag, and the moment he got to her she was quiet and let him saw her horn off and daub the place with tar."

Emil had been watching his sister, his face reflecting the sufferings of the cow. "And then did n't it hurt her any more?" he asked.

Alexandra patted him. "No, not any more. And in two days they could use her milk again."

The road to Ivar's homestead was a very poor one. He had settled in the rough country across the country line, where no one lived but some Russians,—half a dozen families who dwelt together in

4. Many settlers in the Great Plains would live in a dugout—a dwelling cut into a swelling in the land or a gully—before they could construct a sod or log house.

one long house, divided off like barracks. Ivar had explained his choice by saying that the fewer neighbors he had, the fewer temptations. Nevertheless, when one considered that his chief business was horse-doctoring, it seemed rather short-sighted of him to live in the most inaccessible place he could find. The Bergson wagon lurched along over the rough hummocks and grass banks, followed the bottom of winding draws, or skirted the margin of wide lagoons, where the golden coreopsis grew up out of the clear water and the wild ducks rose with a whirr of wings.

Lou looked after them helplessly. "I wish I'd brought my gun, anyway, Alexandra," he said fretfully. "I could have hidden it under the straw in the bottom of the wagon."

"Then we'd have had to lie to Ivar. Besides, they say he can smell dead birds. And if he knew, we would n't get anything out of him, not even a hammock. I want to talk to him, and he won't talk sense if he's angry. It makes him foolish."

Lou sniffed. "Whoever heard of him talking sense, anyhow! I'd rather have ducks for supper than Crazy Ivar's tongue."

Emil was alarmed. "Oh, but, Lou, you don't want to make him mad! He might howl!"

They all laughed again, and Oscar urged the horses up the crumbling side of a clay bank. They had left the lagoons and the red grass behind them. In Crazy Ivar's country the grass was short and gray, the draws deeper than they were in the Bergson's neighborhood, and the land was all broken up into hillocks and clay ridges. The wild flowers disappeared, and only in the bottom of the draws and gullies grew a few of the very toughest and hardiest: shoestring, and ironweed, and snow-on-the-mountain.

"Look, look, Emil, there's Ivar's big pond!" Alexandra pointed to a shining sheet of water that lay at the bottom of a shallow draw. At one end of the pond was an earthen dam, planted with green willow bushes, and above it a door and a single window were set into the hillside. You would not have seen them at all but for the reflection of the sunlight upon the four panes of window-glass. And that was all you saw. Not a shed, not a corral, not a well, not even a path broken in the curly grass. But for the piece of rusty stovepipe sticking up through the sod, you could have walked over the roof of Ivar's dwelling without dreaming that you were near a human habitation. Ivar had lived for three years in the clay bank, without defiling the face of nature any more than the coyote that had lived there before him had done.

When the Bergsons drove over the hill, Ivar was sitting in the doorway of his house, reading the Norwegian Bible. He was a queerly shaped old man, with a thick, powerful body set on short bow-legs. His shaggy white hair, falling in a thick mane about his ruddy cheeks, made him look older than he was. He was barefoot, but he wore a clean shirt of unbleached cotton, open at the neck. He always put on a clean shirt when Sunday morning came round, though he never went to church. He had a peculiar religion of his own and could not get on with any of the denominations. Often he did not see anybody from one week's end to another. He kept a calendar, and every morning he checked off a day, so that he was never in any doubt as to which day of the week it was. Ivar hired himself out in threshing and corn-husking time, and he doctored sick animals when he was sent for. When he was at home, he made hammocks out of twine and committed chapters of the Bible to memory.

Ivar found contentment in the solitude he had sought out for himself. He disliked the litter of human dwellings: the broken food, the bits of broken china, the old wash-boilers and tea-kettles thrown into the sunflower patch. He preferred the cleanness and tidiness of the wild sod. He always said that the badgers had cleaner houses than people, and that when he took a housekeeper her name would be Mrs. Badger. He best expressed his preference for his wild homestead by saying that his Bible seemed truer to him there. If one stood in the doorway of his cave, and looked off at the rough land, the smiling sky, the curly grass white in the hot sunlight; if one listened to the rapturous song of the lark, the drumming of the quail, the burr of the locust against that vast silence, one understood what Ivar meant.

On this Sunday afternoon his face shone with happiness. He closed the book on his knee, keeping the place with his horny finger, and repeated softly:—

> He sendeth the springs into the valleys, which run among the hills;
> They give drink to every beast of the field; the wild asses quench their thirst.
> The trees of the Lord are full of sap; the cedars of Lebanon which he hath planted;
> Where the birds make their nests: as for the stork, the fir trees are her house.
> The high hills are a refuge for the wild goats; and the rocks for the conies.[5]

Before he opened his Bible again, Ivar heard the Bergsons' wagon approaching, and he sprang up and ran toward it.

"No guns, no guns!" he shouted, waving his arms distractedly.

"No, Ivar, no guns," Alexandra called reassuringly.

5. Ivar conflates verses 10, 11, 16, 17, and 18 of Psalm 104.

He dropped his arms and went up to the wagon, smiling amiably and looking at them out of his pale blue eyes.

"We want to buy a hammock, if you have one," Alexandra explained, "and my little brother, here, wants to see your big pond, where so many birds come."

Ivar smiled foolishly, and began rubbing the horses' noses and feeling about their mouths behind the bits. "Not many birds just now. A few ducks this morning; and some snipe come to drink. But there was a crane last week. She spent one night and came back the next evening. I don't know why. It is not her season, of course. Many of them go over in the fall. Then the pond is full of strange voices every night."

Alexandra translated for Carl, who looked thoughtful. "Ask him, Alexandra, if it is true that a sea gull came here once. I have heard so."

She had some difficulty in making the old man understand.

He looked puzzled at first, then smote his hands together as he remembered. "Oh, yes, yes! A big white bird with long wings and pink feet. My! what a voice she had! She came in the afternoon and kept flying about the pond and screaming until dark. She was in trouble of some sort, but I could not understand her. She was going over to the other ocean, maybe, and did not know how far it was. She was afraid of never getting there. She was more mournful than our birds here; she cried in the night. She saw the light from my window and darted up to it. Maybe she thought my house was a boat, she was such a wild thing. Next morning, when the sun rose, I went out to take her food, but she flew up into the sky and went on her way." Ivar ran his fingers through his thick hair. "I have many strange birds stop with me here. They come from very far away and are great company. I hope you boys never shoot wild birds?"

Lou and Oscar grinned, and Ivar shook his bushy head. "Yes, I know boys are thoughtless. But these wild things are God's birds. He watches over them and counts them, as we do our cattle; Christ says so in the New Testament."[6]

"Now, Ivar," Lou asked, "may we water our horses at your pond and give them some feed? It's a bad road to your place."

"Yes, yes, it is." The old man scrambled about and began to loose the tugs. "A bad road, eh, girls? And the bay with a colt at home!"

Oscar brushed the old man aside. "We'll take care of the horses,

6. See Matthew 10.29–31: "Are not two sparrows sold for a farthing? and one of them shall not fall on the ground without your Father. But the very hairs of your head are numbered. Fear ye not therefore, ye are of more value than many sparrows." See also Luke 12.6–7.

Ivar. You'll be finding some disease on them. Alexandra wants to see your hammocks."

Ivar led Alexandra and Emil to his little cave house. He had but one room, neatly plastered and whitewashed, and there was a wooden floor. There was a kitchen stove, a table covered with oilcloth, two chairs, a clock, a calendar, a few books on the window-shelf; nothing more. But the place was as clean as a cupboard.

"But where do you sleep, Ivar?" Emil asked, looking about.

Ivar unslung a hammock from a hook on the wall; in it was rolled a buffalo robe. "There, my son. A hammock is a good bed, and in winter I wrap up in this skin. Where I go to work, the beds are not half so easy as this."

By this time Emil had lost all his timidity. He thought a cave a very superior kind of house. There was something pleasantly unusual about it and about Ivar. "Do the birds know you will be kind to them, Ivar? Is that why so many come?" he asked.

Ivar sat down on the floor and tucked his feet under him. "See, little brother, they have come from a long way, and they are very tired. From up there where they are flying, our country looks dark and flat. They must have water to drink and to bathe in before they can go on with their journey. They look this way and that, and far below them they see something shining, like a piece of glass set in the dark earth. That is my pond. They come to it and are not disturbed. Maybe I sprinkle a little corn. They tell the other birds, and next year more come this way. They have their roads up there, as we have down here."

Emil rubbed his knees thoughtfully. "And is that true, Ivar, about the head ducks falling back when they are tired, and the hind ones taking their place?"

"Yes. The point of the wedge gets the worst of it; they cut the wind. They can only stand it there a little while—half an hour, maybe. Then they fall back and the wedge splits a little, while the rear ones come up the middle to the front. Then it closes up and they fly on, with a new edge. They are always changing like that, up in the air. Never any confusion; just like soldiers who have been drilled."

Alexandra had selected her hammock by the time the boys came up from the pond. They would not come in, but sat in the shade of the bank outside while Alexandra and Ivar talked about the birds and about his housekeeping, and why he never ate meat, fresh or salt.

Alexandra was sitting on one of the wooden chairs, her arms resting on the table. Ivar was sitting on the floor at her feet. "Ivar," she said suddenly, beginning to trace the pattern on the oilcloth with her forefinger, "I came to-day more because I wanted to talk to you than because I wanted to buy a hammock."

"Yes?" The old man scraped his bare feet on the plank floor.

"We have a big bunch of hogs, Ivar. I would n't sell in the spring, when everybody advised me to, and now so many people are losing their hogs that I am frightened. What can be done?"

Ivar's little eyes began to shine. They lost their vagueness.

"You feed them swill and such stuff? Of course! And sour milk? Oh, yes! And keep them in a stinking pen? I tell you, sister, the hogs of this country are put upon! They become unclean, like the hogs in the Bible.[7] If you kept your chickens like that, what would happen? You have a little sorghum patch, maybe? Put a fence around it, and turn the the hogs in. Build a shed to give them shade, a thatch on poles. Let the boys haul water to them in barrels, clean water, and plenty. Get them off the old stinking ground, and do not let them go back there until winter. Give them only grain and clean feed, such as you would give horses or cattle. Hogs do not like to be filthy."

The boys outside the door had been listening. Lou nudged his brother. "Come, the horses are done eating. Let's hitch up and get out of here. He'll fill her full of notions. She'll be for having the pigs sleep with us, next."

Oscar grunted and got up. Carl, who could not understand what Ivar said, saw that the two boys were displeased. They did not mind hard work, but they hated experiments and could never see the use of taking pains. Even Lou, who was more elastic than his older brother, disliked to do anything different from their neighbors. He felt that it made them conspicuous and gave people a chance to talk about them.

Once they were on the homeward road, the boys forgot their ill-humor and joked about Ivar and his birds. Alexandra did not propose any reforms in the care of the pigs, and they hoped she had forgotten Ivar's talk. They agreed that he was crazier than ever, and would never be able to prove up on his land[8] because he worked it so little. Alexandra privately resolved that she would have a talk with Ivar about this and stir him up. The boys persuaded Carl to stay for supper and go swimming in the pasture pond after dark.

That evening, after she had washed the supper dishes, Alexandra sat down on the kitchen doorstep, while her mother was mixing the

7. In the Bible, hogs, swine, and pigs are grouped among "unclean" creatures, and so their flesh cannot be eaten. (Leviticus 11.4: "And the swine, though he divide the hoof, and be cloven-footed, yet he cheweth not the cud; he is unclean to you." See also Deuteronomy 14.8.)

8. According to the Homestead Act, the settler was required both to build a house and to farm the land in order to "prove up" or improve the property.

bread. It was a still, deep-breathing summer night, full of the smell of the hay fields. Sounds of laughter and splashing came up from the pasture, and when the moon rose rapidly above the bare rim of the prairie, the pond glittered like polished metal, and she could see the flash of white bodies as the boys ran about the edge, or jumped into the water. Alexandra watched the shimmering pool dreamily, but eventually her eyes went back to the sorghum patch south of the barn, where she was planning to make her new pig corral.

IV

For the first three years after John Bergson's death, the affairs of his family prospered. Then came the hard times that brought every one on the Divide to the brink of despair; three years of drouth and failure, the last struggle of a wild soil against the encroaching plowshare. The first of these fruitless summers the Bergson boys bore courageously. The failure of the corn crop made labor cheap. Lou and Oscar hired two men and put in bigger crops than ever before. They lost everything they spent. The whole country was discouraged. Farmers who were already in debt had to give up their land. A few foreclosures demoralized the county. The settlers sat about on the wooden sidewalks in the little town and told each other that the country was never meant for men to live in; the thing to do was to get back to Iowa, to Illinois, to any place that had been proved habitable. The Bergson boys, certainly, would have been happier with their uncle Otto, in the bakery shop in Chicago. Like most of their neighbors, they were meant to follow in paths already marked out for them, not to break trails in a new country. A steady job, a few holidays, nothing to think about, and they would have been very happy. It was no fault of theirs that they had been dragged into the wilderness when they were little boys. A pioneer should have imagination, should be able to enjoy the idea of things more than the things themselves.

The second of these barren summers was passing. One September afternoon Alexandra had gone over to the garden across the draw to dig sweet potatoes—they had been thriving upon the weather that was fatal to everything else. But when Carl Linstrum came up the garden rows to find her, she was not working. She was standing lost in thought, leaning upon her pitchfork, her sunbonnet lying beside her on the ground. The dry garden patch smelled of drying vines and was strewn with yellow seed-cucumbers and pumpkins and citrons. At one end, next the rhubarb, grew feathery asparagus, with red berries. Down the middle of the garden was a row of gooseberry and currant bushes. A few tough zenias and marigolds and a row of scarlet sage bore witness to the buckets of water that Mrs. Bergson had carried there after sundown, against the prohibition of her sons. Carl came quietly and slowly up the garden path, looking intently at Alexandra. She did not hear him. She was standing perfectly still, with that serious ease so characteristic of her. Her thick, reddish braids, twisted about her head, fairly burned in the sunlight. The air was cool enough to make the warm sun pleasant on one's back and shoulders, and so clear that the eye could follow a hawk up and up, into the blazing blue depths of the sky. Even Carl, never a very cheerful boy, and considerably darkened by these last two bitter years, loved the country on days like this, felt something strong and young and wild come out of it, that laughed at care.

"Alexandra," he said as he approached her, "I want to talk to you. Let's sit down by the gooseberry bushes." He picked up her sack of potatoes and they crossed the garden. "Boys gone to town?" he asked as he sank down on the warm, sunbaked earth. "Well, we have made up our minds at last, Alexandra. We are really going away."

She looked at him as if she were a little frightened. "Really, Carl? Is it settled?"

"Yes, father has heard from St. Louis, and they will give him back his old job in the cigar factory. He must be there by the first of November. They are taking on new men then. We will sell the place for whatever we can get, and auction the stock. We haven't enough to ship. I am going to learn engraving with a German engraver there, and then try to get work in Chicago."

Alexandra's hands dropped in her lap. Her eyes became dreamy and filled with tears.

Carl's sensitive lower lip trembled. He scratched in the soft earth beside him with a stick. "That's all I hate about it, Alexandra," he said slowly. "You've stood by us through so much and helped father out so many times, and now it seems as if we were running off and leaving you to face the worst of it. But it is n't as if we could really ever be of any help to you. We are only one more drag, one more thing you look out for and feel responsible for. Father was never meant for a farmer, you know that. And I hate it. We'd only get in deeper and deeper."

"Yes, yes, Carl, I know. You are wasting your life here. You are able to do much better things. You are nearly nineteen now, and I wouldn't have you stay. I've always hoped you would get away. But I can't help feeling scared when I think how I will miss you—more than you will ever know." She brushed the tears from her cheeks, not trying to hide them.

"But, Alexandra," he said sadly and wistfully, "I've never been any real help to you, beyond sometimes trying to keep the boys in a good humor."

Alexandra smiled and shook her head. "Oh, it's not that. Nothing like that. It's by understanding me, and the boys, and mother, that you've helped me. I expect that is the only way one person ever really can help another. I think you are about the only one that ever helped me. Somehow it will take more courage to bear your going than everything that has happened before."

Carl looked at the ground. "You see, we've all depended so on you," he said, "even father. He makes me laugh. When anything comes up he always says, 'I wonder what the Bergsons are going to do about that? I guess I'll go and ask her.' I'll never forget that time, when we first came here, and our horse had the colic, and I ran over to your place—your father was away, and you came home with me and showed father how to let the wind out of the horse. You were only a little girl then, but you knew ever so much more about farm work than poor father. You remember how homesick I used to get, and what long talks we used to have coming from school? We've someway always felt alike about things."

"Yes, that's it; we've liked the same things and we've liked them together, without anybody else knowing. And we've had good times, hunting for Christmas trees and going for ducks and making our plum wine together every year. We've never either of us had any other close friend. And now—" Alexandra wiped her eyes with the corner of her apron, "and now I must remember that you are going where you will have many friends, and you will find the work you were meant to do. But you'll write to me, Carl? That will mean a great deal to me here."

"I'll write as long as I live," cried the boy impetuously. "And I'll be working for you as much as for myself, Alexandra. I want to do something you'll like and be proud of. I'm a fool here, but I know I can do something!" He sat up and frowned at the red grass.

Alexandra sighed. "How discouraged the boys will be when they hear. They always come home from town discouraged, anyway. So many people are trying to leave the country, and they talk to our boys and make them low-spirited. I'm afraid they are beginning to feel hard toward me because I won't listen to any talk about going. Sometimes I feel like I'm getting tired of standing up for this country."

"I won't tell the boys yet, if you'd rather not."

"Oh, I'll tell them myself, to-night, when they come home. They'll be talking wild, anyway, and no good comes of keeping bad news. It's all harder on them than it is on me. Lou wants to get married, poor boy, and he can't until times are better. See, there goes the sun, Carl. I must be getting back. Mother will want her potatoes. It's chilly already, the moment the light goes."

Alexandra rose and looked about. A golden afterglow throbbed in the west, but the country already looked empty and mournful. A dark moving mass came over the western hill, the Lee boy was bringing in the herd from the other half-section. Emil ran from the windmill to open the corral gate. From the log house, on the little rise across the draw, the smoke was curling. The cattle lowed and bellowed. In the sky the pale half-moon was slowly silvering. Alexandra and Carl walked together down the potato rows. "I have to keep telling myself what is going to happen," she said softly. "Since you have been here, ten years now, I have never really been lonely. But I can remember what it was like before. Now I shall have nobody but Emil. But he is my boy, and he is tender-hearted."

That night, when the boys were called to supper, they sat down moodily. They had worn their coats to town, but they ate in their striped shirts and suspenders. They were grown men now, and, as Alexandra said, for the last few years they had been growing more and more like themselves. Lou was still the slighter of the two, the quicker and more intelligent, but apt to go off at half-cock. He had a lively blue eye, a thin, fair skin (always burned red to the neck-band of his shirt in summer), stiff, yellow hair that would not lie down on his head, and a bristly little yellow mustache, of which he was very proud. Oscar could not grow a mustache; his pale face was as bare as an egg, and his white eyebrows gave it an empty look. He was a man of powerful body and unusual endurance; the sort of man you could attach to a corn-sheller as you would an engine. He would turn it all day, without hurrying, without slowing down. But he was as indolent of mind as he was unsparing of his body. His love of routine amounted to a vice. He worked like an insect, always doing the same thing over in the same way, regardless of whether it was best or no. He felt that there was a sovereign virtue in mere bodily toil, and he rather liked to do things in the hardest way. If a field had once been in corn, he couldn't bear to put it into wheat. He liked to begin his corn-planting at the same time every year, whether the season were backward or forward. He seemed to feel that by his own irreproachable regularity he would clear himself of blame and reprove the weather. When the wheat crop failed, he threshed the straw at a dead loss to demonstrate how little grain there was, and thus prove his case against Providence.

Lou, on the other hand, was fussy and flighty; always planned to get through two days' work in one, and often got only the least important things done. He liked to keep the place up, but he never got round to doing odd jobs until he had to neglect more pressing work to attend to them. In the middle of the wheat harvest, when the grain was over-ripe and every hand was needed, he would stop to mend fences or to patch the harness; then dash down to the field and over-work and be laid up in bed for a week. The two boys balanced each other, and they pulled well together. They had been good friends since they were children. One seldom went anywhere, even to town, without the other.

To-night, after they sat down to supper, Oscar kept looking at Lou as if he expected him to say something, and Lou blinked his eyes and frowned at his plate. It was Alexandra herself who at last opened the discussion.

"The Linstrums," she said calmly, as she put another plate of hot biscuit on the table, "are going back to St. Louis. The old man is going to work in the cigar factory again."

At this Lou plunged in. "You see, Alexandra, everybody who can crawl out is going away. There's no use of us trying to stick it out, just to be stubborn. There's something in knowing when to quit."

"Where do you want to go, Lou?"

"Any place where things will grow," said Oscar grimly.

Lou reached for a potato. "Chris Arnson has traded his half-section for a place down on the river."

"Who did he trade with?"

"Charley Fuller, in town."

"Fuller the real estate man? You see, Lou, that Fuller has a head on him. He's buying and trading for every bit of land he can get up here. It'll make him a rich man, some day."

"He's rich now, that's why he can take a chance."

"Why can't we? We'll live longer than he will. Some day the land itself will be worth more than all we can ever raise on it."

Lou laughed. "It could be worth that, and still not be worth much. Why, Alexandra, you don't know what you're talking about. Our place wouldn't bring now what it would six years ago. The fellows that settled up here just made a mistake. Now they're beginning to see this high land was n't never meant to grow nothing on, and everybody who ain't fixed to graze cattle is trying to crawl out. It's too high to farm up here. All the Americans are skinning out. That man Percy Adams, north of town, told me that he was going to let Fuller take his land and stuff for four hundred dollars and a ticket to Chicago."

"There's Fuller again!" Alexandra exclaimed. "I wish that man would take me for a partner. He's feathering his nest! If only poor people could learn a little from rich people! But all these fellows who are running off are bad farmers, like poor Mr. Linstrum. They could n't get ahead even in good years, and they all got into debt while father was getting out. I think we ought to hold on as long as we can on father's account. He was so set on keeping this land. He must have seen harder times than this, here. How was it in the early days, mother?"

Mrs. Bergson was weeping quietly. These family discussions always depressed her, and made her remember all that she had been torn away from. "I don't see why the boys are always taking on about going away," she said, wiping her eyes. "I don't want to move again; out to some raw place, maybe, where we'd be worse off than we are here, and all to do over again. I won't move! If the rest of you go, I will ask some of the neighbors to take me in, and stay and be buried by father. I'm not going to leave him by himself on the prairie, for cattle to run over." She began to cry more bitterly.

The boys looked angry. Alexandra put a soothing hand on her mother's shoulder. "There's no question of that, mother. You don't have to go if you don't want to. A third of the place belongs to you by American law, and we can't sell without your consent. We only want you to advise us. How did it use to be when you and father first came? Was it really as bad as this, or not?"

"Oh, worse! Much worse," moaned Mrs. Bergson. "Drouth, chinch-bugs, hail, everything! My garden all cut to pieces like sauerkraut. No grapes on the creek, no nothing. The people all lived just like coyotes."

Oscar got up and tramped out of the kitchen. Lou followed him. They felt that Alexandra had taken an unfair advantage in turning their mother loose on them. The next morning they were silent and reserved. They did not offer to take the women to church, but went down to the barn immediately after breakfast and stayed there all day. When Carl Linstrum came over in the afternoon, Alexandra winked to him and pointed toward the barn. He understood her and went down to play cards with the boys. They believed that a very wicked thing to do on Sunday, and it relieved their feelings.

Alexandra stayed in the house. On Sunday afternoon Mrs. Bergson always took a nap, and Alexandra read. During the week she read only the newspaper, but on Sunday, and in the long evenings of winter, she read a good deal; read a few things over a great many times. She knew long portions of the "Frithjof Saga"[9] by heart, and, like most Swedes who read at all, she was fond of Longfellow's verse,—the ballads and the "Golden Legend" and "The Spanish Student." To-day she sat in the wooden rocking-chair with the Swedish Bible open on her knees, but she was not reading. She was looking thoughtfully away at the point where the upland road dis-

9. *Frithjof's Saga* (1825), a long narrative poem and classic of Swedish literature by Swedish poet Esaias Tegnér that draws on traditional Scandinavian sagas and legends. Sections were translated into English by Henry Wadsworth Longfellow.

appeared over the rim of the prairie. Her body was in an attitude of perfect repose, such as it was apt to take when she was thinking earnestly. Her mind was slow, truthful, steadfast. She had not the least spark of cleverness.

All afternoon the sitting-room was full of quiet and sunlight. Emil was making rabbit traps in the kitchen shed. The hens were clucking and scratching brown holes in the flower beds, and the wind was teasing the prince's feather by the door.

That evening Carl came in with the boys to supper.

"Emil," said Alexandra, when they were all seated at the table, "how would you like to go traveling? Because I am going to take a trip, and you can go with me if you want to."

The boys looked up in amazement; they were always afraid of Alexandra's schemes. Carl was interested.

"I've been thinking, boys," she went on, "that maybe I am too set against making a change. I'm going to take Brigham and the buckboard to-morrow and drive down to the river country and spend a few days looking over what they've got down there. If I find anything good, you boys can go down and make a trade."

"Nobody down there will trade for anything up here," said Oscar gloomily.

"That's just what I want to find out. Maybe they are just as discontented down there as we are up here. Things away from home often look better than they are. You know what your Hans Andersen book says, Carl, about the Swedes liking to buy Danish bread and the Danes liking to buy Swedish bread, because people always think the bread of another country is better than their own.[1] Anyway, I've heard so much about the river farms, I won't be satisfied till I've seen for myself."

Lou fidgeted. "Look out! Don't agree to anything. Don't let them fool you."

Lou was apt to be fooled himself. He had not yet learned to keep away from the shell-game wagons that followed the circus.

After supper Lou put on a necktie and went across the fields to court Annie Lee, and Carl and Oscar sat down to a game of checkers, while Alexandra read "The Swiss Family Robinson" aloud to her mother and Emil. It was not long before the two boys at the table neglected their game to listen. They were all big children together, and they found the adventures of the family in the tree house so absorbing that they gave them their undivided attention.

1. A reference to Hans Christian Andersen's "Holger Danske": "The Danish and the Swedish flags wave, and the Danes and Swedes say 'Good-day,' and 'Thank you' to each other, not with cannons, but with a friendly shake of the hand, and they exchange white bread and biscuits with each other, because foreign articles taste better."

V

Alexandra and Emil spent five days down among the river farms, driving up and down the valley. Alexandra talked to the men about their crops and to the women about their poultry. She spent a whole day with one young farmer who had been away at school, and who was experimenting with a new kind of clover hay. She learned a great deal. As they drove along, she and Emil talked and planned. At last, on the sixth day, Alexandra turned Brigham's head northward and left the river behind.

"There's nothing in it for us down there, Emil. There are a few fine farms, but they are owned by the rich men in town, and couldn't be bought. Most of the land is rough and hilly. They can always scrape along down there, but they can never do anything big. Down there they have a little certainty, but up with us there is a big chance. We must have faith in the high land, Emil. I want to hold on harder than ever, and when you're a man you'll thank me." She urged Brigham forward.

When the road began to climb the first long swells of the Divide, Alexandra hummed an old Swedish hymn, and Emil wondered why his sister looked so happy. Her face was so radiant that he felt shy about asking her. For the first time, perhaps, since that land emerged from the waters of geologic ages, a human face was set toward it with love and yearning. It seemed beautiful to her, rich and strong and glorious. Her eyes drank in the breadth of it, until her tears blinded her. Then the Genius of the Divide, the great, free spirit which breathes across it, must have bent lower than it ever bent to a human will before. The history of every country begins in the heart of a man or a woman.

Alexandra reached home in the afternoon. That evening she held a family council and told her brothers all that she had seen and heard.

"I want you boys to go down yourselves and look it over. Nothing will convince you like seeing with your own eyes. The river land was settled before this, and so they are a few years ahead of us, and have learned more about farming. The land sells for three times as much as this, but in five years we will double it. The rich men down there own all the best land, and they are buying all they can get. The thing to do is to sell our cattle and what little old corn we have, and buy the Linstrum place. Then the next thing to do is to take out two loans on our half-sections, and buy Peter Crow's place; raise every dollar we can, and buy every acre we can."

"Mortgage the homestead again?" Lou cried. He sprang up and began to wind the clock furiously. "I won't slave to pay off another mortgage. I'll never do it. You'd just as soon kill us all, Alexandra, to carry out some scheme!"

Oscar rubbed his high, pale forehead. "How do you propose to pay off your mortgages?"

Alexandra looked from one to the other and bit her lip. They had never seen her so nervous. "See here," she brought out at last. "We borrow the money for six years. Well, with the money we buy a half-section from Linstrum and a half from Crow, and a quarter from Struble, maybe. That will give us upwards of fourteen hundred acres, won't it? You won't have to pay off your mortgages for six years. By that time, any of this land will be worth thirty dollars an acre—it will be worth fifty, but we'll say thirty; then you can sell a garden patch anywhere, and pay off a debt of sixteen hundred dollars. It's not the principal I'm worried about, it's the interest and taxes. We'll have to strain to meet the payments. But as sure as we are sitting here to-night, we can sit down here ten years from now independent landowners, not struggling farmers any longer. The chance that father was always looking for has come."

Lou was pacing the floor. "But how do you *know* that land is going to go up enough to pay the mortgages and—"

"And make us rich besides?" Alexandra put in firmly. "I can't explain that, Lou. You'll have to take my word for it. I *know*, that's all. When you drive about over the country you can feel it coming."

Oscar had been sitting with his head lowered, his hands hanging between his knees. "But we can't work so much land," he said dully, as if he were talking to himself. "We can't even try. It would just lie there and we'd work ourselves to death." He sighed, and laid his calloused fist on the table.

Alexandra's eyes filled with tears. She put her hand on his shoulder. "You poor boy, you won't have to work it. The men in town who are buying up other people's land don't try to farm it. They are the men to watch, in a new country. Let's try to do like the shrewd ones, and not like these stupid fellows. I don't want you boys always to have to work like this. I want you to be independent, and Emil to go to school."

Lou held his head as if it were splitting. "Everybody will say we are crazy. It must be crazy, or everybody would be doing it."

"If they were, we wouldn't have much chance. No, Lou, I was talking about that with the smart young man who is raising the new kind of clover. He says the right thing is usually just what everybody don't do. Why are we better fixed than any of our neighbors? Because father had more brains. Our people were better people than these in the old country. We *ought* to do more than they do, and see further ahead. Yes, mother, I'm going to clear the table now."

Alexandra rose. The boys went to the stable to see to the stock, and they were gone a long while. When they came back Lou played on his *dragharmonika*[2] and Oscar sat figuring at his father's secretary all evening. They said nothing more about Alexandra's project, but she felt sure now that they would consent to it. Just before bedtime Oscar went out for a pail of water. When he did not come back, Alexandra threw a shawl over her head and ran down the path to the windmill. She found him sitting there with his head in his hands, and she sat down beside him.

"Don't do anything you don't want to do, Oscar," she whispered. She waited a moment, but he did not stir. "I won't say any more about it, if you'd rather not. What makes you so discouraged?"

"I dread signing my name to them pieces of paper," he said slowly. "All the time I was a boy we had a mortgage hanging over us."

"Then don't sign one. I don't want you to, if you feel that way."

Oscar shook his head. "No, I can see there's a chance that way. I've thought a good while there might be. We're in so deep now, we might as well go deeper. But it's hard work pulling out of debt. Like pulling a threshing-machine out of the mud; breaks your back. Me and Lou's worked hard, and I can't see it's got us ahead much."

"Nobody knows about that as well as I do, Oscar. That's why I want to try an easier way. I don't want you to have to grub for every dollar."

"Yes, I know what you mean. Maybe it'll come out right. But signing papers is signing papers. There ain't no maybe about that." He took his pail and trudged up the path to the house.

Alexandra drew her shawl closer about her and stood leaning against the frame of the mill, looking at the stars which glittered so keenly through the frosty autumn air. She always loved to watch them, to think of their vastness and distance, and of their ordered march. It fortified her to reflect upon the great operations of nature, and when she thought of the law that lay behind them, she felt a sense of personal security. That night she had a new consciousness of the country, felt almost a new relation to it. Even her talk with the boys had not taken away the feeling that had overwhelmed her when she drove back to the Divide that afternoon. She had never known before how much the country meant to her. The chirping of the insects down in the long grass had been like the sweetest music. She had felt as if her heart were hiding down there, somewhere, with the quail and the plover and all the little wild things that crooned or buzzed in the sun. Under the long shaggy ridges, she felt the future stirring.

2. Concertina.

Part II. Neighboring Fields

I

It is sixteen years since John Bergson died. His wife now lies beside him, and the white shaft that marks their graves gleams across the wheat-fields. Could he rise from beneath it, he would not know the country under which he has been asleep. The shaggy coat of the prairie, which they lifted to make him a bed, has vanished forever. From the Norwegian graveyard one looks out over a vast checker-board, marked off in squares of wheat and corn; light and dark, dark and light. Telephone wires hum along the white roads, which always run at right angles. From the graveyard gate one can count a dozen gayly painted farmhouses; the gilded weather-vanes on the big red barns wink at each other across the green and brown and yellow fields. The light steel windmills tremble throughout their frames and tug at their moorings, as they vibrate in the wind that often blows from one week's end to another across that high, active, resolute stretch of country.

The Divide is now thickly populated. The rich soil yields heavy harvests; the dry, bracing climate and the smoothness of the land make labor easy for men and beasts. There are few scenes more gratifying than a spring plowing in that country, where the furrows of a single field often lie a mile in length, and the brown earth, with such a strong, clean smell, and such a power of growth and fertility in it, yields itself eagerly to the plow; rolls away from the shear, not even dimming the brightness of the metal, with a soft, deep sigh of happiness. The wheat-cutting sometimes goes on all night as well as all day, and in good seasons there are scarcely men and horses enough to do the harvesting. The grain is so heavy that it bends toward the blade and cuts like velvet.

There is something frank and joyous and young in the open face of the country. It gives itself ungrudgingly to the moods of the season, holding nothing back. Like the plains of Lombardy, it seems to rise a little to meet the sun. The air and the earth are curiously mated and intermingled, as if the one were the breath of the other. You feel in the atmosphere the same tonic, puissant quality that is in the tilth, the same strength and resoluteness.

One June morning a young man stood at the gate of the Norwegian graveyard, sharpening his scythe in strokes unconsciously timed to the tune he was whistling. He wore a flannel cap and duck trousers, and the sleeves of his white flannel shirt were rolled back to the elbow. When he was satisfied with the edge of his blade, he slipped the whetstone into his hip pocket and began to swing his scythe, still whistling, but softly, out of respect to the quiet folk about him. Unconscious respect, probably, for he seemed intent upon his own thoughts, and, like the Gladiator's,[3] they were far away. He was a splendid figure of a boy, tall and straight as a young pine tree, with a handsome head, and stormy gray eyes, deeply set under a serious brow. The space between his two front teeth, which were unusually far apart, gave him the proficiency in whistling for which he was distinguished at college. (He also played the cornet in the University band.)

When the grass required his close attention, or when he had to stoop to cut about a headstone, he paused in his lively air,—the "Jewel" song,[4]—taking it up where he had left it when his scythe swung free again. He was not thinking about the tired pioneers over whom his blade glittered. The old wild country, the struggle in which his sister was destined to succeed while so many men broke their hearts and died, he can scarcely remember. That is all among the dim things of childhood and has been forgotten in the brighter pattern life weaves to-day, in the bright facts of being captain of the track team, and holding the interstate record for the high jump, in the all-suffusing brightness of being twenty-one. Yet sometimes, in the pauses of his work, the young man frowned and looked at the ground with an intentness which suggested that even twenty-one might have its problems.

When he had been mowing the better part of an hour, he heard the rattle of a light cart on the road behind him. Supposing that it was his sister coming back from one of her farms, he kept on with his work. The cart stopped at the gate and a merry contralto voice called, "Almost through, Emil?" He dropped his scythe and went toward the fence, wiping his face and neck with his handkerchief. In the cart sat a young woman who wore driving gauntlets and a wide shade hat, trimmed with red poppies. Her face, too, was rather like a poppy, round and brown, with rich color in her

3. The allusion is to Byron's description of the dying gladiator in *Childe Harold's Pilgrimage*: ". . . he is gone, / Ere ceased the inhuman shout which hailed the wretch who won. / He heard it, but he heeded not—his eyes / Were with his heart, and that was far away; . . . where his rude hut by the Danube lay" (IV, stanzas 140–141).

4. Marguerite's aria from the opera *Faust* (1859) by Charles Gounod (1818–1893). As she sings she adorns herself with jewels Mephistopheles has given her in order to aid her seduction by Faust.

cheeks and lips, and her dancing yellow-brown eyes bubbled with gayety. The wind was flapping her big hat and teasing a curl of her chestnut-colored hair. She shook her head at the tall youth.

"What time did you get over here? That's not much of a job for an athlete. Here I've been to town and back. Alexandra lets you sleep late. Oh, I know! Lou's wife was telling me about the way she spoils you. I was going to give you a lift, if you were done." She gathered up her reins.

"But I will be, in a minute. Please wait for me, Marie," Emil coaxed. "Alexandra sent me to mow our lot, but I've done half a dozen others, you see. Just wait till I finish off the Kourdnas'. By the way, they were Bohemians. Why are n't they up in the Catholic graveyard?"

"Free-thinkers," replied the young woman laconically.

"Lots of the Bohemian boys at the University are," said Emil, taking up his scythe again. "What did you ever burn John Huss[5] for, anyway? It's made an awful row. They still jaw about it in history classes."

"We'd do it right over again, most of us," said the young woman hotly. "Don't they ever teach you in your history classes that you'd all be heathen Turks if it hadn't been for the Bohemians?"[6]

Emil had fallen to mowing. "Oh, there's no denying you're a spunky little bunch, you Czechs," he called back over his shoulder.

Marie Shabata settled herself in her seat and watched the rhythmical movement of the young man's long arms, swinging her foot as if in time to some air that was going through her mind. The minutes passed. Emil mowed vigorously and Marie sat sunning herself and watching the long grass fall. She sat with the ease that belongs to persons of an essentially happy nature, who can find a comfortable spot almost anywhere; who are supple, and quick in adapting themselves to circumstances. After a final swish, Emil snapped the gate and sprang into the cart, holding his scythe well out over the wheel. "There," he sighed. "I gave old man Lee a cut or so, too. Lou's wife need n't talk. I never see Lou's scythe over here."

Marie clucked to her horse. "Oh, you know Annie!" She looked at the young man's bare arms. "How brown you've got since you came home. I wish I had an athlete to mow my orchard. I get wet to my knees when I go down to pick cherries."

5. Jan Hus (1369–1415) was a Bohemian religious leader whose teachings influenced the Protestant Reformation. Considered a heretic by the Catholic Church, he was burned at the stake.
6. Celebrating Bohemia's role in opposing the Ottoman Empire's expansion into Eastern Europe during the sixteenth and seventeenth centuries, Marie is romanticizing her country's history. An alliance of European powers defeated the Ottomans at the siege of Vienna in 1683.

"You can have one, any time you want him. Better wait until after it rains." Emil squinted off at the horizon as if he were looking for clouds.

"Will you? Oh, there's a good boy!" She turned her head to him with a quick, bright smile. He felt it rather than saw it. Indeed, he had looked away with the purpose of not seeing it. "I've been up looking at Angélique's wedding clothes," Marie went on, "and I'm so excited I can hardly wait until Sunday. Amédée will be a handsome bridegroom. Is anybody but you going to stand up with him? Well, then it will be a handsome wedding party." She made a droll face at Emil, who flushed. "Frank," Marie continued, flicking her horse, "is cranky at me because I loaned his saddle to Jan Smirka, and I'm terribly afraid he won't take me to the dance in the evening. Maybe the supper will tempt him. All Angélique's folks are baking for it, and all Amédée's twenty cousins. There will be barrels of beer. If once I get Frank to the supper, I'll see that I stay for the dance. And by the way, Emil, you must n't dance with me but once or twice. You must dance with all the French girls. It hurts their feelings if you don't. They think you're proud because you've been away to school or something."

Emil sniffed. "How do you know they think that?"

"Well, you didn't dance with them much at Raoul Marcel's party, and I could tell how they took it by the way they looked at you—and at me."

"All right," said Emil shortly, studying the glittering blade of his scythe.

They drove westward toward Norway Creek, and toward a big white house that stood on a hill, several miles across the fields. There were so many sheds and outbuildings grouped about it that the place looked not unlike a tiny village. A stranger, approaching it, could not help noticing the beauty and fruitfulness of the outlying fields. There was something individual about the great farm, a most unusual trimness and care for detail. On either side of the road, for a mile before you reached the foot of the hill, stood tall osage orange hedges, their glossy green marking off the yellow fields. South of the hill, in a low, sheltered swale, surrounded by a mulberry hedge, was the orchard, its fruit trees knee-deep in timothy grass. Any one thereabouts would have told you that this was one of the richest farms on the Divide, and that the farmer was a woman, Alexandra Bergson.

If you go up the hill and enter Alexandra's big house, you will find that it is curiously unfinished and uneven in comfort. One room is papered, carpeted, over-furnished; the next is almost bare. The pleasantest rooms in the house are the kitchen—where Alexandra's three young Swedish girls chatter and cook and pickle and preserve all summer long—and the sitting-room, in which Alexandra has brought together the old homely furniture that the Bergsons used in their first log house, the family portraits, and the few things her mother brought from Sweden.

When you go out of the house into the flower garden, there you feel again the order and fine arrangement manifest all over the great farm; in the fencing and hedging, in the windbreaks and sheds, in the symmetrical pasture ponds, planted with scrub willows to give shade to the cattle in flytime. There is even a white row of beehives in the orchard, under the walnut trees. You feel that, properly, Alexandra's house is the big out-of-doors, and that it is in the soil that she expresses herself best.

II

Emil reached home a little past noon, and when he went into the kitchen Alexandra was already seated at the head of the long table, having dinner with her men, as she always did unless there were visitors. He slipped into his empty place at his sister's right. The three pretty young Swedish girls who did Alexandra's housework were cutting pies, refilling coffee-cups, placing platters of bread and meat and potatoes upon the red tablecloth, and continually getting in each other's way between the table and the stove. To be sure they always wasted a good deal of time getting in each other's way and giggling at each other's mistakes. But, as Alexandra had pointedly told her sisters-in-law, it was to hear them giggle that she kept three young things in her kitchen; the work she could do herself, if it were necessary. These girls, with their long letters from home, their finery, and their love-affairs, afforded her a great deal of entertainment, and they were company for her when Emil was away at school.

Of the youngest girl, Signa, who has a pretty figure, mottled pink cheeks, and yellow hair, Alexandra is very fond, though she keeps a sharp eye upon her. Signa is apt to be skittish at mealtime, when the men are about, and to spill the coffee or upset the cream. It is supposed that Nelse Jensen, one of the six men at the dinner-table, is courting Signa, though he has been so careful not to commit himself that no one in the house, least of all Signa, can tell just how far the matter has progressed. Nelse watches her glumly as she waits upon the table, and in the evening, he sits on a bench behind the stove with his *dragharmonika*, playing mournful airs and watching her as she goes about her work. When Alexandra asked Signa whether she thought Nelse was in earnest, the poor child hid her hands under her apron and murmured, "I don't know, ma'am. But he scolds me about everything, like as if he wanted to have me!"

At Alexandra's left sat a very old man, barefoot and wearing a long blue blouse, open at the neck. His shaggy head is scarcely whiter than it was sixteen years ago, but his little blue eyes have become pale and watery, and his ruddy face is withered, like an apple that has clung all winter to the tree. When Ivar lost his land through mismanagement a dozen years ago, Alexandra took him in, and he has been a member of her household ever since. He is too old to work in the fields, but he hitches and unhitches the work-teams and looks after the health of the stock. Sometimes of a winter evening Alexandra calls him into the sitting-room to read the Bible aloud to her, for he still reads very well. He dislikes human habitations, so Alexandra has fitted him up a room in the barn, where he is very comfortable, being near the horses and, as he says, further from temptations. No one has ever found out what his temptations are. In cold weather he sits by the kitchen fire and makes hammocks or mends harness until it is time to go to bed. Then he says his prayers at great length behind the stove, puts on his buffalo-skin coat and goes out to his room in the barn.

Alexandra herself has changed very little. Her figure is fuller, and she has more color. She seems sunnier and more vigorous than she did as a young girl. But she still has the same calmness and deliberation of manner, the same clear eyes, and she still wears her hair in two braids wound round her head. It is so curly that fiery ends escape from the braids and make her head look like one of the big double sunflowers that fringe her vegetable garden. Her face is always tanned in summer, for her sunbonnet is oftener on her arm than on her head. But where her collar falls away from her neck, or where her sleeves are pushed back from her wrist, the skin is of such smoothness and whiteness as none but Swedish women ever possess; skin with the freshness of the snow itself.

Alexandra did not talk much at the table, but she encouraged her men to talk, and she always listened attentively, even when they seemed to be talking foolishly.

To-day Barney Flinn, the big red-headed Irishman who had been with Alexandra for five years and who was actually her foreman, though he had no such title, was grumbling about the new silo she had put up that spring. It happened to be the first silo on the Divide, and Alexandra's neighbors and her men were skeptical about it. "To be sure, if the thing don't work, we'll have plenty of feed without it, indeed," Barney conceded.

Nelse Jensen, Signa's gloomy suitor, had his word. "Lou, he says he would n't have no silo on his place if you'd give it to him. He says the feed outen it gives the stock the bloat. He heard of somebody lost four head of horses, feedin' 'em that stuff."

Alexandra looked down the table from one to another. "Well, the only way we can find out is to try. Lou and I have different notions about feeding stock, and that's a good thing. It's bad if all the members of a family think alike. They never get anywhere. Lou can learn by my mistakes and I can learn by his. Is n't that fair, Barney?"

The Irishman laughed. He had no love for Lou, who was always uppish with him and who said that Alexandra paid her hands too much. "I've no thought but to give the thing an honest try, mum. 'T would be only right, after puttin' so much expense into it. Maybe Emil will come out an' have a look at it wid me." He pushed back his chair, took his hat from the nail, and marched out with Emil, who, with his university ideas, was supposed to have instigated the silo. The other hands followed them, all except old Ivar. He had been depressed throughout the meal and had paid no heed to the talk of the men, even when they mentioned cornstalk bloat, upon which he was sure to have opinions.

"Did you want to speak to me, Ivar?" Alexandra asked as she rose from the table. "Come into the sitting-room."

The old man followed Alexandra, but when she motioned him to a chair he shook his head. She took up her workbasket and waited for him to speak. He stood looking at the carpet, his bushy head bowed, his hands clasped in front of him. Ivar's bandy legs seemed to have grown shorter with years, and they were completely misfitted to his broad, thick body and heavy shoulders.

"Well, Ivar, what is it?" Alexandra asked after she had waited longer than usual.

Ivar had never learned to speak English and his Norwegian was quaint and grave, like the speech of the more old-fashioned people. He always addressed Alexandra in terms of the deepest respect, hoping to set a good example to the kitchen girls, whom he thought too familiar in their manners.

"Mistress," he began faintly, without raising his eyes, "the folk have been looking coldly at me of late. You know there has been talk."

"Talk about what, Ivar?"

"About sending me away; to the asylum."

Alexandra put down her sewing-basket. "Nobody has come to me with such talk," she said decidedly. "Why need you listen? You know I would never consent to such a thing."

Ivar lifted his shaggy head and looked at her out of his little eyes. "They say that you cannot prevent it if the folk complain of me, if your brothers complain to the authorities. They say that your brothers are afraid—God forbid!—that I may do you some injury when my spells are on me. Mistress, how can any one think that?—that I could bite the hand that fed me!" The tears trickled down on the old man's beard.

Alexandra frowned. "Ivar, I wonder at you, that you should come bothering me with such nonsense. I am still running my own house, and other people have nothing to do with either you or me. So long as I am suited with you, there is nothing to be said."

Ivar pulled a red handkerchief out of the breast of his blouse and wiped his eyes and beard. "But I should not wish you to keep me if, as they say, it is against your interests, and if it is hard for you to get hands because I am here."

Alexandra made an impatient gesture, but the old man put out his hand and went on earnestly:—

"Listen, mistress, it is right that you should take these things into account. You know that my spells come from God, and that I would not harm any living creature. You believe that every one should worship God in the way revealed to him. But that is not the way of this country. The way here is for all to do alike. I am despised because I do not wear shoes, because I do not cut my hair, and because I have visions. At home, in the old country, there were many like me, who had been touched by God, or who had seen things in the graveyard at night and were different afterward. We thought nothing of it, and let them alone. But here, if a man is different in his feet or in his head, they put him in the asylum. Look at Peter Kralik; when he was a boy, drinking out of a creek, he swallowed a snake, and always after that he could eat only such food as the creature liked, for when he ate anything else, it became enraged and gnawed him. When he felt it whipping about in him, he drank alcohol to stupefy it and get some ease for himself. He could work as good as any man, and his head was clear, but they locked him up for being different in his stomach. That is the way; they have built the asylum for people who are different, and they will not even let us live in the holes with the badgers. Only your great prosperity has protected me so far. If you had had ill-fortune, they would have taken me to Hastings[7] long ago."

As Ivar talked, his gloom lifted. Alexandra had found that she could often break his fasts and long penances by talking to him and letting him pour out the thoughts that troubled him. Sympathy always cleared his mind, and ridicule was poison to him.

"There is a great deal in what you say, Ivar. Like as not they will be wanting to take me to Hastings because I have built a silo; and then I may take you with me. But at present I need you here. Only don't come to me again telling me what people say. Let people go on talking as they like, and we will go on living as we think best. You have been with me now for twelve years, and I have gone to

7. The insane asylum in Hastings, Nebraska.

you for advice oftener than I have ever gone to any one. That ought to satisfy you."

Ivar bowed humbly. "Yes, mistress, I shall not trouble you with their talk again. And as for my feet, I have observed your wishes all these years, though you have never questioned me; washing them every night, even in winter."

Alexandra laughed. "Oh, never mind about your feet, Ivar. We can remember when half our neighbors went barefoot in summer. I expect old Mrs. Lee would love to slip her shoes off now sometimes, if she dared. I'm glad I'm not Lou's mother-in-law."

Ivar looked about mysteriously and lowered his voice almost to a whisper. "You know what they have over at Lou's house? A great white tub, like the stone water-troughs in the old country, to wash themselves in. When you sent me over with the strawberries, they were all in town but the old woman Lee and the baby. She took me in and showed me the thing, and she told me it was impossible to wash yourself clean in it, because, in so much water, you could not make a strong suds. So when they fill it up and send her in there, she pretends, and makes a splashing noise. Then, when they are all asleep, she washes herself in a little wooden tub she keeps under her bed."

Alexandra shook with laughter. "Poor old Mrs. Lee! They won't let her wear nightcaps, either. Never mind; when she comes to visit me, she can do all the old things in the old way, and have as much beer as she wants. We'll start an asylum for old-time people, Ivar."

Ivar folded his big handkerchief carefully and thrust it back into his blouse. "This is always the way, mistress. I come to you sorrowing, and you send me away with a light heart. And will you be so good as to tell the Irishman that he is not to work the brown gelding until the sore on its shoulder is healed?"

"That I will. Now go and put Emil's mare to the cart. I am going to drive up to the north quarter to meet the man from town who is to buy my alfalfa hay."

III

Alexandra was to hear more of Ivar's case, however. On Sunday her married brothers came to dinner. She had asked them for that day because Emil, who hated family parties, would be absent, dancing at Amédée Chevalier's wedding, up in the French country. The table was set for company in the dining-room, where highly varnished wood and colored glass and useless pieces of china were conspicuous enough to satisfy the standards of the new prosperity. Alexandra had put herself into the hands of the Hanover furniture dealer, and he had conscientiously done his best to make her dining-room look like his display window. She said frankly that she knew nothing about such things, and she was willing to be governed by the general conviction that the more useless and utterly unusable objects were, the greater their virtue as ornament. That seemed reasonable enough. Since she liked plain things herself, it was all the more necessary to have jars and punch-bowls and candlesticks in the company rooms for people who did appreciate them. Her guests liked to see about them these reassuring emblems of prosperity.[8]

The family party was complete except for Emil, and Oscar's wife who, in the country phrase, "was not going anywhere just now."[9] Oscar sat at the foot of the table and his four towheaded little boys, aged from twelve to five, were ranged at one side. Neither Oscar nor Lou has changed much; they have simply, as Alexandra said of them long ago, grown to be more and more like themselves. Lou now looks the older of the two; his face is thin and shrewd and wrinkled about the eyes, while Oscar's is thick and dull. For all his dullness, however, Oscar makes more money than his brother, which adds to Lou's sharpness and uneasiness and tempts him to make a show. The trouble with Lou is that he is tricky, and his neighbors have found out that, as Ivar says, he has not a fox's face for nothing. Politics being the natural field for such talents, he neglects his farm to attend conventions and to run for county offices.

Lou's wife, formerly Annie Lee, has grown to look curiously like her husband. Her face has become longer, sharper, more aggressive. She wears her yellow hair in a high pompadour, and is bedecked with rings and chains and "beauty pins." Her tight, high-heeled shoes give her an awkward walk, and she is always more or less preoccupied with her clothes. As she sat at the table, she kept telling her youngest daughter to "be careful now, and not drop anything on mother."

The conversation at the table was all in English. Oscar's wife, from the malaria district of Missouri, was ashamed of marrying a foreigner, and his boys do not understand a word of Swedish. Annie and Lou sometimes speak Swedish at home, but Annie is almost as much afraid of being "caught" at it as ever her mother was of being caught barefoot. Oscar still has a thick accent, but Lou speaks like anybody from Iowa.[1]

8. Allusion to the practice of "conspicuous consumption" first described by sociologist Thorstein Veblen in *The Theory of the Leisure Class* (1899). Members of the newly emerging middle and upper classes displayed success and wealth through material objects.
9. Was pregnant.
1. Reference to the speech of native-born Americans, most likely from New England and the Middle Atlantic states, who emigrated to Iowa in the late nineteenth century.

"When I was in Hastings to attend the convention," he was saying, "I saw the superintendent of the asylum, and I was telling him about Ivar's symptoms. He says Ivar's case is one of the most dangerous kind, and it's a wonder he has n't done something violent before this."

Alexandra laughed good-humoredly. "Oh, nonsense, Lou! The doctors would have us all crazy if they could. Ivar's queer, certainly, but he has more sense than half the hands I hire."

Lou flew at his fried chicken. "Oh, I guess the doctor knows his business, Alexandra. He was very much surprised when I told him how you'd put up with Ivar. He says he's likely to set fire to the barn any night, or to take after you and the girls with an axe."

Little Signa, who was waiting on the table, giggled and fled to the kitchen. Alexandra's eyes twinkled. "That was too much for Signa, Lou. We all know that Ivar's perfectly harmless. The girls would as soon expect me to chase them with an axe."

Lou flushed and signaled to his wife. "All the same, the neighbors will be having a say about it before long. He may burn anybody's barn. It's only necessary for one property-owner in the township to make complaint, and he'll be taken up by force. You'd better send him yourself and not have any hard feelings."

Alexandra helped one of her little nephews to gravy. "Well, Lou, if any of the neighbors try that, I'll have myself appointed Ivar's guardian and take the case to court, that's all. I am perfectly satisfied with him."

"Pass the preserves, Lou," said Annie in a warning tone. She had reasons for not wishing her husband to cross Alexandra too openly. "But don't you sort of hate to have people see him around here, Alexandra?" she went on with persuasive smoothness. "He *is* a disgraceful object, and you're fixed up so nice now. It sort of makes people distant with you, when they never know when they'll hear him scratching about. My girls are afraid as death of him, are n't you, Milly, dear?"

Milly was fifteen, fat and jolly and pompadoured, with a creamy complexion, square white teeth, and a short upper lip. She looked like her grandmother Bergson, and had her comfortable and comfort-loving nature. She grinned at her aunt, with whom she was a great deal more at ease than she was with her mother. Alexandra winked a reply.

"Milly need n't be afraid of Ivar. She's an especial favorite of his. In my opinion Ivar has just as much right to his own way of dressing and thinking as we have. But I'll see that he does n't bother other people. I'll keep him at home, so don't trouble any more about him, Lou. I've been wanting to ask you about your new bathtub. How does it work?"

Annie came to the fore to give Lou time to recover himself. "Oh, it works something grand! I can't keep him out of it. He washes himself all over three times a week now, and uses all the hot water. I think it's weakening to stay in as long as he does. You ought to have one, Alexandra."

"I'm thinking of it. I might have one put in the barn for Ivar, if it will ease people's minds. But before I get a bathtub, I'm going to get a piano for Milly."

Oscar, at the end of the table, looked up from his plate. "What does Milly want of a pianny? What's the matter with her organ? She can make some use of that, and play in church."

Annie looked flustered. She had begged Alexandra not to say anything about this plan before Oscar, who was apt to be jealous of what his sister did for Lou's children. Alexandra did not get on with Oscar's wife at all. "Milly can play in church just the same, and she'll still play on the organ. But practising on it so much spoils her touch. Her teacher says so," Annie brought out with spirit.

Oscar rolled his eyes. "Well, Milly must have got on pretty good if she's got past the organ. I know plenty of grown folks that ain't," he said bluntly.

Annie threw up her chin. "She has got on good, and she's going to play for her commencement when she graduates in town next year."

"Yes," said Alexandra firmly, "I think Milly deserves a piano. All the girls around here have been taking lessons for years, but Milly is the only one of them who can ever play anything when you ask her. I'll tell you when I first thought I would like to give you a piano, Milly, and that was when you learned that book of old Swedish songs that your grandfather used to sing. He had a sweet tenor voice, and when he was a young man he loved to sing. I can remember hearing him singing with the sailors down in the shipyard, when I was no bigger than Stella here," pointing to Annie's younger daughter.

Milly and Stella both looked through the door into the sitting-room, where a crayon portrait of John Bergson hung on the wall. Alexandra had had it made from a little photograph, taken for his friends just before he left Sweden; a slender man of thirty-five, with soft hair curling about his high forehead, a drooping mustache, and wondering, sad eyes that looked forward into the distance, as if they already beheld the New World.

After dinner Lou and Oscar went to the orchard to pick cherries—they had neither of them had the patience to grow an orchard of their own—and Annie went down to gossip with Alexandra's kitchen girls while they washed the dishes. She could always find out more about Alexandra's domestic economy from the prattling maids than from Alexandra herself, and what she discovered she used to her own advantage with Lou. On the Divide, farmers' daughters no longer went out into service, so Alexandra got her girls from Sweden, by paying their fare over. They stayed with her until they married, and were replaced by sisters or cousins from the old country.

Alexandra took her three nieces into the flower garden. She was fond of the little girls, especially of Milly, who came to spend a week with her aunt now and then, and read aloud to her from the old books about the house, or listened to stories about the early days on the Divide. While they were walking among the flower beds, a buggy drove up the hill and stopped in front of the gate. A man got out and stood talking to the driver. The little girls were delighted at the advent of a stranger, some one from very far away, they knew by his clothes, his gloves, and the sharp, pointed cut of his dark beard. The girls fell behind their aunt and peeped out at him from among the castor beans. The stranger came up to the gate and stood holding his hat in his hand, smiling, while Alexandra advanced slowly to meet him. As she approached he spoke in a low, pleasant voice.

"Don't you know me, Alexandra? I would have known you, anywhere."

Alexandra shaded her eyes with her hand. Suddenly she took a quick step forward. "Can it be!" she exclaimed with feeling; "can it be that it is Carl Linstrum? Why, Carl, it is!" She threw out both her hands and caught his across the gate. "Sadie, Milly, run tell your father and Uncle Oscar that our old friend Carl Linstrum is here. Be quick! Why, Carl, how did it happen? I can't believe this!" Alexandra shook the tears from her eyes and laughed.

The stranger nodded to his driver, dropped his suitcase inside the fence, and opened the gate. "Then you are glad to see me, and you can put me up overnight? I could n't go through this country without stopping off to have a look at you. How little you have changed! Do you know, I was sure it would be like that. You simply could n't be different. How fine you are!" He stepped back and looked at her admiringly.

Alexandra blushed and laughed again. "But you yourself, Carl—with that beard—how could I have known you? You went away a little boy." She reached for his suitcase and when he intercepted her she threw up her hands. "You see, I give myself away. I have only women come to visit me, and I do not know how to behave. Where is your trunk?"

"It's in Hanover. I can stay only a few days. I am on my way to the coast."

They started up the path. "A few days? After all these years!" Alexandra shook her finger at him. "See this, you have walked into a trap. You do not get away so easy." She put her hand affectionately on his shoulder. "You owe me a visit for the sake of old times. Why must you go to the coast at all?"

"Oh, I must! I am a fortune hunter. From Seattle I go on to Alaska."

"Alaska?" She looked at him in astonishment. "Are you going to paint the Indians?"

"Paint?" the young man frowned. "Oh! I'm not a painter, Alexandra. I'm an engraver. I have nothing to do with painting."

"But on my parlor wall I have the paintings—"

He interrupted nervously. "Oh, water-color sketches—done for amusement. I sent them to remind you of me, not because they were good. What a wonderful place you have made of this, Alexandra." He turned and looked back at the wide, map-like prospect of field and hedge and pasture. "I would never have believed it could be done. I'm disappointed in my own eye, in my imagination."

At this moment Lou and Oscar came up the hill from the orchard. They did not quicken their pace when they saw Carl; indeed, they did not openly look in his direction. They advanced distrustfully, and as if they wished the distance were longer.

Alexandra beckoned to them. "They think I am trying to fool them. Come, boys, it's Carl Linstrum, our old Carl!"

Lou gave the visitor a quick, sidelong glance and thrust out his hand. "Glad to see you." Oscar followed with "How d' do." Carl could not tell whether their offishness came from unfriendliness or from embarrassment. He and Alexandra led the way to the porch.

"Carl," Alexandra explained, "is on his way to Seattle. He is going to Alaska."

Oscar studied the visitor's yellow shoes. "Got business there?" he asked.

Carl laughed. "Yes, very pressing business. I'm going there to get rich. Engraving's a very interesting profession, but a man never makes any money at it. So I'm going to try the gold-fields."

Alexandra felt that this was a tactful speech, and Lou looked up with some interest. "Ever done anything in that line before?"

"No, but I'm going to join a friend of mine who went out from New York and has done well. He has offered to break me in."

"Turrible cold winters, there, I hear," remarked Oscar. "I thought people went up there in the spring."

"They do. But my friend is going to spend the winter in Seattle and I am to stay with him there and learn something about prospecting before we start north next year."

Lou looked skeptical. "Let's see, how long have you been away from here?"

"Sixteen years. You ought to remember that, Lou, for you were married just after we went away."

"Going to stay with us some time?" Oscar asked.

"A few days, if Alexandra can keep me."

"I expect you'll be wanting to see your old place," Lou observed more cordially. "You won't hardly know it. But there's a few chunks of your old sod house left. Alexandra would n't never let Frank Shabata plough over it."

Annie Lee, who, ever since the visitor was announced, had been touching up her hair and settling her lace and wishing she had worn another dress, now emerged with her three daughters and introduced them. She was greatly impressed by Carl's urban appearance, and in her excitement talked very loud and threw her head about. "And you ain't married yet? At your age, now! Think of that! You'll have to wait for Milly. Yes, we've got a boy, too. The youngest. He's at home with his grandma. You must come over to see mother and hear Milly play. She's the musician of the family. She does pyrography,[2] too. That's burnt wood, you know. You wouldn't believe what she can do with her poker. Yes, she goes to school in town, and she is the youngest in her class by two years."

Milly looked uncomfortable and Carl took her hand again. He liked her creamy skin and happy, innocent eyes, and he could see that her mother's way of talking distressed her. "I'm sure she's a clever little girl," he murmured, looking at her thoughtfully. "Let me see— Ah, it's your mother that she looks like, Alexandra. Mrs. Bergson must have looked just like this when she was a little girl. Does Milly run about over the country as you and Alexandra used to, Annie?"

Milly's mother protested. "Oh, my, no! Things has changed since we was girls. Milly has it very different. We are going to rent the place and move into town as soon as the girls are old enough to go out into company. A good many are doing that here now. Lou is going into business."

Lou grinned. "That's what she says. You better go get your things on. Ivar's hitching up," he added, turning to Annie.

Young farmers seldom address their wives by name. It is always "you," or "she."

Having got his wife out of the way, Lou sat down on the step and began to whittle. "Well, what do folks in New York think of William Jennings Bryan?"[3] Lou began to bluster, as he always did when he

2. Pyrography is the art of "woodburning": creating designs and pictures on wood or leather by using a heated object, such as a poker or a wire.

3. In 1896 William Jennings Bryan (1860–1925), presidential candidate of the Democrats and Populists, antagonized Wall Street bankers and financiers by attacking the gold standard and advocating the revival of the economy through the unlimited coinage of silver (which would have made it easier for farmers to repay their debts and finance mortgages). A popular political figure in Nebraska and the West, he also ran for president in 1900 and 1908.

talked politics. "We gave Wall Street a scare in ninety-six, all right, and we're fixing another to hand them. Silver was n't the only issue," he nodded mysteriously. "There's a good many things got to be changed. The West is going to make itself heard."

Carl laughed. "But, surely, it did do that, if nothing else."

Lou's thin face reddened up to the roots of his bristly hair. "Oh, we've only begun. We're waking up to a sense of our responsibilities, out here, and we ain't afraid, neither. You fellows back there must be a tame lot. If you had any nerve you'd get together and march down to Wall Street and blow it up. Dynamite it, I mean," with a threatening nod.

He was so much in earnest that Carl scarcely knew how to answer him. "That would be a waste of powder. The same business would go on in another street. The street does n't matter. But what have you fellows out here got to kick about? You have the only safe place there is. Morgan himself[4] could n't touch you. One only has to drive through this country to see that you're all as rich as barons."

"We have a good deal more to say than we had when we were poor," said Lou threateningly. "We're getting on to a whole lot of things."

As Ivar drove a double carriage up to the gate, Annie came out in a hat that looked like the model of a battleship.[5] Carl rose and took her down to the carriage, while Lou lingered for a word with his sister.

"What do you suppose he's come for?" he asked, jerking his head toward the gate.

"Why, to pay us a visit. I've been begging him to for years."

Oscar looked at Alexandra. "He did n't let you know he was coming?"

"No. Why should he? I told him to come at any time."

Lou shrugged his shoulders. "He does n't seem to have done much for himself. Wandering around this way!"

Oscar spoke solemnly, as from the depths of a cavern. "He never was much account."

Alexandra left them and hurried down to the gate where Annie was rattling on to Carl about her new dining-room furniture. "You must bring Mr. Linstrum over real soon, only be sure to telephone me first," she called back, as Carl helped her into the carriage. Old Ivar, his white head bare, stood holding the horses. Lou came down the path and climbed into the front seat, took up the reins, and drove off without saying anything further to any one. Oscar picked

4. J. Pierpont Morgan (1837–1913), prominent New York financier and banker.
5. In the late nineteenth and early twentieth centuries, fashionable women's hats became large and elaborate, requiring wired ribbons and ornaments to increase height.

up his youngest boy and trudged off down the road, the other three trotting after him. Carl, holding the gate open for Alexandra, began to laugh. "Up and coming on the Divide, eh, Alexandra?" he cried gayly.

IV

Carl had changed, Alexandra felt, much less than one might have expected. He had not become a trim, self-satisfied city man. There was still something homely and wayward and definitely personal about him. Even his clothes, his Norfolk coat[6] and his very high collars, were a little unconventional. He seemed to shrink into himself as he used to do; to hold himself away from things, as if he were afraid of being hurt. In short, he was more self-conscious than a man of thirty-five is expected to be. He looked older than his years and not very strong. His black hair, which still hung in a triangle over his pale forehead, was thin at the crown, and there were fine, relentless lines about his eyes. His back, with its high, sharp shoulders, looked like the back of an overworked German professor off on his holiday. His face was intelligent, sensitive, unhappy.

That evening after supper, Carl and Alexandra were sitting by the clump of castor beans in the middle of the flower garden. The gravel paths glittered in the moonlight, and below them the fields lay white and still.

"Do you know, Alexandra," he was saying, "I've been thinking how strangely things work out. I've been away engraving other men's pictures, and you've stayed at home and made your own." He pointed with his cigar toward the sleeping landscape. "How in the world have you done it? How have your neighbors done it?"

"We had n't any of us much to do with it, Carl. The land did it. It had its little joke. It pretended to be poor because nobody knew how to work it right; and then, all at once, it worked itself. It woke up out of its sleep and stretched itself, and it was so big, so rich, that we suddenly found we were rich, just from sitting still. As for me, you remember when I began to buy land. For years after that I was always squeezing and borrowing until I was ashamed to show my face in the banks. And then, all at once, men began to come to me offering to lend me money—and I did n't need it! Then I went ahead and built this house. I really built it for Emil. I want you to see Emil, Carl. He is so different from the rest of us!"

"How different?"

"Oh, you'll see! I'm sure it was to have sons like Emil, and to give

6. A tweed jacket, popular in the late Victorian period, of the kind worn by the Prince of Wales for shooting in Norfolk.

them a chance, that father left the old country. It's curious, too; on the outside Emil is just like an American boy,—he graduated from the State University in June, you know,—but underneath he is more Swedish than any of us. Sometimes he is so like father that he frightens me; he is so violent in his feelings like that."

"Is he going to farm here with you?"

"He shall do whatever he wants to," Alexandra declared warmly. "He is going to have a chance, a whole chance; that's what I've worked for. Sometimes he talks about studying law, and sometimes, just lately, he's been talking about going out into the sand hills and taking up more land. He has his sad times, like father. But I hope he won't do that. We have land enough, at last!" Alexandra laughed.

"How about Lou and Oscar? They've done well, have n't they?"

"Yes, very well; but they are different, and now that they have farms of their own I do not see so much of them. We divided the land equally when Lou married. They have their own way of doing things, and they do not altogether like my way, I am afraid. Perhaps they think me too independent. But I have had to think for myself a good many years and am not likely to change. On the whole, though, we take as much comfort in each other as most brothers and sisters do. And I am very fond of Lou's oldest daughter."

"I think I liked the old Lou and Oscar better, and they probably feel the same about me. I even, if you can keep a secret,"—Carl leaned forward and touched her arm, smiling,—"I even think I liked the old country better. This is all very splendid in its way, but there was something about this country when it was a wild old beast that has haunted me all these years. Now, when I come back to all this milk and honey, I feel like the old German song, 'Wo bist du, wo bist du, mein geliebtest Land?'[7]—Do you ever feel like that, I wonder?"

"Yes, sometimes, when I think about father and mother and those who are gone; so many of our old neighbors." Alexandra paused and looked up thoughtfully at the stars. "We can remember the graveyard when it was wild prairie, Carl, and now—"

"And now the old story has begun to write itself over there," said Carl softly. "Is n't it queer: there are only two or three human stories, and they go on repeating themselves as fiercely as if they had never happened before; like the larks in this country, that have been singing the same five notes over for thousands of years."

"Oh, yes! The young people, they live so hard. And yet I sometimes envy them. There is my little neighbor, now; the people who

7. "Where are you, where are you, my dear land?" The lyrics are from "Der Wanderer" (The Wanderer), a *lied* composed by Franz Shubert with words from a poem by Georg Phillip Schmidt.

bought your old place. I would n't have sold it to any one else, but I was always fond of that girl. You must remember her, little Marie Tovesky, from Omaha, who used to visit here? When she was eighteen she ran away from the convent school and got married, crazy child! She came out here a bride, with her father and husband. He had nothing, and the old man was willing to buy them a place and set them up. Your farm took her fancy, and I was glad to have her so near me. I've never been sorry, either. I even try to get along with Frank on her account."

"Is Frank her husband?"

"Yes. He's one of these wild fellows. Most Bohemians are good-natured, but Frank thinks we don't appreciate him here, I guess. He's jealous about everything, his farm and his horses and his pretty wife. Everybody likes her, just the same as when she was little. Sometimes I go up to the Catholic church with Emil, and it's funny to see Marie standing there laughing and shaking hands with people, looking so excited and gay, with Frank sulking behind her as if he could eat everybody alive. Frank's not a bad neighbor, but to get on with him you've got to make a fuss over him and act as if you thought he was a very important person all the time, and different from other people. I find it hard to keep that up from one year's end to another."

"I should n't think you'd be very successful at that kind of thing, Alexandra." Carl seemed to find the idea amusing.

"Well," said Alexandra firmly, "I do the best I can, on Marie's account. She has it hard enough, anyway. She's too young and pretty for this sort of life. We're all ever so much older and slower. But she's the kind that won't be downed easily. She'll work all day and go to a Bohemian wedding and dance all night, and drive the hay wagon for a cross man next morning. I could stay by a job, but I never had the go in me that she has, when I was going my best. I'll have to take you over to see her to-morrow."

Carl dropped the end of his cigar softly among the castor beans and sighed. "Yes, I suppose I must see the old place. I'm cowardly about things that remind me of myself. It took courage to come at all, Alexandra. I would n't have, if I had n't wanted to see you very, very much."

Alexandra looked at him with her calm, deliberate eyes. "Why do you dread things like that, Carl?" she asked earnestly. "Why are you dissatisfied with yourself?"

Her visitor winced. "How direct you are, Alexandra! Just like you used to be. Do I give myself away so quickly? Well, you see, for one thing, there's nothing to look forward to in my profession. Wood-engraving is the only thing I care about, and that had gone out before I began. Everything's cheap metal work nowadays, touching up miserable photographs, forcing up poor drawings, and spoiling good ones. I'm absolutely sick of it all." Carl frowned. "Alexandra, all the way out from New York I've been planning how I could deceive you and make you think me a very enviable fellow, and here I am telling you the truth the first night. I waste a lot of time pretending to people, and the joke of it is, I don't think I ever deceive any one. There are too many of my kind; people know us on sight."

Carl paused. Alexandra pushed her hair back from her brow with a puzzled, thoughtful gesture. "You see," he went on calmly, "measured by your standards here, I'm a failure. I couldn't buy even one of your cornfields. I've enjoyed a great many things, but I've got nothing to show for it all."

"But you show for it yourself, Carl. I'd rather have had your freedom than my land."

Carl shook his head mournfully. "Freedom so often means that one is n't needed anywhere. Here you are an individual, you have a background of your own, you would be missed. But off there in the cities there are thousands of rolling stones like me. We are all alike; we have no ties, we know nobody, we own nothing. When one of us dies, they scarcely know where to bury him. Our landlady and the delicatessen man are our mourners, and we leave nothing behind us but a frock-coat and a fiddle, or an easel, or a typewriter, or whatever tool we got our living by. All we have ever managed to do is to pay our rent, the exorbitant rent that one has to pay for a few square feet of space near the heart of things. We have no house, no place, no people of our own. We live in the streets, in the parks, in the theatres. We sit in restaurants and concert halls and look about at the hundreds of our own kind and shudder."

Alexandra was silent. She sat looking at the silver spot the moon made on the surface of the pond down in the pasture. He knew that she understood what he meant. At last she said slowly, "And yet I would rather have Emil grow up like that than like his two brothers. We pay a high rent, too, though we pay differently. We grow hard and heavy here. We don't move lightly and easily as you do, and our minds get stiff. If the world were no wider than my cornfields, if there were not something beside this, I wouldn't feel that it was much worth while to work. No, I would rather have Emil like you than like them. I felt that as soon as you came."

"I wonder why you feel like that?" Carl mused.

"I don't know. Perhaps I am like Carrie Jensen, the sister of one of my hired men. She had never been out of the cornfields, and a few years ago she got despondent and said life was just the same thing over and over, and she did n't see the use of it. After she had tried to kill herself once or twice, her folks got worried and sent her over to Iowa to visit some relations. Ever since she's come back she's been perfectly cheerful, and she says she's contented to live and work in a world that's so big and interesting. She said that anything as big as the bridges over the Platte and the Missouri reconciled her. And it's what goes on in the world that reconciles me."

V

Alexandra did not find time to go to her neighbor's the next day, nor the next. It was a busy season on the farm, with the corn-plowing going on, and even Emil was in the field with a team and cultivator. Carl went about over the farms with Alexandra in the morning, and in the afternoon and evening they found a great deal to talk about. Emil, for all his track practice, did not stand up under farmwork very well, and by night he was too tired to talk or even to practise on his cornet.

On Wednesday morning Carl got up before it was light, and stole downstairs and out of the kitchen door just as old Ivar was making his morning ablutions at the pump. Carl nodded to him and hurried up the draw, past the garden, and into the pasture where the milking cows used to be kept.

The dawn in the east looked like the light from some great fire that was burning under the edge of the world. The color was reflected in the globules of dew that sheathed the short gray pasture grass. Carl walked rapidly until he came to the crest of the second hill, where the Bergson pasture joined the one that had belonged to his father. There he sat down and waited for the sun to rise. It was just there that he and Alexandra used to do their milking together, he on his side of the fence, she on hers. He could remember exactly how she looked when she came over the close-cropped grass, her skirts pinned up, her head bare, a bright tin pail in either hand, and the milky light of the early morning all about her. Even as a boy he used to feel, when he saw her coming with her free step, her upright head and calm shoulders, that she looked as if she had walked straight out of the morning itself. Since then, when he had happened to see the sun come up in the country or on the water, he had often remembered the young Swedish girl and her milking pails.

Carl sat musing until the sun leaped above the prairie, and in the grass about him all the small creatures of day began to tune their tiny instruments. Birds and insects without number began to chirp, to twitter, to snap and whistle, to make all manner of fresh shrill noises. The pasture was flooded with light; every clump of ironweed and snow-on-the-mountain threw a long shadow, and the golden light seemed to be rippling through the curly grass like the tide racing in.

He crossed the fence into the pasture that was now the Shabatas' and continued his walk toward the pond. He had not gone far, however, when he discovered that he was not the only person abroad. In the draw below, his gun in his hands, was Emil, advancing cautiously, with a young woman beside him. They were moving softly, keeping close together, and Carl knew that they expected to find ducks on the pond. At the moment when they came in sight of the bright spot of water, he heard a whirr of wings and the ducks shot up into the air. There was a sharp crack from the gun, and five of the birds fell to the ground. Emil and his companion laughed delightedly, and Emil ran to pick them up. When he came back, dangling the ducks by their feet, Marie held her apron and he dropped them into it. As she stood looking down at them, her face changed. She took up one of the birds, a rumpled ball of feathers with the blood dripping slowly from its mouth, and looked at the live color that still burned on its plumage.

As she let it fall, she cried in distress, "Oh, Emil, why did you?"

"I like that!" the boy exclaimed indignantly. "Why, Marie, you asked me to come yourself."

"Yes, yes, I know," she said tearfully, "but I did n't think. I hate to see them when they are first shot. They were having such a good time, and we've spoiled it all for them."

Emil gave a rather sore laugh. "I should say we had! I'm not going hunting with you any more. You're as bad as Ivar. Here, let me take them." He snatched the ducks out of her apron.

"Don't be cross, Emil. Only—Ivar's right about wild things. They're too happy to kill. You can tell just how they felt when they flew up. They were scared, but they didn't really think anything could hurt them. No, we won't do that any more."

"All right," Emil assented. "I'm sorry I made you feel bad." As he looked down into her tearful eyes, there was a curious, sharp young bitterness in his own.

Carl watched them as they moved slowly down the draw. They had not seen him at all. He had not overheard much of their dialogue, but he felt the import of it. It made him, somehow, unreasonably mournful to find two young things abroad in the pasture in the early morning. He decided that he needed his breakfast.

VI

At dinner that day Alexandra said she thought they must really manage to go over to the Shabatas' that afternoon. "It's not often I let three days go by without seeing Marie. She will think I have forsaken her, now that my old friend has come back."

After the men had gone back to work, Alexandra put on a white dress and her sun-hat, and she and Carl set forth across the fields. "You see we have kept up the old path, Carl. It has been so nice for me to feel that there was a friend at the other end of it again."

Carl smiled a little ruefully. "All the same, I hope it has n't been *quite* the same."

Alexandra looked at him with surprise. "Why, no, of course not. Not the same. She could not very well take your place, if that's what you mean. I'm friendly with all my neighbors, I hope. But Marie is really a companion, some one I can talk to quite frankly. You would n't want me to be more lonely than I have been, would you?"

Carl laughed and pushed back the triangular lock of hair with the edge of his hat. "Of course I don't. I ought to be thankful that this path has n't been worn by—well, by friends with more pressing errands than your little Bohemian is likely to have." He paused to give Alexandra his hand as she stepped over the stile. "Are you the least bit disappointed in our coming together again?" he asked abruptly. "Is it the way you hoped it would be?"

Alexandra smiled at this. "Only better. When I've thought about your coming, I've sometimes been a little afraid of it. You have lived where things move so fast, and everything is slow here; the people slowest of all. Our lives are like the years, all made up of weather and crops and cows. How you hated cows!" She shook her head and laughed to herself.

"I did n't when we milked together. I walked up to the pasture corners this morning. I wonder whether I shall ever be able to tell you all that I was thinking about up there. It's a strange thing, Alexandra; I find it easy to be frank with you about everything under the sun except—yourself!"

"You are afraid of hurting my feelings, perhaps." Alexandra looked at him thoughtfully.

"No, I'm afraid of giving you a shock. You've seen yourself for so long in the dull minds of the people about you, that if I were to tell you how you seem to me, it would startle you. But you must see that you astonish me. You must feel when people admire you."

Alexandra blushed and laughed with some confusion. "I felt that you were pleased with me, if you mean that."

"And you've felt when other people were pleased with you?" he insisted.

"Well, sometimes. The men in town, at the banks and the county offices, seem glad to see me. I think, myself, it is more pleasant to do business with people who are clean and healthy-looking," she admitted blandly.

Carl gave a little chuckle as he opened the Shabatas' gate for her. "Oh, do you?" he asked dryly.

There was no sign of life about the Shabatas' house except a big yellow cat, sunning itself on the kitchen doorstep.

Alexandra took the path that led to the orchard. "She often sits there and sews. I didn't telephone her we were coming, because I did n't want her to go to work and bake cake and freeze ice-cream. She'll always make a party if you give her the least excuse. Do you recognize the apple trees, Carl?"

Linstrum looked about him. "I wish I had a dollar for every bucket of water I've carried for those trees. Poor father, he was an easy man, but he was perfectly merciless when it came to watering the orchard."

"That's one thing I like about Germans; they make an orchard grow if they can't make anything else. I'm so glad these trees belong to some one who takes comfort in them. When I rented this place, the tenants never kept the orchard up, and Emil and I used to come over and take care of it ourselves. It needs mowing now. There she is, down in the corner. Ma-ria-a-a!" she called.

A recumbent figure started up from the grass and came running toward them through the flickering screen of light and shade.

"Look at her! Is n't she like a little brown rabbit?" Alexandra laughed.

Marie ran up panting and threw her arms about Alexandra. "Oh, I had begun to think you were not coming at all, maybe. I knew you were so busy. Yes, Emil told me about Mr. Linstrum being here. Won't you come up to the house?"

"Why not sit down there in your corner? Carl wants to see the orchard. He kept all these trees alive for years, watering them with his own back."

Marie turned to Carl. "Then I'm thankful to you, Mr. Linstrum. We'd never have bought the place if it had n't been for this orchard, and then I would n't have had Alexandra, either." She gave Alexandra's arm a little squeeze as she walked beside her. "How nice your dress smells, Alexandra; you put rosemary leaves in your chest, like I told you."

She led them to the northwest corner of the orchard, sheltered on one side by a thick mulberry hedge and bordered on the other by a wheatfield, just beginning to yellow. In this corner the ground dipped a little, and the bluegrass, which the weeds had driven out in the upper part of the orchard, grew thick and luxuriant. Wild roses were flaming in the tufts of bunchgrass along the fence. Under a white mulberry tree there was an old wagon-seat. Beside it lay a book and a work-basket.

"You must have the seat, Alexandra. The grass would stain your dress," the hostess insisted. She dropped down on the ground at Alexandra's side and tucked her feet under her. Carl sat at a little distance from the two women, his back to the wheatfield, and watched them. Alexandra took off her shade-hat and threw it on the ground. Marie picked it up and played with the white ribbons, twisting them about her brown fingers as she talked. They made a pretty picture in the strong sunlight, the leafy pattern surrounding them like a net; the Swedish woman so white and gold, kindly and amused, but armored in calm, and the alert brown one, her full lips parted, points of yellow light dancing in her eyes as she laughed and chattered. Carl had never forgotten little Marie Tovesky's eyes, and he was glad to have an opportunity to study them. The brown iris, he found, was curiously slashed with yellow, the color of sunflower honey, or of old amber. In each eye one of these streaks must have been larger than the others, for the effect was that of two dancing points of light, two little yellow bubbles, such as rise in a glass of champagne. Sometimes they seemed like the sparks from a forge. She seemed so easily excited, to kindle with a fierce little flame if one but breathed upon her. "What a waste," Carl reflected. "She ought to be doing all that for a sweetheart. How awkwardly things come about!"

It was not very long before Marie sprang up out of the grass again. "Wait a moment. I want to show you something." She ran away and disappeared behind the low-growing apple trees.

"What a charming creature," Carl murmured. "I don't wonder that her husband is jealous. But can't she walk? does she always run?"

Alexandra nodded. "Always. I don't see many people, but I don't believe there are many like her, anywhere."

Marie came back with a branch she had broken from an apricot tree, laden with pale-yellow, pink-cheeked fruit. She dropped it beside Carl. "Did you plant those, too? They are such beautiful little trees."

Carl fingered the blue-green leaves, porous little blotting-paper and shaped like birch leaves, hung on waxen red stems. "Yes, I think I did. Are these the circus trees, Alexandra?"

"Shall I tell her about them?" Alexandra asked. "Sit down like a good girl, Marie, and don't ruin my poor hat, and I'll tell you a story. A long time ago, when Carl and I were, say, sixteen and twelve, a circus came to Hanover and we went to town in our wagon, with Lou and Oscar, to see the parade. We had n't money enough to go to the circus. We followed the parade out to the circus grounds and hung around until the show began and the crowd went inside the tent. Then Lou was afraid we looked foolish standing outside in the pasture, so we went back to Hanover feeling very sad. There was a man in the streets selling apricots, and we had never seen any before. He had driven down from somewhere up in the French country, and he was selling them twenty-five cents a peck. We had a little money our fathers had given us for candy, and I bought two pecks and Carl bought one. They cheered us a good deal, and we saved all the seeds and planted them. Up to the time Carl went away, they had n't borne at all."

"And now he's come back to eat them," cried Marie, nodding at Carl. "That *is* a good story. I can remember you a little, Mr. Linstrum. I used to see you in Hanover sometimes, when Uncle Joe took me to town. I remember you because you were always buying pencils and tubes of paint at the drug store. Once, when my uncle left me at the store, you drew a lot of little birds and flowers for me on a piece of wrapping-paper. I kept them for a long while. I thought you were very romantic because you could draw and had such black eyes."

Carl smiled. "Yes, I remember that time. Your uncle bought you some kind of a mechanical toy, a Turkish lady sitting on an ottoman and smoking a hookah, was n't it? And she turned her head backwards and forwards."

"Oh, yes! Was n't she splendid! I knew well enough I ought not to tell Uncle Joe I wanted it, for he had just come back from the saloon and was feeling good. You remember how he laughed? She tickled him, too. But when we got home, my aunt scolded him for buying toys when she needed so many things. We wound our lady up every night, and when she began to move her head my aunt used to laugh as hard as any of us. It was a music-box, you know, and the Turkish lady played a tune while she smoked. That was how she made you feel so jolly. As I remember her, she was lovely, and had a gold crescent on her turban."

Half an hour later, as they were leaving the house, Carl and Alexandra were met in the path by a strapping fellow in overalls and a blue shirt. He was breathing hard, as if he had been running, and was muttering to himself.

Marie ran forward, and, taking him by the arm, gave him a little push toward her guests. "Frank, this is Mr. Linstrum."

Frank took off his broad straw hat and nodded to Alexandra. When he spoke to Carl, he showed a fine set of white teeth. He was burned a dull red down to his neckband, and there was a heavy three-days' stubble on his face. Even in his agitation he was handsome, but he looked a rash and violent man.

Barely saluting the callers, he turned at once to his wife and began, in an outraged tone, "I have to leave my team to drive the old woman Hiller's hogs out-a my wheat. I go to take dat old woman to de court if she ain't careful, I tell you!"

His wife spoke soothingly. "But, Frank, she has only her lame boy to help her. She does the best she can."

Alexandra looked at the excited man and offered a suggestion. "Why don't you go over there some afternoon and hog-tight her fences? You'd save time for yourself in the end."

Frank's neck stiffened. "Not-a-much, I won't. I keep my hogs home. Other peoples can do like me. See? If that Louis can mend shoes, he can mend fence."

"Maybe," said Alexandra placidly; "but I've found it sometimes pays to mend other people's fences. Good-bye, Marie. Come to see me soon."

Alexandra walked firmly down the path and Carl followed her.

Frank went into the house and threw himself on the sofa, his face to the wall, his clenched fist on his hip. Marie, having seen her guests off, came in and put her hand coaxingly on his shoulder.

"Poor Frank! You've run until you've made your head ache, now haven't you? Let me make you some coffee."

"What else am I to do?" he cried hotly in Bohemian. "Am I to let any old woman's hogs root up my wheat? Is that what I work myself to death for?"

"Don't worry about it, Frank. I'll speak to Mrs. Hiller again. But, really, she almost cried last time they got out, she was so sorry."

Frank bounced over on his other side. "That's it; you always side with them against me. They all know it. Anybody here feels free to borrow the mower and break it, or turn their hogs in on me. They know you won't care!"

Marie hurried away to make his coffee. When she came back, he was fast asleep. She sat down and looked at him for a long while, very thoughtfully. When the kitchen clock struck six she went out to get supper, closing the door gently behind her. She was always sorry for Frank when he worked himself into one of these rages, and she was sorry to have him rough and quarrelsome with his neighbors. She was perfectly aware that the neighbors had a good deal to put up with, and that they bore with Frank for her sake.

VII

Marie's father, Albert Tovesky, was one of the more intelligent Bohemians who came West in the early seventies. He settled in Omaha and became a leader and adviser among his people there. Marie was his youngest child, by a second wife, and was the apple of his eye. She was barely sixteen, and was in the graduating class of the Omaha High School, when Frank Shabata arrived from the old country and set all the Bohemian girls in a flutter. He was easily the buck of the beer-gardens, and on Sunday he was a sight to see, with his silk hat and tucked shirt and blue frock-coat, wearing gloves and carrying a little wisp of a yellow cane. He was tall and fair, with splendid teeth and close-cropped yellow curls, and he wore a slightly disdainful expression, proper for a young man with high connections, whose mother had a big farm in the Elbe valley. There was often an interesting discontent in his blue eyes, and every Bohemian girl he met imagined herself the cause of that unsatisfied expression. He had a way of drawing out his cambric handkerchief slowly, by one corner, from his breast-pocket, that was melancholy and romantic in the extreme. He took a little flight with each of the more eligible Bohemian girls, but it was when he was with little Marie Tovesky that he drew his handkerchief out most slowly, and, after he had lit a fresh cigar, dropped the match most despairingly. Any one could see, with half an eye, that his proud heart was bleeding for somebody.

One Sunday, late in the summer after Marie's graduation, she met Frank at a Bohemian picnic down the river and went rowing with him all the afternoon. When she got home that evening she went straight to her father's room and told him that she was engaged to Shabata. Old Tovesky was having a comfortable pipe before he went to bed. When he heard his daughter's announcement, he first prudently corked his beer bottle and then leaped to his feet and had a turn of temper. He characterized Frank Shabata by a Bohemian expression which is the equivalent of stuffed shirt.

"Why don't he go to work like the rest of us did? His farm in the Elbe valley, indeed! Ain't he got plenty brothers and sisters? It's his mother's farm, and why don't he stay at home and help her? Have n't I seen his mother out in the morning at five o'clock with her ladle and her big bucket on wheels, putting liquid manure on the cabbages? Don't I know the look of old Eva Shabata's hands? Like an old horse's hoofs they are—and this fellow wearing gloves and rings! Engaged, indeed! You are n't fit to be out of school, and that's what's the matter with you. I will send you off to the Sisters of the Sacred Heart in St. Louis, and they will teach you some sense, *I* guess!"

Accordingly, the very next week, Albert Tovesky took his daughter, pale and tearful, down the river to the convent. But the way to make Frank want anything was to tell him he couldn't have it. He managed to have an interview with Marie before she went away, and whereas he had been only half in love with her before, he now persuaded himself that he would not stop at anything. Marie took with her to the convent, under the canvas lining of her trunk, the results of a laborious and satisfying morning on Frank's part; no less than a dozen photographs of himself, taken in a dozen different love-lorn attitudes. There was a little round photograph for her watch-case, photographs for her wall and dresser, and even long narrow ones to be used as bookmarks. More than once the handsome gentleman was torn to pieces before the French class by an indignant nun.

Marie pined in the convent for a year, until her eighteenth birthday was passed. Then she met Frank Shabata in the Union Station in St. Louis and ran away with him. Old Tovesky forgave his daughter because there was nothing else to do, and bought her a farm in the country that she had loved so well as a child. Since then her story had been a part of the history of the Divide. She and Frank had been living there for five years when Carl Linstrum came back to pay his long deferred visit to Alexandra. Frank had, on the whole, done better than one might have expected. He had flung himself at the soil with savage energy. Once a year he went to Hastings or to Omaha, on a spree. He stayed away for a week or two, and then came home and worked like a demon. He did work; if he felt sorry for himself, that was his own affair.

VIII

On the evening of the day of Alexandra's call at the Shabatas', a heavy rain set in. Frank sat up until a late hour reading the Sunday newspapers. One of the Goulds[8] was getting a divorce, and Frank took it as a personal affront. In printing the story of the young man's marital troubles, the knowing editor gave a sufficiently colored account of his career, stating the amount of his income and the manner in which he was supposed to spend it. Frank read English slowly, and the more he read about this divorce case, the angrier he grew. At last he threw down the page with a snort. He turned to his farm-hand who was reading the other half of the paper.

"By God! if I have that young feller in de hayfield once, I show him someting. Listen here what he do wit his money." And Frank began the catalogue of the young man's reputed extravagances.

Marie sighed. She thought it hard that the Goulds, for whom she had nothing but good will, should make her so much trouble. She hated to see the Sunday newspapers come into the house. Frank was always reading about the doings of rich people and feeling outraged. He had an inexhaustible stock of stories about their crimes and follies, how they bribed the courts and shot down their butlers with impunity whenever they chose. Frank and Lou Bergson had very similar ideas, and they were two of the political agitators of the county.

The next morning broke clear and brilliant, but Frank said the ground was too wet to plough, so he took the cart and drove over to

8. One of the sons of financier and railroad tycoon Jay Gould (1836–1892).

Sainte-Agnes to spend the day at Moses Marcel's saloon. After he was gone, Marie went out to the back porch to begin her butter-making. A brisk wind had come up and was driving puffy white clouds across the sky. The orchard was sparkling and rippling in the sun. Marie stood looking toward it wistfully, her hand on the lid of the churn, when she heard a sharp ring in the air, the merry sound of the whetstone on the scythe. That invitation decided her. She ran into the house, put on a short skirt and a pair of her husband's boots, caught up a tin pail and started for the orchard. Emil had already begun work and was mowing vigorously. When he saw her coming, he stopped and wiped his brow. His yellow canvas leggings and khaki trousers were splashed to the knees.

"Don't let me disturb you, Emil. I'm going to pick cherries. Is n't everything beautiful after the rain? Oh, but I'm glad to get this place mowed! When I heard it raining in the night, I thought maybe you would come and do it for me to-day. The wind wakened me. Did n't it blow dreadfully? Just smell the wild roses! They are always so spicy after a rain. We never had so many of them in here before. I suppose it's the wet season. Will you have to cut them, too?"

"If I cut the grass, I will," Emil said teasingly. "What's the matter with you? What makes you so flighty?"

"Am I flighty? I suppose that's the wet season, too, then. It's exciting to see everything growing so fast,—and to get the grass cut! Please leave the roses till last, if you must cut them. Oh, I don't mean all of them, I mean that low place down by my tree, where there are so many. Are n't you splashed! Look at the spider-webs all over the grass. Good-bye. I'll call you if I see a snake."

She tripped away and Emil stood looking after her. In a few moments he heard the cherries dropping smartly into the pail, and he began to swing his scythe with that long, even stroke that few American boys ever learn. Marie picked cherries and sang softly to herself, stripping one glittering branch after another, shivering when she caught a shower of raindrops on her neck and hair. And Emil mowed his way slowly down toward the cherry trees.

That summer the rains had been so many and opportune that it was almost more than Shabata and his man could do to keep up with the corn; the orchard was a neglected wilderness. All sorts of weeds and herbs and flowers had grown up there; splotches of wild larkspur, pale green-and-white spikes of hoarhound, plantations of wild cotton, tangles of foxtail and wild wheat. South of the apricot trees, cornering on the wheatfield, was Frank's alfalfa, where myriads of white and yellow butterflies were always fluttering above the purple blossoms. When Emil reached the lower corner by the hedge, Marie was sitting under her white mulberry tree, the pailful of cherries beside her, looking off at the gentle, tireless swelling of the wheat.

"Emil," she said suddenly—he was mowing quietly about under the tree so as not to disturb her—"what religion did the Swedes have away back, before they were Christians?"

Emil paused and straightened his back. "I don't know. About like the Germans', was n't it?"

Marie went on as if she had not heard him. "The Bohemians, you know, were tree worshipers before the missionaries came. Father says the people in the mountains still do queer things, sometimes,—they believe that trees bring good or bad luck."

Emil looked superior. "Do they? Well, which are the lucky trees? I'd like to know."

"I don't know all of them, but I know lindens are. The old people in the mountains plant lindens to purify the forest, and to do away with the spells that come from the old trees they say have lasted from heathen times. I'm a good Catholic, but I think I could get along with caring for trees, if I had n't anything else."

"That's a poor saying," said Emil, stooping over to wipe his hands in the wet grass.

"Why is it? If I feel that way, I feel that way. I like trees because they seem more resigned to the way they have to live than other things do. I feel as if this tree knows everything I ever think of when I sit here. When I come back to it, I never have to remind it of anything; I begin just where I left off."

Emil had nothing to say to this. He reached up among the branches and began to pick the sweet, insipid fruit,—long ivory-colored berries, tipped with faint pink, like white coral, that fall to the ground unheeded all summer through. He dropped a handful into her lap.

"Do you like Mr. Linstrum?" Marie asked suddenly.

"Yes. Don't you?"

"Oh, ever so much; only he seems kind of staid and school-teachery. But, of course, he is older than Frank, even. I'm sure I don't want to live to be more than thirty, do you? Do you think Alexandra likes him very much?"

"I suppose so. They were old friends."

"Oh, Emil, you know what I mean!" Marie tossed her head impatiently. "Does she really care about him? When she used to tell me about him, I always wondered whether she was n't a little in love with him."

"Who, Alexandra?" Emil laughed and thrust his hands into his trousers pockets. "Alexandra's never been in love, you crazy!" He laughed again. "She would n't know how to go about it. The idea!"

Marie shrugged her shoulders. "Oh, you don't know Alexandra as well as you think you do! If you had any eyes, you would see that she is very fond of him. It would serve you all right if she walked off with Carl. I like him because he appreciates her more than you do."

Emil frowned. "What are you talking about, Marie? Alexandra's all right. She and I have always been good friends. What more do you want? I like to talk to Carl about New York and what a fellow can do there."

"Oh, Emil! Surely you are not thinking of going off there?"

"Why not? I must go somewhere, must n't I?" The young man took up his scythe and leaned on it. "Would you rather I went off in the sand hills and lived like Ivar?"

Marie's face fell under his brooding gaze. She looked down at his wet leggings. "I'm sure Alexandra hopes you will stay on here," she murmured.

"Then Alexandra will be disappointed," the young man said roughly. "What do I want to hang around here for? Alexandra can run the farm all right, without me. I don't want to stand around and look on. I want to be doing something on my own account."

"That's so," Marie sighed. "There are so many, many things you can do. Almost anything you choose."

"And there are so many, many things I can't do." Emil echoed her tone sarcastically. "Sometimes I don't want to do anything at all, and sometimes I want to pull the four corners of the Divide together,"—he threw out his arm and brought it back with a jerk,—"so, like a table-cloth. I get tired of seeing men and horses going up and down, up and down."

Marie looked up at his defiant figure and her face clouded. "I wish you were n't so restless, and did n't get so worked up over things," she said sadly.

"Thank you," he returned shortly.

She sighed despondently. "Everything I say makes you cross, don't it? And you never used to be cross to me."

Emil took a step nearer and stood frowning down at her bent head. He stood in an attitude of self-defense, his feet well apart, his hands clenched and drawn up at his sides, so that the cords stood out on his bare arms. "I can't play with you like a little boy any more," he said slowly. "That's what you miss, Marie. You'll have to get some other little boy to play with." He stopped and took a deep breath. Then he went on in a low tone, so intense that it was almost threatening: "Sometimes you seem to understand perfectly, and then sometimes you pretend you don't. You don't help things any by pretending. It's then that I want to pull the corners of the Divide together. If you *won't* understand, you know, I could make you!"

Marie clasped her hands and started up from her seat. She had grown very pale and her eyes were shining with excitement and distress. "But, Emil, if I understand, then all our good times are over, we can never do nice things together any more. We shall have to behave like Mr. Linstrum. And, anyhow, there's nothing to understand!" She struck the ground with her little foot fiercely. "That won't last. It will go away, and things will be just as they used to. I wish you were a Catholic. The Church helps people, indeed it does. I pray for you, but that's not the same as if you prayed yourself."

She spoke rapidly and pleadingly, looked entreatingly into his face. Emil stood defiant, gazing down at her.

"I can't pray to have the things I want," he said slowly, "and I won't pray not to have them, not if I'm damned for it."

Marie turned away, wringing her hands. "Oh, Emil, you won't try! Then all our good times are over."

"Yes; over. I never expect to have any more."

Emil gripped the hand-holds of his scythe and began to mow. Marie took up her cherries and went slowly toward the house, crying bitterly.

IX

On Sunday afternoon, a month after Carl Linstrum's arrival, he rode with Emil up into the French country to attend a Catholic fair. He sat for most of the afternoon in the basement of the church, where the fair was held, talking to Marie Shabata, or strolled about the gravel terrace, thrown up on the hillside in front of the basement doors, where the French boys were jumping and wrestling and throwing the discus. Some of the boys were in their white baseball suits; they had just come up from a Sunday practice game down in the ball-grounds. Amédée, the newly married, Emil's best friend, was their pitcher, renowned among the country towns for his dash and skill. Amédée was a little fellow, a year younger than Emil and much more boyish in appearance; very lithe and active and neatly made, with a clear brown and white skin, and flashing white teeth. The Sainte-Agnes boys were to play the Hastings nine in a fortnight, and Amédée's lightning balls were the hope of his team. The little Frenchman seemed to get every ounce there was in him behind the ball as it left his hand.

"You'd have made the battery at the University for sure, 'Médée," Emil said as they were walking from the ballgrounds back to the church on the hill. "You're pitching better than you did in the spring."

Amédée grinned. "Sure! A married man don't lose his head no more." He slapped Emil on the back as he caught step with him. "Oh, Emil, you wanna get married right off quick! It's the greatest thing ever!"

Emil laughed. "How am I going to get married without any girl?"

Amédée took his arm. "Pooh! There are plenty girls will have you. You wanna get some nice French girl, now. She treat you well; always be jolly. See,"—he began checking off on his fingers,—"there is Sévérine, and Alphosen, and Joséphine, and Hectorine, and Louise, and Malvina—why, I could love any of them girls! Why don't you get after them? Are you stuck up, Emil, or is anything the matter with you? I never did know a boy twenty-two years old before that did n't have no girl. You wanna be a priest, maybe? Not-a for me!" Amédée swaggered. "I bring many good Catholics into this world, I hope, and that's a way I help the Church."

Emil looked down and patted him on the shoulder. "Now you're windy, 'Médée. You Frenchies like to brag."

But Amédée had the zeal of the newly married, and he was not to be lightly shaken off. "Honest and true, Emil, don't you want *any* girl? Maybe there's some young lady in Lincoln, now, very grand,"—Amédée waved his hand languidly before his face to denote the fan of heartless beauty,—"and you lost your heart up there. Is that it?"

"Maybe," said Emil.

But Amédée saw no appropriate glow in his friend's face. "Bah!" he exclaimed in disgust. "I tell all the French girls to keep 'way from you. You gotta rock in there," thumping Emil on the ribs.

When they reached the terrace at the side of the church, Amédée, who was excited by his success on the ball-grounds, challenged Emil to a jumping-match, though he knew he would be beaten. They belted themselves up, and Raoul Marcel, the choir tenor and Father Duchesne's pet, and Jean Bordelau, held the string over which they vaulted. All the French boys stood round, cheering and humping themselves up when Emil or Amédée went over the wire, as if they were helping in the lift. Emil stopped at five-feet-five, declaring that he would spoil his appetite for supper if he jumped any more.

Angélique, Amédée's pretty bride, as blonde and fair as her name, who had come out to watch the match, tossed her head at Emil and said:—

" 'Médée could jump much higher than you if he were as tall. And anyhow, he is much more graceful. He goes over like a bird, and you have to hump yourself all up."

"Oh, I do, do I?" Emil caught her and kissed her saucy mouth squarely, while she laughed and struggled and called, " 'Médée! 'Médée!"

"There, you see your 'Médée is n't even big enough to get you away from me. I could run away with you right now and he could only sit down and cry about it. I'll show you whether I have to hump myself!" Laughing and panting, he picked Angélique up in his arms and began running about the rectangle with her. Not until he saw Marie Shabata's tiger eyes flashing from the gloom of the basement doorway did he hand the disheveled bride over to her husband. "There, go to your graceful; I have n't the heart to take you away from him."

Angélique clung to her husband and made faces at Emil over the white shoulder of Amédée's ball-shirt. Emil was greatly amused at her air of proprietorship and at Amédée's shameless submission to it. He was delighted with his friend's good fortune. He liked to see and to think about Amédée's sunny, natural, happy love.

He and Amédée had ridden and wrestled and larked together since they were lads of twelve. On Sundays and holidays they were always arm in arm. It seemed strange that now he should have to hide the thing that Amédée was so proud of, that the feeling which gave one of them such happiness should bring the other such despair. It was like that when Alexandra tested her seed-corn in the spring, he mused. From two ears that had grown side by side, the grains of one shot up joyfully into the light, projecting themselves into the future, and the grains from the other lay still in the earth and rotted; and nobody knew why.

X

While Emil and Carl were amusing themselves at the fair, Alexandra was at home, busy with her account-books, which had been neglected of late. She was almost through with her figures when she heard a cart drive up to the gate, and looking out of the window she saw her two older brothers. They had seemed to avoid her ever since Carl Linstrum's arrival, four weeks ago that day, and she hurried to the door to welcome them. She saw at once that they had come with some very definite purpose. They followed her stiffly into the sitting-room. Oscar sat down, but Lou walked over to the window and remained standing, his hands behind him.

"You are by yourself?" he asked, looking toward the doorway into the parlor.

"Yes. Carl and Emil went up to the Catholic fair."

For a few moments neither of the men spoke.

Then Lou came out sharply. "How soon does he intend to go away from here?"

"I don't know, Lou. Not for some time, I hope." Alexandra spoke in an even, quiet tone that often exasperated her brothers. They felt that she was trying to be superior with them.

Oscar spoke up grimly. "We thought we ought to tell you that people have begun to talk," he said meaningly.

Alexandra looked at him. "What about?"

Oscar met her eyes blankly. "About you, keeping him here so long. It looks bad for him to be hanging on to a woman this way. People think you're getting taken in."

Alexandra shut her account-book firmly. "Boys," she said seriously, "don't let's go on with this. We won't come out anywhere. I can't take advice on such a matter. I know you mean well, but you must not feel responsible for me in things of this sort. If we go on with this talk it will only make hard feeling."

Lou whipped about from the window. "You ought to think a little about your family. You're making us all ridiculous."

"How am I?"

"People are beginning to say you want to marry the fellow."

"Well, and what is ridiculous about that?"

Lou and Oscar exchanged outraged looks. "Alexandra! Can't you see he's just a tramp and he's after your money? He wants to be taken care of, he does!"

"Well, suppose I want to take care of him? Whose business is it but my own?"

"Don't you know he'd get hold of your property?"

"He'd get hold of what I wished to give him, certainly."

Oscar sat up suddenly and Lou clutched at his bristly hair.

"Give him?" Lou shouted. "Our property, our homestead?"

"I don't know about the homestead," said Alexandra quietly. "I know you and Oscar have always expected that it would be left to your children, and I'm not sure but what you're right. But I'll do exactly as I please with the rest of my land, boys."

"The rest of your land!" cried Lou, growing more excited every minute. "Did n't all the land come out of the homestead? It was bought with money borrowed on the homestead, and Oscar and me worked ourselves to the bone paying interest on it."

"Yes, you paid the interest. But when you married we made a division of the land, and you were satisfied. I've made more on my farms since I've been alone than when we all worked together."

"Everything you've made has come out of the original land that us boys worked for, has n't it? The farms and all that comes out of them belongs to us as a family."

Alexandra waved her hand impatiently. "Come now, Lou. Stick to the facts. You are talking nonsense. Go to the county clerk and ask him who owns my land, and whether my titles are good."

Lou turned to his brother. "This is what comes of letting a woman meddle in business," he said bitterly. "We ought to have taken things in our own hands years ago. But she liked to run things, and we humored her. We thought you had good sense, Alexandra. We never thought you'd do anything foolish."

Alexandra rapped impatiently on her desk with her knuckles. "Listen, Lou. Don't talk wild. You say you ought to have taken things into your own hands years ago. I suppose you mean before you left home. But how could you take hold of what was n't there? I've got most of what I have now since we divided the property; I've built it up myself, and it has nothing to do with you."

Oscar spoke up solemnly. "The property of a family really belongs to the men of the family, no matter about the title. If anything goes wrong, it's the men that are held responsible."

"Yes, of course," Lou broke in. "Everybody knows that. Oscar and me have always been easy-going and we've never made any fuss. We were willing you should hold the land and have the good of it, but you got no right to part with any of it. We worked in the fields to pay for the first land you bought, and whatever's come out of it has got to be kept in the family."

Oscar reinforced his brother, his mind fixed on the one point he could see. "The property of a family belongs to the men of the family, because they are held responsible, and because they do the work."

Alexandra looked from one to the other, her eyes full of indignation. She had been impatient before, but now she was beginning to feel angry. "And what about my work?" she asked in an unsteady voice.

Lou looked at the carpet. "Oh, now, Alexandra, you always took it pretty easy! Of course we wanted you to. You liked to manage round, and we always humored you. We realize you were a great deal of help to us. There's no woman anywhere around that knows as much about business as you do, and we've always been proud of that, and thought you were pretty smart. But, of course, the real work always fell on us. Good advice is all right, but it don't get the weeds out of the corn."

"Maybe not, but it sometimes puts in the crop, and it sometimes keeps the fields for corn to grow in," said Alexandra dryly. "Why, Lou, I can remember when you and Oscar wanted to sell this homestead and all the improvements to old preacher Ericson for two thousand dollars. If I'd consented, you'd have gone down to the river and scraped along on poor farms for the rest of your lives. When I put in our first field of alfalfa you both opposed me, just because I first heard about it from a young man who had been to the University. You said I was being taken in then, and all the neighbors said so. You know as well as I do that alfalfa has been the salvation of this country. You all laughed at me when I said our land here was about ready for wheat, and I had to raise three big wheat crops before the neighbors quit putting all their land in corn. Why, I remember you cried, Lou, when we put in the first big wheat-planting, and said everybody was laughing at us."

Lou turned to Oscar. "That's the woman of it; if she tells you to put in a crop, she thinks she's put it in. It makes women conceited to meddle in business. I should n't think you'd want to remind us how hard you were on us, Alexandra, after the way you baby Emil."

"Hard on you? I never meant to be hard. Conditions were hard. Maybe I would never have been very soft, anyhow; but I certainly did n't choose to be the kind of girl I was. If you take even a vine and cut it back again and again, it grows hard, like a tree."

Lou felt that they were wandering from the point, and that in digression Alexandra might unnerve him. He wiped his forehead with a jerk of his handkerchief. "We never doubted you, Alexandra. We never questioned anything you did. You've always had your own way. But you can't expect us to sit like stumps and see you done out of the property by any loafer who happens along, and making yourself ridiculous into the bargain."

Oscar rose. "Yes," he broke in, "everybody's laughing to see you get took in; at your age, too. Everybody knows he's nearly five years younger than you, and is after your money. Why, Alexandra, you are forty years old!"

"All that does n't concern anybody but Carl and me. Go to town and ask your lawyers what you can do to restrain me from disposing of my own property. And I advise you to do what they tell you; for the authority you can exert by law is the only influence you will ever have over me again." Alexandra rose. "I think I would rather not have lived to find out what I have to-day," she said quietly, closing her desk.

Lou and Oscar looked at each other questioningly. There seemed to be nothing to do but to go, and they walked out.

"You can't do business with women," Oscar said heavily as he clambered into the cart. "But anyhow, we've had our say, at last."

Lou scratched his head. "Talk of that kind might come too high, you know; but she's apt to be sensible. You had n't ought to said that about her age, though, Oscar. I'm afraid that hurt her feelings; and the worst thing we can do is to make her sore at us. She'd marry him out of contrariness."

"I only meant," said Oscar, "that she is old enough to know better, and she is. If she was going to marry, she ought to done it long ago, and not go making a fool of herself now."

Lou looked anxious, nevertheless. "Of course," he reflected hopefully and inconsistently, "Alexandra ain't much like other women-folks. Maybe it won't make her sore. Maybe she'd as soon be forty as not!"

XI

Emil came home at about half-past seven o'clock that evening. Old Ivar met him at the windmill and took his horse, and the young man went directly into the house. He called to his sister and she answered from her bedroom, behind the sitting-room, saying that she was lying down.

Emil went to her door.

"Can I see you for a minute?" he asked. "I want to talk to you about something before Carl comes."

Alexandra rose quickly and came to the door. "Where is Carl?"

"Lou and Oscar met us and said they wanted to talk to him, so he rode over to Oscar's with them. Are you coming out?" Emil asked impatiently.

"Yes, sit down. I'll be dressed in a moment."

Alexandra closed her door, and Emil sank down on the old slat lounge and sat with his head in his hands. When his sister came out, he looked up, not knowing whether the interval had been short or long, and he was surprised to see that the room had grown quite dark. That was just as well; it would be easier to talk if he were not under the gaze of those clear, deliberate eyes, that saw so far in some directions and were so blind in others. Alexandra, too, was glad of the dusk. Her face was swollen from crying.

Emil started up and then sat down again. "Alexandra," he said slowly, in his deep young baritone, "I don't want to go away to law school this fall. Let me put it off another year. I want to take a year off and look around. It's awfully easy to rush into a profession you don't really like, and awfully hard to get out of it. Linstrum and I have been talking about that."

"Very well, Emil. Only don't go off looking for land." She came up and put her hand on his shoulder. "I've been wishing you could stay with me this winter."

"That's just what I don't want to do, Alexandra. I'm restless. I want to go to a new place. I want to go down to the City of Mexico to join one of the University fellows who's at the head of an electrical plant. He wrote me he could give me a little job, enough to pay my way, and I could look around and see what I want to do. I want to go as soon as harvest is over. I guess Lou and Oscar will be sore about it."

"I suppose they will." Alexandra sat down on the lounge beside him. "They are very angry with me, Emil. We have had a quarrel. They will not come here again."

Emil scarcely heard what she was saying; he did not notice the sadness of her tone. He was thinking about the reckless life he meant to live in Mexico.

"What about?" he asked absently.

"About Carl Linstrum. They are afraid I am going to marry him, and that some of my property will get away from them."

Emil shrugged his shoulders. "What nonsense!" he murmured. "Just like them."

Alexandra drew back. "Why nonsense, Emil?"

"Why, you've never thought of such a thing, have you? They always have to have something to fuss about."

"Emil," said his sister slowly, "you ought not to take things for granted. Do you agree with them that I have no right to change my way of living?"

Emil looked at the outline of his sister's head in the dim light. They were sitting close together and he somehow felt that she could hear his thoughts. He was silent for a moment, and then said in an embarrassed tone, "Why, no, certainly not. You ought to do whatever you want to. I'll always back you."

"But it would seem a little bit ridiculous to you if I married Carl?"

Emil fidgeted. The issue seemed to him too far-fetched to warrant discussion. "Why, no. I should be surprised if you wanted to. I can't see exactly why. But that's none of my business. You ought to do as you please. Certainly you ought not to pay any attention to what the boys say."

Alexandra sighed. "I had hoped you might understand, a little, why I do want to. But I suppose that's too much to expect. I've had a pretty lonely life, Emil. Besides Marie, Carl is the only friend I have ever had."

Emil was awake now; a name in her last sentence roused him. He put out his hand and took his sister's awkwardly. "You ought to do just as you wish, and I think Carl's a fine fellow. He and I would always get on. I don't believe any of the things the boys say about him, honest I don't. They are suspicious of him because he's intelligent. You know their way. They've been sore at me ever since you let me go away to college. They're always trying to catch me up. If I were you, I would n't pay any attention to them. There's nothing to get upset about. Carl's a sensible fellow. He won't mind them."

"I don't know. If they talk to him the way they did to me, I think he'll go away."

Emil grew more and more uneasy. "Think so? Well, Marie said it would serve us all right if you walked off with him."

"Did she? Bless her little heart! *She* would." Alexandra's voice broke.

Emil began unlacing his leggings. "Why don't you talk to her about it? There's Carl, I hear his horse. I guess I'll go upstairs and get my boots off. No, I don't want any supper. We had supper at five o'clock, at the fair."

Emil was glad to escape and get to his own room. He was a little ashamed for his sister, though he had tried not to show it. He felt that there was something indecorous in her proposal, and she did seem to him somewhat ridiculous. There was trouble enough in the world, he reflected, as he threw himself upon his bed, without people who were forty years old imagining they wanted to get married. In the darkness and silence Emil was not likely to think long about Alexandra. Every image slipped away but one. He had seen Marie in the crowd that afternoon. She sold candy at the fair. *Why* had she ever run away with Frank Shabata, and how could she go on laughing and working and taking an interest in things? Why did she like so many people, and why had she seemed pleased when all the French and Bohemian boys, and the priest himself, crowded round her candy stand? Why did she care about any one but him? Why could he never, never find the thing he looked for in her playful, affectionate eyes?

Then he fell to imagining that he looked once more and found it there, and what it would be like if she loved him,—she who, as Alexandra said, could give her whole heart. In that dream he could lie for hours, as if in a trance. His spirit went out of his body and crossed the fields to Marie Shabata.

At the University dances the girls had often looked wonderingly at the tall young Swede with the fine head, leaning against the wall and frowning, his arms folded, his eyes fixed on the ceiling or the floor. All the girls were a little afraid of him. He was distinguished-looking, and not the jollying kind. They felt that he was too intense and preoccupied. There was something queer about him. Emil's fraternity rather prided itself upon its dances, and sometimes he did his duty and danced every dance. But whether he was on the floor or brooding in a corner, he was always thinking about Marie Shabata. For two years the storm had been gathering in him.

XII

Carl came into the sitting-room while Alexandra was lighting the lamp. She looked up at him as she adjusted the shade. His sharp shoulders stooped as if he were very tired, his face was pale, and there were bluish shadows under his dark eyes. His anger had burned itself out and left him sick and disgusted.

"You have seen Lou and Oscar?" Alexandra asked.

"Yes." His eyes avoided hers.

Alexandra took a deep breath. "And now you are going away. I thought so."

Carl threw himself into a chair and pushed the dark lock back from his forehead with his white, nervous hand. "What a hopeless position you are in, Alexandra!" he exclaimed feverishly. "It is your fate to be always surrounded by little men. And I am no better than the rest. I am too little to face the criticism of even such men as Lou and Oscar. Yes, I am going away; to-morrow. I cannot even ask you to give me a promise until I have something to offer you. I thought, perhaps, I could do that; but I find I can't."

"What good comes of offering people things they don't need?" Alexandra asked sadly. "I don't need money. But I have needed you for a great many years. I wonder why I have been permitted to prosper, if it is only to take my friends away from me."

"I don't deceive myself," Carl said frankly. "I know that I am going away on my own account. I must make the usual effort. I must have something to show for myself. To take what you would give me, I should have to be either a very large man or a very small one, and I am only in the middle class."

Alexandra sighed. "I have a feeling that if you go away, you will not come back. Something will happen to one of us, or to both. People have to snatch at happiness when they can, in this world. It is always easier to lose than to find. What I have is yours, if you care enough about me to take it."

Carl rose and looked up at the picture of John Bergson. "But I can't, my dear, I can't! I will go North at once. Instead of idling about in California all winter, I shall be getting my bearings up there. I won't waste another week. Be patient with me, Alexandra. Give me a year!"

"As you will," said Alexandra wearily. "All at once, in a single day, I lose everything; and I do not know why. Emil, too, is going away." Carl was still studying John Bergson's face and Alexandra's eyes followed his. "Yes," she said, "if he could have seen all that would come of the task he gave me, he would have been sorry. I hope he does not see me now. I hope that he is among the old people of his blood and country, and that tidings do not reach him from the New World."

Part III. Winter Memories

I

Winter has settled down over the Divide again; the season in which Nature recuperates, in which she sinks to sleep between the fruitfulness of autumn and the passion of spring. The birds have gone. The teeming life that goes on down in the long grass is exterminated. The prairie-dog keeps his hole. The rabbits run shivering from one frozen garden patch to another and are hard put to it to find frost-bitten cabbage-stalks. At night the coyotes roam the wintry waste, howling for food. The variegated fields are all one color now; the pastures, the stubble, the roads, the sky are the same leaden gray. The hedgerows and trees are scarcely perceptible against the bare earth, whose slaty hue they have taken on. The ground is frozen so hard that it bruises the foot to walk in the roads or in the ploughed fields. It is like an iron country, and the spirit is oppressed by its rigor and melancholy. One could easily believe that in that dead landscape the germs of life and fruitfulness were extinct forever.

Alexandra has settled back into her old routine. There are weekly letters from Emil. Lou and Oscar she has not seen since Carl went away. To avoid awkward encounters in the presence of curious spectators, she has stopped going to the Norwegian Church and drives up to the Reform Church at Hanover, or goes with Marie Shabata to the Catholic Church, locally known as "the French Church." She has not told Marie about Carl, or her differences with her brothers. She was never very communicative about her own affairs, and when she came to the point, an instinct told her that about such things she and Marie would not understand one another.

Old Mrs. Lee had been afraid that family misunderstandings might deprive her of her yearly visit to Alexandra. But on the first day of December Alexandra telephoned Annie that to-morrow she would send Ivar over for her mother, and the next day the old lady arrived with her bundles. For twelve years Mrs. Lee had always entered Alexandra's sitting-room with the same exclamation, "Now we be yust-a like old times!" She enjoyed the liberty Alexandra gave her, and hearing her own language about her all day long. Here she could wear her nightcap and sleep with all her windows shut, listen to Ivar reading the Bible, and here she could run about among the stables in a pair of Emil's old boots. Though she was bent almost double, she was as spry as a gopher. Her face was as brown as if it had been varnished, and as full of wrinkles as a washerwoman's hands. She had three jolly old teeth left in the front of her mouth, and when she grinned she looked very knowing, as if when you found out how to take it, life was n't half bad. While she and Alexandra patched and pieced and quilted, she talked incessantly about stories she read in a Swedish family paper, telling the plots in great detail; or about her life on a dairy farm in Gottland when she was a girl. Sometimes she forgot which were the printed stories and which were the real stories, it all seemed so far away. She loved to take a little brandy, with hot water and sugar, before she went to bed, and Alexandra always had it ready for her. "It sends good dreams," she would say with a twinkle in her eye.

When Mrs. Lee had been with Alexandra for a week, Marie Shabata telephoned one morning to say that Frank had gone to town for the day, and she would like them to come over for coffee in the afternoon. Mrs. Lee hurried to wash out and iron her new cross-stitched apron, which she had finished only the night before; a checked gingham apron worked with a design ten inches broad across the bottom; a hunting scene, with fir trees and a stag and dogs and huntsmen. Mrs. Lee was firm with herself at dinner, and refused a second helping of apple dumplings. "I ta-ank I save up," she said with a giggle.

At two o'clock in the afternoon Alexandra's cart drove up to the Shabatas' gate, and Marie saw Mrs. Lee's red shawl come bobbing up the path. She ran to the door and pulled the old woman into the house with a hug, helping her to take off her wraps while Alexandra blanketed the horse outside. Mrs. Lee had put on her best black satine dress—she abominated woolen stuffs, even in winter—and a crocheted collar, fastened with a big pale gold pin, containing faded daguerreotypes of her father and mother. She had not worn her apron for fear of rumpling it, and now she shook it out and tied it round her waist with a conscious air. Marie drew back and threw up her hands, exclaiming, "Oh, what a beauty! I've never seen this one before, have I, Mrs. Lee?"

The old woman giggled and ducked her head. "No, yust las' night I ma-ake. See dis tread; verra strong, no wa-ash out, no fade. My sister send from Sveden. I yust-a ta-ank you like dis."

Marie ran to the door again. "Come in, Alexandra. I have been looking at Mrs. Lee's apron. Do stop on your way home and show it to Mrs. Hiller. She's crazy about cross-stitch."

While Alexandra removed her hat and veil, Mrs. Lee went out to the kitchen and settled herself in a wooden rocking-chair by the stove, looking with great interest at the table, set for three, with a white cloth, and a pot of pink geraniums in the middle. "My, a-an't you gotta fine plants; such-a much flower. How you keep from freeze?"

She pointed to the window-shelves, full of blooming fuchsias and geraniums.

"I keep the fire all night, Mrs. Lee, and when it's very cold I put them all on the table, in the middle of the room. Other nights I only put newspapers behind them. Frank laughs at me for fussing, but when they don't bloom he says, 'What's the matter with the darned things?'—What do you hear from Carl, Alexandra?"

"He got to Dawson before the river froze, and now I suppose I won't hear any more until spring. Before he left California he sent me a box of orange flowers, but they didn't keep very well. I have brought a bunch of Emil's letters for you." Alexandra came out from the sitting-room and pinched Marie's cheek playfully. "You don't look as if the weather ever froze you up. Never have colds, do you? That's a good girl. She had dark red cheeks like this when she was a little girl, Mrs. Lee. She looked like some queer foreign kind of a doll. I've never forgot the first time I saw you in Mieklejohn's store, Marie, the time father was lying sick. Carl and I were talking about that before he went away."

"I remember, and Emil had his kitten along. When are you going to send Emil's Christmas box?"

"It ought to have gone before this. I'll have to send it by mail now, to get it there in time."

Marie pulled a dark purple silk necktie from her work-basket. "I knit this for him. It's a good color, don't you think? Will you please put it in with your things and tell him it's from me, to wear when he goes serenading."

Alexandra laughed. "I don't believe he goes serenading much. He says in one letter that the Mexican ladies are said to be very beautiful, but that don't seem to me very warm praise."

Marie tossed her head. "Emil can't fool me. If he's bought a guitar, he goes serenading. Who would n't, with all those Spanish girls dropping flowers down from their windows! I'd sing to them every night, would n't you, Mrs. Lee?"

The old lady chuckled. Her eyes lit up as Marie bent down and opened the oven door. A delicious hot fragrance blew out into the tidy kitchen. "My, somet'ing smell good!" She turned to Alexandra with a wink, her three yellow teeth making a brave show, "I ta-ank dat stop my yaw from ache no more!" she said contentedly.

Marie took out a pan of delicate little rolls, stuffed with stewed apricots, and began to dust them over with powdered sugar. "I hope you'll like these, Mrs. Lee; Alexandra does. The Bohemians always like them with their coffee. But if you don't, I have a coffee-cake with nuts and poppy seeds. Alexandra, will you get the cream jug? I put it in the window to keep cool."

"The Bohemians," said Alexandra, as they drew up to the table, "certainly know how to make more kinds of bread than any other people in the world. Old Mrs. Hiller told me once at the church supper that she could make seven kinds of fancy bread, but Marie could make a dozen."

Mrs. Lee held up one of the apricot rolls between her brown thumb and forefinger and weighed it critically. "Yust like-a fedders," she pronounced with satisfaction. "My, a-an't dis nice!" she exclaimed as she stirred her coffee. "I yust ta-ake a liddle yelly now, too, I ta-ank."

Alexandra and Marie laughed at her forehandedness, and fell to talking of their own affairs. "I was afraid you had a cold when I talked to you over the telephone the other night, Marie. What was the matter, had you been crying?"

"Maybe I had," Marie smiled guiltily. "Frank was out late that night. Don't you get lonely sometimes in the winter, when everybody has gone away?"

"I thought it was something like that. If I had n't had company, I'd have run over to see for myself. If you get down-hearted, what will become of the rest of us?" Alexandra asked.

"I don't, very often. There's Mrs. Lee without any coffee!"

Later, when Mrs. Lee declared that her powers were spent, Marie and Alexandra went upstairs to look for some crochet patterns the old lady wanted to borrow. "Better put on your coat, Alexandra. It's cold up there, and I have no idea where those patterns are. I may have to look through my old trunks." Marie caught up a shawl and opened the stair door, running up the steps ahead of her guest. "While I go through the bureau drawers, you might look in those hat-boxes on the closet-shelf, over where Frank's clothes hang. There are a lot of odds and ends in them."

She began tossing over the contents of the drawers, and Alexandra went into the clothes-closet. Presently she came back, holding a slender elastic yellow stick in her hand.

"What in the world is this, Marie? You don't mean to tell me Frank ever carried such a thing?"

Marie blinked at it with astonishment and sat down on the floor. "Where did you find it? I did n't know he had kept it. I have n't seen it for years."

"It really is a cane, then?"

"Yes. One he brought from the old country. He used to carry it when I first knew him. Is n't it foolish? Poor Frank!"

Alexandra twirled the stick in her fingers and laughed. "He must have looked funny!"

Marie was thoughtful. "No, he did n't, really. It did n't seem out of place. He used to be awfully gay like that when he was a young man. I guess people always get what's hardest for them, Alexandra." Marie gathered the shawl closer about her and still looked hard at the cane. "Frank would be all right in the right place," she said reflectively. "He ought to have a different kind of wife, for one thing. Do you know, Alexandra, I could pick out exactly the right sort of woman for Frank—now. The trouble is you almost have to marry a man before you can find out the sort of wife he needs; and usually it's exactly the sort you are not. Then what are you going to do about it?" she asked candidly.

Alexandra confessed she did n't know. "However," she added, "it seems to me that you get along with Frank about as well as any woman I've ever seen or heard of could."

Marie shook her head, pursing her lips and blowing her warm breath softly out into the frosty air. "No; I was spoiled at home. I like my own way, and I have a quick tongue. When Frank brags, I say sharp things, and he never forgets. He goes over and over it in his mind; I can feel him. Then I'm too giddy. Frank's wife ought to be timid, and she ought not to care about another living thing in the world but just Frank! I did n't, when I married him, but I suppose I was too young to stay like that." Marie sighed.

Alexandra had never heard Marie speak so frankly about her husband before, and she felt that it was wiser not to encourage her. No good, she reasoned, ever came from talking about such things, and while Marie was thinking aloud, Alexandra had been steadily searching the hat-boxes. "Are n't these the patterns, Maria?"

Marie sprang up from the floor. "Sure enough, we were looking for patterns, were n't we? I'd forgot about everything but Frank's other wife. I'll put that away."

She poked the cane behind Frank's Sunday clothes, and though she laughed, Alexandra saw there were tears in her eyes.

When they went back to the kitchen, the snow had begun to fall, and Marie's visitors thought they must be getting home. She went out to the cart with them, and tucked the robes about old Mrs. Lee while Alexandra took the blanket off her horse. As they drove away, Marie turned and went slowly back to the house. She took up the package of letters Alexandra had brought, but she did not read them. She turned them over and looked at the foreign stamps, and then sat watching the flying snow while the dusk deepened in the kitchen and the stove sent out a red glow.

Marie knew perfectly well that Emil's letters were written more for her than for Alexandra. They were not the sort of letters that a young man writes to his sister. They were both more personal and more painstaking; full of descriptions of the gay life in the old Mexican capital in the days when the strong hand of Porfirio Diaz was still strong. He told about bull-fights and cock-fights, churches and *fiestas*, the flower-markets and the fountains, the music and dancing, the people of all nations he met in the Italian restaurants on San Francisco Street. In short, they were the kind of letters a young man writes to a woman when he wishes himself and his life to seem interesting to her, when he wishes to enlist her imagination in his behalf.

Marie, when she was alone or when she sat sewing in the evening, often thought about what it must be like down there where Emil was; where there were flowers and street bands everywhere, and carriages rattling up and down, and where there was a little blind bootblack in front of the cathedral who could play any tune you asked for by dropping the lids of blacking-boxes on the stone steps. When everything is done and over for one at twenty-three, it is pleasant to let the mind wander forth and follow a young adventurer who has life before him. "And if it had not been for me," she thought, "Frank might still be free like that, and having a good time making people admire him. Poor Frank, getting married was n't very good for him either. I'm afraid I do set people against him, as he says. I seem, somehow, to give him away all the time. Perhaps he would try to be agreeable to people again, if I were not around. It seems as if I always make him just as bad as he can be."

Later in the winter, Alexandra looked back upon that afternoon as the last satisfactory visit she had had with Marie. After that day the younger woman seemed to shrink more and more into herself. When she was with Alexandra she was not spontaneous and frank as she used to be. She seemed to be brooding over something, and holding something back. The weather had a good deal to do with their seeing less of each other than usual. There had not been such snowstorms in twenty years, and the path across the fields was drifted deep from Christmas until March. When the two neighbors went to see each other, they had to go round by the wagonroad, which was twice as far. They telephoned each other almost every night, though in January there was a stretch of three weeks when the wires were down, and when the postman did not come at all.

Marie often ran in to see her nearest neighbor, old Mrs. Hiller, who was crippled with rheumatism and had only her son, the lame shoemaker, to take care of her; and she went to the French

Church, whatever the weather. She was a sincerely devout girl. She prayed for herself and for Frank, and for Emil, among the temptations of that gay, corrupt old city. She found more comfort in the Church that winter than ever before. It seemed to come closer to her, and to fill an emptiness that ached in her heart. She tried to be patient with her husband. He and his hired man usually played California Jack[9] in the evening. Marie sat sewing or crocheting and tried to take a friendly interest in the game, but she was always thinking about the wide fields outside, where the snow was drifting over the fences; and about the orchard, where the snow was falling and packing, crust over crust. When she went out into the dark kitchen to fix her plants for the night, she used to stand by the window and look out at the white fields, or watch the currents of snow whirling over the orchard. She seemed to feel the weight of all the snow that lay down there. The branches had become so hard that they wounded your hand if you but tried to break a twig. And yet, down under the frozen crusts, at the roots of the trees, the secret of life was still safe, warm as the blood in one's heart; and the spring would come again! Oh, it would come again!

II

If Alexandra had had much imagination she might have guessed what was going on in Marie's mind, and she would have seen long before what was going on in Emil's. But that, as Emil himself had more than once reflected, was Alexandra's blind side, and her life had not been of the kind to sharpen her vision. Her training had all been toward the end of making her proficient in what she had undertaken to do. Her personal life, her own realization of herself, was almost a subconscious existence; like an underground river that came to the surface only here and there, at intervals months apart, and then sank again to flow on under her own fields. Nevertheless, the underground stream was there, and it was because she had so much personality to put into her enterprises and succeeded in putting it into them so completely, that her affairs prospered better than those of her neighbors.

There were certain days in her life, outwardly uneventful, which Alexandra remembered as peculiarly happy; days when she was close to the flat, fallow world about her, and felt, as it were, in her own body the joyous germination in the soil. There were days, too, which she and Emil had spent together, upon which she loved to look back. There had been such a day when they were down on the river in the dry year, looking over the land. They had made an early

9. Two-handed version of the card game high-low-jack.

start one morning and had driven a long way before noon. When Emil said he was hungry, they drew back from the road, gave Brigham his oats among the bushes, and climbed up to the top of a grassy bluff to eat their lunch under the shade of some little elm trees. The river was clear there, and shallow, since there had been no rain, and it ran in ripples over the sparkling sand. Under the overhanging willows of the opposite bank there was an inlet where the water was deeper and flowed so slowly that it seemed to sleep in the sun. In this little bay a single wild duck was swimming and diving and preening her feathers, disporting herself very happily in the flickering light and shade. They sat for a long time, watching the solitary bird take its pleasure. No living thing had ever seemed to Alexandra as beautiful as that wild duck. Emil must have felt about it as she did, for afterward, when they were at home, he used sometimes to say, "Sister, you know our duck down there—" Alexandra remembered that day as one of the happiest in her life. Years afterward she thought of the duck as still there, swimming and diving all by herself in the sunlight, a kind of enchanted bird that did not know age or change.

Most of Alexandra's happy memories were as impersonal as this one; yet to her they were very personal. Her mind was a white book, with clear writing about weather and beasts and growing things. Not many people would have cared to read it; only a happy few. She had never been in love, she had never indulged in sentimental reveries. Even as a girl she had looked upon men as work-fellows. She had grown up in serious times.

There was one fancy indeed, which persisted through her girlhood. It most often came to her on Sunday mornings, the one day in the week when she lay late abed listening to the familiar morning sounds; the windmill singing in the brisk breeze, Emil whistling as he blacked his boots down by the kitchen door. Sometimes, as she lay thus luxuriously idle, her eyes closed, she used to have an illusion of being lifted up bodily and carried lightly by some one very strong. It was a man, certainly, who carried her, but he was like no man she knew; he was much larger and stronger and swifter, and he carried her as easily as if she were a sheaf of wheat. She never saw him, but, with eyes closed, she could feel that he was yellow like the sunlight, and there was the smell of ripe cornfields about him. She could feel him approach, bend over her and lift her, and then she could feel herself being carried swiftly off across the fields. After such a reverie she would rise hastily, angry with herself, and go down to the bath-house that was partitioned off the kitchen shed. There she would stand in a tin tub and prosecute her bath with vigor, finishing it by pouring buckets of cold well-water over her gleaming white body which no man on the Divide could have carried very far.

As she grew older, this fancy more often came to her when she was tired than when she was fresh and strong. Sometimes, after she had been in the open all day, overseeing the branding of the cattle or the loading of the pigs, she would come in chilled, take a concoction of spices and warm home-made wine, and go to bed with her body actually aching with fatigue. Then, just before she went to sleep, she had the old sensation of being lifted and carried by a strong being who took from her all her bodily weariness.

Part IV. The White Mulberry Tree

I

The French church, properly the Church of Sainte-Agnes, stood upon a hill. The high, narrow, red-brick building, with its tall steeple and steep roof, could be seen for miles across the wheat-fields, though the little town of Sainte-Agnes was completely hidden away at the foot of the hill. The church looked powerful and triumphant there on its eminence, so high above the rest of the landscape, with miles of warm color lying at its feet, and by its position and setting it reminded one of some of the churches built long ago in the wheat-lands of middle France.

Late one June afternoon Alexandra Bergson was driving along one of the many roads that led through the rich French farming country to the big church. The sunlight was shining directly in her face, and there was a blaze of light all about the red church on the hill. Beside Alexandra lounged a strikingly exotic figure in a tall Mexican hat, a silk sash, and a black velvet jacket sewn with silver buttons. Emil had returned only the night before, and his sister was so proud of him that she decided at once to take him up to the church supper, and to make him wear the Mexican costume he had brought home in his trunk. "All the girls who have stands are going to wear fancy costumes," she argued, "and some of the boys. Marie is going to tell fortunes, and she sent to Omaha for a Bohemian dress her father brought back from a visit to the old country. If you wear those clothes, they will all be pleased. And you must take your guitar. Everybody ought to do what they can to help along, and we have never done much. We are not a talented family."

The supper was to be at six o'clock, in the basement of the church, and afterward there would be a fair, with charades and an auction. Alexandra had set out from home early, leaving the house to Signa and Nelse Jensen, who were to be married next week. Signa had shyly asked to have the wedding put off until Emil came home.

Alexandra was well satisfied with her brother. As they drove through the rolling French country toward the westering sun and the stalwart church, she was thinking of that time long ago when she and Emil drove back from the river valley to the still unconquered Divide. Yes, she told herself, it had been worth while; both Emil and the country had become what she had hoped. Out of her father's children there was one who was fit to cope with the world, who had not been tied to the plow, and who had a personality apart from the soil. And that, she reflected, was what she had worked for. She felt well satisfied with her life.

When they reached the church, a score of teams were hitched in front of the basement doors that opened from the hillside upon the sanded terrace, where the boys wrestled and had jumping-matches. Amédée Chevalier, a proud father of one week, rushed out and embraced Emil. Amédée was an only son,—hence he was a very rich young man,—but he meant to have twenty children himself, like his uncle Xavier. "Oh, Emil," he cried, hugging his old friend rapturously, "why ain't you been up to see my boy? You come tomorrow, sure? Emil, you wanna get a boy right off! It's the greatest thing ever! No, no, no! Angel not sick at all. Everything just fine. That boy he come into this world laughin', and he been laughin' ever since. You come an' see!" He pounded Emil's ribs to emphasize each announcement.

Emil caught his arms. "Stop, Amédée. You're knocking the wind out of me. I brought him cups and spoons and blankets and moccasins enough for an orphan asylum. I'm awful glad it's a boy, sure enough!"

The young men crowded round Emil to admire his costume and to tell him in a breath everything that had happened since he went away. Emil had more friends up here in the French country than down on Norway Creek. The French and Bohemian boys were spirited and jolly, liked variety, and were as much predisposed to favor anything new as the Scandinavian boys were to reject it. The Norwegian and Swedish lads were much more self-centred, apt to be egotistical and jealous. They were cautious and reserved with Emil because he had been away to college, and were prepared to take him down if he should try to put on airs with them. The French boys liked a bit of swagger, and they were always delighted to hear about anything new: new clothes, new games, new songs, new dances. Now they carried Emil off to show him the club room they had just fitted up over the post-office, down in the village. They ran down the hill in a drove, all laughing and chattering at once, some in French, some in English.

Alexandra went into the cool, whitewashed basement where the women were setting the tables. Marie was standing on a chair, building a little tent of shawls where she was to tell fortunes. She sprang down and ran toward Alexandra, stopping short and looking at her in disappointment. Alexandra nodded to her encouragingly.

"Oh, he will be here, Marie. The boys have taken him off to show him something. You won't know him. He is a man now, sure enough. I have no boy left. He smokes terrible-smelling Mexican cigarettes and talks Spanish. How pretty you look, child. Where did you get those beautiful earrings?"

"They belonged to father's mother. He always promised them to me. He sent them with the dress and said I could keep them."

Marie wore a short red skirt of stoutly woven cloth, a white bodice and kirtle, a yellow silk turban wound low over her brown curls, and long coral pendants in her ears. Her ears had been pierced against a piece of cork by her great-aunt when she was seven years old. In those germless days she had worn bits of broom-straw, plucked from the common sweeping-broom, in the lobes until the holes were healed and ready for little gold rings.

When Emil came back from the village, he lingered outside on the terrace with the boys. Marie could hear him talking and strumming on his guitar while Raoul Marcel sang falsetto. She was vexed with him for staying out there. It made her very nervous to hear him and not to see him; for, certainly, she told herself, she was not going out to look for him. When the supper bell rang and the boys came trooping in to get seats at the first table, she forgot all about her annoyance and ran to greet the tallest of the crowd, in his conspicuous attire. She did n't mind showing her embarrassment at all. She blushed and laughed excitedly as she gave Emil her hand, and looked delightedly at the black velvet coat that brought out his fair skin and fine blond head. Marie was incapable of being lukewarm about anything that pleased her. She simply did not know how to give a half-hearted response. When she was delighted, she was as likely as not to stand on her tiptoes and clap her hands. If people laughed at her, she laughed with them.

"Do the men wear clothes like that every day, in the street?" She caught Emil by his sleeve and turned him about. "Oh, I wish I lived where people wore things like that! Are the buttons real silver? Put on the hat, please. What a heavy thing! How do you ever wear it? Why don't you tell us about the bull-fights?"

She wanted to wring all his experiences from him at once, without waiting a moment. Emil smiled tolerantly and stood looking down at her with his old, brooding gaze, while the French girls fluttered about him in their white dresses and ribbons, and Alexandra watched the scene with pride. Several of the French girls, Marie knew, were hoping that Emil would take them to supper, and she was relieved when he took only his sister. Marie caught Frank's arm and dragged him to the same table, managing to get seats opposite the Bergsons, so that she could hear what they were talking about. Alexandra made Emil tell Mrs. Xavier Chevalier, the mother of the twenty, about how he had seen a famous matador killed in the bull-ring. Marie listened to every word, only taking her eyes from Emil to watch Frank's plate and keep it filled. When Emil finished his account,—bloody enough to satisfy Mrs. Xavier and to make her feel thankful that she was not a matador,—Marie broke out with a volley of questions. How did the women dress when they went to bull-fights? Did they wear mantillas? Did they never wear hats?

After supper the young people played charades for the amusement of their elders, who sat gossiping between their guesses. All the shops in Sainte-Agnes were closed at eight o'clock that night, so that the merchants and their clerks could attend the fair. The auction was the liveliest part of the entertainment, for the French boys always lost their heads when they began to bid, satisfied that their extravagance was in a good cause. After all the pincushions and sofa pillows and embroidered slippers were sold, Emil precipitated a panic by taking out one of his turquoise shirt studs, which every one had been admiring, and handing it to the auctioneer. All the French girls clamored for it, and their sweethearts bid against each other recklessly. Marie wanted it, too, and she kept making signals to Frank, which he took a sour pleasure in disregarding. He did n't see the use of making a fuss over a fellow just because he was dressed like a clown. When the turquoise went to Malvina Sauvage, the French banker's daughter, Marie shrugged her shoulders and betook herself to her little tent of shawls, where she began to shuffle her cards by the light of a tallow candle, calling out, "Fortunes, fortunes!"

The young priest, Father Duchesne, went first to have his fortune read. Marie took his long white hand, looked at it, and then began to run off her cards. "I see a long journey across water for you, Father. You will go to a town all cut up by water; built on islands, it seems to be, with rivers and green fields all about. And you will visit an old lady with a white cap and gold hoops in her ears, and you will be very happy there."

"Mais, oui," said the priest, with a melancholy smile. "C'est L'Isle-Adam, chez ma mère. Vous êtes très savante, ma fille."[1] He patted her yellow turban, calling, "Venez donc, mes garçons! Il y a ici une véritable clairvoyante!"[2]

Marie was clever at fortune-telling, indulging in a light irony that amused the crowd. She told old Brunot, the miser, that he would lose all his money, marry a girl of sixteen, and live happily on a crust. Sholte, the fat Russian boy, who lived for his stomach, was to be disappointed in love, grow thin, and shoot himself from despon-

1. "Of course. It's my mother's house on L'Isle-Adam. You are very wise, my daughter."
2. "Come here, lads! We're in the presence of a real fortune-teller!"

dency. Amédée was to have twenty children, and nineteen of them were to be girls. Amédée slapped Frank on the back and asked him why he did n't see what the fortune-teller would promise him. But Frank shook off his friendly hand and grunted, "She tell my fortune long ago; bad enough!" Then he withdrew to a corner and sat glowering at his wife.

Frank's case was all the more painful because he had no one in particular to fix his jealousy upon. Sometimes he could have thanked the man who would bring him evidence against his wife. He had discharged a good farm-boy, Jan Smirka, because he thought Marie was fond of him; but she had not seemed to miss Jan when he was gone, and she had been just as kind to the next boy. The farm-hands would always do anything for Marie; Frank could n't find one so surly that he would not make an effort to please her. At the bottom of his heart Frank knew well enough that if he could once give up his grudge, his wife would come back to him. But he could never in the world do that. The grudge was fundamental. Perhaps he could not have given it up if he had tried. Perhaps he got more satisfaction out of feeling himself abused than he would have got out of being loved. If he could once have made Marie thoroughly unhappy, he might have relented and raised her from the dust. But she had never humbled herself. In the first days of their love she had been his slave; she had admired him abandonedly. But the moment he began to bully her and to be unjust, she began to draw away; at first in tearful amazement, then in quiet, unspoken disgust. The distance between them had widened and hardened. It no longer contracted and brought them suddenly together. The spark of her life went somewhere else, and he was always watching to surprise it. He knew that somewhere she must get a feeling to live upon, for she was not a woman who could live without loving. He wanted to prove to himself the wrong he felt. What did she hide in her heart? Where did it go? Even Frank had his churlish delicacies; he never reminded her of how much she had once loved him. For that Marie was grateful to him.

While Marie was chattering to the French boys, Amédée called Emil to the back of the room and whispered to him that they were going to play a joke on the girls. At eleven o'clock, Amédée was to go up to the switchboard in the vestibule and turn off the electric lights, and every boy would have a chance to kiss his sweetheart before Father Duchesne could find his way up the stairs to turn the current on again. The only difficulty was the candle in Marie's tent; perhaps, as Emil had no sweetheart, he would oblige the boys by blowing out the candle. Emil said he would undertake to do that.

At five minutes to eleven he sauntered up to Marie's booth, and the French boys dispersed to find their girls. He leaned over the card-table and gave himself up to looking at her. "Do you think you could tell my fortune?" he murmured. It was the first word he had had alone with her for almost a year. "My luck has n't changed any. It's just the same."

Marie had often wondered whether there was anyone else who could look his thoughts to you as Emil could. To-night, when she met his steady, powerful eyes, it was impossible not to feel the sweetness of the dream he was dreaming; it reached her before she could shut it out, and hid itself in her heart. She began to shuffle her cards furiously. "I'm angry with you, Emil," she broke out with petulance. "Why did you give them that lovely blue stone to sell? You might have known Frank would n't buy it for me, and I wanted it awfully!"

Emil laughed shortly. "People who want such little things surely ought to have them," he said dryly. He thrust his hand into the pocket of his velvet trousers and brought out a handful of uncut turquoises, as big as marbles. Leaning over the table he dropped them into her lap. "There, will those do? Be careful, don't let any one see them. Now, I suppose you want me to go away and let you play with them?"

Marie was gazing in rapture at the soft blue color of the stones. "Oh, Emil! Is everything down there beautiful like these? How could you ever come away?"

At that instant Amédée laid hands on the switchboard. There was a shiver and a giggle, and every one looked toward the red blur that Marie's candle made in the dark. Immediately that, too, was gone. Little shrieks and currents of soft laughter ran up and down the dark hall. Marie started up,—directly into Emil's arms. In the same instant she felt his lips. The veil that had hung uncertainly between them for so long was dissolved. Before she knew what she was doing, she had committed herself to that kiss that was at once a boy's and a man's, as timid as it was tender; so like Emil and so unlike any one else in the world. Not until it was over did she realize what it meant. And Emil, who had so often imagined the shock of this first kiss, was surprised at its gentleness and naturalness. It was like a sigh which they had breathed together; almost sorrowful, as if each were afraid of wakening something in the other.

When the lights came on again, everybody was laughing and shouting, and all the French girls were rosy and shining with mirth. Only Marie, in her little tent of shawls, was pale and quiet. Under her yellow turban the red coral pendants swung against white cheeks. Frank was still staring at her, but he seemed to see nothing. Years ago, he himself had had the power to take the blood from her cheeks like that. Perhaps he did not remember—perhaps he had never noticed! Emil was already at the other end of the hall, walking about with the shoulder-motion he had acquired among the Mexicans, studying the floor with his intent, deep-set eyes. Marie began to take down and fold her shawls. She did not glance up again. The young people drifted to the other end of the hall where the guitar was sounding. In a moment she heard Emil and Raoul singing:—

"Across the Rio Grand-e
There lies a sunny land-e,
My bright-eyed Mexico!"

Alexandra Bergson came up to the card booth. "Let me help you, Marie. You look tired."

She placed her hand on Marie's arm and felt her shiver. Marie stiffened under that kind, calm hand. Alexandra drew back, perplexed and hurt.

There was about Alexandra something of the impervious calm of the fatalist, always disconcerting to very young people, who cannot feel that the heart lives at all unless it is still at the mercy of storms; unless its strings can scream to the touch of pain.

II

Signa's wedding supper was over. The guests, and the tiresome little Norwegian preacher who had performed the marriage ceremony, were saying good-night. Old Ivar was hitching the horses to the wagon to take the wedding presents and the bride and groom up to their new home, on Alexandra's north quarter. When Ivar drove up to the gate, Emil and Marie Shabata began to carry out the presents, and Alexandra went into her bedroom to bid Signa good-bye and to give her a few words of good counsel. She was surprised to find that the bride had changed her slippers for heavy shoes and was pinning up her skirts. At that moment Nelse appeared at the gate with the two milk cows that Alexandra had given Signa for a wedding present.

Alexandra began to laugh. "Why, Signa, you and Nelse are to ride home. I'll send Ivar over with the cows in the morning."

Signa hesitated and looked perplexed. When her husband called her, she pinned her hat on resolutely. "I ta-ank I better do yust like he say," she murmured in confusion.

Alexandra and Marie accompanied Signa to the gate and saw the party set off, old Ivar driving ahead in the wagon and the bride and groom following on foot, each leading a cow. Emil burst into a laugh before they were out of hearing.

"Those two will get on," said Alexandra as they turned back to the house. "They are not going to take any chances. They will feel safer with those cows in their own stable. Marie, I am going to send for an old woman next. As soon as I get the girls broken in, I marry them off."

"I've no patience with Signa, marrying that grumpy fellow!" Marie declared. "I wanted her to marry that nice Smirka boy who worked for us last winter. I think she liked him, too."

"Yes, I think she did," Alexandra assented, "but I suppose she was too much afraid of Nelse to marry any one else. Now that I think of it, most of my girls have married men they were afraid of. I believe there is a good deal of the cow in most Swedish girls. You high-strung Bohemians can't understand us. We're a terribly practical people, and I guess we think a cross man makes a good manager."

Marie shrugged her shoulders and turned to pin up a lock of hair that had fallen on her neck. Somehow Alexandra had irritated her of late. Everybody irritated her. She was tired of everybody. "I'm going home alone, Emil, so you need n't get your hat," she said as she wound her scarf quickly about her head. "Good-night, Alexandra," she called back in a strained voice, running down the gravel walk.

Emil followed with long strides until he overtook her. Then she began to walk slowly. It was a night of warm wind and faint starlight, and the fireflies were glimmering over the wheat.

"Marie," said Emil after they had walked for a while, "I wonder if you know how unhappy I am?"

Marie did not answer him. Her head, in its white scarf, drooped forward a little.

Emil kicked a clod from the path and went on:—

"I wonder whether you are really shallow-hearted, like you seem? Sometimes I think one boy does just as well as another for you. It never seems to make much difference whether it is me or Raoul Marcel or Jan Smirka. Are you really like that?"

"Perhaps I am. What do you want me to do? Sit round and cry all day? When I've cried until I can't cry anymore, then—then I must do something else."

"Are you sorry for me?" he persisted.

"No, I'm not. If I were big and free like you, I would n't let anything make me unhappy. As old Napoleon Brunot said at the fair, I would n't go lovering after no woman. I'd take the first train and go off and have all the fun there is."

"I tried that, but it did n't do any good. Everything reminded me. The nicer the place was, the more I wanted you." They had come to the stile and Emil pointed to it persuasively. "Sit down a moment, I want to ask you something." Marie sat down on the top step and Emil drew nearer. "Would you tell me something that's none of my business if you thought it would help me out? Well, then, tell me, *please* tell me, why you ran away with Frank Shabata!"

Marie drew back. "Because I was in love with him," she said firmly.

"Really?" he asked incredulously.

"Yes, indeed. Very much in love with him. I think I was the one who suggested our running away. From the first it was more my fault than his."

Emil turned away his face.

"And now," Marie went on, "I've got to remember that. Frank is just the same now as he was then, only then I would see him as I wanted him to be. I would have my own way. And now I pay for it."

"You don't do all the paying."

"That's it. When one makes a mistake, there's no telling where it will stop. But you can go away; you can leave all this behind you."

"Not everything. I can't leave you behind. Will you go away with me, Marie?"

Marie started up and stepped across the stile. "Emil! How wickedly you talk! I am not that kind of a girl, and you know it. But what am I going to do if you keep tormenting me like this!" she added plaintively.

"Marie, I won't bother you any more if you will tell me just one thing. Stop a minute and look at me. No, nobody can see us. Everybody's asleep. That was only a firefly. Marie, *stop* and tell me!"

Emil overtook her and catching her by the shoulders shook her gently, as if he were trying to awaken a sleepwalker.

Marie hid her face on his arm. "Don't ask me anything more. I don't know anything except how miserable I am. And I thought it would be all right when you came back. Oh, Emil," she clutched his sleeve and began to cry, "what am I to do if you don't go away? I can't go, and one of us must. Can't you see?"

Emil stood looking down at her, holding his shoulders stiff and stiffening the arm to which she clung. Her white dress looked gray in the darkness. She seemed like a troubled spirit, like some shadow out of the earth, clinging to him and entreating him to give her peace. Behind her the fireflies were weaving in and out over the wheat. He put his hand on her bent head. "On my honor, Marie, if you will say you love me, I will go away."

She lifted her face to his. "How could I help it? Did n't you know?"

Emil was the one who trembled, through all his frame. After he left Marie at her gate, he wandered about the fields all night, till morning put out the fireflies and the stars.

III

One evening, a week after Signa's wedding, Emil was kneeling before a box in the sitting-room, packing his books. From time to time he rose and wandered about the house, picking up stray volumes and bringing them listlessly back to his box. He was packing without enthusiasm. He was not very sanguine about his future. Alexandra sat sewing by the table. She had helped him pack his trunk in the afternoon. As Emil came and went by her chair with his books, he thought to himself that it had not been so hard to leave his sister since he first went away to school. He was going directly to Omaha, to read law in the office of a Swedish lawyer until October, when he would enter the law school at Ann Arbor. They had planned that Alexandra was to come to Michigan—a long journey for her—at Christmas time, and spend several weeks with him. Nevertheless, he felt that this leavetaking would be more final than his earlier ones had been; that it meant a definite break with his old home and the beginning of something new—he did not know what. His ideas about the future would not crystallize; the more he tried to think about it, the vaguer his conception of it became. But one thing was clear, he told himself; it was high time that he made good to Alexandra, and that ought to be incentive enough to begin with.

As he went about gathering up his books he felt as if he were uprooting things. At last he threw himself down on the old slat lounge[3] where he had slept when he was little, and lay looking up at the familiar cracks in the ceiling.

"Tired, Emil?" his sister asked.

"Lazy," he murmured, turning on his side and looking at her. He studied Alexandra's face for a long time in the lamplight. It had never occurred to him that his sister was a handsome woman until Marie Shabata had told him so. Indeed, he had never thought of her as being a woman at all, only a sister. As he studied her bent head, he looked up at the picture of John Bergson above the lamp. "No," he thought to himself, "she did n't get it there. I suppose I am more like that."

"Alexandra," he said suddenly, "that old walnut secretary you use for a desk was father's, was n't it?"

Alexandra went on stitching. "Yes. It was one of the first things he bought for the old log house. It was a great extravagance in those days. But he wrote a great many letters back to the old country. He had many friends there, and they wrote to him up to the time he died. No one ever blamed him for grandfather's disgrace. I can see him now, sitting there on Sundays, in his white shirt, writ-

3. A lounge chair made from slats of wood.

ing pages and pages, so carefully. He wrote a fine, regular hand, almost like engraving. Yours is something like his, when you take pains."

"Grandfather was really crooked, was he?"

"He married an unscrupulous woman, and then—then I'm afraid he was really crooked. When we first came here father used to have dreams about making a great fortune and going back to Sweden to pay back to the poor sailors the money grandfather had lost."

Emil stirred on the lounge. "I say, that would have been worth while, would n't it? Father was n't a bit like Lou or Oscar, was he? I can't remember much about him before he got sick."

"Oh, not at all!" Alexandra dropped her sewing on her knee. "He had better opportunities; not to make money, but to make something of himself. He was a quiet man, but he was very intelligent. You would have been proud of him, Emil."

Alexandra felt that he would like to know there had been a man of his kin whom he could admire. She knew that Emil was ashamed of Lou and Oscar, because they were bigoted and self-satisfied. He never said much about them, but she could feel his disgust. His brothers had shown their disapproval of him ever since he first went away to school. The only thing that would have satisfied them would have been his failure at the University. As it was, they resented every change in his speech, in his dress, in his point of view; though the latter they had to conjecture, for Emil avoided talking to them about any but family matters. All his interests they treated as affectations.

Alexandra took up her sewing again. "I can remember father when he was quite a young man. He belonged to some kind of a musical society, a male chorus, in Stockholm. I can remember going with mother to hear them sing. There must have been a hundred of them, and they all wore long black coats and white neckties. I was used to seeing father in a blue coat, a sort of jacket, and when I recognized him on the platform, I was very proud. Do you remember that Swedish song he taught you, about the ship boy?"

"Yes. I used to sing it to the Mexicans. They like anything different." Emil paused. "Father had a hard fight here, did n't he?" he added thoughtfully.

"Yes, and he died in a dark time. Still, he had hope. He believed in the land."

"And in you, I guess," Emil said to himself. There was another period of silence; that warm, friendly silence, full of perfect understanding, in which Emil and Alexandra had spent many of their happiest half-hours.

At last Emil said abruptly, "Lou and Oscar would be better off if they were poor, would n't they?"

Alexandra smiled. "Maybe. But their children would n't. I have great hopes of Milly."

Emil shivered. "I don't know. Seems to me it gets worse as it goes on. The worst of the Swedes is that they're never willing to find out how much they don't know. It was like that at the University. Always so pleased with themselves! There's no getting behind that conceited Swedish grin. The Bohemians and Germans were so different."

"Come, Emil, don't go back on your own people. Father was n't conceited, Uncle Otto was n't. Even Lou and Oscar were n't when they were boys."

Emil looked incredulous, but he did not dispute the point. He turned on his back and lay still for a long time, his hands locked under his head, looking up at the ceiling. Alexandra knew that he was thinking of many things. She felt no anxiety about Emil. She had always believed in him, as she had believed in the land. He had been more like himself since he got back from Mexico; seemed glad to be at home, and talked to her as he used to do. She had no doubt that his wandering fit was over, and that he would soon be settled in life.

"Alexandra," said Emil suddenly, "do you remember the wild duck we saw down on the river that time?"

His sister looked up. "I often think of her. It always seems to me she's there still, just like we saw her."

"I know. It's queer what things one remembers and what things one forgets." Emil yawned and sat up. "Well, it's time to turn in." He rose, and going over to Alexandra stooped down and kissed her lightly on the cheek. "Good-night, sister. I think you did pretty well by us."

Emil took up his lamp and went upstairs. Alexandra sat finishing his new nightshirt, that must go in the top tray of his trunk.

IV

The next morning Angélique, Amédée's wife, was in the kitchen baking pies, assisted by old Mrs. Chevalier. Between the mixing-board and the stove stood the old cradle that had been Amédée's, and in it was his black-eyed son. As Angélique, flushed and excited, with flour on her hands, stopped to smile at the baby, Emil Bergson rode up to the kitchen door on his mare and dismounted.

" 'Médée is out in the field, Emil," Angélique called as she ran across the kitchen to the oven. "He begins to cut his wheat to-day;

the first wheat ready to cut anywhere about here. He bought a new header, you know, because all the wheat's so short this year. I hope he can rent it to the neighbors, it cost so much. He and his cousins bought a steam thresher on shares. You ought to go out and see that header work. I watched it an hour this morning, busy as I am with all the men to feed. He has a lot of hands, but he's the only one that knows how to drive the header or how to run the engine, so he has to be everywhere at once. He's sick, too, and ought to be in his bed."

Emil bent over Hector Baptiste, trying to make him blink his round, bead-like black eyes. "Sick? What's the matter with your daddy, kid? Been making him walk the floor with you?"

Angélique sniffed. "Not much! We don't have that kind of babies. It was his father that kept Baptiste awake. All night I had to be getting up and making mustard plasters to put on his stomach. He had an awful colic. He said he felt better this morning, but I don't think he ought to be out in the field, overheating himself."

Angélique did not speak with much anxiety, not because she was indifferent, but because she felt so secure in their good fortune. Only good things could happen to a rich, energetic, handsome young man like Amédée, with a new baby in the cradle and a new header in the field.

Emil stroked the black fuzz on Baptiste's head. "I say, Angélique, one of 'Médée's grandmothers, 'way back, must have been a squaw. This kid looks exactly like the Indian babies."

Angélique made a face at him, but old Mrs. Chevalier had been touched on a sore point, and she let out such a stream of fiery *patois* that Emil fled from the kitchen and mounted his mare.

Opening the pasture gate from the saddle, Emil rode across the field to the clearing where the thresher stood, driven by a stationary engine and fed from the header boxes. As Amédée was not on the engine, Emil rode on to the wheatfield, where he recognized, on the header, the slight, wiry figure of his friend, coatless, his white shirt puffed out by the wind, his straw hat stuck jauntily on the side of his head. The six big work-horses that drew, or rather pushed, the header, went abreast at a rapid walk, and as they were still green at the work they required a good deal of management on Amédée's part; especially when they turned the corners, where they divided, three and three, and then swung round into line again with a movement that looked as complicated as a wheel of artillery. Emil felt a new thrill of admiration for his friend, and with it the old pang of envy at the way in which Amédée could do with his might what his hand found to do, and feel that, whatever it was, it was the most important thing in the world. "I'll have to bring Alexandra up to see this thing work," Emil thought; "it's splendid!"

When he saw Emil, Amédée waved to him and called to one of his twenty cousins to take the reins. Stepping off the header without stopping it, he ran up to Emil who had dismounted. "Come along," he called. "I have to go over to the engine for a minute. I gotta green man running it, and I gotta to keep an eye on him."

Emil thought the lad was unnaturally flushed and more excited than even the cares of managing a big farm at a critical time warranted. As they passed behind a last year's stack, Amédée clutched at his right side and sank down for a moment on the straw.

"Ouch! I got an awful pain in me, Emil. Something's the matter with my insides, for sure."

Emil felt his fiery cheek. "You ought to go straight to bed, 'Médée, and telephone for the doctor; that's what you ought to do."

Amédée staggered up with a gesture of despair. "How can I? I got no time to be sick. Three thousand dollars' worth of new machinery to manage, and the wheat so ripe it will begin to shatter next week. My wheat's short, but it's gotta grand full berries. What's he slowing down for? We have n't got header boxes enough to feed the thresher, I guess."

Amédée started hot-foot across the stubble, leaning a little to the right as he ran, and waved to the engineer not to stop the engine.

Emil saw that this was no time to talk about his own affairs. He mounted his mare and rode on to Sainte-Agnes, to bid his friends there good-bye. He went first to see Raoul Marcel, and found him innocently practising the "Gloria" for the big confirmation service on Sunday while he polished the mirrors of his father's saloon.

As Emil rode homewards at three o'clock in the afternoon, he saw Amédée staggering out of the wheatfield, supported by two of his cousins. Emil stopped and helped them put the boy to bed.

V

When Frank Shabata came in from work at five o'clock that evening, old Moses Marcel, Raoul's father, telephoned him that Amédée had had a seizure in the wheatfield, and that Doctor Paradis was going to operate on him as soon as the Hanover doctor got there to help. Frank dropped a word of this at the table, bolted his supper, and rode off to Sainte-Agnes, where there would be sympathetic discussion of Amédée's case at Marcel's saloon.

As soon as Frank was gone, Marie telephoned Alexandra. It was a comfort to hear her friend's voice. Yes, Alexandra knew what there was to be known about Amédée. Emil had been there when they carried him out of the field, and had stayed with him until the doctors operated for appendicitis at five o'clock. They were afraid it was too late to do much good; it should have been done three days ago. Amédée was in a very bad way. Emil had just come home, worn out and sick himself. She had given him some brandy and put him to bed.

Marie hung up the receiver. Poor Amédée's illness had taken on a new meaning to her, now that she knew Emil had been with him. And it might so easily have been the other way—Emil who was ill and Amédée who was sad! Marie looked about the dusky sitting-room. She had seldom felt so utterly lonely. If Emil was asleep, there was not even a chance of his coming; and she could not go to Alexandra for sympathy. She meant to tell Alexandra everything, as soon as Emil went away. Then whatever was left between them would be honest.

But she could not stay in the house this evening. Where should she go? She walked slowly down through the orchard, where the evening air was heavy with the smell of wild cotton. The fresh, salty scent of the wild roses had given way before this more powerful perfume of midsummer. Wherever those ashes-of-rose balls hung on their milky stalks, the air about them was saturated with their breath. The sky was still red in the west and the evening star hung directly over the Bergsons' windmill. Marie crossed the fence at the wheatfield corner, and walked slowly along the path that led to Alexandra's. She could not help feeling hurt that Emil had not come to tell her about Amédée. It seemed to her most unnatural that he should not have come. If she were in trouble, certainly he was the one person in the world she would want to see. Perhaps he wished her to understand that for her he was as good as gone already.

Marie stole slowly, flutteringly, along the path, like a white night-moth out of the fields. The years seemed to stretch before her like the land; spring, summer, autumn, winter, spring; always the same patient fields, the patient little trees, the patient lives; always the same yearning, the same pulling at the chain—until the instinct to live had torn itself and bled and weakened for the last time, until the chain secured a dead woman, who might cautiously be released. Marie walked on, her face lifted toward the remote, inaccessible evening star.

When she reached the stile she sat down and waited. How terrible it was to love people when you could not really share their lives!

Yes, in so far as she was concerned, Emil was already gone. They could n't meet any more. There was nothing for them to say. They had spent the last penny of their small change; there was nothing left but gold. The day of love-tokens was past. They had now only their hearts to give each other. And Emil being gone, what was her life to be like? In some ways, it would be easier. She would not, at least, live in perpetual fear. If Emil were once away and settled at work, she would not have the feeling that she was spoiling his life. With the memory he left her, she could be as rash as she chose. Nobody could be the worse for it but herself; and that, surely, did not matter. Her own case was clear. When a girl had loved one man, and then loved another while that man was still alive, everybody knew what to think of her. What happened to her was of little consequence, so long as she did not drag other people down with her. Emil once away, she could let everything else go and live a new life of perfect love.

Marie left the stile reluctantly. She had, after all, thought he might come. And how glad she ought to be, she told herself, that he was asleep. She left the path and went across the pasture. The moon was almost full. An owl was hooting somewhere in the fields. She had scarcely thought about where she was going when the pond glittered before her, where Emil had shot the ducks. She stopped and looked at it. Yes, there would be a dirty way out of life, if one chose to take it. But she did not want to die. She wanted to live and dream—a hundred years, forever! As long as this sweetness welled up in her heart, as long as her breast could hold this treasure of pain! She felt as the pond must feel when it held the moon like that; when it encircled and swelled with that image of gold.

In the morning, when Emil came downstairs, Alexandra met him in the sitting-room and put her hands on his shoulders. "Emil, I went to your room as soon as it was light, but you were sleeping so sound I hated to wake you. There was nothing you could do, so I let you sleep. They telephoned from Sainte-Agnes that Amédée died at three o'clock this morning."

VI

The church has always held that life is for the living. On Saturday, while half the village of Sainte-Agnes was mourning for Amédée and preparing the funeral black for his burial on Monday, the other half was busy with white dresses and white veils for the great confirmation service to-morrow, when the bishop was to confirm a class of one hundred boys and girls. Father Duchesne divided his time between the living and the dead. All day Saturday the church was a scene of bustling activity, a little hushed by the thought of Amédée. The choir were busy rehearsing a mass of Rossini, which they had studied and practised for this occasion. The women were trimming the altar, the boys and girls were bringing flowers.

On Sunday morning the bishop was to drive overland to Sainte-Agnes from Hanover, and Emil Bergson had been asked to take the place of one of Amédée's cousins in the cavalcade of forty French boys who were to ride across country to meet the bishop's carriage. At six o'clock on Sunday morning the boys met at the church. As they stood holding their horses by the bridle, they talked in low tones of their dead comrade. They kept repeating that Amédée had always been a good boy, glancing toward the red brick church which had played so large a part in Amédée's life, had been the scene of his most serious moments and of his happiest hours. He had played and wrestled and sung and courted under its shadow. Only three weeks ago he had proudly carried his baby there to be christened. They could not doubt that that invisible arm was still about Amédée; that through the church on earth he had passed to the church triumphant,[4] the goal of the hopes and faith of so many hundred years.

When the word was given to mount, the young men rode at a walk out of the village; but once out among the wheat-fields in the morning sun, their horses and their own youth got the better of them. A wave of zeal and fiery enthusiasm swept over them. They longed for a Jerusalem to deliver. The thud of their galloping hoofs interrupted many a country breakfast and brought many a woman and child to the door of the farmhouses as they passed. Five miles east of Sainte-Agnes they met the bishop in his open carriage, attended by two priests. Like one man the boys swung off their hats in a broad salute, and bowed their heads as the handsome old man lifted his two fingers in the episcopal blessing. The horsemen closed about the carriage like a guard, and whenever a restless horse broke from control and shot down the road ahead of the body, the bishop laughed and rubbed his plump hands together. "What fine boys!" he said to his priests. "The Church still has her cavalry."

As the troop swept past the graveyard half a mile east of the town,—the first frame church of the parish had stood there,—old Pierre Séguin was already out with his pick and spade, digging Amédée's grave. He knelt and uncovered as the bishop passed. The boys with one accord looked away from old Pierre to the red church on the hill, with the gold cross flaming on its steeple.

Mass was at eleven. While the church was filling, Emil Bergson waited outside, watching the wagons and buggies drive up the hill. After the bell began to ring, he saw Frank Shabata ride up on horseback and tie his horse to the hitchbar. Marie, then, was not coming. Emil turned and went into the church. Amédée's was the only empty pew, and he sat down in it. Some of Amédée's cousins were there, dressed in black and weeping. When all the pews were

4. In Roman Catholic theology, the church triumphant is the souls of the faithful in heaven.

full, the old men and boys packed the open space at the back of the church, kneeling on the floor. There was scarcely a family in town that was not represented in the confirmation class, by a cousin, at least. The new communicants, with their clear, reverent faces, were beautiful to look upon as they entered in a body and took the front benches reserved for them. Even before the Mass began, the air was charged with feeling. The choir had never sung so well and Raoul Marcel, in the "Gloria," drew even the bishop's eyes to the organ loft. For the offertory he sang Gounod's "Ave Maria,"—always spoken of in Sainte-Agnes as "the Ave Maria."

Emil began to torture himself with questions about Marie. Was she ill? Had she quarreled with her husband? Was she too unhappy to find comfort even here? Had she, perhaps, thought that he would come to her? Was she waiting for him? Overtaxed by excitement and sorrow as he was, the rapture of the service took hold upon his body and mind. As he listened to Raoul, he seemed to emerge from the conflicting emotions which had been whirling him about and sucking him under. He felt as if a clear light broke upon his mind, and with it a conviction that good was, after all, stronger than evil, and that good was possible to men. He seemed to discover that there was a kind of rapture in which he could love forever without faltering and without sin. He looked across the heads of the people at Frank Shabata with calmness. That rapture was for those who could feel it; for people who could not, it was nonexistent. He coveted nothing that was Frank Shabata's. The spirit he had met in music was his own. Frank Shabata had never found it; would never find it if he lived beside it a thousand years; would have destroyed it if he had found it, as Herod slew the innocents,[5] as Rome slew the martyrs.

San—cta Mari-i-i-a,

wailed Raoul from the organ loft;

O—ra pro no-o-bis![6]

And it did not occur to Emil that any one had ever reasoned thus before, that music had ever before given a man this equivocal revelation.

The confirmation service followed the Mass. When it was over, the congregation thronged about the newly confirmed. The girls, and even the boys, were kissed and embraced and wept over. All the aunts and grandmothers wept with joy. The housewives had much ado to tear themselves away from the general rejoicing and hurry

5. The story of Herod's massacre of the Hebrew children is told in Matthew 2.16–17.
6. "Holy Mary, pray for us!"

back to their kitchens. The country parishioners were staying in town for dinner, and nearly every house in Sainte-Agnes entertained visitors that day. Father Duchesne, the bishop, and the visiting priests dined with Fabien Sauvage, the banker. Emil and Frank Shabata were both guests of old Moïse Marcel. After dinner Frank and old Moïse retired to the rear room of the saloon to play California Jack and drink their cognac, and Emil went over to the banker's with Raoul, who had been asked to sing for the bishop.

At three o'clock, Emil felt that he could stand it no longer. He slipped out under cover of "The Holy City,"[7] followed by Malvina's wistful eye, and went to the stable for his mare. He was at that height of excitement from which everything is foreshortened, from which life seems short and simple, death very near, and the soul seems to soar like an eagle. As he rode past the graveyard he looked at the brown hole in the earth where Amédée was to lie, and felt no horror. That, too, was beautiful, that simple doorway into forgetfulness. The heart, when it is too much alive, aches for that brown earth, and ecstasy has no fear of death. It is the old and the poor and the maimed who shrink from that brown hole; its wooers are found among the young, the passionate, the gallant-hearted. It was not until he had passed the graveyard that Emil realized where he was going. It was the hour for saying good-bye. It might be the last time that he would see her alone, and to-day he could leave her without rancor, without bitterness.

Everywhere the grain stood ripe and the hot afternoon was full of the smell of the ripe wheat, like the smell of bread baking in an oven. The breath of the wheat and the sweet clover passed him like pleasant things in a dream. He could feel nothing but the sense of diminishing distance. It seemed to him that his mare was flying, or running on wheels, like a railway train. The sunlight, flashing on the window-glass of the big red barns, drove him wild with joy. He was like an arrow shot from the bow. His life poured itself out along the road before him as he rode to the Shabata farm.

When Emil alighted at the Shabatas' gate, his horse was in a lather. He tied her in the stable and hurried to the house. It was empty. She might be at Mrs. Hiller's or with Alexandra. But anything that reminded him of her would be enough, the orchard, the mulberry tree . . . When he reached the orchard the sun was hanging low over the wheat-field. Long fingers of light reached through the apple branches as through a net; the orchard was riddled and shot with gold; light was the reality, the trees were merely interferences that reflected and refracted light. Emil went softly down between the cherry trees toward the wheatfield. When he came to the

7. Sacred song by English composer Michael Maybrick (1844–1913).

corner, he stopped short and put his hand over his mouth. Marie was lying on her side under the white mulberry tree, her face half hidden in the grass, her eyes closed, her hands lying limply where they had happened to fall. She had lived a day of her new life of perfect love, and it had left her like this. Her breast rose and fell faintly, as if she were asleep. Emil threw himself down beside her and took her in his arms. The blood came back to her cheeks, her amber eyes opened slowly, and in them Emil saw his own face and the orchard and the sun. "I was dreaming this," she whispered, hiding her face against him, "don't take my dream away!"

VII

When Frank Shabata got home that night, he found Emil's mare in his stable. Such an impertinence amazed him. Like everybody else, Frank had had an exciting day. Since noon he had been drinking too much, and he was in a bad temper. He talked bitterly to himself while he put his own horse away, and as he went up the path and saw that the house was dark he felt an added sense of injury. He approached quietly and listened on the doorstep. Hearing nothing, he opened the kitchen door and went softly from one room to another. Then he went through the house again, upstairs and down, with no better result. He sat down on the bottom step of the box stairway and tried to get his wits together. In that unnatural quiet there was no sound but his own heavy breathing. Suddenly an owl began to hoot out in the fields. Frank lifted his head. An idea flashed into his mind, and his sense of injury and outrage grew. He went into his bedroom and took his murderous 405 Winchester[8] from the closet.

When Frank took up his gun and walked out of the house, he had not the faintest purpose of doing anything with it. He did not believe that he had any real grievance. But it gratified him to feel like a desperate man. He had got into the habit of seeing himself always in desperate straits. His unhappy temperament was like a cage; he could never get out of it; and he felt that other people, his wife in particular, must have put him there. It had never more than dimly occurred to Frank that he made his own unhappiness. Though he took up his gun with dark projects in his mind, he would have been paralyzed with fright had he known that there was the slightest probability of his ever carrying any of them out.

Frank went slowly down to the orchard gate, stopped and stood for a moment lost in thought. He retraced his steps and looked through the barn and the hayloft. Then he went out to the road,

8. The most powerful commercial rifle available in the United States in the late nineteenth and early twentieth centuries, famously used by Teddy Roosevelt in hunting big game.

where he took the footpath along the outside of the orchard hedge. The hedge was twice as tall as Frank himself, and so dense that one could see through it only by peering closely between the leaves. He could see the empty path a long way in the moonlight. His mind traveled ahead to the stile, which he always thought of as haunted by Emil Bergson. But why had he left his horse?

At the wheatfield corner, where the orchard hedge ended and the path led across the pasture to the Bergsons', Frank stopped. In the warm, breathless night air he heard a murmuring sound, perfectly inarticulate, as low as the sound of water coming from a spring, where there is no fall, and where there are no stones to fret it. Frank strained his ears. It ceased. He held his breath and began to tremble. Resting the butt of his gun on the ground, he parted the mulberry leaves softly with his fingers and peered through the hedge at the dark figures on the grass, in the shadow of the mulberry tree. It seemed to him that they must feel his eyes, that they must hear him breathing. But they did not. Frank, who had always wanted to see things blacker than they were, for once wanted to believe less than he saw. The woman lying in the shadow might so easily be one of the Bergsons' farm-girls. . . . Again the murmur, like water welling out of the ground. This time he heard it more distinctly, and his blood was quicker than his brain. He began to act, just as a man who falls into the fire begins to act. The gun sprang to his shoulder, he sighted mechanically and fired three times without stopping, stopped without knowing why. Either he shut his eyes or he had vertigo. He did not see anything while he was firing. He thought he heard a cry simultaneous with the second report, but he was not sure. He peered again through the hedge, at the two dark figures under the tree. They had fallen a little apart from each other, and were perfectly still—No, not quite; in a white patch of light, where the moon shone through the branches, a man's hand was plucking spasmodically at the grass.

Suddenly the woman stirred and uttered a cry, then another, and another. She was living! She was dragging herself toward the hedge! Frank dropped his gun and ran back along the path, shaking, stumbling, gasping. He had never imagined such horror. The cries followed him. They grew fainter and thicker, as if she were choking. He dropped on his knees beside the hedge and crouched like a rabbit, listening; fainter, fainter; a sound like a whine; again—a moan—another—silence. Frank scrambled to his feet and ran on, groaning and praying. From habit he went toward the house, where he was used to being soothed when he had worked himself into a frenzy, but at the sight of the black, open door, he started back. He knew that he had murdered somebody, that a woman was bleeding and moaning in the orchard, but he had not realized before that it was his wife. The gate stared him in the face. He threw his hands over his head. Which way to turn? He lifted his tormented face and looked at the sky. "Holy Mother of God, not to suffer! She was a good girl—not to suffer!"

Frank had been wont to see himself in dramatic situations; but now, when he stood by the windmill, in the bright space between the barn and the house, facing his own black doorway, he did not see himself at all. He stood like the hare when the dogs are approaching from all sides. And he ran like a hare, back and forth about that moonlit space, before he could make up his mind to go into the dark stable for a horse. The thought of going into a doorway was terrible to him. He caught Emil's horse by the bit and led it out. He could not have buckled a bridle on his own. After two or three attempts, he lifted himself into the saddle and started for Hanover. If he could catch the one o'clock train, he had money enough to get as far as Omaha.

While he was thinking dully of this in some less sensitized part of his brain, his acuter faculties were going over and over the cries he had heard in the orchard. Terror was the only thing that kept him from going back to her, terror that she might still be she, that she might still be suffering. A woman, mutilated and bleeding in his orchard—it was because it was a woman that he was so afraid. It was inconceivable that he should have hurt a woman. He would rather be eaten by wild beasts than see her move on the ground as she had moved in the orchard. Why had she been so careless? She knew he was like a crazy man when he was angry. She had more than once taken that gun away from him and held it, when he was angry with other people. Once it had gone off while they were struggling over it. She was never afraid. But, when she knew him, why had n't she been more careful? Did n't she have all summer before her to love Emil Bergson in, without taking such chances? Probably she had met the Smirka boy, too, down there in the orchard. He did n't care. She could have met all the men on the Divide there, and welcome, if only she had n't brought this horror on him.

There was a wrench in Frank's mind. He did not honestly believe that of her. He knew that he was doing her wrong. He stopped his horse to admit this to himself the more directly, to think it out the more clearly. He knew that he was to blame. For three years he had been trying to break her spirit. She had a way of making the best of things that seemed to him a sentimental affectation. He wanted his wife to resent that he was wasting his best years among these stupid and unappreciative people; but she had seemed to find the people quite good enough. If he ever got rich he meant to buy her pretty clothes and take her to California in a Pullman car,[9] and treat her like a lady; but in the mean time he wanted her to feel that life was as ugly and as unjust as he felt it. He had tried to make her life ugly. He had refused to share any of the little pleasures she was so plucky about making for herself. She could be gay about the least thing in the world; but she must be gay! When she first came to him, her faith in him, her adoration—Frank struck the mare with his fist. Why had Marie made him do this thing; why had she brought this upon him? He was overwhelmed by sickening misfortune. All at once he heard her cries again—he had forgotten for a moment. "Maria," he sobbed aloud, "Maria!"

When Frank was halfway to Hanover, the motion of his horse brought on a violent attack of nausea. After it had passed, he rode on again, but he could think of nothing except his physical weakness and his desire to be comforted by his wife. He wanted to get into his own bed. Had his wife been at home, he would have turned and gone back to her meekly enough.

VIII

When old Ivar climbed down from his loft at four o'clock the next morning, he came upon Emil's mare, jaded and lather-stained, her bridle broken, chewing the scattered tufts of hay outside the stable door. The old man was thrown into a fright at once. He put the mare in her stall, threw her a measure of oats, and then set out as fast as his bow-legs could carry him on the path to the nearest neighbor.

"Something is wrong with that boy. Some misfortune has come upon us. He would never have used her so, in his right senses. It is not his way to abuse his mare," the old man kept muttering, as he scuttled through the short, wet pasture grass on his bare feet.

While Ivar was hurrying across the fields, the first long rays of the sun were reaching down between the orchard boughs to those two dew-drenched figures. The story of what had happened was written plainly on the orchard grass, and on the white mulberries that had fallen in the night and were covered with dark stain. For Emil the chapter had been short. He was shot in the heart, and had rolled over on his back and died. His face was turned up to the sky and his brows were drawn in a frown, as if he had realized that something had befallen him. But for Marie Shabata it had not been so easy. One ball had torn through her right lung, another had shattered the carotid artery. She must have started up and gone toward

9. A luxurious passenger railcar featuring sleeping compartments and a lavishly furnished lounge.

the hedge, leaving a trail of blood. There she had fallen and bled. From that spot there was another trail, heavier than the first, where she must have dragged herself back to Emil's body. Once there, she seemed not to have struggled any more. She had lifted her head to her lover's breast, taken his hand in both her own, and bled quietly to death. She was lying on her right side in an easy and natural position, her cheek on Emil's shoulder. On her face there was a look of ineffable content. Her lips were parted a little; her eyes were lightly closed, as if in a day-dream or a light slumber. After she lay down there, she seemed not to have moved an eyelash. The hand she held was covered with dark stains, where she had kissed it.

But the stained, slippery grass, the darkened mulberries, told only half the story. Above Marie and Emil; two white butterflies from Frank's alfalfa-field were fluttering in and out among the interlacing shadows; diving and soaring, now close together, now far apart; and in the long grass by the fence the last wild roses of the year opened their pink hearts to die.

When Ivar reached the path by the hedge, he saw Shabata's rifle lying in the way. He turned and peered through the branches, falling upon his knees as if his legs had been mowed from under him. "Merciful God!" he groaned; "merciful, merciful God!"

Alexandra, too, had risen early that morning, because of her anxiety about Emil. She was in Emil's room upstairs when, from the window, she saw Ivar coming along the path that led from the Shabatas'. He was running like a spent man, tottering and lurching from side to side. Ivar never drank, and Alexandra thought at once that one of his spells had come upon him, and that he must be in a very bad way indeed. She ran downstairs and hurried out to meet him, to hide his infirmity from the eyes of her household. The old man fell in the road at her feet and caught her hand, over which he bowed his shaggy head. "Mistress, mistress," he sobbed, "it has fallen! Sin and death for the young ones! God have mercy upon us!"

Part V. Alexandra

I

Ivar was sitting at a cobbler's bench in the barn, mending harness by the light of a lantern and repeating to himself the 101st Psalm.[1] It was only five o'clock of a mid-October day, but a storm had come up in the afternoon, bringing black clouds, a cold wind and torrents of rain. The old man wore his buffalo-skin coat, and occasionally stopped to warm his fingers at the lantern. Suddenly a woman burst into the shed, as if she had been blown in, accompanied by a shower of rain-drops. It was Signa, wrapped in a man's overcoat and wearing a pair of boots over her shoes. In time of trouble Signa had come back to stay with her mistress, for she was the only one of the maids from whom Alexandra would accept much personal service. It was three months now since the news of the terrible thing that had happened in Frank Shabata's orchard had first run like a fire over the Divide. Signa and Nelse were staying on with Alexandra until winter.

"Ivar," Signa exclaimed as she wiped the rain from her face, "do you know where she is?"

The old man put down his cobbler's knife. "Who, the mistress?"

"Yes. She went away about three o'clock. I happened to look out of the window and saw her going across the fields in her thin dress and sun-hat. And now this storm has come on. I thought she was going to Mrs. Hiller's, and I telephoned as soon as the thunder stopped, but she had not been there. I'm afraid she is out somewhere and will get her death of cold."

Ivar put on his cap and took up the lantern. "*Ja, ja*, we will see. I will hitch the boy's mare to the cart and go."

Signa followed him across the wagon-shed to the horses' stable. She was shivering with cold and excitement. "Where do you suppose she can be, Ivar?"

The old man lifted a set of single harness carefully from its peg. "How should I know?"

"But you think she is at the graveyard, don't you?" Signa per-

1. The psalm begins "I will sing of mercy and judgment: unto thee, O Lord, will I sing."

sisted. "So do I. Oh, I wish she would be more like herself! I can't believe it's Alexandra Bergson come to this, with no head about anything. I have to tell her when to eat and when to go to bed."

"Patience, patience, sister," muttered Ivar as he settled the bit in the horse's mouth. "When the eyes of the flesh are shut, the eyes of the spirit are open. She will have a message from those who are gone, and that will bring her peace. Until then we must bear with her. You and I are the only ones who have weight with her. She trusts us."

"How awful it's been these last three months." Signa held the lantern so that he could see to buckle the straps. "It don't seem right that we must all be so miserable. Why do we all have to be punished? Seems to me like good times would never come again."

Ivar expressed himself in a deep sigh, but said nothing. He stooped and took a sandburr from his toe.

"Ivar," Signa asked suddenly, "will you tell me why you go barefoot? All the time I lived here in the house I wanted to ask you. Is it for a penance, or what?"

"No, sister. It is for the indulgence of the body. From my youth up I have had a strong, rebellious body, and have been subject to every kind of temptation. Even in age my temptations are prolonged. It was necessary to make some allowances; and the feet, as I understand it, are free members. There is no divine prohibition for them in the Ten Commandments. The hands, the tongue, the eyes, the heart, all the bodily desires we are commanded to subdue; but the feet are free members. I indulge them without harm to any one, even to trampling in filth when my desires are low. They are quickly cleaned again."

Signa did not laugh. She looked thoughtful as she followed Ivar out to the wagon-shed and held the shafts up for him, while he backed in the mare and buckled the hold-backs. "You have been a good friend to the mistress, Ivar," she murmured.

"And you, God be with you," replied Ivar as he clambered into the cart and put the lantern under the oilcloth lap-cover. "Now for a ducking, my girl," he said to the mare, gathering up the reins.

As they emerged from the shed, a stream of water, running off the thatch, struck the mare on the neck. She tossed her head indignantly, then struck out bravely on the soft ground, slipping back again and again as she climbed the hill to the main road. Between the rain and the darkness Ivar could see very little, so he let Emil's mare have the rein, keeping her head in the right direction. When the ground was level, he turned her out of the dirt road upon the sod, where she was able to trot without slipping.

Before Ivar reached the graveyard, three miles from the house, the storm had spent itself, and the downpour had died into a soft, dripping rain. The sky and the land were a dark smoke color, and seemed to be coming together, like two waves. When Ivar stopped at the gate and swung out his lantern, a white figure rose from beside John Bergson's white stone.

The old man sprang to the ground and shuffled toward the gate calling, "Mistress, mistress!"

Alexandra hurried to meet him and put her hand on his shoulder. "*Tyst!*[2] Ivar. There's nothing to be worried about. I'm sorry if I've scared you all. I did n't notice the storm till it was on me, and I could n't walk against it. I'm glad you've come. I am so tired I did n't know how I'd ever get home."

Ivar swung the lantern up so that it shone in her face. "*Gud!*[3] Y ou are enough to frighten us, mistress. You look like a drowned woman. How could you do such a thing!"

Groaning and mumbling he led her out of the gate and helped her into the cart, wrapping her in the dry blankets on which he had been sitting.

Alexandra smiled at his solicitude. "Not much use in that, Ivar. You will only shut the wet in. I don't feel so cold now; but I'm heavy and numb. I'm glad you came."

Ivar turned the mare and urged her into a sliding trot. Her feet sent back a continual spatter of mud.

Alexandra spoke to the old man as they jogged along through the sullen gray twilight of the storm. "Ivar, I think it has done me good to get cold clear through like this, once. I don't believe I shall suffer so much any more. When you get so near the dead, they seem more real than the living. Worldly thoughts leave one. Ever since Emil died, I've suffered so when it rained. Now that I've been out in it with him, I shan't dread it. After you once get cold clear through, the feeling of the rain on you is sweet. It seems to bring back feelings you had when you were a baby. It carries you back into the dark, before you were born; you can't see things, but they come to you, somehow, and you know them and are n't afraid of them. Maybe it's like that with the dead. If they feel anything at all, it's the old things, before they were born, that comfort people like the feeling of their own bed does when they are little."

"Mistress," said Ivar reproachfully, "those are bad thoughts. The dead are in Paradise."

Then he hung his head, for he did not believe that Emil was in Paradise.

When they got home, Signa had a fire burning in the sitting-room stove. She undressed Alexandra and gave her a hot footbath,

2. *Quiet!*
3. *God!*

while Ivar made ginger tea in the kitchen. When Alexandra was in bed, wrapped in hot blankets, Ivar came in with his tea and saw that she drank it. Signa asked permission to sleep on the slat lounge outside her door. Alexandra endured their attentions patiently, but she was glad when they put out the lamp and left her. As she lay alone in the dark, it occurred to her for the first time that perhaps she was actually tired of life. All the physical operations of life seemed difficult and painful. She longed to be free from her own body, which ached and was so heavy. And longing itself was heavy: she yearned to be free of that.

As she lay with her eyes closed, she had again, more vividly than for many years, the old illusion of her girlhood, of being lifted and carried lightly by some one very strong. He was with her a long while this time, and carried her very far, and in his arms she felt free from pain. When he laid her down on her bed again, she opened her eyes, and, for the first time in her life, she saw him, saw him clearly, though the room was dark, and his face was covered. He was standing in the doorway of her room. His white cloak was thrown over his face, and his head was bent a little forward. His shoulders seemed as strong as the foundations of the world. His right arm, bared from the elbow, was dark and gleaming, like bronze, and she knew at once that it was the arm of the mightiest of all lovers. She knew at last for whom it was she had waited, and where he would carry her. That, she told herself, was very well. Then she went to sleep.

Alexandra wakened in the morning with nothing worse than a hard cold and a stiff shoulder. She kept her bed for several days, and it was during that time that she formed a resolution to go to Lincoln to see Frank Shabata. Ever since she last saw him in the courtroom, Frank's haggard face and wild eyes had haunted her. The trial had lasted only three days. Frank had given himself up to the police in Omaha and pleaded guilty of killing without malice and without premeditation. The gun was, of course, against him, and the judge had given him the full sentence,—ten years. He had now been in the State Penitentiary for a month.

Frank was the only one, Alexandra told herself, for whom anything could be done. He had been less in the wrong than any of them, and he was paying the heaviest penalty. She often felt that she herself had been more to blame than poor Frank. From the time the Shabatas had first moved to the neighboring farm, she had omitted no opportunity of throwing Marie and Emil together. Because she knew Frank was surly about doing little things to help his wife, she was always sending Emil over to spade or plant or carpenter for Marie. She was glad to have Emil see as much as possible of an intelligent, city-bred girl like their neighbor; she noticed that it improved his manners. She knew that Emil was fond of Marie, but it had never occurred to her that Emil's feeling might be different from her own. She wondered at herself now, but she had never thought of danger in that direction. If Marie had been unmarried,—oh, yes! Then she would have kept her eyes open. But the mere fact that she was Shabata's wife, for Alexandra, settled everything. That she was beautiful, impulsive, barely two years older than Emil, these facts had had no weight with Alexandra. Emil was a good boy, and only bad boys ran after married women.

Now, Alexandra could in a measure realize that Marie was, after all, Marie; not merely a "married woman." Sometimes, when Alexandra thought of her, it was with an aching tenderness. The moment she had reached them in the orchard that morning, everything was clear to her. There was something about those two lying in the grass, something in the way Marie had settled her cheek on Emil's shoulder, that told her everything. She wondered then how they could have helped loving each other; how she could have helped knowing that they must. Emil's cold, frowning face, the girl's content—Alexandra had felt awe of them, even in the first shock of her grief.

The idleness of those days in bed, the relaxation of body which attended them, enabled Alexandra to think more calmly than she had done since Emil's death. She and Frank, she told herself, were left out of that group of friends who had been overwhelmed by disaster. She must certainly see Frank Shabata. Even in the courtroom her heart had grieved for him. He was in a strange country, he had no kinsmen or friends, and in a moment he had ruined his life. Being what he was, she felt, Frank could not have acted otherwise. She could understand his behavior more easily than she could understand Marie's. Yes, she must go to Lincoln to see Frank Shabata.

The day after Emil's funeral, Alexandra had written to Carl Linstrum; a single page of note-paper, a bare statement of what had happened. She was not a woman who could write much about such a thing, and about her own feelings she could never write very freely. She knew that Carl was away from post-offices, prospecting somewhere in the interior. Before he started he had written her where he expected to go, but her ideas about Alaska were vague. As the weeks went by and she heard nothing from him, it seemed to Alexandra that her heart grew hard against Carl. She began to wonder whether she would not do better to finish her life alone. What was left of life seemed unimportant.

II

Late in the afternoon of a brilliant October day, Alexandra Bergson, dressed in a black suit and traveling-hat, alighted at the Burlington depot in Lincoln. She drove to the Lindell Hotel, where she had stayed two years ago when she came up for Emil's Commencement. In spite of her usual air of sureness and self-possession, Alexandra felt ill at ease in hotels, and she was glad, when she went to the clerk's desk to register, that there were not many people in the lobby. She had her supper early, wearing her hat and black jacket down to the dinning-room and carrying her handbag. After supper she went out for a walk.

It was growing dark when she reached the university campus. She did not go into the grounds, but walked slowly up and down the stone walk outside the long iron fence, looking through at the young men who were running from one building to another, at the lights shining from the armory and the library. A squad of cadets were going through their drill behind the armory, and the commands of their young officer rang out at regular intervals, so sharp and quick that Alexandra could not understand them. Two stalwart girls came down the library steps and out through one of the iron gates. As they passed her, Alexandra was pleased to hear them speaking Bohemian to each other. Every few moments a boy would come running down the flagged walk and dash out into the street as if he were rushing to announce some wonder to the world. Alexandra felt a great tenderness for them all. She wished one of them would stop and speak to her. She wished she could ask them whether they had known Emil.

As she lingered by the south gate she actually did encounter one of the boys. He had on his drill cap and was swinging his books at the end of a long strap. It was dark by this time; he did not see her and ran against her. He snatched off his cap and stood bareheaded and panting. "I'm awfully sorry," he said in a bright, clear voice, with a rising inflection, as if he expected her to say something.

"Oh, it was my fault!" said Alexandra eagerly. "Are you an old student here, may I ask?"

"No, ma'am. I'm a Freshie, just off the farm. Cherry County. Were you hunting somebody?"

"No, thank you. That is—" Alexandra wanted to detain him. "That is, I would like to find some of my brother's friends. He graduated two years ago."

"Then you'd have to try the Seniors, would n't you? Let's see; I don't know any of them yet, but there'll be sure to be some of them around the library. That red building, right there," he pointed.

"Thank you, I'll try there," said Alexandra lingeringly.

"Oh, that's all right! Good-night." The lad clapped his cap on his head and ran straight down Eleventh Street. Alexandra looked after him wistfully.

She walked back to her hotel unreasonably comforted. "What a nice voice that boy had, and how polite he was. I know Emil was always like that to women." And again, after she had undressed and was standing in her nightgown, brushing her long, heavy hair by the electric light, she remembered him and said to herself: "I don't think I ever heard a nicer voice than that boy had. I hope he will get on well here. Cherry County; that's where the hay is so fine, and the coyotes can scratch down to water."

At nine o'clock the next morning Alexandra presented herself at the warden's office in the State Penitentiary. The warden was a German, a ruddy, cheerful-looking man who had formerly been a harness-maker. Alexandra had a letter to him from the German banker in Hanover. As he glanced at the letter, Mr. Schwartz put away his pipe.

"That big Bohemian, is it? Sure, he's gettin' along fine," said Mr. Schwartz cheerfully.

"I am glad to hear that. I was afraid he might be quarrelsome and get himself into more trouble. Mr. Schwartz, if you have time, I would like to tell you a little about Frank Shabata, and why I am interested in him."

The warden listened genially while she told him briefly something of Frank's history and character, but he did not seem to find anything unusual in her account.

"Sure, I'll keep an eye on him. We'll take care of him all right," he said, rising. "You can talk to him here, while I go to see to things in the kitchen. I'll have him sent in. He ought to be done washing out his cell by this time. We have to keep 'em clean, you know."

The warden paused at the door, speaking back over his shoulder to a pale young man in convicts' clothes who was seated at a desk in the corner, writing in a big ledger.

"Bertie, when 1037 is brought in, you just step out and give this lady a chance to talk."

The young man bowed his head and bent over his ledger again.

When Mr. Schwartz disappeared, Alexandra thrust her black-edged handkerchief nervously into her handbag. Coming out on the street-car she had not had the least dread of meeting Frank. But since she had been here the sounds and smells in the corridor, the look of the men in convicts' clothes who passed the glass door of the warden's office, affected her unpleasantly.

The warden's clock ticked, the young convict's pen scratched busily in the big book, and his sharp shoulders were shaken every few seconds by a loose cough which he tried to smother. It was easy to see that he was a sick man. Alexandra looked at him timidly, but he did not once raise his eyes. He wore a white shirt under his striped jacket, a high collar, and a necktie, very carefully tied. His hands were thin and white and well cared for, and he had a seal ring on his little finger. When he heard steps approaching in the corridor, he rose, blotted his book, put his pen in the rack, and left the room without raising his eyes. Through the door he opened a guard came in, bringing Frank Shabata.

"You the lady that wanted to talk to 1037? Here he is. Be on your good behavior, now. He can set down, lady," seeing that Alexandra remained standing. "Push that white button when you're through with him, and I'll come."

The guard went out and Alexandra and Frank were left alone.

Alexandra tried not to see his hideous clothes. She tried to look straight into his face, which she could scarcely believe was his. It was already bleached to a chalky gray. His lips were colorless, his fine teeth looked yellowish. He glanced at Alexandra sullenly, blinked as if he had come from a dark place, and one eyebrow twitched continually. She felt at once that this interview was a terrible ordeal to him. His shaved head, showing the conformation of his skull, gave him a criminal look which he had not had during the trial.

Alexandra held out her hand. "Frank," she said, her eyes filling suddenly, "I hope you'll let me be friendly with you. I understand how you did it. I don't feel hard toward you. They were more to blame than you."

Frank jerked a dirty blue handkerchief from his trousers pocket. He had begun to cry. He turned away from Alexandra. "I never did mean to do not'ing to dat woman," he muttered. "I never mean to do not'ing to dat boy. I ain't had not'ing ag'in' dat boy. I always like dat boy fine. An' then I find him—" He stopped. The feeling went out of his face and eyes. He dropped into a chair and sat looking stolidly at the floor, his hands hanging loosely between his knees, the handkerchief lying across his striped leg. He seemed to have stirred up in his mind a disgust that had paralyzed his faculties.

"I have n't come up here to blame you, Frank. I think they were more to blame than you." Alexandra, too, felt benumbed.

Frank looked up suddenly and stared out of the office window. "I guess dat place all go to hell what I work so hard on," he said with a slow, bitter smile. "I not care a damn." He stopped and rubbed the palm of his hand over the light bristles on his head with annoyance. "I no can t'ink without my hair," he complained. "I forget English. We not talk here, except swear."

Alexandra was bewildered. Frank seemed to have undergone a change of personality. There was scarcely anything by which she could recognize her handsome Bohemian neighbor. He seemed, somehow, not altogether human. She did not know what to say to him.

"You do not feel hard to me, Frank?" she asked at last.

Frank clenched his fist and broke out in excitement. "I not feel hard at no woman. I tell you I not that kind-a man. I never hit my wife. No, never I hurt her when she devil me something awful!" He struck his fist down on the warden's desk so hard that he afterward stroked it absently. A pale pink crept over his neck and face. "Two, t'ree years I know dat woman don' care no more 'bout me, Alexandra Bergson. I know she after some other man. I know her, oo-oo! An' I ain't never hurt her. I never would-a done dat, if I ain't had dat gun along. I don' know what in hell make me take dat gun. She always say I ain't no man to carry gun. If she been in dat house, where she ought-a been— But das a foolish talk."

Frank rubbed his head and stopped suddenly, as he had stopped before. Alexandra felt that there was something strange in the way he chilled off, as if something came up in him that extinguished his power of feeling or thinking.

"Yes, Frank," she said kindly. "I know you never meant to hurt Marie."

Frank smiled at her queerly. His eyes filled slowly with tears. "You know, I most forgit dat woman's name. She ain't got no name for me no more. I never hate my wife, but dat woman what make me do dat— Honest to God, but I hate her! I no man to fight. I don' want to kill no boy and no woman. I not care how many men she take under dat tree. I no care for not'ing but dat fine boy I kill, Alexandra Bergson. I guess I go crazy sure 'nough."

Alexandra remembered the little yellow cane she had found in Frank's clothes-closet. She thought of how he had come to this country a gay young fellow, so attractive that the prettiest Bohemian girl in Omaha had run away with him. It seemed unreasonable that life should have landed him in such a place as this. She blamed Marie bitterly. And why, with her happy, affectionate nature, should she have brought destruction and sorrow to all who had loved her, even to poor old Joe Tovesky, the uncle who used to carry her about so proudly when she was a little girl? That was the strangest thing of all. Was there, then, something wrong in being warm-hearted and impulsive like that? Alexandra hated to think so. But there was Emil, in the Norwegian graveyard at home, and here was Frank Shabata. Alexandra rose and took him by the hand.

"Frank Shabata, I am never going to stop trying until I get you pardoned. I'll never give the Governor any peace. I know I can get you out of this place."

Frank looked at her distrustfully, but he gathered confidence from her face. "Alexandra," he said earnestly, "if I git out-a here, I not trouble dis country no more. I go back where I come from; see my mother."

Alexandra tried to withdraw her hand, but Frank held on to it nervously. He put out his finger and absently touched a button on her black jacket. "Alexandra," he said in a low tone, looking steadily at the button, "you ain' t'ink I use dat girl awful bad before—"

"No, Frank. We won't talk about that," Alexandra said, pressing his hand. "I can't help Emil now, so I'm going to do what I can for you. You know I don't go away from home often, and I came up here on purpose to tell you this."

The warden at the glass door looked in inquiringly. Alexandra nodded, and he came in and touched the white button on his desk. The guard appeared, and with a sinking heart Alexandra saw Frank led away down the corridor. After a few words with Mr. Schwartz, she left the prison and made her way to the street-car. She had refused with horror the warden's cordial invitation to "go through the institution." As the car lurched over its uneven roadbed, back toward Lincoln, Alexandra thought of how she and Frank had been wrecked by the same storm and of how, although she could come out into the sunlight, she had not much more left in her life than he. She remembered some lines from a poem she had liked in her schooldays:—

> Henceforth the world will only be[4]
> A wider prison-house to me,—

and sighed. A disgust of life weighed upon her heart; some such feeling as had twice frozen Frank Shabata's features while they talked together. She wished she were back on the Divide.

When Alexandra entered her hotel, the clerk held up one finger and beckoned to her. As she approached his desk, he handed her a telegram. Alexandra took the yellow envelope and looked at it in perplexity, then stepped into the elevator without opening it. As she walked down the corridor toward her room, she reflected that she was, in a manner, immune from evil tidings. On reaching her room she locked the door, and sitting down on a chair by the dresser, opened the telegram. It was from Hanover, and it read:—

> Arrived Hanover last night. Shall wait here until you come. Please hurry.
>
> CARL LINSTRUM.

Alexandra put her head down on the dresser and burst into tears.

4. "And the whole earth would henceforth be / A wider prison unto me." Byron, "The Prisoner of Chillon," lines 322–23.

III

The next afternoon Carl and Alexandra were walking across the fields from Mrs. Hiller's. Alexandra had left Lincoln after midnight, and Carl had met her at the Hanover station early in the morning. After they reached home, Alexandra had gone over to Mrs. Hiller's to leave a little present she had bought for her in the city. They stayed at the old lady's door but a moment, and then came out to spend the rest of the afternoon in the sunny fields.

Alexandra had taken off her black traveling-suit and put on a white dress; partly because she saw that her black clothes made Carl uncomfortable and partly because she felt oppressed by them herself. They seemed a little like the prison where she had worn them yesterday, and to be out of place in the open fields. Carl had changed very little. His cheeks were browner and fuller. He looked less like a tired scholar than when he went away a year ago, but no one, even now, would have taken him for a man of business. His soft, lustrous black eyes, his whimsical smile, would be less against him in the Klondike than on the Divide. There are always dreamers on the frontier.

Carl and Alexandra had been talking since morning. Her letter had never reached him. He had first learned of her misfortune from a San Francisco paper, four weeks old, which he had picked up in a saloon, and which contained a brief account of Frank Shabata's trial. When he put down the paper, he had already made up his mind that he could reach Alexandra as quickly as a letter could; and ever since he had been on the way; day and night, by the fastest boats and trains he could catch. His steamer had been held back two days by rough weather.

As they came out of Mrs. Hiller's garden they took up their talk again where they had left it.

"But could you come away like that, Carl, without arranging things? Could you just walk off and leave your business?" Alexandra asked.

Carl laughed. "Prudent Alexandra! You see, my dear, I happen to have an honest partner. I trust him with everything. In fact, it's been his enterprise from the beginning, you know. I'm in it only because he took me in. I'll have to go back in the spring. Perhaps you will want to go with me then. We have n't turned up millions yet, but we've got a start that's worth following. But this winter I'd like to spend with you. You won't feel that we ought to wait longer, on Emil's account, will you, Alexandra?"

Alexandra shook her head. "No, Carl; I don't feel that way about it. And surely you need n't mind anything Lou and Oscar say now. They are much angrier with me about Emil, now, than about you.

They say it was all my fault. That I ruined him by sending him to college."

"No, I don't care a button for Lou or Oscar. The moment I knew you were in trouble, the moment I thought you might need me, it all looked different. You've always been a triumphant kind of person." Carl hesitated, looking sidewise at her strong, full figure. "But you do need me now, Alexandra?"

She put her hand on his arm. "I needed you terribly when it happened, Carl. I cried for you at night. Then everything seemed to get hard inside of me, and I thought perhaps I should never care for you again. But when I got your telegram yesterday, then—then it was just as it used to be. You are all I have in the world, you know."

Carl pressed her hand in silence. They were passing the Shabatas' empty house now, but they avoided the orchard path and took one that led over by the pasture pond.

"Can you understand it, Carl?" Alexandra murmured. "I have had nobody but Ivar and Signa to talk to. Do talk to me. Can you understand it? Could you have believed that of Marie Tovesky? I would have been cut to pieces, little by little, before I would have betrayed her trust in me!"

Carl looked at the shining spot of water before them. "Maybe she was cut to pieces, too, Alexandra. I am sure she tried hard; they both did. That was why Emil went to Mexico, of course. And he was going away again, you tell me, though he had only been home three weeks. You remember that Sunday when I went with Emil up to the French Church fair? I thought that day there was some kind of feeling, something unusual, between them. I meant to talk to you about it. But on my way back I met Lou and Oscar and got so angry that I forgot everything else. You must n't be hard on them, Alexandra. Sit down here by the pond a minute. I want to tell you something."

They sat down on the grass-tufted bank and Carl told her how he had seen Emil and Marie out by the pond that morning, more than a year ago, and how young and charming and full of grace they had seemed to him. "It happens like that in the world sometimes, Alexandra," he added earnestly. "I've seen it before. There are women who spread ruin around them through no fault of theirs, just by being too beautiful, too full of life and love. They can't help it. People come to them as people go to a warm fire in winter. I used to feel that in her when she was a little girl. Do you remember how all the Bohemians crowded round her in the store that day, when she gave Emil her candy? You remember those yellow sparks in her eyes?"

Alexandra sighed. "Yes. People could n't help loving her. Poor Frank does, even now, I think; though he's got himself in such a tangle that for a long time his love has been bitterer than his hate. But if you saw there was anything wrong, you ought to have told me, Carl."

Carl took her hand and smiled patiently. "My dear, it was something one felt in the air, as you feel the spring coming, or a storm in summer. I did n't *see* anything. Simply, when I was with those two young things, I felt my blood go quicker, I felt—how shall I say it?—an acceleration of life. After I got away, it was all too delicate, too intangible, to write about."

Alexandra looked at him mournfully. "I try to be more liberal about such things than I used to be. I try to realize that we are not all made alike. Only, why could n't it have been Raoul Marcel, or Jan Smirka? Why did it have to be my boy?"

"Because he was the best there was, I suppose. They were both the best you had here."

The sun was dropping low in the west when the two friends rose and took the path again. The straw-stacks were throwing long shadows, the owls were flying home to the prairie-dog town. When they came to the corner where the pastures joined, Alexandra's twelve young colts were galloping in a drove over the brow of the hill.

"Carl," said Alexandra, "I should like to go up there with you in the spring. I have n't been on the water since we crossed the ocean, when I was a little girl. After we first came out here I used to dream sometimes about the shipyard where father worked, and a little sort of inlet, full of masts." Alexandra paused. After a moment's thought she said, "But you would never ask me to go away for good, would you?"

"Of course not, my dearest. I think I know how you feel about this country as well as you do yourself." Carl took her hand in both his own and pressed it tenderly.

"Yes, I still feel that way, though Emil is gone. When I was on the train this morning, and we got near Hanover, I felt something like I did when I drove back with Emil from the river that time, in the dry year. I was glad to come back to it. I've lived here a long time. There is great peace here, Carl, and freedom. . . . I thought when I came out of that prison, where poor Frank is, that I should never feel free again. But I do, here." Alexandra took a deep breath and looked off into the red west.

"You belong to the land," Carl murmured, "as you have always said. Now more than ever."

"Yes, now more than ever. You remember what you once said about the graveyard, and the old story writing itself over? Only it is we who write it, with the best we have."

They paused on the last ridge of the pasture, overlooking the house and the windmill and the stables that marked the site of

John Bergson's homestead. On every side the brown waves of the earth rolled away to meet the sky.

"Lou and Oscar can't see those things," said Alexandra suddenly. "Suppose I do will my land to their children, what difference will that make? The land belongs to the future, Carl; that's the way it seems to me. How many of the names on the county clerk's plat[5] will be there in fifty years? I might as well try to will the sunset over there to my brother's children. We come and go, but the land is always here. And the people who love it and understand it are the people who own it—for a little while."

Carl looked at her wonderingly. She was still gazing into the west, and in her face there was that exalted serenity that sometimes came to her at moments of deep feeling. The level rays of the sinking sun shone in her clear eyes.

"Why are you thinking of such things now, Alexandra?"

"I had a dream before I went to Lincoln—But I will tell you about that afterward, after we are married. It will never come true, now, in the way I thought it might." She took Carl's arm and they walked toward the gate. "How many times we have walked this path together, Carl. How many times we will walk it again! Does it seem to you like coming back to your own place? Do you feel at peace with the world here? I think we shall be very happy. I have n't any fears. I think when friends marry, they are safe. We don't suffer like—those young ones." Alexandra ended with a sigh.

They had reached the gate. Before Carl opened it, he drew Alexandra to him and kissed her softly, on her lips and on her eyes.

She leaned heavily on his shoulder. "I am tired," she murmured. "I have been very lonely, Carl."

They went into the house together, leaving the Divide behind them, under the evening star. Fortunate country, that is one day to receive hearts like Alexandra's into its bosom, to give them out again in the yellow wheat, in the rustling corn, in the shining eyes of youth!

THE END

5. Land map showing the names of landowners and their properties.

CONTEXTS AND BACKGROUNDS

Railroad circular advertising farmland in Nebaska, distributed in Bohemia in the 1880s. (Nebraska State Historical Society)

Lincoln, Nebraska, 1880s. The University of Nebraska is in the background. (Nebaska State Historical Society)

Lincoln in the late 1880s. The University of Nebraska is the large building on the left. (Nebraska State Historical Society)

Prairie landscape, Nebraska, 1880s. (Nebraska State Historical Society)

Willa Cather, age seventeen (1890 or 1891). Philip L. and Helen Cather Southwick Collection, Archives and Special Collections, University of Nebraska–Lincoln Libraries.

Willa Cather during her editorship at *McClure's Magazine*, about 1910. Philip L. and Helen Cather Southwick Collection, Archives and Special Collections, University of Nebraska–Lincoln Libraries.

Willa Cather, about 1924. Philip L. and Helen Cather Southwick Collection, Archives and Special Collections, University of Nebraska–Lincoln Libraries.

Uriah and Mattie Oblinger with their daughter Ella, 1874. (Nebraska State Historical Society)

Sod house, Custer Country, Nebraska, 1903. (Nebraska State Historical Society)

Dugout, Custer County, Nebraska, 1892. (Nebraska State Historical Society)

Four sisters on their claim in Custer County, Nebraska, 1886. (Nebraska State Historical Society)

Autobiographical and Biographical Essays

ELIZABETH SHEPLEY SERGEANT

From Willa Cather: A Memoir†

Chapter III. The Golden Year, 1912

Galloping growth, sure forward movement, are fine things to observe and share. In 1912, after a long period of submission to a daily job hard for a creative writer to carry, Willa Cather's own literary life began to burgeon and bear fruit. She had been working joyously at Cherry Valley—all through the autumn and early winter of 1911 with a release from *McClure's* to do her own writing. After the turn of the New Year she began to make occasional lively reappearances in New York and Boston. The first sign of new work was her novel (the one which she many years later described as her "first first novel"). It began to appear in *McClure's* in February, 1912, under the title, later discarded, *Alexander's Masquerade*. In the book published by Houghton Mifflin in June of this year the magazine title was changed to *Alexander's Bridge*, and in the simultaneous English edition to *Alexander's Bridges*.

Naturally, I turned to the first number with avidity, and saw at once that it had a Jamesian touch as to backgrounds (Boston and London). As I remember it, Willa intervened, when she heard that I was reading the serial, and begged me, instead, to read the book proofs, in which she had made changes. We did this, I remember, in Boston. I took the galleys to Brookline, brooded over them, returned them to Willa, with timid suggestions that she surprised me by honoring. I had never before seen a galley and it was an exciting business but to my discomfiture the story seemed conventional. (This feeling was enhanced by the frontispiece both to the serial

† Chapters 3 and 4, pp. 74–97, from *Willa Cather: A Memoir* by Elizabeth Shepley Sergeant. Copyright © 1953 by Elizabeth Shepley Sergeant. Reprinted by permission of HarperCollins Publishers.

and the book. Two lovers in evening dress in one another's arms and the actress saying: "Are you going to let me love you a little, Bartley?")

Bartley Alexander, the hero, a Westerner and a bridgebuilder with a correct Boston wife, was in the midst of a personal predicament of an insoluble kind. He wanted, even under Beacon Hill, to eat his cake and have it too. He wanted marriage, success in his work, but he also wanted Hilda Burgoyne, a warm, gay little Irish actress in London who led him to a rediscovery of self and youth. So the intemperate Bartley recklessly plied back and forth across the Atlantic. There was a fourth character, a pale, wise, observant professorial friend, the first of a line of Cather observers,—though I could not know this in 1912—who was a bit squeamish about the whole business.

A vital theme and delicate writing; but somehow spun out into finesse. I could not find in the story the author of strength and latent power I valued in life. When Bartley's bridge went down, and he with it, in a sort of cosmic if not moralistic splash, sending Bartley back to the "element" that in himself seemed unredeemed and of the wilds, the death was minor, the great chorus of tragedy failed to sound.

Willa, rather depressed, pulled my uncomfortable disappointment out of me—and more or less agreed with it. She said that though Mrs. Fields[1] was all praise and delight, she was through with Bartley. In his book she had for the first time in her life tried to be literary and she feared that she had come a cropper. But in Cherry Valley she had been working on two little Western stories. One was a Swedish thing: chill and grey, not ready to show.[2] The other was a Bohemian story she would like me to see. It was different from anything she'd ever written, in an entirely new vein. She was convinced that no magazine would consider it. But she somehow liked it herself.

That I was responsive to the more fertile process that was now established in Willa's mind led her to send me, before long, the manuscript of "The Bohemian Girl." It had exactly the potential I had divined in her and had not found in the bridge-builder's story, where her pen had been guided by a fashionable pattern. Here, at last, was a Willa Cather story that was true to the person. To the woman of essential vision—generous, sure, writing of a region she knew and the public didn't—about those Swedes and Bohemians who cropped up in her talk of her youth. I was so excited that I rushed over to see Willa in New York. She remained incredulous at

1. Annie Adams Fields (1834–1915), Boston literary figure and hostess.
2. "Alexandra," the story that became the source of "The Wild Land" and "Neighboring Fields" sections of *O Pioneers!*

my certainty that *this was it.* We spent the better part of two days arguing about it at the Brevoort, on the bus, and in the Park, though the season was March. As I took my Boston train I hoped she had ceased her self-queries, and was offering the piece to Cameron Mackenzie, S. S. McClure's son-in-law, then business manager of the magazine.

All the way along the reaches of Connecticut and Massachusetts on the railroad, I thought about the return to Nebraska of Nils Ericson, the wanderer in a big family of brothers, the rest of whom had stuck to the farm. The wind had whispered to Nils names out of the geography books, they had suggested the sea, or something "trying to tear loose." Off he had gone and done well for himself. But his favorite Bohemian girl, Clara Vavrika, who had meanwhile married the dumbest of his brothers, "teased him like a wild tune." Clara was at odds with her environment and "pulled Nils out of his boots." He persuaded her to run off with him. These European Midwesterners, so lacking in guilt, so equal in maturity—not always true of lovers in Cather novels—were welcome after Ethan Frome and his girl and Bartley and his doubts. Then I found a fine quality of conviction in the relationship of the people to the country, and a great beauty of sensuous style in describing it.

> The moonlight flooded that great, silent land. The reaped fields lay yellow in it. The straw stacks and popular windbreaks threw sharp black shadows. The roads were white rivers of dust. Everything seemed to have succumbed, to have sunk to sleep, under the great, golden, tender, midsummer moon. . . . The senses were too feeble to take it in, and every time one looked up to the sky, one felt unequal to it, as if one were sitting deaf under the waves of a great river of melody.

Next day came a letter from Willa. Mackenzie had lunched her and taken possession of the manuscript, then asked her to tea at the Brevoort, and simply floored her by offering $750 for "The Bohemian Girl." To which she had briskly replied that, as she knew far better than he, no story was worth more than $500 to *McClure's*. He told her she was a goose and made her promise to take more for the next story. Everybody in the office, even those she did not expect to please, spoke up about it. That was puzzling. What did they see in it? And how could she ever resign from this devoted *McClure's*?

But the big news was that she was on the edge of her first trip Southwest to visit her brother Douglas in Winslow, Arizona. Now that her hero, Alexander, was on his way and Clara Vavrika[3] on

3. The heroine of Cather's short story "The Bohemian Girl" (1912).

hers, she could go with a clear conscience. Life was splendid. It had been splendid to have those days together.

So at last I saw my friend at the jumping-off place for the writer's life. "The Bohemian Girl" was the springboard. But where with her abounding vitality, and her royal gifts, would she dive to? She refused to say. She was off to rest and travel, not to write.

The first news of her came from 1180 Murray Hill Avenue, Pittsburgh. The McClungs stood for "family" in Willa's Eastern life and she struck a serious family event when she arrived there. Mrs. McClung had had a sudden critical illness, and Willa must, for a bit, stay on, in the stilled household.

She was keeping normal by long walks in the damp, smoky air and reading the third volume of Michelet's *History of France*. She urged upon me Wagner's autobiography: he didn't stop to plead his own cause, or pause to meditate—just recorded action, and this she admired.

Then I heard from Red Cloud, where she had stopped to see her father and mother. She had written a new scene into "The Bohemian Girl" in Pittsburgh, and, to be frank, the story seemed right when she again made human connection with the region. It was like the people and had taken the shape of the land. Again, she thanked me warmly for backing her in this story.

But the general effect of the West had been overpowering—she had run into the same old shock she used to suffer at the mere size of it. When she was in the East, she forgot everything but the sharp, specific flavor. Once there, an unreasoning fear of being swallowed by the distances between herself and anything else jumped out at her—as in childhood, again. On the plains the wind is a soporific. She was afraid to drowse and to dream. Why did she have such feelings if she were to write about the country—unsuitable, wasn't it?

In North Carolina, where I was recovering from flu and riding horseback, I pondered this comment. So Willa preferred detachment and discontent, as far as Red Cloud was concerned? Maybe she needed them, to keep her contented in New York? Or just to enable her to write of her childhood world?

Soon came vivid, uncensored descriptions of Winslow, Arizona, where she was feeling fit, if baffled. The little house where her brother hoped she would write was a shell, and the town an ugly little railroad and trading settlement surrounded by vast spaces of rubbish. But beyond—ah beyond!—began the red sand of the desert, with its dull green rabbit brush and sage. Across the tracks was a most alluring little foreign settlement—Spanish Mexican—

which redeemed the boredom of the desert and the crassness of the frontier by its whole gentle, homely, free-handed atmosphere.

As Willa's brother went off for several days at a time with a railroad construction gang, she would be left alone in the *casa*—quite in line with the *mores* of Winslow—with an irreproachable brakeman, who had mined and prospected in Mexico and looked just like Henry Miller in William Vaughn Moody's *The Great Divide*. He was a devotee of Ralph Waldo Emerson, and bought a magazine at every station—so he was replete with useless information which he expressed in bi-syllabic Latin words. If he, too, was off on a "run," she always had the companionship of an English Cockney housekeeper-and-cook her brother had rescued from starvation. The Londoner spoke queer French and, when drunk, which was most of the time, sang sentimental ditties about "them fair deceivin' eyes." So she had had to fall back on the Mexican village.

She had found there a string trio of Mexicans, who often came to play for her delight: two section hands and a bartender. Also, a young Antinous of a singer from Vera Cruz, with a mellifluous name and a few simple thoughts and feelings. His golden skin, his ancient race, his eyes with their tragic gleam—well, he reminded Willa of some antique sculpture in the Naples Museum. Being with him was like living in a classic age.

Here she interrupted herself to apologize. Nothing bored *her* more than to hear ecstatic accounts from friends about the charm of Venetian gondoliers and Sicilian donkey boys. But this one was different. His words seemed to come from the Breviary, they were so full of simple piety and directness. He would go anywhere to find wild flowers, or hunt a spring of water, as she would do as a child in Nebraska. But when asked to visit cliff dwellers he was indifferent—*"por qué los muertos, pobrecitos?"* Mrs. Bell, Mrs. Fields' witty Bostonian friend, used to say that after the motor-car came, there were only the quick and the dead. The Mexican singer saw things similarly—you say Masses for the dead and forget them. Only the living matter.

Besides, he had told her a story of an Aztec Cleopatra, called "The Forty Lovers of the Queen." (This sounded like a Rider Haggard story.) Willa would write it down when she could go to the place where it happened—she did not work from an imaginary base. (Nevertheless, the rather sadistic story was told to the heroine of "Coming, Aphrodite!" by her artist lover.)

Will you go to *Madre Mexicana* with me sometime?

In fact, she was suggesting now that I come to Albuquerque where she was sure I could work—not Winslow: I was over-civilized for Winslow. (Did she mean too finicky?) Albuquerque had a Spanish feel, and was set in the most beautiful country she'd ever seen—something like the country between Marseilles and Nice but more luminous. Even finer than the Rhône Valley. She would come over to see me: a night on the train was nothing in the West. She described Indian villages set around Spanish Mission churches built in Queen Elizabeth's time; talked of a priest who had driven her about to them. In this Rio Grande region the grandiose and historical scale of things seemed to forecast some great spiritual event—something like a Crusade, perhaps; something certainly that had nothing to do with the appalling mediocrity and vulgarity of the industrial civilization.

Having thrown off a prophetic idea, which was, in a sense, to flower in one of her greater books, Willa moved on to the Grand Canyon, which she described by understatement as the most alluring and let-alone Wonder in these United States. But geology cannot long be endured without human beings: one had to come to the desert to know how fascinating they are. Douglass, declaring that his sister was wearing him to the bones, was a fine companion—always had been. The well-read brakeman, too, in the upper canyons where they camped, shed his Emersonian altitude—became the kind of resourceful Westerner formed by the sheep camps, who could tell you a story or companion you down a cliff one hundred and fifty feet high, at an angle of forty-five degrees.

One more trip was planned with Douglass before she left Arizona: to hunt cliff dwellings along the Little Colorado. (It was as if they were again tomboy kids inventing prehistoric adventures along the muddy Republican River.) Then she had promised the Spanish trio and the troubadour (she enclosed a Serenata of his, for *vox contralto*, which must be sung only by a married woman, either to her husband or her lover) to attend a Mexican *baile* (ball) in Winslow. All those gentle, dark-skinned people who lived south of the railroad tracks would be there. . . . There would be fine folk dancing and she would be the only white. . . .

I am willing to wager that the staid editor of *McClure's* never, in her most bohemian hour, attended an artist ball in Greenwich Village, but it was not hard to imagine Willa's Western self, her youthful, resilient, tough, gay-hearted prairie self, now set free and moving with the current, whirling around a whitewashed dance hall, with small-waisted, red-sashed Mexican partners, who took their pleasures from their roots. Such men, whose hearts knew well what reason knoweth not, respected and loved her because in a frontier town, where "Mexicans" were misprized, she put the joys and the music they gave her above the prejudices of the white ruling class. Naturally they spun Willa Cather around and around, like a top, and then seated her by their lean angular wives and their dolorous *madres*, shawled and patient as Goyas, on the long adobe benches, while they displayed, on the floor, the intricacies of a native dance. They gave her a new Spanish world to think of—and eventually to write of—and added their share to the golden elixir distilled by the Arizona desert in two months' time.

Two months was all she wanted, apparently. She told me how, suddenly, after she went on to New Mexico, she was hit by a cold gloom. It happened at the pueblo of Santo Domingo, a large old-style village west of Santa Fe, where the law of the white man is scarcely accepted and a white lady sitting by the sluggish, ruddy Rio Grande, *reflecting*, is an object of suspicion.

There, however, Willa sat, and suddenly a bitter wind seemed to arise from the peaks and she saw, written before her in the dust, a sentence from Balzac she had long forgotten:

> Duns le désert, voyez-vous, il y a tout et il n'y a rien—Dieu, sans les hommes.

Everything and nothing—God without men!

So that was what was wrong! Not even her brother, not all the brakemen and troubadours of the desert, certainly not the Indians, could replace a civilization—her civilization. *Her own*. Panic seized her—it said the West is consuming you, make tracks for home.

She did, and by mid-June was back in Nebraska seeing the wheat harvest in the Bohemian country for the first time in many years. There was a great sound of cymbals in the air, for all at once—as if her journey had been taken for no other purpose—she had a new story in mind.

It would be called "The White Mulberry Tree," and would, she feared, terrify Mr. Greenslet.[4] In two weeks she would be in Pittsburgh and start working. Meanwhile she enclosed the carbon of a poem which showed how the wheat country had seemed when she returned from the Southwest.

> Evening and the flat land,
> Rich and sombre and always silent;
> The miles of fresh-plowed soil,
> Heavy and black, full of strength and harshness;
> The growing wheat, the growing weeds,
> The toiling horses, the tired men;
> The long empty roads,
> Sullen fires of sunset, fading,
> The eternal, unresponsive sky.
> Against all this, Youth,
> Flaming like the wild roses,

4. Ferris Greenslet, Willa Cather's editor at the Houghton Mifflin publishing company.

Singing like the larks over the plowed fields,
Flashing like a star out of the twilight;
Youth with its insupportable sweetness,
Its fierce necessity,
Its sharp desire,
Singing and singing,
Out of the lips of silence,
Out of the earthy dusk.

This is the poem—entitled "Prairie Spring"—that stands at the beginning of *O Pioneers!* It suggests that Willa Cather was suddenly in control of inner creative forces which had tended to swamp her and make her dismal so long as she could not use them. The vast solitude of the Southwest, its bald magnificence, brilliant light and physical impact, too, had the effect of toning up her spirit, and made available a path in which a new artistic method could evolve from familiar Nebraska subject matter.

After all, it had been in the little undistinguished prairie town, which she had left at twenty-two in a cloud of dust, that she had had the appointment to meet the rest of herself, and the literary fate she harbored, which she still knew very little about.

Willa was deeply involved with her book when I next heard from her in August, from the McClungs' in Pittsburgh, a shut-in place where, established in emotional security with a sympathetic woman friend, the spirit of her inner music could imperceptibly change from the *crescendo, crescendo* of the Southwest to the *molto moderato* of Pittsburgh's wet and somber skies.

She was working three hours a day—for her a normal day's work. She was getting a lot of sleep. She and Isabelle[5] were reading aloud the ninth volume of Michelet—six volumes further on than in March. They also read my French sketch "Standards of a Bourgeois Family" in the August *Scribner's*, and had good things to say of it. "The Bohemian Girl" had come out in the August *McClure's*. One reader wrote in to the effect that Willa Sibert Cather was Procuress to the Lords of Hell (quoting Tennyson).[6] But on the whole the letters to the magazine about this story, and the serial also, were so warm, and the new work went so amazingly well that she was freed from her editorial servitude, this time for six months—which, in fact, proved sufficient for the completion of *O Pioneers!*

I had gone to England by autumn and then to Paris, where I lived on the rue de Sèvres, *chez* Madame Gaston Paris, the widow of a

5. Isabelle McClung, beloved lifelong friend of Willa Cather.
6. The reference is to Alfred Lord Tennyson's elegy *In Memoriam*: "Hold thou the good; define it well; / For fear divine Philosophy / Should push beyond her mark, and be / Procuress to the Lords of Hell."

great mediaevalist, who had been succeeded by Joseph Bedier at the Collège de France. In this intellectual and aesthetic environment, huddled over a *boulet* fire, looking out on a closed garden where roses still hung and chrysanthemums scattered their petals, I heard from Willa that she was on the last lap of her novel. The cold Swedish story she had written in the autumn of 1911, Alexandra's story, had entwined itself with the Bohemian story, "The White Mulberry Tree," and somehow she had on her hands a two-part pastoral: the most foolish endeavor imaginable, she mourned. She now thought of calling the book by Whitman's line: "*O Pioneers!*"

She knew, as she proceeded, that it was much better than "The Bohemian Girl." She spoke of a murder—she was three days killing off the lovers, she mentioned rather lightly. The reference was to that moment under the mulberry trees, when the wild Bohemian farmer, Frank Shabata, shoots his wife Marie in the arms of the tender, frustrated young Swede Emil, favorite young brother of Alexandra—a scene that by its passion and its tragic restraint has taken its place as a lasting passage in American literature.

So 1912 ended for Willa with the knowledge of an inner achievement. Once this was reached, she had made the turn, as if unconsciously, and found herself at a new level of the spiral of work and living.

Chapter IV. O Pioneers! 1913

As 1913 opened, Willa settled herself, for many years, as it proved, into an apartment at Number Five Bank Street; so she always wrote it, in her firm, level, succinct, small longhand. A letter from her was a personal thing, and with its even margins and fine script, a pleasure to the eye, as well as to the mind. She never typed personal letters. Her handwriting looked open as her face, at first sight. When one hit an obscure spot, it was worth puzzling over.

At this time, Bank Street was in a quiet demure almost soundless corner of Greenwich Village. No big arteries brought traffic coursing by, no movie houses intruded. Willa was fanatical about noise; but in 1913, peace and security reigned.

Miss Edith Lewis, now Willa Cather's literary executor, who companioned a genius through many books and years, had made the happy "find" of the apartment. It had good woodwork and good windows and fireplaces and a number of pleasant rooms. Her last stay in Pittsburgh had been shadowed by Mrs. McClung's illness; she looked forward to a home of her own that satisfied her. Miss Lewis had a magazine job that took her out early in the morning. Willa did the marketing (Jefferson Market was close by), and then, in perfect solitude, her stint of work before the maid came to get the lunch. She was, indeed, "all set," in more ways than one. The Society Library was only across Fifth Avenue, the Metropolitan Opera just up Broadway. Her book was nearly done, and it had started her on the way of no return.

Though *Alexander's Bridge* was doing well enough, Willa Cather's lady-like Jamesian days of writing about the best people in merely sophisticated settings were over. Gone was her bitterness about the Anglo-Saxons of Red Cloud and their limitations—at least for the present. "You must know the world before you can know the village," Miss Jewett had said. Well, now she did know the world and her pen, of its own volition, started unwinding the Swedish, Bohemian and French lives of the Divide, as memory presented them from pristine childhood fortunes. Inspiration, says Santayana,[7] comes from the heart and is, at the outset, as blameless and courageous as life itself.

Willa did not tell me that she had written of these foreign neighbors for college periodicals. She was, when interrogated about early work, transformed into a wooden image. Her beginnings just did not count. We know that her little room in "The Rose Bower" in her parents' home was locked when she went to college—something hard to enforce in a large family in a town where everybody was interested in everybody else's business. The Cather parents had unusual insight into a rebel daughter. Willa's great friendliness, her contrasting susceptibility, her drive, her perplexing secretiveness and detachment made her no easy girl to raise. Surely they suspected that their eldest child had a special destiny waiting for her.

Some time before I went abroad I had seen my friend during a moment of convalescence and consequent gloom and self-disparagement. Indeed, I had shepherded her back from Boston on a Pullman in this typical down-hearted state of mind in which, through physical illness, she had, in a way that was baffling to me, lost her own self-respect. With our chairs turned toward the moving landscape, we watched the flying fields and blue bays, till at last sentiency took over in her, she cast her mood like an old skin, and accepted the world as good again.

Suddenly she remarked: "Now *you* must write a novel."

I said timidly that I lacked the imagination. But, she replied in her positive, assured, blunt way, *imagination is not necessary*—all you need is the insight and the style you give evidence of in your French sketches. But, I said, those were *French* people—if I wrote about neighbors, friends, or New England family I should hurt their feelings—what does one do about that?

7. George Santayana (1863–1952), Spanish-born philosopher and essayist who lived in the United States.

Willa said she did not like hurting people's feelings either—we all want to be liked. She implied that her characters were largely composites. How "close to life" the characters in *O Pioneers!* were I was never to know with exactitude from herself, in spite of our many talks about the book.

Though Willa had apparently not conceived "The White Mulberry Tree" when she started for the Southwest in March, 1912, she did have, in first draft as I have said, Alexandra Bergson's story—the story of the vital young Swedish pioneer woman who took on the master work of producing a successful farm out of land largely untilled and with stupid brothers who could not see or feel the future in the untamed prairie. The Swedish manuscript ended, Miss Lewis has told me, with Alexandra's dream which came to her when she was overtired: the fantasy of being lifted and carried bodily, like a sheaf of wheat, by a man she never saw, great in stature, yellow as the sunlight, with the smell of ripe cornfields about him. This man relieved Alexandra of all weariness.

Since the Alexandra of the story married that rather weak, sensitive man who, in the pioneer world—and even in these United States in general—does often marry the strong matriarchal woman, we may divine, if we please, that the man of the cornfields was simply a psychological figure that gave a writer the lifting courage to become a great novelist—no matter what Red Cloud thought of it or how many feelings were hurt.

Willa sent to me in Paris early in 1913, shortly after New Year's, the typescript of her new story. The book was more than twice as long as *Alexander's Bridge*. She noted, too, some hasty writing in it—and a lot about crops and farming. But it was either a fair success or an utter calamity. Maybe it had too much the tempo of *The Swiss Family Robinson?*

Anyhow, she had done what she cared to do without concern for consequences or critics, submitted herself humbly to her own creative impulse, dismissing all preconceived ideas as to what a novel "ought" to be. She had let the story run along at its own pace and length, without trimming it to pattern. The country insisted on being the Hero and she did not interfere, for the story came out of the long grasses, she felt, like Dvořak's *New World Symphony* which program notes always said was based on Negro melodies. She knew better.[8]

8. The Czech composer Antonin Dvořák visited the United States from 1892 to 1895 and composed his Symphony No. 9, "From the New World" (Op. 95) during this time. He was interested in both Native American music and African-American spirituals, and some music commentators found these influences in Dvořák's symphony. In writing to Sergeant, however, Willa Cather claims that she "knew better"—that Dvořák had been inspired by the time he spent in Nebraska, as she had been.

Dvořak had actually spent several weeks in Nebraska, in the early eighties. Yes, her themes were all there, but something had to happen to herself before they could rise up and reach her ear, and take form in her mind.

But, she quickly recanted, she was just boasting, because she really felt low and tense, as always when she finished something and got separated from it. Exposed to a cold, windy world. Not more than half a dozen people in the United States would be concerned. Yet it was the story that had teased her for years and she could not bear to fail.

Since, she said, there were just three people whose judgment she valued (naturally, this went to my head), she begged me to hand her the unvarnished truth. She was given to emotional writing—if I found any, come down on it hard. She was not one who took offense—she could be detached from something she had created. Should "The Bohemian Girl" be published in the same volume or did this stand best alone?

I was to pass the story on to an agent in Paris who might get a translation for it.

Since *O Pioneers!* had to me the sobriety, force, and freshness of a literary discovery, I decided to try it out on the French cultivated mind. After *déjeuner, chez* Madame Gaston Paris, the family gathered about the salon fire for an hour of fine needlework and conversation. So it was that the old mother of ninety, Madame Paris in her sixties, a young daughter in her early twenties, listened with poised attention to the reading of *O Pioneers!* They had all read *Piers Plowman*, Chaucer, and Walt Whitman in English, and were genuinely thrilled by the emergence of an indigenous American novelist.

Très original! Alexandra interested them. No French-woman for centuries had seen virgin soil. Alexandra's return from the river farms singing a Swedish song, sure of the future of the wheat on the Divide, was poetry and legend. For the first time, Willa Cather wrote, since the land emerged from the waters of a geologic age, a human face was set toward it with love and yearning. "The history of every country begins in the heart of a man or a woman." The French listeners thought the history of Nebraska had now found the right heart to come to birth in.

"We French who love the land, have it in our bones, can see the quality of her writing. . . ." They thought the American agent who had refused *O Pioneers!* for French translation asinine; they prophesied that this American friend of mine, with her acute poetic sensibility, would be known to the cultivated French reader in the end. . . .

In the grey, wet months that follow Christmas in Paris, I

arranged to go to the South of France with a friend who came from London to join me—Mrs. James F. Muirhead, wife of the Scotch editor of the Baedeker for the United States, and author of *The Land of Contrasts.* Helen Quincy Muirhead was an "old" Bostonian with a difference. Whether one stayed with her near Hampstead Heath, or was drawn into her circle in Cambridge, Massachusetts, one was offered the varied fruits of a rare intellectual curiosity and detachment. H.Q.M. had a generous and eclectic literary taste, a compassionate, searching interest in many kinds of human beings.

My first knowledge of the works of Henry Adams had appropriately come from this Quincy. She loaned me, soon after I left Bryn Mawr, his *Mont-Saint-Michel and Chartres* in some privately printed form, and later his autobiography. Since we were both Jamesians, H.Q.M. had taken me with her to the stately home of Miss Grace Norton, the Queen Victoria of Irving Street, opposite neighbor of William James and Josiah Royce, and sister of Professor Charles Eliot Norton of Shady Hill.

It delighted H.Q.M. that Henry James had chosen as a confidante for some of the early inner questionings he lived through in deciding to become an expatriate, this now dumpy, scholarly, old Cambridge lady who was a good friend of his. Miss Norton had worn caps since she was thirty, learned Greek at seventy, and even now rose at six to carry on her literary correspondence before breakfast, in order to devote the morning to her work on Montaigne.

Max Beerbohm's cartoon of Lord Tennyson reading *In Memoriam* to His Sovereign suggests the tiny, plump, authoritative figure we gazed at across her Victorian carpet. In this instance it was the Sovereign who benignantly read to her subjects, H.Q.M. and me. In spite of Miss Norton's maternal excisions of revelatory subjective passages, the matter we heard made clear to us just why the first fiction writer of his American time had had to leave the land where an *Atlantic Monthly* editor, W. D. Howells himself, urged the "happy ending." In Europe, Turgenev and George Eliot were still there, to sanction H.J. if in a story, as in life, Fate showed a dark wing.

Willa had inquired eagerly about these early James letters. She had met H.Q.M.'s witty sister Fanny (Mrs. Mark Howe) at Mrs. Fields' and I divined that I might venture to show Mrs. Muirhead the manuscript of *O Pioneers!* on our Riviera trip. Willa was still in need of reassurance about her new story—wasn't it heavy and earthbound? She said she had written it only for herself—then I had unaccountably liked it, and Ferris Greenslet had too, against all her expectations—he was rushing it to publication in June. But somehow she was down about it now, and would welcome more comment from me while there was yet time.

H.Q.M. reacted to Willa Cather's spontaneous unpatterned novel as Justice Holmes, much later on, did to *My Ántonia*. It made her sense the core of her own Americanism, and feel prouder of her country that these people of European stock, who brought their *mores* and their hopes to the Nebraska Divide, so quickly blended their lives with its deep red stains.

The story of the pioneer Puritans, "our over-rated progenitors" (after all they were middle-class malcontents, chock-full of narrow prejudice) had been a hundred times told, H.Q.M. said, like the story of the covered-wagon days. But this fiercely untamed, untrammelled, sweeping natural world of the Divide, of which the author gave such rare and measured visual images, had new, almost cosmic vistas, overtones and undertones. Though the story unfolded with deceptive simplicity, it had majesty, even terror. The author seemed to be looking through objective lenses at something new God had made.

After H.Q.M. went back to London, I journeyed north up the Rhône, still with *O Pioneers!* in a bag I kept under my eye, and settled myself for the spring in Avignon, which happened to be one of Willa's favorite towns in all the world. Springtime really is merry, sensuous, expansive in Provence; one has to give in to it and merge with it—harsh one day with bitter biting cold mistral, warm rioting and expanding the next, like the speech of the Provençaux who always "languish" for everything, as I wrote Willa. *Je languis de te revoir, je languis de me promener avec toi, dans les Alpilles.*

Willa replied, mourning that she was not with me drinking a *petit verre* in the Place de la République and catching the jolly come-on-with-you gleam in a French soldier's eye. . . . If I wrote her of the yellow irises flaming in the ditches, and the tall black cypresses piercing the blue like arrows, she matched me with the yellow mustard in the tragic theatre at Arles and the little willows of Avignon resting their elbows in the flooded Rhône. Her most splendid memory was of the Rocher des Doms and its Virgin, golden above the great river, finest in the world, maybe. Did the same swirling mighty current rush past the old Pont d'Avignon?

How Willa loved all that was potent, mighty in nature! My first view of her at *McClure's* had brought that vision of red earth. Her future might prove as broad as the windy spaces of her state which, thanks to her gifts of memory and description, now lived in my mind as a concrete backdrop for her Eastern life.

When I let her know that the only flaw I could find in *O Pioneers!* was that it had no sharp skeleton, she swiftly replied, true enough I had named a weakness. But the land has no sculptured lines or features. The soil is soft, light, fluent, black, for the grass of the plains creates this type of soil as it decays. This influences the mind and memory of the author and so the composition of the story. Some time, Willa promised, there would be a story with sharp clear definite lines like the country in which I then was. . . .

More, more, tell her *more* about Provence. Like the Southwest it was a land that made one mad with delight. There *was* plenty more, especially about the Provençal poets, artists and writers whom I met through my French literary friends in Paris; or through my Scotch hosts at the Avignon pension. Through staying with the Soeurs Gardes Malades in Arles I had also fallen into a little nest of Catholic clergy, red-cheeked, devoted, hearty men in black *soutanes* who loved good living and shot quail and grouse in the Camargue. It was in company of two curés and a Sister Superior that I went to Maillane, that green village on a dusty plain where the old poet Mistral, with his goatee, and his sombrero on the back of his head, was drinking *eau sucrée* in his garden. He did so closely resemble "Boofalo," as he called Buffalo Bill, that the two of them had once bowed low and exchanged hats in a Paris café.

The curés presented me as an Arlésienne, taking much pleasure in this innocent deception. The Sisters had made me into a perfect counterfeit of the native article, headdress, fichu, black bodice, full skirt and Roman nose included. Mistral was so pleased that he promptly invited me to attend the forthcoming fêtes of his literary group, the Félibrige, who wrote in the native dialect.

I must have written Willa about all this light-hearted initiation into the poetry and legend of the land; about my walks with Provençal artists and writers in the dry Alpilles; and how my portrait was painted by a Cubist from a vineyard—*un sauvage*, a wild man, he called himself, a "*Fauve*," who had already exhibited in New York.

Willa was intrigued, especially by the Cubist. She determined I should expound modern art to her. She had been urging me to stop with her at Number Five Bank Street when I landed in late June and this was now arranged.

She hoped I would like her new home . . . I would find that she had had to become separated from *O Pioneers!*; get it out of her system by seeing it through proofs and into press, before she could be clear enough to admit to herself that she really wanted to do a very different kind of story!

This surprising remark undermined all my ideas about Willa's treading in the footsteps of Sarah Jewett, and writing of a region. What next then? She talked more and more of a new enthusiasm of hers, the Metropolitan Opera star Olive Fremstad. I had certainly heard Fremstad sing Kundry, Isolde and other Wagnerian rôles? Fremstad, born in Sweden, grew up in Minnesota, but she had the rebellious dubious eyes, far-scanning and keen, of the pioneer woman on the Divide—and an intelligence that challenged you and put you sharply and brusquely on your mettle. Willa wanted to tell me more about Fremstad when I got to Bank Street.

She ended by thanking me for caring for her book, for wanting to care for it, but even more for caring about the whole thing—that is, the art of creative writing.

Willa Cather Talks of Work†

Miss Willa Sibert Cather, whose new novel, *O Pioneers!* has just placed her in the foremost rank of American novelists, began to do newspaper work on the *Nebraska State Journal* while she was still an undergraduate in the University at Lincoln. From Lincoln Miss Cather came East as far as Pittsburgh, to go on the regular staff of the *Daily Leader.*

Leaving the newspaper life, while still very young, Miss Cather then accepted a position to teach, first Latin and afterward English, in the Pittsburgh High School. It was during this time that she wrote the verse and short stories which secured her the post of associate editor of *McClure's Magazine* and took her finally to New York.

Miss Cather's new novel, *O Pioneers!* is of special interest to Philadelphians—this magnificently grave and simple and poetic picture of early days on the uplands of Nebraska—if only for the strong influence of Whitman which the writing shows. There is the wise, clean-earthed philosophy of Whitman in the selection of the book's theme, too, and Miss Cather quotes her title direct from our superb white-bearded old lover of the world.

Though Miss Cather no longer spends all her time in the McClure Publications offices, on Fourth Avenue (she was managing editor of *McClure's Magazine* for four years), she is still connected with that publishing house; and I was eager to have her opinion of modern short-story writing in the United States.

"My own favorite American writers? said Miss Cather. "Well, I've never changed in that respect much since I was a girl at school. There were great ones I liked best then and still like—Mark Twain, Henry James and Sarah Orne Jewett."

"You must have read a lot of work by new people while you were editor of *McClure's*?" I suggested.

"Yes," smiled Miss Cather, "I suppose I read a good many thousand stories, some good and some bad."

† Interview by F. H. in the *Philadelphia Record*, August 10, 1913.

"And what seemed to you to be the trouble with most of the mediocre ones?"

"Simply this," replied Miss Cather unhesitatingly, "that the writer had not felt them strongly enough before he wrote them. Like everything else in the world, this is a question of—how far. No one person knows much more about writing than another. I expect that when people think they know anything about it, then their case is hopeless. But in my course of reading thousands of stories, I was strengthened in the conclusion that I had come to before; that nothing was really worth while that did not cut pretty deep, and that the main thing always was to be honest.

"So many of the stories that come into magazines are a combination of the genuine and the fake. A writer has really a story to tell, and he has evidently tried to make it fit the outline of some story that he admires, or that he believes has been successful. You can not always tell just where a writer stops being himself and begins to attitudinize in a story, but when you finish it, you have a feeling that he has been trying to fool himself. I think a writer ought to get into his copy as he really is, in his everyday clothes. His readers are thrown with him in a personal relation, just as if they were traveling with him; and if he is not sincere, there is no possibility of any sort of comradeship.

"I think many story writers try to multiply their ideas instead of trying to simplify them; that is, they often try to make a story out of every idea they have, to get returns on every situation that suggests itself. And, as a result, their work is entertaining, journalistic and thin. Whether it is a pianist, or a singer, or a writer, art ought to simplify—that seems to me to be the whole process. Millet[1] did hundreds of sketches of peasants sowing grain, some of them very complicated, but when he came to paint 'The Sower,' the composition is so simple that it seems inevitable. It was probably the hundred sketches that went before that made the picture what it finally became—a process of simplifying all the time—of sacrificing many things that were in themselves interesting and pleasing, and all the time getting closer to the one thing—It.

"Of course I am talking now about the kind of writing that interests me most—I take it that is what you want me to do. There is *The Three Guardsmen*[2] kind, which is, perhaps, quite as fine in its way, where the whole zest of the thing is the rapid multiplication of fancies and devices. That kind of writing, at its best, is like fencing

1. Jean-François Millet (1814–1875), French realist painter of peasant and farm life.
2. Also known as *The Three Musketeers*, an adventure novel by French writer Alexandre Dumas (1802–1870).

and dancing, the games that live forever. But the other kind, the kind that I am talking about, is pretty well summed up in a letter of Miss Sarah Orne Jewett's, that I found among some of her papers in South Berwick after her death:

"'Ah, it is things like that, which haunt the mind for years, and at last write themselves down, that belong, whether little or great, to literature.'

"It is that kind of honesty, that earnest endeavor to tell truly the thing that haunts the mind, that I love in Miss Jewett's own work. Reading her books from the beginning one finds that often she tried a character or a theme over and over, first in one story and then in another, before she at last realized it completely on the page. That wonderful story, 'Martha's Lady,' for instance, was hinted at and felt for in several of her earlier stories. And so was the old woman in 'The Queen's Twin.'

"I dedicated my novel *O Pioneers!* to Miss Jewett because I had talked over some of the characters in it with her one day at Manchester, and in this book I tried to tell the story of the people as truthfully and simply as if I were telling it to her by word of mouth."

"How did you come to write about that flat part of the prairie west, Miss Cather, which not many people find interesting?"

"I happen to be interested in the Scandinavian and Bohemian pioneers of Nebraska," said the young novelist, "because I lived among them when I was a child. When I was eight years old, my father moved from the Shenandoah Valley in Virginia to that Western country. My grandfather and grandmother had moved to Nebraska eight years before we left Virginia; they were among the real pioneers.

"But it was still wild enough and bleak enough when we got there. My grandfather's homestead was about eighteen miles from Red Cloud—a little town on the Burlington, named after the old Indian chief[3] who used to come hunting in that country, and who buried his daughter on the top of one of the river bluffs south of the town. Her grave had been looted for her rich furs and beadwork long before my family went West, but we children used to find arrowheads there and some of the bones of her pony that had been strangled above her grave."

"What was the country like when you got there?"

"I shall never forget my introduction to it. We drove out from Red Cloud to my grandfather's homestead one day in April. I was sitting

3. Makhpiya-Luta or Red Cloud (1822–1909) was one of the most important Lakota warriors and leaders in nineteenth-century America, fighting to preserve Indian autonomy and rights.

on the bay in the bottom of a Studebaker wagon, holding on to the side of the wagon box to steady myself—the roads were mostly faint trails over the bunch grass in those days. The land was open range and there was almost no fencing. As we drove further and further out into the country, I felt a good deal as if we had come to the end of everything—it was a kind of erasure of personality.

"I would not know how much a child's life is bound up in the woods and hills and meadows around it, if I had not been jerked away from all these and thrown out into a country as bare as a piece of sheet iron. I had heard my father say you had to show grit in a new country, and I would have got on pretty well during that ride if it had not been for the larks. Every now and then one flew up and sang a few splendid notes and dropped down into the grass again. That reminded me of something—I don't know what, but my one purpose in life just then was not to cry, and every time they did it, I thought I should go under.

"For the first week or two on the homestead I had that kind of contraction of the stomach which comes from homesickness. I didn't like canned things anyhow, and I made an agreement with myself that I would not eat much until I got back to Virginia and could get some fresh mutton. I think the first thing that interested me after I got to the homestead was a heavy hickory cane with a steel tip which my grandmother always carried with her when she went to the garden to kill rattlesnakes. She had killed a good many snakes with it, and that seemed to argue that life might not be so flat as it looked there.

"We had very few American neighbors—they were mostly Swedes and Danes, Norwegians and Bohemians. I liked them from the first and they made up for what I missed in the country. I particularly liked the old women, they understood my homesickness and were kind to me. I had met 'traveled' people in Virginia and in Washington, but these old women on the farms were the first people who ever gave me the real feeling of an older world across the sea. Even when they spoke very little English, the old women somehow managed to tell me a great many stories about the old country. They talk more freely to a child than to grown people, and I always felt as if every word they said to me counted for twenty.

"I have never found any intellectual excitement any more intense than I used to feel when I spent a morning with one of those old women at her baking or butter making. I used to ride home in the most unreasonable state of excitement; I always felt as if they told me so much more than they said—as if I had actually got inside another person's skin. If one begins that early, it is the story of the maneating tiger over again—no other adventure ever carries one quite so far."

"Some of your early short stories were about these people, were they not?"

"Yes, but most of them were poor. It is always hard to write about the things that are near to your heart, from a kind of instinct of self-protection you distort them and disguise them. Those stories were so poor that they discouraged me. I decided that I wouldn't write any more about the country and people for which I had such personal feeling.

"Then I had the good fortune to meet Sarah Orne Jewett, who had read all of my early stories and had very clear and definite opinions about them and about where my work fell short. She said, 'Write it as it is, don't try to make it like this or that. You can't do it in anybody else's way—you will have to make a way of your own. If the way happens to be new, don't let that frighten you. Don't try to write the kind of short story that this or that magazine wants—write the truth, and let them take it or leave it.'

"I was not at all sure, however, that my feeling about the Western country and my Scandinavian friends was the truth—I thought perhaps that going among them so young I had a romantic personal feeling about them. I thought that Americans in general must see only the humorous side of the Scandinavian—the side often presented in vaudeville dialect sketches[4] because nobody had ever tried to write about the Swedish settlers seriously.

"What has pleased me most in the cordial reception the West has given this new book of mine, is that the reviewers in all those Western States say the thing seems to them true to the country and the people. That is a great satisfaction. The reviews have concerned themselves a good deal more with the subject matter of the story than with my way of telling it, and I am glad of that. I care a lot more about the country and the people than I care about my own way of writing or anybody else's way of writing."

ETHEL M. HOCKETT

The Vision of a Successful Fiction Writer†

For the benefit of the many young people who have literary ambitions and to whom the pinnacle of success attained by this Nebraska novelist appears as the most desirable thing to be gained in the world, Miss [Willa] Cather was persuaded to give the time from

4. Swedish vaudeville humor used the stereotypes of "Ole" and "Lena," a rustic (and not too bright) farm couple who spoke in heavily accented English.

† Article in the *Lincoln Daily Star*, October 24, 1915.

her busy hours in Lincoln of living over school days with old acquaintances, to give a number of valuable suggestions from her rich fund of experiences.

"The business of writing is a personal problem and must be worked out in an individual way," said Miss Cather. "A great many people ambitious to write, fall by the wayside, but if they are the discourageable kind it is better that they drop out. No beginner knows what he has to go through with or he would never begin.

"When I was in college and immediately after graduation, I did newspaper work. I found that newspaper writing did a great deal of good for me in working off the purple flurry of my early writing. Every young writer has to work off the 'fine writing' stage. It was a painful period in which I overcame my florid, exaggerated, foamy-at-the-mouth, adjective-spree period. I knew even then it was a crime to write like I did, but I had to get the adjectives and the youthful fervor worked off.

"I believe every young writer must write whole books of extravagant language to get it out. It is agony to be smothered in your own florescence, and to be forced to dump great carloads of your posies out in the road before you find one posy that will fit in the right place. But it must be done, just as a great singer must sacrifice so many lovely lyrical things in herself to be a great interpreter."

Miss Cather is pre-eminently qualified to give advice to young writers, not only from her own experiences in traveling the road which led her to literary success, but because she has had opportunities to study the writings of others from the viewpoint of a buyer.

After she had worked on Lincoln newspapers, one of which was edited by Mrs. Sarah Harris Dorris whom she visited last week, Miss Cather went to Pittsburgh where she worked on a newspaper for several years. She tired of newspaper work and became the head of the English department in the Allegheny high school in Pittsburgh where she remained three years. It was while teaching that she wrote the verses which appeared in the book *April Twilights*, and the short stories which made up the book *The Troll Garden*. These stories and verses were published by McClure's, most of them appearing in the *McClure's* magazine. A year after their publication, Mr. McClure went to Pittsburgh and offered Miss Cather a position on his magazine which she accepted. Exceptional opportunities were shortly afterward afforded Miss Cather, as Miss Ida Tarbell, Mr. Phillips, Mr. Baker and several other prominent writers, left *McClure's* and bought the *American* magazine. Within two years, therefore, Miss Cather was managing editor of *McClure's*. She held that position for six years. Although life as managing editor was stimulating, affording Miss Cather opportunity for travel abroad and in this country, she could do no creative work, so left in order to produce the stories pent up in her mind. She says the material used in her stories was all collected before she was twenty years old.

"Aside from the fact that my duties occupied much of my time, when you are buying other writers' stuff, it simply isn't the graceful thing to do to do any writing yourself," she said.

Leaving *McClure's*, Miss Cather moved to a suburb of New York and wrote *Alexander's Bridge* and *The Bohemian Girl*. She went to Arizona for the summer and returned to New York to write *O Pioneers!*

Miss Cather's books all have western settings, in Nebraska, Colorado and Arizona, and she spends part of each year in the west reviewing the early impressions and stories which go to make up her books.

"No one without a good ear can write good fiction," was a surprising statement made by Miss Cather. "It is an essential to good writing to be sensitive to the beauty of language and speech, and to be able to catch the tone, phrase, length of syllables, enunciation, etc., of persons of all types that cross a writer's path. The successful writer must also be sensitive to accomplishment to others.

"Writers have such hard times if they just have rules and theories. Things that make for integrity in writing are quite as unnameable as the things that make the difference between an artist and a near-artist in music. And it is the longest distance in the world between the artist and the near-artist.

"It is up to the writer and no one else. He must spend thousands of uncounted hours at work. He must strive untiringly while others eat and sleep and play. Some people are more gifted than others, but it takes brains in the most gifted to make a success. Writing has to be gone at like any other trade. One trouble is that people aren't honest with themselves; they are awfully unfrank about sizing themselves up. They have such queer ways of keeping half-done things stored by and inconsistently saying to themselves that they will finish them after a while, and never admitting they shrink from that work because they are not qualified for it.

"One trouble with young writers is that they imitate too much, often unconsciously," said Miss Cather. "Ninety-nine out of every hundred stories received by magazines are imitations of some former success. This is a natural mistake for young people to make. The girl or boy of 24 or 25 is not strong though to digest experiences in the raw, therefore they take them pre-digested from things they read. That is why young writing does not as a rule amount to much. These young writers can sometimes give cries of pain and of rapture and even the cry from a baby sometimes moves.

"Young writers must care vitally, fiercely, absurdly about the trickery and the arrangement of words, the beauty and power of phrases. But they must go on and on until they get more out of life itself than out of anything written. Then a writer reaches the stage where a tramp on a rail pile in Arizona fills him with as many thrills as the greatest novel ever written, he has well begun on his career.

"William Jones[1] once expressed this idea well when he told me great minds like Balzac or Shakespeare got thousands and thousands more of distinct impressions and mental pictures in every single day of life than the average man got in all his life.

"I can remember when Kipling's *Jungle Tales* meant more to me than a tragic wreck or big fire in the city. But I passed through that stage. If I hadn't again grasped the thrills of life, I would have been too literary and academic to ever write anything worth while.

"There are a great many young people who like good literature and go to work on a magazine or newspaper with the idea of reforming it and showing it what to print. It is all right to have ideas, but they should be kept locked up, for the beginner should do the things in his employer's way. If his ideas are worth anything, they will come out untarnished; if they are not, they will get mixed up with crooked things and he will be disillusioned and soured.

"I have seen a great many western girls and boys come to New York and make a living around magazines and newspapers, and many rise to very good positions. They must be wide awake, adaptable and not afraid to work. A beginner can learn a lot about magazine requirements and style by proof-reading, or doing other jobs other than writing the leading editorials. Every magazine has its individual style.

"Most people have the idea that magazines are like universities—existing to pass on the merits of productions. They think if stories and articles are accepted, it is an honor, and if they are refused, it is a disgrace. They do not realize the magazine is in the business of buying and selling.

"The truth is that many good stories are turned down every day in a magazine office. If the editor has twenty-five children's stories in the safe and a twenty-sixth good children's story comes in with one poor adventure story, he must buy the poor adventure story and return the good children's story. It is just like being overstocked in anything else. The magazine editor must have variety, and it is sometimes maddening the way the stories come in in flocks of like kinds.

"The young writer must learn to deal with subjects he really knows about. No matter how commonplace a subject may be, if it

1. Will Owen Jones (1862–1928), managing editor of the Lincoln *Journal*, was a long-time friend of Willa Cather.

is one with which the author is thoroughly familiar it makes a much better story than the purely imaginational.

"Imagination, which is a quality writers must have, does not mean the ability to weave pretty stories out of nothing. In the right sense, imagination is a response to what is going on—a sensitiveness to which outside things appeal. It is a composition of sympathy and observation."

Miss Cather makes the comparison between learning to write and learning to play the piano. If there is no talent to begin with, the struggler can never become an artist. But no matter what talent there is, the writer must spend hours and years of practice in writing just as the musician must drudge at his scales.

Miss Cather laughed merrily as she said that her old friends in Lincoln insist on dragging up what she pleased to call her "shady past," and reminding her of her rhetorical and reformative flights of her youth. It was recalled by one friend that she led the last cane rush in the university, that she wore her hair cropped short and a stiff hat and that the boys among whom she was very popular, called her "Billy." Miss Cather graduated from the University of Nebraska in 1895.

ELEANOR HINMAN

Interview with Willa Cather†

"The old fashioned farmer's wife is nearer to the type of the true artist and the prima donna than is the culture enthusiast," declared Miss Willa Cather, author of *The Song of the Lark*, *O Pioneers!*, *My Ántonia*, *Youth and the Bright Medusa*, who has earned the title of one of the foremost American novelists by her stories of prima donnas and pioneers. She was emphasizing that the two are not so far apart in type as most people seem to imagine.

Miss Cather had elected to take her interview out-of-doors in the autumnal sunshine, walking. The fact is characteristic. She is an outdoor person, not far different in type from the pioneers and prima donnas whom she exalts.

She walks with the gait of one who has been used to the saddle. Her complexion is firm with an outdoor wholesomeness. The red in her cheeks is the red that comes from the bite of the wind. Her voice is deep, rich, and full of color; she speaks with her whole body, like a singer.

† *Lincoln Sunday Star*, November 6, 1921.

"Downright" is the word that comes most often to the mind in thinking of her. Whatever she does is done with every fibre. There is no pretense in her, and no conventionality. In conversation she is more stimulating than captivating. She has ideas and is not afraid to express them. Her mind scintillates and sends rays of light down many avenues of thought.

When the interviewer was admitted to her, she was pasting press clippings on a huge sheet of brown wrapping paper, as whole-heartedly as though it were the most important action of her life.

"This way you get them all together," she explained, "and you can see who it is that really likes you, who that really hates you, and who that actually hates you but pretends to like you. I don't mind the ones that hate me; I don't doubt they have good reasons, but I despise the ones that pretend."

When she had finished, she went to her room and almost immediately came out of it again, putting on her hat and coat as she came down the stairs, and going out without a glance at the mirror. She dresses well, yet she is clearly one of the women to whom the chief requirement of clothes is that they should be clean and comfortable.

Although she is very fond of walking, it is evidently strictly subordinate in her mind to conversation. The stroll was perpetually slowing down to a crawl and stopping short at some point which required emphasis. She has a characteristic gesture to bring out a cardinal point; it commences as though it would be a hearty clap upon the shoulder of the person whom she is addressing, but it checks itself and ends without even a touch.

I had intended to interview her on how she gathers the material for her writings; but walking leads to discursiveness and it would be hard to assemble the whole interview under any more definite topic than that bugbear of authors, "an author's views on art." But the longer Miss Cather talks, the more one is filled with the conviction that life is a fascinating business and one's own experience more fascinating than one had ever suspected it of being. Some persons have this gift of infusing their own abundant vitality into the speaker, as Roosevelt is said to have done.

"I don't gather the material for my stories," declared Miss Cather. "All my stories have been written with material that was gathered—no, God save us! not gathered but absorbed—before I was fifteen years old. Other authors tell me it is the same way with them. Sarah Orne Jewett insisted to me that she has used nothing in all her short stories which she did not remember before she was eight years old.

"People will tell you that I come west to get ideas for a new novel, or material for a new novel, as though a novel could be conceived by running around with a pencil and [paper] and jotting down phrases and suggestions. I don't even come west for local color.

"I could not say, however, that I don't come west for inspiration. I do get freshened up by coming out here. I like to go back to my home town, Red Cloud, and get out among the folk who like me for myself, who don't know and don't care a thing about my books, and who treat me just as they did before I published any of them. It makes me feel just like a kid!" cried Willa Cather, writer of finely polished prose.

"The ideas for all my novels have come from things that happened around Red Cloud when I was a child. I was all over the country then, on foot, on horseback and in our farm wagons. My nose went poking into nearly everything. It happened that my mind was constructed for the particular purpose of absorbing impressions and retaining them. I always intended to write, and there were certain persons I studied. I seldom had much idea of the plot or the other characters, but I used my eyes and my ears."

Miss Cather described in detail the way in which the book *My Ántonia* took form in her mind. This is the most recent of her novels; its scene is laid in Nebraska, and it is evidently a favorite of hers.

"One of the people who interested me most as a child was the Bohemian hired girl of one of our neighbors, who was so good to me. She was one of the truest artists I ever knew in the keenness and sensitiveness of her enjoyment, in her love of people and in her willingness to take pains. I did not realize all this as a child, but Annie fascinated me, and I always had it in mind to write a story about her.

"But from what point of view should I write it up? I might give her a lover and write from his standpoint. However, I thought my Ántonia deserved something better than the *Saturday Evening Post* sort of stuff in her book. Finally I concluded that I would write from the point of a detached observer, because that was what I had always been.

"Then, I noticed that much of what I knew about Annie came from the talks I had with young men. She had a fascination for them, and they used to be with her whenever they could. They had to manage it on the sly, because she was only a hired girl. But they respected and admired her, and she meant a good deal to some of them. So I decided to make my observer a young man.

"There was the material in that book for a lurid melodrama. But I decided that in writing it I would dwell very lightly upon those things that a novelist would ordinarily emphasize and make up my story of the little, every-day happenings and occurrences that form the greatest part of everyone's life and happiness.

"After all, it is the little things that really matter most, the unfinished things, the things that never quite come to birth. Sometimes a man's wedding day is the happiest day in his life, but usually he likes most of all to look back upon some quite simple, quite uneventful day when nothing in particular happened but all the world seemed touched with gold. Sometimes it is a man's wife who sums up to him his ideal of all a woman can be; but how often it is some girl whom he scarcely knows, whose beauty and kindliness have caught at his imagination without cloying it!"

It was many years after the conception of the story that it was written. This story of Nebraska was finally brought to birth in the White Mountains.[1] And Miss Cather's latest novel, which will be published next fall, and which alone of all her prairie stories deals with the Nebraska of the present, was written largely on the Mediterranean coast in southern France, where its author has been during the past spring and summer.

It is often related that Miss Cather draws the greater part of her characters from the life, that they are actual portraits of individual people. This statement she absolutely denies.

"I have never drawn but one portrait of an actual person. That was the mother of the neighbor family, in *My Ántonia*. She was the mother of my childhood chums in Red Cloud. I used her so for this reason: While I was getting under way with the book in the White Mountains, I received the word of her death. One clings to one's friends so—I don't know why it was—but the resolve came over me that I would put her into that book as nearly drawn from the life as I could do it. I had not seen her for years.

"I have always been so glad that I did so, because her daughters were so deeply touched. When the book was published it recalled to them little traits of hers that they had not remembered of themselves—as, for example, that when she was vexed she used to dig her heels into the floor as she walked and go clump! clump! clump! across the floor. They cannot speak of the book without weeping.

"All my other characters are drawn from life, but they are all composites of three or four persons. I do not quite understand it, but certain persons seem to coalesce naturally when one is working up a story. I believe most authors shrink from actual portrait painting. It seems so cold-blooded, so heartless, so indecent almost, to present an actual person in that intimate fashion, stripping his very soul."

Although Miss Cather's greatest novels all deal with Nebraska, and although it has been her work which has first put Nebraska

1. Willa Cather wrote most of *My Ántonia* while staying at the Shattuck Inn in Jaffrey, near the White Mountains of New Hampshire.

upon the literary map, this seems to have been more a matter of necessity with her than of choice. For when she was asked to give her reflections about Nebraska as a storehouse of literary or artistic material, her answer was not altogether conciliatory.

"Of course Nebraska is a storehouse of literary material. Everywhere is a storehouse of literary material. If a true artist was born in a pigpen and raised in a sty, he would still find plenty of inspiration for his work. The only need is the eye to see.

"Generally speaking, the older and more established the civilization, the better a subject it is for art. In an old community there has been time for associations to gather and for interesting types to develop. People do not feel that they all must be exactly alike.

"At present in the west there seems to be an idea that we all must be like somebody else, as much as if we had all been cast in the same mold. We wear exactly similar clothes, drive the same make of car, live in the same part of town, in the same style of house. It's deadly! Not long ago one of my dear friends said to me that she was about to move.

" 'Oh,' I cried, 'how can you leave this beautiful old house!'

" 'Well,' she said, 'I don't really want to go, but all our friends have moved to the other end of town, and we have lived in this house for forty years.'

"What better reason can you want for staying in a house than that you have lived there for forty years?

"New things are always ugly. New clothes are always ugly. A prima donna will never wear a new gown upon the stage. She wears it first around her apartment until it shapes itself to her figure; or if she hasn't time to do that, she hires an understudy to wear it. A house can never be beautiful until it has been lived in for a long time. An old house built and furnished in miserable taste is more beautiful than a new house built and furnished in correct taste. The beauty lies in the associations that cluster around it, the way in which the house has fitted itself to the people.

"This rage for newness and conventionality is one of the things which I deplore in the present-day Nebraska. The second is the prevalence of a superficial culture. These women who run about from one culture club to another studying Italian art out of a textbook and an encyclopedia and believing that they are learning something about it by memorizing a string of facts, are fatal to the spirit of art. The nigger boy who plays by ear on his fiddle airs from *Traviata* without knowing what he is playing, or why he likes it, has more real understanding of Italian art than these esthetic creatures with a head and a larynx, and no organs that they get any use of, who reel you off the life of Leonardo da Vinci.

"Art is a matter of enjoyment through the five senses. Unless you can see the beauty all around you everywhere, and enjoy it, you can never comprehend art. Take the cottonwood, for example, the most beautiful tree on the plains. The people of Paris go crazy about them. They have planted long boulevards with them. They hold one of their fetes when the cotton begins to fly; they call it 'summer snow.' But people of Red Cloud and Hastings chop them down.

"Take our Nebraska wild flowers. There is no place in the world that has more beautiful ones. But they have no common names. In England, in any European country, they would all have beautiful names like eglantine, primrose, and celandine. As a child I gave them all names of my own. I used to gather great armfuls of them and sit and cry over them. They were so lovely, and no one seemed to care for them at all! There is one book that I would rather have produced than all my novels. That is the Clemens botany[2] dealing with the wild flowers of the west.

"But why am I taking so many examples from one sense? Esthetic appreciation begins with the enjoyment of the morning bath. It should include all the activities of life. There is real art in cooking a roast just right, so that it is brown and dripping and odorous and 'saignant.'[3]

"The farmer's wife who raises a large family and cooks for them and makes their clothes and keeps house and on the side runs a truck garden and a chicken farm and a canning establishment, and thoroughly enjoys doing it all, and doing it well, contributes more to art than all the culture clubs. Often you find such a woman with all the appreciation of the beautiful bodies of her children, of the order and harmony of her kitchen, of the real creative joy of all her activities, which marks the great artist.

"Most of the women artists I have known—the prima donnas, novelists, poets, sculptors—have been women of this same type. The very best cooks I have ever known have been prima donnas. When I visited them the way to their hearts was the same as to the hearts of the pioneer rancher's wife in my childhood—I must eat a great deal, and enjoy it.

"Many people seem to think that art is a luxury to be imported and tacked on to life. Art springs out of the very stuff that life is made of. Most of our young authors start to write a story and make a few observations from nature to add local color. The results are invariably false and hollow. Art must spring out of the fullness and the richness of life."

This glorification of the old-fashioned housewife came very natu-

2. Frederic E. Clements, *Rocky Mountain Flowers; An Illustrated Guide for Plantlovers and Plant-users* (New York: Wilson, 1914).
3. "Rare."

rally from Willa Cather, chronicler of women with careers. What does Miss Cather think of the present movement of women into business and the arts?

"It cannot help but be good," was her reply. "It at least keeps the woman interested in something real.

"As for the choice between a woman's home and her career, is there any reason why she cannot have both? In France the business is regarded as a family affair. It is taken for granted that Madame will be the business partner of her husband; his bookkeeper, cashier, or whatever she fits best. Yet the French women are famous housekeepers and their children do not suffer for lack of care.

"The situation is similar if the woman's business is art. Her family life will be a help rather than a hinderance to her; and if she has a quarter of the vitality of her prototype on the farm she will be able to fulfill the claims of both."

Miss Cather, however, deplores heartily the drift of the present generation away from the land.

"All the farmer's sons and daughters seem to want to get into the professions where they think they may find a soft place. 'I'm sure not going to work the way the old man did,' seems to be the slogan of today. Soon only the Swedes and Germans will be left to uphold the prosperity of the country."

She contrasts the university of the present with that in the lean days of the nineties, "when," as she says, "the ghosts walked in this country." She came to Lincoln, a child barely in her teens, with her own way to make absolutely. She lived on thirty dollars a month, worked until 1 or 2 o'clock every night, ate no breakfast in the morning by way of saving time and money, never really had enough to eat, and carried full college work. "And many of the girls I was with were much worse off than I." Yet the large majority of the famous alumni of the university date from precisely this period of hard work and little cash.

In making her way into the literary world she never had, she declares, half the hardships that she endured in this battle for an education. Her first book of short stories, to be sure, was a bitter disappointment. Few people bought it, and her Nebraska friends could find no words bad enough for it. "They wanted me to write propaganda for the commercial club," she explained.

"An author is seldom sensitive except about his first volume. Any criticism of that hurts. Not criticism of its style—that only spurs one on to improve it. But the root-and-branch kind of attack is hard to forget. Nearly all very young authors write sad stories and very many of them write their first stories in revolt against everything. Humor, kindliness, tolerance come later."

LATROBE CARROLL

Willa Sibert Cather†

On the Nebraska prairie some years ago, a little girl rode about on her pony, among settlements of Scandinavians and Bohemians, listening to their conversation, fascinated by their personalities. She was Willa Sibert Cather, who, as a woman, was to give in her novels the story of their struggle with the soil. Ever since those early years, she has been studying people, until she is today one of that small group of American writers who tell of life with beauty and entire earnestness. She has won the praise of those critics whose standards are highest, whose condemnation of insincerity and distortion is severest. Listen to Randolph Bourne:[1] "She has outgrown provincialism and can now be reckoned among those who are richly interpreting youth all over the world." And to H. L. Mencken:[2] "There is no other American author of her sex, now in view, whose future promises so much."

Miss Cather's reputation is of recent growth. Though her first novel, "Alexander's Bridge", was published in 1912, she remained comparatively unknown until about five years ago. Then critics realized that every successive book of hers had shown an advance, and began to look forward with interest to her future work. She is, however, still unknown to large sections of the American reading public.

Not long ago, she sat in her New York apartment in Greenwich Village, and talked to me about her books. She seems just the one to have written them. She is sincere, vigorous, self-controlled. There is no flippancy about her. She has not made herself the heroine of any of her novels, but she is akin to her own heroines. In "The Song of the Lark", one of the characters remarks that Thea Kronborg, the central figure, "doesn't sigh every time the wind blows". Miss Cather herself is that sort. She has a mental sturdiness.

She spoke of the beginnings of her impulse to write.

"When I was about nine," she said, "father took me from our place near Winchester, Virginia, to a ranch in Nebraska. Few of our neighbors were Americans—most of them were Danes, Swedes, Norwegians, and Bohemians. I grew fond of some of these immi-

† *Bookman*, May 3, 1921.
1. Cultural critic and writer (1886–1918) and early admirer of Cather's fiction.
2. One of the most influential editors, critics, and men of letters in early twentieth-century America, H. L. Mencken (1880–1956) championed Willa Cather's early novels and contributed to her growing literary reputation.

grants—particularly the old women, who used to tell me of their home country. I used to think them underrated, and wanted to explain them to their neighbors. Their stories used to go round and round in my head at night. This was, with me, the initial impulse. I didn't know any writing people. I had an enthusiasm for a kind of country and a kind of people, rather than ambition.

"I've always had a habit of remembering mannerisms, turns of speech," she explained. "The phraseology of those people stuck in my mind. If I had made notes, or should make them now, the material collected would be dead. No, it's memory—the memory that goes with the vocation. When I sit down to write, turns of phrase I've forgotten for years come back like white ink before fire. I think that most of the basic material a writer works with is acquired before the age of fifteen. That's the important period: when one's not writing. Those years determine whether one's work will be poor and thin or rich and fine."

After a high school preparation, Miss Cather entered the University of Nebraska. She said, of this time:

"Back in the files of the college magazine, there were once several of my perfectly honest but very clumsy attempts to give the story of some of the Scandinavian and Bohemian settlers who lived not far from my father's farm. In these sketches, I simply tried to tell about the people, without much regard for style. These early stories were bald, clumsy, and emotional. As I got toward my senior year, I began to admire, for the first time, writing for writing's sake. In those days, no one seemed so wonderful as Henry James; for me, he was the perfect writer."

When Willa Cather graduated at nineteen, her instructors and friends expected her to become a "writer" in a few months, and achieve popular success. But they were disappointed. For almost nine years she wrote little besides a volume of verse, the experimental "April Twilights", and a dozen stories for magazines. Most of these stories she now dismisses as "affected" and "bad".

"It wasn't that I didn't want to write," she said of this period. "But I was too interested in trying to find out something about the world and about people. I worked on the Pittsburg 'Leader', taught English in the Allegheny High School, went abroad for long periods, and traveled in the west. I couldn't have got as much out of those nine years if I'd been writing."

In 1905 there was published a collection of her stories, "The Troll Garden". Largely by reason of these, she was offered a position on "McClure's Magazine", of which she was managing editor from 1908 until 1912.

"I took a salaried position," she said, "because I didn't want to write directly to sell. I didn't want to compromise. Not that the magazine demands were wrong. But they were definite. I had a delightful sense of freedom when I'd saved up enough to take a house in Cherry Valley, New York, and could begin work on my first novel, 'Alexander's Bridge'.

"In 'Alexander's Bridge' I was still more preoccupied with trying to write well than with anything else. It takes a great deal of experience to become natural. People grow in honesty as they grow in anything else. A painter or writer must learn to distinguish what is his *own* from that which he admires. I never abandoned trying to make a compromise between the kind of matter that my experience had given me and the manner of writing which I admired, until I began my second novel, 'O Pioneers!' And from the first chapter, I decided not to 'write' at all—simply to give myself up to the pleasure of recapturing in memory people and places I had believed forgotten. This was what my friend Sarah Orne Jewett had advised me to do. She said to me that if my life had lain in a part of the world that was without a literature, and I couldn't tell about it truthfully in the form I most admired, I'd have to make a kind of writing that would tell it, no matter what I lost in the process."

"O Pioneers!" placed Miss Cather definitely among the writers who count. It is an epic of the early struggles of Swedish and Bohemian settlers in Nebraska—a book of beauty and power. In taking for a title the name of one of Walt Whitman's poems, the author drew attention to his influence upon the mood of her narrative.

* * *

"I work from two and a half to three hours a day," Miss Cather [said]. I don't hold myself to longer hours; if I did, I wouldn't gain by it. The only reason I write is because it interests me more than any other activity I've ever found. I like riding, going to operas and concerts, travel in the west; but on the whole writing interests me more than anything else. If I made a chore of it, my enthusiasm would die. I make it an adventure every day. I get more entertainment from it than any I could buy, except the privilege of hearing a few great musicians and singers. To listen to them interests me as much as a good morning's work.

"For me, the morning is the best time to write. During the other hours of the day I attend to my housekeeping, take walks in Central Park, go to concerts, and see something of my friends. I try to keep myself fit, fresh: one has to be in as good form to write as to sing. When not working, I shut work from my mind."

At present Miss Cather is writing a new novel[3]—she says of it:

"What I always want to do is to make the 'writing' count for less and less and the people for more. In this new novel I'm trying to

3. *One of Ours* (1922).

cut out all analysis, observation, description, even the picture-making quality, in order to make things and people tell their own story simply by juxtaposition, without any persuasion or explanation on my part.

"Just as if I put here on the table a green vase, and beside it a yellow orange. Now, those two things affect each other. Side by side, they produce a reaction which neither of them will produce alone. Why should I try to say anything clever, or by any colorful rhetoric detract attention from those two objects, the relation they have to each other and the effect they have upon each other? I want the reader to see the orange and the vase—beyond that, *I* am out of it. Mere cleverness must go. I'd like the writing to be so lost in the object, that it doesn't exist for the reader—except for the reader who knows how difficult it is to lose writing in the object. One must choose one's audience, and the audience I try to write for is the one interested in the effect the green vase brings out in the orange, and the orange in the green vase."

* * *

DOROTHY CANFIELD FISHER

Daughter of the Frontier†

Scientists seem to think there is no better entertainment than to set up a hypothesis in the intellectual bowling alley and see how much of it is standing after the evidence is in. Why leave all the fun to them? I offer you a hypothesis about Willa Cather's work: that the one real subject of all her books is the effect new country—our new country—has on people transplanted to it from the old traditions of a stable complex civilisation.

Such a hypothesis, if true, would show her as the only American author who has concentrated on the only unique quality of our national life, on the one element which is present, more or less, in every American life and unknown and unguessable to Europeans or European colonials. For Americans (whether originally from Norway, Scotland, Poland or Bohemia) are the only people who have given to the shift from the old to the new life the stern dignity of the irrevocable.

English and French colonists seem to take the attitude of those married people who can't bear to give up thinking of themselves as

† "Willa Cather, Daughter of the Frontier" from the *New York Herald Tribune*, 5/28/33; © 1933, New York Herald Tribune, Inc. All rights reserved. Reproduced by permission. Dorothy Canfield Fisher (1879–1958), a lifelong friend of Willa Cather, was a best-selling novelist and woman of letters.

somebody's children rather than as grown-ups: for whom not their own, but their parents' house is home. Psychologists tell us that the definite break with the past and the assuming of adult responsibility involved in marriage is too much for many people who for no matter how many years after their weddings continue to long for mother's pies and father's protection.

Americans have no choice but to accept the definite break with the past. They are like people who have married against their parents' wishes, and know they must make the best of their bargain. Every American finds himself shut out from the home of his father and married to a new country, with no arrangement made for divorce if he does not like his bride.

Is there one of Miss Cather's novels which is not centered around the situation of a human being whose inherited traits come from centuries of European or English forebears, but who is set down in a new country to live a new life which is not European or English, whatever else it may be? Isn't Miss Cather's chief interest what happens to him in this country, as opposed to what might have happened to him if his family had stayed on the other side of the Atlantic?

This hypothesis cannot be fully examined without looking to see what Miss Cather herself has made out of being an American. For it is not only in her books but in her own experience that she has wrestled with the grave problems and perplexities of transplantation. In her own person she lived through the typical American experience of going from a stable old society to live in a new world. She was born in Virginia of a family who had been farmers for generations, and lived where she was born till she was eight years old. That means she was born and lived for what is traditionally the period of life which most influences personality in a state which had the tradition of continuity and stability as far as they could exist in this country, and in a class which more than any other is always stubbornly devoted to the old ways of doing things.

By the time she was a child of eight Nebraska was being settled by one of the greatest floodtides of rural immigration in the history of the United States. In one decade half a million people pulled their roots from the soil—Danish, German, Norwegian, Bohemian, Virginian—where they had been for centuries and transplanted themselves to a new country where, strangers not only to the land but to one another, they had the full responsibility of creating whatever communal life was to be.

Along with the half million, out to a ranch near Red Cloud went the Cathers. Their sensitive, intelligent, gifted little girl, marked to the marrow of her bones by her experience of life lived according to an old, stable, orderly and unquestioned tradition, found herself in what from this distance looks rather like social chaos and anarchy.

But the sight of chaos is, everybody knows, the most potent stimulus the creative impulse can encounter: and anarchy taking away the props supplied to the weak in settled societies gives infinitely more elbow room for the strong.

Our little Virginia girl was not only sensitive and gifted, she was endowed with wonderful vitality and with what I feel to be a prime virtue, perhaps *the* prime virtue—the will and the ability to enjoy life. And what vital young creature could fail to respond to the stirring drama of hope enacted in those first years of the new settlements? Nothing being yet done, everything was still possible. The pioneers had left behind them stability and tradition, but they had also left social barriers and class inhibitions. They might live in sod houses and have few and plain possessions, but horses—old Aryan symbol of the ruling class—were cheap and, symbolically again, there were no fences.

The women of the little girl's family probably were sometimes homesick; most pioneer women were. But the child with a pony of her own to ride in a world without fences probably enjoyed life very much indeed; most frontier children did. No matter how widely she rode, in all that unfenced prairie, the only people for her to see were transplants; and for the first few years most of them half drunk with the exquisite and unforgettable elixir of frontier hopefulness.

The tragic souring of that wine coincided with her growing up. By the time she was twelve the tide had begun to turn. Successive droughts had brought terrible crop failures to those farmers from rainy climates, pitifully unprepared for a hot, dry land. In one decade the population of Nebraska increased more rapidly than that of any other state west of the Mississippi; but in the decade following, so violent was the revulsion of feeling, the increase was not only less than in any other state of the entire Union, but an actual numerical decrease took place in half of the counties.

This dismal period, full of disappointment and bitterness as dramatic as the preceding hope, began when Willa Cather was about twelve. Till she was twenty—twenty-one—out of college, out of the state, she lived in the midst of one of the greatest disillusions the American pioneer movement has ever known. She had lived through years of hope so blinding that the defects of frontier life could not be seen; she had lived through years of reaction so bleak and black that its fine qualities were invisible. Is it surprising that her writing centers around the theme of the varying ways in which new life in a new country affects those transplanted to it?

Now she was not merely a wonderfully sensitive instrument for recording accurately and storing away all these impressions. She was also a vigorous individual in her own right, who wanted what she wanted with the invincible energy of health. Nebraska might, as people sometimes then gloomily prophesied it would, crumble into deserted desolation; she was twenty-one years old, as intelligent as they come, fearless, determined, eager. From deep roots the sap of life poured up into her young heart. She intended to live, not to brood over a communal heartbreak she could not help. She put out a strong hand and began to take what she wanted. Why not? What she wanted was hers by right. She took it away from no man.

She had already taken something of what she wanted from her student days. When she came up from Red Cloud to the State University, Lincoln was a new little prairie city, the university a rough approximation to an institution of learning. But they offered the brilliant young freshman something different from what she had had.

Sharp-set, fortunate owner of one of the finest appetites mortal ever had for the best in art and life, the girl from Red Cloud fell ravenously on the new opportunities. She amazed and sometimes abashed some of her professors by caring much more fiercely about their subjects than they did. Especially French. There seemed to be a natural affinity between her mind and French forms of art. During her undergraduate years she made it a loving duty to read every French literary masterpiece she could lay her hands on. Judge how disconcerting she was to the head of the French department! When she graduated it was the general conviction of those who knew her that she was the most brilliant student the university had ever had, and was destined for more striking success than any other member of her class.

Then, full of love and hate for the frontier, she moved eastward, to a job on a Pittsburgh newspaper. Being eminently natural and vigorous, she went right on wanting what she wanted and what she had not had; that is, what farm, ranch and small town life and state university education had not been able to give her: she wanted the best music, the best plays, personal contact with artists and actors and other interesting creative-minded people out of the common run; she wanted knowledge of the niceties of fine food and good wine and good service and of the work of the great painters and the great writers of the world, of where to go and what to see in Europe—but, above all, she wanted then, and always, to write.

I don't live where I hear much of what is said in literary chat, but I understand a legend is going the rounds which presents Willa Cather as a pale victim sacrificed to art. It is true that her art has always been first and foremost in her life, center and core and meaning of her existence; but she has sacrificed herself to it as much as a person who enjoys good eating sacrifices himself in eating good meals. Of course, he can't do other things at the same time; but what of it when he is already doing what he likes best? As well sympathise with Tilden[1] for the fancy dress parties and bridge playing he has missed because of his tennis; as well sympathise with a fish for being in water instead of gasping in the dust, as sympathise with Willa Cather for what she hasn't done while she has been writing.

In no time (as such things go—say, in ten years) she had her diploma from the University of the World, again with very high standing. She had worked on that Pittsburgh newspaper. She had changed from that to teaching in a public high school (which she did extremely well). She had read ever so many more first-rate books. She had heard much good music. She knew interesting people, as many as she liked. She knew Europe. She moved from Pittsburgh to New York to edit a magazine and met more stimulating people. Presently, having had the best out of various kinds of life, she was what she set out to be—an accomplished woman of the world and an accomplished writer.

Then, feeling her power ripe within her, she set herself at the business of writing. What did she write about? Why, about what but the different ways in which life in a new country affects different personalities exposed to it. About human lives in which the qualities coming from heredity must be adapted to an environment slowly evolved. Isn't that the thread of unity tying all the beautiful and various Cather works into one whole?

You will hear people say, commenting on what they call the disconnectedness of her work. 'The unity of Balzac's work comes from the fact that he is mostly concerned with showing how people react to the presence or absence of money in their lives; Hardy concentrates on the reaction of human beings to the brute element of chance which so often wrecks their lives: Thackeray's main interest is in the action of worldly and social ambitions on naturally noble and disinterested impulses. But what common element is there in Willa Cather's work? Show me one thing in common between *A Lost Lady* and *Shadows on the Rock*.'

There is, of course, everything in common; they are two treatments of the same theme. Any one wishing to depict marriage as an institution would naturally show cases where it succeeded and others where it failed. Miss Cather shows that the institution of America also varies in its results. Cécile[2] finds that she can be and is happily married to her new country, bringing a grand dowry of fine traditions with her. But America fairly breaks *A Lost Lady* on the

1. Bill Tilden, (1893–1953) American championship tennis player.
2. Cécile Auclair, a character in *Shadows on the Rock* (1931).

wheel. What is Mrs Forrester but Mme Recamier in Red Cloud?[3] As Miss Cather presents her, her tragedy is not universal, like the clash of Richard Mahoney's temperament against human existence in general. It is a tragedy not of life but of frontier life, which needs so sorely other qualities than charm in its women that it has not the tradition of delight in charm that would have made Mrs Forrester a joyous and joy-giving woman in an eighteenth century French salon.

But my space limit is more than passed. Why don't you go on testing this hypothesis on the Cather novels? It will not by any means cover everything. What hypothesis does? But I think that you'll see at once that *My Ántonia*, like Cécile, is one who makes a rich and fruitful success out of her union with the new world: and that Claude[4] is one of those who would have done infinitely better if his family had never left the old countries. Claude's going to war is only an escape from a hated marriage (both with his country and with his flesh-and-blood wife who is perhaps its symbol). What the war really gives him is a glimpse, that makes his heart ache, of a country where he could have developed innate qualities of taste and skill and discrimination and power which his America would have none of. And the Archbishop—but I was going to leave the rest of this to you.

Still, space or no space, I must not close without pointing out that if this hypothesis is true, it explains, among other things, the otherwise inexplicable lack of general enthusiasm abroad about her splendid books. Her name is well known, but she is not as much read as many authors of half her worth. Intelligent and fair-minded English critics have said, 'Yes, I recognise that hers is fine work. But somehow it doesn't interest me.' Such comment has always reduced us to the sort of speechless indignation felt by lovers of A.E. Houseman's poetry for people who 'can't see so much as all that in those little verses.' Our hypothesis would suggest, you see, a perfectly simple explanation for this British obtuseness—namely, that Miss Cather's work is all about an experience which no one but an American can have had: that, like Dante, she is the first to write in the true folk language of her country,[5] which naturally is not understood by outsiders; that she is deeply and mystically our own.

3. Mrs. Forrester, the central character in *A Lost Lady* (1925), tries, ultimately unsuccessfully, to host lively dinner parties in small-town Nebraska. Madame de Recamier (1777–1849) was a French hostess whose fashionable salon attracted important politicians and writers in early nineteenth-century Paris.
4. Claude Wheeler, the hero of Cather's novel *One of Ours* (1922), finds Midwestern materialism and small-mindedness stifling.
5. Dante was the first major poet to write in Italian rather than Latin.

WILLA CATHER

Preface†

It is difficult to comply with the publisher's request that I write a preface for this new edition of an early book.[1] "Alexander's Bridge" was my first novel, and does not deal with the kind of subject-matter in which I now find myself most at home. The people and the places of the story interested me intensely at the time when it was written, because they were new to me and were in themselves attractive. "Alexander's Bridge" was written in 1911, and "O Pioneers!" the following year. The difference in quality in the two books is an illustration of the fact that it is not always easy for the inexperienced writer to distinguish between his own material and that which he would like to make his own. Everything is new to the young writer, and everything seems equally personal. That which is outside his deepest experience, which he observes and studies, often seems more vital than that which he knows well, because he regards it with all the excitement of discovery. The things he knows best he takes for granted, since he is not continually thrilled by new discoveries about them. They lie at the bottom of his consciousness, whether he is aware of it or no, and they continue to feed him, but they do not stimulate him.

There is a time in a writer's development when his "life line"[2] and the line of his personal endeavor meet. This may come early or late, but after it occurs his work is never quite the same. After he has once or twice done a story that formed itself, inevitably, in his mind, he will not often turn back to the building of external stories again. The inner feeling produces for him a deeper excitement than the thrill of novelty or the glitter of the passing show.

The writer, at the beginning of his career, is often more interested in his discoveries about his art than in the homely truths which have been about him from his cradle. He is likely to feel that writing is one of the most important things, if not the most important thing, in the world, and that what he learns about it is his one really precious possession. He understands, of course, that he must know a great deal about life, but he thinks this knowledge is something he can get by going out to look for it, as one goes to a theatre. Perhaps it is just as well for him to believe this until he has ac-

† Written for the 1922 edition of *Alexander's Bridge*.

1. Ferris Greenslet, Willa Cather's editor at Houghton Mifflin, asked her to write a preface for the novel's republication in 1922.
2. In palmistry, the "life line"—the line stretching from the base of the thumb toward the base of the index finger—represents vitality, longevity, and quality of life.

quired a little facility and strength of hand; to work through his youthful vanities and gaudy extravagances before he comes to deal with the material that is truly his own. One of the few really helpful words I ever heard from an older writer, I had from Sarah Orne Jewett when she said to me: "Of course, one day you will write about your own country. In the meantime, get all you can. One must know the world *so well* before one can know the parish."

There have been notable and beautiful exceptions, but I think usually the young writer must have his affair with the external material he covets; must imitate and strive to follow the masters he most admires, until he finds he is starving for reality and cannot make this go any longer. Then he learns that it is not the adventure he sought, but the adventure that sought him, which has made the enduring mark upon him.

When a writer once begins to work with his own material, he realizes that, no matter what his literary excursions may have been, he has been working with it from the beginning—by living it. With this material he is another writer. He has less and less power of choice about the moulding of it. It seems to be there of itself, already moulded. If he tries to meddle with its vague outline, to twist it into some categorical shape, above all if he tries to adapt or modify its mood, he destroys its value. In working with this material he finds that he need have little to do with literary devices; he comes to depend more and more on something else—the thing by which our feet find the road home on a dark night, accounting of themselves for roots and stones which we had never noticed by day. This guide is not always with him, of course. He loses it and wanders. But when it is with him it corresponds to what Mr. Bergson[3] calls the wisdom of intuition as opposed to that of intellect. With this to shape his course, a writer contrives and connives only as regards mechanical details, and questions of effective presentation, always debatable. About the essential matter of his story he cannot argue this way or that; he has seen it, has been enlightened about it in flashes that are as unreasoning, often as unreasonable, as life itself.

Willa Cather

Whale Cove Cottage[4]
Grand Manan, N.B.
September, 1922

3. Willa Cather admired the writings of French philosopher Henri Bergson (1859–1941), in particular his work on time and memory, *Matter and Memory* (1911).
4. Whale Cove Cottage, the cabin Willa Cather and Edith Lewis built on Grand Manan Island, New Brunswick, was Cather's writing and vacation retreat in the 1920s and 1930s.

WILLA CATHER

My First Novels†

[There Were Two]

My first novel, *Alexander's Bridge*, was very like what painters call a studio picture. It was the result of meeting some interesting people in London. Like most young writers, I thought a book should be made out of "interesting material," and at that time I found the new more exciting than the familiar. The impressions I tried to communicate on paper were genuine, but they were very shallow. I still find people who like that book because it follows the most conventional pattern, and because it is more or less laid in London. London is supposed to be more engaging than, let us say, Gopher Prairie;[1] even if the writer knows Gopher Prairie very well and London very casually. Soon after the book was published I went for six months to Arizona and New Mexico. The longer I stayed in a country I really did care about, and among people who were a part of the country, the more unnecessary and superficial a book like *Alexander's Bridge* seemed to me. I did no writing down there, but I recovered from the conventional editorial point of view.

When I got back to Pittsburgh I began to write a book entirely for myself; a story about some Scandinavians and Bohemians who had been neighbours of ours when I lived on a ranch in Nebraska, when I was eight or nine years old. I found it a much more absorbing occupation than writing *Alexander's Bridge*; a different process altogether. Here there was no arranging or "inventing"; everything was spontaneous and took its own place, right or wrong. This was like taking a ride through a familiar country on a horse that knew the way, on a fine morning when you felt like riding. The other was like riding in a park, with someone not altogether congenial, to whom you had to be talking all the time. Since I wrote this book for myself, I ignored all the situations and accents that were then generally thought to be necessary. The "novel of the soil" had not then come into fashion in this country. The drawing-room was considered the proper setting for a novel, and the only characters worth reading about were smart people or clever people. "O. Henry"[2] had made the

1. The fictional Minnesota small town that is the setting for Sinclair Lewis's novel *Main Street* (1920).
2. The pen name of popular American short story writer William Sydney Porter (1862–1910).

short story go into the world of the cheap boarding-house and the shop-girl and the truck-driver. But Henry James and Mrs. Wharton were our most interesting novelists, and most of the younger writers followed their manner, without having their qualifications.

O Pioneers! interested me tremendously, because it had to do with a kind of country I loved, because it was about old neighbours, once very dear, whom I had almost forgotten in the hurry and excitement of growing up and finding out what the world was like and trying to get on in it. But I did not in the least expect that other people would see anything in a slow-moving story, without "action," without "humour," without a "hero"; a story concerned entirely with heavy farming people, with cornfields and pasture lands and pig yards,—set in Nebraska, of all places! As everyone knows, Nebraska is distinctly déclassé as a literary background; its very name throws the delicately atuned critic into a clammy shiver of embarrassment. Kansas is almost as unpromising. Colorado, on the contrary, is considered quite possible. Wyoming really has some class, of its own kind, like well-cut riding breeches. But a New York critic voiced a very general opinion when he said: "I simply don't care a damn what happens in Nebraska, no matter who writes about it."

O Pioneers! was not only about Nebraska farmers; the farmers were Swedes! At that time, 1912, the Swede had never appeared on the printed page in this country except in broadly humorous sketches; and the humour was based on two peculiarities: his physical strength, and his inability to pronounce the letter "j." I had certainly good reasons for supposing that the book I had written for myself would remain faithfully with me, and continue to be exclusively my property. I sent it to Mr. Ferris Greenslet, of Houghton Mifflin, who had published *Alexander's Bridge*, and was truly astonished when he wrote me they would publish it.

I was very much pleased when William Heinemann decided to publish it in England. I had met Mr. Heinemann in London several times, when I was on the editorial staff of *McClure's Magazine*, and I had the highest opinion of his taste and judgment. His personal taste was a thing quite apart from his business, and it was uncompromising. The fact that a second-rate book sold tremendously never made him hedge and insist that there must be something pretty good in it after all. Most publishers, like most writers, are ruined by their successes.

When my third book, *The Song of the Lark*, came along, Heinemann turned it down. I had never heard from him directly that he liked *O Pioneers!* but now I had a short hand-written letter from him, telling me that he admired it very much; that he was declining *The Song of the Lark* because he thought in that book I had taken the wrong road, and that the full-blooded method, which told everything about everybody, was not natural to me and was not the one in which I would ever take satisfaction. "As for myself," he wrote, "I always find the friendly, confidential tone of writing of this sort distressingly familiar, even when the subject matter is very fine."

At that time I did not altogether agree with Mr. Heinemann, nor with Randolph Bourne, in this country, who said in his review almost the same thing. One is always a little on the defensive about one's last book. But when the next book, *My Ántonia*, came along, quite of itself and with no direction from me, it took the road of *O Pioneers!*—not the road of *The Song of the Lark*. Too much detail is apt, like any other form of extravagance, to become slightly vulgar; and it quite destroys in a book a very satisfying element analogous to what painters call "composition."

Literary Contexts

WILLA CATHER

Peter†

"No, Antone, I have told thee many times, no, thou shalt not sell it until I am gone."

"But I need money; what good is that old fiddle to thee? The very crows laugh at thee when thou art trying to play. Thy hand trembles so thou canst scarce hold the bow. Thou shalt go with me to the Blue to cut wood tomorrow. See to it thou art up early."

"What, on the Sabbath, Antone, when it is so cold? I get so very cold, my son, let us not go tomorrow."

"Yes, tomorrow, thou lazy old man. Do not I cut wood upon the Sabbath? Care I how cold it is? Wood thou shalt cut, and haul it too, and as for the fiddle, I tell thee I will sell it yet." Antone pulled his ragged cap down over his low heavy brow, and went out. The old man drew his stool up nearer the fire, and sat stroking his violin with trembling fingers and muttering, "Not while I live, not while I live."

Five years ago they had come here, Peter Sadelack, and his wife, and oldest son Antone, and countless smaller Sadelacks, here to the dreariest part of southwestern Nebraska, and had taken up a homestead. Antone was the acknowledged master of the premises, and people said he was a likely youth, and would do well. That he was mean and untrustworthy every one knew, but that made little difference. His corn was better tended than any in the county, and his wheat always yielded more than other men's.

Of Peter no one knew much, nor had any one a good word to say for him. He drank whenever he could get out of Antone's sight long enough to pawn his hat or coat for whisky. Indeed there were but two things he would not pawn, his pipe and his violin. He was a lazy, absent-minded old fellow, who liked to fiddle better than to plow, though Antone surely got work enough out of them all, for that mat-

† "Peter" (1892), written while Willa Cather was a student at the University of Nebraska, was her first published work of fiction.

ter. In the house of which Antone was master there was no one, from the little boy three years old, to the old man of sixty, who did not earn his bread. Still people said that Peter was worthless, and was a great drag on Antone, his son, who never drank, and was a much better man than his father had ever been. Peter did not care what people said. He did not like the country, nor the people, least of all he liked the plowing. He was very homesick for Bohemia. Long ago, only eight years ago by the calendar, but it seemed eight centuries to Peter, he had been a second violinist in the great theatre at Prague. He had gone into the theatre very young, and had been there all his life, until he had a stroke of paralysis, which made his arm so weak that his bowing was uncertain. Then they told him he could go. Those were great days at the theatre. He had plenty to drink then, and wore a dress coat every evening, and there were always parties after the play. He could play in those days, ay, that he could! He could never read the notes well, so he did not play first; but his touch, he had a touch indeed, so Herr Mikilsdoff, who led the orchestra, had said. Sometimes now Peter thought he could plow better if he could only bow as he used to. He had seen all the lovely women in the world there, all the great singers and the great players. He was in the orchestra when Rachel played, and he heard Liszt play when the Countess d'Agoult sat in the stage box and threw the master white lilies. Once, a French woman came and played for weeks, he did not remember her name now.[1] He did not remember her face very well either, for it changed so, it was never twice the same. But the beauty of it, and the great hunger men felt at the sight of it, that he remembered. Most of all he remembered her voice. He did not know French, and could not understand a word she said, but it seemed to him that she must be talking the music of Chopin. And her voice, he thought he should know that in the other world. The last night she played a play in which a man touched her arm, and she stabbed him. As Peter sat among the smoking gas jets down below the footlights with his fiddle on his knee, and looked up at her, he thought he would like to die too, if he could touch her arm once, and have her stab him so. Peter went home to his wife very drunk that night. Even in those days he was a foolish fellow, who cared for nothing but music and pretty faces.

It was all different now. He had nothing to drink and little to eat, and here, there was nothing but sun, and grass, and sky. He had forgotten almost everything, but some things he remembered well enough. He loved his violin and the holy Mary, and above all else he feared the Evil One, and his son Antone.

The fire was low, and it grew cold. Still Peter sat by the fire re-

1. Sarah Bernhardt (1845–1923) in Victorien Sardou's *La Tosca* (1887).

membering. He dared not throw more cobs on the fire; Antone would be angry. He did not want to cut wood tomorrow, it would be Sunday, and he wanted to go to mass. Antone might let him do that. He held his violin under his wrinkled chin, his white hair fell over it, and he began to play "Ave Maria." His hand shook more than ever before, and at last refused to work the bow at all. He sat stupefied for a while, then arose, and taking his violin with him, stole out into the old sod stable. He took Antone's shotgun down from its peg, and loaded it by the moonlight which streamed in through the door. He sat down on the dirt floor, and leaned back against the dirt wall. He heard the wolves howling in the distance, and the night wind screaming as it swept over the snow. Near him he heard the regular breathing of the horses in the dark. He put his crucifix above his heart, and folding his hands said brokenly all the Latin he had ever known, "*Pater noster, qui in coelum est.*"[2] Then he raised his head and sighed, "Not one kreutzer will Antone pay them to pray for my soul, not one kreutzer, he is so careful of his money, is Antone, he does not waste it in drink, he is a better man than I, but hard sometimes. He works the girls too hard, women were not made to work so. But he shall not sell thee, my fiddle, I can play thee no more, but they shall not part us. We have seen it all together, and we will forget it together, the French woman and all." He held his fiddle under his chin a moment, where it had lain so often, then put it across his knee and broke it through the middle. He pulled off his old boot, held the gun between his knees with the muzzle against his forehead, and pressed the trigger with his toe.

In the morning Antone found him stiff, frozen fast in a pool of blood. They could not straighten him out enough to fit a coffin, so they buried him in a pine box. Before the funeral Antone carried to town the fiddle-bow which Peter had forgotten to break. Antone was very thrifty, and a better man than his father had been.

WILLA CATHER

A Wagner Matinee†

I received one morning a letter, written in pale ink on glassy, blue-lined note-paper, and bearing the postmark of a little Nebraska vil-

2. "Our Father, who art in heaven."

† The story first appeared in *Everybody's Magazine* in February 1904 and was one of the seven stories collected in *The Troll Garden* (1905). "A Wagner Matinee" disturbed some friends and family in Nebraska because of its bleak portrayal of farm life and because the character of Aunt Georgiana was based on Cather's Aunt Franc (Franc Smith Cather).

lage. This communication, worn and rubbed, looking as though it had been carried for some days in a coat pocket that was none too clean, was from my Uncle Howard and informed me that his wife had been left a small legacy by a bachelor relative who had recently died, and that it would be necessary for her to go to Boston to attend to the settling of the estate. He requested me to meet her at the station and render her whatever services might be necessary. On examining the date indicated as that of her arrival, I found it no later than to-morrow. He had characteristically delayed writing until, had I been away from home for a day, I must have missed the good woman altogether.

The name of my Aunt Georgiana called up not alone her own figure, at once pathetic and grotesque, but opened before my feet a gulf of recollection so wide and deep, that, as the letter dropped from my hand, I felt suddenly a stranger to all the present conditions of my existence, wholly ill at ease and out of place amid the familiar surroundings of my study. I became, in short, the gangling farmer-boy my aunt had known, scourged with chilblains and bashfulness, my hands cracked and sore from the corn husking. I felt the knuckles of my thumb tentatively, as though they were raw again. I sat again before her parlour organ, fumbling the scales with my stiff, red hands, while she, beside me, made canvas mittens for the huskers.

The next morning, after preparing my landlady somewhat, I set out for the station. When the train arrived I had some difficulty in finding my aunt. She was the last of the passengers to alight, and it was not until I got her into the carriage that she seemed really to recognize me. She had come all the way in a day coach; her linen duster had become black with soot and her black bonnet grey with dust during the journey. When we arrived at my boarding-house the landlady put her to bed at once and I did not see her again until the next morning.

Whatever shock Mrs. Springer experienced at my aunt's appearance, she considerately concealed. As for myself, I saw my aunt's misshapen figure with that feeling of awe and respect with which we behold explorers who have left their ears and fingers north of Franz-Josef-Land, or their health somewhere along the Upper Congo. My Aunt Georgiana had been a music teacher at the Boston Conservatory, somewhere back in the latter sixties. One summer, while visiting in the little village among the Green Mountains where her ancestors had dwelt for generations, she had kindled the callow fancy of the most idle and shiftless of all the village lads, and had conceived for this Howard Carpenter one of those extravagant passions which a handsome country boy of twenty-one sometimes inspires in an angular, spectacled woman of thirty.

When she returned to her duties in Boston, Howard followed her, and the upshot of this inexplicable infatuation was that she eloped with him, eluding the reproaches of her family and the criticisms of her friends by going with him to the Nebraska frontier. Carpenter, who, of course, had no money, had taken a homestead in Red Willow County, fifty miles from the railroad. There they had measured off their quarter section themselves by driving across the prairie in a wagon, to the wheel of which they had tied a red cotton handkerchief, and counting off its revolutions. They built a dugout in the red hillside, one of those cave dwellings whose inmates so often reverted to primitive conditions. Their water they got from the lagoons where the buffalo drank, and their slender stock of provisions was always at the mercy of bands of roving Indians. For thirty years my aunt had not been further than fifty miles from the homestead.

But Mrs. Springer knew nothing of all this, and must have been considerably shocked at what was left of my kinswoman. Beneath the soiled linen duster which, on her arrival, was the most conspicuous feature of her costume, she wore a black stuff dress, whose ornamentation showed that she had surrendered herself unquestioningly into the hands of a country dressmaker. My poor aunt's figure, however, would have presented astonishing difficulties to any dressmaker. Originally stooped, her shoulders were now almost bent together over her sunken chest. She wore no stays, and her gown, which trailed unevenly behind, rose in a sort of peak over her abdomen. She wore ill-fitting false teeth, and her skin was as yellow as a Mongolian's from constant exposure to a pitiless wind and to the alkaline water which hardens the most transparent cuticle into a sort of flexible leather.

I owed to this woman most of the good that ever came my way in my boyhood, and had a reverential affection for her. During the years when I was riding herd for my uncle, my aunt, after cooking the three meals—the first of which was ready at six o'clock in the morning—and putting the six children to bed, would often stand until midnight at her ironing-board, with me at the kitchen table beside her, hearing me recite Latin declensions and conjugations, gently shaking me when my drowsy head sank down over a page of irregular verbs. It was to her, at her ironing or mending, that I read my first Shakespeare, and her old text-book on mythology was the first that ever came into my empty hands. She taught me my scales and exercises, too—on the little parlour organ, which her husband had bought her after fifteen years, during which she had not so much as seen any instrument, but an accordion that belonged to one of the Norwegian farmhands. She would sit beside me by the hour, darning and counting while I struggled with the "Joyous

Farmer," but she seldom talked to me about music, and I understood why. She was a pious woman; she had the consolations of religion and, to her at least, her martyrdom was not wholly sordid. Once when I had been doggedly beating out some easy passages from an old score of *Euryanthe*[1] I had found among her music books, she came up to me and, putting her hands over my eyes, gently drew my head back upon her shoulder, saying tremulously, "Don't love it so well, Clark, or it may be taken from you. Oh! dear boy, pray that whatever your sacrifice may be, it be not that."

When my aunt appeared on the morning after her arrival, she was still in a semi-somnambulant state. She seemed not to realize that she was in the city where she had spent her youth, the place longed for hungrily half a lifetime. She had been so wretchedly train-sick throughout the journey that she had no recollection of anything but her discomfort, and, to all intents and purposes, there were but a few hours of nightmare between the farm in Red Willow County and my study on Newbury Street. I had planned a little pleasure for her that afternoon, to repay her for some of the glorious moments she had given me when we used to milk together in the straw-thatched cowshed and she, because I was more than usually tired, or because her husband had spoken sharply to me, would tell me of the splendid performance of the *Huguenots*[2] she had seen in Paris, in her youth. At two o'clock the Symphony Orchestra was to give a Wagner programme, and I intended to take my aunt; though, as I conversed with her, I grew doubtful about her enjoyment of it. Indeed, for her own sake, I could only wish her taste for such things quite dead, and the long struggle mercifully ended at last. I suggested our visiting the Conservatory and the Common[3] before lunch, but she seemed altogether too timid to wish to venture out. She questioned me absently about various changes in the city, but she was chiefly concerned that she had forgotten to leave instructions about feeding half-skimmed milk to a certain weakling calf, "old Maggie's calf, you know, Clark," she explained, evidently having forgotten how long I had been away. She was further troubled because she had neglected to tell her daughter about the freshly-opened kit of mackerel in the cellar, which would spoil if it were not used directly.

I asked her whether she had ever heard any of the Wagnerian operas, and found that she had not, though she was perfectly familiar with their respective situations, and had once possessed the piano score of *The Flying Dutchman*. I began to think it would have been

1. Opera (1823) by Karl Maria von Weber.
2. Opera (1836) by Giacomo Meyerbeer.
3. The Boston Common, a large public park in the heart of the city.

best to get her back to Red Willow County without waking her, and regretted having suggested the concert.

From the time we entered the concert hall, however, she was a trifle less passive and inert, and for the first time seemed to perceive her surroundings. I had felt some trepidation lest she might become aware of the absurdities of her attire, or might experience some painful embarrassment at stepping suddenly into the world to which she had been dead for a quarter of a century. But, again, I found how superficially I had judged her. She sat looking about her with eyes as impersonal, almost as stony, as those with which the granite Rameses in a museum watches the froth and fret that ebbs and flows about his pedestal—separated from it by the lonely stretch of centuries. I have seen this same aloofness in old miners who drift into the Brown hotel at Denver, their pockets full of bullion, their linen soiled, their haggard faces unshaven; standing in the thronged corridors as solitary as though they were still in a frozen camp on the Yukon, conscious that certain experiences have isolated them from their fellows by a gulf no haberdasher could bridge.

We sat at the extreme left of the first balcony, facing the arc of our own and the balcony above us, veritable hanging gardens, brilliant as tulip beds. The matinée audience was made up chiefly of women. One lost the contour of faces and figures, indeed any effect of line whatever, and there was only the colour of bodices past counting, the shimmer of fabrics soft and firm, silky and sheer; red, mauve, pink, blue, lilac, purple, ecru, rose, yellow, cream, and white, all the colours that an impressionist finds in a sunlit landscape, with here and there the dead shadow of a frock coat. My Aunt Georgiana regarded them as though they had been so many daubs of tube-paint on a palette.

When the musicians came out and took their places, she gave a little stir of anticipation and looked with quickening interest down over the rail at that invariable grouping, perhaps the first wholly familiar thing that had greeted her eye since she had left old Maggie and her weakling calf. I could feel how all those details sank into her soul, for I had not forgotten how they had sunk into mine when I came fresh from ploughing forever and forever between green aisles of corn, where, as in a treadmill, one might walk from daybreak to dusk without perceiving a shadow of change. The clean profiles of the musicians, the gloss of their linen, the dull black of their coats, the beloved shapes of the instruments, the patches of yellow light thrown by the green shaded lamps on the smooth, varnished bellies of the 'cellos and the bass viols in the rear, the restless, wind-tossed forest of fiddle necks and bows—I recalled how, in the first orchestra I had ever heard, those long bow strokes seemed to draw the heart out of me, as a conjurer's stick reels out yards of paper ribbon from a hat.

The first number was the *Tannhauser* overture. When the horns drew out the first strain of the Pilgrim's chorus, my Aunt Georgiana clutched my coat sleeve. Then it was I first realized that for her this broke a silence of thirty years; the inconceivable silence of the plains. With the battle between the two motives, with the frenzy of the Venusberg theme and its ripping of strings, there came to me an overwhelming sense of the waste and wear we are so powerless to combat; and I saw again the tall, naked house on the prairie, black and grim as a wooden fortress; the black pond where I had learned to swim, its margin pitted with sun-dried cattle tracks; the rain gullied clay banks about the naked house, the four dwarf ash seedlings where the dish-cloths were always hung to dry before the kitchen door. The world there was the flat world of the ancients; to the east, a cornfield that stretched to daybreak; to the west, a corral that reached to sunset; between, the conquests of peace, dearer bought than those of war.

The overture closed, my aunt released my coat sleeve, but she said nothing. She sat staring at the orchestra through a dullness of thirty years, through the films made little by little by each of the three hundred and sixty-five days in every one of them. What, I wondered, did she get from it? She had been a good pianist in her day I knew, and her musical education had been broader than that of most music teachers of a quarter of a century ago. She had often told me of Mozart's operas and Meyerbeer's, and I could remember hearing her sing, years ago, certain melodies of Verdi's. When I had fallen ill with a fever in her house she used to sit by my cot in the evening—when the cool, night wind blew in through the faded mosquito netting tacked over the window and I lay watching a certain bright star that burned red above the cornfield—and sing "Home to our mountains, O, let us return!"[4] in a way fit to break the heart of a Vermont boy near dead of homesickness already.

I watched her closely through the prelude to *Tristan and Isolde*, trying vainly to conjecture what that seething turmoil of strings and winds might mean to her, but she sat mutely staring at the violin bows that drove obliquely downward, like the pelting streaks of rain in a summer shower. Had this music any message for her? Had she enough left to at all comprehend this power which had kindled the world since she had left it? I was in a fever of curiosity, but Aunt Georgiana sat silent upon her peak in Darien.[5] She preserved this

4. Popular song derived from an aria in Verdi's *Il Trovatore*.
5. In his sonnet "On First Looking into Chapman's Homer" (1816), John Keats compares his reaction as a reader to that of the explorer Cortez, who is "silent upon a peak in

utter immobility throughout the number from *The Flying Dutchman*, though her fingers worked mechanically upon her black dress, as though, of themselves, they were recalling the piano score they had once played. Poor old hands! They had been stretched and twisted into mere tentacles to hold and lift and knead with; the palms unduly swollen, the fingers bent and knotted—on one of them a thin, worn band that had once been a wedding ring. As I pressed and gently quieted one of those groping hands, I remembered with quivering eyelids their services for me in other days.

Soon after the tenor began the "Prize Song,"[6] I heard a quick drawn breath and turned to my aunt. Her eyes were closed, but the tears were glistening on her cheeks, and I think, in a moment more, they were in my eyes as well. It never really died, then—the soul that can suffer so excruciatingly and so interminably; it withers to the outward eye only; like that strange moss which can lie on a dusty shelf half a century and yet, if placed in water, grows green again. She wept so throughout the development and elaboration of the melody.

During the intermission before the second half of the concert, I questioned my aunt and found that the "Prize Song" was not new to her. Some years before there had drifted to the farm in Red Willow County a young German, a tramp cow puncher, who had sung the chorus at Bayreuth,[7] when he was a boy, along with the other peasant boys and girls. Of a Sunday morning he used to sit on his gingham-sheeted bed in the hands' bedroom which opened off the kitchen, cleaning the leather of his boots and saddle, singing the "Prize Song," while my aunt went about her work in the kitchen. She had hovered about him until she had prevailed upon him to join the country church, though his sole fitness for this step, in so far as I could gather, lay in his boyish face and his possession of this divine melody. Shortly afterward he had gone to town on the Fourth of July, been drunk for several days, lost his money at a faro table, ridden a saddled Texan steer on a bet, and disappeared with a fractured collar-bone. All this my aunt told me huskily, wanderingly, as though she were talking in the weak lapses of illness.

"Well, we have come to better things than the old *Trovatore*[8] at any rate, Aunt Georgie?" I queried, with a well meant effort at jocularity.

Her lip quivered and she hastily put her handkerchief up to her mouth. From behind it she murmured, "And you have been hearing

Darien" when he first sights the Pacific Ocean. (Keats confused Cortez with Balboa, who crossed the Isthmus of Darien, now Panama, in 1513.)

6. Courtship song that concludes Wagner's opera *Die Meistersinger von Nurnberg* (1867).
7. A city in Bavaria, Germany, known for its annual Wagner festival, a tradition that began in 1882.
8. Giuseppe Verdi's opera *Il Trovatore (The Troubador)* (1853).

this ever since you left me, Clark?" Her question was the gentlest and saddest of reproaches.

The second half of the programme consisted of four numbers from the *Ring*, and closed with Siegfried's funeral march. My aunt wept quietly, but almost continuously, as a shallow vessel overflows in a rainstorm. From time to time her dim eyes looked up at the lights which studded the ceiling, burning softly under their dull glass globes; doubtless they were stars in truth to her. I was still perplexed as to what measure of musical comprehension was left to her, she who had heard nothing but the singing of Gospel Hymns at Methodist services in the square frame school-house on Section Thirteen for so many years. I was wholly unable to gauge how much of it had been dissolved in soapsuds, or worked into bread, or milked into the bottom of a pail.

The deluge of sound poured on and on; I never knew what she found in the shining current of it; I never knew how far it bore her, or past what happy islands. From the trembling of her face I could well believe that before the last numbers she had been carried out where the myriad graves are, into the grey, nameless burying grounds of the sea; or into some world of death vaster yet, where, from the beginning of the world, hope has lain down with hope and dream with dream and, renouncing, slept.

The concert was over; the people filed out of the hall chattering and laughing, glad to relax and find the living level again, but my kinswoman made no effort to rise. The harpist slipped its green felt cover over his instrument; the flute-players shook the water from their mouthpieces; the men of the orchestra went out one by one, leaving the stage to the chairs and music stands, empty as a winter cornfield.

I spoke to my aunt. She burst into tears and sobbed pleadingly. "I don't want to go, Clark, I don't want to go!"

I understood. For her, just outside the door of the concert hall, lay the black pond with the cattle-tracked bluffs; the tall, unpainted house, with weather-curled boards; naked as a tower, the crook-backed ash seedlings where the dish-cloths hung to dry; the gaunt, moulting turkeys picking up refuse about the kitchen door.

WILLA CATHER

Review of Kate Chopin's *The Awakening*†

A creole "Bovary" is this little novel of Miss Chopin's. Not that the heroine is a creole exactly, or that Miss Chopin is a Flaubert—save the mark!—but the theme is similar to that which occupied Flaubert.[1] There was, indeed, no need that a second "Madame Bovary" should be written, but an author's choice of themes is frequently as inexplicable as his choice of a wife. It is governed by some innate temperamental bias that cannot be diagrammed. This is particularly so in women who write, and I shall not attempt to say why Miss Chopin has devoted so exquisite and sensitive, well-governed a style to so trite and sordid a theme. She writes much better than it is ever given to most people to write, and hers is a genuinely literary style; of no great elegance or solidity; but light, flexible, subtle and capable of producing telling effects directly and simply. The story she has to tell in the present instance is new neither in matter nor treatment. "Edna Pontellier," a Kentucky girl, who, like "Emma Bovary," had been in love with innumerable dream heroes before she was out of short skirts, married "Leonce Pontellier" as a sort of reaction from a vague and visionary passion for a tragedian whose unresponsive picture she used to kiss. She acquired the habit of liking her husband in time, and even of liking her children. Though we are not justified in presuming that she ever threw articles from her dressing table at them, as the charming "Emma" had a winsome habit of doing, we are told that "she would sometimes gather them passionately to her heart, she would sometimes forget them." At a creole watering place, which is admirably and deftly sketched by Miss Chopin, "Edna" met "Robert Lebrun," son of the landlady, who dreamed of a fortune awaiting him in Mexico while he occupied a petty clerical position in New Orleans. "Robert" made it his business to be agreeable to his mother's boarders, and "Edna," not being a creole, much against his wish and will, took him seriously. "Robert" went to Mexico but found that fortunes were no easier to make there than in New Orleans. He returns and does not even call to pay his respects to her. She encounters him at the home of a friend and takes him home with her. She wheedles him into staying for dinner, and we are told she sent the maid off "in search of some delicacy she had not thought

† From the *Pittsburg Leader*, July 8, 1899.

1. *Madame Bovary* (1857), by French author Gustave Flaubert (1821–1880), tells the story of a romantic, dissatisfied woman who has an adulterous affair, is abandoned, and suffers a painful death.

of for herself, and she recommended great care in the dripping of the coffee and having the omelet done to a turn."

Only a few pages back we were informed that the husband, "M. Pontellier," had cold soup and burnt fish for his dinner. Such is life. The lover of course disappointed her, was a coward and ran away from his responsibilities before they began. He was afraid to begin a chapter with so serious and limited a woman. She remembered the sea where she had first met "Robert." Perhaps from the same motive which threw "Anna Keraninna" under the engine wheels,[2] she threw herself into the sea, swam until she was tired and then let go.

> "She looked into the distance, and for a moment the old terror flamed up, then sank again. She heard her father's voice, and her sister Margaret's. She heard the barking of an old dog that was chained to the sycamore tree. The spurs of the cavalry officer clanged as he walked across the porch. There was a hum of bees, and the musky odor of pinks filled the air."

"Edna Pontellier" and "Emma Bovary" are studies in the same feminine type; one a finished and complete portrayal, the other a hasty sketch, but the theme is essentially the same. Both women belong to a class, not large, but forever clamoring in our ears, that demands more romance out of life than God put into it. Mr. G. Bernard Shaw would say that they are the victims of the over-idealization of love. They are the spoil of the poets, the Iphigenias of sentiment.[3] The unfortunate feature of their disease is that it attacks only women of brains, at least of rudimentary brains, but whose development is one-sided; women of strong and fine intuitions, but without the faculty of observation, comparison, reasoning about things. Probably, for emotional people, the most convenient thing about being able to think is that it occasionally gives them a rest from feeling. Now with women of the "Bovary" type, this relaxation and recreation is impossible. They are not critics of life, but, in the most personal sense, partakers of life. They receive impressions through the fancy. With them everything begins with fancy, and passions rise in the brain rather than in the blood, the poor, neglected, limited one-sided brain that might do so much better things than badgering itself into frantic endeavors to love. For these are the people who pay with their blood for the fine ideals of the poets, as Marie Delclasse paid for Dumas' great cre-

2. The adulterous heroine of the novel *Anna Karenina* by Russian author Leo Tolstoy (1828–1910) commits suicide by throwing herself in the path of a train.
3. In Greek myth, Iphigenia is the daughter of Agamemnon. Misled by the false promise that she is to marry the warrior Achilles, she travels to Aulis, where her father intends to sacrifice her to the goddess Artemis.

ation, "Marguerite Gauthier."[4] These people really expect the passion of love to fill and gratify every need of life, whereas nature only intended that it should meet one of many demands. They insist upon making it stand for all the emotional pleasures of life and art, expecting an individual and self-limited passion to yield infinite variety, pleasure and distraction, to contribute to their lives what the arts and the pleasurable exercise of the intellect gives to less limited and less intense idealists. So this passion, when set up against Shakespeare, Balzac, Wagner, Raphael, fails them. They have staked everything on one hand, and they lose. They have driven the blood until it will drive no further, they have played their nerves up to the point where any relaxation short of absolute annihilation is impossible. Every idealist abuses his nerves, and every sentimentalist brutally abuses them. And in the end, the nerves get even. Nobody ever cheats them, really. Then "the awakening" comes. Sometimes it comes in the form of arsenic, as it came to "Emma Bovary," sometimes it is carbolic acid taken covertly in the police station, a goal to which unbalanced idealism not infrequently leads. "Edna Pontellier," fanciful and romantic to the last, chose the sea on a summer night and went down with the sound of her first lover's spurs in her ears, and the scent of pinks about her. And next time I hope that Miss Chopin will devote that flexible, iridescent style of hers to a better cause.

WILLA CATHER

[On Henry James]†

Their mania for careless and hasty work is not confined to the lesser men. Howells and Hardy have gone with the crowd. Now that Stevenson is dead I can think of but one English-speaking author who is really keeping his self-respect and sticking for perfection. Of course I refer to that mighty master of language and keen student of human actions and motives, Henry James. In the last four years he has published, I believe, just two small volumes, *The Lesson of the Master* and *Terminations*,[1] and in those two little volumes of short stories he who will may find out something of what it means to be really an artist. The framework is perfect and the pol-

4. Marguerite Gauthier, who dies of tuberculosis, is the heroine of the popular novel *La Dame aux Camelias* (1852) by Alexandre Dumas *fils* (1824–1895). Dumas based the story on the death of his lover Marie Duplessis (whom Cather refers to as "Marie Delclasse").

† From the *Lincoln Courier*, November 16, 1895.

1. *The Lesson of the Master* was published in 1892, *Terminations* in 1895.

ish is absolutely without flaw. They are sometimes a little hard, always calculating and dispassionate, but they are perfect. I wish James would write about modern society, about "degeneracy"[2] and the new woman[3] and all the rest of it. Not that he would throw any light on it. He seldom does; but he would say such awfully clever things about it, and turn on so many side-lights. And then his sentences! If his character novels were all wrong one could read him forever for the mere beauty of his sentences. He never lets his phrases run away with him. They are never dull and never too brilliant. He subjects them to the general tone of his sentence and has his whole paragraph partake of the same predominating color. You are never startled, never surprised, never thrilled or never enraptured; always delighted by that masterly prose that is as correct, as classical, as calm and as subtle as the music of Mozart.

HENRY JAMES

From The Lesson of the Master†

He had been informed that the ladies were at church, but that was corrected by what he saw from the top of the steps (they descended from a great height in two arms, with a circular sweep of the most charming effect) at the threshold of the door which, from the long, bright gallery, overlooked the immense lawn. Three gentlemen, on the grass, at a distance, sat under the great trees; but the fourth figure was not a gentleman, the one in the crimson dress which made so vivid a spot, told so as a "bit of colour" amid the fresh, rich green. The servant had come so far with Paul Overt to show him the way and had asked him if he wished first to go to his room. The young man declined this privilege, having no disorder to repair after so short and easy a journey and liking to take a general perceptive possession of the new scene immediately, as he always did. He stood there a little with his eyes on the group and on the admirable picture—the wide grounds of an old country house near London (that only made it better,) on a splendid Sunday in June. "But that lady, who is she?" he said to the servant before the man went away.

"I think it's Mrs. St. George, sir."

"Mrs. St. George, the wife of the distinguished——" Then Paul

2. The cultural belief, widespread in the 1890s and early twentieth century, that civilization was declining or deteriorating instead of progressing.
3. The ideology of the "New Woman," prominent in late nineteenth- and early twentieth-century America and linked to the ideas of the women's suffrage movement, promoted female autonomy and liberation.
† From Henry James, *The Lesson of the Master* (New York and London: Macmillan, 1892).

Overt checked himself, doubting whether the footman would know.

"Yes, sir—probably, sir," said the servant, who appeared to wish to intimate that a person staying at Summersoft would naturally be, if only by alliance, distinguished. His manner, however, made poor Overt feel for the moment as if he himself were but little so.

"And the gentlemen?" he inquired.

"Well, sir, one of them is General Fancourt."

"Ah yes, I know; thank you." General Fancourt was distinguished, there was no doubt of that, for something he had done, or perhaps even had not done (the young man could not remember which) some years before in India. The servant went away, leaving the glass doors open into the gallery, and Paul Overt remained at the head of the wide double staircase, saying to himself that the place was sweet and promised a pleasant visit, while he leaned on the balustrade of fine old ironwork which, like all the other details, was of the same period as the house. It all went together and spoke in one voice—a rich English voice of the early part of the eighteenth century. It might have been church-time on a summer's day in the reign of Queen Anne; the stillness was too perfect to be modern, the nearness counted so as distance and there was something so fresh and sound in the originality of the large smooth house, the expanse of whose beautiful brickwork, which had been kept clear of messy creepers (as a woman with a rare complexion disdains a veil,) was pink rather than red. When Paul Overt perceived that the people under the trees were noticing him he turned back through the open doors into the great gallery which was the pride of the place. It traversed the mansion from end to end and seemed—with its bright colours, its high panelled windows, its faded, flowered chintzes, its quickly recognised portraits and pictures, the blue and white china of its cabinets and the attenuated festoons and rosettes of its ceiling—a cheerful upholstered avenue into the other century.

The young man was slightly nervous; that belonged in general to his disposition as a student of fine prose, with his dose of the artist's restlessness; and there was a particular excitement in the idea that Henry St. George might be a member of the party. For the younger writer he had remained a high literary figure, in spite of the lower range of production to which he had fallen after his three first great successes, the comparative absence of quality in his later work. There had been moments when Paul Overt almost shed tears upon this, but now that he was near him (he had never met him,) he was conscious only of the fine original source and of his own immense debt. After he had taken a turn or two up and down the gallery he came out again and descended the steps. He was but slenderly supplied with a certain social boldness (it was really a weakness in him,) so that, conscious of a want of acquaintance with the four persons in the distance, he indulged in a movement as to which he had a certain safety in feeling that it did not necessarily appear to commit him to an attempt to join them. There was a fine English awkwardness in it—he felt this too as he sauntered vaguely and obliquely across the lawn, as if to take an independent line. Fortunately there was an equally fine English directness in the way one of the gentlemen presently rose and made as if to approach him, with an air of conciliation and reassurance. To this demonstration Paul Overt instantly responded, though he knew the gentleman was not his host. He was tall, straight and elderly, and had a pink, smiling face and a white moustache. Our young man met him half way while he laughed and said: "A——Lady Watermouth told us you were coming; she asked me just to look after you." Paul Overt thanked him (he liked him without delay,) and turned round with him, walking toward the others. "They've all gone to church—all except us," the stranger continued as they went; "we're just sitting here—it's so jolly." Overt rejoined that it was jolly indeed—it was such a lovely place; he mentioned that he had not seen it before—it was a charming impression.

"Ah, you've not been here before?" said his companion. "It's a nice little place—not much to *do*, you know." Overt wondered what he wanted to "do"—he felt as if he himself were doing a good deal. By the time they came to where the others sat he had guessed his initiator was a military man, and (such was the turn of Overt's imagination,) this made him still more sympathetic. He would naturally have a passion for activity—for deeds at variance with the pacific, pastoral scene. He was evidently so good-natured, however, that he accepted the inglorious hour for what it was worth. Paul Overt shared it with him and with his companions for the next twenty minutes; the latter looked at him and he looked at them without knowing much who they were, while the talk went on without enlightening him much as to what it was about. It was indeed about nothing in particular, and wandered, with casual, pointless pauses and short terrestrial flights, amid the names of persons and places—names which, for him, had no great power of evocation. It was all sociable and slow, as was right and natural on a warm Sunday morning.

Overt's first attention was given to the question, privately considered, of whether one of the two younger men would be Henry St. George. He knew many of his distinguished contemporaries by their photographs, but he had never, as it happened, seen a portrait of the great misguided novelist. One of the gentlemen was out of the question—he was too young; and the other scarcely looked clever enough, with such mild, undiscriminating eyes. If those eyes were St. George's the problem presented by the ill-matched parts of his genius was still more difficult of solution. Besides, the deportment of the personage possessing them was not, as regards the lady in the red dress, such as could be natural, towards his wife, even to a writer accused by several critics of sacrificing too much to manner. Lastly, Paul Overt had an indefinite feeling that if the gentleman with the sightless eyes bore the name that had set his heart beating faster (he also had contradictory, conventional whiskers—the young admirer of the celebrity had never in a mental vision seen *his* face in so vulgar a frame), he would have given him a sign of recognition or of friendliness—would have heard of him a little, would know something about *Ginistrella*, would have gathered at least that that recent work of fiction had made an impression on the discerning. Paul Overt had a dread of being grossly proud, but it seemed to him that his self-consciousness took no undue license in thinking that the authorship of *Ginistrella* constituted a degree of identity. His soldierly friend became clear enough; he was "Fancourt," but he was also the General; and he mentioned to our young man in the course of a few moments that he had but lately returned from twenty years' service abroad.

"And do you mean to remain in England?" Overt asked.

"Oh yes, I have bought a little house in London."

"And I hope you like it," said Overt, looking at Mrs. St. George.

"Well, a little house in Manchester Square—there's a limit to the enthusiasm that that inspires."

"Oh, I meant being at home again—being in London."

"My daughter likes it—that's the main thing. She's very fond of art and music and literature and all that kind of thing. She missed it in India and she finds it in London, or she hopes she will find it. Mr. St. George has promised to help her—he has been awfully kind to her. She has gone to church—she's fond of that too—but they'll all be back in a quarter of an hour. You must let me introduce you to her—she will be so glad to know you. I dare say she has read every word you have written."

"I shall be delighted—I haven't written very many," said Overt, who felt without resentment that the General at least was very vague about that. But he wondered a little why, since he expressed this friendly disposition, it did not occur to him to pronounce the word which would put him in relation with Mrs. St. George. If it was a question of introductions Miss Fancourt (apparently she was unmarried,) was far away and the wife of his illustrious *confrère*[1] was almost between them. This lady struck Paul Overt as a very pretty woman, with a surprising air of youth and a high smartness

1. Colleague.

of aspect which seemed to him (he could scarcely have said why,) a sort of mystification. St. George certainly had every right to a charming wife, but he himself would never have taken the important little woman in the aggressively Parisian dress for the domestic partner of a man of letters. That partner in general, he knew, was far from presenting herself in a single type: his observation had instructed him that she was not inveterately, not necessarily dreary. But he had never before seen her look so much as if her prosperity had deeper foundations than an ink-spotted study-table littered with proof-sheets. Mrs. St. George might have been the wife of a gentleman who "kept" books rather than wrote them, who carried on great affairs in the City[2] and made better bargains than those that poets make with publishers. With this she hinted at a success more personal, as if she had been the most characteristic product of an age in which society, the world of conversation, is a great drawing-room with the City for its antechamber. Overt judged her at first to be about thirty years of age; then, after a while, he perceived that she was much nearer fifty. But she juggled away the twenty years somehow—you only saw them in a rare glimpse, like the rabbit in the conjurer's sleeve. She was extraordinarily white, and everything about her was pretty—her eyes, her ears, her hair, her voice, her hands, her feet (to which her relaxed attitude in her wicker chair gave a great publicity,) and the numerous ribbons and trinkets with which she was bedecked. She looked as if she had put on her best clothes to go to church and then had decided that they were too good for that and had stayed at home. She told a story of some length about the shabby way Lady Jane had treated the Duchess, as well as an anecdote in relation to a purchase she had made in Paris (on her way back from Cannes,) for Lady Egbert, who had never refunded the money. Paul Overt suspected her of a tendency to figure great people as larger than life, until he noticed the manner in which she handled Lady Egbert, which was so subversive that it reassured him. He felt that he should have understood her better if he might have met her eye; but she scarcely looked at him. "Ah, here they come—all the good ones!" she said at last; and Paul Overt saw in the distance the return of the churchgoers—several persons, in couples and threes, advancing in a flicker of sun and shade at the end of a large green vista formed by the level grass and the overarching boughs.

"If you mean to imply that we are bad, I protest," said one of the gentlemen—"after making oneself agreeable all the morning!"

"Ah, if they've found you agreeable!" Mrs. St. George exclaimed, smiling. "But if we are good the others are better."

2. The business center of London.

"They must be angels then," observed the General.

"Your husband was an angel, the way he went off at your bidding," the gentleman who had first spoken said to Mrs. St. George.

"At my bidding?"

"Didn't you make him go to church?"

"I never made him do anything in my life but once, when I made him burn up a bad book. That's all!" At her "That's all!" Paul broke into an irrepressible laugh; it lasted only a second, but it drew her eyes to him. His own met them, but not long enough to help him to understand her; unless it were a step towards this that he felt sure on the instant that the burnt book (the way she alluded to it!) was one of her husband's finest things.

"A bad book?" her interlocutor repeated.

"I didn't like it. He went to church because your daughter went," she continued, to General Fancourt. "I think it my duty to call your attention to his demeanour to your daughter."

"Well, if you don't mind it, I don't," the General laughed.

"*Il s'attache à ses pas.*[3] But I don't wonder—she's so charming."

"I hope she won't make him burn any books!" Paul Overt ventured to exclaim.

"If she would make him write a few it would be more to the purpose," said Mrs. St. George. "He has been of an indolence this year!"

Our young man stared—he was so struck with the lady's phraseology. Her "Write a few" seemed to him almost as good as her "That's all." Didn't she, as the wife of a rare artist, know what it was to produce *one* perfect work of art? How in the world did she think they were turned off? His private conviction was that admirably as Henry St. George wrote, he had written for the last ten years, and especially for the last five, only too much, and there was an instant during which he felt the temptation to make this public. But before he had spoken a diversion was effected by the return of the absent guests. They strolled up dispersedly—there were eight or ten of them—and the circle under the trees rearranged itself as they took their place in it. They made it much larger; so that Paul Overt could feel (he was always feeling that sort of thing, as he said to himself,) that if the company had already been interesting to watch it would now become a great deal more so. He shook hands with his hostess, who welcomed him without many words, in the manner of a woman able to trust him to understand—conscious that, in every way, so pleasant an occasion would speak for itself. She offered him no particular facility for sitting by her, and when they had all subsided again he found himself still next General Fancourt, with an unknown lady on his other flank.

3. He follows her every step.

"That's my daughter—that one opposite," the General said to him without loss of time. Overt saw a tall girl, with magnificent red hair, in a dress of a pretty grey-green tint and of a limp silken texture, in which every modern effect had been avoided. It had therefore somehow the stamp of the latest thing, so that Overt quickly perceived she was eminently a contemporary young lady.

"She's very handsome—very handsome," he repeated, looking at her. There was something noble in her head, and she appeared fresh and strong.

Her father surveyed her with complacency; then he said: "She looks too hot—that's her walk. But she'll be all right presently. Then I'll make her come over and speak to you."

"I should be sorry to give you that trouble; if you were to take me over there—" the young man murmured.

"My dear sir, do you suppose I put myself out that way? I don't mean for you, but for Marian," the General added.

"*I* would put myself out for her, soon enough," Overt replied; after which he went on: "Will you be so good as to tell me which of those gentlemen is Henry St. George?"

"The fellow talking to my girl. By Jove, he *is* making up to her—they're going off for another walk."

"Ah, is that he, really?" The young man felt a certain surprise, for the personage before him contradicted a preconception which had been vague only till it was confronted with the reality. As soon as this happened the mental image, retiring with a sigh, became substantial enough to suffer a slight wrong. Overt, who had spent a considerable part of his short life in foreign lands, made now, but not for the first time, the reflection that whereas in those countries he had almost always recognised the artist and the man of letters by his personal "type," the mould of his face, the character of his head, the expression of his figure and even the indications of his dress, in England this identification was as little as possible a matter of course, thanks to the greater conformity, the habit of sinking the profession instead of advertising it, the general diffusion of the air of the gentleman—the gentleman committed to no particular set of ideas. More than once, on returning to his own country, he had said to himself in regard to the people whom he met in society: "One sees them about and one even talks with them; but to find out what they *do* one would really have to be a detective." In respect to several individuals whose work he was unable to like (perhaps he was wrong) he found himself adding, "No wonder they conceal it—it's so bad!" He observed that oftener than in France and in Germany his artist looked like a gentleman (that is, like an English one,) while he perceived that outside of a few exceptions his gentleman didn't look like an artist. St. George was not one of the exceptions; that circumstance he definitely apprehended before the great man had turned his back to walk off with Miss Fancourt. He certainly looked better behind than any foreign man of letters, and beautifully correct in his tall black hat and his superior frock coat. Somehow, all the same, these very garments (he wouldn't have minded them so much on a weekday,) were disconcerting to Paul Overt, who forgot for the moment that the head of the profession was not a bit better dressed than himself. He had caught a glimpse of a regular face, with a fresh colour, a brown moustache and a pair of eyes surely never visited by a fine frenzy, and he promised himself to study it on the first occasion. His temporary opinion was that St. George looked like a lucky stock-broker—a gentleman driving eastward every morning from a sanitary suburb in a smart dog-cart. That carried out the impression already derived from his wife. Paul Overt's glance, after a moment, travelled back to this lady, and he saw that her own had followed her husband as he moved off with Miss Fancourt. Overt permitted himself to wonder a little whether she were jealous when another woman took him away. Then he seemed to perceive that Mrs. St. George was not glaring at the indifferent maiden—her eyes rested only on her husband, and with unmistakable serenity. That was the way she wanted him to be—she liked his conventional uniform. Overt had a great desire to hear more about the book she had induced him to destroy.

EDITH WHARTON

From The House of Mirth†

Book I

I

Selden paused in surprise. In the afternoon rush of the Grand Central Station his eyes had been refreshed by the sight of Miss Lily Bart.

It was a Monday in early September, and he was returning to his work from a hurried dip into the country; but what was Miss Bart doing in town at that season? If she had appeared to be catching a train, he might have inferred that he had come on her in the act of transition between one and another of the country-houses which disputed her presence after the close of the Newport[1] season, but

† From Edith Wharton, *The House of Mirth* (New York: Scribner's 1905).

1. A town on the Rhode Island coast that became a fashionable summer resort for the wealthy and leisure classes in the late nineteenth and early twentieth centuries.

her desultory air perplexed him. She stood apart from the crowd, letting it drift by her to the platform or the street, and wearing an air of irresolution which might, as he surmised, be the mask of a very definite purpose. It struck him at once that she was waiting for some one, but he hardly knew why the idea arrested him. There was nothing new about Lily Bart, yet he could never see her without a faint movement of interest: it was characteristic of her that she always roused speculation, that her simplest acts seemed the result of far-reaching intentions.

An impulse of curiosity made him turn out of his direct line to the door, and stroll past her. He knew that if she did not wish to be seen she would contrive to elude him; and it amused him to think of putting her skill to the rest.

"Mr. Selden—what good luck!"

She came forward smiling, eager almost, in her resolve to intercept him. One or two persons, in brushing past them, lingered to look; for Miss Bart was a figure to arrest even the suburban traveller rushing to his last train.

Selden had never seen her more radiant. Her vivid head, relieved against the dull tints of the crowd, made her more conspicuous than in a ball-room, and under her dark hat and veil she regained the girlish smoothness, the purity of tint, that she was beginning to lose after eleven years of late hours and indefatigable dancing. Was it really eleven years, Selden found himself wondering, and had she indeed reached the nine-and-twentieth birthday with which her rivals credited her?

"What luck!" she repeated. "How nice of you to come to my rescue!"

He responded joyfully that to do so was his mission in life, and asked what form the rescue was to take.

"Oh, almost any—even to sitting on a bench and talking to me. One sits out a cotillion—why not sit out a train? It is n't a bit hotter here than in Mrs. Van Osburgh's conservatory—and some of the women are not a bit uglier."

She broke off, laughing, to explain that she had come up to town from Tuxedo, on her way to the Gus Trenors' at Bellomont, and had missed the three-fifteen train to Rhinebeck.

"And there is n't another till half-past five." She consulted the little jewelled watch among her laces. "Just two hours to wait. And I don't know what to do with myself. My maid came up this morning to do some shopping for me, and was to go on to Bellomont at one o'clock, and my aunt's house is closed, and I don't know a soul in town." She glanced plaintively about the station. "It *is* hotter than Mrs. Van Osburgh's, after all. If you can spare the time, do take me somewhere for a breath of air."

He declared himself entirely at her disposal: the adventure struck him as diverting. As a spectator, he had always enjoyed Lily Bart; and his course lay so far out of her orbit that it amused him to be drawn for a moment into the sudden intimacy which her proposal implied.

"Shall we go over to Sherry's for a cup of tea?"

She smiled assentingly, and then made a slight grimace.

"So many people come up to town on a Monday—one is sure to meet a lot of bores. I 'm as old as the hills, of course, and it ought not to make any difference; but if *I 'm* old enough, you're not," she objected gaily. "I 'm dying for tea—but is n't there a quieter place?"

He answered her smile, which rested on him vividly. Her discretions interested him almost as much as her imprudences: he was so sure that both were part of the same carefully-elaborated plan. In judging Miss Bart, he had always made use of the "argument from design."[2]

"The resources of New York are rather meagre," he said; "but I'll find a hansom first, and then we'll invent something."

He led her through the throng of returning holiday makers, past swallow-faced girls in preposterous hats, and flat-chested women struggling with paper bundles and palm-leaf fans. Was it possible that she belonged to the same race? The dinginess, the crudity of this average section of womanhood made him feel how highly specialized she was.

A rapid shower had cooled the air, and clouds still hung refreshingly over the moist street.

"How delicious! Let us walk a little," she said as they emerged from the station.

They turned into Madison Avenue and began to stroll northward. As she moved beside him, with her long light step, Selden was conscious of taking a luxurious pleasure in her nearness: in the modelling of her little ear, the crisp upward wave of her hair—was it ever so slightly brightened by art?—and the thick planting of her straight black lashes. Everything about her was at once vigorous and exquisite, at once strong and fine. He had a confused sense that she must have cost a great deal to make, that a great many dull and ugly people must, in some mysterious way, have been sacrificed to produce her. He was aware that the qualities distinguishing her from the herd of her sex were chiefly external: as though a fine glaze of beauty and fastidiousness had been applied to vulgar clay. Yet the analogy left him unsatisfied, for a coarse texture will not take a high finish; and was it not possible that the material

2. A theory of the existence of God, developed in the eighteenth century, positing that the beauty and order of the universe required a divine creator.

was fine, but that circumstance had fashioned it into a futile shape?

As he reached this point in his speculations the sun came out, and her lifted parasol cut off his enjoyment. A moment or two later she paused with a sigh.

"Oh, dear, I'm so hot and thirsty—and what a hideous place New York is!" She looked despairingly up and down the dreary thoroughfare. "Other cities put on their best clothes in summer, but New York seems to sit in its shirt-sleeves." Her eyes wandered down one of the side-streets. "Some one has had the humanity to plant a few trees over there. Let us go into the shade."

"I am glad my street meets with your approval," said Selden as they turned the corner.

"Your street? Do you live here?"

She glanced with interest along the new brick and limestone house-fronts, fantastically varied in obedience to the American craving for novelty, but fresh and inviting with their awnings and flower-boxes.

"Ah, yes—to be sure: *The Benedick*. What a nice-looking building! I don't think I 've ever seen it before." She looked across at the flat-house with its marble porch and pseudo-Georgian façade. "Which are your windows? Those with the awnings down?"

"On the top floor—yes."

"And that nice little balcony is yours? How cool it looks up there!"

He paused a moment. "Come up and see," he suggested. "I can give you a cup of tea in no time—and you won't meet any bores."

Her colour deepened—she still had the art of blushing at the right time—but she took the suggestion as lightly as it was made.

"Why not? It's too tempting—I'll take the risk," she declared.

"Oh, I'm not dangerous," he said in the same key. In truth, he had never liked her as well as as that moment. He knew she had accepted without afterthought: he could never be a factor in her calculations, and there was a surprise, a refreshment almost, in the spontaneity of her consent.

On the threshold he paused a moment, feeling for his latch-key.

"There's no one here; but I have a servant who is supposed to come in the mornings, and it's just possible he may have put out the tea-things and provided some cake."

He ushered her into a slip of a hall hung with old prints. She noticed the letters and notes heaped on the table among his gloves and sticks; then she found herself in a small library, dark but cheerful, with its walls of books, a pleasantly faded Turkey rug, a littered desk, and, as he had foretold, a tea-tray on a low table near the window. A breeze had sprung up, swaying inward the muslin curtains, and bringing a fresh scent of mignonette and petunias from the flower-box on the balcony.

Lily sank with a sigh into one of the shabby leather chairs.

"How delicious to have a place like this all to one's self! What a miserable thing it is to be a woman." She leaned back in a luxury of discontent.

Selden was rummaging in a cupboard for the cake.

"Even women," he said, "have been known to enjoy the privileges of a flat."

"Oh, governesses—or widows. But not girls—not poor, miserable, marriageable girls!"

"I even know a girl who lives in a flat."

She sat up in surprise. "You do?"

"I do," he assured her, emerging from the cupboard with the sought-for cake.

"Oh, I know—you mean Gerty Farish." She smiled a little unkindly. "But I said *marriageable*—and besides, she has a horrid little place, and no maid, and such queer things to eat. Her cook does the washing and the food tastes of soap. I should hate that, you know."

"You should n't dine with her on wash-days." said Selden, cutting the cake.

They both laughed, and he knelt by the table to light the lamp under the kettle, which she measured out the tea into a little tea-pot of green glaze. As he watched her hand, polished as a bit of old ivory, with its slender pink nails, and the sapphire bracelet slipping over her wrist, he was struck with the irony of suggesting to her such a life as his cousin Gertrude Farish had chosen. She was so evidently the victim of the civilization which had produced her, that the links of her bracelet seemed like manacles chaining her to her fate.

She seemed to read his thought. "It was horrid of me to say that of Gerty," she said with charming compunction. "I forgot she was your cousin. But we 're so different, you know: she likes being good, and I like being happy. And besides, she is free and I am not. If I were, I daresay I could manage to be happy even in her flat. It must be pure bliss to arrange the furniture just as one likes, and give all the horrors to the ash-man. If I could only do over my aunt's drawing-room I know I should be a better woman."

"Is it so very bad?" he asked sympathetically.

She smiled at him across the tea-pot which she was holding up to be filled.

"That shows how seldom you come there. Why don't you come oftener?"

"When I do come, it 's not to look at Mrs. Peniston's furniture."

"Nonsense," she said, "You don't come at all—and yet we get on so well when we meet."

"Perhaps that 's the reason," he answered promptly. "I 'm afraid I have n't any cream, you know—shall you mind a slice of lemon instead?"

"I shall like it better." She waited while he cut the lemon and dropped a thin disk into her cup. "But that is not the reason," she insisted.

"The reason for what?"

"For your never coming." She leaned forward with a shade of perplexity in her charming eyes. "I wish I knew—I wish I could make you out. Of course I know there are men who don't like me—one can tell that at a glance. And there are others who are afraid of me: they think I want to marry them." She smiled up at him frankly. "But I don't think you dislike me—and you can't possibly think I want to marry you."

"No—I absolve you of that," he agreed.

"Well, then—?"

He had carried his cup to the fireplace, and stood leaning against the chimney piece and looking down on her with an air of indolent amusement. The provocation in her eyes increased his amusement—he had not supposed she would waste her powder on such small game; but perhaps she was only keeping her hand in; or perhaps a girl of her type had no conversation but of the personal kind. At any rate, she was amazingly pretty, and he had asked her to tea and must live up to his obligations.

"Well, then," he said with a plunge, "perhaps *that's* the reason."

"What?"

"The fact that you don't want to marry me. Perhaps I don't regard it as such a strong inducement to go and see you." He felt a slight shiver down his spine as he ventured this, but her laugh reassured him.

"Dear Mr. Selden, that was n't worthy of you. It's stupid of you to make love to me, and it is n't like you to be stupid." She leaned back, sipping her tea with an air so enchantingly judicial that, if they had been in her aunt's drawing-room, he might almost have tried to disprove her deduction.

"Don't you see," she continued, "that there are men enough to say pleasant things to me, and that what I want is a friend who won't be afraid to say disagreeable ones when I need them? Sometimes I have fancied you might be that friend—I don't know why, except that you are neither a prig nor a bounder, and that I should n't have to pretend with you or be on my guard against you." Her voice had dropped to a note of seriousness, and she sat gazing up at him with the troubled gravity of a child.

"You don't know how much I need such a friend," she said. "My aunt is full of copy-book axioms, but they were all meant to apply to conduct in the early fifties. I always feel that to live up to them would include wearing book-muslin with gigot sleeves. And the other women—my best friends—well, they use me or abuse me; but they don't care a straw what happens to me. I've been about too long—people are getting tired of me, they are beginning to say I ought to marry."

There was a moment's pause, during which Selden meditated one or two replies calculated to add a momentary zest to the situation; but he rejected them in favour of the simple question: "Well, why don't you?"

She coloured and laughed. "Ah, I see you *are* a friend after all, and that is one of the disagreeable things I was asking for."

"It was n't meant to be disagreeable," he returned amicably. "Is n't marriage your vocation? Is n't it what you 're all brought up for?"

She sighed. "I suppose so. What else is there?"

"Exactly. And so why not take the plunge and have it over?"

She shrugged her shoulders. "You speak as if I ought to marry the first man who came along."

"I did n't mean to imply that you are as hard put to it as that. But there must be some one with the requisite qualifications."

She shook her head wearily. "I threw away one or two good chances when I first came out—I suppose every girl does; and you know I am horribly poor—and very expensive. I must have a great deal of money."

Selden had turned to reach for a cigarette-box on the mantelpiece.

"What's become of Dillworth?" he asked.

"Oh, his mother was frightened—she was afraid I should have all the family jewels reset. And she wanted me to promise that I would n't do over the drawing-room."

"The very thing you are marrying for!"

"Exactly. So she packed him off to India."

"Hard luck—but you can do better than Dillworth."

He offered the box, and she took out three or four cigarettes, putting one between her lips and slipping the others into a little gold case attached to her long pearl chain.

"Have I time? Just a whiff, then." She leaned forward, holding the tip of her cigarette to his. As she did so, he noted, with a purely impersonal enjoyment, how evenly the black lashes were set in her smooth white lids, and how the purplish shade beneath them melted into the pure pallour of the cheek.

She began to saunter about the room, examining the bookshelves between the puffs of her cigarette smoke. Some of the volumes had the ripe tints of good tooling and old morocco, and her eyes lingered on them caressingly, not with the appreciation of the expert, but with the pleasure in agreeable tones and textures that was one of her inmost susceptibilities. Suddenly her expression changed from desultory enjoyment to active conjecture, and she turned to Selden with a question.

"You collect, don't you—you know about first editions and things?"

"As much as a man may who has no money to spend. Now and then I pick up something in the rubbish heap; and I go and look on at the big sales."

She had again addressed herself to the shelves, but her eyes now swept them inattentively, and he saw that she was preoccupied with a new idea.

"And Americana—do you collect Americana?"

Selden stared and laughed.

"No, that 's rather out of my line. I'm not really a collector, you see; I simply like to have good editions of the books I am fond of."

She made a slight grimace. "And Americana are horribly dull, I suppose?"

"I should fancy so—except to the historian. But your real collector values a thing for its rarity. I don't suppose the buyers of Americana sit up reading them all night—old Jefferson Gryce certainly did n't."

She was listening with keep attention. "And yet they fetch fabulous prices, don't they? It seems so odd to want to pay a lot for an ugly badly printed book that one is never going to read! And I suppose most of the owners of Americana are not historians either?"

"No; very few of the historians can afford to buy them. They have to use those in the public libraries or in private collections. It seems to be the mere rarity that attracts the average collector."

He had seated himself on an arm of the chair near which she was standing, and she continued to question him, asking which were the rarest volumes, whether the Jefferson Gryce collection was really considered the finest in the world, and what was the largest price ever fetched by a single volume.

It was so pleasant to sit there looking up at her, as she lifted now one book and then another from the shelves, fluttering the pages between her fingers, while her drooping profile was outlined against the warm background of old bindings, that he talked on without pausing to wonder at her sudden interest in so unsuggestive a subject. But he could never be long with her without trying to find a reason for what she was doing, and as she replaced his first edition of La Bruyère[3] and turned away from the book-

3. Jean de la Bruyère (1645–1696), a French writer.

cases, he began to ask himself what she had been driving at. Her next question was not of a nature to enlighten him. She paused before him with a smile which seemed at once designed to admit him to her familiarity, and to remind him of the restrictions it imposed.

"Don't you ever mind," she asked suddenly, "not being rich enough to buy all the books you want?"

He followed her glance about the room, with its worn furniture and shabby walls.

"Don't I just? Do you take me for a saint on a pillar?"

"And having to work—do you mind that?"

"Oh, the work itself is not so bad—I'm rather fond of the law."

"No; but the being tied down: the routine—don't you ever want to get away, to see new places and people?"

"Horribly—especially when I see all my friends rushing to the steamer."

She drew a sympathetic breath. "But do you mind enough—to marry to get out of it?"

Selden broke into a laugh. "God forbid!" he declared.

She rose with a sigh, tossing her cigarette into the grate.

"Ah, there 's the difference—a girl must, a man may if he chooses." She surveyed him critically. "Your coat 's a little shabby—but who cares? It does n't keep people from asking you to dine. If I were shabby no one would have me: a woman is asked out as much for her clothes as for herself. The clothes are the background, the frame, if you like: they don't make success, but they are a part of it. Who wants a dingy woman? We are expected to be pretty and well-dressed till we drop—and if we can't keep it up alone, we have to go into partnership."

Selden glanced at her with amusement: it was impossible, even with her lovely eyes imploring him, to take a sentimental view of her case.

"Ah, well, there must be plenty of capital on the look-out for such an investment. Perhaps you 'll meet your fate tonight at the Trenors'."

She returned his look interrogatively.

"I thought you might be going there—oh, not in that capacity! But there are to be a lot of your set—Gwen Van Osburgh, the Wetheralls, Lady Cressida Raith—and the George Dorsets."

She paused a moment before the last name, and shot a query through her lashes; but he remained imperturbable.

"Mrs. Trenor asked me; but I can't get away till the end of the week; and those big parties bore me."

"Ah, so they do me," she exclaimed.

"Then why go?"

"It 's part of the business—you forget! And besides, if I did n't, I should be playing bézique with my aunt at Richfield Springs."

"That 's almost as bad as marrying Dillworth," he agreed, and they both laughed for pure pleasure in their sudden intimacy.

She glanced at the clock.

"Dear me! I must be off. It's after five."

She paused before the mantelpiece, studying herself in the mirror while she adjusted her veil. The attitude revealed the long slope of her slender sides, which gave a kind of wild-wood grace to her outline—as though she were a captured dryad subdued to the conventions of the drawing-room; and Selden reflected that it was the same streak of sylvan freedom in her nature that lent such savour to her artificiality.

He followed her across the room to the entrance-hall; but on the threshold she held out her hand with a gesture of leave-taking.

"It's been delightful; and now you will have to return my visit."

"But don't you want me to see you to the station?"

"No; good bye here, please."

She let her hand lie in his a moment, smiling up at him adorably.

"Good bye, then—and good luck at Bellomont!" he said, opening the door for her.

On the landing she paused to look about her. There were a thousand chances to one against her meeting anybody, but one could never tell, and she always paid for her rare indiscretions by a violent reaction of prudence. There was no one in sight, however, but a char-woman who was scrubbing the stairs. Her own stout person and its surrounding implements took up so much room that Lily, to pass her, had to gather up her skirts and brush against the wall. As she did so, the woman paused in her work and looked up curiously, resting her clenched red fists on the wet cloth she had just drawn from her pail. She had a broad sallow face, slightly pitted with small-pox, and thin straw-coloured hair through which her scalp shone unpleasantly.

"I beg your pardon," said Lily, intending by her politeness to convey a criticism of the other's manner.

The woman, without answering, pushed her pail aside, and continued to stare as Miss Bart swept by with a murmur of silken linings. Lily felt herself flushing under the look. What did the creature suppose? Could one never do the simplest, the most harmless thing, without subjecting one's self to some odious conjecture? Half way down the next flight, she smiled to think that a charwoman's stare should so perturb her. The poor thing was probably dazzled by such as unwonted apparition. But *were* such apparitions unwonted on Selden's stairs? Miss Bart was not familiar with the moral code of bachelors' flat-houses, and her colour rose again as it occurred to her that the woman's persistent gaze implied a groping among past associations. But she put aside the thought with a smile at her own fears, and hastened downward, wondering if she should find a cab short of Fifth Avenue.

Under the Georgian porch she paused again, scanning the street for a hansom. None was in sight, but as she reached the sidewalk she ran against a small glossy-looking man with a gardenia in his coat, who raised his hat with a surprised exclamation.

"Miss Bart? Well—of all people! This *is* luck," he declared; and she caught a twinkle of amused curiosity between his screwed-up lids.

"Oh, Mr. Rosedale—how are you?" she said, perceiving that the irrepressible annoyance on her face was reflected in the sudden intimacy of his smile.

Mr. Rosedale stood scanning her with interest and approval. He was a plump rosy man of the blond Jewish type, with smart London clothes fitting him like upholstery, and small sidelong eyes which gave him the air of appraising people as if they were bric-a-brac. He glanced up interrogatively at the porch of the Benedick.

"Been up to town for a little shopping, I suppose?" he said, in a tone which had the familiarity of a touch.

Miss Bart shrank from it slightly, and then flung herself into precipitate explanations.

"Yes—I came up to see my dress-maker. I am just on my way to catch the train to the Trenors'."

"Ah—your dress-maker; just so," he said blandly. "I did n't know there were any dress-makers in the Benedick."

"The Benedick?" She looked gently puzzled. "Is that the name of this building?"

"Yes, that's the name: I believe it 's an old word for bachelor,[4] is n't it? I happen to own the building—that 's the way I know." His smile deepened as he added with increasing assurance: "But you must let me take you to the station. The Trenors are at Bellomont, of course? You 've barely time to catch the five-forty. The dress-maker kept you waiting, I suppose."

Lily stiffened under the pleasantry.

"Oh, thanks," she stammered; and at that moment her eye caught a hansom drifting down Madison Avenue, and she hailed it with a desperate gesture.

"You 're very kind; but I could n't think of troubling you," she said, extending her hand to Mr. Rosedale; and heedless of his

4. "Benedick" is a confirmed bachelor in Shakespeare's *Much Ado About Nothing* who finally succumbs to his love for Beatrice and then to marriage. The word "benedick" or "benedict" came to signify a newly married man who had previously been a confirmed bachelor.

protestations, she sprang into the rescuing vehicle, and called out a breathless order to the driver.

WILLA CATHER

The Willing Muse†

Various opinions were held among Kenneth Gray's friends regarding his approaching marriage, but on the whole it was considered a hopeful venture, and, what was with some of us much more to the point, a hopeful indication. From the hour his engagement was an assured relation, he had seemed to gain. There was now a certain intention in his step, an eager, almost confident flash behind his thick glasses, which cheered his friends like indications of recovery after long illness. Even his shoulders seemed to droop less despondently and his head to sit upon them more securely. Those of us who knew him best drew a long sigh of relief that Kenneth had at last managed to get right with the current.

If, on the insecurity of a meager income and a career at its belated dawn, he was to marry at all, we felt that a special indulgence of destiny had allowed him to fix his choice upon Bertha Torrence. If there was anywhere a woman who seemed able to give him what he needed, to play upon him a continual stream of inspiriting confidence, to order the very simple affairs which he had so besottedly bungled, surely Bertha was the woman.

There were certain of his friends in Olympia who held out that it was a mistake for him to marry a woman who followed his own profession; who was, indeed, already much more within the public consciousness than Kenneth himself. To refute such arguments, one had only to ask what was possible between that and a housekeeper. Could any one conceive of Kenneth's living in daily intercourse with a woman who had no immediate and personal interest in letters, bitten to the bone as he was by his slow, consuming passion?

Perhaps, in so far as I was concerned, my personal satisfaction at Kenneth's projected marriage was not without its alloy of selfishness, and I think more than one of us counted upon carrying lighter hearts to his wedding than we had known in his company for some time. It was not that we did not believe in him. Hadn't it become a fixed habit to believe? But we, perhaps, felt slightly aggrieved that our faith had not wrought for him the miracles we

† First published in *Century*, 74 (August 1907).

could have hoped. We were, we found, willing enough to place the direct administration, the first responsibility, upon Bertha's firm young shoulders.

With Harrison, the musical critic, and me, Kenneth was an old issue. We had been college classmates of his, out in Olympia, Ohio, and even then no one had questioned his calling and election, unless it was Kenneth himself. But he had taxed us all sorely, the town and the college, and he had continued to tax us long afterward. As Harrison put it, he had kept us all holding our breath for years. There was never such a man for getting people into a fever of interest and determination for him, for making people (even people who had very vague surmises as to the particular eminence toward which he might be headed) fervidly desire to push him and for refusing, on any terms, to be pushed. There was nothing more individual about Kenneth than his inability to be exploited. Coercion and encouragement spent themselves upon him like summer rain.

He was thirty-five when his first book, *Charles de Montpensier*, was published, and the work was, to those who knew its author intimately, a kind of record of his inverse development. It was first conceived and written as a prose drama, then amplified into an historical novel, and had finally been compressed into a psychological study of two hundred pages, in which the action was hushed to a whisper and the teeming pageantry of his background, which he had spent years in developing and which had cost him several laborious summers in France and Italy, was reduced to a shadowy atmosphere, suggestive enough, doubtless, but presenting very little that was appreciable to the eyes of the flesh. The majority of Kenneth's readers, even those baptized into his faith, must have recalled the fable of the mouse and the mountain. As for those of us who had travailed with him, confident as we were of the high order of the ultimate production, we had a baffled feeling that there had been a distressing leakage of power. However, when this study of the High Constable of Bourbon was followed by an exquisite prose idyl, *The Wood of Ronsard*, we began to take heart, and when we learned that a stimulus so reassuring as a determination to marry had hurried this charming bit of romance into the world, we felt that Kenneth had at last entered upon the future that had seemed for so long only a step before him.

Since Gray's arrival in New York, Harrison and I had had more than ever the feeling of having him on our hands. He had been so long accustomed to the respectful calm of Olympia that he was unable to find his way about in a new environment. He was incapable of falling in with any of the prevailing attitudes, and even of civilly tolerating them in other people. Commercialism wounded him, flippancy put him out of countenance, and he clung stubbornly to certain fond, Olympian superstitions regarding his profession. One by one his new acquaintances chilled, offended by his arrogant reception of their genial efforts to put him in the way of things. Even those of us who had known him at his best, and who remembered the summer evenings in his garden at Olympia, found his seriousness and punctilious reservations tedious in the broad glare of short, noisy working days.

Some weeks before the day set for Kenneth's marriage, I learned that it might be necessary for me to go to Paris for a time to take the place of our correspondent there, who had fallen into precarious health, and I called at Bertha's apartment for a serious talk with her. I found her in the high tide of work; but she made a point of accepting interruptions agreeably, just as she made a point of looking astonishingly well, of being indispensable in an appalling number of "circles," and of generally nullifying the traditional reproach attaching to clever women.

"In all loyalty to you both," I remarked, "I feel that I ought to remind you that you are accepting a responsibility."

"His uncertainty, you mean?"

"Oh, I mean all of them—the barriers which are so intangible he cannot climb them and so terrifying he can't jump them, which lie between him and everything."

Bertha looked at me thoughtfully out of her candid blue eyes. "But what he needs is, after all, so little compared with what he has."

"What he has," I admitted, "is inestimably precious; but the problem is to keep it from going back into the ground with him."

She shot a glance of alarm at me from under her blond lashes. "But certainly he is endlessly more capable of doing than any of us. With such depth to draw from, how can he possibly fail?"

"Perhaps it's his succeeding that I fear more than anything. I think the fair way to measure Kenneth is by what he simply can't do."

"The cheap, you mean?" she asked reflectively. "Oh, that he will never do. We may just eliminate that from our discussion. The problem is simply to make him mine his vein, even if, from his fanciful angle of vision, it's at first a losing business."

"Ah, my dear young lady, but it's just his fanciful angle, as you so happily term it, that puts a stop to everything, and I've never quite dared to urge him past his scruples, though I'm not saying I could if I would. If there is anything at all in the whole business, any element of chosenness, of a special call, any such value in individual tone as he fancies, then, the question is, dare one urge him?"

"Nonsense!" snapped Bertha, drawing up her slender shoulders with decision—I had purposely set out to exhaust her patience—

"you have all put a halo about him until he daren't move for fear of putting it out. What he needs is simply to keep at it. How much satisfaction do you suppose he gets out of hanging back?"

"The point, it seems to me, my dear Bertha, is not that, but the remarkableness of any one's having the conviction, the moral force, just now and under the circumstances, to hang back at all. There must be either very much or very little in a man when he refuses to make the most of his vogue and sell out on a rising market. If he would rather bring up a little water out of the well than turn the river across his lands, has one a right to coerce him?" I put my shaft home steadily, and Bertha caught fire with proper spirit.

"All I can say is, that it's a miracle he's as adaptable as he is. I simply can't understand what you meant, you and Harrison, by keeping him out there in Ohio so long."

"But we didn't," I expostulated. "We didn't keep him there. We only did not succeed in getting him away. We, too, had our scruples. He had his old house there, and his garden, his friends, and the peace of God. And then, Olympia isn't a bad sort of place. It kept his feeling fresh, at least, and in fifteen years or so you'll begin to know the value of that. There everything centers about the college, and every one reads, just as every one goes to church. It's a part of the decent, comely life of the place. In Olympia there is a deep seated, old-fashioned respect for the printed page, and Kenneth naturally found himself in the place of official sanctity. The townswomen reverently attended his college lectures, along with their sons and daughters, and, had he been corruptible, he might have established a walled supremacy of personal devotion behind which he could have sheltered himself to the end of his days."

"But he didn't, you see," said Bertha, triumphantly; "which is proof that he was meant for the open waters. Oh, we shall do fine things, I promise you! I can just fancy the hushed breath of the place for wonder at him. And his rose garden! Will people never have done with his rose garden! I remember you and Harrison told me of it, with an air, before I had met Kenneth at all. I wonder that you didn't keep him down there forever from a pure sense of the picturesque. What sort of days and nights do you imagine he passed in his garden, in his miserably uncertain state? I suppose we should all like well enough to grow roses, if we had nothing else to do."

I felt that Bertha was considerably keeping her eyes from the clock, and I rose to go.

"Well, Bertha, I suppose the only reason we haven't brought him to a worse pass than we have, is just the fact that he happens to have been born an anachronism, and such a stubborn one that we leave him pretty much where we found him."

II

After Kenneth's wedding, I left immediately for Paris, and during the next four years I knew of the Grays only what I could sense from Kenneth's labored letters, ever more astonishing in their aridity, and from the parcels I received twice a year by book-post, containing Bertha's latest work. I never picked up an American periodical that Bertha's name was not the first to greet my eye on the advertising pages. She surpassed all legendary accounts of phenomenal productiveness, and I could feel no anxiety for the fortunes of the pair while Bertha's publishers thought her worth such a display of heavy type. There was scarcely a phase of colonial life left untouched by her, and her last, *The Maid of Domremy*, showed that she had fairly crowded herself out of her own field.

The real wonder was, that, making so many, she could make them so well—should make them, indeed, rather better and better. Even were one so unreasonable as to consider her gain a loss, there was no denying it. I read her latest, one after another, as they arrived, with growing interest and amazement, wholly unable to justify my first suspicion. There was every evidence that she had absorbed from Kenneth like a water plant, but none that she had used him more violently than a clever woman may properly use her husband. Knowing him as I did, I could never accredit him with having any hand in Bertha's intrepid, wholehearted, unimpeachable conventionality. One could not exactly call her unscrupulous; one could observe only that no predicament embarrassed her; that she went ahead and pulled it off.

When I returned to New York, I found a curious state of feeling prevalent concerning the Grays. Bertha was *la fille du régiment*[1] more than ever. Every one championed her, every one went to her teas, every one was smilingly and conspicuously present in her triumph. Even those who had formerly stood somewhat aloof, now found no courage to dissent. With Bertha herself so gracious, so eager to please, the charge of pettiness, of jealousy, even, could be too easily incurred. She quite floated the sourest and heaviest upon her rising tide.

There was, however, the undertow. I felt it even before I had actually made sure of it—in the peculiar warmth with which people spoke of Kenneth. In him they saw their own grievances magnified until he became symbolic. Publicly every one talked of Bertha; but behind closed doors it was of Kenneth they spoke—*sotto voce* and

1. The daughter of the regiment (French). *La Fille du Régiment* is a comic opera by Gaetano Donizetti, first performed in 1840, in which the heroine Marie is adopted by an entire regiment of soldiers.

with a shake of the head. As he had published nothing since his marriage, this smothered feeling had resulted in a new and sumptuous edition of *Montpensier* and *The Wood of Ronsard*; one of those final, votive editions, suggestive of the bust and the catafalque.

I called upon the Grays at the first opportunity. They had moved from their downtown flat into a new apartment house on Eighty-fifth street. The servant who took my card did not return, but Kenneth himself stumbled into the reception hall, overturning a gilt chair in his haste, and gripped my hands as if he would never let them go. He held on to my arm as he took me to his study, telling me again and again that I couldn't possibly know what pleasure it gave him to see me. When he dropped limply into his desk chair, he seemed really quite overcome with excitement. It was not until I asked him about his wife that he collected himself and began to talk coherently.

"I'm sorry I can't speak to her now," he explained, rapidly twirling a paper cutter between his long fingers. "She won't be free until four o'clock. She will be so pleased that I'm almost tempted to call her at once. But she's so overworked, poor girl, and she will go out so much."

"My dear Kenneth, how does she ever manage it all? She must have nerves of iron."

"Oh, she's wonderful, wonderful!" he exclaimed, brushing his limp hair back from his forehead with a perplexed gesture. "As to how she does it, I really don't know much more than you. It all gets done, somehow." He glanced quickly toward the partition, through which we heard the steady clicking of a typewriter. "I scarcely know what she is up to until her proofs come in. I usually go at those with her." He darted a piercing look at me, and I wondered whether he had got a hint of the malicious stories which found their way about concerning his varied usefulness to Bertha.

"If you'll excuse me for a moment, Philip," he went on, "I'll finish a letter that must go out this afternoon, and then I shall be quite free."

He turned in his revolving chair to a desk littered deep with papers, and began writing hurriedly. I could see that the simplest kind of composition still perplexed and disconcerted him. He stopped, hesitated, bit his nails, then scratched desperately ahead, darting an annoyed glance at the partition as if the sharp, regular click of the machine bewildered him.

He had grown older, I noticed, but it was good to see him again—his limp, straight hair, which always hung down in a triangle over his high forehead; his lean cheek, loose under lip, and long whimsical chin; his faded, serious eyes, which were always peering inquiringly from behind his thick glasses; his long, tremulous fingers, which handled a pen as uncertainly as ever. There was a general looseness of articulation about his gaunt frame that made his every movement seem more or less haphazard.

On the desk lay a heap of letters, the envelopes marked "answered" in Kenneth's small, irregular hand, and all of them, I noticed, addressed to Bertha. In the open drawer at his left were half a dozen manuscript envelopes, addressed to her in as many different hands.

"What on earth!" I gasped. "Does Bertha conduct a literary agency as well?"

Kenneth swung round in his chair, and made a wry face as he glanced at the contents of the drawer. "It's almost as bad as that. Really, it's the most abominable nuisance. But we're the victims of success, as Bertha says. Sometimes a dozen manuscripts come in to her for criticism in one week. She dislikes to hurt any one's feelings, so one of us usually takes a look at them."

"Bertha's correspondence must be something of a responsibility in itself," I ventured.

"Oh, it is, I assure you. People are most inconsiderate. I'm rather glad, though, when it piles up like this and I can take a hand at it. It gives me an excuse for putting off my own work, and you know how I welcome any pretext," he added, with a flushed, embarrassed smile.

"What are you doing, anyhow? I don't know where you'll ever learn industry if Bertha can't teach you."

"I'm working, I'm working," he insisted, hurriedly crossing out the last sentence of his letter and blotting it carefully. "You know how reprehensibly slow I am. It seems to grow on me. I'm finishing up some studies in the French Renaissance. They'll be ready by next fall, I think." As he spoke, he again glanced hurriedly over the closely written page before him; then, stopping abruptly, he tore the sheet across the middle. "Really, you've quite upset me. Tell me about yourself, Philip. Are you going out to Olympia?"

"That depends upon whether I remain here or decamp immediately for China, which prospect is in the cards. Olympia is greatly changed, Harrison tells me."

Kenneth sighed and sank deeper into his chair, reaching again for the paper cutter. "Ruined completely. Capital and enterprise have broken in even there. They've all sorts of new industries, and the place is black with smoke and thick with noise from sunrise to sunset. I still own my house there, but I seldom go back. I don't know where we're bound for, I'm sure. There must be places, somewhere in the world, where a man can take a book or two and drop behind the procession for an hour; but they seem impossibly far from here."

I could not help smiling at the deeply despondent gaze which he fixed upon the paper cutter. "But the procession itself is the thing we've got to enjoy," I suggested, "the mere sense of speed."

"I suppose so, I suppose so," he reiterated, wiping his forehead with his handkerchief. "The six-day bicycle race seems to be what we've all come to, and doubtless one form of it's as much worth while as another. We don't get anywhere, but we go. We certainly go; and that's what we're after. You'll be lucky if you are sent to China. There must be calm there as yet, I imagine."

Our conversation went on fitfully, with interruptions, irrelevant remarks, and much laughter, as talk goes between two persons who have once been frank with each other, and who find that frankness has become impossible. My coming had clearly upset him, and his agitation of manner visibly increased when he spoke of his wife. He wiped his forehead and hands repeatedly, and finally opened a window. He fairly wrested the conversation out of my hands and was continually interrupting and forestalling me, as if he were apprehensive that I might say something he did not wish to hear. He started and leaned forward in his chair whenever I approached a question.

At last we were aware of a sudden slack in the tension; the typewriter had stopped. Kenneth looked at his watch, and disappeared through a door into his wife's study. When he returned, Bertha was beside him, her hand on his shoulder, taller, straighter, younger than I had left her—positively childlike in her freshness and candor.

"Didn't I tell you," she cried, "that we should do fine things?"

III

A few weeks later I was sent to Hong Kong, where I remained for two years. Before my return to America, I was ordered into the interior for eight months, during which time my mail was to be held for me at the consul's office in Canton, the port where I was to take ship for home. Once in the Sze Chuen province, floods and bad roads delayed me to such an extent that I barely reached Canton on the day my vessel sailed. I hurried on board with all my letters unread, having had barely time to examine the instructions from my paper.

We were well out at sea when I opened a letter from Harrison in which he gave an account of Kenneth Gray's disappearance. He had, Harrison stated, gone out to Olympia to dispose of his property there which, since the development of the town, had greatly increased in value. He completed his business after a week's stay, and left for New York by the night train, several of his friends accompanying him to the station. Since that night he had not been seen or heard of. Detectives had been at work; hospitals and morgues had been searched without result.

The date of this communication put me beside myself. It had awaited me in Canton for nearly seven months, and Gray had last been seen on the tenth of November, four months before the date of Harrison's letter, which was written as soon as the matter was made public. It was eleven months, then, since Kenneth Gray had been seen in America. During my long voyage I went through an accumulated bulk of American newspapers, but found nothing more reassuring than occasional items to the effect that the mystery surrounding Gray's disappearance remained unsolved. In a "literary supplement" of comparatively recent date, I came upon a notice to the effect that the new novel by Bertha Torrence Gray, announced for spring publication, would, owing to the excruciating experience through which the young authoress had lately passed, be delayed until the autumn.

I bore my suspense as best I could across ocean and continent. When I arrived in New York, I went from the ferry to the *Messenger* office, and, once there, directly to Harrison's room.

"What's all this," I cried, "about Kenneth Gray? I tell you I saw Gray in Canton ten months ago."

Harrison sprang to his feet and put his finger to his lip.

"Hush! Don't say another word! There are leaky walls about here. Go and attend to your business, and then come back and go to lunch with me. In the meantime, be careful not to discuss Gray with any one."

Four hours later, when we were sitting in a quiet corner of a café, Harrison dismissed the waiter and turned to me. "Now," he said, leaning across the table, "if you can be sufficiently guarded, you may tell me what you know about our friend."

"Well," I replied, "it would have been, under ordinary circumstances, a commonplace thing enough. On the day before I started for the interior, I was in Canton, making some last purchases to complete my outfit. I stepped out of a shop on one of the crooked streets in the old part of the city, and I saw him as plainly as I see you, being trundled by in a jinrikisha,[2] got up in a helmet and white duck, a fat white umbrella across his knees, peering hopefully out through his glasses. He was so like himself, his look and attitude, his curious chin poked forward, that I simply stood and stared until he had passed me and turned a corner, vanishing like a stereopticon picture traveling across the screen. I hurried to the banks, the big hotels, to the consul's, getting no word of him, but leaving let-

2. Rickshaw.

ters for him everywhere. My party started the next day, and I was compelled to leave for an eight-months' nightmare in the interior. I got back to Canton barely in time to catch my steamer, and did not open your letter until we were down the river and losing sight of land. Either I saw Kenneth, or I am a subject for the Society for Psychical Research."

"Just so," said Harrison, peering mysteriously above his coffee cup. "And now forget it. Simply disabuse yourself of any notion that you've seen him since we crossed the ferry with you three years ago. It's your last service to him, probably."

"Speak up," I cried, exasperated. "I've had about all of this I can stand. I came near wiring the story in from San Francisco. I don't know why I didn't."

"Well, here's to whatever withheld you! When a man comes to the pass where he wants to wipe himself off the face of the earth, when it's the last play he can make for his self-respect, the only decent thing is to let him do it. You know the yielding stuff he's made of well enough to appreciate the amount of pressure it must have taken to harden him to such an exit. I'm sure I never supposed he had it in him."

"But what, short of insanity—"

"Insanity? Nonsense! I wonder that people don't do it oftener. The pressure simply got past the bearing-point. His life was going, and going for nothing—worse than nothing. His future was chalked out for him, and whichever way he turned he was confronted by his unescapable destiny. In the light of Bertha's splendid success, he couldn't be churlish or ungracious; he had to play his little part along with the rest of us. And Bertha, you know, has passed all the limits of nature, not to speak of decorum. They come as certainly as the seasons, her new ones, each cleverer and more damnable than the last. And yet there is nothing that one can actually put one's finger on—not, at least, without saying the word that would lay us open to a charge which as her friends we are none of us willing to incur, and which no one would listen to if it were said.

"I tell you," Harrison continued, "the whole thing sickened him. He had dried up like a stockfish.[3] His brain was beaten into torpidity by the mere hammer of her machine, as by so many tiny mallets. He had lived to help lessen the value of all that he held precious, to disprove all that he wanted to believe. Having ridden to victory under the banners of what he most despised, there was nothing for him but to live in the blaze of her conquest, and that was the very measure of his fall. His usefulness to the world was over when he had done what he did for Bertha. I don't believe he even knew

3. An unsalted fish, such as cod, dried in open air on wooden racks.

where he stood; the thing had gone so, seemed to answer the purpose so wonderfully well, and there was never anything that one could really put one's finger on—except all of it. It was a trial of faith, and Bertha had won out so beautifully. He had proved the fallacy of his own position. There was nothing left for him to say. I'm sure I don't know whether he had anything left to think."

"Do you remember," I said slowly, "I used to hold that, in the end, Kenneth would be measured by what he didn't do, by what he couldn't do? What a wonder he was at not being able to do it. Surely, if Bertha couldn't convince him, fire and faggots couldn't."

"For, after all," sighed Harrison, as we rose to go, "Bertha is a wonderful woman—a woman of her time and people; and she has managed, in spite of her fatal facility, to be enough sight better than most of us."

SARAH ORNE JEWETT

Letters to Willa Cather†

My Dear Willa,—I was glad to get your letter last night, and I was sorry to miss the drive to the station and a last talk about the story and other things; but I was too tired—"spent quite bankrupt!" It takes but little care about affairs, and almost less true pleasure, to make me feel overdone, and I have to be careful—it is only stupid and disappointing, but *there it is*, as an old friend of mine often says dolefully. And I knew that I was disappointing you, besides disappointing and robbing myself, which made it all the harder. It would have been such a good piece of a half hour! Emerson[1] was very funny once, Mrs. Fields[2] has told me, when he said to a friend, "You formerly bragged of ill-health, sir!" But indeed I don't brag, I only deplore and often think it is a tiresome sort of mortification. I begin to think this is just what makes old age so trying to many persons. It seemed a very long little journey, and I could hardly sit up in my place in the car. I have never been very strong, but always capable of "great pulls."

I expect to be here until Monday the seventh, unless dear Mrs. Fields should need me. I have just had a most dear and cheerful note from her, and we spoke by telephone last evening. She wrote me about the pink roses.

† From *Letters of Sarah Orne Jewett*, ed. Annie Fields (Boston: Houghton Mifflin, 1911), pp. 245–50.

1. Ralph Waldo Emerson (1803–1882), philosopher, poet, and essayist.
2. Annie Adams Fields, writer and Boston literary figure who became Sarah Orne Jewett's companion after the death of her husband, Boston publisher James Fields.

And now I wish to tell you—the first of this letter being but a preface—with what deep happiness and recognition I have read the "McClure" story,[3]—night before last I found it with surprise and delight. It made me feel very near to the writer's young and loving heart. You have drawn your two figures of the wife and her husband with unerring touches and wonderful tenderness for her. It makes me the more sure that you are far on your road toward a fine and long story of very high class. The lover is as well done as he could be when a woman writes in the man's character,—it must always, I believe, be something of a masquerade. I think it is safer to write about him as you did about the others, and not try to be he! And you could almost have done it as yourself—a woman could love her in that same protecting way—a woman could even care enough to wish to take her away from such a life, by some means or other. But oh, how close—how tender—how true the feeling is! the sea air blows through the very letters on the page. Do not hurry too fast in these early winter days,—a quiet hour is worth more to you than anything you can do in it.

148 Charles Street, BOSTON, MASS.,
Sunday, 13th of *December*.

MY DEAR WILLA,—I have been thinking about you and hoping that things are going well. I cannot help saying what I think about your writing and its being hindered by such incessant, important, responsible work as you have in your hands now. I do think that it is impossible for you to work so hard and yet have your gifts mature as they should—when one's first working power has spent itself nothing ever brings it back just the same, and I do wish in my heart that the force of this very year could have gone into three or four stories. In the "Troll-Garden" the Sculptor's Funeral[4] stands alone a head higher than the rest, and it is to that level you must hold and take for a starting-point. You are older now than that book in general; you have been living and reading and knowing new types; but if you don't keep and guard and mature your force, and above all, have time and quiet to perfect your work, you will be writing things not much better than you did five years ago. This you are anxiously saying to yourself! but I am wondering how to get at the right conditions. I want you to be surer of your backgrounds,—you have your Nebraska life,—a child's Virginia, and now an intimate knowledge of what we are pleased to call the "Bohemia" of newspaper and magazine-office life. These are uncommon equipment, but you

3. Willa Cather's "On the Gull's Road" (1908), in which the male narrator falls in love with a dying woman.
4. "The Sculptor's Funeral" is a story in Cather's first published book of fiction, a collection of short stories (*The Troll Garden* [1905]).

don't see them yet quite enough from the outside,—you stand right in the middle of each of them when you write, without having the standpoint of the looker-on who takes them each in their relations to letters, to the world. Your good schooling and your knowledge of "the best that has been thought and said in the world,"[5] as Matthew Arnold put it, have helped you, but these you wish and need to deepen and enrich still more. You must find a quiet place near the best companions (not those who admire and wonder at everything one does, but those who know the good things with delight!). You do need reassurance,—every artist does!—but you need still more to feel "responsible for the state of your conscience" (your literary conscience, we can just now limit that quotation to), and you need to dream your dreams and go on to new and more shining ideals, to be aware of "the gleam" and to follow it; your vivid, exciting companionship in the office must not be your audience, you must find your own quiet centre of life, and write from that to the world that holds offices, and all society, all Bohemia; the city, the country—in short, you must write to the human heart, the great consciousness that all humanity goes to make up. Otherwise what might be strength in a writer is only crudeness, and what might be insight is only observation; sentiment falls to sentimentality—you can write about life, but never write life itself. And to write and work on this level, we must live on it—we must at least recognize it and defer to it at every step. We must be ourselves, but we must be our best selves. If we have patience with cheapness and thinness, as Christians must, we must know that it *is* cheapness and not make believe about it. To work in silence and with all one's heart, that is the writer's lot; he is the only artist who must be a solitary, and yet needs the widest outlook upon the world. But you have been growing I feel sure in the very days when you felt most hindered, and this will be counted to you. You need to have time to yourself and time to read and add to your recognitions. I do not know when a letter has grown so long and written itself so easily, but I have been full of thought about you. You will let me hear again from you before long?

5. The quotation is from Matthew Arnold's essay "Culture and Anarchy" (1882).

WILLA CATHER

Miss Jewett†

I

In reading over a package of letters from Sarah Orne Jewett, I find this observation: *"The thing that teases the mind over and over for years, and at last gets itself put down rightly on paper—whether little or great, it belongs to Literature."* Miss Jewett was very conscious of the fact that when a writer makes anything that belongs to Literature (limiting the term here to imaginative literature, which she of course meant), his material goes through a process very different from that by which he makes merely a good story. No one can define this process exactly; but certainly persistence, survival, recurrence in the writer's mind, are highly characteristic of it. The shapes and scenes that have "teased" the mind for years, when they do at last get themselves rightly put down, make a much higher order of writing, and a much more costly, than the most vivid and vigorous transfer of immediate impressions.

In some of Miss Jewett's earlier books, *Deep-haven, Country By-ways, Old Friends and New,* one can find first sketches, first impressions, which later crystallized into almost flawless examples of literary art. One can, as it were, watch in process the two kinds of making: the first, which is full of perception and feeling but rather fluid and formless; the second, which is tightly built and significant in design. The design is, indeed, so happy, so right, that it seems inevitable; the design is the story and the story is the design. The "Pointed Fir"[1] sketches are living things caught in the open, with light and freedom and airspaces about them. They melt into the land and the life of the land until they are not stories at all, but life itself.

A great many stories were being written upon New England themes at the same time that Miss Jewett was writing; stories that to many contemporary readers may have seemed more interesting than hers, because they dealt with more definite "situations" and were more heavily accented. But they are not very interesting to reread today; they have not the one thing that survives all arresting

† From *Not Under Forty* by Willa Cather, copyright © 1936 by Willa S. Cather, renewed 1964 by Edith Lewis and the City Bank Farmers Trust Co. Used by permission of Alfred A. Knopf, an imprint of the Knopf Doubleday Publishing Group, a division of Penguin Random House LLC. [Much of Part I of this sketch was originally written as a preface to a two-volume collection of Miss Jewett's stories published by Houghton Mifflin in 1925—Cather's note.]

1. Sarah Orne Jewett, *The Country of the Pointed Firs* (Boston: Houghton Mifflin, 1896).

situations, all good writing and clever story-making—inherent, individual beauty.

Walter Pater said that every truly great drama must, in the end, linger in the reader's mind as a sort of ballad. One might say that every fine story must leave in the mind of the sensitive reader an intangible residuum of pleasure; a cadence, a quality of voice that is exclusively the writer's own, individual, unique. A quality which one can remember without the volume at hand, can experience over and over again in the mind but can never absolutely define, as one can experience in memory a melody, or the summer perfume of a garden. The magnitude of the subject-matter is not of primary importance, seemingly. An idyll of Theocritus, concerned with sheep and goats and shade and pastures, is today as much alive as the most dramatic passages of the *Iliad*—stirs the reader's feeling quite as much, perhaps.

It is a common fallacy that a writer, if he is talented enough, can achieve this poignant quality by improving upon his subject-matter, by using his "imagination" upon it and twisting it to suit his purpose. The truth is that by such a process (which is not imaginative at all!) he can at best produce only a brilliant sham, which, like a badly built and pretentious house, looks poor and shabby after a few years. If he achieves anything noble, anything enduring, it must be by giving himself absolutely to his material. And this gift of sympathy is his great gift; is the fine thing in him that alone can make his work fine.

The artist spends a lifetime in pursuing the things that haunt him, in having his mind "teased" by them, in trying to get these conceptions down on paper exactly as they are to him and not in conventional poses supposed to reveal their character; trying this method and that, as a painter tries different lightings and different attitudes with his subject to catch the one that presents it more suggestively than any other. And at the end of a lifetime he emerges with much that is more or less happy experimenting, and comparatively little that is the very flower of himself and his genius.

The best of Miss Jewett's work, read by a student fifty years from now, will give him the characteristic flavour, the spirit, the cadence, of an American writer of the first order,—and of a New England which will then be a thing of the past.

Even in the stories which fall short of being Miss Jewett's best, one has the pleasure of her society and companionship—if one likes that sort of companionship. I remember she herself had a fondness for "The Hiltons' Holiday,"[2]—the slightest of stories: a

2. "The Hiltons' Holiday" appeared first in *Century Magazine* (24) in September 1893 and was collected in the *The Life of Nancy* (Boston: Houghton Mifflin, 1895).

hard-worked New England farmer takes his two little girls to town, some seventeen miles away (a long drive by wagon), for a treat. That is all, yet the story is a little miracle. It simply *is the look*—shy, kind, a little wistful—which shines out at one from good country faces on remote farms; it is the look *itself*. To have got it down upon the printed page is like bringing the tenderest of early spring flowers from the deep wood into the hot light of noon without bruising its petals.

To note an artist's limitations is but to define his talent. A reporter can write equally well about everything that is presented to his view, but a creative writer can do his best only with what lies within the range and character of his deepest sympathies. These stories of Miss Jewett's have much to do with fisher-folk and seaside villages; with juniper pastures and lonely farms, neat grey country houses and delightful, well-seasoned men and women. That, when one thinks of it in a flash, is New England. I remember hearing an English actor say that until he made a motor trip through the New England country he had supposed that the Americans killed their aged in some merciful fashion, for he saw none in the cities where he played.

There are many kinds of people in the State of Maine, and neighbouring States, who are not found in Miss Jewett's books. There may be Othellos and Iagos and Don Juans; but they are not highly characteristic of the country, they do not come up spontaneously in the juniper pastures as the everlasting does. Miss Jewett wrote of everyday people who grew out of the soil, not about exceptional individuals at war with their environment. This was not a creed with her, but an instinctive preference.

Born within the scent of the sea but not within sight of it, in a beautiful old house full of strange and lovely things brought home from all over the globe by seafaring ancestors, she spent much of her childhood driving about the country with her old doctor father on his professional rounds among the farms. She early learned to love her country for what it was. What is quite as important, she saw it as it was. She happened to have the right nature, the right temperament, to see it so—and to understand by intuition the deeper meaning of what she saw.

She had not only the eye, she had the ear. From her early years she must have treasured up those pithy bits of local speech, of native idiom, which enrich and enliven her pages. The language her people speak to each other is a native tongue. No writer can invent it. It is made in the hard school of experience, in communities where language has been undisturbed long enough to take on colour and character from the nature and experiences of the people. The "sayings" of a community, its proverbs, are its characteristic comment upon life; they imply its history, suggest its attitude toward the world and its way of accepting life. Such an idiom makes the finest language any writer can have; and he can never get it with a notebook. He himself must be able to think and feel in that speech—it is a gift from heart to heart.

Much of Miss Jewett's delightful humour comes from her delicate and tactful handling of this native language of the waterside and countryside, never overdone, never pushed a shade too far; from this, and from her own fine attitude toward her subject-matter. This attitude in itself, though unspoken, is everywhere felt, and constitutes one of the most potent elements of grace and charm in her stories. She had with her own stories and her own characters a very charming relation; spirited, gay, tactful, noble in its essence and a little arch in its expression. In this particular relationship many of our most gifted writers are unfortunate. If a writer's attitude toward his characters and his scene is as vulgar as a showman's, as mercenary as an auctioneer's, vulgar and meretricious will his product for ever remain.

II

"The distinguished outward stamp"[3]—it was that one felt immediately upon meeting Miss Jewett: a lady, in the old high sense. It was in her face and figure, in her carriage, her smile, her voice, her way of greeting one. There was an ease, a graciousness, a light touch in conversation, a delicate unobtrusive wit. You quickly recognized that her gift with the pen was one of many charming personal attributes. In the short period when I knew her, 1908 and 1909, she was not writing at all, and found life full enough without it. Some six years before, she had been thrown from a carriage on a country road (sad fate for an enthusiastic horsewoman) and suffered a slight concussion. She recovered, after a long illness, but she did not write again—felt that her best working power was spent.

She had never been one of those who "live to write." She lived for a great many things, and the stories by which we know her were one of many preoccupations. After the carriage accident she was not strong enough to go out into the world a great deal; before that occurred her friendships occupied perhaps the first place in her life. She had friends among the most interesting and gifted people of her time, and scores of friends among the village and country people of her own State—people who knew her as Doctor Jewett's daughter and regarded "Sarah's writing" as a ladylike accomplishment. These country friends, she used to say, were the wisest of all,

3. The phrase is Henry James's in speaking of Jewett. (See note 9 on p. 232).

because they could never be fooled about fundamentals. Even after her long illness she was at home to a few visitors almost every afternoon; friends from England and France were always coming and going. Small dinner-parties and luncheons were part of the regular routine when she was with Mrs. Fields on Charles Street or at Manchester-by-the-Sea.[4] When she was at home, in South Berwick, there were the old friends of her childhood to whom she must be always accessible. At the time I knew her she had, as she said, forgone all customary exercises—except a little gardening in spring and summer. But as a young woman she devoted her mornings to horseback riding in fine weather, and was skilful with a sailboat. Every day, in every season of the year, she enjoyed the beautiful country in which she had the good fortune to be born. Her love of the Maine country and seacoast was the supreme happiness of her life. Her stories were but reflections, quite incidental, of that peculiar and intensely personal pleasure. Take, for instance, that clear, daybreak paragraph which begins "By the Morning Boat":[5]

> "On the coast of Maine, where many green islands and salt inlets fringe the deep-cut shore line; where balsam firs and bayberry bushes send their fragrance far seaward, and song-sparrows sing all day, and the tide runs plashing in and out among the weedy ledges; where cowbells tinkle on the hills and herons stand in the shady coves—on the lonely coast of Maine stood a small gray house facing the morning light."

Wherever Miss Jewett might be in the world, in the Alps, the Pyrenees, the Apennines, she carried the Maine shore-country with her. She loved it by instinct, and in the light of wide experience, from near and from afar.

"You must know the world before you can know the village," she once said to me. Quoted out of its context this remark sounds like a wise pronouncement, but Miss Jewett never made wise pronouncements. Her personal opinions she voiced lightly, half-humorously; any expression of them was spontaneous, the outgrowth of the immediate conversation. This remark was a supplementary comment, apropos of a story we had both happened to read: a story about a mule, introduced by the magazine which published it with an editorial note to the effect that (besides being "fresh" and "promising") it was authentic, as the young man who

4. Annie Adams Fields (1834–1915), the widow of James T. Fields of Ticknor and Fields publishers and for many years Sarah Orne Jewett's life partner. A writer herself, Mrs. Fields held a literary salon in her Beacon Hill home, which Cather describes in her essay "148 Charles Street," also collected in *Not under Forty*. Mrs. Fields also entertained at her seaside home in Manchester, a small town on the coast north of Boston.
5. The story first appeared in *Strangers and Wayfarers* (Boston: Houghton Mifflin, 1890).

wrote it was a mule-driver and had never been anything else. When I asked Miss Jewett if she had seen it, she gave no affirmative but a soft laugh, rather characteristic of her, something between amusement and forbearance, and exclaimed:

"Poor lad! But his mule could have done better! A mule, by God's grace, is a mule, with the mettle of his kind. Besides, the mule would be grammatical. It's not in his sure-footed nature to slight syntax. A horse might tangle himself up in his sentences or his picket rope, but never a mule."

III

Miss Jewett had read too widely, and had too fine a literary sense, to overestimate her own performance. Every Sunday book section of the New York dailies announces half a dozen "great" books, and calls our attention to more great writers than the Elizabeth age and the nineteenth century put together could muster. Miss Jewett applied that adjective very seldom (to Tolstoi, Flaubert, and a few others), certainly never to herself or to anything of her own. She spoke of "the Pointed Fir papers" or "the Pointed Fir sketches"; I never heard her call them stories. She had, as Henry James said of her, "a sort of elegance of humility, or fine flame of modesty." She was content to be slight, if she could be true. The closing sentences of "Marsh Rosemary"[6] might stand as an unconscious piece of self-criticism,—or perhaps as a gentle apology for the art of all new countries, which must grow out of a thin soil and bear its fate:

> "Who can laugh at my Marsh Rosemary, or who can cry, for that matter? The gray primness of the plant is made up from a hundred colors if you look close enough to find them. This Marsh Rosemary stands in her own place, and holds her dry leaves and tiny blossoms steadily toward the same sun that the pink lotus blooms for, and the white rose."

For contemporary writers of much greater range than her own, she had the most reverent and rejoicing admiration. She was one of the first Americans to see the importance of Joseph Conrad. Indeed, she was reading a new volume of Conrad, late in the night, when the slight cerebral hemorrhage occurred from which she died some months later.

At a time when machine-made historical novels were the literary fashion in the United States, when the magazines were full of dreary dialect stories, and the works of John Fox, Jr.,[7] were consid-

6. The story first appeared in *Tales of New England* (Boston: Houghton Mifflin, 1890).
7. Novelist and short-story writer (1862–1919) from Kentucky, a prolific producer of regional fiction set in Appalachia.

ered profound merely because they were very dull and heavy as clay, Miss Jewett quietly developed her own medium and confined herself to it. At that time Henry James was the commanding figure in American letters, and his was surely the keenest mind any American ever devoted to the art of fiction. But it was devoted almost exclusively to the study of other and older societies than ours. He was interested in his countrymen chiefly as they appeared in relation to the European scene. As an American writer he seems to claim, and richly to deserve, a sort of personal exemption. Stephen Crane came upon the scene, a young man of definite talent, brilliant and brittle,—dealing altogether with the surfaces of things, but in a manner all his own. He died young, but he had done something real. One can read him today. If we glance back over the many novels which have challenged our attention since Crane's time, it is like taking a stroll through a World's Fair grounds some years after the show is over. Palaces with the stucco peeling off, oriental villages stripped to beaver-board and cement, broken fountains, lakes gone to mud and weeds. We realize that whatever it is that makes a book hold together, most of these hadn't it.

Among those glittering novelties which have now become old-fashioned Miss Jewett's little volumes made a small showing. A taste for them must always remain a special taste,—but it will remain. She wrote for a limited audience, and she still has it, both here and abroad. To enjoy her the reader must have a sympathetic relation with the subject-matter and a sensitive ear; especially must he have a sense of "pitch" in writing. He must recognize when the quality of feeling comes inevitably out of the theme itself; when the language, the stresses, the very structure of the sentences are imposed upon the writer by the special mood of the piece.

It is easy to understand why some of the young students who have turned back from the present to glance at Miss Jewett find very little on her pages. Imagine a young man, or woman, born in New York City, educated at a New York university, violently inoculated with Freud, hurried into journalism, knowing no more about New England country people (or country folk anywhere) than he has caught from motor trips or observed from summer hotels: what is there for him in *The Country of the Pointed Firs?*

This hypothetical young man is perhaps of foreign descent: German, Jewish, Scandinavian. To him English is merely a means of making himself understood, of communicating his ideas. He may write and speak American English correctly, but only as an American may learn to speak French correctly. It is a surface speech: he clicks the words out as a bank clerk clicks out silver when you ask for change. For him the language has no emotional roots. How could he find the talk of the Maine country people anything but "dialect"? Moreover, the temper of the people which lies behind the language is incomprehensible to him. He can see what these Yankees have not (hence an epidemic of "suppressed desire" plays and novels), but what they *have*, their actual preferences and their fixed scale of values, are absolutely dark to him. When he tries to put himself in the Yankee's place, he attempts an impossible substitution.

But the adopted American is not alone in being cut off from an instinctive understanding of "the old moral harmonies." There is the new American, whom Mr. Santayana describes as "the untrained, pushing, cosmopolitan orphan, cocksure in manner but none too sure in his morality, to whom the old Yankee, with his sour integrity, is almost a foreigner."[8]

When we find ourselves on shipboard, among hundreds of strangers, we very soon recognize those who are sympathetic to us. We find our own books in the same way. We like a writer much as we like individuals; for what he is, simply, underneath his accomplishments. Oftener than we realize, it is for some moral quality, some ideal which he himself cherishes, though it may be little discernible in his behaviour in the world. It is the light behind his books and is the living quality in his sentences.

It is this very personal quality of perception, a vivid and intensely personal experience of life, which make a "style"; Mark Twain had it, at his best, and Hawthorne. But among fifty thousand books you will find very few writers who ever achieved a style at all. The distinctive thing about Miss Jewett is that she had an individual voice; "a sense for the finest kind of truthful rendering, the sober, tender note, the temperately touched, whether in the ironic or pathetic," as Henry James said of her.[9] During the twenty-odd clamorous years since her death "masterpieces" have been bumping down upon us like trunks pouring down the baggage chutes from an overcrowded ocean steamer. But if you can get out from under them and go to a quiet spot and take up a volume of Miss Jewett, you will

8. George Santayana, *Character and Opinion in the United States* (New York: Charles Scribner's Sons, 1920). (Willa Cather's note [Editor].)
9. James wrote an appreciation of Jewett in the *Atlantic Monthly* from which Cather took the quotation:

> Her admirable gift, that artistic sensibility in her which rivaled the rare personal, that sense for the finest kind of truthful rendering, the sober and tender note, the temperately touched, whether in the ironic or the pathetic, would have deserved some more pointed commemoration than I judge her beautiful little quantum of achievement, her free and high, yet all so generously subdued character, a sort of elegance of humility or fine flame of modesty, with her remarkably distinguished outward stamp, to have called forth before the premature and overdarkened close of her young course of production. (Quoted in Francis Otto Matthiessen, *Sarah Orne Jewett* (Boston: Houghton Mifflin, 1929), pp. 136–137.

find the voice still there, with a quality which any ear trained in literature must recognize.

SARAH ORNE JEWETT

A White Heron†

I

The woods were already filled with shadows one June evening, just before eight o'clock, though a bright sunset still glimmered faintly among the trunks of the trees. A little girl was driving home her cow, a plodding, dilatory, provoking creature in her behavior, but a valued companion for all that. They were going away from the western light, and striking deep into the dark woods, but their feet were familiar with the path, and it was no matter whether their eyes could see it or not.

There was hardly a night the summer through when the old cow could be found waiting at the pasture bars; on the contrary, it was her greatest pleasure to hide herself away among the high huckleberry bushes, and though she wore a loud bell she had made the discovery that if one stood perfectly still it would not ring. So Sylvia had to hunt for her until she found her, and call Co'! Co'! with never an answering Moo, until her childish patience was quite spent. If the creature had not given good milk and plenty of it, the case would have seemed very different to her owners. Besides, Sylvia had all the time there was, and very little use to make of it. Sometimes in pleasant weather it was a consolation to look upon the cow's pranks as an intelligent attempt to play hide and seek, and as the child had no playmates she lent herself to this amusement with a good deal of zest. Though this chase had been so long that the wary animal herself had given an unusual signal of her whereabouts, Sylvia had only laughed when she came upon Mistress Moolly at the swamp-side, and urged her affectionately homeward with a twig of birch leaves. The old cow was not inclined to wander farther, she even turned in the right direction for once as they left the pasture, and stepped along the road at a good pace. She was quite ready to be milked now, and seldom stopped to browse. Sylvia wondered what her grandmother would say because

† From *The Best Stories of Sarah Orne Jewett,* selected and arranged with a preface by Willa Cather, Vol. II (Boston: Houghton Mifflin, 1925), pp. 1–21.

they were so late. It was a a great while since she had left home at half past five o'clock, but everybody knew the difficulty of making this errand a short one. Mrs. Tilley had chased the hornéd torment too many summer evenings herself to blame any one else for lingering, and was only thankful as she waited that she had Sylvia, nowadays, to give such valuable assistance. The good woman suspected that Sylvia loitered occasionally on her own account; there never was such a child for straying about out-of-doors since the world was made! Everybody said that it was a good change for a little maid who had tried to grow for eight years in a crowded manufacturing town, but, as for Sylvia herself, it seemed as if she never had been alive at all before she came to live at the farm. She thought often with wistful compassion of a wretched dry geranium that belonged to a town neighbor.

" 'Afraid of folks,' " old Mrs. Tilley said to herself, with a smile, after she had made the unlikely choice of Sylvia from her daughter's houseful of children, and was returning to the farm. " 'Afraid of folks,' they said! I guess she won't be troubled no great with 'em up to the old place!" When they reached the door of the lonely house and stopped to unlock it, and the cat came to purr loudly, and rub against them, a deserted pussy, indeed, but fat with young robins, Sylvia whispered that this was a beautiful place to live in, and she never should wish to go home.

The companions followed the shady woodroad, the cow taking slow steps, and the child very fast ones. The cow stopped long at the brook to drink, as if the pasture were not half a swamp, and Sylvia stood still and waited, letting her bare feet cool themselves in the shoal water, while the great twilight moths struck softly against her. She waded on through the brook as the cow moved away, and listened to the thrushes with a heart that beat fast with pleasure. There was a stirring in the great boughs overhead. They were full of little birds and beasts that seemed to be wide-awake, and going about their world, or else saying good-night to each other in sleepy twitters. Sylvia herself felt sleepy as she walked along. However, it was not much farther to the house, and the air was soft and sweet. She was not often in the woods so late as this, and it made her feel as if she were a part of the gray shadows and the moving leaves. She was just thinking how long it seemed since she first came to the farm a year ago, and wondering if everything went on in the noisy town just the same as when she was there; the thought of the great red-faced boy who used to chase and frighten her made her hurry along the path to escape from the shadow of the trees.

Suddenly this little woods-girl is horror-stricken to hear a clear whistle not very far away. Not a bird's whistle, which would have a sort of friendliness, but a boy's whistle, determined, and somewhat aggressive. Sylvia left the cow to whatever sad fate might await her, and stepped discreetly aside into the bushes, but she was just too late. The enemy had discovered her, and called out in a very cheerful and persuasive tone, "Halloa, little girl, how far is it to the road?" and trembling Sylvia answered almost inaudibly, "A good ways."

She did not dare to look boldly at the tall young man, who carried a gun over his shoulder, but she came out of her bush and again followed the cow, while he walked alongside.

"I have been hunting for some birds," the stranger said kindly, "and I have lost my way, and need a friend very much. Don't be afraid," he added gallantly. "Speak up and tell me what your name is, and whether you think I can spend the night at your house, and go out gunning early in the morning."

Sylvia was more alarmed than before. Would not her grandmother consider her much to blame? But who could have foreseen such an accident as this? It did not appear to be her fault, and she hung her head as if the stem of it were broken, but managed to answer "Sylvy," with much effort when her companion again asked her name.

Mrs. Tilley was standing in the doorway when the trio came into view. The cow gave a loud moo by way of explanation.

"Yes, you'd better speak up for yourself, you old trial! Where'd she tucked herself away this time, Sylvy?" Sylvia kept an awed silence; she knew by instinct that her grandmother did not comprehend the gravity of the situation. She must be mistaking the stranger for one of the farmer-lads of the region.

The young man stood his gun beside the door, and dropped a heavy game-bag beside it; then he bade Mrs. Tilley good-evening, and repeated his wayfarer's story, and asked if he could have a night's lodging.

"Put me anywhere you like," he said. "I must be off early in the morning, before day; but I am very hungry, indeed. You can give me some milk at any rate, that's plain."

"Dear sakes, yes," responded the hostess, whose long slumbering hospitality seemed to be easily awakened. "You might fare better if you went out on the main road a mile or so, but you're welcome to what we've got. I'll milk right off, and you make yourself at home. You can sleep on husks or feathers," she proffered graciously. "I raised them all myself. There's good pasturing for geese just below here towards the ma'sh. Now step round and set a plate for the gentleman, Sylvy!" And Sylvia promptly stepped. She was glad to have something to do, and she was hungry herself.

It was a surprise to find so clean and comfortable a little dwelling in this New England wilderness. The young man had known the horrors of its most primitive housekeeping, and the dreary squalor of that level of society which does not rebel at the companionship of hens. This was the best thrift of an old-fashioned farmstead, though on such a small scale that it seemed like a hermitage. He listened eagerly to the old woman's quaint talk, he watched Sylvia's pale face and shining gray eyes with ever growing enthusiasm, and insisted that this was the best supper he had eaten for a month; then, afterward, the new-made friends sat down in the doorway together while the moon came up.

Soon it would be berry-time, and Sylvia was a great help at picking. The cow was a good milker, though a plaguy thing to keep track of, the hostess gossiped frankly, adding presently that she had buried four children, so that Sylvia's mother, and a son (who might be dead) in California were all the children she had left. "Dan, my boy, was a great hand to go gunning," she explained sadly. "I never wanted for pa'tridges or gray squer'ls while he was to home. He's been a great wand'rer, I expect, and he's no hand to write letters. There, I don't blame him, I'd ha' seen the world myself if it had been so I could.

"Sylvia takes after him," the grandmother continued affectionately, after a minute's pause. "There ain't a foot o' ground she don't know her way over, and the wild creatur's counts her one o' themselves. Squer'ls she'll tame to come an' feed right out o' her hands, and all sorts o' birds. Last winter she got the jay-birds to bangeing here, and I believe she'd 'a' scanted herself of her own meals to have plenty to throw out amongst 'em, if I had n't kep' watch. Anything but crows, I tell her, I'm willin' to help support,—though Dan he went an' tamed one o' them that did seem to have reason same as folks. It was round here a good spell after he went away. Dan an' his father they did n't hitch,—but he never held up his head ag'in after Dan had dared him an' gone off."

The guest did not notice this hint of family sorrows in his eager interest in something else.

"So Sylvy knows all about birds, does she?" he exclaimed, as he looked round at the little girl who sat, very demure but increasingly sleepy, in the moonlight. "I am making a collection of birds myself. I have been at it ever since I was a boy." (Mrs. Tilley smiled.) "There are two or three very rare ones I have been hunting for these five years. I mean to get them on my own ground if they can be found."

"Do you cage 'em up?" asked Mrs. Tilley doubtfully, in response to this enthusiastic announcement.

"Oh, no, they're stuffed and preserved, dozens and dozens of them," said the ornithologist, "and I have shot or snared every one myself. I caught a glimpse of a white heron three miles from here on Saturday, and I have followed it in this direction. They have never been found in this district at all. The little white heron, it is," and he turned again to look at Sylvia with the hope of discovering that the rare bird was one of her acquaintances.

But Sylvia was watching a hop-toad in the narrow footpath.

"You would know the heron if you saw it," the stranger continued eagerly. "A queer tall white bird with soft feathers and long thin legs. And it would have a nest perhaps in the top of a high tree, made of sticks, something like a hawk's nest."

Sylvia's heart gave a wild beat; she knew that strange white bird, and had once stolen softly near where it stood in some bright green swamp grass, away over at the other side of the woods. There was an open place where the sunshine always seemed strangely yellow and hot, where tall, nodding rushes grew, and her grandmother had warned her that she might sink in the soft black mud underneath and never be heard of more. Not far beyond were the salt marshes and beyond those was the sea, the sea which Sylvia wondered and dreamed about, but never had looked upon, though its great voice could often be heard above the noise of the woods on stormy nights.

"I can't think of anything I should like so much as to find that heron's nest," the handsome stranger was saying. "I would give ten dollars to anybody who could show it to me," he added desperately, "and I mean to spend my whole vacation hunting for it if need be. Perhaps it was only migrating, or had been chased of out its own region by some bird of prey."

Mrs. Tilley gave amazed attention to all this, but Sylvia still watched the toad, not divining, as she might have done at some calmer time, that the creature wished to get to its hole under the doorstep, and was much hindered by the unusual spectators at that hour of the evening. No amount of thought, that night, could decide how many wished-for treasures the ten dollars, so lightly spoken of, would buy.

The next day the young sportsman hovered about the woods, and Sylvia kept him company, having lost her first fear of the friendly lad, who proved to be most kind and sympathetic. He told her many things about the birds and what they knew and where they lived and what they did with themselves. And he gave her a jack-knife, which she thought as great a treasure as if she were a desert-islander. All day long he did not once make her troubled or afraid except when he brought down some unsuspecting singing creature from its bough. Sylvia would have liked him vastly better without his gun; she could not understand why he killed the very birds he seemed to like so much. But as the day waned, Sylvia still watched the young man with loving admiration. She had never seen anybody so charming and delightful; the woman's heart, asleep in the child, was vaguely thrilled by a dream of love. Some premonition of that great power stirred and swayed these young foresters who traversed the solemn woodlands with soft-footed silent care. They stopped to listen to a bird's song; they pressed forward again eagerly, parting the branches,—speaking to each other rarely and in whispers; the young man going first and Sylvia following, fascinated, a few steps behind, with her gray eyes dark with excitement.

She grieved because the longed-for white heron was elusive, but she did not lead the guest, she only followed, and there was no such thing as speaking first. The sound of her own unquestioned voice would have terrified her,—it was hard enough to answer yes or no when there was need of that. At last evening began to fall, and they drove the cow home together, and Sylvia smiled with pleasure when they came to the place where she heard the whistle and was afraid only the night before.

II

Half a mile from home, at the farther edge of the woods, where the land was highest, a great pine-tree stood, the last of its generation. Whether it was left for a boundary mark, or for what reason, no one could say; the woodchoppers who had felled its mates were dead and gone long ago, and a whole forest of sturdy trees, pines and oaks and maples, had grown again. But the stately head of this old pine towered above them all and made a landmark for sea and shore miles and miles away. Sylvia knew it well. She had always believed that whoever climbed to the top of it could see the ocean; and the little girl had often laid her hand on the great rough trunk and looked up wistfully at those dark boughs that the wind always stirred, no matter how hot and still the air might be below. Now she thought of the tree with a new excitement, for why, if one climbed it at break of day, could not one see all the world, and easily discover whence the white heron flew, and mark the place, and find the hidden nest?

What a spirit of adventure, what wild ambition! What fancied triumph and delight and glory for the later morning when she could make known the secret! It was almost too real and too great for the childish heart to bear.

All night the door of the little house stood open, and the whippoorwills came and sang upon the very step. The young sportsman and his old hostess were sound asleep, but Sylvia's great design kept her broad awake and watching. She forgot to think of sleep. The short summer night seemed as long as the winter darkness, and at last when the whippoorwills ceased, and she was afraid the morning would after all come too soon, she stole out of the house and followed the pasture path through the woods, hastening toward the open ground beyond, listening with a sense of comfort and companionship to the drowsy twitter of a half-awakened bird, whose perch she had jarred in passing. Alas, if the great wave of human interest which flooded for the first time this dull little life should sweep away the satisfactions of an existence heart to heart with nature and the dumb life of the forest!

There was the huge tree asleep yet in the paling moonlight, and small and hopeful Sylvia began with utmost bravery to mount to the top of it, with tingling, eager blood coursing the channels of her whole frame, with her bare feet and fingers, that pinched and held like bird's claws to the monstrous ladder reaching up, up, almost to the sky itself. First she must mount the white oak tree that grew alongside, where she was almost lost among the dark branches and the green leaves heavy and wet with dew; a bird fluttered off its nest, and a red squirrel ran to and fro and scolded pettishly at the harmless housebreaker. Sylvia felt her way easily. She had often climbed there, and knew that higher still one of the oak's upper branches chafed against the pine trunk, just where its lower boughs were set close together. There, when she made the dangerous pass from one tree to the other, the great enterprise would really begin.

She crept out along the swaying oak limb at last, and took the daring step across into the old pine-tree. The way was harder than she thought; she must reach far and hold fast, the sharp dry twigs caught and held her and scratched her like angry talons, the pitch made her thin little fingers clumsy and stiff as she went round and round the tree's great stem, higher and higher upward. The sparrows and robins in the woods below were beginning to wake and twitter to the dawn, yet it seemed much lighter there aloft in the pine-tree, and the child knew that she must hurry if her project were to be of any use.

The tree seemed to lengthen itself out as she went up, and to reach farther and farther upward. It was like a great main-mast to the voyaging earth; it must truly have been amazed that morning through all its ponderous frame as it felt this determined spark of human spirit creeping and climbing from higher branch to branch. Who knows how steadily the least twigs held themselves to advantage this light, weak creature on her way! The old pine must have loved his new dependent. More than all the hawks, and bats, and moths, and even the sweet-voiced thrushes, was the brave, beating heart of the solitary gray-eyed child. And the tree stood still and held away the winds that June morning while the dawn grew bright in the east.

Sylvia's face was like a pale star, if one had seen it from the ground, when the last thorny bough was past, and she stood trembling and tired but wholly triumphant, high in the tree-top. Yes, there was the sea with the dawning sun making a golden dazzle over it, and toward that glorious east flew two hawks with slow-moving pinions. How low they looked in the air from that height when before one had only seen them far up, and dark against the blue sky. Their gray feathers were as soft as moths; they seemed only a little way from the tree, and Sylvia felt as if she too could go flying away among the clouds. Westward, the woodlands and farms reached miles and miles into the distance; here and there were church steeples, and white villages; truly it was a vast and awesome world.

The birds sang louder and louder. At last the sun came up bewilderingly bright. Sylvia could see the white sails of ships out at sea, and the clouds that were purple and rose-colored and yellow at first began to fade away. Where was the white heron's nest in the sea of green branches, and was this wonderful sight and pageant of the world the only reward for having climbed to such a giddy height? Now look down again, Sylvia, where the green marsh is set among the shining birches and dark hemlocks; there where you saw the white heron once you will see him again; look, look! a white spot of him like a single floating feather comes up from the dead hemlock and grows larger, and rises, and comes close at last, and goes by the landmark pine with steady sweep of wing and outstretched slender neck and crested head. And wait! wait! do not move a foot or a finger, little girl, do not send an arrow of light and consciousness from your two eager eyes, for the heron has perched on a pine bough not far beyond yours, and cries back to his mate on the nest, and plumes his feathers for the new day!

The child gives a long sigh a minute later when a company of shouting cat-birds comes also to the tree, and vexed by their fluttering and lawlessness the solemn heron goes away. She knows his secret now, the wild, light, slender bird that floats and wavers, and goes back like an arrow presently to his home in the green world beneath. Then Sylvia, well satisfied, makes her perilous way down again, not daring to look far below the branch she stands on, ready to cry sometimes because her fingers ache and her lamed feet slip. Wondering over and over again what the stranger would say to her, and what he would think when she told him how to find his way straight to the heron's nest.

"Sylvy, Sylvy!" called the busy old grandmother again and again, but nobody answered, and the small husk bed was empty, and Sylvia had disappeared.

The guest waked from a dream, and remembering his day's pleasure hurried to dress himself that it might sooner begin. He was sure from the way the shy little girl looked once or twice yesterday that she had at least seen the white heron, and now she must really be persuaded to tell. Here she comes now, paler than ever, and her worn old frock is torn and tattered, and smeared with pine pitch. The grandmother and the sportsman stand in the door together and question her, and the splendid moment has come to speak of the dead hemlock-tree by the green marsh.

But Sylvia does not speak after all, though the old grandmother fretfully rebukes her, and the young man's kind appealing eyes are looking straight in her own. He can make them rich with money; he has promised it, and they are poor now. He is so well worth making happy, and he waits to hear the story she can tell.

No, she must keep silence! What is it that suddenly forbids her and makes her dumb? Has she been nine years growing, and now, when the great world for the first time puts out a hand to her, must she thrust it aside for a bird's sake? The murmur of the pine's green branches is in her ears, she remembers how the white heron came flying through the golden air and how they watched the sea and the morning together, and Sylvia cannot speak; she cannot tell the heron's secret and give its life away.

Dear loyalty, that suffered a sharp pang as the guest went away disappointed later in the day, that could have served and followed him and loved him as a dog loves! Many a night Sylvia heard the echo of his whistle haunting the pasture path as she came home with the loitering cow. She forgot even her sorrow at the sharp report of his gun and the piteous sight of thrushes and sparrows dropping silent to the ground, their songs hushed and their pretty feathers stained and wet with blood. Were the birds better friends than their hunter might have been,—who can tell? Whatever treasures were lost to her, woodlands and summer-time, remember! Bring your gifts and graces and tell your secrets to this lonely country child!

WILLA CATHER

From Alexander's Bridge†

Chapter III

The next evening Alexander dined alone at a club, and at about nine o'clock he dropped in at the Duke of York's.[1] The house was sold out and he stood through the second act. When he returned to his hotel, he examined the new directory, and found Miss Burgoyne's address still given as off Bedford Square, though at a new number. He remembered that, in so far as she had been brought up at all, she had been brought up in Bloomsbury.[2] Her father and mother played in the provinces most of the year, and she was left a great deal in the care of an old aunt who was crippled by rheumatism and who had had to leave the stage altogether.

In the days when Alexander knew her, Hilda always managed to have a lodging of some sort about Bedford Square, because she clung tenaciously to such scraps and shreds of memories as were connected with it. The mummy room of the British Museum had been one of the chief delights of her childhood. That forbidding pile was the goal of her truant fancy, and she was sometimes taken there for a treat, as other children are taken to the theatre. It was long since Alexander had thought of any of these things, but now they came back to him quite fresh, and had a significance they did not have when they were first told him in his restless twenties. So she was still in the old neighborhood, near Bedford Square. The new number probably meant increased prosperity. He hoped so. He would like to know that she was snugly settled. He looked at his watch. It was a quarter past ten; she would not be home for a good two hours yet, and he might as well walk over and have a look at the place. He remembered the shortest way.

It was a warm, smoky evening, and there was a grimy moon. He went through Covent Garden to Oxford Street, and as he turned into Museum Street he walked more slowly, smiling at his own nervousness as he approached the sullen grey mass at the end. He had not been inside the Museum, actually, since he and Hilda used to meet there; sometimes to set out for gay adventures at Twicken-

† (Boston: Houghton Mifflin, 1912).
1. A well-known theater in London.
2. In the early twentieth century, Bloomsbury—a fashionable area in London's West End—became known for the "Bloomsbury group," a coterie of artists and writers who often met there to discuss political, aesthetic, and social issues.

ham or at Richmond,[3] sometimes to linger about the place for a while and to ponder by Lord Elgin's marbles[4] upon the lastingness of some things, or, in the mummy room, upon the awful brevity of others.

Since then Bartley had always thought of the British Museum as the ultimate repository of mortality, where all the dead things in the world were assembled to make one's hour of youth the more precious. One trembled lest before he got out it might somehow escape him, lest he might drop the glass from overeagerness and see it shivered on the stone floor at his feet. How one hid his youth under his coat and hugged it!

And how good it was to turn one's back upon all that vaulted cold, to take Hilda's arm and hurry out of the great door and down the steps into the sunlight among the pigeons—to know that the warm and vital thing within him was still there and had not been snatched away to flush Caesar's lean cheek or to feed the veins of some bearded Assyrian king. They in their day had carried the flaming liquor, but to-day was his! So the song used to run in his head those summer mornings a dozen years ago. Alexander walked by the place very quietly, as if he were afraid of waking someone.

He crossed Bedford Square and found the number he was looking for. The house, a comfortable, well-kept place enough, was dark except for the four front windows on the second floor, where a low, even light was burning behind the white muslin sash curtains. Outside there were window-boxes, painted white and full of flowers.

Bartley was making a third round of the Square when he heard the far-flung hoof-beats of a hansom-cab horse, driven rapidly. He looked at his watch, and was astonished to find that it was a few minutes after twelve. He turned and walked back along the iron railing as the cab came up to Hilda's number and stopped. The hansom must have been one that she employed regularly, for she did not stop to pay the driver. She stepped out quickly and lightly. He heard her cheerful 'Good night, cabby,' as she ran up the steps and opened the door with a latchkey. In a few moments the lights flared up brightly behind the white curtains, and as he walked away he heard a window raised. But he had gone too far to look up without turning round. He went back to his hotel, feeling that he had had a good evening, and he slept well.

For the next few days Alexander was very busy. He took a desk in

3. In the nineteenth century, Twickenham and Richmond, Thames-side villages southwest of London, were favorite sites for boating parties and picknickers.
4. In the early nineteenth century, Thomas Bruce, seventh Earl of Elgin (1766–1841) and ambassador to Constantinople, had many sculptures from Athens (including friezes from the Parthenon) removed to England. Placed on display in the British Museum, these became known as the "Elgin marbles."

the office of a Scotch engineering firm on Henrietta Street, and was at work almost constantly. He avoided the clubs and usually dined alone at his hotel. One afternoon, after he had tea, he started for a walk down the Embankment toward Westminster, intending to end his stroll at Bedford Square and to ask whether Miss Burgoyne would let him take her to the theatre. But he did not go so far. When he reached the Abbey, he turned back and crossed Westminster Bridge and sat down to watch the trails of smoke behind the Houses of Parliament catch fire with the sunset. The slender towers were washed by a rain of golden light and licked by little flickering flames; Somerset House and the bleached grey pinnacles about Whitehall were floated in a luminous haze. The yellow light poured through the trees and the leaves seemed to burn with soft fires. There was a smell of acacias in the air everywhere, and the laburnums were dripping gold over the walls of the gardens. It was a sweet, lonely kind of summer evening. Remembering Hilda as she used to be was doubtless more satisfactory than seeing her as she must be now—and, after all, Alexander asked himself, what was it but his own young years that he was remembering?

He crossed back to Westminster, went up to the Temple, and sat down to smoke in the Middle Temple[5] gardens, listening to the thin voice of the fountain and smelling the spice of the sycamores that came out heavily in the damp evening air. He thought, as he sat there, about a great many things: about his own youth and Hilda's; above all, he thought of how glorious it had been, and how quickly it had passed; and, when it had passed, how little worth while anything was. None of the things he had gained in the least compensated. In the last six years his reputation had become, as the saying is, popular. Four years ago he had been called to Japan to deliver, at the Emperor's request, a course of lectures at the Imperial University, and had instituted reforms throughout the islands, not only in the practice of bridge-building, but in drainage and road-making. On his return he had undertaken the bridge at Moorlock, in Canada, the most important piece of bridge-building going on in the world—a test, indeed, of how far the latest practice in bridge-structure could be carried. It was a spectacular undertaking by reason of its very size, and Bartley realized that, whatever else he might do, he would probably always be known as the engineer who designed the great Moorlock Bridge, the longest cantilever in existence. Yet it was to him the least satisfactory thing he had ever done. He was cramped in every way to a niggardly commission, and was using lighter structural material than he thought proper. He

5. Temple and Middle Temple are two of the four Inns of Court (societies for the study of law), located on the south side of Fleet Street in London.

had vexations enough, too, with his work at home. He had several bridges under way in the United States, and they were always being held up by strikes and delays resulting from a general industrial unrest.

Though Alexander often told himself he had never put more into his work than he had done in the last few years, he had to admit that he had never got so little out of it. He was paying for success, too, in the demands made on his time by boards of civic enterprise and committees of public welfare. The obligations imposed by his wife's fortune and position were sometimes distracting to a man who followed his profession, and he was expected to be interested in a great many worthy endeavours on her account as well as on his own. His existence was becoming a network of great and little details. He had expected that success would bring him freedom and power; but it had brought only power that was in itself another kind of restraint. He had always meant to keep his personal liberty at all costs, as old MacKeller, his first chief, had done, and not, like so many American engineers, to become a part of a professional movement, a cautious board member, a Nestor *de pontibus*.[6] He happened to be engaged in work of public utility, but he was not willing to become what is called a public man.

He found himself living exactly the kind of life he had determined to escape. What, he asked himself, did he want with these genial honours and substantial comforts? Hardships and difficulties he had carried lightly; overwork had not exhausted him; but this dead calm of middle life which confronted him—of that he was afraid. He was not ready for it. It was like being buried alive. In his youth he would not have believed such a thing possible. The one thing he had really wanted all his life was to be free; and there was still something unconquered in him, something besides the strong work-horse that his profession had made of him. He felt rich tonight in the possession of that unstultified survival; in the light of his experience, it was more precious than honours or achievement. In all those busy, successful years there had been nothing so good as this hour of wild light-heartedness. This feeling was the only happiness that was real to him, and such hours were the only ones in which he could feel his own continuous identity—feel the boy he had been in the rough days of the old West, feel the youth who had worked his way across the ocean on a cattle-ship and gone to study in Paris without a dollar in his pocket.

The man who sat in his offices in Boston was only a powerful machine. Under the activities of that machine the person who, at

6. In Greek mythology, Nestor is a wise counselor, too old for combat. "*De pontibus*": of bridges.

such moments as this, he felt to be himself, was fading and dying. He remembered how, when he was a little boy and his father called him in the morning, he used to leap from his bed into the full consciousness of himself. That consciousness was Life itself. Whatever took its place, action, reflection, the power of concentrated thought, were only functions of a mechanism useful to society; things that could be bought in the market. There was only one thing that had an absolute value for each individual, and it was just that original impulse, that internal heat, that feeling of one's self in one's own breast.

When Alexander walked back to his hotel, the red and green lights were blinking along the docks on the farther shore, and the soft white stars were shining in the wide sky above the river.

The next night, and the next, Alexander repeated this same foolish performance. It was always Miss Burgoyne whom he started out to find, and he got no farther than the Temple gardens and the Embankment. It was a pleasant kind of loneliness. To a man who was so little given to reflection, whose dreams always took the form of definite ideas, reaching into the future, there was a seductive excitement in renewing old experiences in imagination. He started out upon these walks half-guiltily, with a curious longing and expectancy which were wholly gratified by solitude. Solitude, but not solitariness; for he walked shoulder to shoulder with a shadowy companion—not little Hilda Burgoyne, by any means, but someone vastly dearer to him than she had ever been—his own young self, the youth who had waited for him upon the steps of the British Museum that night, and who, though he had tried to pass so quietly, had known him and come down and linked an arm in his.

It was not until long afterward that Alexander learned that for him this youth was the most dangerous of companions.

* * *

WILLA CATHER

The Bohemian Girl†

The transcontinental express swung along the windings of the Sand River Valley, and in the rear seat of the observation car a young man sat greatly at his ease, not in the least discomfited by the fierce

† Cather wrote this story of the Nebraska Divide in 1912, when she was just beginning work on *O Pioneers!* "The Bohemian Girl" was published in *McClure's* in August 1912.

sunlight which beat in upon his brown face and neck and strong back. There was a look of relaxation and of great passivity about his broad shoulders, which seemed almost too heavy until he stood up and squared them. He wore a pale flannel shirt and a blue silk necktie with loose ends. His trousers were wide and belted at the waist, and his short sack coat hung open. His heavy shoes had seen good service. His reddish-brown hair, like his clothes, had a foreign cut. He had deep-set, dark blue eyes under heavy reddish eyebrows. His face was kept clean only by close shaving, and even the sharpest razor left a glint of yellow in the smooth brown of his skin. His teeth and the palms of his hands were very white. His head, which looked hard and stubborn, lay indolently in the green cushion of the wicker chair, and as he looked out at the ripe summer country a teasing, not unkindly smile played over his lips. Once, as he basked thus comfortably, a quick light flashed in his eyes, curiously dilating the pupils, and his mouth became a hard, straight line, gradually relaxing into its former smile of rather kindly mockery. He told himself, apparently, that there was no point in getting excited; and he seemed a master hand at taking his ease when he could. Neither the sharp whistle of the locomotive nor the brakeman's call disturbed him. It was not until after the train had stopped that he rose, put on a Panama hat, took from the rack a small valise and a flute case, and stepped deliberately to the station platform. The baggage was already unloaded, and the stranger presented a check for a battered sole-leather steamer trunk.

"Can you keep it here for a day or two?" he asked the agent. "I may send for it, and I may not."

"Depends on whether you like the country, I suppose?" demanded the agent in a challenging tone.

"Just so."

The agent shrugged his shoulders, looked scornfully at the small trunk, which was marked "N. E.," and handed out a claim check without further comment. The stranger watched him as he caught one end of the trunk and dragged it into the express room. The agent's manner seemed to remind him of something amusing. "Doesn't seem to be a very big place," he remarked, looking about.

"It's big enough for us," snapped the agent, as he banged the trunk into a corner.

That remark, apparently, was what Nils Ericson had wanted. He chuckled quietly as he took a leather strap from his pocket and swung his valise around his shoulder. Then he settled his Panama securely on his head, turned up his trousers, tucked the flute case under his arm, and started off across the fields. He gave the town, as he would have said, a wide berth, and cut through a great fenced pasture, emerging, when he rolled under the barbed wire at the farther corner, upon a white dusty road which ran straight up from the river valley to the high prairies, where the ripe wheat stood yellow and the tin roofs and weathercocks were twinkling in the fierce sunlight. By the time Nils had done three miles, the sun was sinking and the farm wagons on their way home from town came rattling by, covering him with dust and making him sneeze. When one of the farmers pulled up and offered to give him a lift, he clambered in willingly. The driver was a thin, grizzled old man with a long lean neck and a foolish sort of beard, like a goat's. "How fur ye goin'?" he asked, as he clucked to his horses and started off.

"Do you go by the Ericson place?"

"Which Ericson?" The old man drew in his reins as if he expected to stop again.

"Preacher Ericson's."

"Oh, the Old Lay Ericson's!" He turned and looked at Nils. "La, me! If you're goin' out there you might 'a' rid out in the automobile. That's a pity, now. The Old Lady Ericson was in town with her auto. You might 'a' heard it snortin' anywhere about the post office er the butcher shop."

"Has she a motor?" asked the stranger absently.

" 'Deed an' she has! She runs into town every night about this time for her mail and meat for supper. Some folks say she's afraid her auto won't get exercise enough, but I say that's jealousy."

"Aren't there any other motors about here?"

"Oh, yes! we have fourteen in all. But nobody else gets around like the Old Lady Ericson. She's out, rain er shine, over the whole county, chargin' into town and out amongst her farms, an' up to her sons' places. Sure you ain't goin' to the wrong place?" He craned his neck and looked at Nils' flute case with eager curiosity. "The old woman ain't got any piany that I knows on. Olaf, he has a grand. His wife's musical; took lessons in Chicago."

"I'm going up there tomorrow," said Nils imperturbably. He saw that the driver took him for a piano tuner.

"Oh, I see!" The old man screwed up his eyes mysteriously. He was a little dashed by the stranger's noncommunicativeness, but he soon broke out again.

"I'm one o' Mis' Ericson's tenants. Look after one of her places. I did own the place myself oncet, but I lost it a while back, in the bad years just after the World's Fair.[1] Just as well, too, I say. Lets you out o' payin' taxes. The Ericsons do own most of the country now. I remember the old preacher's fav'rite text used to be, 'To them that hath shall be given.'[2] They've spread something wonderful—run

1. The year 1893 marked both the Chicago World's Fair (the "World's Columbian Exposition") and the beginning of a devastating economic depression (the Panic of 1893).
2. Cf. Matthew 13.12, 25.29, Mark 4.25, Luke 8.18.

over this here country like bindweed. But I ain't one that begretches it to 'em. Folks is entitled to what they kin git; and they're hustlers. Olaf, he's in the Legislature now, and a likely man fur Congress. Listen, if that ain't the old woman comin' now. Want I should stop her?"

Nils shook his head. He heard the deep chug-chug of a motor vibrating steadily in the clear twilight behind them. The pale lights of the car swam over the hill, and the old man slapped his reins and turned clear out of the road, ducking his head at the first of three angry snorts from behind. The motor was running at a hot, even speed, and passed without turning an inch from its course. The driver was a stalwart woman who sat at ease in the front seat and drove her car bareheaded. She left a cloud of dust and a trail of gasoline behind her. Her tenant threw back his head and sneezed.

"Whew! I sometimes say I'd as lief be *before* Mrs. Ericson as behind her. She does beat all! Nearly seventy, and never lets another soul touch that car. Puts it into commission herself every morning, and keeps it tuned up by the hitch-bar all day. I never stop work for a drink o' water that I don't hear her a-churnin' up the road. I reckon her darter-in-laws never sets down easy nowadays. Never know when she'll pop in. Mis' Otto, she says to me: 'We're so afraid that thing'll blow up and do Ma some injury yet, she's so turrible venturesome.' Says I: 'I wouldn't stew, Mis' Otto; the old lady'll drive that car to the funeral of every darter-in-law she's got.' That was after the old woman had jumped a turrible bad culvert."

The stranger heard vaguely what the old man was saying. Just now he was experiencing something very much like homesickness, and he was wondering what had brought it about. The mention of a name or two, perhaps; the rattle of a wagon along a dusty road; the rank, resinous smell of sunflowers and ironweed, which the night damp brought up from the draws and low places; perhaps, more than all, the dancing lights of the motor that had plunged by. He squared his shoulders with a comfortable sense of strength.

The wagon, as it jolted westward, climbed a pretty steady upgrade. The country, receding from the rough river valley, swelled more and more gently, as if it had been smoothed out by the wind. On one of the last of the rugged ridges, at the end of a branch road, stood a grim square house with a tin roof and double porches. Behind the house stretched a row of broken, wind-racked poplars, and down the hill slope to the left straggled the sheds and stables. The old man stopped his horses where the Ericsons' road branched across a dry sand creek that wound about the foot of the hill.

"That's the old lady's place. Want I should drive in?"

"No, thank you. I'll roll out here. Much obliged to you. Good night."

His passenger stepped down over the front wheel, and the old man drove on reluctantly, looking back as if he would like to see how the stranger would be received.

As Nils was crossing the dry creek he heard the restive tramp of a horse coming toward him down the hill. Instantly he flashed out of the road and stood behind a thicket of wild plum bushes that grew in the sandy bed. Peering through the dusk, he saw a light horse, under tight rein, descending the hill at a sharp walk. The rider was a slender woman—barely visible against the dark hill-side—wearing an old-fashioned derby hat and a long riding skirt. She sat lightly in the saddle, with her chin high, and seemed to be looking into the distance. As she passed the plum thicket her horse snuffed the air and shied. She struck him, pulling him in sharply, with an angry exclamation, "*Blázne!*" in Bohemian.[3] Once in the main road, she let him out into a lope, and they soon emerged upon the crest of high land, where they moved along the skyline, silhouetted against the band of faint color that lingered in the west. This horse and rider, with their free, rhythmical gallop, were the only moving things to be seen on the face of the flat country. They seemed, in the last sad light of evening, not to be there accidentally, but as an inevitable detail of the landscape.

Nils watched them until they had shrunk to a mere moving speck against the sky, then he crossed the sand creek and climbed the hill. When he reached the gate the front of the house was dark, but a light was shining from the side windows. The pigs were squealing in the hog corral, and Nils could see a tall boy, who carried two big wooden buckets, moving about among them. Halfway between the barn and the house, the windmill wheezed lazily. Following the path that ran around to the back porch, Nils stopped to look through the screen door into the lamplit kitchen. The kitchen was the largest room in the house; Nils remembered that his older brothers used to give dances there when he was a boy. Beside the stove stood a little girl with two light yellow braids and a broad, flushed face, peering anxiously into a frying pan. In the dining room beyond, a large, broad-shouldered woman was moving about the table. She walked with an active, springy step. Her face was heavy and florid, almost without wrinkles, and her hair was black at seventy. Nils felt proud of her as he watched her deliberate activity; never a momentary hesitation, or a movement that did not tell. He

3. *Damn!*

waited until she came out into the kitchen and, brushing the child aside, took her place at the stove. Then he tapped on the screen door and entered.

"It's nobody but Nils, Mother. I expect you weren't looking for me."

Mrs. Ericson turned away from the stove and stood staring at him. "Bring the lamp, Hilda, and let me look."

Nils laughed and unslung his valise. "What's the matter, Mother? Don't you know me?"

Mrs. Ericson put down the lamp. "You must be Nils. You don't look very different, anyway."

"Nor you, Mother. You hold your own. Don't you wear glasses yet?"

"Only to read by. Where's your trunk, Nils?"

"Oh, I left that in town. I thought it might not be convenient for you to have company so near threshing-time."

"Don't be foolish, Nils." Mrs. Ericson turned back to the stove. "I don't thresh now. I hitched the wheat land onto the next farm and have a tenant. Hilda, take some hot water up to the company room, and go call little Eric."

The tow-haired child, who had been standing in mute amazement, took up the tea kettle and withdrew, giving Nils a long, admiring look from the door of the kitchen stairs.

"Who's the youngster?" Nils asked, dropping down on the bench behind the kitchen stove.

"One of your Cousin Henrik's."

"How long has Cousin Henrik been dead?"

"Six years. There are two boys. One stays with Peter and one with Anders. Olaf is their guardeen."

There was a clatter of pails on the porch, and a tall, lanky boy peered wonderingly in through the screen door. He had a fair, gentle face and big gray eyes, and wisps of soft yellow hair hung down under his cap. Nils sprang up and pulled him into the kitchen, hugging him and slapping him on the shoulders. "Well, if it isn't my kid! Look at the size of him! Don't you know me, Eric?"

The boy reddened under his sunburn and freckles, and hung his head. "I guess it's Nils," he said shyly.

"You're a good guesser," laughed Nils giving the lad's hand a swing. To himself he was thinking: "That's why the little girl looked so friendly. He's taught her to like me. He was only six when I went away, and he's remembered for twelve years."

Eric stood fumbling with his cap and smiling. "You look just like I thought you would," he ventured.

"Go wash your hands, Eric," called Mrs. Ericson. "I've got cob corn for supper, Nils. You used to like it. I guess you don't get much of that in the old country. Here's Hilda; she'll take you up to your room. You'll want to get the dust off you before you eat."

Mrs. Ericson went into the dining room to lay another plate, and the little girl came up and nodded to Nils as if to let him know that his room was ready. He put out his hand and she took it, with a startled glance up at his face. Little Eric dropped his towel, threw an arm about Nils and one about Hilda, gave them a clumsy squeeze, and then stumbled out to the porch.

During supper Nils heard exactly how much land each of his eight grown brothers farmed, how their crops were coming on, and how much live stock they were feeding. His mother watched him narrowly as she talked. "You've got better looking, Nils," she remarked abruptly, whereupon he grinned and the children giggled. Eric, although he was eighteen and as tall as Nils, was always accounted a child, being the last of so many sons. His face seemed childlike, too, Nils thought, and he had the open, wandering eyes of a little boy. All the others had been men at his age.

After supper Nils went out to the front porch and sat down on the step to smoke a pipe. Mrs. Ericson drew a rocking chair up near him and began to knit busily. It was one of the few Old World customs she had kept up, for she could not bear to sit with idle hands.

"Where's little Eric, Mother?"

"He's helping Hilda with the dishes. He does it of his own will; I don't like a boy to be too handy about the house."

"He seems like a nice kid."

"He's very obedient."

Nils smiled a little in the dark. It was just as well to shift the line of conversation. "What are you knitting there, Mother?"

"Baby stockings. The boys keep me busy." Mrs. Ericson chuckled and clicked her needles.

"How many grandchildren have you?"

"Only thirty-one now. Olaf lost his three. They were sickly, like their mother."

"I supposed he had a second crop by this time!"

"His second wife has no children. She's too proud. She tears about on horseback all the time. But she'll get caught up with, yet. She sets herself very high, though nobody knows what for. They were low enough Bohemians she came of. I never thought much of Bohemians; always drinking."

Nils puffed away at his pipe in silence, and Mrs. Ericson knitted on. In a few moments she added grimly: "She was down here tonight, just before you came. She'd like to quarrel with me and come between me and Olaf, but I don't give her the chance. I suppose you'll be bringing a wife home some day."

"I don't know. I've never thought much about it."

"Well, perhaps it's best as it is," suggested Mrs. Ericson hopefully. "You'd never be contented tied down to the land. There was roving blood in your father's family, and it's come out in you. I expect your own way of life suits you best." Mrs. Ericson had dropped into a blandly agreeable tone which Nils well remembered. It seemed to amuse him a good deal and his white teeth flashed behind his pipe. His mother's strategies had always diverted him, even when he was a boy—they were so flimsy and patent, so illy proportioned to her vigor and force. "They've been waiting to see which way I'd jump," he reflected. He felt that Mrs. Ericson was pondering his case deeply as she sat clicking her needles.

"I don't suppose you've ever got used to steady work," she went on presently. "Men ain't apt to if they roam around too long. It's a pity you didn't come back the year after the World's Fair. Your father picked up a good bit of land cheap then, in the hard times, and I expect maybe he'd have give you a farm. It's too bad you put off comin' back so long, for I always thought he meant to do something by you."

Nils laughed and shook the ashes out of his pipe. "I'd have missed a lot if I had come back then. But I'm sorry I didn't get back to see father."

"Well, I suppose we have to miss things at one end or the other. Perhaps you are as well satisfied with your own doings, now, as you'd have been with a farm," said Mrs. Ericson reassuringly.

"Land's a good thing to have," Nils commented, as he lit another match and sheltered it with his hand.

His mother looked sharply at his face until the match burned out. "Only when you stay on it!" she hastened to say.

Eric came round the house by the path just then, and Nils rose, with a yawn. "Mother, if you don't mind, Eric and I will take a little tramp before bedtime. It will make me sleep."

"Very well; only don't stay long. I'll sit up and wait for you. I like to lock up myself."

Nils put his hand on Eric's shoulder, and the two tramped down the hill and across the sand creek into the dusty highroad beyond. Neither spoke. They swung along at an even gait, Nils puffing at his pipe. There was no moon, and the white road and the wide fields lay faint in the starlight. Over everything was darkness and thick silence, and the smell of dust and sunflowers. The brothers followed the road for a mile or more without finding a place to sit down. Finally, Nils perched on a stile over the wire fence, and Eric sat on the lower step.

"I began to think you never would come back, Nils," said the boy softly.

"Didn't I promise you I would?"

"Yes; but people don't bother about promises they make to babies. Did you really know you were going away for good when you went to Chicago with the cattle that time?"

"I thought it very likely, if I could make my way."

"I don't see how you did it, Nils. Not many fellows could." Eric rubbed his shoulder against his brother's knee.

"The hard thing was leaving home—you and father. It was easy enough, once I got beyond Chicago. Of course I got awful homesick; used to cry myself to sleep. But I'd burned my bridges."

"You had always wanted to go, hadn't you?"

"Always. Do you still sleep in our little room? Is that cottonwood still by the window?"

Eric nodded eagerly and smiled up at his brother in the gray darkness.

"You remember how we always said the leaves were whispering when they rustled at night? Well, they always whispered to me about the sea. Sometimes they said names out of the geography books. In a high wind they had a desperate sound, like something trying to tear loose."

"How funny, Nils," said Eric dreamily, resting his chin on his hand. "That tree still talks like that, and 'most always it talks to me about you."

They sat a while longer, watching the stars. At last Eric whispered anxiously: "Hadn't we better go back now? Mother will get tired waiting for us." They rose and took a short cut home, through the pasture.

II

The next morning Nils woke with the first flood of light that came with dawn. The white-plastered walls of his room reflected the glare that shone through the thin window shades, and he found it impossible to sleep. He dressed hurriedly and slipped down the hall and up the back stairs to the half-story room which he used to share with his little brother. Eric, in a skimpy nightshirt, was sitting on the edge of the bed, rubbing his eyes, his pale yellow hair standing up in tufts all over his head. When he saw Nils, he murmured something confusedly and hustled his long legs into his trousers. "I didn't expect you'd be up so early, Nils," he said, as his head emerged from his blue shirt.

"Oh, you thought I was a dude, did you?" Nils gave him a playful tap which bent the tall boy up like a clasp knife. "See here; I must teach you to box." Nils thrust his hands into his pockets and walked about. "You haven't changed things much up here. Got most of my old traps, haven't you?"

He took down a bent, withered piece of sapling that hung over the dresser. "If this isn't the stick Lou Sandberg killed himself with!"

The boy looked up from his shoe-lacing.

"Yes; you never used to let me play with that. Just how did he do it, Nils? You were with father when he found Lou, weren't you?"

"Yes. Father was going off to preach somewhere, and, as we drove along, Lou's place looked sort of forlorn, and we thought we'd stop and cheer him up. When we found him father said he'd been dead a couple days. He'd tied a piece of binding twine round his neck, made a noose in each end, fixed the nooses over the ends of a bent stick, and let the stick spring straight; strangled himself."

"What made him kill himself such a silly way?"

The simplicity of the boy's question set Nils laughing. He clapped little Eric on the shoulder. "What made him such a silly as to kill himself at all, I should say!"

"Oh, well! But his hogs had the cholera, and all up and died on him, didn't they?"

"Sure they did; but he didn't have cholera; and there were plenty of hogs left in the world, weren't there?"

"Well, but, if they weren't his, how could they do him any good?" Eric asked, in astonishment.

"Oh, scat! He could have had lots of fun with other people's hogs. He was a chump, Lou Sandberg. To kill yourself for a pig—think of that, now!" Nils laughed all the way downstairs, and quite embarrassed little Eric, who fell to scrubbing his face and hands at the tin basin. While he was parting his wet hair at the kitchen looking glass, a heavy tread sounded on the stairs. The boy dropped his comb. "Gracious, there's Mother. We must have talked too long." He hurried out to the shed, slipped on his overalls, and disappeared with the milking pails.

Mrs. Ericson came in, wearing a clean white apron, her black hair shining from the application of a wet brush.

"Good morning, Mother. Can't I make the fire for you?"

"No, thank you, Nils. It's no trouble to make a cob fire, and I like to manage the kitchen stove myself." Mrs. Ericson paused with a shovel full of ashes in her hand. "I expect you will be wanting to see your brothers as soon as possible. I'll take you up to Anders' place this morning. He's threshing, and most of our boys are over there."

"Will Olaf be there?"

Mrs. Ericson went on taking out the ashes, and spoke between shovels. "No; Olaf's wheat is all in, put away in his new barn. He got six thousand bushel this year. He's going to town today to get men to finish roofing his barn."

"So Olaf is building a new barn?" Nils asked absently.

"Biggest one in the country, and almost done. You'll likely be here for the barn-raising. He's going to have a supper and a dance as soon as everybody's done threshing. Says it keeps the voters in a good humor. I tell him that's all nonsense; but Olaf has a long head for politics."

"Does Olaf farm all Cousin Henrik's land?"

Mrs. Ericson frowned as she blew into the faint smoke curling up about the cobs. "Yes; he holds it in trust for the children, Hilda and her brothers. He keeps strict account of everything he raises on it, and puts the proceeds out at compound interest for them."

Nils smiled as he watched the little flames shoot up. The door of the back stairs opened, and Hilda emerged, her arms behind her, buttoning up her long gingham apron as she came. He nodded to her gaily, and she twinkled at him out of her little blue eyes, set far apart over her wide cheekbones.

"There, Hilda, you grind the coffee—and just put in an extra handful; I expect your Cousin Nils likes his strong," said Mrs. Ericson, as she went out to the shed.

Nils turned to look at the little girl, who gripped the coffee grinder between her knees and ground so hard that her two braids bobbed and her face flushed under its broad spattering of freckles. He noticed on her middle finger something that had not been there last night, and that had evidently been put on for company: a tiny gold ring with a clumsily set garnet stone. As her hand went round and round he touched the ring with the tip of his finger, smiling.

Hilda glanced toward the shed door through which Mrs. Ericson had disappeared. "My Cousin Clara gave me that," she whispered bashfully. "She's Cousin Olaf's wife."

III

Mrs. Olaf Ericson—Clara Vavrika, as many people still called her—was moving restlessly about her big bare house that morning. Her husband had left for the country town before his wife was out of bed—her lateness in rising was one of the many things the Ericson family had against her. Clara seldom came downstairs before eight o'clock, and this morning she was even later, for she had dressed with unusual care. She put on, however, only a tight-fitting black dress, which people thereabouts thought very plain. She was a tall, dark woman of thirty, with a rather sallow complexion and a touch of dull salmon red in her cheeks, where the blood seemed to burn under her brown skin. Her hair, parted evenly above her low forehead, was so black that there were distinctly blue lights in it. Her black eyebrows were delicate half-moons and her lashes were long and heavy. Her eyes slanted a little, as if she had a strain of Tartar or gypsy blood, and were sometimes full of fiery determination and sometimes dull and opaque. Her expression was never altogether amiable; was often, indeed, distinctly sullen, or, when she was animated, sarcastic. She was most attractive in profile, for then one saw to advantage her small, well-shaped head and delicate ears, and felt at once that here was a very positive, if not an altogether pleasing, personality.

The entire management of Mrs. Olaf's household devolved upon her aunt, Johanna Vavrika, a superstitious, doting woman of fifty. When Clara was a little girl her mother died, and Johanna's life had been spent in ungrudging service to her niece. Clara, like many self-willed and discontented persons, was really very apt, without knowing it, to do as other people told her, and to let her destiny be decided for her by intelligences much below her own. It was her Aunt Johanna who had humored and spoiled her in her girlhood, who had got her off to Chicago to study piano, and who had finally persuaded her to marry Olaf Ericson as the best match she would be likely to make in that part of the country. Johanna Vavrika had been deeply scarred by smallpox in the old country. She was short and fat, homely and jolly and sentimental. She was so broad, and took such short steps when she walked, that her brother, Joe Vavrika, always called her his duck. She adored her niece because of her talent, because of her good looks and masterful ways, but most of all because of her selfishness.

Clara's marriage with Olaf Ericson was Johanna's particular triumph. She was inordinately proud of Olaf's position, and she found a sufficiently exciting career in managing Clara's house, in keeping it above the criticism of the Ericsons, in pampering Olaf to keep him from finding fault with his wife, and in concealing from every one Clara's domestic infelicities. While Clara slept of a morning, Johanna Vavrika was bustling about, seeing that Olaf and the men had their breakfast, and that the cleaning or the butter-making or the washing was properly begun by the two girls in the kitchen. Then, at about eight o'clock, she would take Clara's coffee up to her, and chat with her while she drank it, telling her what was going on in the house. Old Mrs. Ericson frequently said that her daughter-in-law would not know what day of the week it was if Johanna did not tell her every morning. Mrs. Ericson despised and pitied Johanna, but did not wholly dislike her. The one thing she hated in her daughter-in-law above everything else was the way in which Clara could come it over people. It enraged her that the affairs of her son's big, barnlike house went on as well as they did, and she used to feel that in this world we have to wait overlong to see the guilty punished. "Suppose Johanna Vavrika died or got sick?" the old lady used to say to Olaf. "Your wife wouldn't know where to look for her own dishcloth." Olaf only shrugged his shoulders. The fact remained that Johanna did not die, and, although Mrs. Ericson often told her she was looking poorly, she was never ill. She seldom left the house, and she slept in a little room off the kitchen. No Ericson, by night or day, could come prying about there to find fault without her knowing it. Her one weakness was that she was an incurable talker, and she sometimes made trouble without meaning to.

This morning Clara was tying a wine-colored ribbon about her throat when Johanna appeared with her coffee. After putting the tray on a sewing table, she began to make Clara's bed, chattering the while in Bohemian.

"Well, Olaf got off early, and the girls are baking. I'm going down presently to make some poppy-seed bread for Olaf. He asked for prune preserves at breakfast, and I told him I was out of them, and to bring some prunes and honey and cloves from town."

Clara poured her coffee. "Ugh! I don't see how men can eat so much sweet stuff. In the morning, too!"

Her aunt chuckled knowingly. "Bait a bear with honey, as we say in the old country."

"Was he cross?" her niece asked indifferently.

"Olaf? Oh, no! He was in fine spirits. He's never cross if you know how to take him. I never knew a man to make so little fuss about bills. I gave him a list of things to get a yard long, and he didn't say a word; just folded it up and put it in his pocket."

"I can well believe he didn't say a word," Clara remarked with a shrug. "Some day he'll forget how to talk."

"Oh, but they say he's a grand speaker in the Legislature. He knows when to keep quiet. That's why he's got such influence in politics. The people have confidence in him." Johanna beat up a pillow and held it under her fat chin while she slipped on the case. Her niece laughed.

"Maybe we could make people believe we were wise, Aunty, if we held our tongues. Why did you tell Mrs. Ericson that Norman threw me again last Saturday and turned my foot? She's been talking to Olaf."

Johanna fell into great confusion. "Oh, but, my precious, the old lady asked for you, and she's always so angry if I can't give an excuse. Anyhow, she needn't talk; she's always tearing up something with that motor of hers."

When her aunt clattered down to the kitchen, Clara went to dust the parlor. Since there was not much there to dust, this did not take very long. Olaf had built the house new for her before their marriage, but her interest in furnishing it had been short-lived. It went, indeed, little beyond a bathtub and her piano. They had disagreed about almost every other article of furniture, and Clara had said she would rather have her house empty than full of things she didn't want. The house was set in a hillside, and the west windows of the parlor looked out above the kitchen yard thirty feet below. The east windows opened directly into the front yard. At one of the latter, Clara, while she was dusting, heard a low whistle. She did not turn at once, but listened intently as she drew her cloth slowly along the round of a chair. Yes, there it was:

I dreamt that I dwelt in ma-a-arble halls.[4]

She turned and saw Nils Ericson laughing in the sunlight, his hat in his hand, just outside the window. As she crossed the room he leaned against the wire screen. "Aren't you at all surprised to see me, Clara Vavrika?"

"No; I was expecting to see you. Mother Ericson telephoned Olaf last night that you were here."

Nils squinted and gave a long whistle. "Telephoned? That must have been while Eric and I were out walking. Isn't she enterprising? Lift this screen, won't you?"

Clara lifted the screen, and Nils swung his leg across the window sill. As he stepped into the room she said: "You didn't think you were going to get ahead of your mother, did you?"

He threw his hat on the piano. "Oh, I do sometimes. You see, I'm ahead of her now. I'm supposed to be in Anders' wheat field. But, as we were leaving, Mother ran her car into a soft place beside the road and sank up to the hubs. While they were going for horses to pull her out, I cut away behind the stacks and escaped." Nils chuckled. Clara's dull eyes lit up as she looked at him admiringly.

"You've got them guessing already. I don't know what your mother said to Olaf over the telephone, but he came back looking as if he'd seen a ghost, and he didn't go to bed until a dreadful hour—ten o'clock, I should think. He sat out on the porch in the dark like a graven image. It had been one of his talkative days, too." They both laughed, easily and lightly, like people who have laughed a great deal together; but they remained standing.

"Anders and Otto and Peter looked as if they had seen ghosts, too, over in the threshing field. What's the matter with them all?"

4. A song from *The Bohemian Girl* (1843), a popular opera by the Irish composer Michael Balfe, with the libretto by Alfred Bunn. All the other songs mentioned in the story are from this opera.

Clara gave him a quick, searching look. "Well, for one thing, they've always been afraid you have the other will."

Nils looked interested. "The other will?"

"Yes. A later one. They knew your father made another, but they never knew what he did with it. They almost tore the old house to pieces looking for it. They always suspected that he carried on a clandestine correspondence with you, for the one thing he would do was to get his own mail himself. So they thought he might have sent the new will to you for safekeeping. The old one, leaving everything to your mother, was made long before you went away, and it's understood among them that it cuts you out—that she will leave all the property to the others. Your father made the second will to prevent that. I've been hoping you had it. It would be such fun to spring it on them." Clara laughed mirthfully, a thing she did not often do now.

Nils shook his head reprovingly. "Come, now, you're malicious."

"No, I'm not. But I'd like something to happen to stir them all up, just for once. There never was such a family for having nothing ever happen to them but dinner and threshing. I'd almost be willing to die, just to have a funeral. *You* wouldn't stand it for three weeks."

Nils bent over the piano and began pecking at the keys with the finger of one hand. "I wouldn't? My dear young lady, how do you know what I can stand? *You* wouldn't wait to find out."

Clara flushed darkly and frowned. "I didn't believe you would ever come back—" she said defiantly.

"Eric believed I would, and he was only a baby when I went away. However, all's well that ends well, and I haven't come back to be a skeleton at the feast. We mustn't quarrel. Mother will be here with a search warrant pretty soon." He swung round and faced her; thrusting his hands into his coat pockets. "Come, you ought to be glad to see me, if you want something to happen. I'm something, even without a will. We can have a little fun, can't we? I think we can!"

She echoed him, "I think we can!" They both laughed and their eyes sparkled. Clara Vavrika looked ten years younger than when she had put the velvet ribbon about her throat that morning.

"You know, I'm so tickled to see mother," Nils went on. "I didn't know I was so proud of her. A regular pile driver. How about little pigtails, down at the house? Is Olaf doing the square thing by those children?"

Clara frowned pensively. "Olaf has to do something that looks like the square thing, now that he's a public man!" She glanced drolly at Nils. "But he makes a good commission out of it. On Sundays they all get together here and figure. He lets Peter and Anders put in big bills for the keep of the two boys, and he pays them out of the estate. They are always having what they call accountings.

Olaf gets something out of it, too. I don't know just how they do it, but it's entirely a family matter, as they say. And when the Ericsons say that—" Clara lifted her eyebrows.

Just then the angry *honk-honk* of an approaching motor sounded from down the road. Their eyes met and they began to laugh. They laughed as children do when they can not contain themselves, and can not explain the cause of their mirth to grown people, but share it perfectly together. When Clara Vavrika sat down at the piano after he was gone, she felt that she had laughed away a dozen years. She practised as if the house were burning over her head.

When Nils greeted his mother and climbed into the front seat of the motor beside her, Mrs. Ericson looked grim, but she made no comment upon his truancy until she had turned her car and was retracing her revolutions along the road that ran by Olaf's big pasture. Then she remarked dryly:

"If I were you I wouldn't see too much of Olaf's wife while you are here. She's the kind of woman who can't see much of men without getting herself talked about. She was a good deal talked about before he married her."

"Hasn't Olaf tamed her?" Nils asked indifferently.

Mrs. Ericson shrugged her massive shoulders. "Olaf don't seem to have much luck, when it comes to wives. The first one was meek enough, but she was always ailing. And this one has her own way. He says if he quarreled with her she'd go back to her father, and then he'd lose the Bohemian vote. There are a great many Bohunks in this district. But when you find a man under his wife's thumb you can always be sure there's a soft spot in him somewhere."

Nils thought of his own father, and smiled. "She brought him a good deal of money, didn't she, besides the Bohemian vote?"

Mrs. Ericson sniffed. "Well, she has a fair half section[5] in her own name, but I can't see as that does Olaf much good. She will have a good deal of property some day, if old Vavrika don't marry again. But I don't consider a saloonkeeper's money as good as other people's money."

Nils laughed outright. "Come, Mother, don't let your prejudices carry you that far. Money's money. Old Vavrika's a mighty decent sort of saloonkeeper. Nothing rowdy about him."

Mrs. Ericson spoke up angrily: "Oh, I know you always stood up for them! But hanging around there when you were a boy never did you any good, Nils, nor any of the other boys who went there. There weren't so many after her when she married Olaf, let me tell you. She knew enough to grab her chance."

5. A 320-acre piece of land. In the Midwest, public lands were divided into "sections," each of 640 acres.

Nils settled back in his seat. "Of course I liked to go there, Mother, and you were always cross about it. You never took the trouble to find out that it was the one jolly house in this country for a boy to go to. All the rest of you were working yourselves to death, and the houses were mostly a mess, full of babies and washing and flies. Oh, it was all right—I understand that; but you are young only once, and I happened to be young then. Now, Vavrika's was always jolly. He played the violin, and I used to take my flute, and Clara played the piano, and Johanna used to sing Bohemian songs. She always had a big supper for us—herrings and pickles and poppy-seed bread, and lots of cake and preserves. Old Joe had been in the army in the old country, and he could tell lots of good stories. I can see him cutting bread, at the head of the table, now. I don't know what I'd have done when I was a kid if it hadn't been for the Vavrikas, really."

"And all the time he was taking money that other people had worked hard in the fields for," Mrs. Ericson observed.

"So do the circuses, Mother, and they're a good thing. People ought to get fun for some of their money. Even father liked old Joe."

"Your father," Mrs. Ericson said grimly, "liked everybody."

As they crossed the sand creek and turned into her own place, Mrs. Ericson observed, "There's Olaf's buggy. He's stopped on his way from town." Nils shook himself and prepared to greet his brother, who was waiting on the porch.

Olaf was a big, heavy Norwegian, slow of speech and movement. His head was large and square, like a block of wood. When Nils, at a distance, tried to remember what his brother looked like, he could recall only his heavy head, high forehead, large nostrils, and pale blue eyes, set far apart. Olaf's features were rudimentary: the thing one noticed was the face itself, wide and flat and pale, devoid of any expression, betraying his fifty years as little as it betrayed anything else, and powerful by reason of its very stolidness. When Olaf shook hands with Nils he looked at him from under his light eyebrows, but Nils felt that no one could ever say what that pale look might mean. The one thing he had always felt in Olaf was a heavy stubbornness, like the unyielding stickiness of wet loam against the plow. He had always found Olaf the most difficult of his brothers.

"How do you do, Nils? Expect to stay with us long?"

"Oh, I may stay forever," Nils answered gaily. "I like this country better than I used to."

"There's been some work put into it since you left," Olaf remarked.

"Exactly. I think it's about ready to live in now—and I'm about ready to settle down." Nils saw his brother lower his big head. ("Exactly like a bull," he thought.) "Mother's been persuading me to slow down now, and go in for farming," he went on lightly.

Olaf made a deep sound in his throat. "Farming ain't learned in a day," he brought out, still looking at the ground.

"Oh, I know! But I pick things up quickly." Nils had not meant to antagonize his brother, and he did not know now why he was doing it. "Of course," he went on, "I shouldn't expect to make a big success, as you fellows have done. But then, I'm not ambitious. I won't want much. A little land, and some cattle, maybe."

Olaf still stared at the ground, his head down. He wanted to ask Nils what he had been doing all these years, that he didn't have a business somewhere he couldn't afford to leave; why he hadn't more pride than to come back with only a little sole-leather trunk to show for himself, and to present himself as the only failure in the family. He did not ask one of these questions, but he made them all felt distinctly.

"Humph!" Nils thought. "No wonder the man never talks, when he can butt his ideas into you like that without ever saying a word. I suppose he uses that kind of smokeless powder on his wife all the time. But I guess she has her innings." He chuckled, and Olaf looked up. "Never mind me, Olaf. I laugh without knowing why, like little Eric. He's another cheerful dog."

"Eric," said Olaf slowly, "is a spoiled kid. He's just let his mother's best cow go dry because he don't milk her right. I was hoping you'd take him away somewhere and put him into business. If he don't do any good among strangers, he never will." This was a long speech for Olaf, and as he finished it he climbed into his buggy.

Nils shrugged his shoulders. "Same old tricks," he thought. "Hits from behind you every time. What a whale of a man!" He turned and went round to the kitchen, where his mother was scolding little Eric for letting the gasoline get low.

IV

Joe Vavrika's saloon was not in the county seat, where Olaf and Mrs. Ericson did their trading, but in a cheerfuller place, a little Bohemian settlement which lay at the other end of the country, ten level miles north of Olaf's farm. Clara rode up to see her father almost every day. Vavrika's house was, so to speak, in the back yard of his saloon. The garden between the two buildings was inclosed by a high board fence as tight as a partition, and in summer Joe kept beer tables and wooden benches among the gooseberry bushes under his little cherry tree. At one of these tables Nils Ericson was seated in the late afternoon, three days after his return home. Joe had gone in to serve a customer, and Nils was lounging on his elbows, looking rather mournfully into his half-emptied pitcher, when he heard a laugh across the little garden. Clara, in her riding habit, was standing at the back door of the house, under the grapevine trellis that old Joe had grown there long ago. Nils rose.

"Come out and keep your father and me company. We've been gossiping all afternoon. Nobody to bother us but the flies."

She shook her head. "No, I never come out here any more. Olaf doesn't like it. I must live up to my position, you know."

"You mean to tell me you never come out and chat with the boys, as you used to? He *has* tamed you! Who keeps up these flower beds?"

"I come out on Sundays, when father is alone, and read the Bohemian papers to him. But I am never here when the bar is open. What have you two been doing?"

"Talking, as I told you. I've been telling him about my travels. I find I can't talk much at home, not even to Eric."

Clara reached up and poked with her riding-whip at a white moth that was fluttering in the sunlight among the vine leaves. "I suppose you will never tell me about all those things."

"Where can I tell them? Not in Olaf's house, certainly. What's the matter with our talking here?" He pointed persuasively with his hat to the bushes and the green table, where the flies were singing lazily above the empty beer glasses.

Clara shook her head weakly. "No, it wouldn't do. Besides, I am going now."

"I'm on Eric's mare. Would you be angry if I overtook you?"

Clara looked back and laughed. "You might try and see. I can leave you if I don't want you. Eric's mare can't keep up with Norman."

Nils went into the bar and attempted to pay his score. Big Joe, six feet four, with curly yellow hair and mustache, clapped him on the shoulder. "Not a God-damn a your money go in my drawer, you hear? Only next time you bring your flute, te-te-te-te-te-ty." Joe wagged his fingers in imitation of the flute player's position. "My Clara, she come all-a-time Sundays an' play for me. She not like to play at Ericson's place." He shook his yellow curls and laughed. "Not a God-damn a fun at Ericson's. You come a Sunday. You like-a fun. No forget de flute." Joe talked very rapidly and always tumbled over his English. He seldom spoke it to his customers, and had never learned much.

Nils swung himself into the saddle and trotted to the west end of the village, where the houses and gardens scattered into prairie land and the road turned south. Far ahead of him, in the declining light, he saw Clara Vavrika's slender figure, loitering on horseback. He touched his mare with the whip, and shot along the white, level road, under the reddening sky. When he overtook Olaf's wife he saw that she had been crying. "What's the matter, Clara Vavrika?" he asked kindly.

"Oh, I get blue sometimes. It was awfully jolly living there with father. I wonder why I ever went away."

Nils spoke in a low, kind tone that he sometimes used with women: "That's what I've been wondering these many years. You were the last girl in the country I'd have picked for a wife for Olaf. What made you do it, Clara?"

"I suppose I really did it to oblige the neighbors"—Clara tossed her head. "People were beginning to wonder."

"To wonder?"

"Yes—why I didn't get married. I suppose I didn't like to keep them in suspense. I've discovered that most girls marry out of consideration for the neighborhood."

Nils bent his head toward her and his white teeth flashed. "I'd have gambled that one girl I knew would say, 'Let the neighborhood be damned.' "

Clara shook her head mournfully. "You see, they have it on you, Nils; that is, if you're a woman. They say you're beginning to go off. That's what makes us get married: we can't stand the laugh."

Nils looked sidewise at her. He had never seen her head droop before. Resignation was the last thing he would have expected of her. "In your case, there wasn't something else?"

"Something else?"

"I mean, you didn't do it to spite somebody? Somebody who didn't come back?"

Clara drew herself up. "Oh, I never thought you'd come back. Not after I stopped writing to you, at least. *That* was all over, long before I married Olaf."

"It never occurred to you, then, that the meanest thing you could do to me was to marry Olaf?"

Clara laughed. "No; I didn't know you were so fond of Olaf."

Nils smoothed his horse's mane with his glove. "You know, Clara Vavrika, you are never going to stick it out. You'll cut away some day, and I've been thinking you might as well cut away with me."

Clara threw up her chin. "Oh, you don't know me as well as you think. I won't cut away. Sometimes, when I'm with father, I feel like it. But I can hold out as long as the Ericsons can. They've never got the best of me yet, and one can live, so long as one isn't beaten. If I go back to father, it's all up with Olaf in politics. He knows that, and he never goes much beyond sulking. I've as much wit as the Ericsons. I'll never leave them unless I can show them a thing or two."

"You mean unless you can come it over them?"

"Yes—unless I go away with a man who is cleverer than they are, and who has more money."

Nils whistled. "Dear me, you are demanding a good deal. The Ericsons, take the lot of them, are a bunch to beat. But I should think the excitement of tormenting them would have worn off by this time."

"It has, I'm afraid," Clara admitted mournfully.

"Then why don't you cut away? There are more amusing games than this in the world. When I came home I thought it might amuse me to bully a few quarter sections[6] out of the Ericsons; but I've almost decided I can get more fun for my money somewhere else."

Clara took in her breath sharply. "Ah, you have got the other will! That was why you came home!"

"No, it wasn't. I came home to see how you were getting on with Olaf."

Clara struck her horse with the whip, and in a bound she was far ahead of him. Nils dropped one word, "Damn!" and whipped after her; but she leaned forward in her saddle and fairly cut the wind. Her long riding skirt rippled in the still air behind her. The sun was just sinking behind the stubble in a vast, clear sky, and the shadows drew across the fields so rapidly that Nils could scarcely keep in sight the dark figure on the road. When he overtook her he caught her horse by the bridle. Norman reared, and Nils was frightened for her; but Clara kept her seat.

"Let me go, Nils Ericson!" she cried. "I hate you more than any of them. You were created to torture me, the whole tribe of you—to make me suffer in every possible way."

She struck her horse again and galloped away from him. Nils set his teeth and looked thoughtful. He rode slowly home along the deserted road, watching the stars come out in the clear violet sky. They flashed softly into the limpid heavens, like jewels let fall into clear water. They were a reproach, he felt, to a sordid world. As he turned across the sand creek, he looked up at the North Star and smiled, as if there were an understanding between them. His mother scolded him for being late for supper.

6. 160-acre pieces of land.

V

On Sunday afternoon Joe Vavrika, in his shirtsleeves and carpet slippers, was sitting in his garden, smoking a long-tasseled porcelain pipe with a hunting scene painted on the bowl. Clara sat under the cherry tree, reading aloud to him from the weekly Bohemian papers. She had worn a white muslin dress under her riding habit, and the leaves of the cherry tree threw a pattern of sharp shadows over her skirt. The black cat was dozing in the sunlight at her feet, and Joe's dachshund was scratching a hole under the scarlet geraniums and dreaming of badgers. Joe was filling his pipe for the third time since dinner, when he heard a knocking on the fence. He broke into a loud guffaw and unlatched the little door that led into the street. He did not call Nils by name, but caught him by the hand and dragged him in. Clara stiffened and the color deepened under her dark skin. Nils, too, felt a little awkward. He had not seen her since the night when she rode away from him and left him alone on the level road between the fields. Joe dragged him to the wooden bench beside the green table.

"You bring de flute," he cried, tapping the leather case under Nils' arm. "Ah, das-a good! Now we have some liddle fun like old times. I got somet'ing good for you." Joe shook his finger at Nils and winked his blue eye, a bright clear eye, full of fire, though the tiny bloodvessels on the ball were always a little distended. "I got somet'ing for you from"—he paused and waved his hand—"Hongarie. You know Hongarie? You wait!" He pushed Nils down on the bench, and went through the back door of his saloon.

Nils looked at Clara, who sat frigidly with her white skirts drawn tight about her. "He didn't tell you he had asked me to come, did he? He wanted a party and proceeded to arrange it. Isn't he fun? Don't be cross; let's give him a good time."

Clara smiled and shook out her skirt. "Isn't that like father? And he has sat here so meekly all day. Well, I won't pout. I'm glad you came. He doesn't have very many good times now any more. There are so few of his kind left. The second generation are a tame lot."

Joe came back with a flask in one hand and three wine glasses caught by the stems between the fingers of the other. These he placed on the table with an air of ceremony, and, going behind Nils, held the flask between him and the sun, squinting into it admiringly. "You know dis, Tokai? A great friend of mine, he bring dis to me, a present out of Hongarie. You know how much it cost, dis wine? Chust so much what it weigh in gold. Nobody but de nobles drink him in Bohemie. Many, many years I save him up, dis Tokai." Joe whipped out his official corkscrew and delicately removed the cork. "De old man die what bring him to me, an' dis wine he lay on his belly in my cellar an' sleep. An' now," carefully pouring out the heavy yellow wine, "an' now he wake up; and maybe he wake us up, too!" He carried one of the glasses to his daughter and presented it with great gallantry.

Clara shook her head, but, seeing her father's disappointment, relented. "You taste it first. I don't want so much."

Joe sampled it with a beatific expression, and turned to Nils. "You drink him slow, dis wine. He very soft, but he go down hot. You see!"

After a second glass Nils declared that he couldn't take any more without getting sleepy. "Now get your fiddle, Vavrika," he said as he opened his flute case.

But Joe settled back in his wooden rocker and wagged his big carpet slipper. "No-no-no-no-no-no-no! No play fiddle now any more: too much ache in de finger," waving them, "all-a-time rheumatiz. You play de flute, te-tety-te-tety-te. Bohemie songs."

"I've forgotten all the Bohemian songs I used to play with you and Johanna. But here's one that will make Clara pout. You remember how her eyes used to snap when we called her the Bohemian Girl?" Nils lifted his flute and began "When Other Lips and Other Hearts," and Joe hummed the air in a husky baritone, waving his carpet slipper. "Oh-h-h, das-a fine music," he cried, clapping his hands as Nils finished. "Now 'Marble Halls, Marble Halls'! Clara, you sing him."

Clara smiled and leaned back in her chair, beginning softly:

> "I dreamt that I dwelt in ma-a-arble halls,
> With vassals and serfs at my knee,"

and Joe hummed like a big bumblebee.

"There's one more you always played," Clara said quietly; "I remember that best." She locked her hands over her knee and began "The Heart Bowed Down," and sang it through without groping for the words. She was singing with a good deal of warmth when she came to the end of the old song:

> For memory is the only friend
> That grief can call its own.

Joe flashed out his red silk handkerchief and blew his nose, shaking his head. "No-no-no-no-no-no-no! Too sad, too sad! I not like-a dat. Play quick somet'ing gay now."

Nils put his lips to the instrument, and Joe lay back in his chair, laughing and singing, "Oh, Evelina, Sweet Evelina!" Clara laughed, too. Long ago, when she and Nils went to high school, the model student of their class was a very homely girl in thick spectacles. Her name was Evelina Oleson; she had a long, swinging walk which somehow suggested the measure of that song, and they used mercilessly to sing it at her.

"Dat ugly Oleson girl, she teach in de school," Joe gasped, "an' she still walk chust like dat, yup-a, yup-a, yup-a, chust like a camel she go! Now, Nils, we have some more li'l drink. Oh, yes-yes-yes-yes-yes-yes-*yes!* Dis time you haf to drink, and Clara she haf to, so she show she not jealous. So, we all drink to your girl. You not tell her name, eh? No-no-no, I no make you tell. She pretty, eh? She make good sweetheart? I bet!" Joe winked and lifted his glass. "How soon you get married?"

Nils screwed up his eyes. "That I don't know. When she says."

Joe threw out his chest. "Das-a way boys talks. No way for mans. Mans say, 'You come to de church, an' get a hurry on you.' Das-a way mans talks."

"Maybe Nils hasn't got enough to keep a wife," put in Clara ironically. "How about that, Nils?" she asked him frankly, as if she wanted to know.

Nils looked at her coolly, raising one eyebrow. "Oh, I can keep her, all right."

"The way she wants to be kept?"

"With my wife, I'll decide that," replied Nils calmly. "I'll give her what's good for her."

Clara made a wry face. "You'll give her the strap, I expect, like old Peter Oleson gave his wife."

"When she needs it," said Nils lazily, locking his hands behind his head and squinting up through the leaves of the cherry tree. "Do you remember the time I squeezed the cherries all over your clean dress, and Aunt Johanna boxed my ears for me? My gracious, weren't you mad! You had both hands full of cherries, and I squeezed 'em and made the juice fly all over you. I liked to have fun with you; you'd get so mad."

"We *did* have fun, didn't we? None of the other kids ever had so much fun. We knew how to play."

Nils dropped his elbows on the table and looked steadily across at her. "I've played with lots of girls since, but I haven't found one who was such good fun."

Clara laughed. The late afternoon sun was shining full in her face, and deep in the back of her eyes there shone something fiery, like the yellow drops of Tokai in the brown glass bottle. "Can you still play, or are you only pretending?"

"I can play better than I used to, and harder."

"Don't you ever work, then?" She had not intended to say it. It slipped out because she was confused enough to say just the wrong thing.

"I work between times." Nils' steady gaze still beat upon her. "Don't you worry about my working, Mrs. Ericson. You're getting like all the rest of them." He reached his brown, warm hand across the table and dropped it on Clara's, which was cold as an icicle. "Last call for play, Mrs. Ericson!" Clara shivered, and suddenly her hands and cheeks grew warm. Her fingers lingered in his a moment, and they looked at each other earnestly. Joe Vavrika had put the mouth of the bottle to his lips and was swallowing the last drops of the Tokai, standing. The sun, just about to sink behind his shop, glistened on the bright glass, on his flushed face and curly yellow hair. "Look," Clara whispered; "that's the way I want to grow old."

VI

On the day of Olaf Ericson's barn-raising, his wife, for once in a way, rose early. Johanna Vavrika had been baking cakes and frying and boiling and spicing meats for a week beforehand, but it was not until the day before the party was to take place that Clara showed any interest in it. Then she was seized with one of her fitful spasms of energy, and took the wagon and little Eric and spent the day on Plum Creek, gathering vines and swamp goldenrod to decorate the barn.

By four o'clock in the afternoon buggies and wagons began to arrive at the big unpainted building in front of Olaf's house. When Nils and his mother came at five, there were more than fifty people in the barn, and a great drove of children. On the ground floor stood six long tables, set with the crockery of seven flourishing Ericson families, lent for the occasion. In the middle of each table was a big yellow pumpkin, hollowed out and filled with woodbine. In one corner of the barn, behind a pile of green-and-white-striped watermelons, was a circle of chairs for the old people; the younger guests sat on bushel measures or barbed-wire spools, and the children tumbled about in the haymow. The box stalls Clara had converted into booths. The framework was hidden by goldenrod and sheaves of wheat, and the partitions were covered with wild grapevines full of fruit. At one of these Johanna Vavrika watched over her cooked meats, enough to provision an army; and at the next her kitchen girls had ranged the ice-cream freezers, and Clara was already cutting pies and cakes against the hour of serving. At the third stall, little Hilda, in a bright pink lawn dress, dispensed lemonade throughout the afternoon. Olaf, as a public man, had thought it inadvisable to serve beer in his barn; but Joe Vavrika had come over with two demijohns concealed in his buggy, and after his arrival the wagon shed was much frequented by the men.

"Hasn't Cousin Clara fixed things lovely?" little Hilda whispered, when Nils went up to her stall and asked for lemonade.

Nils leaned against the booth, talking to the excited little girl and watching the people. The barn faced the west, and the sun, pouring in at the big doors, filled the whole interior with a golden light, through which filtered fine particles of dust from the haymow, where the children were romping. There was a great chattering from the stall where Johanna Vavrika exhibited to the admiring women her platters heaped with fried chicken, her roasts of beef, boiled tongues, and baked hams with cloves stuck in the crisp brown fat and garnished with tansy and parsley. The older women, having assured themselves that there were twenty kinds of cake, not counting cookies, and three dozen fat pies, repaired to the corner behind the pile of watermelons, put on their white aprons, and fell to their knitting and fancywork. They were a fine company of old women, and a Dutch painter would have loved to find them there together, where the sun made bright patches on the floor and sent long, quivering shafts of gold through the dusky shade up among the rafters. There were fat, rosy old women who looked hot in their best black dresses; spare, alert old women with brown, dark-veined hands; and several of almost heroic frame, not less massive than old Mrs. Ericson herself. Few of them wore glasses, and old Mrs. Svendsen, a Danish woman, who was quite bald, wore the only cap among them. Mrs. Oleson, who had twelve big grandchildren, could still show two braids of yellow hair as thick as her own wrists. Among all these grandmothers there were more brown heads than white. They all had a pleased, prosperous air, as if they were more than satisfied with themselves and with life. Nils, leaning against Hilda's lemonade stand, watched them as they sat chattering in four languages, their fingers never lagging behind their tongues.

"Look at them over there," he whispered, detaining Clara as she passed him. "Aren't they the Old Guard? I've just counted thirty hands. I guess they've wrung many a chicken's neck and warmed many a boy's jacket for him in their time."

In reality he fell into amazement when he thought of the Herculean labors those fifteen pairs of hands had performed: of the cows they had milked, the butter they had made, the gardens they had planted, the children and grandchildren they had tended, the brooms they had worn out, the mountains of food they had cooked. It made him dizzy. Clara Vavrika smiled a hard, enigmatical smile at him and walked rapidly away. Nils' eyes followed her white figure as she went toward the house. He watched her walking alone in the sunlight, looked at her slender, defiant shoulders and her little hard-set head with its coils of blue-black hair. "No," he reflected;

"she'd never be like them, not if she lived here a hundred years. She'd only grow more bitter. You can't tame a wild thing; you can only chain it. People aren't all alike. I mustn't lose my nerve." He gave Hilda's pigtail a parting tweak and set out after Clara. "Where to?" he asked, as he came upon her in the kitchen.

"I'm going to the cellar for preserves."

"Let me go with you. I never get a moment alone with you. Why do you keep out of my way?"

Clara laughed. "I don't usually get in anybody's way."

Nils followed her down the stairs and to the far corner of the cellar, where a basement window let in a stream of light. From a swinging shelf Clara selected several glass jars, each labeled in Johanna's careful hand. Nils took up a brown flask. "What's this? It looks good."

"It is. It's some French brandy father gave me when I was married. Would you like some? Have you a corkscrew? I'll get glasses."

When she brought them, Nils took them from her and put them down on the window sill. "Clara Vavrika, do you remember how crazy I used to be about you?"

Clara shrugged her shoulders. "Boys are always crazy about somebody or other. I dare say some silly has been crazy about Evelina Oleson. You got over it in a hurry."

"Because I didn't come back, you mean? I had to get on, you know, and it was hard sledding at first. Then I heard you'd married Olaf."

"And then you stayed away from a broken heart," Clara laughed.

"And then I began to think about you more than I had since I first went away. I began to wonder if you were really as you had seemed to me when I was a boy. I thought I'd like to see. I've had lots of girls, but no one ever pulled me the same way. The more I thought about you, the more I remembered how it used to be—like hearing a wild tune you can't resist, calling you out at night. It had been a long while since anything had pulled me out of my boots, and I wondered whether anything ever could again." Nils thrust his hands into his coat pockets and squared his shoulders, as his mother sometimes squared hers, as Olaf, in a clumsier manner, squared his. "So I thought I'd come back and see. Of course the family have tried to do me, and I rather thought I'd bring out father's will and make a fuss. But they can have their old land; they've put enough sweat into it." He took the flask and filled the two glasses carefully to the brim. "I've found out what I want from the Ericsons. Drink *skoal*, Clara." He lifted his glass, and Clara took hers with downcast eyes. "Look at me, Clara Vavrika. *Skoal!*"

She raised her burning eyes and answered fiercely: "*Skoal!*"

The barn supper began at six o'clock and lasted for two hilarious hours. Yense Nelson had made a wager that he could eat two whole fried chickens, and he did. Eli Swanson stowed away two whole custard pies, and Nick Hermanson ate a chocolate layer cake to the last crumb. There was even a cooky contest among the children, and one thin, slablike Bohemian boy consumed sixteen and won the prize, a gingerbread pig which Johanna Vavrika had carefully decorated with red candies and burnt sugar. Fritz Sweiheart, the German carpenter, won in the pickle contest, but he disappeared soon after supper and was not seen for the rest of the evening. Joe Vavrika said that Fritz could have managed the pickles all right, but he had sampled the demijohn in his buggy too often before sitting down to the table.

While the supper was being cleared away the two fiddlers began to tune up for the dance. Clara was to accompany them on her old upright piano, which had been brought down from her father's. By this time Nils had renewed old acquaintances. Since his interview with Clara in the cellar, he had been busy telling all the old women how young they looked, and all the young ones how pretty they were, and assuring the men that they had here the best farmland in the world. He had made himself so agreeable that old Mrs. Ericson's friends began to come up to her and tell how lucky she was to get her smart son back again, and please to get him to play his flute. Joe Vavrika, who could still play very well when he forgot that he had rheumatism, caught up a fiddle from Johnny Oleson and played a crazy Bohemian dance tune that set the wheels going. When he dropped the bow every one was ready to dance.

Olaf, in a frock coat and a solemn made-up necktie, led the grand march with his mother. Clara had kept well out of *that* by sticking to the piano. She played the march with a pompous solemnity which greatly amused the prodigal son, who went over and stood behind her.

"Oh, aren't you rubbing it into them, Clara Vavrika? And aren't you lucky to have me here, or all your wit would be thrown away."

"I'm used to being witty for myself. It saves my life."

The fiddles struck up a polka, and Nils convulsed Joe Vavrika by leading out Evelina Oleson, the homely schoolteacher. His next partner was a very fat Swedish girl, who, although she was an heiress, had not been asked for the first dance, but had stood against the wall in her tight, high-heeled shoes, nervously fingering a lace handkerchief. She was soon out of breath, so Nils led her, pleased and panting, to her seat, and went over to the piano, from which Clara had been watching his gallantry. "Ask Olena Yenson," she whispered. "She waltzes beautifully."

Olena, too, was rather inconveniently plump, handsome in a

smooth, heavy way, with a fine color and good-natured, sleepy eyes. She was redolent of violet sachet powder, and had warm, soft, white hands, but she danced divinely, moving as smoothly as the tide coming in. "There, that's something like," Nils said as he released her. "You'll give me the next waltz, won't you? Now I must go and dance with my little cousin."

Hilda was greatly excited when Nils went up to her stall and held out his arm. Her little eyes sparkled, but she declared that she could not leave her lemonade. Old Mrs. Ericson, who happened along at this moment, said she would attend to that, and Hilda came out, as pink as her pink dress. The dance was a schottische,[7] and in a moment her yellow braids were fairly standing on end. "Bravo!" Nils cried encouragingly. "Where did you learn to dance so nicely?"

"My Cousin Clara taught me," the little girl panted.

Nils found Eric sitting with a group of boys who were too awkward or too shy to dance, and told him that he must dance the next waltz with Hilda.

The boy screwed up his shoulders. "Aw, Nils, I can't dance. My feet are too big; I look silly."

"Don't be thinking about yourself. It doesn't matter how boys look."

Nils had never spoken to him so sharply before, and Eric made haste to scramble out of his corner and brush the straw from his coat.

Clara nodded approvingly. "Good for you, Nils. I've been trying to get hold of him. They dance very nicely together; I sometimes play for them."

"I'm obliged to you for teaching him. There's no reason why he should grow up to be a lout."

"He'll never be that. He's more like you than any of them. Only he hasn't your courage." From her slanting eyes Clara shot forth one of those keen glances, admiring and at the same time challenging, which she seldom bestowed on any one, and which seemed to say, "Yes, I admire you, but I am your equal."

Clara was proving a much better host than Olaf, who, once the supper was over, seemed to feel no interest in anything but the lanterns. He had brought a locomotive headlight from town to light the revels, and he kept skulking about it as if he feared the mere light from it might set his new barn on fire. His wife, on the contrary, was cordial to every one, was animated and even gay. The deep salmon color in her cheeks burned vividly, and her eyes were full of life. She gave the piano over to the fat Swedish heiress,

7. A partnered Bohemian folk dance.

pulled her father away from the corner where he sat gossiping with his cronies, and made him dance a Bohemian dance with her. In his youth Joe had been a famous dancer, and his daughter got him so limbered up that every one sat round and applauded them. The old ladies were particularly delighted, and made them go through the dance again. From their corner where they watched and commented, the old women kept time with their feet and hands, and whenever the fiddles struck up a new air old Mrs. Svendsen's white cap would begin to bob.

Clara was waltzing with little Eric when Nils came up to them, brushed his brother aside, and swung her out among the dancers. "Remember how we used to waltz on rollers at the old skating rink in town? I suppose people don't do that any more. We used to keep it up for hours. You know, we never did moon around as other boys and girls did. It was dead serious with us from the beginning. When we were most in love with each other, we used to fight. You were always pinching people; your fingers were like little nippers. A regular snapping turtle, you were. Lord, how you'd like Stockholm! Sit out in the streets in front of cafés and talk all night in summer. Just like a reception—officers and ladies and funny English people. Jolliest people in the world, the Swedes, once you get them going. Always drinking things—champagne and stout mixed, half-and-half; serve it out of big pitchers, and serve plenty. Slow pulse, you know; they can stand a lot. Once they light up, they're glowworms, I can tell you."

"All the same, you don't really like gay people."

"*I* don't?"

"No; I could see that when you were looking at the old women there this afternoon. They're the kind you really admire, after all; women like your mother. And that's the kind you'll marry."

"Is it, Miss Wisdom? You'll see who I'll marry, and she won't have a domestic virtue to bless herself with. She'll be a snapping turtle, and she'll be a match for me. All the same, they're a fine bunch of old dames over there. You admire them yourself."

"No, I don't; I detest them."

"You won't, when you look back on them from Stockholm or Budapest. Freedom settles all that. Oh, but you're the real Bohemian Girl, Clara Vavrika!" Nils laughed down at her sullen frown and began mockingly to sing:

> "Oh, how could a poor gypsy maiden like me
> Expect the proud bride of a baron to be?"

Clara clutched his shoulder. "Hush, Nils; every one is looking at you."

"I don't care. They can't gossip. It's all in the family, as the Ericsons say when they divide up little Hilda's patrimony amongst them. Besides, we'll give them something to talk about when we hit the trail. Lord, it will be a godsend to them! They haven't had anything so interesting to chatter about since the grasshopper year. It'll give them a new lease of life. And Olaf won't lose the Bohemian vote, either. They'll have the laugh on him so that they'll vote two apiece. They'll send him to Congress. They'll never forget his barn party, or us. They'll always remember us as we're dancing together now. We're making a legend. Where's my waltz, boys?" he called as they whirled past the fiddlers.

The musicians grinned, looked at each other, hesitated, and began a new air; and Nils sang with them, as the couples fell from a quick waltz to a long, slow glide:

"When other lips and other hearts
  Their tale of love shall tell,
In language whose excess imparts
  The power they feel so well."

The old women applauded vigorously. "What a gay one he is, that Nils!" And old Mrs. Svendsen's cap lurched dreamily from side to side to the flowing measure of the dance.

Of days that have as ha-a-p-py been,
  And you'll remember me.

VII

The moonlight flooded that great, silent land. The reaped fields lay yellow in it. The straw stacks and poplar windbreaks threw sharp black shadows. The roads were white rivers of dust. The sky was a deep, crystalline blue, and the stars were few and faint. Everything seemed to have succumbed, to have sunk to sleep, under the great, golden, tender, midsummer moon. The splendor of it seemed to transcend human life and human fate. The senses were too feeble to take it in, and every time one looked up at the sky one felt unequal to it, as if one were sitting deaf under the waves of a great river of melody. Near the road, Nils Ericson was lying against a straw stack in Olaf's wheat field. His own life seemed strange and unfamiliar to him, as if it were something he had read about, or dreamed, and forgotten. He lay very still, watching the white road that ran in front of him, lost itself among the fields, and then, at a distance, reappeared over a little hill. At last, against this white band he saw something moving rapidly, and he got up and walked to the edge of the field. "She is passing the row of poplars now," he thought. He heard the padded beat of hoofs along the dusty road, and as she came into sight he stepped out and waved his arms.

Then, for fear of frightening the horse, he drew back and waited. Clara had seen him, and she came up at a walk. Nils took the horse by the bit and stroked his neck.

"What are you doing out so late, Clara Vavrika? I went to the house, but Johanna told me you had gone to your father's."

"Who can stay in the house on a night like this? Aren't you out yourself?"

"Ah, but that's another matter."

Nils turned the horse into the field.

"What are you doing? Where are you taking Norman?"

"Not far, but I want to talk to you tonight; I have something to say to you. I can't talk to you at the house, with Olaf sitting there on the porch, weighing a thousand tons."

Clara laughed. "He won't be sitting there now. He's in bed by this time, and asleep—weighing a thousand tons."

Nils plodded on across the stubble. "Are you really going to spend the rest of your life like this, night after night, summer after summer? Haven't you anything better to do on a night like this than to wear yourself and Norman out tearing across the country to your father's and back? Besides, your father won't live forever, you know. His little place will be shut up or sold, and then you'll have nobody but the Ericsons. You'll have to fasten down the hatches for the winter then."

Clara moved her head restlessly. "Don't talk about that. I try never to think of it. If I lost father I'd lose everything, even my hold over the Ericsons."

"Bah! You'd lose a good deal more than that. You'd lose your race, everything that makes you yourself. You've lost a good deal of it now."

"Of what?"

"Of your love of life, your capacity for delight."

Clara put her hands up to her face. "I haven't, Nils Ericson, I haven't! Say anything to me but that. I won't have it!" she declared vehemently.

Nils led the horse up to a straw stack, and turned to Clara, looking at her intently, as he had looked at her that Sunday afternoon at Vavrika's. "But why do you fight for that so? What good is the power to enjoy, if you never enjoy? Your hands are cold again; what are you afraid of all the time? Ah, you're afraid of losing it; that's what's the matter with you! And you will, Clara Vavrika, you will! When I used to know you—listen; you've caught a wild bird in your hand, haven't you, and felt its heart beat so hard that you were afraid it would shatter its little body to pieces? Well, you used to be just like that, a slender, eager thing with a wild delight inside you. That is how I remembered you. And I come back and find you—a bitter woman. This is a perfect ferret fight here; you live by biting and being bitten. Can't you remember what life used to be? Can't you remember that old delight? I've never forgotten it, or known its like, on land or sea."

He drew the horse under the shadow of the straw stack. Clara felt him take her foot out of the stirrup, and she slid softly down into his arms. He kissed her slowly. He was a deliberate man, but his nerves were steel when he wanted anything. Something flashed out from him like a knife out of a sheath. Clara felt everything slipping away from her; she was flooded by the summer night. He thrust his hand into his pocket, and then held it out at arm's length. "Look," he said. The shadow of the straw stack fell sharp across his wrist, and in the palm of his hand she saw a silver dollar shining. "That's my pile," he muttered; "will you go with me?"

Clara nodded, and dropped her forehead on his shoulder.

Nils took a deep breath. "Will you go with me tonight?"

"Where?" she whispered softly.

"To town, to catch the midnight flyer."

Clara lifted her head and pulled herself together. "Are you crazy, Nils? We couldn't go away like that."

"That's the only way we ever will go. You can't sit on the bank and think about it. You have to plunge. That's the way I've always done, and it's the right way for people like you and me. There's nothing so dangerous as sitting still. You've only got one life, one youth, and you can let it slip through your fingers if you want to; nothing easier. Most people do that. You'd be better off tramping the roads with me than you are here." Nils held back her head and looked into her eyes. "But I'm not that kind of a tramp, Clara. You won't have to take in sewing. I'm with a Norwegian shipping line; came over on business with the New York offices, but now I'm going straight back to Bergen. I expect I've got as much money as the Ericsons. Father sent me a little to get started. They never knew about that. There, I hadn't meant to tell you; I wanted you to come on your own nerve."

Clara looked off across the fields. "It isn't that, Nils, but something seems to hold me. I'm afraid to pull against it. It comes out of the ground, I think."

"I know all about that. One has to tear loose. You're not needed here. Your father will understand; he's made like us. As for Olaf, Johanna will take better care of him than ever you could. It's now or never, Clara Vavrika. My bag's at the station; I smuggled it there yesterday."

Clara clung to him and hid her face against his shoulder. "Not tonight," she whispered. "Sit here and talk to me tonight. I don't want to go anywhere tonight. I may never love you like this again."

Nils laughed through his teeth. "You can't come that on me. That's not my way, Clara Vavrika. Eric's mare is over there behind the stacks, and I'm off on the midnight. It's goodbye, or off across the world with me. My carriage won't wait. I've written a letter to Olaf; I'll mail it in town. When he reads it he won't bother us—not if I know him. He'd rather have the land. Besides, I could demand an investigation of his administration of Cousin Henrik's estate, and that would be bad for a public man. You've no clothes, I know; but you can sit up tonight, and we can get everything on the way. Where's your old dash, Clara Vavrika? What's become of your Bohemian blood? I used to think you had courage enough for anything. Where's your nerve—what are you waiting for?"

Clara drew back her head, and he saw the slumberous fire in her eyes. "For you to say one thing, Nils Ericson."

"I never say that thing to any woman, Clara Vavrika." He leaned back, lifted her gently from the ground, and whispered through his teeth: "But I'll never, never let you go, not to any man on earth but me! Do you understand me? Now, wait here."

Clara sank down on a sheaf of wheat and covered her face with her hands. She did not know what she was going to do—whether she would go or stay. The great, silent country seemed to lay a spell upon her. The ground seemed to hold her as if by roots. Her knees were soft under her. She felt as if she could not bear separation from her old sorrows, from her old discontent. They were dear to her, they had kept her alive, they were a part of her. There would be nothing left of her if she were wrenched away from them. Never could she pass beyond that skyline against which her restlessness had beat so many times. She felt as if her soul had built itself a nest there on that horizon at which she looked every morning and every evening, and it was dear to her, inexpressibly dear. She pressed her fingers against her eyeballs to shut it out. Beside her she heard the tramping of horses in the soft earth. Nils said nothing to her. He put his hands under her arms and lifted her lightly to her saddle. Then he swung himself into his own.

"We shall have to ride fast to catch the midnight train. A last gallop, Clara Vavrika. Forward!"

There was a start, a thud of hoofs along the moonlit road, two dark shadows going over the hill; and then the great, still land stretched untroubled under the azure night. Two shadows had passed.

VIII

A year after the flight of Olaf Ericson's wife, the night train was steaming across the plains of Iowa. The conductor was hurrying through one of the day coaches, his lantern on his arm, when a lank, fair haired boy sat up in one of the plush seats and tweaked him by the coat.

"What is the next stop, please, sir?"

"Red Oak, Iowa. But you go through to Chicago, don't you?" He looked down, and noticed that the boy's eyes were red and his face was drawn, as if he were in trouble.

"Yes. But I was wondering whether I could get off at the next place and get a train back to Omaha."

"Well, I suppose you could. Live in Omaha?"

"No. In the western part of the State. How soon do we get to Red Oak?"

"Forty minutes. You'd better make up your mind, so I can tell the baggageman to put your trunk off."

"Oh, never mind about that! I mean, I haven't got any," the boy added, blushing.

"Run away," the conductor thought, as he slammed the coach door behind him.

Eric Ericson crumpled down in his seat and put his brown hand to his forehead. He had been crying, and he had had no supper, and his head was aching violently. "Oh, what shall I do?" he thought, as he looked dully down at his big shoes. "Nils will be ashamed of me; I haven't got any spunk."

Ever since Nils had run away with his brother's wife, life at home had been hard for little Eric. His mother and Olaf both suspected him of complicity. Mrs. Ericson was harsh and faultfinding, constantly wounding the boy's pride; and Olaf was always setting her against him.

Joe Vavrika heard often from his daughter. Clara had always been fond of her father, and happiness made her kinder. She wrote him long accounts of the voyage to Bergen, and of the trip she and Nils took through Bohemia to the little town where her father had grown up and where she herself was born. She visited all her kinsmen there, and sent her father news of his brother, who was a priest; of his sister, who had married a horse-breeder—of their big farm and their many children. These letters Joe always managed to read to little Eric. They contained messages for Eric and Hilda. Clara sent presents, too, which Eric never dared to take home and which poor little Hilda never even saw, though she loved to hear Eric tell about them when they were out getting the eggs together. But Olaf once saw Eric coming out of Vavrika's house—the old man had never asked the boy to come into his saloon—and Olaf went straight to his mother and told her. That night Mrs. Ericson came to Eric's room after he was in bed and made a terrible scene. She could be very terrifying when she was really angry. She forbade him ever to speak to Vavrika again, and after that night she would not allow him to go to town alone. So it was a long while before Eric got any more news of his brother. But old Joe suspected what was going on, and he carried Clara's letters about in his pocket. One Sunday he drove out to see a German friend of his, and chanced to catch sight of Eric, sitting by the cattle pond in the big pasture. They went together into Fritz Oberlies' barn, and read the letters and talked things over. Eric admitted that things were getting hard for him at home. That very night old Joe sat down and laboriously penned a statement of the case to his daughter.

Things got no better for Eric. His mother and Olaf felt that, however closely he was watched, he still, as they said, "heard." Mrs. Ericson could not admit neutrality. She had sent Johanna Vavrika packing back to her brother's, though Olaf would much rather have kept her than Anders' eldest daughter, whom Mrs. Ericson installed in her place. He was not so highhanded as his mother, and he once sulkily told her that she might better have taught her granddaughter to cook before she sent Johanna away. Olaf could have borne a good deal for the sake of prunes spiced in honey, the secret of which Johanna had taken away with her.

At last two letters came to Joe Vavrika: one from Nils, inclosing a postal order for money to pay Eric's passage to Bergen, and one from Clara, saying that Nils had a place for Eric in the offices of his company, that he was to live with them, and that they were only waiting for him to come. He was to leave New York on one of the boats of Nils' own line; the captain was one of their friends, and Eric was to make himself known at once.

Nils' directions were so explicit that a baby could have followed them, Eric felt. And here he was, nearing Red Oak, Iowa, and rocking backward and forward in despair. Never had he loved his brother so much, and never had the big world called to him so hard. But there was a lump in his throat which would not go down. Ever since nightfall he had been tormented by the thought of his mother, alone in that big house that had sent forth so many men. Her unkindness now seemed so little, and her loneliness so great. He remembered everything she had ever done for him: how frightened she had been when he tore his hand in the cornsheller, and how she wouldn't let Olaf scold him. When Nils went away he didn't leave his mother all alone, or he would never have gone. Eric felt sure of that.

The train whistled. The conductor came in, smiling not unkindly. "Well, young man, what are you going to do? We stop at Red Oak in three minutes."

"Yes, thank you. I'll let you know." The conductor went out, and the boy doubled up with misery. He couldn't let his one chance go like this. He felt for his breast pocket and crackled Nils' kind letter to give him courage. He didn't want Nils to be ashamed of him. The train stopped. Suddenly he remembered his brother's kind, twinkling eyes, that always looked at you as if from far away. The lump in his throat softened. "Ah, but Nils, Nils would *understand!*" he thought. "That's just it about Nils; he always understands."

A lank, pale boy with a canvas telescope stumbled off the train to the Red Oak siding, just as the conductor called, "All aboard!"

The next night Mrs. Ericson was sitting alone in her wooden rocking chair on the front porch. Little Hilda had been sent to bed and had cried herself to sleep. The old woman's knitting was in her lap, but her hands lay motionless on top of it. For more than an hour she had not moved a muscle. She simply sat, as only the Ericsons and the mountains can sit. The house was dark, and there was no sound but the croaking of the frogs down in the pond of the little pasture.

Eric did not come home by the road, but across the fields, where no one could see him. He set his telescope down softly in the kitchen shed, and slipped noiselessly along the path to the front porch. He sat down on the step without saying anything. Mrs. Ericson made no sign, and the frogs croaked on. At last the boy spoke timidly.

"I've come back, Mother."

"Very well," said Mrs. Ericson.

Eric leaned over and picked up a little stick out of the grass.

"How about the milking?" he faltered.

"That's been done, hours ago."

"Who did you get?"

"Get? I did it myself. I can milk as good as any of you."

Eric slid along the step nearer to her. "Oh, Mother, why did you?" he asked sorrowfully. "Why didn't you get one of Otto's boys?"

"I didn't want anybody to know I was in need of a boy," said Mrs. Ericson bitterly. She looked straight in front of her and her mouth tightened. "I always meant to give you the home farm," she added.

The boy started and slid closer. "Oh, Mother," he faltered, "I don't care about the farm. I came back because I thought you might be needing me, maybe." He hung his head and got no further.

"Very well," said Mrs. Ericson. Her hand went out from her suddenly and rested on his head. Her fingers twined themselves in his soft, pale hair. His tears splashed down on the boards; happiness filled his heart.

WILLA CATHER

[On Walt Whitman]†

Speaking of monuments reminds one that there is more talk about a monument to Walt Whitman, "the good, gray poet."[1] Just why the adjective good is always applied to Whitman it is difficult to discover, probably because people who could not understand him at all took it for granted that he meant well. If ever there was a poet who had no literary ethics at all beyond those of nature, it was he. He was neither good nor bad, any more than are the animals he continually admired and envied. He was a poet without an exclusive sense of the poetic, a man without the finer discriminations, enjoying everything with the unreasoning enthusiasm of a boy. He was the poet of the dung hill as well as of the mountains, which is admirable in theory but excruciating in verse. In the same paragraph he informs you that, "The pure contralto sings in the organ loft," and that "The malformed limbs are tied to the table, what is removed drop horribly into a pail." No branch of surgery is poetic, and that hopelessly prosaic word "pail" would kill a whole volume of sonnets. Whitman's poems are reckless rhapsodies over creation in general, some times sublime, some times ridiculous. He declares that the ocean with its "imperious waves, commanding" is beautiful, and that the fly-specks on the walls are also beautiful. Such catholic taste may go in science, but in poetry their results are sad. The poet's task is usually to select the poetic. Whitman never bothers to do that, he takes everything in the universe from fly-specks to the fixed stars. His "Leaves of Grass" is a sort of dictionary of the English language, and in it is the name of everything in creation set down with great reverence but without any particular connection.

But however ridiculous Whitman may be there is a primitive elemental force about him. He is so full of hardiness and of the joy of life. He looks at all nature in the delighted, admiring way in which the old Greeks and the primitive poets did. He exults so in the red blood in his body and the strength in his arms. He has such a passion for the warmth and dignity of all that is natural. He has no code but to be natural, a code that this complex world has so long outgrown. He is sensual, not after the manner of Swinbourne and Gautier,[2] who are always seeking for perverted and bizarre effects

† *Nebraska State Journal*, January 19, 1896.

1. The widely used label "the good gray poet" originated in a pamphlet of that title published in 1886 by William Douglas O'Connor (1832–1889), a staunch defender of Whitman.
2. Algernon Swinburne (1837–1909), late Victorian poet; Theophile Gautier (1811–1872), French poet and novelist.

on the senses, but in the frank fashion of the old barbarians who ate and slept and married and smacked their lips over the mead horn. He is rigidly limited to the physical, things that quicken his pulses, please his eyes or delight his nostrils. There is an element of poetry in all this, but it is by no means the highest. If a joyous elephant should break forth into song, his lay would probably be very much like Whitman's famous "song of myself." It would have just about as much delicacy and deftness and discriminations. He says:

"I think I could turn and live with the animals. They are so placid and self-contained, I stand and look at them long and long. They do not sweat and whine about their condition. They do not lie awake in the dark and weep for their sins. They do not make me sick discussing their duty to God. Not one is dissatisfied nor not one is demented with the mania of many things. Not one kneels to another nor to his kind that lived thousands of years ago. Not one is respectable or unhappy, over the whole earth." And that is not irony on nature, he means just that, life meant no more to him. He accepted the world just as it is and glorified it, the seemly and unseemly, the good and the bad. He had no conception of a difference in people or in things. All men had bodies and were alike to him, one about as good as another. To live was to fulfil all natural laws and impulses. To be comfortable was to be happy. To be happy was the ultimatum. He did not realize the existence of a conscience or a responsibility. He had no more thought of good or evil than the folks in Kipling's Jungle book.[3]

And yet there is an undeniable charm about this optimistic vagabond who is made so happy by the warm sunshine and the smell of spring fields. A sort of good fellowship and wholeheartedness in every line he wrote. His veneration for things physical and material, for all that is in water or air or land, is so real that as you read him you think for the moment that you would rather like to live so if you could. For the time you half believe that a sound body and a strong arm are the greatest things in the world. Perhaps no book shows so much as "Leaves of Grass" that keen senses do not make a poet. When you read it you realize how spirited a thing poetry really is and how great a part spiritual perceptions play in apparently sensuous verse, if only to select the beautiful from the gross.

3. The "folks" in *The Jungle Book* are the child Mowgli's animal mentors and enemies, including a panther, orangutan, bear, python, and tiger.

WALT WHITMAN

Pioneers! O Pioneers!†

Come my tan-faced children,
Follow well in order, get your weapons ready,
Have you your pistols? have you your sharp-edged axes?
Pioneers! O pioneers!

For we cannot tarry here,
We must march my darlings, we must bear the brunt of danger,
We the youthful sinewy races, all the rest on us depend,
Pioneers! O pioneers!

O you youths, Western youths,
So impatient, full of action, full of manly pride and friendship,
Plain I see you Western youths, see you tramping with the
foremost,
Pioneers! O pioneers!

Have the elder races halted?
Do they droop and end their lesson, wearied over there beyond the
seas?
We take up the task eternal, and the burden and the lesson,
Pioneers! O pioneers!

All the past we leave behind,
We debouch upon a newer mightier world, varied world,
Fresh and strong the world we seize, world of labor and the march,
Pioneers! O pioneers!

We detachments steady throwing,
Down the edges, through the passes, up the mountains steep,
Conquering, holding, daring, venturing as we go the unknown
ways,
Pioneers! O pioneers!

We primeval forests felling,
We the rivers stemming, vexing we and piercing deep the mines
within,

† First published in *Drum-Taps* (1865), the poem was included in the 1881 edition of *Leaves of Grass*.

We the surface broad surveying, we the virgin soil upheaving,
Pioneers! O pioneers!

Colorado men are we,
From the peaks gigantic, from the great sierras and the high plateaus,
From the mine and from the gully, from the hunting trail we come,
Pioneers! O pioneers!

From Nebraska, from Arkansas,
Central inland race are we, from Missouri, with the continental blood intervein'd,
All the hands of comrades clasping, all the Southern, all the Northern,
Pioneers! O pioneers!

O resistless restless race!
O beloved race in all! O my breast aches with tender love for all!
O I mourn and yet exult, I am rapt with love for all,
Pioneers! O pioneers!

Raise the mighty mother mistress,
Waving high the delicate mistress, over all the starry mistress, (bend your heads all,)
Raise the fang'd and warlike mistress, stern, impassive, weapon'd mistress,
Pioneers! O pioneers!

See my children, resolute children,
By those swarms upon our rear we must never yield or falter,
Ages back in ghostly millions frowning there behind us urging,
Pioneers! O pioneers!

On and on the compact ranks,
With accessions ever waiting, with the places of the dead quickly fill'd,
Through the battle, through defeat, moving yet and never stopping,
Pioneers! O pioneers!

O to die advancing on!
Are there some of us to droop and die? has the hour come?
Then upon the march we fittest die, soon and sure the gap is fill'd.
Pioneers! O pioneers!

All the pulses of the world,
Falling in they beat for us, with the Western movement beat,
Holding single or together, steady moving to the front, all for us,
Pioneers! O pioneers!

Life's involv'd and varied pageants,
All the forms and shows, all the workmen at their work,
All the seamen and the landsmen, all the masters with their slaves,
Pioneers! O pioneers!

All the hapless silent lovers,
All the prisoners in the prisons, all the righteous and the wicked,
All the joyous, all the sorrowing, all the living, all the dying,
Pioneers! O pioneers!

I too with my soul and body,
We, a curious trio, picking, wandering on our way,
Through these shores amid the shadows, with the apparitions pressing,
Pioneers! O pioneers!

Lo, the darting bowling orb!
Lo, the brother orbs around, all the clustering suns and planets,
All the dazzling days, all the mystic nights with dreams,
Pioneers! O pioneers!

These are of us, they are with us,
All for primal needed work, while the followers there in embryo wait behind,
We to-day's procession heading, we the route for travel clearing,
Pioneers! O pioneers!

O you daughters of the West!
O you young and elder daughters! O you mothers and you wives!
Never must you be divided, in our ranks you move united,
Pioneers! O pioneers!

Minstrels latent on the prairies!
(Shrouded bards of other lands, you may rest, you have done your work,)
Soon I hear you coming warbling, soon you rise and tramp amid us,
Pioneers! O pioneers!

Not for delectations sweet,
Not the cushion and the slipper, not the peaceful and the
 studious,
Not the riches safe and palling, not for us the tame enjoyment,
Pioneers! O pioneers!

Do the feasters gluttonous feast?
Do the corpulent sleepers sleep? have they lock'd and bolted
 doors?
Still be ours the diet hard, and the blanket on the ground,
Pioneers! O pioneers!

Has the night descended?
Was the road of late so toilsome? did we stop discouraged nodding
 on our way?
Yet a passing hour I yield you in your tracks to pause oblivious,
Pioneers! O pioneers!

Till with sound of trumpet,
Far, far off the daybreak call-hark! how loud and clear I hear it
 wind,
Swift! to the head of the army! swift! spring to your places,
Pioneers! O pioneers!

The American West

Letters of Mattie and Uriah Oblinger†

The following letters are taken from *Prairie Settlement: Nebraska Photographs and Family Letters 1862–1912*, a digital collection on the American Memory Web site of the Library of Congress. This important collection of primary materials describing the settlement of the Great Plains combines two holdings from the Nebraska State Historical Society: the Solomon D. Butcher photographs and the letters of the Uriah W. Oblinger and Mattie Oblinger family. Uriah Oblinger first came from Indiana to Fillmore County, Nebraska, in 1872 to claim a homestead for his family. (Fillmore County is in south-central Nebraska, approximately sixty miles northeast of Webster County, the home of Willa Cather's family and the setting for *O Pioneers!*)

The letters included here are those Uriah wrote to his wife, Mattie, who was waiting in Indiana until he had staked his claim and built a dwelling. She joined him in Nebraska in May 1873. The couple homesteaded in Nebraska for seven years; Mattie died in childbirth in 1880, leaving Uriah with three young daughters. He then moved to Minnesota to be near his family.

The *Prairie Settlement* collection contains approximately three thousand pages of Oblinger family letters; the ones selected here concentrate on the early emigration and settlement experience of Uriah and Mattie—in particular their struggle to establish a farm and a home on the prairie in the 1870s.

† The Oblinger letters on the *Prairie Settlement* Web site exist in two forms: scanned original texts and transcriptions. They are catalogued by subject, by correspondent, and by date. The transcriptions record all the deletions and substitutions made by the writer and preserve the unparagraphed format of the original letters. For ease of reading, I have created paragraphs and eliminated the editorial references to additions and deletions. Readers can find the original letters and their transcriptions at http://memory.loc.gov/ammem/award98/nbhihtml/pshome.html.

Uriah W. Oblinger to Mattie V. Oblinger, Ella Oblinger, February 9, 1873

Fillmore Co Neb
Sabbath Feb 9th 1873

Dear Wife & Baby
I have just been looking Over all or nearly all the letters rec'd since we separated & it seems as though today we ought to be together talking instead of using the silent but ever faithful pen but so it is Ma[1] we are apart & the pen will ever do its faithful work wheth to record blessings or curses but thank high Heaven ours does not record anything but love & blessings for one another, & may it never be otherwise. My <u>dear Child</u>[2] how I should love to see you and hold you in my arms. there are children here one that can nearly walk where we are staying this winter and others in the neighborhood that I have nursed but they do not fill the place of my own <u>darling baby</u>. and Ma & baby both must take good care of themselves so that they will be in good health & able to stand the trip when the time comes for you to start for I think the looks of this country will be an agreeable surprise to you to see the beauties of it in the spring.

ma I would love to be with you & baby & go to church today but our lot is cast otherwise it seems as though we are destined to help make (what was once called the great american desert) blossom as the rose.

Within the memory of men now living, all this vast extent of land from the missouri river to the foot of the Rocky Mountains was covered with nothing but what is called buffalo grass & inhabited by nothing but wild beasts and wilder men. but now for nearly 200 miles west of the Missouri River the occasional spot of buffalo grass is pointed out by the pioneer as the waymark of a vegetation that but a few years ago flourished luxuriantly but now is being replaced by that more useful prairie grass called bluejoint which is the pioneers hay & fodder. & the wild animals & wild men that but a few years ago reigned supreme all over this beautiful extent of country are fast passing away before the approaching civilization of the 'pale face' (as the red man is wont to call him) and in a few years will be numbered among the things that were. and what was once known as the great 'American desert' will blossom as the rose. surely the hand of Providence must be in this, as it seems this desert as it has been termed so long has been specially reserved for the poor of our land to find a place to dwell in and where they can

1. Uriah addresses his wife as "Ma" [Editor].
2. Uriah and Mattie's baby daughter Ella [Editor].

find a home for themselves & families and where they can enjoy the companionship of their loved ones undisturbed by those that have hertofore held them under their almost exclusive control. but enough of this and we will now set about answering some of the questions I can remember of your asking in your previous letters first neither of the VanDoren girls are married and drawing water out of the well is accomplished just as it is in Ind[3] in the absence of pumps.

if it is a well that has been bored it is drawn with a rope & windlass & a galvanized Iron bucket about 5 in' wide and 2 ft long that will go inside the tubing conveniently if a dug well it is drawn with a rope passing over a pulley with a bucket fast to each end just as you have seen many a one in Ind this is much the best we have of drawing water yet until we get further along so we can afford to get wind mill pumps there is a great many of them on the prairies but I suppose you never seen one. well when you start out here next spring just watch and you will see one at almost every water station along the rail road as they use them very extensively you will see a large wheel mounted high up in the air on a large frame and when you see one of them just set it down it is a wind pump

as to Indians there is no more danger here in this locality than there is at your fathers for they never pass nearer than six miles of here on their hunting trips & when they get this far into settlements they are afraid to bother any one. beside it is only those living on reservations east of here that ever pass this way the wild Indians is not nearer than 150 mi west of here.

as to what we are doing just now this paper speaks for me Sam is laying on the bed in a deep study. Giles is reading in the bible & Mr Dewolf & wife are in the other room enjoying themselves with their baby[4] Mr Dewolfs enjoyment is somewhat mared by being a little sick as to sickness there is little here I think it is much healthier than Ind what would you think of seeing the dust fly there today or what would you think of camping all through the winter in Ind well that is just what they do here and the dust has been flying for a week and the weather warm & plasant with the exception of the wind it is blowing pretty hard all day from the south and about camping out the neighbors go down to the little Blue River 24 miles south of here for wood & poles to build with & camp out all night as they cannot make the trip there & back in a day and camp out without suffering too if we can we are going tomorrow to the

3. Indiana [Editor].
4. Sam and Giles Thomas were Mattie's brothers who went with Uriah to homestead in Nebraska. George Dewolf and his wife Eliza were farmers who homesteaded near Sam and Giles [Editor].

Blue for some poles I am going to get up something to build me a house out of for to coop ma & Baby in when I get them here.

* * *

did I tell you in my other letter that I traded Jenny so that I could get here colt the first of Sept well if I did not you know it when you read this I felt like taking a good boo hoo when I let her go but I could not help myself my Wife & Baby were dearer to me than Jenny was & I could see no other way of raising the money to get them here & take care of them after they were here so I guess it was for the best. and you know I dont want to go in debt any more if it can be helped for then a person is a slave ma have you sold your chickens yet if so what did you get for them. dont put off telling next time that Ella is sick till she gets well for I fell uneasey all the time as it seems to be so sickly there as to sickness here there is none at all to speak of

* * *

I think I have rec'd all the letters you have writte and the questions that I did not answer is an oversight merely, it is not because I did not want to answer them sam got a letter from Jeff Burch he talks as though he would like to come out here and I think it the best thing he can do I think a person just starting in life had better come here and grow up with the country the man that I traded Jenny to came here five years ago with himsef and wife and had but 50 cts left when he got here and now he has 80 acres of good land 3 children & team beside 6 head of cattle and 4 or 5 hogs and owes no one a cent. this is only one of a hundred such cases now they are independent & dont have to rent

Your loving Husband

Uriah W Oblinger

Page 85 Pure Gold[5] Learn it I love to sing it when lonesome

Uriah W. Oblinger to Mattie V. Oblinger and Ella Oblinger, March 9, 1873

Fillmore Co Nebraska
Mar 9th 1873

Dear Wife And Baby

* * *

Ma you must make up your mind to see a very naked looking home at first nothing but the land covered with grass and a sod

5. Uriah is probably referring to a songbook or hymnal, possibly one that Mattie had at home. Mattie also mentions it in a letter dated July 5, 1874.

house to live in. the prospect will no doubt look monotonous enough to you at first no fences (as none is needed) in sight but we have a soil rich as the richest river bottoms of Ind and no clay hills of course there is some poor land but it is the shape of sand & gravel knobs you do not see here as in Ind a rich black piece of ground and clay all around it, but the land is even all black soil I do not believe there is an acre of clay soil in Fillmore co. you must not build your hopes to high for "there's many a slip twixt cup & lip" but if we have health and luck we will have a beautiful home in a few years for we have a nice pattern to make one out of one thing we wont have to do here is clear land before we can put up a house all we have to do is plow up some sod (which will hang together for a half mile without breaking) cut in lengths to suit and lay up a wall & cover it and you have a house. to one who never seen one of our houses built of Nebraska brick it would seem as though they were a dirty house but they are warmer & cleaner than our hosier[6] log cabins ever were unless duble pains were taken with them for there is no daubing to fall out nor cracks for the wind to sift dust through there are some here who wish they had built sod houses in place of frame ones until they were able to build permanent.

* * *

Well it is past 2 P.M. and I must have some slapjacks.

Well Ma slapjacks is over and here I am talking at you again well you no doubt think so many slapjacks are not good well we are all getting fat on them any way. as every body that comes here get fat I hope *you* will not be an exception to the rule but get *fat* too. now dont box my ears for saying so till you and by that time you will be over your mad and then there will be no danger.

Ma be careful of Ella and dont get her exposed to the measles or whooping cough at this time if you can help it

* * *

Well Ella I dont think it is good for little girls to eat much candy it is better for them to have little books and larn to read and write beside candy money will be scarce for a year or two it will take all we can rake and scrape to get Bread, Meat, & potatoes but nevertheless we will try and get what my little needs to make a useful woman of her. Ma you talk of not wanting nice clothes till we can afford them from present appearances we will be able to afford them sooner here than if we had staid in Ind but a home of our own is far more preferable at present than nice clothes, or rather fine clothes for good common clothes is good enough for anybody

Mother wanted to know how our butter was keeping it is doing well. the first jar we opened is at any rate we have just commenced

6. Hoosier [Editor].

on the second we have about half of the sack of dried fruit yet that we started with and a few of the beans and one piece of the meat that come in the box and one can of the apple butter yet

your loving Husband

Uriah W Oblinger

Uriah W. Oblinger to Mattie V. Oblinger and Ella Oblinger, March 30, 1873

March 30th 1873
Fillmore Co Nebraska

Dear Wife & Baby
Your letter of 23rd Mar' is rec'd & it bears news that I do not like to hear but nothing more than I expected since the measles have been so near but probably it is all for the best as my baby could not have them in a better time the only thing that I regret is the lateness of the season it will come right in the best breaking season when I will have to go after you.[7] but Ma take good care of her so she will get over them soon and without leaving any serious effects.

* * *

well it is nearly sunset & I must quit and water my Oxens and then I will tell some more

Well Buck & Bright are watered and here I am talking to you again like I used to on sunday evening only this is with the pen & that used to be with the mouth, just like I wish this was. I am glad Uriah Cook[8] is coming with you for it will be company for you & in his pocket also I am watching for land for him. I am keeping myself posted as well as I can about all the vacant lands about here but land is being taking up very fast emigration is coming in very fast yesterday in sutton I seen 5 teams go through in less than an hour all going to settle in Adams county just west of Clay and every train is bringing some so you can tell the folks that what used to be called the great american desert is pretty thickly settled already & more coming and it will support hundreds yet from it soil which is all as black as Ind's richest river bottoms. Uriah Cook wants to fetch all the money he can for money is a big object here as every one that comes must depend on the pocket book till they can raise something to live on although we can live cheaper here than we can in an older country. when one buys all the living it counts up pretty fast now you may wonder why we can live cheaper here but

7. Mattie would be arriving in May, the optimum sod-breaking season for spring planting [Editor].
8. Uriah Cook was Uriah Oblinger's cousin [Editor].

we can be sociable here without so many Nick Nacks or such fine clothes as is required back there. but it will not be long if we have health till we can afford some of the comforts & luxuries of life as well as the bare necessities.

if I can just have luck to get my home improved as I want to the rest of the world will have no charms for me if my family are spared to me with health, then my ambition will be filled so far as this world is concerned. for I would rather have a good nice home all paid for and live happy with my family than to have what the world calls honor piled on me till I would be heard of all over the world.

well the weather now our equinoxial storm came off this week it comenced monday about noon by snowing and then got pretty cold but was warm enough till thursday to go to the blue[9] but was very windy but today is beautiful here no rain yet roads dusty again as the snow only lasted a little while and was just a skim any way

good night ma & baby with a kiss and take good care of baby through the measles

Uriah W Oblinger

Uriah W. Oblinger to Mattie V. Oblinger and Ella Oblinger, April 6, 1873

Bachelors Hall Neb' Fillmore County
April 6th 1873

Dear Wife & Baby
Giles & Sam have just finished each of them a letter and have gone in the other room to visit the folks in the east end of the house and here I am now at the table hurrying my <u>pen</u> over the paper talking to those I love through its silent medium.

I commenced my sod mansion last Monday and took some of the material on the ground such as brush & poles tuesday it misted rain some so I could not work at it, Wednesday I broke sod & commenced laying the walls, hauling the sod about 80 rods off of R.R. land. Why don't you get it on your own you ask, well we are not going to use our own soil to build with when the R.R. owns every other section around here. I am building my walls 2 1/2 ft thick and have got them 3 1/2 ft high, but the weather today and tonight looks as though I would not do much at it tomorrow this morning when we got up it was misting rain and this afternoon it snowed some and tonight (for I am writing by candle light) the wind is

9. Uriah could be referring either to the West Fork of the Big Blue River, which runs through the northern part of Fillmore county about five to seven miles north of Uriah's homestead, or to the Little Blue River, about twenty-five miles south in Thayer County, Nebraska. (Willa Cather refers to the Little Blue River in *O Pioneers!* [Editor].)

blowing from the north and looks as though it would freeze some befor morning. well if it will give us a good rain it would do us good for it is dry here so that the dust blows my eyes full and makes my face all dirty. now I expect you think being so dry the sod would all break to pieces. not a bit of it you can grab a piece 10 ft long and strart off with it and wear it out dragging and not tear it. I cut my sod 2 1/2 ft long and plowed about 4 1/2 in' deep & 10 in' wide and it is pretty heavy work to handle them.

* * *

Ma I got no letter yesterday and I wanted one so bad for I fell a little anxious about my little Pet since she is going to have the measles. if the weather is such tomorrow that I cannot work at my house I will go to the P.O. and ask the P. M. about it and mail this one also. I am in hopes this is almost the last letter I will have to write for I want you and baby to answer in person pretty soon. if you get to come at the time appointed it will only be two more sundays till we will be together if delayed a week it will be three, but dont risk starting with Ella till it is perfecly safe.

Now Ma just fasten your head on good for the wind will blow it off if you dont. Sundowns[1] like you used to wear would be good in this country for they would develop the body running after them. and fix your eyes to quit looking at fences for we have none here only little pig pens and very few of them yet.

* * *

I have realized this winter more than ever before that it is not good for man to be alone. you say I have had two men with me, well thats true but 20 men cannot fill the place of one woman. but I suppose you think just to the contrary, well we wont quarrel abot that till we get in quarreling distance I am getting a little tired of Sapjacks for once. I begin to want some bread that tastes like if a womans fingers had been in it. When I went to the Blue after wood I would get Mrs Dewolf to bake me some biscuit and it tasted awful good I tell you, but then it would taste better seasoned with Matties fingers and then her & Baby to pour my coffee & help eat it. you see I am writing this part of my letter in a whisper for fear some one will hear me.

* * *

Ma if all goes well you will get to see jenny when we start from Crete to *my* homestead (not ours till you get here) for I will be there hauling off my corn right where she is. now Ma dont get mad for saying mine not ours for you know every body in this country is called a bachelor till he gets a woman to live with him whether he is married or not some try to make me believe I am not married

1. Broad-brimmed straw hats [Editor].

they tell me they dont believe I have a wife for if had I would have her with me. they tell me they dont believe if I had a woman I could stand it away from her so long, they are only joking you know

I have lots to tell you when you get here so just make up your mind to listen and dont bring any deaf ears out here with you but enough of this nonsense

I am enjoying excellent health at present and hope you and Baby and all the friends are doing the same thing no more for tonight but remain your affectionate Husband & baby's happy Father

Uriah W Oblinger

Uriah W. Oblinger to Mattie V. Oblinger and Ella Oblinger, April 13–18, 1873

Bachelors Hall Neb' Fillmore Co
Apr' 13th 1873

Dear Wife and Baby
here I am at my old trade again, the boys have each of them just been writing a letter and now I am in the business. Sam wrote to Jeff Burch I do not know who Giles has written to for I did not see. Well, Ma I got your letter yesterday that was mailed Apr' 1st while Sam got one from will[2] mailed the day, last monday, why this was I cannot tell I should have got one yesterday written last Sunday but did not. yours of March 30th I was very anxious about as I did not get on saturday I walked to Sutton monday expecting to get it but was disappointed but Giles & I went into Sam's letter to find the news from home and that relieved my anxiety considerable. I was afraid Ella had the Measles bad and you would not write on that account but after reading Wills letter I felt easier but I was sorry to hear that Nettie[3] was sick. She had better come with you to Neb' where there is no chills only along the streams (where we have settled there has been none known yet and I hope never will be) then if she was to come here she might stand a chance of making some of these young bach's happy well enough of this

The measles are here too but not so plenty as Ind has them because there is not so many to have them. I think Geo' Reed has but little concern for his family but if they can stand it I can. if Ella is as long taking the measles after being exposed as I was it will be a good while for I was with them all the time for about 5 weeks before I took them but I hope she will not have them as hard as I did.

* * *

2. William Thomas, younger brother of Mattie [Editor].
3. Nettie Thomas, Mattie's sister [Editor].

Well Ma I will soon have a house done I have the walls all up the door frame in the pole up in the middle the ridge pole on and the rafters up now I have the roof to put on yet, and a window to put in and the floor to level off and then it is ready to move into it is 14 by 16 ft inside the walls are 2 1/2 ft thick I have worked a little over 9 days at it & hauled the sod and done every bit of the work alone no one even coming to look at me work till yesterday afternoon Mr Ferguson our nearest neighbor came over to look at it and pronounced it a good job and done quickly it took two of them 9 days to build his house. about 3 oclock yesterday afternoon Sam came to see it and brough me 2 letters one from Mrs Oblinger mailed Apr 1st and one from mr Huck the man that owns Jenny he says she has a colt and is all right so I have that much toward a horse team again. now I will try and buy a match for it this fall and will soon have a young team again.

If you can make the arrangements with Uriah Cook to pay your way it will save me a good deal of trouble for I cannot get a draft without going or sending to a bank and there is none nearer than Crete and if I send I would have to go to Fairmont (16 miles) and get a man there who is doing business for the Bank to send to it for me and then when it came back I would have to remail all of which would be a good deal of trouble which would be avoided if you can make such arrangements with cousin Uriah.

* * *

The weather still continues dry here yesterday evening it threatened rain but we did not get it and this evening again I hope it will come for we need it bad enough the wheat that was sowed a month ago is just barely up while some that was put in two weeks ago is harly sprouted I sent to town yesterday for a 1/2 bush of early rose potatoes to plant I told Giles if he would furnish the ground & raise them I would furnish the potatoes as he has ground that was broke last year and mine is all prairie unbroken yet & they would not do well on it.

Ma you must make up your mind to stand a good deal of wind for Neb' does a heap of blowing and since it is so dry there is lots of dust flying. yesterday and today have been terrible windy it nearly blew me off the walls of my house yesterday when I would be carrying a sod on the wall a gust of wind would come and blow my hat over my eyes and nearly capsize me my sods for my wall were pretty heavy they were from 2 1/2 to 4 ft long 4 in thick and from 10 to 12 in wide now you may think a sod of that size would not hold together but if I could have handled them I could have 10 ft without breaking. the whole furrow as longh as I plowed it all hung together unbroken so you see we have some pretty tough sod here but when once entirely subdued it is like a pile of ashes. Oh yes I have quite a wood pile up I have wood plentier here than I had at Jake murrays if he does live in a timbered country and me where there is none in sight there is one consolation here you wont have to burn old rotten fence rails

* * *

Your Affectionate Husband

Uriah W Oblinger

perhaps you can read this my arms are so numb & tired handling heavy Sod that it is hard work for me to write

from your loving Husband

Uriah Oblinger

Friday Apr' 18th
Dear Wife & Baby

I thought my letter finished Sunday evening. I spoke about looking for rain in that & raining a little, but now I can tell you of one of the most terrible storms I ever witnessed Language fails to describe so that one may know just how it seemed to one in the storm. It struck us at sunset sunday evening with wind & rain & rained nearly all night the wind increaseing all the time monday morning it turned to snow (very fine article) & snow & wind increasing all the time all though it seemed as though the wind was doing it best. the storm lasted from sunset Sunday evening till near midnight Wednesday night making near 80 hours storm. when we would go out to try to do anything for the stock we could not see other more than from 5 to 10 ft & to be heard we had to shout at the top of the voice on account of the wind blowing such a gale.

one could harly keep his feet at all we had to dig snow about 1/2 hr whenever we undertook to feed anything in order to get to the stable door. the snow streamed through every crevice I say streamed through for it just almost blinded one to get to the corn pile we had to shovel in short it was shovel to utmost of ones strength to do anything or get anything. Mr Wards were at mr Elliots visiting and did not get home & Sam was going to ride home with them so him & Giles were caught there too but about 9 oclock sunday night Giles & Sam & Mr Ward came up here to stay all night on monday morning Mr Elliots stove smoked them out on account of the stove pipe being defective and we had to bring them all up here, 2 women 4 children & 5 men all here. Mr DeWolfs being gone to his wifes sisters 18 miles southeast of here, & left all of his things for us to tend, 2 cows 5 calves hogs & yoke of oxen and chickens.

by hard work we saved every thing for him but 4 pigs 1 chicken & 2 calves the third calf probably will die. the calves were in a small stable very open where for us to have tried any more than we would have perished *us*. one of his cows had a young calf right in the midst of the storm in the stable half full of snow where there were 2 yoke of oxen and another cow & I gathered it up & carried that in the cellar and saved it. Mr Elliotts fed their horses & mr Wards monday morn and the storm was so fearful that we could not venture dow to his stable to see after them till tuesday evening although not more than 80 rd

tuesday evening we concluded to venture and when we got there we found the entrance to the house door banked full to the top and his stable door being in the north and considerably open we found 2 calves 1 cow & six head of horses all snowed in as the storm came from a little west of North the stable full from one end to the other entirely to the roof except right at the door where there was just room for 2 horses to stand by being literally crammed together the rest all down, well the next thing was to get them out. two of the men Mr Ward & Ellott commenced digging to get the house door open while the rest of us wen to getting horses out I took an open knife and went in to 2 of the horses and cut the halters & came near getting under as they were nearly crazy to get out

we got them in the house carpet & all on the floor. then commenced digging to get the rest out we saved all but one of Mr Wards & she died in 1/2 hour after we got her out we dug through the roof and found her packed in snow laying on her side with the snow so tight around her she could only move her head a little we dug the side of the stable down about half way and dragged the mare over the side as there was 20 feet of snow betwen her & the door. the next morning (wednesday) we dug mr Elliotts cow out she will probably live but is not able to get up yet but 2 calves that were in the stable perished making 4 calves 1 5 year old mare[4] & 4 pigs that perished right here at 2 stables with us.

the loss of stock has been fearful & I am afraid human life, as there were numbers of emigrants on the road though I have heard of none yet. there was a woman about a mile from here with 4 children whose husband was away from home and I knew she had but little wood if any so Wednesday afternoon I concluded to make the effort to reach her and see how they were getting along & I had to go right aganst the strom. just as I was starting Sam hollowed at me to come back that I would get lost and perish but I did not come back nor perish either. I would proceed abut 5 rd then turn and get a little breath then try it again in this way I succeeded in reaching

4. Uriah probably meant one five-year-old mare not a fifteen-year-old mare.

the house & she was mighty glad to see me as they were out of wood and the ax buried under the snow. they had been in bed for 2 days only as she would break up something in the house to burn & cook something for the children to eat the oldest was only 7 years old. I dug the ax from under the snow hunted my way to a pig pen got a couple of poles and cut wood enough to do till next day.

then started home again but the storm had commenced abating so that I could by spells see nearly 1/2 mile on the way back I got a prairie chicken his feather were so icy he could not go very fast & threw the shovel after him (I had taken one with me) and knocked it over yesterday was beautiful & today also the snow by night will be all gone except in the ravines and the snow banks. over 1/2 the prairie is bare already and good walking. Sam lost his hat monday morning so I willed him my old one. his started near cut over the prairies for Kansas. Sam seems some little discouraged since witnessing the storm but there is no use of that for it is the most terrible storm ever witnessed here and may never occur again.

what made the storm so destructive to the life of stock was the time of year that it occurred the stables or a great many of them have nothing but hay for roof with poles thrown on to hold them down and they had considerably blown to pieces and people thought there was no use to fix them as summer was just here I heard of one man had 30 head and another 60 head of cattle go off in the storm and has not found but few yet and they were dead. another had 15 hed perish in one pile when stock was turned loose to shif for themselves they would just go with the storm.

Now Ma dont get discouraged discouraged [*sic*] because we have had a terrible storm here for I am not

* * *

you can tell the folks they never seen a storm in Ind only playthings

Love to all

Uriah W Oblinger

Uriah W. Oblinger to Mattie V. Oblinger and Ella Oblinger, April 27, 1873

Bachelors Hall Fillmore Co Neb'
April 27th 1873

Dear Wife & Baby
As I have been straining myself so long to write you a long letter almost every week since we have been separated I will "<u>make</u> this one <u>short</u>" as I hope the next will be delivered by the word of mouth with a smack to it. Yesterday Giles cleaned house again for church

but was not disappointed this time, we had preaching this time, although it has favored rain considerable all day and has rained very gently by spells and is raining very much so at present nearly sunset. since easter we have had worse weather than we have had all winter for work first came the storm spoken of in my last, then came a few beautiful days as nice as heart could wish but tuesday it was cool and snowed some in the afternoon and has been cool all week till today it is warm with the rain it was froze part of the time so I could not break prairie

I broke the first ground on my claim last monday I just surrounded 20 acres exactly measured off and have about 4 1/2 of it plowed Mr Dewolf & I measured off the 40 acres that he is to break for me last Monday and I plowed about 1 acre of it the same day with buck & bright & a right hand plow & it went pretty awkward at first the reason I got a right hand plow is because I could not get a left hand one at all at the time. but now I have a good excuse to take it back they give 2 shares with every plow and the extra one will not fit at all and tomorrow I am going to Sutton to see if I cant exchange for a left hand one. My house is not done yet I got it all ready to put the roof on the day before the storm commenced and the storm left it too wet inside to put it on till it dried out some so I have been breaking.

I bught 1/2 bush. Early Rose P's[5] and Giles planted them on the halves last monday I am going to get 2 or 3 bush more & let him plant them on the same terms as his ground was broke last year and mine is all sod. Ma we will have water near the house for washing and watering stock but for drinking and cooking I will have to haul a little over 1/4 of a mile till I get time to dig a well.

* * *

I am doing just the best I know how to get along I come here with almost nothing and I am holding my own well, so you may not get angry for trading my team off I have <u>determined to get my land</u> on some terms, I am not going back to Ind to rent until I bust entirely and have to walk back now you can just set that down & set on it. I did not set down & do nothing this winter I put off & went to work at some price I had some bad luck tis true, but it was better to make an effort than to sit here and suck my fingers. and when I could make nothing at work I had to do the next best thing & when I got a chance to better my condition by trading I did and I intend to make every turn I can that will help me get a home

I have just as much land as I desire and now I want to fix it up so that I can live on it comfortable and happy, and it will do no one

5. Early Rose potatoes. Uriah also mentions them in letters written April 13–18, 1873, and June 16, 1873.

any good to throw any thing in my way for I am running my own machine now and if I keep my health I am going to succeed now mind, ma dont come with, I cant, for it will do no good I come to get a home, and I want you to come determined on a home too you may get some homesick but make up your mind for the worst and we will succeed

from your affectionate Husband
Uriah W Oblinger

Mattie V. Oblinger to Thomas Family, May 19, 1873

May 19th 1873

At Home in our own house and a sod at that And just eat dinner

* * *

We moved in to our house last Wednesday (U. W. O birthday) I suppose you would like to see us in our sod house It is not quite so convenient as a nice frame[6] but I would as soon live in it as the cabins I have lived in and then we are at home which makes it more comfortable I ripped our Waggon sheet in too have it arround too sides and have several papers up so the boys think it looks real well the Uriahs[7] made a bed stead and a Lounge so could have some thing to sleep on The only objection I have we have no floor yet will be better this fall I got one tea cup & saucer and the corner of the glass on the little hero picture broken Pretty good luck I think my goods got here two days before I did Uriah had taken them out to Mr Houks

Uriah was plowing sod this fore noon talks of planting some this after noon he has twenty acres surounded have ten of it broke Doc & Billie & Uriah C stayed with us I know you would have laughed to see us fixing their bed we set boxes to the side of the Lounge and enlarged Uriahs bed for all of them We enjoyed the fun and they enjoyed their bed as much as if they had been in a nice parlor bed room U. C.[8] & Doc sung while I got supper They call Doc Sam out here sounds very odd to me wish you could see his whiskers shaved all off but what is on his chin an lip I told him I wanted some to send you but he could not see it

* * *

I am washing to day This after noon is little cloudy with the sun shineing occasionaly Ella is as hearty as she can be and has an ap-

6. A house built around a wooden frame, considered more comfortable than a sod house and a sign of prosperity [Editor].
7. Uriah Oblinger and his cousin, Uriah A. Cook, the son of Eliza and John Cook, Uriah Oblinger's paternal aunt and uncle. Uriah Cook escorted Mattie and Ella to Nebraska in 1873, then went to Rice County, Minnesota.
8. The initials stand for Uriah Cook.

petite like a little horse I never cooked for such appetites as I have since I been here some times I think I will cook enough of some things for two meals but the boys clean them every time

We are all well I must close for this time I am as ever your sister & daughter Our love to all

M V O

Mattie V. Oblinger to George W. Thomas, Grizzie B. Thomas, and Wheeler Thomas Family, June 16, 1873

Fillmore County Neb
June 16th 1873

Dear Brother & Sister & all of Uncle Wheelers
Thinking you would like to hear from us and hear how we are prospering I thought I must write you a letter and to fulfill the promise I made when I last saw you

* * *

I think there will be a methodist preaching place established in the neighborhood before long as there was a methodist preacher around a few days ago hunting up the scattered members in the country He said the conference had sent him here so you see we are not entirely out of civilization I know if you was here you would not think so I have just as good neighbors as I ever had any where and they are very sociable I was never in a neighborhood where all was as near on equality as they are here Those that have been here have a little the most they all have cows and that is quite a help here I get milk & butter from Mrs Furgison who lives 1/4 of a mile from us get the milk for nothing and pay twelve cents a pound for butter she makes good butter

Most all of the people here live in Sod houses and dug outs I like the sod house the best they are the most convenient I expect you think we live miserable because we are in a sod house but I tell you in solid earnest I never enjoyed my self better but George I expect you are ready to say It is because it is somthing new No this not the case it is because we are on our own and the thoughts of moveing next spring does not bother me and every lick we strike is for our selves and not half for some one else I tell you this is quite a consolation to us who have been renters so long there are no renters here every one is on his own and doing the best he can and not much a head yet for about all that are here was renters and it took about all they had to get here Some come here and put up temporary frame houses thought they could not live in a sod house This fall they are going to build sod houses so they can live live [*sic*] comfortable this winter a temporary frame house here is a poor thing a house that is not plastered the wind and dust goes right through and they are very cold A sod house can be built so they are real nice and comfortable build nice walls and then plaster and lay a floor above and below and then they are nice Uriah is going to build one after that style this fall

The one we are in at present is 14 by 16 and a dirt floor Uriah intends takeing it for a stable this winter I will be a nice comfortable stable A little ways from the door is a small pond that has watter the year round we use out of it for all purposes but drinking and cooking We have the drinking water cary about 1/4 of a mile and the best of water We have two neighbors only 1/4 of a mile from us

I must stop and get supper

Supper is over and dishes washed I wish I had a cow or two to milk I would feel quite proud then think will get one after harvest

* * *

Almost every man here does his own work yet for they are not able to hire I think it will be quite different in a few years Uriah has 23 acres of sod corn planted it looks real well I tell you it is encourageing to have out a lot of corn and all your own We have a nice lot of Squashes and Cucumbers & Mellons & Beans comeing on There was a striped bug worked some on our squashes but did not bother our other vines

We have our Potatoes and cabbage up at Giles as they do not so well on sod I set a hundred & thirty cabbages last week they are every one growing We have the nicest patch of early rose potatoes in the neighborhood will not be long until we will have new potatoes We have fared pretty well in the potato line as Uriah bought ten bushel when I come to Crete he bought for seed and to use we will have plenty until new potatoes come If nothing happens we will have a nice lot this fall I have nice Tomato plants comeing on I want to set more Tomatoes and Cabbage this week I get Garden vegetables in Giles garden

I could not make garden here as we had no sod subdued and I have such good neighbors they said they would divide their garden vegetables I planted a lot of beet seed in Mrs Alkires garden they look real nice Uriah is breaking sod to day he will soon have 40 acres turned over then it will be ready to go into right next Spring It looks like it was fun to turn the sod over here there are no roots or stpumps to be jerkinking the plows out

* * *

we had the hardest storm saturday night or evening that has been since I come the wind blew very hard I do not know how long it lasted for I went to sleep and the wind was blowing yet We can not notice the wind so much in a sod house as in a frame

* * *

The prarie looks beautiful now as the grass is so nice and green and the most pretty flowers I can not tell how many different kinds I have noticed I have seen three Antelopes one Jack Rabbit and one swift and lots of prarie squirrels I thought when I left the timber I would not see any more birds but there are lots of them here some that are entirely different to any I ever saw in Ind There is more Rattle snakes here than there are garter snakes in Ind Uriah has killed two on our place there are not so plent right in our neighborhood as they are three miles east of here near a prarie dog town some men over there have killed as high 18 & 20

* * *

Now Geo I send this in your name but I want you to besure and give it Uncle Wheels too as postage is scarce I thoughgt this would do all I want you all to besure and write soon We send our love and best wishes from

U W O & M V Oblinger

Direct to Sutton Clay County Neb Excuse letter paper

Mattie V. Oblinger to Thomas Family, April 12, 1874

Sunday forenoon Aprile 12th 1872[9]
Fillmore Co Neb

Dear Father & Mother & Bros & Sister

To day finds me converseing with you through the silent medium of the pen What a blessed prvalege that we can converse in this way when we are deprived of converseing with each other verbaly How I would love to see you all to day if it was so that I could Nett I think we would have considerable of gabbing to do I fancy I would see you trying to tell me every thing and getting dinner too I would like to be there to keep the fire punched up and keep the meat frying while you are trotting out to the milk house and down in the cellar say you may just bring up some of that caned fruit for dinner but what would I care for can fruit if I had two or three big apples to eat just throw one over

* * *

If we could drive up to the the [*sic*] gate I wonder who would be the first one to meet us Nett I imagine I would see you comeing makeing about two jumps from the door to the gate Charlie[1] I dont

9. This letter was misdated 1872 instead of 1874. Mattie and Ella did not come to Nebraska until May 1873, so Mattie could not have written it in 1872. The letter can also be internally dated to 1874, because Mattie wrote, "When I think of the changes there has been already [in Indiana] and not quite a year."
1. Charles Thomas, Mattie's youngest brother [Editor].

believe you would take time to get your hat and then stick your hands in your pockets and walk out Well I would not care how all of you would cut your extras if I could only see you Now I am not home sick and have not been since I have been here but you know it is natural for friends to have a great anxiety to see each other after they have been separated awhile Uriah says when we go back he intends to rent out the farm and stay a year for he wants to go to Minnesota and Ind both

Some that have been here three years are going to visit their friend this fall Those that have been here that long are the first settlers in this neighborhood When they came here there was any amount of vacant land and now there is non near here only the RR land how I wish all of it would go back to the Gov all the RR land around here would be taken in a very short time There are some comeing in that have money and are buying it Doc there was some more dutch come from Ill and bought 3/4 of section 7 Town 6 & Range 3 east they wanted eleven but it belongs to the land that has been reserved for some purpose Those that are acquainted with them say they seem like very nice people They are building farame buildings all together even frame stables you know that is stylish for Fillmore

* * *

We had nice Easter here was pleasent all day quite different to what last Easter was here We had snow the day before consequently we had a white Easter moring Nett you said if I would set a day and let you know you would come over & bring the machine and wash my bed clothes Well I can set the day easier than you can come any day will suit me that you can come Giles says he did not write last week I thought he certainly would write We try to write every other week and think he will do the same I expect you think we are carless when we do not write every week but it is so expensive that we can hardly stand to write oftener Nett I think you was full when you wrote your last letter

When we get a letter from home the work is vey quick laid to one side and read but I have not received those papers and pattern and seeds that you spoke of Net did you forget I sent for a few Onions if you think you can send them I should think you could send them as easy as any other bulbs my plants are looking nicely I have not made garden yet will make some tomorrow if it does rain it has the appearance of rain this eveing I would have made some this last week but the ground was not ready and Uiah wanted to finish his wheat I feel like killing my old hens they will not go to setting I expect when they do take a notion to set they will all want to set at one time I have made two table clothes & two shirts for Uriah & one for my self out of our waggon sheet Dont you think I will have a good time washing them this summer Uriah looks so odd with an everday white shirt on

I have commenced peicing a quilt I know no name for it it is peiced of dark & light calico I did think I would peice an Ocean wave but when I peice that I want it for a nice quilt I have seen some scrap quilts peiced that way here and they look real well I do not need the white yarn there was a little ball of my white yarn at Elliotts I had forgot it so I did not have to borrow Nett I tried a new way to make bread custard I use water instead of milk and it does real well If you doubt it why just try it & see

If you was living in Neb you would try a great many projects that you never think of in Ind

* * *

Oh yes I suppose we will live high now as Uriah has taken a step toward the white house He was selected School director last Monday and voted a five dollar sallary for him guess he will not have to work now I torment him considerable about it Nett how do you do up your hair now days Does the boys hurry you as they use to when you go to comb I do mine up just as I use to for sunday and every day too for my old net is played out if I had a braid I could do my hair up as you use to

I suppose you know by this time who your preacher is I am anxious to hear if we get the Journal a Wednesday we will know Well I am getting sleepy so I will close and send this to the Office if I get a chance tomorrow I am as ever yours truly

M V Oblinger

Monday morning

rained a little last night and very much the appearance of a rainy day I wish it would rain we have had no rain yet this spring

Mattie V. Oblinger to Thomas Family, April 25, 1874

Saturday forenoon 11 Oclock Aprl 25th 1874
Fillmore Co Neb

Dear Father & Mother & Bros & Sister
To day finds Ella & I alone as the boys (Giles & Uriah have gone to Sutton I have finished my Saturdays work and thought I would write until the boys come for their dinner Nett my Saturdays work does not amount to much To day I give the house a general sweeping & brushing cleaned out the cupboard and washed off all my dishes then washed down the windows & doors Last Wednesday I washed & then scoured my tin ware so we will live bright for a few days Now Mother are you ready to say well Marth what do you

scour tin ware with away out in Neb Well I use sand just as I use to in Ind but I can not go to the Creek here and get it for we are not near any runing stream the sand I useed come out of Mr Powells Well it was some Mrs Allkire give me Then I give the table a genuine scouring with it I had scoured it frequently with ashes but it would never look the way I wanted it to

* * *

We had a little thunder last evening the first we have had this year but I did not burn my bed ticks we had a little shower To day is a very beautiful day a little too windy from the North to make it real pleasent out of doors but I have had the door open all day You ask what kind of a day Easter was here It was quite different to what it was with you It was a very pleasent and beautiful all day with a south wind some anticipated a storm as they had such a dreadful one last easter guess they expected another We have not had much snow since but some cool days for this time of the year but I think hardly so much as you have had We have had some very warm pleasent days The spring is considered very backward here for this state

I have mad some garden planted some of nearly all kinds but beans Mother I suppose next Friday will be the day for them I planted peas last Tuesday guess the sign was right as it was in the Twins but I had no twins[2] to plant them as you use to I remember when you would have Giles & George to plant your peas I planted about the half of what I had will plant again in a few days we have planted our Early Rose & Peerless potatoes have quite a good sized patch of them have some more of all kinds to plant Uriah has got his Wheat & Flax sowed and considerable plowed for corn some are going to plant corn a Monday several will plant during the week I have quite a nice lot of horse raddish & sage roots and Rhubarb my Honey suckel is growing nicely and most all of my rose bushes are alive I can not tell yet about the little forest shrubery yet I fear they will not do much my Pinroes and Dialetre grew nicely for awhile and then died I wish you would try and save some Peonies seed this season I believe we can get them that way best I know they have seed Now dont forget it I do not as you can get any seed of the Dialetre There is lots of flowers I want to get after the sod is once subdued so they will grow

* * *

What a pleasure it is to work on ones own farm a person has some heart to go ahead and fix up for you can feel that it is ours

2. Mattie may be referring to a "sign" in the constellation Gemini, the Twins, as an indicator for planting. The second reference is a play on the word twins, as Mattie's twin brothers, Giles and George, had helped their mother plant in the past.

and not for some one else to come along and say well you will have to hunt anothe place I want to get another man on here I would rather live as we do than to have to rent and have some one bossing us and telling us when to move and be bothered moveing as we use to

* * *

Uriahs Father sent him 25 dollars to homestead his land When Uriah jumped this claim he did not have money enough to homestead so he just put a Fileing on it When he Filed on it they said it was just as good as a homestead for 33 months if you would stay on it and improve it Sometime ago there was quite a trouble in the Beatrice district about the fileings they said they were no account and several men around here put out for Beatrice and put homestead papers on their land

* * *

We have heard of no trouble in the Lincon district some thinks the fileings that have been jumped has been done by a set of land sharks that is watching the land office to make money without work

* * *

Well this sheet is full and my brain is not empty yet neither has Uriah wrote any and there is none wrote for Ella I believe I will try another peice with this for three cents

I thought when I comenced I would not have much to write and I did not double the lines[3] I wish now I had but it makes such tedious writing to double the lines Uriah is reading the Journal and Ella is crying for me to take her and put her to bed she likes to be nursed as well as ever she runs so much during the day that when night comes she is nearly pegged out so I will close for to night I am as ever

Mattie Oblinger
Sutton Clay Co Neb

Sunday fore noon April 26th

Well as I said last evening I was not done writing I will try now to finish

* * *

Father I guess we can manage to get through with out that money now unless something happens us at the time I ask things looked a little scaly but we was not suffering and never have been discouraged yet I expect as you are building you need all the money you can get but I tell you what I do wish and that is that you would write to us occasionly how gladly we would receive it I expect you

3. To "double the lines" meant to write vertically as well as horizontally so that lines crossed each other—a way to save paper [Editor].

think because Nett writes so much you would not have any thing to write well I know you can tell us something and let Nett skip one week I love to get Netts letters but they are not from Father or Mother when you do not write it seems as though you have nearly forgotten us I know though that you have not nor I dont think you ever will

* * *

Charlie how is your mustache or have you got any sprouts yet I think when a boys goes with the girls he aught to be old enough to have a mustache I suppose you set up to the glass as big as any of them now on saturday night and <u>Lather & Shave</u> but it hardly seems possible to us I would like for you to be cutting some more flourishes with your pen soon Will has your ink bottle dried up or why is it we get no letters from you any more We had intended to go up to Giles to day but it is so windy we thought we would feel best at home & it threatened rain this moring Well if you was all here I would dispense of this writing

* * *

Uriah has quit reading has laid on the Lounge for a nap but I will spoil that for I am going to get dinner We are all well We are as ever yours truly

M V Oblinger

* * *

Uriah W. Oblinger and Mattie V. Oblinger to Thomas Family, December 14, 1874

Monday evening Dec 14th 1874
Fillmore County Neb

Dear Father & Mother & Bro & Sister
We have just eat our suppers and now we will try to answer your letter we recd this morning I have eat so much mush & butter & milk that I can hardly write Well I expect you wonder what I make mush out of well I make it of Graham flour it makes splendid mush to eat with milk & butter & much better fried White flour almost goes a begging at our house since we have been using Graham The money you sent come all righ

We heard a Saturday afternoon that the letter was in the office This mornig Morgan come by going up after a barrel of things that had been sent them by Mrs Morgans folks so Uriah went with him to get the letter but the barrel has not come yet Morgans barrel weighed 80 lbs & come from Coshockton Ohio and then only six dollars Uriah went over home with him he said there was lots of nice & good things in it

Mrs Morgan she sent Ella some Chestnuts & 4 nice large green Apples & sent me a half gallon or more of the nicest dried peaches I do think she is a splendid woman but I guess we will loose her this spring as her folks have been writing & pleading of her to come to Ohio to live ever since she has been here & I guess they have accomplished it I am real sorry of it too She will go back in may or June & Morgan will go next fall and rent out his farm here I dont he will be satisfied there as well as here for her people do not like him very well just because he was a poor boy when he set out for himself He is a man that is well thought of here and could not be any better man to a woman Sam can tell you some thing about them

Ella is very busy writing to Grandpa & Grandma says she think Grandpa & Grandma will have a good time makeing out part of her writing I expect it will have to be sent or there will be a cry she thinks her letters are of much importance She is very anxious for the barrel to come so she can see what her presents are (& I guess there are others in the same fix) She was much pleased with what Grandpa said to her in the letter she made me read it to her two or three times & then she took the letter and read it almost as it was written

* * *

Indeed if she was there Grandpa nor no one else would get lonesome she would keep you busy answering questions and telling her how to read & reading for her and pronounceing for her when she spells wish you could see her when she reads in her 1st reader she has several peices almost memorised The Lazy sheep and Butterflies she can say with but little telling her Pa thinks she would make a good peddler she will come to her Pa with her book when he is busy reading & he will try to make her wait or go away & the first thing he knows She has him looking at a picture or telling her how to pronounce a word & the firsth thing he knows she has him reading for her

* * *

The last cards you sent her it was not more than ten minutes until she had them memorised & she can repeat the verses now any time She can say the childs evenig prayer & nearly all of the Lords prayer It is no trouble for her to memorise She has finished her letter & is sitting on her Pas knee hearing him sing wish you could hear her sing Old Santa claus & Weaver John she is very anxious for Christmas to come she is quite sure Santaclaus will bring her something

* * *

Well Charlie you certainly went to the barn and caught an old hen and soused her in the dye pot and then pulled her across the paper backwards by the tail If you dont do better next time I will not claim you for any kin or say that I have a daughter that has a nose exactly like yours or is any thing like you Your mind must have been wondering and it is hard to tell what your pen was doing only putting a word or two on one line You did not answer the questions I ask you at all now I want you to try again you say you will try & do better next time I think there is room for great improvement

* * *

I know we have to live close & very saveing to get along but we enjoy health & happiness & a plenty to eat as long as it last will try to make it reach the next crop We could have lived nicely this winter if Mr Grass hopper had not come indeed we are thankful for what they did leave Well Uriah wants to write some so I guess I will have to stop he is singing Yankeedoodle for Ella my love to all we are all well

M Oblinger

* * *

Mattie V. Oblinger to Thomas Family, August 8, 1876

Fillmore County Neb
Tuesday afternoon August 8th 1876

Dear Father & Mother & Bro & Sister
This afternoon I will try to write you a few lines I do not remember when I wrote last but I believe it was in june I dont think you have had a letter from Neb since the 4th We have been very busy and most of the time with out stamps and money We havemanaged to keep ourselves in groceries such as we were compelled to have by selling butter and a few vegetables we have had an abundance of Peas Beans Reddishes and other garden truck It has kept us scrapeing and gathering pretty close to keep a going but we have managed so far not to go in debt one cent this summer

Uriah is going to town tomorrow afternoon and I want to send a littile butter and Potatoes and corn and pickles to get some groceries <u>credit</u> is pretty hard for anyone to get in Sutton and we have learned he is a poor customer to deal with and the least we have to do with him that much better off we are Every inch of dry goods we have got this summer was 6 1/2 yds of calico for the girls[4] dresses but we will have to get some pretty soon or we will have to grease and go naked

* * *

We had our barley threshed about two weeks ago thinking we could sell it right away so we could get us some things and get a

4. Mattie had given birth to her second daughter, Stella [Editor].

well we need a well so bad it has been almost impossible to get along this summer with out one haveing two head of horses and 4 head of cattle to watter I find it pretty hard to get along and take care of milk with little watter but I have made butter to sell all the sumer off of our heiffers and have had to use butter to shorten and grease every thing I think they do well for comon cows I do not know what we would have done if we had not got them for we have not had a mess of meat in the house since last winter until the other day our neighbor (Geor Smith) killed a hog and we got 39[5] lbs to have for threshers & well diggers I fried it and packed it down to keep until they come

* * *

Uriah has 13 1/2 acres of corn he thinks will yield 60 bushels per arce and 4 acres that looks well but will not yield so much as it was panted late our cane looks well we will have our share of squashes again and some pumpkins our Wattermellons are not so plenty as last year was planted too late Potatoes are not near so good a yield as lat year as the bugs are so bad we will have more than we can make use of as we have quite a lot planted Some vines are entirely Striped[6] ours are not hurt much yet We will feast on Fried chicken & sweet potatoes after while as both chickens and sweett potatoes are doing well I had a huge mess of cabbage yesterday for dinner will have plenty from now on I have the best cabbage in the neighborhood you bet I worked for it

* * *

Well I will stop writing about harversting and crops or my letter will all be taken up for that Oh yes Giles will start with the thresher now soon Sade will stay here most of the time or she thinks so and at Sams part the time I have had lots of pie plant to use had enough to make eight pies for threshers have had eight Raspberries one bush of them you sent us is growing the blackberries all died

* * *

Well Stella is our baby and will be for a long time she likes her niny[7] as well as ever but I have threatened to take it from her next month if it is cool and she keeps well and I expect I will have a dreadful time of it for she is so bad after it Ella is trying to feed her pup we have another to raise but I expect will be like all the rest when we get it raised we will loose it She calls it Jo Turk she says Jo is its gviven name I named it Turk

5. Mattie overwrote this number in the original letter; it is possible she intended it to be 49 not 39.
6. Stripped clean (by grasshoppers, most likely) [Editor].
7. Child's language either for breast milk or a woman's breast. Frederic G. Cassidy, ed., *Dictionary of American Regional English*, 3 vols. (Cambridge: Belknap Press, 1996), 3, p. 810.

* * *

Nett we recd your letter containing your pictures[8] I dont think your picture is near as good the one you sent me married life certainly can not agree with you You look nearly as old and peaked and lantern jawed[9] as I do What in the land ailed you any how you look as though you was in deep distress was your dress pinching you or is that a kind of style you have got to putting on It dont fit you if it is I dont believe you are fattening up on Peaches this fall Stright[1] looks very much as I thought he would But I dont beleive he is any better looking than my on man I feel just lik takeing hold of tha goatee and pulling him across the house Well I guess there will be no danger of beauty killing either of our men nor will we qarrel over their good look for as pretty is pretty does but I shall look for Strights picture soon besure and send me a peice of your wedding dress this fall for my log cabbin[2] I am working at it and all the peices of the worsted dresses you can get

* * *

Mother you said in your letter for us to keep a stif upper lip that would get some fruit this fall Well that is no trouble for us any more for we have had to keep a stiff upper lip so much since we have been here that they have about grown stiff Wish you could see the girls Ella has been riding Stella in the grain scoop but she has up set her and Stella is mad as a wet hen you better think they are wild but there they go again Write soon

M V & U W Oblinger

Mattie V. Oblinger to Thomas Family, September 10, 1876

Fillmore Co Neb
Sept 10th 1876

Dear Father & Mother & Bros & Sister

I suppose you think it is time you was hearing from us again Sam we recd- your letter this morning I was wondering what had become of all of you for I think the last letter we had was dated July 9th and it seemed like a long time to be with out a letter I had about concluded you were all sick or had run out of Stamps as we do sometimes I guess if you would try you could send us letters oftener Charlie I would like to know why you do not write to us any more I

8. Portraits of Nettie [16372t.jpg] and Stright Bailey [16373t.jpg], which may be the pictures Mattie describes here, are available for viewing [on the *Prairie Settlement* web site (Editor)].
9. Having long, thin jaws, giving a hollow appearance to the cheek. *The Compact Oxford English Dictionary*, 2d ed. (New York: Oxford University Press, 1991), p. 940.
1. Nettie's husband [Editor].
2. A quilt pattern [Editor].

do not think strange of Father & Mother not writing oftener for I do not suppos they have time only on sunday and then they want rest and do not feel like witing but an occasional letter is very acceptable

I suppose you would like to know if we have been Grasshoppered again They were here several days pretty thick and injured the corn considerable Some fields they striped the blades all off and other peices striped partly They nibbled the ends of most all the ears and eat of all the silks so it will not fill out and be as good Neb would have had a splendid corn crop if the hoppers had stayed away awhile It looked rather gloomy when they begin to light on the corn They were not so large nor did not eat near so fast as they did two years ago They eat nearly all of my cabbage The country is nothing like as destitute as two years ago there will be corn but will not be near so good as it would have been The corn and cabbage is about all they hurt this time some cabbage patches they did not leave a head standing They left egges here by the millions do not know how or what damage they will do Giles was about the bluest man you ever seen when they come I guess he was as low in the valley as Uriah ever got The other time he did not lose enough for him to feel the effects of them for he only lost the 1/3 of 7 acres of corn that was nothing like us loseing 27 acres and had a famly to keep too he has a famly to keep now and he finds out a half dollars worth of coffee will not last six months

* * *

I do wish you could see our girls Ella has lost two of her lower teeth you aught to hear her talk I know you would laugh to hear Stella talk she is sitting on top the stove now I believe she is worse to get in michief than Ella ever was when she wants any thing she says I do She will say I want my niny[3] I do and I want dinny I do and I want on bed I do I want brea buer and Guger[4] I do she always closes with I do If she keeps well I intend to wean her the last of this month When a youngone can ask as she does they are old enough to do with out it she will be 20 months old the 4th of next month and Ella was 18 months when I weaned her They have been well all summer so far I would rather be grasshoppered a little than to have the chills every fall

* * *

I think you had better try Nebraska for your health we have no riches yet but waht does riches amount to with out health

* * *

as ever yours

M V Oblinger

3. See note 7, p. 314 [Editor].
4. Mattie is probably trying to write phonetically how Stella says "bread, butter, and sugar."

Mattie V. Oblinger and Uriah W. Oblinger to Thomas Family, September 1–20, 1878

At Home in Fillmore Co Neb[5]
Sept 1st 1878

Dear folks at home
We received your letter yesterday, and this morning while "Ma" is dressing up these naughty "Bug Eaters"[6] of ours I will try and speak my part of the answer. It is difficult for me to write as I have a gathering on the middle knuckle of one of my pen fingers. I am sorry to hear of Father being afflicted the way he is, have you let your notion of a trip to Nebraska fall to the ground, I think a sojourn in our healthy atmosphere would do your cough more good than all the medicine you could take, coughing is so rare here that I cannot remember when I heard any one cough.

My health has not been very good this summer. I took the piles the last week in may and have not been entirely clear of them since, and have had to work very hard, and the hot weather along with the other made me so weak part of the time, that I was hardly able to navigate. I was so weakened down that while stacking my grain I came very near having a sunstroke I felt myself giving way and got off the stack and went to the house only 8 or 10 rods off and if it had been 20 steps more would not have reached it without help as I got very faint & weak, everything turned dark and my head got very dizzy and I had to lay down in the door Matt applied cold water to head & face and brough me around, but since I have had to be careful, for when I would get very warm I would feel dizzy & faint and would have to rest for awhile.

I cut 31 acres of a harvest with the help of man beside myself I hired a man that had a self rake machine to cut it down, and a Swede that is boarding with us & myself bound it all & stacked it all. I have threshed part of wheat, 14 acres made 240 bu, and a little less than 4 1/2 acres that shattered and fell to the ground last year when I cut it, and grew on the stubble without cultivation of any kind made 45 bu of splendid wheat and that too after letting 5 head of cattle run on it whenever they pleased till spring. have a little wheat to thresh yet and all of my barley & oats.

* * *

5. Mattie and Uriah share this letter. Uriah writes first.
6. A resident of Nebraska. The term was applied derisively to inhabitants of Nebraska by travelers on account of the poverty-stricken appearance of many parts of the state due to the crop devastation brought about by the grasshopper invasions of the 1860s and 1870s. Its earliest known use in publication was an 1872 *Harper's Magazine* article, which listed nicknames for people of various states in the country. Frederic G. Cassidy, ed., *Dictionary of American Regional English*, 3 vols. (Cambridge: The Belknap Press, 1985), 1, p. 435.

U W Oblinger

[7]Sept 8th and this letter not finished yet

while it rains & Uriah does his chores & the Children sleeps & Clauses reads his bible I will write a few lines After Uriah wrote I did not have time to write for the same evening we recd'. your letter we recd'. one fome Nett requesting me to write immediately & tell how to use that whooping cough medicine she said Orin had the whooping cough or would have for he had been exposed We are haveing quite a rain this vening we were needing rain very much

Sept 15th

* * *

Ella says tell Grandma they are sitting in the cradle they are all three[8] in the cradle & it is about full well I must go and milk well now I will finish or try to Maggie runs evry where she could run evey where when only 9 1/2 months old she is the wildest chap I ever seen she is in all the mischief there is agoing she climbs on to the chairs and on the beds & is in to every thing and only weighs 18 pounds and only eleven months old have you a hoosier that can beat that

Sep 20th

* * *

Our Fair is over we attended two days had good time only we got rained on last evening comeing home I think my work will not crowd me so much now I had to make some new clothes for the girls to wear to the fair and I was very much hurried as I done it all by hand Mother I often wish I was close to your machine for three girls makes lots of sewing

* * *

I am so tired I will go to bed I am as ever

M V Oblinger

* * *

Giles S. Thomas to Thomas Family, February 27, 1880

Sutton Neb.
Feb. 27" 1880

My Dear, dear Parents
With Sad thoughts I take my pen you a few lines—The Lord called for sister *Matt* this evening at 4.15 Oclok She inded was taken

7. At this point, Mattie begins writing.
8. Mattie has given birth to her third daughter, Maggie [Editor].

away unexpected to us but her master said come and she now is resting with the angels in heaven.

She was confined[9] Tuesday evening about 4 Oclock and a bout 8 Oclock She took a fit very suden and never Spoke after the first one—the spasems come on about every hour and lasted until about 18 hours before her death. The doctors were compelled to perform a Surgical operation by relieveing her of the child the child is also dead and will be buried with her some time Sunday. There has been nothing left undone that could be done in her case the doctors worked with great skill but to no good. I cant write more at this time but will write again. Uriah Said he could not stand[1] it to write now. dont know what he will do yet. its left his three little girls in a sad condition—with out a Mother.

* * *

my Dear Parents, keep in good courage—Look to Jessus for aid and he will shurely suport you. May the Lord bless you is my sincere Prayer.

Giles S. Thomas.

Uriah W. Oblinger to Thomas Family, September 26, 1880[2]

Fillmore Co' Neb'
Sept 26th 1880

Dear Father & Mother
It has been sometime since we exchanged greetings, so tonight I will try and write you a short letter, and tell you how we are getting along. Today there was no appointments of any kind in the neighborhood and I have occupied part of the time writing letters, haveing written two before this one, one of them to Nettie. Perhaps you may wonder why I have not written sooner, but if you knew how nearly every moment of my time is taken up you would not wonder. I now have my children all with me again and it makes some more trouble on my hands, but they are mine own flesh & blood & I try to bear the trouble cheerfully, although the task is hard at times. The past week they have not been very well but are better now.

* * *

I fear I will not be able to take my trip east this winter on account of not having means enough. Crops & prices are so poor that it is making times pretty close here. and my misfortunes during the past year has put me back badly. I hardly know how to manage, I

9. To be in child-bed; to be brought to bed; to be delivered of a child. *The Compact Oxford English Dictionary,* 2d ed. (New York: Oxford University Press, 1991), 312
1. Giles replaced the words "bear it" with "stand it" [Editor].
2. This is the first letter Uriah wrote to Mattie's parents after her death [Editor].

feel that it is not possible or right for me to go through another season as I have this one, for I cannot do justice to myself or family this way & I feel as though it will be hard to separate my children or separate from them, but if I have to do so I would like for you to take part of them at least. If I have to put each one out separate I would like for you to take one, & Nettie one, & Uncle John Cooks one.[3] I can find places for them here & good ones too, but our school advantages are not as good as yours & I fear their education will be neglected.

* * *

I tried to hire help in the house this summer, but I could not, such as I wanted I could not get, & such as I could I did not want for I have a choice what kind of an example is before my children & when I am not with them it does not do to have just any one with them on account of the influence they would exert.

You need not look very much for us for fear we cannot come, although we have not given it up entirely yet. I hope these few lines may find you all enjoying good health temporally & spiritually.

No more but remain as ever Your Son and well wisher for time and eternity

U W Oblinger

EVERETT DICK

Nature Frowns on Mankind†

To the poverty stricken homesteader, struggling to wrest a competence from the face of the virgin plains, all nature seemed hostile. In the spring, floods menaced the cabin or dugout built close to the stream; in summer, drought and hot winds withered the promising crop, and insects everywhere took a terrible toll on the scanty cultivated areas; in the autumn; the prairie fires swept furiously across the plains, jumping creeks and sweeping everything before them, destroying crops, fuel, food for man and beast, homes, and even whole towns; in the winter came the dreaded blizzards and unbear-

3. Uriah did send his daughters to live with relatives and moved to Minnesota in 1881. There he remarried, and moved back to Nebraska with his wife and three daughters in 1883. He would have three more daughters with his second wife and move to Kansas and Missouri before returning to Nebraska in 1894, where he died on March 27, 1901 [Editor].

† From *The Sod-House Frontier 1854–1890: A Social History of the Northern Plains from the Creation of Kansas and Nebraska to the Admission of the Dakotas* (Lincoln, Nebraska: Johnson, 1954), pp. 202–31. By permission of the University of Nebraska Press. Copyright 1937, 1954 by Everett Dick. All notes are by the author.

able sub-zero temperature. These manifestatic inflicted damage all the greater because the pioneers in a new and strange country were unprepared to meet such difficulties.

When the first small areas were broken and planted, the cultivated crops were much more succulent than the native plants and prairie grasses. Hence insects flocked to the patches of the homesteaders and greatly damaged or completely destroyed the crops. Again and again they visited the frontier region, wreaking havoc with the cultivated vegetation. As early as 1857 the grasshopper or Rocky Mountain locusts as they were called, made incursion into the little cultivated area along the Missouri River.[1] At Ponca Nebraska, on August 3 of that year a party of men going home from an election, saw a dark cloud approaching rapidly from the North. As it drew near they saw it was neither a rain nor a dust cloud. Someone suggested that it might be a collection of cottonwood seed floating together high in the air. When near, part of the cloud came to the earth and the hungry grasshoppers devoured everything. Again in 1866 Richardson observed them. They darkened the air like great flakes of snow and in a column one hundred and fifty miles wide and one hundred miles deep they appeared near Fort Kearney, Nebraska, and passed southwest. In the same year they appeared in such vast quantities as to stop the horse races at Fort Scott, Kansas. They covered the track from one to three inches deep. In 1867 they made a raid on the harvest in Dakota and nearly destroyed it in a single day.

The great calamity of the year 1874, however, surpassed anything before or since and caused such great damage that on the plains it is generally called the grasshopper year. The grasshoppers came suddenly. They traveled with a strong wind, coming with it and leaving with it. Rising high in the air with their wings spread, they were carried along with very little effort; they appeared from the North. Their ravages reached from the Dakotas to northern Texas and penetrated as far east as Sedalia, Missouri.

The spring and early summer of the grasshopper year had been very favorable for growing crops. Small grain such as wheat and oats were mostly in the shock. Late in July, according to S. C. Bassett, a keen observer in Buffalo County, Nebraska, the family had sat down to dinner on a bright sunny day. Gradually the sun was slightly darkened by a cloud in the northwest which looked like smoke or dust, and it was remarked that it looked as though an April squall might be in the offing. Presently one of the family who

1. As early as 1818 a swarm of grasshoppers descended upon the Red River Valley, Pembina County, North Dakota, and devoured all trace of vegetation at the Hudson's Bay settlement. Linda W. Slaughter, "Leaves from Northwestern History," *Collections*, State Historical Society of North Dakota, Vol. I, p. 209.

had gone to the well for a pitcher of fresh water cried, "Grasshoppers!" The meal so happily begun was never finished. At first there was no thought of the destruction of the crops. All looked upon the insects with astonishment. They came like a driving snow in winter, filling the air, covering the earth, the buildings, the shocks of grain, and everything. According to one observer their alighting on the roofs and sides of the houses sounded like a continuous hail storm. They alighted on trees in such great numbers that their weight broke off large limbs. The chickens and turkeys at first were frightened and ran to hide from them. On recovering from their fright, they tried to eat all the insects. At first when a hopper alighted, a hen rushed forward and gobbled it up and then without moving she ate another and another until her crop was distended to an unusual size and she could hold no more. Then when a hopper flew near her, she would instinctively make a dash for it, then pause and cock her head as if to say, "Can I possibly hold another"?[2] The turkeys and chickens ate themselves sick. One pioneer reported that a herd of forty hogs and a flock of fifty turkeys fattened themselves by eating nothing but grasshoppers and a little prairie hay. The pork and turkey both had a peculiar taste of grasshoppers.

At times the insects were four to six inches deep on the ground and continued to alight for hours. Men were obliged to tie strings around their pants legs to keep the pests from crawling up their legs. In the cool of the evening the hoppers gathered so thick on the warm rails of the railroad that the Union Pacific trains were stopped.[3] Section men were called out to shovel the grasshoppers off the track near the spot where Kearney, Nebraska, now stands, so that the trains could get through. The track was so oily and greasy that the wheels spun and would not pull a train.[4]

When people began to see the danger of the destruction of their crops, they brought out bed-clothes and blankets to cover the most valuable garden crops. Yet the insects ate holes in the bedclothes or crawled under the edge and destroyed everything; even hay piled on the plants seldom availed much. Smudges of dry hay and litter were tried. In Dakota old straw was piled around a field and set on fire. Some put a salt solution on the grain, all to no avail. A heavy rain was best; it drowned millions of them. Men with clubs walked down

2. A. J. Leach, *History of Antelope County* (Chicago, 1909), p. 58; S. C. Bassett, *Ravenna News*, July 1, 1910.
3. This seems like a piece of fiction, but so many witnesses testify to the occurrence that it must be so.
4. Apparently in this particular case the reason for the great drifts of grasshoppers was because the insects met a storm and heavy wind. The trains were stopped in North Dakota in 1873 by the same cause and could be moved only after the tracks had been sanded. Clement A. Lounsberry, "Popular History of North Dakota," *North Dakota Magazine*, Vol. II, No. 4, p. 54.

the corn rows knocking the hoppers off, but on looking behind them they saw that the insects were as numerous as ever. The grasshoppers alighted in such large numbers on the corn that the stalks bent toward the ground. The potato vines were mashed flat. The sound of their feeding was like a herd of cattle eating in a corn field.

Every green thing except castor beans, cane, and native grass, and the leaves of certain native trees, was eaten. Onions seemed to have been a favorite food for the hoppers. They ate the tops and the onions right down into the ground to the end of the roots leaving little hollow holes where the succulent bulbs had been. One observer claimed in all seriousness that when a large number of these insects flew past his cabin door, their breath was rank with the odor of onions. Turnips were likewise eaten out of the ground. They seemed to have been very fond of tobacco, red peppers, and tansy. Trees, denuded of their leaves and having the bark stripped from their smaller trunks, died.[5]

The water in the creeks, stained with the excrement of the insects, assumed the color of strong coffee. The cattle refused to drink until compelled by extreme thirst. One writer reported that it was his daily task to climb down into the well and clear the hoppers out to keep them from polluting the water. Even the fish in the streams tasted like grasshoppers.

The grasshoppers cut the bands of the sheaves and let the grain shell out on the ground. A piece of harness or a garment left on the ground was quickly ruined. Fork handles, scythe snathes, and such things were so roughened as to become uncomfortable to the hands. The weather-beaten boards on the houses and fences were so eaten that within a few hours they looked as though the structure had been built of new lumber. If any of the creatures were tramped underfoot, their companions quickly devoured them. They ate the mosquito bar off the windows and even invaded the house and ate the window curtains in at least one place in Kansas. A lady with her small children was caught out in the deluge of grasshoppers. The insects crawled inside the children's clothing, frightening them until they were almost distracted. When the insects left a few hours later, the whole country was a scene of vast ruin and desolation. The jaunty waving fields of corn in twelve hours' time were reduced to bent-over stalks entirely denuded of their leaves. Even the large weeds were destroyed. The grasshoppers usually stayed from two days to a week and then on a fair day left with the wind. They came in 1875, 1876, and 1877, but never again did they become the scourge they were in 1874.

5. One observer said the willow hedges were peeled so clean of their bark that one would think a basket maker had done it.

* * *

Storms of various kinds added to the discomforts of frontier life. Electric storms which completely filled the air with the smell of sulphur and lurid flashes of lightning, brought fear to the hearts of the uninitiated. Those caught in these storms never forgot the electrified air which caused balls of fire to jump off the horns of the oxen or roll along the prairie. These storms were frequently accompanied by hail which beat down on the traveler so mercilessly that he was obliged to crawl under his wagon or take the saddle off and cover his head to escape injury from the infuriated elements. In the seventies Mr. Zedekiah Blake was driving to Fort Riley, Kansas, with a lot of garden truck when a storm came up and hail stones, some of them the size of eggs, rattled down so furiously that he was obliged to empty out his wooden tub of vegetables and get under the receptacle himself.

Of all these indications of displeasure on the part of nature, perhaps the most trying were the blizzards. Too often man and beast were poorly prepared to parry winter's icy thrusts. Certain winters stand out in the minds of frontiersmen as particularly "hard winters." Certain storms in these winters, and others, are remembered as particularly severe.

* * *

The Easter storm of 1873 was one long remembered on the plains. The morning of April 13, 1873, dawned bright and clear and was welcomed as the first day of spring. Toward noon the sky became overcast, the wind changed to sleet, and hail was reported in some places. It soon became almost impossible for pedestrians to make their way about town. In Hastings, Nebraska, a rope was tied from a store to the well and people guided themselves in that way. Business ceased. Only the most daring and foolhardy ventured out. Homesteaders in town had to stay until the storm was over, causing a world of anxiety on the part of the women who waited at home. A boy left a hotel in Central City, Nebraska, to go to a print shop one block away, but got lost and was found three days later frozen. Drifts were as high as houses.

Live stock, much of it bought with borrowed money, perished by the thousands. Some animals died endeavoring to cross streams, some in stables and corrals while their owners were unable to give relief, and some in cars on the railroad sidings, for railway traffic was abandoned. Some sought shelter in depressions and perished beneath the snow drifts many feet deep. It was not the intense cold which filled man and beast with terror, but the fine particles of snow, driven by the furious wind, which wet to the skin and chilled living things to the bone.

In Antelope County, Nebraska, a man named Al Wolfe lived

alone in his dugout on the south side of a big hill. The hill furnished some shelter but made the snow drift badly. After the storm one of his neighbors went to hunt him up and see how he was faring, but could find no trace of his dugout. The location of the dwelling was marked by a smooth snowdrift. The friend got a number of neighbors together and started digging. They found the man insensible; in a very short time he would have died. His door opened outward, preventing him from working his way out alone, and the snow packed almost as solid as ice, encased him like a tomb.

During this same Easter storm of 1873 a man of Clay County, Nebraska, housed in the same room his family of eight persons, one hog, one dog, all his chickens, and four head of cattle. It was a frequent occurrence for the barns to be so completely covered with snow and for the snow to drift in such a fashion, that it was impossible to open the barn door. In this event a hole was made through the flimsy hay roof, and hay and grain were thrown down into the stable. Occasionally snow was thrown down for the animals to eat instead of water. This was seldom necessary, for the fine snow penetrated every nook and crevice of the ordinary frontier barn. One man fed his cattle in this way for two weeks, traveling between the house and barn guided by a lariat rope. In one county alone in Kansas eight people perished in this storm.

In Turner County, Dakota Territory, a party was in progress at the pastor's home and the group was snowed in for three days. The days were jolly but the nights were uncomfortable. The men spread their buffalo robes and blankets on the floor and slept there. The women and girls placed chairs along the side of the bed and a half dozen crawled into it, sleeping crossways with their pillows arranged on the chairs. In this manner, crowded to suffocation, they managed to get through the nights.

* * *

The great blizzard of 1888 is sometimes called the "school children's storm." The morning of January twelfth dawned clear warm, and bright. The children started cheerfully off to school. Before long a fifty-six mile wind was blowing and the temperature dropped to thirty-six degrees below zero in Nebraska. Children coming home from school were caught. Parents coming after their children lost their way and were frozen. Many heroic deeds of school teachers are recorded. Many, knowing the children could not reach their homes, stayed in the school-house for one or two nights. There they encouraged their little flock and cared for them through the long weary hours until relief came. Others had the members of their groups hold hands and, forming a living chain, guided the little ones to a neighboring home.

The Knieriem school-house in Jerauld County, Dakota Territory, was about one hundred and forty yards from a settler's home. Thirty yards beyond the house was a stack of flax straw. All day the storm raged and by four o'clock the fuel supply in the little school-house was exhausted. Fred Weeks, the oldest boy, was sent out to see whether the road was clear and the journey to the nearest house possible. When he returned, the group joined hands and with Fred in the lead, started toward the haven of refuge. They lost the path, missed a foot bridge, and plunged into a little ravine. One child's wraps that were tied about her shoes were lost. When just at the point of exhaustion, the group struck the straw pile. Fortunately they found a fork and a lath at the stack, and clearing away the snow, they dug a hole in the side of the pile and teacher and pupils crowded in out of the death-dealing blasts of the frigid wind. They had missed the house by only about six feet. They tore the little girls' aprons in strips and made a long string. Fred took one end and went out into the storm in the hope of finding the house. This was impossible. The storm raged furiously, blinding, suffocating, bewildering. He returned to the straw pile. Fruitlessly they called, shouted, and screamed singly and in unison. They made preparations for the night. They dug back farther into the stack and Fred took his place at the entrance. They kept all awake, made them sing, talk, move about, and laugh between the periods of tears. They told stories, sang, and called the roll every few minutes, anything to keep the little ones from falling into the grip of that sleep which never wakes. About four o'clock in the morning the storm abated sufficiently for them to see the house through the flying snow. Teacher and pupils were taken there. All were more or less frost-bitten; one girl's feet were frozen so badly that they had to be amputated. Fred Weeks's feet were so badly frozen the flesh dropped off, but he finally recovered.

In Buffalo County, Dakota Territory, one man and his wife perished in their own dooryard searching for one another. Another man and his wife tried to reach the school-house in an attempt to take food and clothing to their children. They lost their way and, having a shovel with them, the man buried his wife in a large snowdrift and he tramped in a circle about the spot all day and all night. They called to each other occasionally, greatly encouraging one another. Many parents were frozen while seeking their children.

Etta Shattuck, a school-teacher, near O'Neill, Nebraska, got lost in going home and remained seventy-four hours in a haystack before she was found with both feet frozen. The whole plains region was under a tremendous nervous strain. After three days the tension was broken by the reappearance of the sun. Parents separated from children and husbands from wives, were reunited in happy family circles. But not all circles were unbroken. Over two hundred persons, many of them little children, had lost their lives.[6]

* * *

FREDERICK JACKSON TURNER

From The Significance of the Frontier in American History†

In a recent bulletin of the Superintendent of the Census for 1890 appear these significant words: "Up to and including 1880 the country had a frontier of settlement, but at present the unsettled area has been so broken into by isolated bodies of settlement that there can hardly be said to be a frontier line. In the discussion of its extent, its westward movement, etc., it can not, therefore, any longer have a place in the census reports." This brief official statement marks the closing of a great historic movement. Up to our own day American history has been in a large degree the history of the colonization of the Great West. The existence of an area of free land, its continuous recession, and the advance of American settlement westward, explain American development.

Behind institutions, behind constitutional forms and modifications, lie the vital forces that call these organs into life and shape them to meet changing conditions. The peculiarity of American institutions is, the fact that they have been compelled to adapt themselves to the changes of an expanding people—to the changes involved in crossing a continent, in winning a wilderness, and in developing at each area of this progress out of the primitive economic and political conditions of the frontier into the complexity of city life. Said Calhoun[1] in 1817, "We are great, and rapidly—I was about to say fearfully—growing!" So saying, he touched the distinguishing feature of American life. All peoples show development; the germ theory of politics has been sufficiently emphasized. In the case of most nations, however, the development has occurred in a limited area; and if the nation has expanded, it has met other growing peoples whom it has conquered. But in the case of the United States we have a different phenomenon. Limiting our attention to the Atlantic coast, we have the familiar phenomenon of the evolution of institutions in a limited area, such as the rise of representive

6. The authentic death list carried the names of one hundred and nine known Dakotans; over one hundred perished in Nebraska, besides a large number in Kansas.

† American Historical Association, *Annual Report for 1893* (Washington, 1894), 199–227.

1. John C. Calhoun (1782–1850), politician from South Carolina.

government; the differentiation of simple colonial governments into complex organs; the progress from primitive industrial society, without division of labor, up to manufacturing civilization. But we have in addition to this a recurrence of the process of evolution in each western area reached in the process of expansion. Thus American development has exhibited not merely advance along a single line, but a return to primitive conditions on a continually advancing frontier line, and a new development for that area. American social development has been continually beginning over again on the frontier. This perennial rebirth, this fluidity of American life, this expansion westward with its new opportunities, its continuous touch with the simplicity of primitive society, furnish the forces dominating American character. The true point of view in the history of this nation is not the Atlantic coast, it is the Great West. Even the slavery struggle, which is made so exclusive an object of attention by writers like Professor von Holst,[2] occupies its important place in American history because of its relation to westward expansion.

In this advance, the frontier is the outer edge of the wave—the meeting point between savagery and civilization. Much has been written about the frontier from the point of view of border warfare and the chase, but as a field for the serious study of the economist and the historian it has been neglected.

The American frontier is sharply distinguished from the European frontier—a fortified boundary line running through dense populations. The most significant thing about the American frontier is, that it lies at the hither edge of free land. In the census reports it is treated as the margin of that settlement which has a density of two or more to the square mile. The term is an elastic one, and for our purposes does not need sharp definition. We shall consider the whole frontier belt, including the Indian country and the outer margin of the "settled area" of the census reports. This paper will make no attempt to treat the subject exhaustively; its aim is simply to call attention to the frontier as a fertile field for investigation, and to suggest some of the problems which arise in connection with it.

In the settlement of America we have to observe how European life entered the continent, and how America modified and developed that life and reacted on Europe. Our early history is the study of European germs developing in an American environment. Too exclusive attention has been paid by institutional students to the Germanic origins, too little to the American factors. The frontier is

2. Hermann von Holst (1841–1904), German-American historian who wrote from an antislavery perspective.

the line of most rapid and effective Americanization. The wilderness masters the colonist. It finds him a European in dress, industries, tools, modes of travel, and thought. It takes him from the railroad car and puts him in the birch canoe. It strips off the garments of civilization and arrays him in the hunting shirt and the moccasin. It puts him in the log cabin of the Cherokee and Iroquois and runs an Indian palisade[3] around him. Before long he has gone to planting Indian corn and plowing with a sharp stick; he shouts the war cry and takes the scalp in orthodox Indian fashion. In short, at the frontier the environment is at first too strong for the man. He must accept the conditions which it furnishes, or perish, and so he fits himself into the Indian clearings and follows the Indian trails. Little by little he transforms the wilderness, but the outcome is not the old Europe, not simply the development of Germanic germs, any more than the first phenomenon was a case of reversion to the Germanic mark. The fact is, that here is a new product that is American. At first, the frontier was the Atlantic coast. It was the frontier of Europe in a very real sense. Moving westward, the frontier became more and more American. As successive terminal moraines result from successive glaciations, so each frontier leaves its traces behind it, and when it becomes a settled area the region still partakes of the frontier characteristics. Thus the advance of the frontier has meant a steady movement away from the influence of Europe, a steady growth of independence on American lines. And to study this advance, the men who grew up under these conditions, and the political, economic, and social results of it, is to study the really American part of our history.

* * *

Obviously the immigrant was attracted by the cheap lands of the frontier, and even the native farmer felt their influence strongly. Year by year the farmers who lived on soil whose returns were diminished by unrotated crops were offered the virgin soil of the frontier at nominal prices. Their growing families demanded more lands, and these were dear. The competition of the unexhausted, cheap, and easily tilled prairie lands compelled the farmer either to go west and continue the exhaustion of the soil on a new frontier, or to adopt intensive culture. Thus the census in 1890 shows, in the Northwest,[4] many counties in which there is an absolute or a relative decrease of population. These States have been sending farmers to advance the frontier on the plains, and have themselves

3. Fence.
4. The original Northwest Territory included the area that became the states of Ohio, Indiana, Illinois, Michigan, Wisconsin, and Minnesota.

begun to turn to intensive farming and to manufacture. A decade before this, Ohio had shown the same transition stage. Thus the demand for land and the love of wilderness freedom drew the frontier ever onward.

* * *

But the most important effect of the frontier has been in the promotion of democracy here and in Europe. As has been indicated, the frontier is productive of individualism. Complex society is precipitated by the wilderness into a kind of primitive organization based on the family. The tendency is anti-social. It produces antipathy to control, and particularly to any direct control. The taxgatherer is viewed as a representative of oppression.

* * *

From the conditions of frontier life came intellectual traits of profound importance. The works of travelers along each frontier from colonial days onward describe certain common traits, and these traits have, while softening down, still persisted as survivals in the place of their origin, even when a higher social organization succeeded. The result is that to the frontier the American intellect owes its striking characteristics. That coarseness and strength combined with acuteness and inquisitiveness; that practical, inventive turn of mind, quick to find expedients; that masterful grasp of material things, lacking in the artistic but powerful to effect great ends; that restless, nervous energy; that dominant individualism, working for good and for evil, and withal that buoyancy and exuberance which comes with freedom—these are traits of the frontier, or traits called out elsewhere because of the existence of the frontier. Since the days when the fleet of Columbus sailed into the waters of the New World, America has been another name for opportunity, and the people of the United States have taken their tone from the incessant expansion which has not only been open but has even been forced upon them. He would be a rash prophet who should assert that the expansive character of American life has now entirely ceased. Movement has been its dominant fact, and, unless this training has no effect upon a people, the American energy will continually demand a wider field for its exercise. But never again will such gifts of free land offer themselves. For a moment, at the frontier, the bonds of custom are broken and unrestraint is triumphant. There is not *tabula rasa*. The stubborn American environment is there with its imperious summons to accept its conditions; the inherited ways of doing things are also there; and yet, in spite of environment, and in spite of custom, each frontier did indeed furnish a new field of opportunity, a gate of escape from the bondage of the past; and freshness, and confidence, and scorn of older society, impatience of its restraints and its ideas, and indifference to its lessons, have accompanied the frontier. What the Mediterranean Sea was to the Greeks, breaking the bond of custom, offering new experiences, calling out new institutions and activities, that, and more, the ever retreating frontier has been to the United States directly, and to the nations of Europe more remotely. And now, four centuries from the discovery of America, at the end of a hundred years of life under the Constitution, the frontier has gone, and with its going has closed the first period of American history.

WILLA CATHER

Nebraska: The End of the First Cycle†

The State of Nebraska is part of the great plain which stretches west of the Missouri River, gradually rising until it reaches the Rocky Mountains. The character of all this country between the river and the mountains is essentially the same throughout its extent: a rolling, alluvial plain, growing gradually more sandy toward the west, until it breaks into the white sand-hills of western Nebraska and Kansas and eastern Colorado. From east to west this plain measures something over five hundred miles; in appearance it resembles the wheat lands of Russia, which fed the continent of Europe for so many years. Like Little Russia it is watered by slow-flowing, muddy rivers, which run full in the spring, often cutting into the farm lands along their banks; but by midsummer they lie low and shrunken, their current split by glistening white sand-bars half overgrown with scrub willows.

The climate, with its extremes of temperature, gives to this plateau the variety which, to the casual eye at least, it lacks. There we have short, bitter winters; windy, flower-laden springs; long, hot summers; triumphant autumns that last until Christmas—a season of perpetual sunlight, blazing blue skies, and frosty nights. In this newest part of the New World autumn is the season of beauty and sentiment, as spring is in the Old World.

Nebraska is a newer State than Kansas. It was a State before there were people in it. Its social history falls easily within a period of sixty years, and the first stable settlements of white men were made within the memory of old folk now living. The earliest of these settlements—Bellevue, Omaha, Brownville, Nebraska City—were founded along the Missouri River, which was at that time a pathway for small steamers. In 1855–60 these four towns were

† "Nebraska: The End of the First Cycle" by Willa Cather from the September 5, 1923 issue of *The Nation*. Reprinted by permission.

straggling groups of log houses, hidden away along the wooded river banks.

Before 1860 civilization did no more than nibble at the eastern edge of the State, along the river bluffs. Lincoln, the present capital, was open prairie; and the whole of the great plain to the westward was still a sunny wilderness, where the tall red grass and the buffalo and the Indian hunter were undisturbed. Fremont, with Kit Carson, the famous scout, had gone across Nebraska in 1842, exploring the valley of the Platte. In the days of the Mormon persecution fifteen thousand Mormons camped for two years, 1845–46, six miles north of Omaha, while their exploring parties went farther west, searching for fertile land outside of government jurisdiction. In 1847 the entire Mormon sect, under the leadership of Brigham Young, went with their wagons through Nebraska and on to that desert beside the salty sea which they have made so fruitful.

In forty-nine and the early fifties, gold hunters, bound for California, crossed the State in thousands, always following the old Indian trail along the Platte valley. The State was a highway for dreamers and adventurers; men who were in quest of gold or grace, freedom or romance. With all these people the road led out, but never back again.

While Nebraska was a camping-ground for seekers outward bound, the wooden settlements along the Missouri were growing into something permanent. The settlers broke the ground and began to plant the fine orchards which have ever since been the pride of Otoe and Nemaha counties. It was at Brownville that the first telegraph wire was brought across the Missouri River. When I was a child I heard ex-Governor Furness relate how he stood with other pioneers in the log cabin where the Morse instrument had been installed, and how, when it began to click, the men took off their bats as if they were in church. The first message flashed across the river into Nebraska was not a market report, but a line of poetry: 'Westward the course of empire takes its way.' The Old West was like that.

The first back-and-forth travel through the State was by way of the Overland Mail, a monthly passenger-and-mail-stage service across the plains from Independence to the newly founded colony at Salt Lake—a distance of twelve hundred miles.

When silver ore was discovered in the mountains of Colorado near Cherry Creek—afterward Camp Denver and later the city of Denver—a picturesque form of commerce developed across the great plain of Nebraska: the transporting of food and merchandise from the Missouri to the Colorado mining camps, and on to the Mormon settlement at Salt Lake. One of the largest freighting companies, operating out of Nebraska City, in the six summer months of

1860 carried nearly three million pounds of freight across Nebraska, employing 515 wagons, 5,687 oxen, and 600 drivers.

The freighting began in the early spring, usually about the middle of April, and continued all summer and through the long, warm autumns. The oxen made from ten to twenty miles a day. I have heard the old freighters say that, after embarking on their six-hundred mile trail, they lost count of the days of the week and the days of the month. While they were out in that sea of waving grass, one day was like another; and, if one can trust the memory of these old men, all the days were glorious. The buffalo trails still ran north and south then; deep, dusty paths the bison wore when, single file, they came north in the spring for the summer grass, and went south again in the autumn. Along these trails were the buffalo 'wallows'—shallow depressions where the rain water gathered when it ran off the tough prairie sod. These wallows the big beasts wore deeper and packed hard when they rolled about and bathed in the pools, so that they held water like a cement bottom. The freighters lived on game and shot the buffalo for their hides. The grass was full of quail and prairie chickens, and flocks of wild ducks swam about on the lagoons. These lagoons have long since disappeared, but they were beautiful things in their time; long stretches where the rain water gathered and lay clear on a grassy bottom without mud. From the lagoons the first settlers hauled water to their homesteads, before they had dug their wells. The freighters could recognise the lagoons from afar by the clouds of golden coreopsis which grew up out of the water and waved delicately above its surface. Among the pioneers the coreopsis was known simply as 'the lagoon flower.'

As the railroads came in, the freighting business died out. Many a freight-driver settled down upon some spot he had come to like on his journeys to and fro, homesteaded it, and wandered no more. The Union Pacific, the first transcontinental railroad, was completed in 1869. The Burlington entered Nebraska in the same year, at Platsmouth, and began construction westward. It finally reached Denver by an indirect route, and went on extending and ramifying through the State. With the railroads came the home-seeking people from overseas.

When the first courageous settlers came straggling out through the waste with their oxen and covered wagons, they found open range all the way from Lincoln to Denver; a continuous, undulating plateau, covered with long, red, shaggy grass. The prairie was green only where it had been burned off in the spring by the new settlers or by the Indians, and toward autumn even the new grass became a coppery brown. This sod, which had never been broken by the plow, was so tough and strong with the knotted grass roots of many years, that the home-seekers were able to peel it off the earth like peat, cut it up into bricks, and make of it warm, comfortable, durable houses. Some of these sod houses lingered on until the open range was gone, and the grass was gone, and the whole face of the country had been changed.

Even as late as 1885 the central part of the State, and everything to the westward, was, in the main, raw prairie. The cultivated fields and broken land seemed mere scratches in the brown, running steppe that never stopped until it broke against the foothills of the Rockies. The dugouts and sod farm-houses were three or four miles apart, and the only means of communication was the heavy farm wagon, drawn by heavy work horses. The early population of Nebraska was largely transatlantic. The county in which I grew up, in the south-central part of the State, was typical. On Sunday we could drive to a Norwegian church and listen to a sermon in that language, or to a Danish or a Swedish church. We could go to the French Catholic settlement in the next county and hear a sermon in French, or into the Bohemian township and hear one in Czech, or we could go to church with some German Lutherans. There were, of course, American congregations also.

There is a Prague in Nebraska as well as in Bohemia. Many of our Czech immigrants were people of a very superior type. The political emigration resulting from the revolutionary disturbances of 1848 was distinctly different from the emigration resulting from economic causes, and brought to the United States brilliant young men both from Germany and Bohemia. In Nebraska our Czech settlements were large and very prosperous. I have walked about the streets of Wilber, the county seat of Saline County, for a whole day without hearing a word of English spoken. In Wilber, in the old days, behind the big, friendly brick saloon—it was not a 'saloon,' properly speaking, but a beer garden, where the farmers ate their lunch when they came to town—there was a pleasant little theater where the boys and girls were trained to give the masterpieces of Czech drama in the Czech language. 'Americanization' has doubtless done away with all this. Our lawmakers have rooted conviction that a boy can be a better American if he speaks only one language than if he speaks two. I could name a dozen Bohemian towns in Nebraska where one used to be able to go into a bakery and buy better pastry than is to be had anywhere except in the best pastry shops of Prague or Vienna. The American lard pie never corrupted the Czech.

Cultivated, restless young men from Europe made incongruous figures among the hard-handed breakers of the soil. Frederick Amiel's[1] nephew lived for many years and finally died among the

1. Henri Frederic Amiel (1821–1881), Swiss philosopher and writer.

Nebraska farmers. Amiel's letters to his kinsman were published in the *Atlantic Monthly* of March, 1921, under the title 'Amiel in Nebraska.' Camille Saint-Saëns's[2] cousin lived just over the line, in Kansas. Knut Hamsun, the Norwegian writer who was awarded the Nobel Prize for 1920, was a 'hired hand' on a Dakota farm to the north of us. Colonies of European people, Slavonic, Germanic, Scandinavian, Latin, spread across our bronze prairies like the daubs of color on a painter's palette. They brought with them something that this neutral new world needed even more than the immigrants needed land.

Unfortunately, their American neighbors were seldom open-minded enough to understand the Europeans, or to profit by their older traditions. Our settlers from New England, cautious and convinced of their own superiority, kept themselves insulated as much as possible from foreign influences. The incomers from the South—from Missouri, Kentucky, the two Virginias—were provincial and utterly without curiosity. They were kind neighbors—lent a hand to help a Swede when he was sick or in trouble. But I am quite sure that Knut Hamsun might have worked a year for any one of our Southern farmers, and his employer would never have discovered that there was anything unusual about the Norwegian. A New England settler might have noticed that his chore-boy had a kind of intelligence, but he would have distrusted and stonily disregarded it. If the daughter of a shiftless West Virginia mountaineer married the nephew of a professor at the University of Upsala, the native family felt disgraced by such an alliance.

Nevertheless, the thrift and intelligence of its preponderant European population have been potent factors in bringing about the present prosperity of the State. The census of 1910 showed that there were then 228,648 foreign-born and native-born Germans living in Nebraska; 103,503 Scandinavians; 50,680 Czechs. The total foreign population of the State was then 900,571, while the entire population was 1,192,214. That is, in round numbers, there were about nine hundred thousand foreign Americans in the State, to three hundred thousand native stock. With such a majority of foreign stock, nine to three, it would be absurd to say that the influence of the European does not cross the boundary of his own acres, and has had nothing to do with shaping the social ideals of the commonwealth.

When I stop at one of the graveyards in my own county, and see on the headstones the names of fine old men I used to know: *'Eric Ericson, born Bergen, Norway . . . died Nebraska,' 'Anton Pucelik, born Prague, Bohemia . . . died Nebraska,'* I have always the hope

2. French composer (1835–1921).

that something went into the ground with those pioneers that will one day come out again. Something that will come out not only in sturdy traits of character, but in elasticity of mind, in an honest attitude toward the realities of life, in certain qualities of feeling and imagination. Some years ago a professor at the University of Nebraska happened to tell me about a boy in one of his Greek classes who had a very unusual taste for the classics—intuitions and perceptions in literature. This puzzled him, he said, as the boy's parents had no interest in such things. I knew what the professor did not: that, though this boy had an American name, his grandfather was a Norwegian, a musician of high attainment, a fellow-student and life-long friend of Edvard Grieg.[3] It is in that great cosmopolitan country known as the Middle West that we may hope to see the hard molds of American provincialism broken up; that we may hope to find young talent which will challenge the pale proprieties, the insincere, conventional optimism of our art and thought.

The rapid industrial development of Nebraska, which began in the latter eighties, was arrested in the years 1893–97 by a succession of crop failures and by the financial depression which spread over the whole country at that time—the depression which produced the People's Party and the Free Silver agitation. These years of trial, as everyone now realizes, had a salutary effect upon the new State. They winnowed out the settlers with a purpose from the drifting malcontents who are ever seeking a land where man does not live by the sweat of his brow. The slack farmer moved on. Superfluous banks failed, and money lenders who drove hard bargains with desperate men came to grief. The strongest stock survived, and within ten years those who had weathered the storm came into their reward. What that reward is, you can see for yourself if you motor through the State from Omaha to the Colorado line. The country has no secrets; it is as open as an honest human face.

The old, isolated farms have come together. They rub shoulders. The whole State is a farm. Now it is the pasture lands that look little and lonely, crowded in among so much wheat and corn. It is scarcely an exaggeration to say that every farmer owns an automobile. I believe the last estimate showed that there is one motor car for every six inhabitants in Nebraska. The great grain fields are plowed by tractors. The old farm houses are rapidly being replaced by more cheerful dwellings, with bathrooms and hardwood floors, heated by furnaces or hot-water plants. Many of them are lighted by electricity, and every farm house has its telephone. The country towns are clean and well kept. On Saturday night the main street is

3. Norwegian composer (1843–1907) whose works include the *Peer Gynt Suites* and *Piano Concerto in A Minor.*

a long black line of parked motor cars; the farmers have brought their families to town to see the moving-picture show. When the school bell rings on Monday morning, crowds of happy looking children, well nourished—for the most part well mannered, too,—flock along the shady streets. They wear cheerful, modern clothes, and the girls, like the boys, are elastic and vigorous in their movements. These thousands and thousands of children—in the little towns and in the country schools—these, of course, ten years from now, will be the State.

In this time of prosperity any farmer boy who wishes to study at the State University can do so. A New York lawyer who went out to Lincoln to assist in training the university students for military service in war time exclaimed when he came back: 'What splendid young men! I would not have believed that any school in the world could get together so many boys physically fit, and so few unfit.'

Of course, there is the other side of the medal, stamped with the ugly crest of materialism, which has set its seal upon all of our most productive commonwealths. Too much prosperity, too many moving-picture shows, too much gaudy fiction have colored the taste and manners of so many of these Nebraskans of the future. There, as elsewhere, one finds the frenzy to be showy; farmer boys who wish to be spenders before they are earners, girls who try to look like the heroines of the cinema screen; a coming generation which tries to cheat its aesthetic sense by buying things instead of making anything. There is even danger that that fine institution, the University of Nebraska, may become a gigantic trade school. The men who control its destiny, the regents and the lawmakers, wish their sons and daughters to study machines, mercantile processes, 'the principles of business'; everything that has to do with the game of getting on in the world—and nothing else. The classics, the humanities, are having their dark hour. They are in eclipse. Studies that develop taste and enrich personality are not encouraged. But the 'Classics' have a way of revenging themselves. One may venture to hope that the children, or the grandchildren, of a generation that goes to a university to select only the most utilitarian subjects in the course of study—among them, salesmanship and dressmaking—will revolt against all the heaped-up, machine-made materialism about them. They will go back to the old sources of culture and wisdom—not as a duty, but with burning desire.

In Nebraska, as in so many other States, we must face the fact that the splendid story of the pioneers is finished, and that no new story worthy to take its place has yet begun. The generation that subdued the wild land and broke up the virgin prairie is passing, but it is still there, a group of rugged figures in the background which inspire respect, compel admiration. With these old men and women the attainment of material prosperity was a moral victory, because it was wrung from hard conditions, was the result of a struggle that tested character. They can look out over those broad stretches of fertility and say: 'We made this, with our backs and hands.' The sons, the generation now in middle life, were reared amid hardships, and it is perhaps natural that they should be very much interested in material comfort, in buying whatever is expensive and ugly. Their fathers came into a wilderness and had to make everything, had to be as ingenious as shipwrecked sailors. The generation now in the driver's seat hates to make anything, wants to live and die in an automobile, scudding past those acres where the old men used to follow the long corn-rows up and down. They want to buy everything ready-made: clothes, food, education, music, pleasure. Will the third generation—the full-blooded, joyous one just coming over the hill—will it be fooled? Will it believe that to live easily is to live happily?

The wave of generous idealism, of noble seriousness, which swept over the State of Nebraska in 1917 and 1918,[4] demonstrated how fluid and flexible is any living, growing, expanding society. If such 'conversions' do not last, they at least show of what men and women are capable. Surely the materialism and showy extravagance of this hour are a passing phase! They will mean no more in half a century from now than will the 'hard times' of twenty-five years ago—which are already forgotten. The population is as clean and full of vigor as the soil; there are no old grudges, no heritages of disease or hate. The belief that snug success and easy money are the real aims of human life has settled down over our prairies, but it has not yet hardened into molds and crusts. The people are warm, mercurial, impressionable, restless, over-fond of novelty and change. These are not the qualities which make the dull chapters of history.

JOSEPH ALEXIS

Swedes in Nebraska†

For the following I am indebted to church reports, histories of Swedish immigration, and the *Omaha-Posten*, which four years ago devoted an extra number to the story of the settlements.

The Swedes left the old country for the same reason that their

4. Years when the United States was engaged in the First World War.
† A paper read at the annual meeting of the Nebraska State Historical Society, January 22, 1914.

forefathers in the Viking age set out for foreign shores. The fatherland was not productive enough to support a large population. Since the founding of the Swedish colony on the Delaware in April, 1638, Swedes have been migrating to America, though the number of immigrants was wellnigh insignificant until the middle of the nineteenth century.

* * *

There have always been people of an adventurous spirit who struck out over the western seas for America, and there are traces to be found of individuals from Sweden who roamed about as far south as Texas and Mexico. These adventurers founded no settlements in the early years of the last century, but they doubtless interested their friends in America. In the latter part of the forties immigration of Swedes in America increased, and families came in search of free land. To find such land it was necessary to continue the journey from New York westward. The usual course was by canal boat to Buffalo and then by steamer to Chicago. Large colonies settled in Illinois, and ere many years had passed that state was well filled, and then the immigrants found it necessary to proceed still farther to the west.

It is not known at what time the first Swede arrived in Nebraska. In the sixties considerable numbers reached Omaha either directly from Europe or from the eastern states. Some remained in Omaha, while others took homesteads or bought cheap railway land and then settled down on the lonesome prairie. The building of the Union Pacific shops in Omaha, in 1865, afforded work for many newcomers, and at this time the Swedes began to come to Nebraska in considerable numbers. There was a great demand for machinists, blacksmiths, carpenters and other tradesmen. The building of the railroad bridge in 1871 also called for laborers. Ever since that time there has been a large colony of Swedes in the metropolis of our state. From Omaha the stream of migration turned to Saunders county and Burt county. Rev. S. G. Larson perhaps did more than any one else toward settling the country east, west and south of Wahoo. He conducted several parties of immigrants from Omaha to Mead, Malmo and Swedeburg.

* * *

Among the first Swedes to settle in the Swedeburg vicinity was N. A. Aspengren. He speaks of the event as follows:

> When we looked over these bare hills for the first time June 23, 1869, there was not a human dwelling to be found. We each took our homestead and at once prepared to build some sort of shelter against wind and rain. The usual method was to dig a hole in a hillside and cover it with grass and

brush, which had been brought from a neighboring ravine. Jan. 22, 1870, the settlement received its first visit by Rev. S. G. Larson of Omaha, and the first sermon was delivered in Olof Olson's home in section 6. In 1871, there were few newcomers, but in 1872 and 1873 larger numbers arrived.

* * *

In 1871 a committee was sent out from Altona, Illinois, to study conditions in Nebraska, in the hope that a colony might be founded somewhere in the state. The committee came by railroad to Lincoln and then went, partly by wagon and partly on foot, to the vicinity where Stromsburg is now situated. The land was to their liking, and they took homesteads and urged their friends to do likewise Stromsburg was founded in 1872, and a steady stream of migration to Polk county followed. The town is strikingly Swedish, as the number of Swedish churches indicates. The Lutherans, the Mission Friends, the Baptists, the Methodists, and the Free Mission are all represented. A little to the northwest of Stromsburg is the large rural settlement of Swedehome. The railroad did not happen to come that way, and so the Swedehome settlement did not become a town.

* * *

There are many other places that might have been mentioned in connection with Swedish immigration to Nebraska, but time and space forbid. I have named only the most important points. As time goes on our interest in the beginnings of our state will be all the keener, and we shall all be the more desirous to know who our pioneers were. We are yet so near the beginning that we may not grasp fully the significance of pioneer days. I hope, however, that our state may succeed well in preserving the records of the past and that there may be written on the pages of history at least a few chapters dealing with the Swedish element in Nebraska.

SARKA B. HRBKOVA

Bohemians in Nebraska†

* * *

While every county of Nebraska has Bohemian inhabitants, the largest numbers are in Douglas, Colfax, Saline, Saunders, and Butler. Cities and towns which have a generous percentage of Bohemians are Omaha, South Omaha, Wilber, Crete, Clarkson, Milligan

† From *Publications of the Nebraska State Historical Society,* Vol. XIX, ed. Albert Watkins (Lincoln, NE: Nebraska State Historical Society, 1919), pp. 143–49. Hrbkova was Professor of Slavonic Languages at the University of Nebraska. All notes are by the editor.

Schuyler, and Prague. In the main, however, Bohemians in Nebraska are settled on farms rather than in towns, in small communities rather than in cities, and in the eastern, rather than in the western part of the state.

A large majority of the Bohemians of this state are in agricultural pursuits; and as farmers are the real backbone of the great West, it may be said that the Bohemian farmers are the mainstay of the Czechs in Nebraska, despite the fact that business and the professions each year gain more accessions from them.

First Bohemians in Nebraska

The first Bohemian who came to Nebraska, so far as can be learned, was Libor Alois Slesinger, who was born October 28, 1806, in Usti above the Orlice River, Bohemia. It is noteworthy that this first Bohemian immigrant to this state came to America for political liberty, which the absolutism prevailing in Austria after the uprising of 1848 had stifled in his own country. Slesinger left Bohemia in November, 1856, and in January, 1857, arrived in Cedar Rapids, Iowa, which was a sort of stopping place for most of the Bohemian immigrants *en route* for the great, attractive, beaming West beyond the Missouri. The trip from Cedar Rapids to Omaha, Slesinger made by wagon. A little later he settled near the Winnebago reservation. His experiences were as picturesque and adventurous as those of other early comers, if not more so. Joseph Horsky, who arrived in 1857 and also came by the Cedar Rapids route, was the second, and the now famous Edward Rosewater the third, Czech to settle in the Cornhusker state.

The homestead act[1] attracted to the West many Bohemians who had already become citizens or were about to swear allegiance to the "starry flag".

* * *

The first wave of Bohemian immigration to Nebraska consisted of men seeking political and religious freedom. Subsequent waves comprised men escaping enforced military service in the Austrian army or seeking economic betterment. Though large numbers of Bohemians came to America to avoid serving in the army at home, yet these same Bohemians, who had but just fled from enforced militarism, of their own will enlisted here to save the Union.

* * *

1. The Homestead Act of 1862 offered a quarter section (160 acres) to anyone who would settle and develop the land for five years.

Religious Life of Czechs in Nebraska

From the domain of Roman Catholic Austria to unpledged Nebraska is a step of many thousands of miles. The difference in the religious attitude of many Czechs who have taken that long step is as great and is likewise analogous. Bohemia's greatest trials and sufferings were a result of religious struggles, both internal and with neighboring states. From the introduction of Christianity into Bohemia in 863 by Cyril and Methodius, the nation's brand of religion has been different from that of her neighbors. Bohemia accepted Christianity from two Greek Priests of Constantinople, who at once introduced the Slavic Bible and preaching in the mother tongue. Bohemia's neighbors received their Christian missionaries from Rome, which required the Latin service.

The burning of John Huss,[2] who preceded the German Luther by a decade more than a hundred years, lighted the way for the reformation, which would not have been possible without the work and martyrdom of the Bohemian reformer. The smoldering dissensions which burst again into flame in 1620, when the Bohemian and Moravian Brethren were exiled and the country was depopulated and plundered, have ever and anon crackled and thrust out gleaming tongues. But the days of crucifixions and martyrdoms are memories of the middle ages. A clearer, whiter light now shines for those who think on things religious.

Perhaps no other people think or write so much on the various phases of religious controversies as Bohemians. And yet the charge of infidelism is too often wrongfully made against them. A people who are thinking, debating, arguing on religious questions and meanwhile trying to live according to the golden rule are much nearer certain professed ideals of conduct than some of the pharisaical "professors" themselves.

The Bohemians of Nebraska may be roughly classified into three general groups—Roman Catholics, Protestants, and Liberal Thinkers. There are Bohemian churches and priests in forty-four towns and villages. The church at Brainard is a very fine structure, costing over $40,000, exclusive of interior decorations, and is the pride of the community. Parochial schools are maintained in connection with some of the churches. For instance, there is a fine building in Dodge where 140 children attend the instruction of Sisters of Our Lady. There are some twenty Bohemian Protestant churches in the state, mainly Methodist and Presbyterian. The Liberal Thinkers are but recently organized, so there are only five societies in Nebraska,

2. John Huss (also spelled Jan Hus) was a Bohemian religious leader whose teachings influenced the Protestant Reformation.

four of them located in Omaha, and only one of them exclusively devoted to the object of the organization. The others are lodges of different orders which have signified approval of the purposes of the Svobodna Obec or Liberal Thinkers League.

Organized Life of Czechs of Nebraska

The Bohemian people in the United States are unusually strong on organization. Judging alone by Nebraska's Bohemian lodge membership one might easily believe they were inveterate "joiners". It is well known that as members of labor unions they are "stickers". They believe thoroughly in the adhesive value of organization to gain a point. However, it is as organizers of social and fraternal protective societies that the Bohemians excel. Practically every man of Bohemian birth or parentage belongs to one or more associations which have for their object insurance, protection in sickness and death, as well as the development of social life. There are also a number of organizations offering no insurance but, instead, opportunities for education along gymnastic, musical, literary or related lines. The lodges of the fraternal class afford cheap insurance, the assessments in nearly every instance being much lower than in other orders.

* * *

It is especially significant that this oldest organization of Bohemians in Saline county [the Bohemian Reading Society], and which was among the oldest in the state, was effected for the purpose of meeting to read and discuss books and magazines. Even in those difficult times, when life was mainly a matter of preserving existence in the hard, rough conditions of the day, these recent immigrants from a foreign land to the prairies of Nebraska held to the social and educational ideals of the mother land, bringing into the sordid commonplace of existence the rosy poetry of song, music, the dance, the theatre, and communion with books.

Music, either vocal or instrumental, always had to be present in any gathering of Bohemians, whether it were a meeting of neighbors or a formal session of a lodge. The Czechs are not without warrant called "the nation of musicians", as the Smetanas, Dvoraks, Kubeliks, Kocians, Ondriceks and Destinns fully attest. If a wager were to be made that every Bohemian community in Nebraska today had its own band or orchestra, it is safe to say that the bettor would win.

ROSE ROSICKY

Bohemian Cemeteries in Nebraska†

Like others of the earliest pioneers in any land, quite a number of our people were buried individually, on their farms, before cemeteries were established. These solitary graves, here and there, were marked by wooden crosses and fences, long fallen into decay and obliterated. The hands of those who sleep in them planted the first kernels of corn in the virgin sod, with the aid of a hatchet, and now, after comparatively a short span, the roar of the tractor and automobile resounds, as it sweeps over these forgotten graves.

Willa Cather tells of such a grave, that of the unfortunate, hapless Bohemian pioneer Shimerda, in her story "My Ántonia":

"Years afterward, when the open-grazing days were over, and the red grass had been ploughed under and under until it had almost disappeared from the prairie; when all the fields were under fence, and roads no longer ran about like wild things, but followed surveyed section lines, Mr. Shimerda's grave was still there, with a sagging wire fence around it, and an unpainted wooden cross. As grandfather had predicted, Mrs. Shimerda never saw the roads go over his head. The road from the north curved a little to the east just there, and the road from the west swung out a little to the south; so that the grave, with its tall red grass that was never mowed, was like a little island; and at twilight, under a new moon or the clear evening star, the dusty roads used to look like soft gray rivers flowing past it. I never came upon the place without emotion, and in all that country it was the spot most dear to me. I loved the dim superstition, the propitiatory intent, that had put the grave there; and still more I loved the spirit that could not carry out the sentence—the error from the surveyed lines, the clemency of the soft earth roads along which the home-coming wagons rumbled after sunset. Never a tired driver passed the wooden cross, I am sure, without wishing well to the sleeper."

Within a very few years after a settlement had established itself, cemeteries were provided. Life intertwines with death, the need for cemeteries is as pressing as for shelter. In time, as with all other material evidences in our state, they have been improved and beautified. Inasmuch as those listed here are entirely Bohemian, they will, in the future, be the only purely Bohemian records, visible to the passer-by, of our people in Nebraska. This truth was in the

† From Rosicky, *A History of Czechs (Bohemians) in Nebraska* (Omaha, NE: Czech Historical Society of Nebraska, 1929), pp. 431–32. Reprinted by permission of the Eastern Nebraska Genealogical Society. All notes are the editor's.

mind of Jeffrey Doležal Hrbek,[1] when he wrote his poem given below, which was published in "The Pulse"[2] in March, 1906:

THE BOHEMIAN CEMETERY

Yonder, the southward hills rise, fair,
  And pleasant green fields bask in the sun.
The view is broad and lovely there,
  Where the dusty road doth upward run.

On the very crown of the highest hill
  Where the tallest oaks lift their arms toward God
Above the clatter and din of lathe and mill
  White marbles gleam athwart the sod.

'Tis the burial ground of a foreign race,
  A race from the heart of Europe sprung,
Men and women of open face
  That speak in the strange Bohemian tongue.

Down in the city that gleams below
  With its streets and lanes and its roofs and domes,
In its southern corner row on row
  They have built their garden-bordered homes.

But here on the hill is the burial ground
  Where the sainted dead in their last long sleep
'Neath many a verdant, flowery mound
  The eternal watches keep.

Snowy marble and granite brown
  And blooming urns of bronze and stone.
Carved and graven with cross and crown
  And with soft green moss o'ergrown.

And the epitaphs and wreathed rhymes
  In the Chechish tongue are writ,
That the men and women of future times
  May muse and wonder a bit.

For, the dialect sweet of the pioneers old
  Is giving slowly but surely way
To the plain smooth speech of the Saxon bold
  The Chechish weakens day by day.

1. Jeffrey Hrbek (1882–1907), Nebraska scholar and poet who chaired the first Slavonic Department at the University of Nebraska.
2. Literary magazine established by Jeffrey Hrbek.

Some day these stone-carved tearful rhymes
Shall be a riddle—a puzzle—nay
Folk will doubt that in by-gone times
Many could read each tombstone's lay.

Still, here on the hill in the burial ground
The Chechish dead in their last long sleep
'Neath grass-o'rgrown, forgotten mound
The eternal watch will keep.

MIKE FISCHER

From Pastoralism and Its Discontents: Willa Cather and the Burden of Imperialism†

Willa Cather's fiction has recently been subjected to a number of revisionist readings, most notably by feminist critics of *My Ántonia* who have exposed both the various sexist stereotypes that underlie Jim Burden's archetypal eulogizing of "his" protagonist and the narrative strategies whereby he attempts to expropriate his female muse. Unfortunately, in doing so they have overlooked the fact that it is not only the history of women on the Plains that is being "rewritten" by Jim but also the conquest of the Plains Indians that is being rewritten by Willa Cather.

Jim initially describes the Nebraskan land upon which he will write his story as "not a country at all, but the material out of which countries are made" (7); and he imagines himself as writing in the tradition of the *Georgics*, Virgil's pastoral account of the founding of the patria. Factually, however, the history of the Plains has more in common with the brutal imperialism recorded in the *Aeneid*; the development of Nebraska is a pastoral story only in the sense of "pastor(al)ization." *My Ántonia* is a story of origins for whites only; its account of conflicts between various selves and their others—an important theme in the novel—ignores the most significant Other in Nebraskan history: the Native Americans whose removal was seen as a *sine qua non* for successful white settlement.

Essential to an "idyllic" view of Plains history is the premise that what the first settlers had to clear was merely the land, and here one begins to see in a new light Cather's repeated description of the Nebraska which preceded white settlement as a prairie that was "empty." Equally revealing, in turn, is the way Cather's feminist

† From "Willa Cather and the Conquest of the West" by Mike Fischer. Originally published in *Mosaic* 23.1 (1990): 31–44. Reprinted by permission.

critics have followed her lead. For all her valuable insights into Jim's sexism, for example, Jean Schwind describes the Nebraska territory that the Shimmerdas subsequently occupy as "new virgin land" (61). Similarly, Sharon O'Brien, perhaps Cather's best feminist critic, refers to the Nebraskan landscape into which Cather moved in 1883 as an "empty world" "uninscribed in a literary as well as a topographical sense," a "new landscape" in which Cather might concern herself "with the human drive to create culture and civilization by making marks in a new landscape"—"taming . . . the wild land" (74).

The land on which Cather inscribed her story, however, was not a *tabula rasa,* even if, as in *O Pioneers!,* she conceives of "the feeble scratches on stone left by prehistoric races [as] so indeterminate that they may, after all, be only the markings of glaciers, and not a record of human strivings" (18–19). In a powerful demonstration of circular logic, Cather's reading of such "feeble scratches" as "indeterminate" allows her to relegate the people who made them to a time before writing—to prehistory.

Cather's appropriation of the land's materials for her own purposes—so that she might build a "country"—required that those contexts and peoples which did not accommodate her textual strategy be marginalized or naturalized so that their stories would not contradict her own. As such, her works confirm what Fredric Jameson has observed with respect to the ideological nature of the esthetic act, which invents "imaginary or formal 'solutions' to unresolvable social contradictions" (79). This is not to accuse Cather of conscious duplicity or racism, any more than it is to indict those feminist critics who ignore her failure to recognize Nebraska's first inhabitants. Instead, the kind of naturalization of which I speak is indicative of the cultural limitations—Jameson's "political unconscious"—that condition the historical interpretations of any epoch and which register the blindspots in any period's texts (74–83). Such ways of perceiving result from an individual's incremental and almost unnoticed absorption of the cultural assumptions of his or her particular group or class.

At the same time, however, the "real" history that such assumptions exclude does not—cannot—just go away. The social contradictions that narrative seeks to resolve, because they are intrinsic to the social infrastructures such narratives depict, have a habit of reappearing at inopportune moments. This "notion of contradiction," writes Jameson, "is central to any Marxist cultural analysis" and it explains why history, in the sense of a grand narrative of human events, will not disappear and cannot be erased; "it happened" (80). There can be no cultural text, however apparently blind to the political preconditions assuring its provenance, that fails to record the traces of those preconditions, in spite of itself. Any story of the (white) settlement of Nebraska—or "America"—will inevitably find itself referring to those peoples whose "removal" preceded that settlement. The function of criticism, accordingly, is to uncover these traces. Or as Tony Bennett argues in corroboration of Jameson's "notion of contradiction," an active and critical intervention "works" upon such texts and serves to expose contradictions that they and their author(s), given their own historical context, could not have seen (141).

While it is true that cultural context inevitably limits the perceptions of any critic, the political struggles of the sixties and seventies—such as the Black Arts and Black Power movements, the American Indian Movement (AIM), and the Chicano Youth Movement's "Plan of Aztlan"—place us today in an especially advantageous position for "working" on texts so as to excavate the buried stories in U.S. history. While the most important part of this project must and will remain the recuperation and celebration of these peoples' own texts, a critical explanation of how such stories are embedded within canonical narratives might help us recognize the degree to which suppressed histories are integral not only to the establishment of canons but also to the idea of "Western Civilization" that canons celebrate.

Before proceeding, perhaps I can make clearer the nature of the interpretive act with an example. Bernice Slote, trying to explain the absence of non-European ethnic groups in much of Cather's early fiction, offers the following picture of the young Cather's Nebraska: "She lived in Nebraska in the 1880s and 1890s, when Indians were noticed in the newspapers chiefly as warring tribes with dirty living habits. In any case, they were far from Red Cloud, and Wounded Knee was only a column or so of print. Literary views in Nebraska were composed in highly romanticized legends, some in Hiawatha style . . ." (98–99). Slote's passage underscores an important contradiction in the (white) Nebraskan perceptions it describes. On the one hand, "columns of print" describing the Indians did in fact exist. On one level, some late-nineteenth-century Nebraskans were still aware of the Indians, as they could not help being, given how recently—as late as the 1870s—much of western Nebraska had still been under Sioux control. On the other hand, the Indians, in Cather's Red Cloud, were reduced from their cultural complexity to "warring tribes with dirty habits." As James Olson has demonstrated in his history of Nebraska, early Nebraskan newspapers, often little more than advertising sheets for the companies that owned them, were far more concerned with the price and yield of land than they were with drawing sensitive or accurate portraits of those peoples being thrown off the land (93). As far as such newspapers were concerned, the Wounded Knee massacre[1] had nothing to do with an agrarian Nebraska economy; it, and the Indians who died there, existed "far away." They simply did not matter.

They were not so far away, however, either temporally or geographically, as Cather might have wanted—and successfully managed—to believe. Red Cloud itself, established in 1870 as the first permanent town in what had been one of the Indians' last buffalo hunting grounds south of the Platte River, was named after the Sioux chief of that name, who was reputed to have held a war council on the site where the town was platted (Perkey 198; J. Olson 171–72).

As recently as 1868, Red Cloud's war councils had been aimed at expelling white settlers from the lands north of the Platte River—guaranteed the Sioux in perpetuity as part of the 1851 Laramie Treaty[2]—in western Nebraska, northern Wyoming and Montana. That year a second Laramie Treaty[3] initiated the process that would eventually force Red Cloud to accept semi-reservation status in northwestern Nebraska and that, finally, after the illegal white incursions into the Black Hills in the mid-1870s, would lead to his expulsion from Nebraska altogether.

Nonetheless, in 1870 the Black Hills catastrophe, originally provoked by the discovery there of gold, could not be foreseen; names like Sitting Bull, Crazy Horse and Custer were relatively unknown. In the very months that Red Cloud, Nebraska, was being founded, Chief Red Cloud was completing a treaty in Washington, D.C. In exchange for peace along Nebraska's Platte River Valley—with its just completed trans-continental railroad that the Indians had successfully sabotaged in the 1866–68 war—the Oglalla Sioux were guaranteed possession of the Black Hills and the Powder River country. The "warring tribes with dirty habits" would be placed in the margins of Nebraska's text; they could continue to "harass" settlers elsewhere as long as Nebraska prospered. Chief Red Cloud's treaty symbolized this compromise; Red Cloud, Nebraska, opening

1. The Wounded Knee Massacre (1890) in South Dakota was the last major battle between Indians and United States troops. The Indian dead included women and children. Later Wounded Knee would become an important site of memory and resistance for Indian activists [Editor].
2. The Fort Laramie Treaty of 1851 between the United States and several Indian nations guaranteed the Indians control of the Great Plains in return for safe passage of settlers on the Oregon Trail and permission to build roads and forts [Editor].
3. The Fort Laramie Treaty of 1868 between the United States and the Lakota nation, forced by Chief Red Cloud's successful military actions against U.S. troops, gave Lakotas ownership of the Black Hills and control of other territories in South Dakota, Wyoming, and Montana. Within ten years the treaty would be violated as white settlers entered these areas, protected by the U.S. military. The defeated Red Cloud was exiled to Pine Ridge Reservation in South Dakota [Editor].

up what had been Indian territory, profited from its provisions (Brown, chapters 5,6,8,12; Baltensperger 37–52; J. Olson 128–41).

The settlers of Red Cloud under Silas Garber—soon to become governor of the state—may have believed that the name they chose for their town could serve as an emblem for the peace that Chief Red Cloud had made—had been forced to make—possible. That peace, however, was tenuous; provoked by continued white expansion into their territory, the Sioux continued a resistance which James Olson has argued was "the most serious opposition they [the whites] encountered in the whole of America's westward expansion" (128–29). The events of 1876, and in particular Custer's astonishing defeat—the most serious blow the U.S. Army suffered in all of the Indian Wars—demonstrated anew at what cost such "peace" had to be won. The hopes generated by Red Cloud's 1870 Washington visit had dissipated amidst a series of bloody wars that, within twenty years, would see the systematic genocide of Red Cloud's people and the deaths of hundreds of white soldiers. Red Cloud became a reminder, for those who chose to remember, that its prosperity and security were predicated upon the removal and elimination of the people for whose chief it was named—people who still occupied most of Nebraska as late as the American Civil War, as Cather herself admitted in a 1923 *Nation* article: "Before 1860 civilization did no more than nibble at the eastern edge of the State, along the river bluffs. Lincoln, the present capital, was open prairie; and the whole of the great plain to the westward was still a sunny wilderness, where the tall red grass and the buffalo and the Indian hunter were undisturbed" (236).

Despite the implications of her *Nation* article, Cather usually chose not to remember the presence of Native Americans in Nebraska, or, perhaps more accurately, she literally seemed to forget their existence. While her short history of Nebraska does acknowledge the Indians' erstwhile presence, it does not try to account for their removal—nor explain how the peoples who roamed the prairies "undisturbed" were eventually disturbed enough to disappear and make possible the agricultural paradise that she proclaims Nebraska to be.

* * *

Cather herself, in the middle of an article celebrating the comforts of the Burlington Railroad—the road that runs through Black Hawk in *My Ántonia* and which runs through the actual town of Red Cloud—recognized that the "sudden transition" from the harsh western prairie to the comforts of a railroad dining car had "something of the black art about it and seemed altogether unnatural" (*World* 838). We can see just how unnatural—and the extent, consequently, to which Cather's narrative "railroads" its readers—

by reviewing the history of how Nebraska was wrested from the Plains Indians.

When Andrew Jackson stole parts of the southeastern United States from the Indians in 1830, he initiated a process that resulted, in 1834, in the Indian Intercourse Act, which guaranteed the Indians possession of most American lands west of the Mississippi, including all of the present state of Nebraska (J. Olson 67). Though subsequent territorial adjustments appropriated substantial portions of this "Indian land," including most of the spaces between the Mississippi and Missouri Rivers, the Indians were still in possession of all of Nebraska when Stephen Douglas, recently elected congressman from Illinois, arose from the floor of the House in 1844 and proposed his first bill to organize Nebraska as a territory (J. Olson 69–70).

Douglas's initiative was, to say the least, peculiar, since territorial organization was supposed to follow an accumulation of white settlers in a region. Not surprisingly, however, given the 1834 agreement with the Indians, the only whites in Nebraska in the mid-1840s were a few missionaries, traders and advance squatters, none of whom was very concerned with his/her official position (92). Douglas's real reason for proposing the Bill was less concerned with these few white transients than with the possibility of placing the eastern terminus of the newly proposed transcontinental railroad in Chicago and running it through Nebraska's easily traversable Platte River valley. With this in mind, Douglas had recently invested in Chicago real estate (Limerick 92). Still, as long as he and his constituency were confronted with the lingering fiction of a permanent Indian territory, the proposed routes would begin elsewhere—as indeed all four of the routes proposed during the 1840s did (J. Olson 68–69).

With the introduction of his Bill and his decade-long fight for the creation of a Nebraska territory, Douglas served notice to Secretary of War Jefferson Davis that no more Indians should be allowed into Nebraska. "The Indian barrier must be removed," he wrote; otherwise the United States would sacrifice its "immense interests and possessions on the Pacific" to a "vast wilderness fifteen hundred miles in breadth, filled with hostile savages, and cutting off all direct communication" (qtd. in Limerick 93). Douglas got his wish. The Nebraska Territory was created in 1854, even though a census taken in November of that year showed only twenty-seven hundred whites living in the state—most of them either residing on the eastern fringe of the territory along the Missouri or transients who actually lived in Kansas (J. Olson 88).

Many of the Indian tribes living in eastern Nebraska were either confined to reservations or forced to "trade" their ancient lands for trinkets and new guarantees of lands further West. The success of this program of removal, combined with the dramatic rise in population as a result of the Homestead Act (intended to consolidate control of these lands) and with the American Civil War, which effectively removed the proposed southern routes from contention, led President Lincoln, in 1863, to choose the Platte River valley as the route that the railroad would follow. The first track was laid that year; by 1867, the rails had reached western Nebraska.

Here, the Sioux, Cheyenne and Arapaho peoples proved more difficult to "remove" than their eastern neighbors had been. As Chief Spotted Tail of the Brûlé Sioux said to President Grant during the 1870 visit of Red Cloud's delegation, "The Great Father has made roads stretching east and west. Those roads are the cause of all our troubles . . . . The country where we live is overrun by whites. All our game is gone . . . . If you stop your roads we can get our game" (qtd. in Brown 138). Spotted Tail was complaining specifically about white incursions into the Powder River country; by 1870, after all, the transcontinental railroad had been finished for a year. Building it was not easy, however, partly because, from the time of the Sand Creek massacre of 1864, the Indians of western Nebraska systematically tore up tracks and raided supply wagons carrying building materials (J. Olson 114, 137–38).

The outcome of this struggle was inevitable. The whites were too powerful, and there were too many of them. From less than three thousand settlers in 1854, white Nebraskan population rose to thirty thousand by 1860, fifty thousand by 1867, when Nebraska became a state, and one hundred twenty-five thousand by 1870, the year of Red Cloud's eastern visit, the year that Red Cloud, Nebraska, was settled. By 1890, just before the economic depression, drought years and emigration that would characterize the nineties, Nebraska had over one million white settlers, almost all of them first generation pioneers (J. Olson 88).

If, as Governor John Thayer of Nebraska claimed in his inaugural address of 1887, the railroads led to Nebraska's settlement a quarter to half century sooner than might otherwise have been expected (Combs 21), one of the reasons was the aggressive propaganda campaign the railroads waged in Europe to lure immigrants to Nebraska. Moreover, the railroads dictated both settlement patterns and the government policy toward the Indians that made settlement feasible.

In 1865, for example, the southern Cheyenne and Arapaho peoples, displaced by the Colorado Gold Rush (1858) and the ensuing Sand Creek massacre (1864), met with representatives of the government to negotiate the site for a reservation. The Indians elected the area between the Smoky Hill River in central Kansas and the Republican River—running through what would become Red Cloud—in southern Nebraska. The government denied their request, knowing as they did that the Burlington planned to open this area for settlement and build a railroad there (Brown 96).

The Cheyenne and Arapaho were forced to move to the Oklahoma territory; Red Cloud was established five years later. Though Indians refusing to accept the 1865 treaty had successfully stymied the first attempt to settle the Republican River valley in 1869, and though they periodically disrupted other attempts at settling the region, such as that at Red Willow in 1871, the prospect of a railroad in the valley—and the railroad's ability to provide the people for settlement—encouraged settlers to believe that if they could hold on for a few years, their ventures into the area would prove successful (J. Olson 170–73). The Burlington dutifully built a spur line through the valley, beginning work in 1878. The line was completed by 1882—a year before Cather traveled it, along with countless immigrant families like the Shimerdas,[4] to Nebraska.

"The real West to Willa Cather," writes Slote, "was the West of settlement, of the immigration of peoples from many parts of the world" (96). It would be misleading to ignore Cather's celebration of these immigrant peoples in novels such as *O Pioneers!* or *My Ántonia*. *My Ántonia* was published in a year of intense xenophobia provoked by the United States government's entry into World War I; on 26 March 1918, Governor Neville of Nebraska successfully engineered the repeal of a law designed to guarantee foreign language instruction in Nebraska's schools as "vicious, undemocratic, and un-American" (J. Olson 265). In this context, Cather's sensitive portrayal and vigorous defense of immigrant peoples such as the Czechs and the Norwegians can and should be seen as the courageous act that it was.

At the same time, however, one must keep in mind Patricia Nelson Limerick's recent admonition that "In race relations, the West could make the turn-of-the-century Northeastern urban confrontation between European immigrants and American nativists look like a family reunion" (27). Without taking anything away from Cather's significant achievement, it is nevertheless true that her conception of western history as the story of immigrant settlers blinded her to the effects of such immigration on the West's native populations.

* * *

4. The Shimerdas are the Bohemian immigrant family in Willa Cather's *My Ántonia* (1918), which is set in a fictionalized version of Red Cloud, Nebraska [Editor].

WORKS CITED

Baltensperger, Bradley H. *Nebraska: A Geography.* London: Westview, 1985.
Bennett, Tony. *Formalism and Marxism.* London: Methuen, 1979.
Brown, Dee. *Bury My Heart at Wounded Knee: An Indian History of the American West.* New York: Washington Square, 1970.
Cather, Willa. *O Pioneers!* Boston: Houghton, 1913.
———. *My Ántonia.* Boston: Houghton, 1926.
———. *Death Comes for the Archbishop.* New York: Modern Library, 1927.
———. "Nebraska: The End of the First Cycle." *The Nation* 117 (1923): 236–38.
———. *The World and the Parish: Willa Cather's Articles and Reviews, 1893–1902.* Ed. William M. Curtin. 2 vols. Lincoln: U of Nebraska P, 1970.
Combs, Barry B. "The Union Pacific Railroad and the Early Settlement of Nebraska." *Nebraska History* 50 (1969): 1–26.
Jameson, Fredric. *The Political Unconscious: Narrative as a Socially Symbolic Act.* Ithaca: Cornell UP, 1981.
Limerick, Patricia Nelson. *The Legacy of Conquest: The Unbroken Past of the American West.* New York: Norton, 1987.
Olson, James C. *History of Nebraska.* Lincoln: U of Nebraska P, 1966.
Perkey, Elton A. *Perkey's Nebraska Place Names.* Lincoln: Nebraska State Historical Society Publications 28, 1982.
Schwind, Jean. "The Benda Illustrations to *My Ántonia*: Cather's 'Silent' Supplement to Jim Burden's Narrative." *PMLA* 100 (1985): 51–67.
Slote, Bernice. "Willa Cather and Plains Culture." *Vision and Refuge: Essays on the Literature of the Great Plains.* Ed. Virginia Faulkner with Frederick C. Luebke. Lincoln: U of Nebraska P. 1982. 93–105.
Slotkin, Richard. *Regeneration Through Violence: The Mythology of the American Frontier: 1600–1860.* Middletown: Wesleyan UP, 1973.
Stouck, David. "Perspective as Structure and Theme in *My Ántonia.*" *Texas Studies in Language and Literature* 12 (1970): 285–94.

CRITICISM

Contemporary Reviews

E. U. S.

O Pioneers! A New Heroine and a New Country Appear†

A new heroine and a new country appear in *O Pioneers!* Miss Cather's second novel. The story is created from the sturdy lives of the Scandinavian and Bohemian pioneers of the Middle West, and is filled with courage, endurance and final triumph. The publisher's announcement aptly characterizes it as "the very voice of those vast plains between the Missouri River and the Rocky Mountains, and of the hope and faith and power that made that country what it is today." . . .

The novel has great dramatic power; it is deep, thrilling, intense—and this intensity comes through the simplicity—one might almost say severity, of treatment. The reader, surfeited by the many-paragraphed conversations of the ordinary novel, finds his imagination unusually roused by the magnificent sufficiency of the book. The subject is not one which can be expressed in a pen and ink sketch; it needs the broad brush lines—and in such a way has Miss Cather treated it. Yet there is great delicacy of touch, particularly in the descriptive passages in which Marie and Emil—her lover and Alexandra's brother—appear. . . .

That Miss Cather knows and appreciates her people is self evident. It would be impossible for anyone who had not lived on unbroken farm land, who had not seen these purposeful immigrants, to catch so completely the spirit of a foreign race renewing the old ideals in a strange country. *O Pioneers!* has many missions: it is a disclosure of the splendid resources in our immigrant population; it is the revelation of a changed and changing country; it is, indirectly perhaps, an embodiment of the feminist theory; and, finally, it is more than worth reading for its literary value.

† *Boston Evening Transcript,* July 16, 1913.

FLOYD DELL

A Good Novel†

This book provides an opportunity for the American Academy of Arts and Letters to justify its existence. One of the functions of an academy—a function which the recently created British Academy has not hesitated to assume—is the discovery and recognition of genius. A committee including Bernard Shaw not long since selected a certain prose work for the honor of a prize, as containing that specific and peculiar promise which attaches to the early productions of genius. Well! It would be a gratifying result of the enterprise of our American academicians if a committee headed by W. D. Howells should discover this novel by Willa Sibert Cather. It has that specific and peculiar quality. It is touched with genius. It is worthy of being recognized as the most vital, subtle and artistic piece of the year's fiction.

Why is it all that? I despair of being able to show why. The book does not deal with any of the large ideas which rightly enough agitate this generation. It has no palpable finesse of style. It does not stun nor dazzle. It only tells the story of a girl and her younger brothers who live on a Nebraska farm: the story of their struggle with a stubborn land which almost crushed them to death before it suddenly smiled and yielded; the story, moreover, of such friendship and love as came, sometimes with wistful autumnal sweetness and again with tragic passion, into their lives. It is not an extraordinary story. Everyone knows a dozen like it.

The book opens rather unpropitiously in the little town of Hanover, anchored on a windy Nebraska tableland, and "trying not to be blown away." The Swedish and Bohemian farmers who are engaged in the fierce and almost despairing effort to reclaim the land from its prairie wildness—it was thirty years ago—are in to trade at the general store. Among them is the girl Alexandra, a fine, resolute, man-minded, thoughtful young creature, with her little brother Emil; and Carl Lindstrum, a thin, frail boy with an artist's sensitiveness and skepticism in his face; and the little Bohemian girl, Marie Tovesky, a pretty child with a coaxing little red mouth and eyes with golden glints in the brown iris.

These are seen for a moment in a setting of men drinking raw alcohol to protect themselves against the cold, and women pinning red shawls about their heads, and all talking loudly in a room reeking with tobacco smoke and kerosene. Then they set out, and the

† *Chicago Evening Post,* July 25, 1913.

town vanishes behind them "as if it had never been." Alexandra goes back to the side of a father who is dying in the shadow of debt and failure, to her brothers to whom she must bear the difficult part of a mother, to a friendship that is cut short by separation, and to the terrible struggle with the land.

That is all there is in the whole first part of the book. And yet one does not stop reading. There is something in her calm yet vivid narrative that seems so profoundly true, a faithfulness not merely to the exterior of life, but to its intimate soul, that it has an extraordinary zest. And there is something more. One feels thru this narrative the spirit of the author, and comes to trust oneself completely in her hands. It is a spirit, an attitude toward life, that in its large and simple honesty has a kind of nobleness. Life, the course of events, as traced by such a mind, loses the taint of commonplace and becomes invested with dignity.

* * *

Either I have conveyed some sense of the richness, the charm and the dignity of this novel, or I have not. But I have done all I can, and—now it [is] up to the Academy.

GARDNER W. WOOD

Books of the Day†

The West seems inexhaustible. Here is a totally new kind of story come out of the prairies—*O Pioneers!* by Willa Sibert Cather. There have been plenty of realistic studies of the West, but this book is not a study—it is the West in action, a great romantic novel, written with striking brilliancy and power, in which one sees emerge a new country and a new people.

Miss Cather's story deals with the Norwegian and Bohmeian pioneers who planted the first seed on the prairies east of Colorado. Alexandra Bergson, a young Swedish girl, is left, at the age of eighteen, to take care of her mother and three younger brothers, and to hold the homestead which her father has vanquished at the cost of his life in the dark early days of the Divide. The figure of this young girl, steadfast, unflinching, self-contained, with her fierce pride and her uncompromising idealism, dominates the whole book. Alexandra is triumphant womanhood—a sort of Nebraska Valkyr, with the daring and confidence of one who carries a new message. The forces of the New World have freed her from the old tradition of

† *McClure's Magazine*, 41 (July 1913).

woman as a dependent drudge, pouring out her life in self-sacrifice and submission. In the quarrel between Alexandra and her brothers, Oscar and Lou, blindly contending for the proprietorship of their sister, are like voices of another generation, repeating a magic formula that has lost its power.

There is another heroine in the story—little Marie Shabata, the Bohemian girl, beautiful, eager, impulsive, so full of "go" that she can dance all night and drive a hay-cart for her cross husband next morning; too young and high-spirited to step aside and let her life go past her. Frank Shabata, her handsome, sullen husband, resents the youth and gaiety of his young wife; embittered himself, he finds something exasperating in her eager responsiveness to life; and Marie turns to young Emil Bergson.

Throughout the story one has the sense of great spaces; of the soil dominating everything, even the human drama that takes place upon it; renewing itself while the generations come and pass away.

FREDERICK TABER COOPER

Review of *O Pioneers!*†

O Pioneers! by Willa Sibert Cather, is quite as local in theme and in characters as any volume that Mr. Fox[1] ever wrote. It is a study of the struggles and privations of the foreign emigrant in the herculean task of subduing the untamed prairie land of the Far West and making it yield something more than a starvation income. Miss Cather has an unquestioned gift of observation, a keen eye for minute details and an instinctive perception of their relative significance. Every character and every incident in this slow-moving and frankly depressing tale give the impression of having been acquired directly through personal contact, and reproduced almost with the fidelity of a kodak picture or a graphonola record. And yet the net result strikes one, on second thought, as rather futile. . . . Now, the story of how Alexandra fought her battle and won it might have been well worth the telling; but this is precisely the part of her history which Miss Cather has neglected to chronicle. Instead, she has passed over it in leaps and bounds, and when we once more meet Alexandra, it is in the midst of prosperity, with all her brothers save the youngest happily married, her land increased by hundreds of acres, all yielding fabulous harvests, and Alexandra herself on

† *Bookman* 37 (August 1913).

1. John Fox, Jr. (1862–1915), best-selling novelist who drew on his native Kentucky as the setting for many of his novels.

the threshold of her fortieth year, and, with all her success, keenly conscious of the emptiness of her life, the craving for the love of husband and of children. Of course, it requires no keen guess-work to foresee that the young neighbour of her youth will ultimately return and the discrepancy of their ages will be forgotten. But somehow the reader cannot bring himself to care keenly whether the young neighbour returns or not, whether Alexandra is eventually happy or not,—whether, indeed, the farm itself prospers or not. The conscious effort required to read to a finish is something like the voluntary pinch that you give yourself in church during an especially somnolent sermon. The book does have its one big moment; but it is due to an incident that lies outside of the main thread of the story. Alexandra's youngest brother falls in love with Marie Shabata, the wife of a big, hot-tempered Bohemian; and one night the two forget discretion and are found in the orchard by the infuriated husband, who wreaks prompt vengeance. The swift, sharp picture which follows has a touch of Maupassant in it.[2]

CELIA HARRIS

Review of *O Pioneers!*†

Early last fall a story by Willa Cather in *McClure's Magazine* startled a good many of us into remembering that there are other ways of looking at the west than the slangily humorous, the obviously picturesque or the drearily realistic ways of prevalent fiction. "The Bohemian Girl" was a story of the prosperous Scandinavians and Bohemians of our rich Nebraska farm country of today, now that the older generation has conquered the prairie and the younger generation has leisure to be temperamental. It was a rare, troubling, important story, for while it was warmly appreciative of its own middle-western soil, it was at the same time reflective of the intellectual and poetic influences of northern Europe. One saw Nebraska under a brilliantly quivering, modern light. Miss Cather's Swedes and Czechs, for all their Americanism, sent one across the sea to their melancholy or complacent or passionate brothers in European literature. Her style, like her Nebraskans, was both American and European.

The effect was beautiful but disturbing. One wondered just where "The Bohemian Girl" would lead Miss Cather. For after all, in interpreting America, even a European neighborhood in Amer-

2. Guy de Maupassant (1850–1893), French short-story writer.

† *Lincoln Sunday State Journal,* August 3, 1913.

ica, it would be a bad thing to let oneself be possessed by a European mood. It was evident that this was a transition story. She had not only found a new vein of material but in developing it she was showing a surer sense of life than she had shown before. "The Bohemian Girl" had all of her old stylistic brilliancy, her old sympathy with intellectual rebels and appreciation of human exotics; but in addition it had a new sympathy with the simpler types of human character and a feeling for productive land that is more usual in older countries than in the United States where apple orchards are given away as subscription premiums. Miss Cather has sometimes seemed hampered by an inclination to write of people who have what we rather sweepingly call the artistic temperament. She has always had a directness of outlook and an intellectual vitality which would seem to demand a wider human field. Of the younger writers she has been one of the few who have allowed themselves to produce slowly and to keep their artistic seriousness. And in "The Bohemian Girl" there were unmistakable signs that she was casting off those shackles of temperament which have kept her from coming into her own high place.

O Pioneers! Miss Cather's new novel of the Nebraska prairie, is an answer to most of the speculations which "The Bohemian Girl" aroused. She is in no danger of exoticism. The book is so deeply, unaffectedly American in style and inspiration that it may disappoint some of Miss Cather's readers by its very simplicity. It stirred me like a trumpet call.

It is a story of the taming of the prairie by the Nebraska pioneers. It tells of the courage and endurance and faith which struggled with a hostile waste, held to it, believed in it and changed it into the smiling, benignant mother land that it is today. In *O Pioneers!* the prairie is given an energy of its own. At first it resists man savagely; then it tries his faith; then it yields to him; then it blesses him. Through all the circumstances of the story one is conscious of the prairie; of the frozen ridges of winters; of the fresh brown furrow of spring; the rabbits that bob across it; the forces that wait under it.

The book produces an extraordinary effect of reality. It is at once homely and beautiful and strange. Its characters seem in true relation not only with their own prairie soil and sky but with those older home soils from which they originally came. There are many people in the book, and they are all drawn with comprehending tenderness. Miss Cather has stripped her style of cleverness, and has found a new warm simplicity of phrase.

* * *

Alexandra's own story moves quietly; it is merely part of the history of the evolving race. She marries Carl Linstrum without knowing that she does not love him and probably journeys with him to serene old age without once finding it out. She is a great relief in an age that is obsessed by the idea of sex. Her deepest, most personal experiences have been what others would call impersonal. Her struggle has been with the natural forces of a new, unbroken country. She has become part of the prairie. In comparison with pulsating Marie Shabata, sullen Frank, introspective Carl and all the other astonishingly vivid folk of this life-like book she seems like a great, calm, kindly, elemental fact. She could not possibly be dramatized. She creates her impression by triumph of actual existence, by character and that individual coloring which the inner life gives to a personality. She is infinitely restful, infinitely mysterious and infinitely lonely.

It is curious that in this almost passionately American book which takes its title from the most exaltantly American of poets, there are, as I remember it, just three characters whom one could even remotely suspect of being of native stock. One is Fuller, a real estate agent, who does not even have a speaking part; another is a little drummer who once meets Alexandra on the street and exclaims, "My God, girl, what a head of hair!" The third is a pale young penitentiary convict named Bertie. In Miss Cather's melting pot there are Swedes, Norwegians, Germans and French but there is no sign that native Americans played any personal part in the lives of these pioneers from the old world. Now, Nebraska lands were first taken up in large part by union soldiers released from the civil war, and by enterprising young men from the eastern states; the foreign immigrants came later. And I can not help thinking that in a community where people of many nationalities were neighboring so naturally, where Swedes were going to French Catholic fairs, and Bohemians were telling Russian fortunes and being buried in Norwegian cemeteries—in such a neighborhood, which can be found only in a new, wonderful, forward moving country, I am sure there were a few friendly American farmers rubbing shoulders with the rest. I wish that Miss Cather had put one or two of these into *O Pioneers*! For the book breathes of Nebraska. It is impossible to take it as an isolated story. And I am jealous of the fact that the native Americans have not a single significant representative.

Review of O *Pioneers!*†

Few American novels of recent years have impressed us so strongly as this. There are two perils by which our fiction on the larger scale

† *Nation*, 97 (September 4, 1913).

is beset—on one hand a self-conscious cultivation of the "literary" quality, and on the other an equally self-conscious avoidance of it. The point may be illustrated by the work of two "late" novelists of native force, Frank Norris and David Graham Phillips. There was no doubt about the Americanism of either of them, so far as their subject-matter was concerned. It was the newer Americanism which has displaced the New Englandism of our nineteenth-century fiction. These men saw American life on a larger scale. Its scope and variety, its promise rather than its accomplishment, absorbed them. The big spaces and big emotions of Western life seemed to them far more interesting and more significant than the smug theory and languid practices of society in the smaller sense of the word. But Norris could not forget the books he had admired, and died before he had outgrown the influence of the French masters of "realism." Phillips, on the other hand, failed to shake off the pose of the plain blunt man, who thinks that the amenities of life are symptoms of weakness and that all Harvard men are snobs.

Now (in writing this story at least) it is the same big primitive fecund America which engages Miss Cather's imagination. She dwells with unforced emotion upon the suffering and the glory of those who have taught a desert to feed the world. The scene is laid in the prairie land of thirty years ago. The settlement to which we are taken is of some years' standing. The rough work has been done, the land cleared and broken up, sod homesteads built, crops planted—and then (the great test of courage and faith in that land) a succession of dry seasons. The weaker have already abandoned their claims, or lost them by mortgage. Only here and there a strong heart, like that of the heroine of the story, refuses to be discouraged, persists in believing that country has a future. Her father, though defeated, has died in this faith, bequeathing it to her; so that when the stupid brothers wish to give up the fight, it is she who insists not only upon holding the land they have, but upon buying every acre they can in the thinning neighborhood. The years justify her, bringing wealth to her and to her beloved country. She prospers beyond her dull and penny-wise elder brothers, who nurse a grudge against her accordingly. Her heart she lavishes upon her younger brother, the baby of the family, and she procures for him the advantages of education which will give him a larger horizon, more flexible interests, than her own. He is a fine lad, manly and responsive, but youth and circumstance prepare a dreadful end for him and for the hapless object of his love. The familiar matter of "rural tragedy" is here. Whether its detail is dwelt upon too ruthlessly is a question which readers will decide according to temperament and individual taste. To us the treatment of the episode seems justified by the mood of tragic emotion which underlies it. As for the bereaved sister, if loneliness has shadowed her youth and tragedy darkened her maturity, there still remains the quiet fulfillment of a long-dreamt-of happiness. The sureness of feeling and touch, the power without strain, which mark this book, lift it far above the ordinary product of contemporary novelists.

A Novel without a Hero†

The hero of the American novel very often starts on the farm, but he seldom stays there; instead, he uses it as a spring-board from which to plunge into the mysteries of politics or finance. Probably the novel reflects a national tendency. To be sure, after we have carefully separated ourselves from the soil, we are apt to talk a lot about the advantages of a return to it, but in most cases it ends there. The average American does not have any deep instinct for the land, or vital consciousness of the dignity and value of the life that may be lived upon it.

O Pioneers! is filled with this instinct and this consciousness. It is a tale of the old wood-and-field-worshipping races, Swedes and Bohemians, transplanted to Nebraskan uplands, of their struggle with the untamed soil, and their final conquest of it. Miss Cather has written a good story, we hasten to assure the reader who cares for good stories, but she has achieved something even finer. Through a direct, human tale of love and struggle and attainment, a tale that is American in the best sense of the word, there runs a thread of symbolism. It is practically a novel without a hero. There are men in it, but the interest centres in two women—not rivals, but friends, and more especially in the splendid blonde farm-woman, Alexandra.

In this new mythology, which is the old, the goddess of fertility once more subdues the barren and stubborn earth. Possibly some might call it a feminist novel, for the two heroines are stronger, cleverer and better balanced than their husbands and brothers—but we are sure Miss Cather had nothing so inartistic in mind. It is a natural growth, feminine because it is only an expansion of the very essence of femininity. Instead of calling *O Pioneers!* a novel without a hero, it might be more accurate to call it a novel with three heroines—Alexandra, the harvest-goddess, Marie, poor little spirit of love and youth snatched untimely from her poppy-fields, and the Earth, itself, patient and bountiful source of all things.

† *New York Times Book Review,* September 14, 1913.

Modern Critical Views

DAVID STOUCK

[Willa Cather and the Epic]†

When Willa Cather put together her novel *O Pioneers!* she was again working with materials taken directly from her own experience, so that if we continue to use the classification of C. S. Lewis the heroic qualities of the book are those of primary epic.[1] The imagination in primary epic expresses itself in the creation of public myths. The artist articulates in his work his society's most fundamental and cherished values, giving voice to the quest and aspirations of a whole people. An epic is nationalistic for it makes its appeal to a whole people by defining a common enemy; consequently, it tends to be simplistic in terms of both the struggle it presents and the moral values it affirms. Primary epics generally appear in the earlier, more creative phases of a culture's development, at a time when the artist can most effectively participate in the growth of his country (or a popular new art form) by giving expression and endorsement to those values which are its source of strength and growth. The urge to be a vital part of the dynamic young American democracy informs all of Whitman's epic poetry.

* * *

The focus in epic rests on the figure of the strong man or woman who defends the people and their values against forces which threaten chaos. Such a figure tends to be one-dimensional because the imagination responds to him largely in terms of his strength as a leader. Consider the larger-than-life but static characterizations of traditional epic heroes such as Odysseus, Beowulf, or Milton's Christ. Sometimes the artist embodies himself in his work in the form of a weaker figure needing the protection and guidance of the

† From *Willa Cather's Imagination* by David Stouck, by permission of the University of Nebraska Press. Copyright © 1975 by the University of Nebraska Press. Copyright © renewed 2003 by the University of Nebraska Press.

1. David Stouck uses C. S. Lewis's definition of a primary epic as one—like *Beowulf*—that "is drawn from the legends and experiences of the artist and his society and is informed by a cyclical vision of human existence" (p. 13) [Editor].

strong leader. This weaker figure may suggest a depth of character and a measure of inner conflict, but the epic hero himself seldom develops or changes. The struggle in which he is engaged serves finally only to heighten our admiration for his strength and moral virtue.

Because its appeal is to people of every class (but particularly the common man), epic is highly rhetorical and conventional in style. The fundamental human emotions expressed in epic are most effectively aroused by heavily rhythmic patterns and by set pieces which call forth a familiar and uncritical response. The concrete physical realism of epic also derives from this demand for the familiar and uncomplicated, while the catalogues and repetitive enumerations (the single image multiplied as in serried ranks of arms and warriors) fulfill a vision of the identity and equality of a united people. We have already seen an example of this aspect of the epic style in "The Bohemian Girl" where Willa Cather describes the great quantities of food prepared for the barn-raising dance and the rows of old pioneer women who had performed such "Herculean" labors during their lifetime. Finally, because epic evokes a simplistic response to life that suppresses all critical distinctions, its tone is humble and eulogistic and its vision (that of the people) is sentimental.

In writing about the settling of the Midwest in *O Pioneers!* Willa Cather chose her subject, as Melville had earlier, from the classical matter for American epic—the struggle of man against nature. As much as from revolution and civil war, America came into being and achieved its identity from the struggle of the common man to subdue the lonely and terrifying wilderness around him. Miss Cather herself apparently referred to the novel as a "two-part pastoral" (Alexandra's story and the romance of "The White Mulberry Tree"),[2] but doubtless she meant simply to indicate the rural subject of her book. For her novel eschews the return to childhood and self-analysis of pastoral writing; her focus is on the struggle of the earliest pioneer settlers of the prairie and on the embodiment of their most heroic gestures in the stalwart figure of Alexandra Bergson. That we respond to Alexandra as an epic heroine there can be little question. She is introduced to us in the first chapter as "a tall, strong girl" who "walked rapidly and resolutely, as if she knew exactly where she was going and what she was going to do next" (p. 6).[3] Her character and her role are defined early in the novel when her dying father turns over the responsibility of the farm and the family to his daughter rather than to his two grown sons. Alexandra

2. See Sergeant, *Willa Cather: A Memoir*, p. 11.
3. All quotations are from the Sentry edition of *O Pioneers!* (Boston: Houghton Mifflin, 1962).

is not only strong in body (at one point she is described as "Amazonian"), but also her father recognizes in her a strength of will and dependability which are wanting in his sons. That initial image of Alexandra taking up the heavy burden of a man's life does not change during the course of the novel; eventually Alexandra becomes the most successful landowner on the Divide, and in effect the leader of the Swedish pioneer community.

Epic focuses on the struggle of a people against a hostile force—here it is the "Genius" of the land, a force unfriendly to man, "like a horse that no one knows how to break to harness, that runs wild and kicks things to pieces" (p. 22). Those with some imagination sense that "the land wanted to be let alone, to preserve its own fierce strength, its peculiar, savage kind of beauty, its uninterrupted mournfulness" (p. 15). But from the beginning Alexandra is resolute in her determination to prevail over the wild country. She promises her father on his death bed that she will never lose the land, and she not only suffers through the harshness of its seasons, but through three long years of drouth and failure. Many families give up and move away, but Alexandra endures and ultimately triumphs, for those years were "the last struggle of a wild soil against the encroaching plowshare" (p. 47). Because Alexandra's vision is to do something big, the landscape and the heroine begin to merge in identification and purpose. Riding across the prairie she reflects on how beautiful, rich, and strong the land seems: "Her eyes drank in the breadth of it, until her tears blinded her. Then the Genius of the Divide, the great, free spirit which breathes across it, must have bent lower than it ever bent to a human will before" (p. 65). Later that same day she resolves to stay on in spite of the drouth and her brothers' wish to move down by the river, realizing that her own destiny is one with that of the land.

While Alexandra as a woman is a particularized character, her struggle to prevail over the landscape and prepare the way for generations to come is representative of the race of early pioneers who settled the American prairie. Our attention is frequently directed in the epic manner to the activities of a whole people. In the prefatory poem, "Prairie Spring," the labors of the pioneers are described in the "miles of fresh-plowed soil," and in "The growing wheat, the growing weeds, / The toiling horses, the tired men." In the first chapter of the novel, despite its particular concerns, we are made aware from the continual reference to people in the background of the typicality of the scene and of the concerns that the people hold in common: "The farm people were making preparations to start for home. The women were checking over their groceries and pinning their big red shawls about their heads. The men were buying tobacco and candy with what money they had left, were showing each other new boots and gloves and blue flannel shirts" (p. 13). When Part II begins we see the fruit of their labors not just in the Bergson farm, but throughout the countryside:

> From the Norwegian graveyard one looks out over a vast checker-board, marked off in squares of wheat and corn; light and dark, dark and light. Telephone wires hum along the white roads, which always run at right angles. From the graveyard gate one can count a dozen gayly painted farmhouses; the gilded weather-vanes on the big red barns wink at each other across the green and brown and yellow fields. The light steel windmills tremble throughout their frames and tug at their moorings. [P. 75]

We are reminded of the movements of a whole people in those conventional set pieces (the French church fair, the grain harvesting, the great confirmation service, the mourning of the people for Amédée Chevalier), which expand the novel's focus to include those joys and sorrows which are communal. A visually striking epic sequence (the single image multipled) describes the cavalcade of forty French boys riding across the plains to meet the bishop; it is charged with the extremes of fundamental human emotions, the ecstatic zeal of high animal spirits tempered by the somber fact of a young friend's death. But always in the foreground remains the figure of Alexandra whose valor and foresight embody the essence of the heroic spirit.

As epic heroine Alexandra's character never changes—her strength of purpose, her dependability and kindness, are constant throughout. We are told that "her mind was slow, truthful, steadfast" (p. 61) and that she was without cleverness, perhaps like the heroic figures of the "Frithjof Saga," an old Swedish legend she has in part committed to memory. She is a woman who feels deeply (she is not without tears in her eyes at moments of crisis), but not one who can show or express her feelings very freely. Moreover, she is always able to control her emotions and proceed with the business of everyday life. When old Ivar finds her alone in the graveyard in the rain she reassures him immediately that everything is all right: " '*Tyst*! Ivar. There's nothing to be worried about. I'm sorry if I've scared you all' " (p. 280). But consequently Alexandra is essentially a flat, one-dimensional character. While she suffers through many disappointments and losses (most agonizing is the death of Emil and Marie), there is never any question as to how she will respond; her character is constant and predictable. It is to Alexandra that everyone else turns with his or her troubles: she protects the old people like Crazy Ivar and Mrs. Lee from the indifference of youth; she advises her family and neighbors in their struggles to tame the wild land; she gives guidance and love to the younger people around her—the Swedish working girls from the old country, Emil and Marie, and her brothers' children. Her strength and compassion are such that she instinctively forgives Frank Shabata, who has destroyed almost everything she has loved. In the courtroom "her heart had grieved for him" (p. 285) and at the novel's close she goes to Lincoln to see what she can do to lighten his punishment.

Alexandra wears a man's coat, but ultimately it is the maternal protection of a strong woman that she offers to those around her; and it is this quality—that of a larger-than-life mother figure—that is at the heart of the imaginative conception of her character. Alexandra is one-dimensional because as epic heroine she is idealized, and accordingly we can feel only a limited sense of identification with her. Her sorrows and her triumphs are those of someone stronger than we are. We hold her strength and virtue in high esteem and yet we cannot really share or emulate them. Rather our imaginative involvement is with that maternal protection she affords those around her.

* * *

In any work of art certain images stand out more than others and remain fixed in our memory—these images have clearly involved the imagination of the artist most deeply. In *O Pioneers!* the image of Alexandra Bergson taking up the heroic task of cultivating the stubborn soil is at the center of our response to the novel—that epic response being reinforced by the Whitman poem of the book's title, with its eulogy to those who have conquered the wild country. Our sense of Alexandra's heroic stature is greatly enhanced by a number of visual images, like Carl's memory of her at dawn, in which her figure is adorned with light and radiates calm strength. When her father is dying and makes her his chief heir, she comes to him, a tall figure with the light of a lamp behind her. When she is working on the farm, the braids of reddish-gold hair about her head burn in the sunlight (the image suggests a gleaming Germanic helmet) and the fiery ends of hair make her head look like a big sunflower. In the sunlight of Marie's garden she is described as "the Swedish woman so white and gold, kindly and amused, but armored in calm" (p. 135).

But almost equally as engaging as Alexandra is the image of the garden, the enclosed, safe place, which is most fully dramatized in Marie Shabata's orchard with its protective mulberry hedge. The expansion of the novel by developing the love story (Miss Cather clearly felt Alexandra's story was not dramatic enough) may seem a gratuitous and unconvincing digression from the central theme of Alexandra and the land. And yet the image of the garden is as integral a part of the novel's imaginative structure as the figure of its stalwart heroine because it is that desire for an enclosed retreat, with its guarantee of maternal protection, which draws the imagination in this novel to its epic heroine. Significantly, Miss Cather dedicated *O Pioneers!* to the memory of Sarah Orne Jewett, a writer whose work was similarly motivated by a search for a green, protected place—realized fictionally in *The Country of the Pointed Firs,* with its half-forgotten village of Dunnet Landing presided over by the maternal, sybillike figure of the herb-gatherer, Mrs. Todd. Much of our instinctive pleasure in reading *O Pioneers!* must derive from our sharing in that wish to find a sheltered place, a refuge carved out of a hostile terrain. Mrs. Bergson's house and garden in which she tries to retain the order and routine of her life in the old country is an image of such a refuge maintained against formidable odds. Her garden survives the long drouth because of the water she carries to the plants despite the prohibition of her sons. Part III of the novel, "Winter Memories," is conceived of almost entirely as a kind of refuge—as an image of physical refuge against the cold of winter, and as an emotional refuge for those women whose men are far away. In one sequence Alexandra takes old Mrs. Lee for an afternoon's visit with Marie Shabata; the fuchsias and geraniums in bloom on the window sill, the coffee and sweet cakes, the exchange of crochet patterns are all redolent of the cozy domesticity of women together. Although Emil is in Mexico and Carl in the Far North, the scene is imaginatively complete, as the refuge desired is a maternal and innocent one.

The story of the lovers is at first wholly romantic and idealized. The idyllic description of the orchard after the rain (with its ripe cherries, its fragrant wild roses, the waving fields of ripening grain outside the hedge) and the description of the young lovers themselves (Emil with his scythe and Marie with the sparkling light in her playful brown eyes) are suggestive of the conventions of medieval art—like scenes from a "book of hours" or the sad, poignant "lais" of Marie de France. But their love is illicit and when Marie's garden becomes a place of erotic fulfillment it is destroyed because the epic vision which prevails, with its apotheosis in the "mother country," is maternal and innocent. The marriage between Carl and Alexandra will fulfill an old friendship rather than sexual passion; that way Alexandra feels they will be "safe."

Earlier in the novel when Carl comes back to the Divide and views what Alexandra and his old neighbors have made out of the land, he says: " 'Isn't it queer: there are only two or three human stories, and they go on repeating themselves as fiercely as if they had never happened before' " (p. 119). The two stories woven together in *O Pioneers!* stretch back to Genesis. Alexandra's is the story of creation, the story of a human civilization being shaped out of a land as flat and formless as the sea. Emil and Marie's is the story of lovers cast from the earth's garden through sin. The timeless, ever-recurring nature of these stories is secured by literary allusion. Alexandra's heroic character and actions are enriched by her connection with the old Swedish legends. Emil and Marie's story acquires a universal pathos by its association with classical tales of lovers who die. When old Ivar comes to the despoiled orchard at dawn he sees two white butterflies fluttering over the dead bodies, like metamorphosed lovers in Ovid's tales. The staining of the white mulberries with the lover's blood recalls specifically the story of Pyramus and Thisbe. While their romance is still innocent Marie tells Emil of her love for the trees in her orchard and of the old Bohemian belief in the power of the linden's virtue to purify the forest. The innocent, domestic love of Baucis and Philemon is perhaps remembered here, for those faithful lovers, wishing to die together, were changed into trees, an oak and a linden. And there is a suggestion of the Endymion story when Marie resolves in the moonlight that to dream of her love will henceforward be enough.[4] The two stories of the novel are brought together in a nexus of creation and destruction as Ivar repeats to himself Psalm 101 from the Bible, a song of "mercy and judgment" in which the psalmist promises to remember the faithful of the land and to destroy all wicked doers.

In terms of the novel's epic theme—and it is the epic note which prevails at the end—the death of the lovers is necessary to give Alexandra's story a tragic depth and to allow her old antagonist, nature, to reassert its power. Marie's garden represents that order of life that Alexandra has worked so arduously to create out of the uncultivated landscape. Alexandra thinks of her struggle on the Divide as ensuring a better life for her brother, her "boy"; she loves both Emil and Marie, and without looking ahead to the possible consequences she encourages their friendship, much as if they were still young children. Their death gives Alexandra's life a tragic quality because they represent essentially everything for which she has lived and fought. At the novel's close she consents to marry Carl and yet it is the land which still has possession of her. Carl agrees that they must come back to the Divide after they are married: " 'You belong to the land,' Carl murmured, 'as you have always said. Now more than ever' " (p. 307). Alexandra, looking out over the great plains under an autumn sunset, concedes that in their struggle with the land there has been only a truce, that it is she who will ultimately be the one possessed: " 'We come and go, but the land is

4. Since Willa Cather was a classicist at university, it is not unlikely that other Ovidian stories of lovers came to her mind as well as that of Pyramus and Thisbe.

always here. And the people who love it and understand it are the people who own it—for a little while' " (p. 308). However, there is a sober triumph in the novel's conclusion, for here the epic view of nature as universal foe gives way to a cyclical and reassuring vision of mutability, and here the author can express once more those feelings of love and admiration for her heroine and for her people:

> They went into the house together, leaving the Divide behind them, under the evening star. Fortunate country, that is one day to receive hearts like Alexandra's into its bosom, to give them out again in the yellow wheat, in the rustling corn, in the shining eyes of youth! [P. 309]

JOHN J. MURPHY

[Biblical and Literary Contexts in O *Pioneers!*]†

The Genesis Dimension

O Pioneers! opens on a January day in 1883 with a description of the embryonic settlement of Hanover, Nebraska, trying not to be blown away in the wind. The sea of prairie and sky are gray and dwarf the place, and snowflakes curl and eddy about haphazardly scattered dwellings "straying off by themselves, headed straight for the open plain."[1] The suggestion of chaos as described in Genesis is obvious: "the earth was without form and void, with darkness over the face of the abyss, and a mighty wind that swept over the surface of the waters."[2] This atmosphere established, Cather introduces her principals. Five-year-old Emil cries for his kitten and is given sweets by seven-year-old Marie, who has "tiger-eye" streaks in her eyes. Fifteen-year-old Carl Linstrum comes to the aid of Alexandra, four years his senior, already matronly and capable of Amazonian fierceness. While Marie flirts with Emil and her uncle's cronies, Alexandra and Carl share their loneliness and sustain each other. The relationships Cather will develop she thus defines within the context of the creation theme. The first chapter concludes with Alexandra, burdened with the sad knowledge that her father will

† From John J. Murphy, "A Comprehensive View of Cather's O *Pioneers!*" in John J. Murphy, ed., *Critical Essays on Willa Cather* (Boston: G. K. Hall, 1984), pp. 113–27.

1. Willa Cather, O *Pioneers*!, Sentry Edition (Boston: Houghton Mifflin, 1962), p. 3; hereafter cited in the text.
2. Genesis 1:1–2, subsequent references are to *The New English Bible with the Apocrypha: Oxford Study Edition*, ed. Samuel Sandmel, M. Jack Suggs, and Arnold J. Tkacik (New York: Oxford Univ. Press, 1976).

soon die, rattling through the swirling darkness in a wagon with a lamp at her feet, making "a moving point of light along the highway, going deeper and deeper into the dark country" (18). She will be the creative force, bringing order to chaos. "God said, 'Let their be light,' and there was light; and God saw that the light was good, and he separated light from darkness" (Genesis 1:3–4).

In a low log homestead on a wintry waste without human landmarks patriarch John Bergson lies on his deathbed contemplating the futility of his efforts to make a country out of the wild land. So far, "[t]he record of the plow was insignificant, like the feeble scratches on stone left by prehistoric races, so indeterminate that they may, after all, be only the markings of glaciers. . . . [The land] was still a wild thing that had its ugly moods. . . . Its genius was unfriendly to man" (19–20). Yet Bergson believes in the land's potential and recognizes Alexandra as the "one among his children to whom he could entrust the future of his family and the possibilities of his hard-won land" (24). He sees her outlined in the light of a lamp behind her and has her pledge to keep her brothers on the land—a pledge that will determine and limit her life. Unlike Isaac, who was tricked by his wife, Bergson deliberately entrusts the heritage to the unexpected one, his daughter rather than his eldest son, Oscar. In light too dim for him to see their faces, he tells Oscar and his younger brother Lou to be guided by their sister. They will bear a grudge against her like Esau bore against Jacob "because of the blessing which his father had given him. . . ." (Genesis 27:41).

Six months after Bergson's death, Alexandra, her brothers, and Carl make their way to Crazy Ivar's to buy a hammock and get advice on hog raising. As they enter rough and less populated country, "all broken up with hillocks and clay ridges" (35), they discuss Ivar's fits and communings with the Lord, and his gifts for doctoring animals. A powerful dwarflike man with a face shining with happiness as he contemplates Psalm 104 (a creation hymn), Ivar resembles Noah. Gentle and protective toward all God's creatures, he is especially solicitous about the shooting of birds and warns the boys that "these wild things are God's birds. He watches over them and counts them . . ." (41). As Alexandra approaches Ivar's cave, its single window and door visible at the end of a broad, flooded pond suggest the ark; indeed, in describing a visit from a sea gull, Ivar explains, "Maybe she thought my house was a boat, she was such a wild thing" (40). God gave Noah charge over "all wild animals on earth" and "all birds of heaven" after the flood, and in establishing the covenant with Noah and "living things of every kind" discouraged the eating of meat (Genesis 9:1–17).[3] Ivar "never ate meat,

3. Ibid., notes to Genesis 9:1–17, pp. 8–9.

fresh or salt" (43). As an otherworldly man in communion with universal rhythms, Ivar will be used to contrast with the family bickering of the ensuing domestic drama and recall the cosmic atmosphere of the novel's opening.

Three years go by; harder times come to the Divide, and people are selling out, including the Linstrums. When Carl brings Alexandra the news that he will no longer be around to comfort her, she is standing in a dry garden patch, "[h]er thick, reddish braids, twisted about her head, fairly [burning] in the sunlight" (49). Still the creative force, she is distinguished from her neighbors and her brothers by her tenacity in staying: "Like most of their neighbors, [the Bergson boys] were meant to follow in paths already marked out for them, not to break trails in a new country. . . . A pioneer should have imagination, should be able to enjoy the idea of things more than the things themselves" (47–48). Alexandra possesses this pioneer imagination, and after convincing her brothers not to leave with the others, she experiences what Edward and Lillian Bloom term "mystic insight into divine causes,"[4] enabling her to persuade her brothers to invest in more land and fulfill their father's dreams. Her face is radiant and turned toward that land "with love and yearning"—perhaps the first human face to so respond "since that land emerged from the waters of geologic ages. . . . It seemed beautiful to her, rich and strong and glorious. Her eyes drank in the breadth of it, until her tears blinded her" (65). The Genius of the Divide, previously "unfriendly to man" (20), now "bent lower than it ever bent to a human will before." The creative order Alexandra represents is now obvious in the comfort she takes in the stars, in "their vastness and distance, and . . . ordered march" (70).

In part 2, "Neighboring Fields," set thirteen years later, order has indeed come to the wild land—creation is complete and the earth fruitful. The drab land and sky have been replaced by a colorful checker-board of wheat and corn that "seems to rise a little to meet the sun" (76). The chaos evident in the opening section has developed into the geometrical precision of Midwestern roadways, complete with corresponding telephone wires. The wind has been harnessed to serve the new order: "light steel windmills tremble throughout their frames and tug at their moorings, as they vibrate in the wind that often blows from one week's end to another. . . ." The earth itself responds to the plow "with a soft, deep sigh of happiness" (75–76). "Then God said, 'Let the earth produce fresh growth, let there be on the earth plants bearing seed, fruit-trees bearing fruit each with seed according to its kind.' So it was; the

4. Edward A. and Lillian D. Bloom, *Willa Cather's Gift of Sympathy* (Carbondale: Southern Illinois Univ. Press, Arcturus Books, 1964), p. 18.

earth yielded fresh growth, plants bearing seed according to their kind and trees bearing fruit each with seed according to its kind; and God saw that it was good" (Genesis 1:11–12).

Carl returns in this section to focus on Alexandra's character and accomplishments, and it is through him that Cather manages the transition from the story of creation to that of the fall. Rising one morning before dawn, he climbs the hill where he and Alexandra used to milk together and recalls his favorite image of her—one he renews each time he sees the sunrise with "her skirts pinned up, her head bare, a bright pail in either hand and the milky light of the early morning all about her . . . she looked as if she had walked straight out of the morning itself" (126). Like the generating light God made to govern the day, the sympathy evident in Alexandra's radiant face has made the wild land prolific, and the field Carl sits in is teeming with life: "Birds and insects without number begin to chirp, to twitter, to snap and whistle, to make all manner of shrill noises. The pasture was flooded with light . . ." (126–27). Carl then walks toward a pasture pond and sees Marie and Emil, who is breaking Crazy Ivar's law by shooting ducks. The bloody birds, "too happy to kill" (128), prefigure the violent deaths of the lovers. In this way Cather directs us toward the love story which will dominate part 4, "The White Mulberry Tree." The Genesis implications of this story are simple and obvious—the lovers sin beneath a tree in an orchard and are then killed by Marie's jealous husband. Earlier, when Emil came to cut grass in the orchard, Marie joined him there and then left his side to pick cherries, saying "I'll call you if I see a snake" (151). The destruction of Alexandra's Eden is announced by Ivar after he discovers the bodies: "Mistress, mistress, . . . it has fallen! Sin and death for the young ones! God have mercy upon us!" (271).

* * *

The Whitman Dimension

The fireflies, wheatfields, mulberries, wild roses, and lush grass surrounding Marie and Emil's lovemaking also suggest inevitablity and naturalism. The dark stains on the orchard grass and the attitudes of the bodies in death tell "only half the story. Above Marie and Emil, two white butterflies from Frank's alfalfa field were fluttering in and out among the interlacing shadows, diving and soaring, now close together, now far apart, and in the long grass by the fence the last wild roses of the year opened their pink hearts to die" (270). This other half of the story is one of instinct and necessity. Marie's prayers and religion are powerless before the attraction she and Emil feel for each other. Although Ivar cries sin as he brings

Alexandra the news that shatters her world, the lovers are finally absolved by Carl, who compares their relationship to "something one felt in the air, as you feel the spring coming, or a storm in summer" (305). Attempting to soften Alexandra's bitterness toward Marie, he explains that she and Emil tried hard to control their feelings but that some women "spread ruin around them through no fault of theirs, just by being too beautiful, too full of life and love. They can't help it. People come to them as people go to a warm fire in winter" (304). Cather's passionate romance thus dramatizes the natural law, while the story of Alexandra framing it celebrates the law of restraint. The same kind of sympathetic dualism is evident throughout *The Scarlet Letter*. When his lovers decide to flee and the sun floods the forest, Hawthorne comments on the two laws: "Such was the sympathy of Nature—that wild, heathen Nature of the forest, never subjugated by human law, nor illumined by higher truth—with the bliss of these two spirits!"[5]

The cosmic vision advanced by the tragic circumstances in *O Pioneers!* and ultimately by Carl is unquestionably informed by the poetry of Walt Whitman. Not only did Cather take her title from Whitman's "Pioneers! O Pioneers!," but her prose approximates his free verse in lyric passages devoted to what he describes in paragraph 3 in "Song of Myself" as "The procreant urge of the world. / Out of the dimness opposite equals advance, always substance and increase, always sex. . . ."[6] At the beginning of "Neighboring Fields," for example, air and earth "are curiously mated and intermingled, as if the one were the breath of the other" (77); also, the responsive earth "yields itself eagerly to the plow; rolls away from the shear, not even dimming the brightness of the metal, with a soft, deep sigh of happiness" (76). This creative urge explains Alexandra's sensation of germinating soil, her fantasy of being carried across the fields by a gigantic earth figure, and her spiritual communion with the Genius of the Divide. The "love and yearning" she feels for the "free spirit which breathes across" the land (65) resembles the intercourse between poet and soul in Whitman's paragraph 5, which concludes with the insight that creation is one, "that the spirit of God is the brother of my own," and relates the universal spirit to the common grass "sprouting alike in broad zones and narrow zones . . . " (91–109).

Alexandra's consciousness of social ostracism and death as well as illicit passion is managed through other people, as in Whitman's

5. Nathaniel Hawthorne, *The Scarlet Letter: A Norton Critical Edition*, 2nd ed., ed. Sculley Bradley et al. (New York: W. W. Norton, 1978), pp. 145–56.
6. Walt Whitman, "Song of Myself" (II. 45–46), in *Leaves of Grass: A Norton Critical Edition*, ed. Sculley Bradley and Harold W. Blodgett (New York: W. W. Norton, 1973); hereafter cited in the text.

poem, where the persona first observes and then becomes those involved in a full range of life experiences. During her visit to the graveyard a few months after Emil's death Alexandra feels carried back into the dark before birth: "Maybe it's like that with the dead," she tells Ivar. "If they feel anything at all, it's the old things, before they were born . . . " (281). Her realization that death is not painful or frightening results from Whitmanlike introjection, as in "The Sleepers," where the persona identifies with the dead state: "A shroud I see and I am the shroud, I wrap a body and lie in the coffin, / It is dark here under ground, it is not evil or pain here, it is blank here, for reasons" (66–67). Alexandra's conjoining of birth and death is a major insight in paragraph 49 in "Song of Myself," although reversed:

> To his work without flinching the accoucheur comes,
> I see the elder-hand pressing receiving supporting,
> I recline by the sills of the exquisite flexible doors,
> And mark the outlet, and mark the relief and escape. (1289–93)

The earth lover of Alexandra's fantasy is revealed after the graveyard episode. As he stands in the doorway of her room with his head covered she recognizes him as Death, "the mightiest of all lovers" (283). Such conjoining of love and death is a favorite Whitman theme, basic to "Song of Myself" and the particular subject of "Out of the Cradle Endlessly Rocking," where the poet fuses the love song of the grieving bird with the "strong and delicious word" death whispered by the sea (174–83).

Having identified Death, Alexandra decides to visit Frank Shabata in the State Penitentiary in Lincoln, where she experiences his revulsion at his deed, his confusion between the wife he loved and the woman who wronged him, and the guilt he feels for neglecting Marie. Alexandra is able to identify, with this changed, not altogether human prisoner, and share his lack of future and feeling of imprisonment: "A disgust of life weighed upon her heart . . . " (298). In spite of her despair, however, she will petition for the release of this man who killed her brother. As when she protects Ivar from those who would have committed him, she uplifts and speaks for the downtrodden, the ostracized, as the poet in paragraph 24 of "Song of Myself": "Through me many long dumb voices, / . . . of prisoners and slaves, / . . . of thieves and dwarfs . . . " (508–10).

Carl returns to Nebraska to rescue Alexandra from her dark night of the soul and help her toward the cosmic vision for which her experiences have prepared her. After changing from mourning clothes to a white dress, she walks the sunny fields with him and discusses the inevitability of passion and the future. She reveals that on the train from Lincoln she felt again the spirit of the land, its comfort and freedom. She realizes now that the land has a wider future than the Bergson family, that her efforts were not confined to Emil: "We come and go, but the land is always here. And those who love it and understand it are the people who own it—for a little while" (308). Cather's final words, that the land will receive hearts like Alexandra's to give them out again in various forms of life, echo the conclusion of Whitman's great poem: "I bequeath myself to the dirt to grow from the grass I love, / If you want me again look for me under your boot-soles" (1339–40).

Alexandra Bergson, then, unifies *O Pioneers!* Hers is the creative force bringing wild land to productive order. Aside from pampering Emil, she remains uncorrupted by the materialism of success evident in Lou and Oscar. Her blindness toward her own accomplishments and toward relationships beyond friendship between men and women is challenged by the tragic affair which deprives her of Emil and exposes Marie's destructive passion. Finally, passing through a dark night of the soul and sharing Frank's horror, she is led by Carl to a new, universal vision of the land and its people.

SHARON O'BRIEN

[Gender and Creativity in *O Pioneers!*]†

In the 1890s Willa Cather had only one solution for the woman writer who wished to revise the "one string" of women's fiction: write men's fiction, using male plots and genres (*KA*, p. 449). But in *O Pioneers!* Cather does not conceive the pioneer adventure as a "manly battle yarn." A conqueror who wins by yielding, Cather's female Alexander tames the land not through force but through "love and yearning" (p. 65). Nor is Alexandra a male-identified woman, one of Cather's romantic heroes in female garb. Although Alexandra possesses the seemingly contradictory traits American society divides between men and women—strength and pragmatism as well as intuition and compassion—she is not a male in disguise. Cather represents her heroine's inner complexity by the outer signs of dress and physical appearance—signs which teach us how to read the novel as a whole.

In the first few pages we see Alexandra wearing a "round plush cap, tied down with a thick veil" and a "man's long ulster," which

† From Sharon O'Brien, *Willa Cather: The Emerging Voice* (New York: Oxford UP, 1987), pp. 429–51. Reprinted by permission of the publisher.

she carries comfortably, like a "young soldier." Yet if we now assume that she is mannish, Cather suddenly confuses us when this "young soldier" takes off her veil to reveal a sign of female beauty, a "shining mass of hair . . . two thick braids, pinned about her head in the German way, with a fringe of reddish-yellow curls" (pp. 6–8). Later Cather grants the mature woman a physical presence that is not conventionally feminine but is still female. "Sunnier" and "more vigorous" than she had been as a girl, Alexandra still has the same unruly, "fiery" hair that makes her resemble "one of the big double sunflowers" in her garden. Her face is "always tanned" in summer, because she neglects to wear her sunbonnet, but where "her collar falls away from her neck" or where "her sleeves are pushed back from her wrist," her skin has the "smoothness and whiteness as none but Swedish women ever possess; skin with the freshness of the snow itself" (pp. 87–88).

As these oppositions—tanned/white, sun/snow—suggest, Alexandra cannot be easily categorized. . . . Both descriptions of Alexandra begin with images that might be considered masculine by conventional viewers (the man's coat, the military bearing, the "calmness and deliberation of manner"), but end with unveilings of female beauty—the beautiful hair hidden under the veil, the smooth, white skin exposed when the collar or the sleeves are pushed back. So this is a woman, Cather tells us, who cannot be understood if we apply our polarized categories of gender. On the surface she may seem unfeminine, but if we wait to see what is unveiled we discover our mistake. This progression reflects the narative structure of the novel as a whole: at first we see Alexandra solely as a strong, heroic, and unemotional figure; later we learn of her need for human attachment when she despairs of life after her brother's death.

In reading the novel we also have to wait to see that the story Cather is telling is unconventional. At first we appear to be in the same wasteland of deprivation that mirrored Aunt Georgianna's defeats and assume we are about to encounter another failed woman artist. Settling the Nebraska Divide in the 1880s, the novel's Swedish and Bohemian farmers face an inhospitable landscape:

> A mist of fine snowflakes was curling and eddying about the cluster of low drab buildings huddled on the gray prairie, under a gray sky. The dwelling-houses were set about haphazard on the tough prairie sod; some of them looked as if they had been moved in overnight, and others as if they were straying off by themselves, headed straight for the open plain. None of them had any appearance of permanence, and the howling wind blew under them as well as over them. . . . The great fact was the land itself, which seemed to overwhelm the little be-

> ginnings of human society that struggled in its sombre wastes. (pp. 3, 15)

This "stern frozen country" is neither the bountiful mother nor the yielding virgin dear to the American imagination, but a genderless "fact" unresponsive to human desire or will. Recalling the harsh plains of her early stories as well as the grim land "as bare as a piece of sheet iron" Cather confronted as a young girl in 1883, this "disheartening" landscape without "human landmarks" is a world where human beings have not yet been able to write their story:

> The roads were but faint tracks in the grass, and the fields were scarcely noticeable. The record of the plow was insignificant, like the feeble scratches in stone left by prehistoric races, so indeterminate that they may, after all, be only the markings of glaciers, and not a record of human strivings. (p. 20)

The unwritten land is an "enigma" to men like Alexandra's father who can only interpret its resistance to cultivation as hostility: "Its Genius was unfriendly to man" (pp. 22, 20). After eleven years of homesteading, John Bergson has "made but little impression upon the wild land he had come to tame" (p. 20). Depressed and sick, defeated by years of crop failures, blizzards, and mischance, Bergson is dying. Meanwhile many of his neighbors have given up the fight and are moving to the city. Bergson does sense, however, that the land is not infertile; instead, he concludes, "no one understood how to farm it properly" (p. 22). Knowing that his daughter Alexandra understands more about farming than his unimaginative sons Lou and Oscar, Bergson leaves the land to her, and she pledges that she will never give it up.

Although the unmarked land can be disheartening to settlers who leave only "indeterminate" scratches in the soil, it can also be inspiring to a farmer who wants not to follow others' patterns but to create her own. "A pioneer should have imagination," Cather observes, "should be able to enjoy the idea of things more than the things themselves" (p. 48). Alexandra is such a pioneer. Gifted with imagination, able to see possibilities in the soil that no one else has glimpsed, she triumphs because she combines a mystic faith in the Divide with a pragmatic willingness to experiment with new farming techniques. After she inherits her father's land, she spends several days among the more fertile river farms, talking "to the men about their crops and to the women about their poultry," conferring with a young farmer who was experimenting with "a new kind of clover hay. She learned a great deal" (p. 64). Returning to the high plains of the Divide, she tells her brothers that they must buy the land others are deserting and mortgage their farm to expand their holdings. Although Alexandra has carefully thought over the financial complexities of this venture, ultimately she can only answer her brothers' question—How does she know that land will increase in crops and value?—with what Cather termed the "wisdom of intuition": "I *know*, that's all. When you drive about over the country you can feel it coming" (p. 67).

Cather ends "The Wild Land" with Alexandra's commitment to the future and opens "Neighboring Fields" after a sixteen-year gap with this description of the inscribed land:

> From the Norwegian graveyard one looks out over a vast checker-board, marked off in squares of wheat and corn; light and dark, dark and light . . . . From the graveyard gate one can count a dozen gayly painted farmhouses; the gilded weather-vanes on the big red barns wink at each other across the green and brown and yellow fields. . . . The Divide is now thickly populated. The rich soil yields heavy harvests; the dry, bracing climate and the smoothness of the land make labor easy for men and beasts. There are few scenes more gratifying than a spring plowing in that country, where . . . the brown earth, with such a strong, clean smell, and such a power of growth and fertility in it, yields itself eagerly to the plow. (pp. 75–76)

Cather then moves from these signs of human presence to the author of this profound transformation. The narrator is also our guide to Alexandra's farm, taking us through unfamiliar country and telling us that a "stranger"—or an Eastern reader, perhaps someone like us—could not help "noticing the beauty and fruitfulness of the outlying fields." As we got closer in this cinematic focusing, we learn that there is something "individual" about Alexandra's farm, something distinguishing; "a most unusual trimness and care for detail." Then we are allowed to see some of the details—osage orange hedges, their "glossy green" marking off a yellow field; a "low sheltered swale"; an orchard, its "fruit trees knee-deep in timothy grass." After this sumptuous introduction we can only agree with the narrator: "Any one thereabouts would have told you that this was one of the richest farms on the Divide, and that the farmer was a woman, Alexandra Bergson" (p. 83).

After passing through this Edenic landscape the narrator allows us to enter Alexandra's "big house," but immediately wants us to leave; the house is "curiously unfinished and uneven in comfort," some rooms overfurnished and others not. This woman farmer is not, we learn, a conventional woman whose home is her sphere. And so, with a sense of relief, the narrator guides us back outside:

> When you go out of the house into the flower garden, there you feel again the order and fine arrangement manifest all over

> the great farm; in the fencing and hedging, in the windbreaks and sheds, in the symmetrical pasture ponds, planted with scrub willows to give shade to the cattle in fly-time. There is even a white row of beehives in the orchard, under the walnut trees. You feel that, properly, Alexandra's house is the big out-of-doors, and that it is in the soil that she expresses herself best. (pp. 83–94)

* * *

As Gilbert and Gubar observe, most Western literary genres "are, after all essentially male—devised by male authors to tell male stories about the world."[1] In telling their stories about American culture and the American self, male American writers have drawn most heavily on the themes and conventions of the pastoral and the epic. Both have seemed most adaptable to narrating what we think of as the American experience: the creation of a new culture in a new world and the formation of an Adamic self, cleansed of European imperfections and reborn in the land of spiritual and economic opportunity.[2] The hero of the new American story, as R. W. B. Lewis describes him in his classic study *The American Adam*, is

> an individual emancipated from history, happily bereft of ancestry, untouched and undefiled by the usual inheritances of family and race; an individual standing alone, self-reliant and self-propelling, ready to confront whatever awaited him with the aid of his own unique and inherent resources.

Given the religious background most nineteenth-century Americans shared, it is not surprising, notes Lewis, that the new hero became identified with "Adam before the Fall," who was both the "first, the archetypal man" and the poet invested with Adam's power of naming. Although, as Lewis observes, this new hero was supposed to embody a "new set of ideal *human* attributes" (emphasis mine), feminist critics have pointed out that this representative American self is male.[3]

1. Sandra M. Gilbert and Susan Gubar, *The Madwoman in the Attic: The Woman Writer and the Nineteenth-Century Literary Imagination* (New Haven: Yale University Press, 1979), p. 67.
2. Although both genres seem to reflect and shape American experience, the pastoral has been a more enduring part of the American literary imagination. As Leo Marx observes, the "pastoral ideal has been used to define the meaning of America since the age of discovery" because the genre's story of withdrawal from a corrupt civilization to a virginal landscape seemed attainable on the new continent (*The Machine in the Garden: Technology and the Pastoral Ideal in America* [New York: Oxford University Press, 1964; rpt., 1969], p. 3).
3. R. W. B. Lewis, *The American Adam: Innocence, Tragedy and Tradition in the Nineteenth Century* (Chicago: University of Chicago Press, 1955), p. 5. The ways in which the Adamic myth both stereotypes and excludes women have been explored by Annette Kolodny in *The Lay of the Land: Metaphor as Experience and History in American Life and Letters* (Chapel Hill: University of North Carolina Press, 1975), and by Nina Baym in "Melodramas of Beset Manhood: How Theories of American Fiction Exclude Women Writers," *American Quarterly* 33, no. 2 (Summer 1981): 123–39.

In her articulation of the myth of America, Nina Baym argues that the "essential quality of America comes to reside in its unsettled wilderness" rather than in society and in "the opportunities that such a wilderness offers to the individual as the medium on which he may inscribe, unhindered, his own destiny and his own nature." As Baym observes, although there is no reason why a woman could not identify with this mythic protagonist, the fact that the other participants in his story—the "entrammeling society and the promising landscape"—are imagined as female makes it difficult for a woman to insert herself into this engendered narrative and to accept its "misogynist implications."[4]

In *O Pioneers!*, however, Cather both uses and transforms this central myth, suggesting that the "essential quality of America" resides not in the unsettled land but in the transformation from "The Wild Land" to "Neighboring Fields," the process of inhabitation that made writers like Cooper and Twain uneasy but that provided, in her view, a more accurate representation of the immigrants' desires and accomplishments. In doing so, she removes the misogyny from the Adamic myth as well as the valorization of the isolated, self-reliant individual; by inscribing herself in the land, Alexandra writes her community's story as well as her own.

Cather was able to challenge the implications of the American pastoral, in which the masculine self flourishes separate from society, by drawing on the epic, in which the hero's triumph is also that of his culture.[5] Wishing to portray Alexandra as a gardener on an epic scale, Cather begins both "The Wild Land" and "Neighboring Fields" with a description of the land and the community before she focuses on her protagonist, placing her in a larger cultural context. Throughout the novel Cather surrounds her heroine with communal events—the farmers buying supplies in town, the forty French boys riding to meet the Bishop, the church fair—that integrate her story with that of her society. Cather's decision to make Alexandra a representative figure is evident in the title change: "Alexandra" became *O Pioneers!* In borrowing her novel's title from Whitman, Cather both connected Alexandra's story to the pioneer

4. Baym, pp. 132–33. As Baym observes, women can rewrite the male-centered American myth in many ways, and she suggests that Cather does so in *O Pioneers!* by casting the land as male, thus reversing the traditional gender roles. But although Alexandra's dream-figure is male, the land is described as feminine and maternal—and hence Cather is rewriting the traditional story in a more complicated way, suggesting that the land—like her heroine—cannot be easily categorized by applying socially derived notions of gender. (Baym, p. 136.)
5. Paul A. Olson explores Cather's use of epic conventions to describe the settling of the Midwest in "The Epic and the Great Plains Literature: Rolvaag, Cather, and Neihardt," *Prairie Schooner* 55 (Spring/Summer 1981): 263–85. As he observes, Cather draws primarily on the *Aeneid.* Olson argues, however, that *My Ántonia* depends most heavily on Virgil's story of the founding of a civilization; in my view *O Pioneers!* is Cather's attempt to write a pastoral epic, *My Ántonia* her attempt to write a myth.

experience and declared that her novel was not an isolated text but part of a shared endeavor by American writers to understand American history and culture.

* * *

Alexandra's role as artist is evident in her visionary imagination, her combination of creative ability and technical skill, her discovery of self-expression in the soil, and in the emergence of the fertile, ordered landscape. Cather, however, wanted to be sure that her readers would not overlook the alliance of the pioneer and the artist, so she has Carl announce it directly. Returning from his sixteen-year absence and seeing the wilderness transformed into settled land, he acknowledges that his is the imitative and Alexandra's the creative sensibility: "I've been away engraving other men's pictures, and you've stayed at home and made your own" (p. 116). Carl's imagination is inspired by others' texts: as a boy he dreams over the illustrated paper, studies patterns for china-painting in the drug store, and collects slides for his magic lantern, preparing for his adult career as the engraver who copies others' designs.[6] Meanwhile Alexandra sees pictures no one has ever viewed before in the land.

In responding with passion and imagination to the Divide—which is her muse, her medium, her subject—Alexandra experiences the creative process in the way Cather later described the composition of *O Pioneers!*: as a yielding to inspiration, as an intermingling of self and other. Erasing subject-object dichotomies and hierarchies, Cather once again rejects the "manly" vision of creativity as a struggle to dominate nature; simultaneously in her "two-part pastoral" she criticizes the power relationship between a male protagonist and a feminine landscape that informs the traditional American pastoral, in which nature is an object—either the virgin land to be raped or the bountiful mother to be sought—against which the male self is defined.[7] In Cather's vision, both the female hero and the maternal land are subjects, and Alexandra defines herself in relation to—instead of against—the natural world. Challenging the traditional culture-nature dichotomy in which men are aligned with culture, women with nature, Cather portrays Alexandra both as connected to nature and as separate from it, a subject with will, imagination, and desire who shapes the land as she is shaped by it.[8] Hence it is she, rather than her father, who succeeds.

6. Early in the novel Carl tells Alexandra that he wants to "paint some slides" for his magic lantern "out of the Hans Andersen book" (p. 17).
7. See Kolodny, pp. 3–9.
8. Sherry Ortner, "Is Female to Male as Nature Is to Culture?" in *Women, Culture and Society,* ed. Michelle Zimbalist Rosaldo and Louise Lamphere (Stanford: Stanford University Press, 1974), pp. 67–87.

* * *

Like other American Adams, John Bergson wants to make his mark on the soil by imposing his will upon it; he views the wild land as something he "had come to tame," as a horse not yet broken to harness (p. 20). Feeling no connection or similarity between himself and his environment, Bergson projects his own thwarted aggression onto the land, viewing it as "unfriendly to man" just as Ahab construes Moby Dick as evil (p. 20). His sons Lou and Oscar, concerned with their own power, wealth, and status, regard the land only as a source of profit. Like the mean-spirited farmers Thoreau attacks in "The Bean-Field" chapter of *Walden*, they do not recognize that "husbandry was once a sacred art" and define the soil "as property, or the means of acquiring property."[9] The violence submerged in John Bergson's struggle to dominate nature emerges in his sons: Lou and Oscar enjoy hunting wild birds and are disgruntled when they cannot bring their guns with them to Crazy Ivar's house.

With Frank Shabata and Emil Bergson Cather draws a clear relationship between man's violence to nature and to women. Emil foreshadows the lovers' deaths when he shoots the wild ducks, laughing "delightedly" as he transforms vivid wildlife into a "rumpled ball of feathers with the blood dripping slowly from its mouth" (pp. 127–28). Husband and lover are not so different, Cather suggests; Frank Shabata also uses a gun to kill both Emil and the wife who has betrayed him. Such violence is possible because the hunter objectifies what he destroys, separating himself from the object he wants to possess and control; but such possession, as Cather demonstrates, kills the object of desire.[1] Although throughout her fiction Cather would connect the human urge to dominate and to destroy with masculine forces (as in *A Lost Lady*), she creates many individual male characters who deviate from this pattern, rejecting the social definition of masculinity as aggressive and competitive. Cather knew that such traits were not inherently male: she had destroyed innocent life herself when she was dissecting Red Cloud's dogs and cats in pursuit of scientific truth.

In *O Pioneers!* two male characters differ from the masculine stereotype in their relationship to nature: Carl Linstrum and Crazy Ivar. A "thin, frail boy" whose mouth was "too sensitive for a boy's," Carl abandons the struggle with the land. But when he returns, he suddenly realizes that he has missed the beauty of the wild country;

9. Henry David Thoreau, *Walden*, ed. Sherman Paul (Boston: Houghton Mifflin [Riverside ed]) 1959, p. 114.
1. Frank's killing of his wife is linked with his urge to dominate her: his idea of love is based on the memories of their first days of marriage, when she had been his "slave" (p. 222).

even though he had found farming uncongenial, memories of the "wild old beast" haunted him during his years in the city (p. 118). Ivar, the hermit and mystic who views nature as sacred, is even more opposed to the men who destroy life. He doctors sick animals, prohibits guns on his land, and unites himself so fully with nature that his home is indistinguishable from the landscape: "But for the piece of rusty stovepipe sticking up through the sod, you could have walked over the roof of Ivar's dwelling without dreaming that you were near a human habitation" (p. 36). Dissolving the boundaries between himself and the natural world, Ivar does not separate himself from the animals he cares for: "They say when horses have distemper he takes the medicine himself, and then prays over the horses" (p. 33). The identity Ivar experiences between self and world makes him protect life but prevents him from marking his environment: he does no harm, but he does not create.

Alexandra mediates between these polarities of dominance and submission; she views the external world neither as completely separate from nor as coextensive with the self. Her relationship with the land dissolves boundaries between self and other, but with the soil she can both erase the self and create it. Cather first describes the reciprocal bond Alexandra will have with nature when she is returning from her scouting trip to the river farms. Her face seems "radiant" to her brother Emil, and Cather tells us why:

> For the first time, perhaps, since that land emerged from the waters of geologic ages, a human face was set toward it with love and yearning. It seemed beautiful to her, rich and strong and glorious. Her eyes drank in the breadth of it, until her tears blinded her. Then the Genius of the Divide, the great, free spirit which breathes across it, must have bent lower than it ever bent to a human will before. The history of every country begins in the heart of a man or a woman. (p. 65)

This is an image of mutual submission, not of power and domination: the "free spirit" of the land bends low to Alexandra's will because her heart has been overwhelmed by its beauty, her eyes "blinded" by its breadth.

In a later passage, Cather develops the same paradox, linking Alexandra's discovery of self-expression in the soil with her abandonment of self: "Her personal life, her own realization of herself, was almost a subconscious existence; like an underground river that came to the surface only here and there . . . and then sank to flow on under her own fields" (p. 203). The metaphor of the underground stream conveys the fertilizing power of Alexandra's unconscious creativity, which nourishes her crops even if hidden from view.

Like an artist who draws on deep and hidden energies, Alexandra takes the external world into the self and returns the self to the world. The times when she was "peculiarly happy" are days when she feels "close to the flat, fallow world about her" and senses in "her own body the joyous germination in the soil" (p. 204). At other times it seems as if her own body extends into the land, as when she feels as if "her heart were hiding" along with the "little wild things that crooned or buzzed in the sun." During these moments of connection she receives her vision of the land's transformation: "Under the long shaggy ridges, she felt the future stirring" (p. 71). In discovering the land's power, she releases her own creative force, which comes out of hiding along with the wheat and corn.

Unlike Ivar, however, Alexandra wants to shape the soil. Just as Cather knew that writing demanded technique, form, and hard work as well as the "wisdom of intuition," so Alexandra studies crop rotation and irrigation, experiments with silos and pig corrals, and consults with other farmers. Cather does not attribute her success solely to mystic moments of communion with the Genius of the Divide: "It was Alexandra who read the papers and followed the markets, and who learned by the mistakes of their neighbors" (p. 23). And at times pragmatic concerns draw her away from romantic contemplation: one summer evening as she "dreamily" watches her brothers swimming in a "shimmering pool," her eyes cannot help but drift "back to the sorghum patch south of the barn, where she was planning to make her new pig corral" (p. 46).

In her bond with the land—a female presence in the novel, although one filled with "strength and resoluteness" like Alexandra herself (p. 77)—she can both assert the self and give it up, playing the roles of both mother and daughter, creator and created. Cather offers an ideal model of feminine development: Alexandra discovers herself in relationship to a maternal presence that allows separation as well as connection.

* * *

Yet Alexandra's daydream of the powerful male figure who lifts her up and carries her off raises the disturbing aspects of self-abandonment. A recurrent fantasy Alexandra finds alluring as well as distressing, it emerges when her conscious mind relinquishes control and she lies in bed in the morning in a trancelike state of reverie, hovering between sleep and wakefulness:

> Sometimes, as she lay thus luxuriously idle, her eyes closed, she used to have an illusion of being lifted up bodily and carried lightly by some one very strong. It was a man, certainly, who carried her, but he was like no man she knew; he was much larger and stronger and swifter, and he carried her as easily as if she were a sheaf of wheat. She never saw him, but,

> with eyes closed, she could feel that he was yellow like the sunlight, and there was the smell of ripe cornfields about him. She could feel herself being carried swiftly off across the fields. After such a reverie she would rise hastily, angry with herself, and go down to the bath-house that was partitioned off the kitchen shed. There she would stand in a tin tub and prosecute her bath with vigor, finishing it by pouring buckets of cold well-water over her gleaming white body which no man on the Divide could have carried very far. (pp. 205–6)

Cather's critics have been intrigued by this enigmatic passage and not surprisingly have offered varied interpretations, seeing the male figure as a vegetation god, the animus, the Genius of the Divide. If we fix his identity in this way, however, we run into one problem: Cather does not portray the land as male. In the earlier passage describing Alexandra's response to the "Genius of the Divide" with "love and yearning," Cather is careful to refer to the spirit as "it," leaving gender indeterminate; and her actual descriptions of the soil create a strong, pro-creative, maternal presence. Moreover, trying to establish the dream-figure's identity is difficult since he changes as the dream changes over time, suggesting that his "meaning" can be found only in relationship to his author, the dreamer Alexandra.

This version of Alexandra's fantasy—for which she wants to "prosecute" her body with cold water—occurs most often during her "girlhood" (p. 205). But as she grows older and takes on more responsibilities, the fantasy changes, occurring at night when she is tired rather than in the morning when she is "fresh and strong." Sometimes after a day of work on the farm, her body "aching with fatigue," just before she falls asleep, Alexandra will feel "the old sensation of being lifted and carried by a strong being who took from her all her bodily weariness" (p. 207). Here the "strong being" does not possess the same erotic power as does the godlike man "yellow like the sunlight"; not given a specific gender, this "being" is a parental figure who soothes and comforts the child's weary body. Later in the novel the dream changes once more. Depressed, lonely, and hopeless after the deaths of Emil and Marie, Alexandra again experiences "the old illusion of her girlhood, of being lifted and carried lightly by some one very strong." But this is, we discover, a death wish: Alexandra, "tired of life," longing to escape consciousness, imagines herself being carried off by the "mightiest of all lovers" to a place where she will be "free from pain" (pp. 282–83).

Although Alexandra feels that death is the true identity of the male figure (whom she can at last see "clearly" [p. 282]), we have to question her interpretation. He has no "clear" coherent identity;

constructed by Alexandra, he is a character whose manifestation and meaning depend on her psychological and emotional state. She creates the erotic god when she is lying in bed "luxuriously idle," the hooded death-figure when she longs to be "free from her own body" and the memories of her loss. Like an author creating two characters or a dreamer splitting herself among the various actors in a dream, Alexandra projects herself both into the figure who lifts and the one who is lifted.

Although the male figure's meaning and function change over time, the dream always involves the woman's yielding and submission. In this fantasy Alexandra thus expresses feelings she enacts only with the land but never, in reality, with another person. On the contrary, she is the strong parent-figure for everyone in the novel, the mother/father who either cares for or controls others: in addition to managing the farm, she protects Ivar, watches out for Mrs. Lee, helps Emil to escape the cornfields, advises Marie, organizes her brothers' work. No one takes care of her. Carl Linstrum is the only character who does not place her in a parental role, but he must leave her and the Divide to prove himself a man. Only in the dream does she create a figure stronger than herself, one who can lift her up, remove bodily weariness, and release her from pain.

The repressed part of the self that Alexandra expresses in the dream is thus not the male figure upon which most critical attention has been focused, but the version of herself who is lifted and borne away. Alexandra both fears and wants to release the yielding, passive, regressive aspects of the self, those she at first expresses only with the land. Once the land is tamed and her artistic project completed, however, she does not have that form of release, and so the fantasy becomes more threatening and self-destructive.

Yet Alexandra does not yield to the final version of her fantasy; when Carl Linstrum returns she begins to express her suppressed needs for support, companionship, and tenderness with him. Carl is not a titanic male figure who will lift her away from all human trials, but he offers her human-scale support that Cather regards positively: "She leaned heavily on his shoulder. 'I am tired,' she murmured. 'I have been very lonely, Carl.' " (p. 309). A childhood friend rather than an imaginary lover, Carl will live on Alexandra's land instead of carrying her away from it; his love will support but not engulf her. "Lean[ing] heavily" on someone else rather than finding relief for fatigue and loneliness only in her day-dreams, Alexandra finds in Carl a human version of her mythic bond with the Divide.

By the end of the novel, Alexandra has thus established two strong and enduring relationships: with Carl and with the land. In forming bonds with both a male and a female presence, Alexandra reflects a larger pattern in the novel, for Cather wants to attribute her character's success as farmer and artist to her receiving a patrilineal and a matrilineal inheritance. Simultaneously Cather connects her own emergence as a writer to the male and female literary traditions.

Interweaving these two inheritances, both Alexandra and Cather can write a new story, a parallel Cather suggests by the many similarities she draws between Alexandra's role as daughter in the Bergson family and her own role as daughter in a literary family headed by Walt Whitman and Sarah Orne Jewett. Whereas the male Adamic self must be "happily bereft of ancestry, untouched and undefiled by the usual inheritances of family" to achieve autonomous existence and original expression, it is precisely because these two daughters receive inheritances that they can become originators.

At first Cather emphasizes Alexandra's continuity with her male "strain of blood" (*MME*, p. 82). She is said to resemble both her father and grandfather in her intellegence, directness, and strength of will. Although John Bergson would have preferred to see these family likenesses in one of his sons, he knows "it was not a question of choice" and is grateful that in his daughter he has an heir "to whom he could entrust the future of his family and the possibilities of his hard-won land" (p. 24). And so he wills his daughter the land, thereby passing on his will to her just as he hopes that the strength that has vanished from his hands will flow into Alexandra's "strong ones" (p. 25). Cather thus opens her novel with a traditional scene: the dying patriarch choosing an heir. But she reverses the patrilineal inheritance of land, the pattern in her own family as in the larger society, by having the father give power and authority to the daughter. Bergson gives his daughter not a family estate but the injunction to continue the struggle to create one. His work is not finished, and so this is a liberating gift: she will have to complete the work he has begun, thus making it her own.

And Alexandra does make the land her own, cultivating it with "love and yearning" rather than her father's will to dominate. Yet the inheritance from her father remains important; in choosing her as his heir, Bergson gives her the public legitimacy and authority the daughter needs in a patriarchal society. So when Lou and Oscar challenge their sister's right to the land, asserting the patrilineal rights of inheritance ("The property of a family really belongs to the men of the family, no matter about the title" [p. 169]), Alexandra does not have to rely on her spiritual and emotional affinity with the Divide to refute them. Thanks to her father, she has patriarchal law on her side, represented by her legal title to the land: she is entitled to it. "You are talking nonsense," she tells her brothers impatiently. "Go to the country clerk and ask him who owns my land, and whether my titles are good" (p. 168).

So titles do matter: they grant a woman publicly recognized authority and ownership. Cather claimed a similar authority for herself—the authority of authorship—when she chose the title for her book, thus declaring that her subject belonged to her. Simultaneously she was declaring herself Whitman's heir, an even bolder act than Alexandra's accepting the gift of her father's land: the literary daughter was appropriating her father's literary mission, to write the story of America—in effect staking a claim to his land.

If we look at the poem that gave Cather her title, her literary relationship to the paternal figure becomes even more complex. *** In *O Pioneers!* Cather was being rebellious as well as respectful in alluding to Whitman. Her novel radically revises the vision of pioneering and settlement Whitman advances in "Pioneers! O Pioneers!," a jingoistic hymn to progress, manifest destiny, and the Westward Movement.

Whitman imagines his pioneers as male, referring to them as "Colorado men" and "Western youths" filled with "manly pride and friendship." Surrounding them with images of violence, war, and penetration, he describes the course of empire as a masculine triumph over a feminine land:

> Come my tan-faced children,
> Follow well in order, get your weapons ready,
> Have you your pistols? Have you your sharp-edged axes?
> Pioneers! O Pioneers!

The connection between such weaponry and the violation of nature's body emerges more fully later in the poem:

> We primeval forest felling,
> We the rivers stemming, vexing we and piercing deep the mines within,
> We the surface broad surveying, we the virgin soil upheaving,
>
> Pioneers! O Pioneers![2]

Whitman thus celebrates what Cather condemns, the masculine urge to subdue and to violate: his land is to be tamed by pioneers brandishing the guns that Cather, like Ivar, would like to exclude from her territory. And so in her novel she offers another vision of the taming of the land, one erasing the polarities and hierarchies in the Whitman poem: male/female, culture/nature, subject/object.

But "Pioneers! O Pioneers!" expresses only one aspect of Whit-

2. Walt Whitman, *Leaves of Grass*, ed. Harold W. Blodgett and Sculley Bradley (New York: Norton, 1965), pp. 229–32.

man, the strident, heartily patriotic poet enraptured with America's progress and power. There was another side to Whitman that is quite consistent with Cather's vision in *O Pioneers!*—the mystic, yielding, erotic speaker of "Song of Myself" who integrates body and soul, male and female, self and other and becomes an artist fueled by this integration of opposites.[3] The likelihood that Cather had "Song of Myself" in mind as well as "Pioneers! O Pioneers!" is suggested by the parallels between the endings of "Song" and *O Pioneers!* Whitman ends his poem envisioning himself reincarnated in the grass, both nature's grass and his own *Leaves of Grass* ("I bequeath myself to the dirt to grow from the grass I love,/ If you want me again look for me under your boot-soles"). Similarly, in the last paragraph of her novel Cather imagines Alexandra becoming part of a continuous cycle of life, one day returning to the "bosom" of the Divide, to be reborn in the "yellow wheat, in the rustling corn, in the shining eyes of youth"—eyes that will read Alexandra's story in Nebraska's "leaves of grass," the wheat and corn she helped the land to produce (p. 309).[4]

While Alexandra and her creator both rewrite the inheritances they receive from their fathers, absorbing what they can use and altering what they cannot, they draw more directly on their mothers' gifts. "Thinking back through their mothers," to paraphrase Virginia Woolf, they imagine themselves.[5] Alexandra's inheritance from her mother is private and unofficial. Mrs. Bergson cannot give her the authority to cultivate the land, but she shows her daughter how to farm it by the model of creativity she exemplifies. "Alexandra often said that if her mother were cast upon a desert island, she would thank God for her deliverance, make a garden, and find something to preserve." By making a garden in the desert, Mrs. Bergson both adapts to the land and expresses creativity and ingenuity as she tries to make the preserves she loves with new materials:

> Preserving was almost a mania with Mrs. Bergson. . . . She made a yellow jam of the insipid ground-cherries that grew on

3. As Paul Zweig observes, before he became a "poet in full possession of his powers," Walt Whitman would integrate opposites within the self—active and passive, masculine and feminine. Whitman represents this union symbolically in the marriage described in the opening stanzas of "Song of Myself," his great poem which records his own creative emergence: another parallel between "Song and Myself" and *O Pioneers!*, which also records the process of its own composition (*Walt Whitman: The Making of a Poet* [New York: Basic Books, 1984], p. 87). The connections Zweig makes between Whitman's experience of the creative process and its representation in "Song of Myself" have several parallels in Cather's literary evolution. See in particular Chapter 7, "Song of Myself."
4. John J. Murphy develops several parallels between *O Pioneers!* and *Leaves of Grass* in "A Comprehensive View of Cather's *O Pioneers!*" in *Critical Essays on Willa Cather*, ed. John J. Murphy (Boston: G. K. Hall, 1984), pp. 113–27, esp. pp. 124–26.
5. Virginia Woolf, *A Room of One's Own* (New York: Harcourt, Brace, 1929), p. 79.

> the prairie, flavoring it with lemon peel; and she made a sticky dark conserve of garden tomatoes. She had experimented even with the rank buffalo-pea. . . . When there was nothing more to preserve, she began to pickle. (p. 29)

Alexandra's mother preserves on a symbolic level as well, continuing traditions and customs from the Old World that give her family a sense of "household order" and ritual in the new (p. 20).

Even before the daughter takes over the family land, then, the mother has made her mark on the soil: evidence of "human striving" is in her log house, her garden, her glass jars of preserves. Although she does not make the mother-daughter relationship a prominent feature in the book, the link between Mrs. Bergson and Alexandra reveals Cather's new recognition of artistry among the rituals of domesticity. When Alexandra extends her mother's efforts and transforms the wilderness into a fruitful, orderly garden, she gains the public recognition her mother lacked. But since the daughter is in a sense carrying on and expanding the work her mother began, the two women are collaborators, not competitors: the seeds of the daughter's achievement are in the mother's garden.

Although Alexandra never pays direct tribute to her mother's example—the bond between the two women is only briefly suggested—Cather publicly acknowledged the influence of Sarah Orne Jewett on her novel when she dedicated *O Pioneers!* to her mentor. Jewett's literary advice and supportive friendship had been important to Cather, but the dedication calls our attention in particular to the links between Jewett's fiction and Cather's novel.

The American pastoral was not completely a male-dominated genre, and Cather may have wanted to associate her own pastoral with Jewett's *The Country of the Pointed Firs,* which also portrays rural people living harmoniously within their environment. Somewhat concerned that the two parts of her pastoral might not have been perfectly integrated, Cather may also have found consolation in remembering that *The Country of the Pointed Firs* also intertwined separate stories which, taken together, painted the portrait of a community. Moreover, the mother-daughter bond between Mrs. Todd and the narrator in *Country* and that between Mrs. Bergson and Alexandra share an important characteristic—in both texts daughter/artists receive a creative inheritance from mothers whose arts are domestic.

Even stronger parallels exist, however, between *O Pioneers!* and "A White Heron," one of the short stories Cather included in her edition of Jewett's fiction. In Jewett's story a young girl's peaceful union with nature is disrupted by an intrusive male who brings sexuality and violence to her secluded rural world. In asking her to reveal the white heron's hidden nest, the hunter threatens not only Sylvia's bond with nature but also her autonomy, her very self. Even though this girl's "woman's heart" is "vaguely thrilled by a dream of love" inspired by the handsome intruder, the "piteous sighs of thrushes and sparrows dropping silent to the ground, their songs hushed and their pretty feathers stained and wet with blood" warn her to protect the heron, nature, and herself, and she refuses to "tell the heron's secret and give its life away" (*CPF*, pp. 161–171). The imagery recalls the scene where Emil shoots the wild ducks, in which Cather is similarly condemning male violence to nature (and symbolically to women).

Sylvia's respectful bond with the natural world suggests Alexandra's. The "happiest day of her life" occurs when she, like Sylvia, discovers a bird's secret hiding place: one day she and Emil come upon an inlet protected by overhanging willows where a wild duck "was swimming and diving and preening her feathers, disporting herself very happily in the flickering light and shade." The two watch the bird for a long time, and years later Alexandra thinks of the duck "as still there, swimming and diving all by herself in the sunlight, a kind of enchanted bird that did not know age or change" (pp. 204–5). She assumes that Emil shares her appreciation, but as we learn he does not: Emil wants to kill the ducks to possess them, whereas—like the artist—Alexandra possesses the duck in memory, where she grants it enduring life. The references to "A White Heron" thus signify both Cather's and Jewett's joint effort to revise the male-authored story of woman and nature as well as the younger writer's willingness to acknowledge her debt to her precursor.

Cather may have found it easy to honor Jewett in *O Pioneers!* because, like Alexandra, she also extends her mother's range. Going beyond Jewett's sketches to write her first successful "long story," giving her novel a title that does not limit it to a region, associating herself with Whitman's epic mode, Cather announces her intention to represent a central pattern in American history and culture.

* * *

C. SUSAN WIESENTHAL

Female Sexuality in Willa Cather's *O Pioneers!* and the Era of Scientific Sexology: A Dialogue between Frontiers†

Perhaps the most critical issue which immediately confronts any discussion of Willa Cather's fictional portrayal of sexuality is the nature of the relationship between the author's life and her work, between biography and art. For it is primarily on biographical bases such as Cather's adolescent rejection of femininity—her masquerade as the short-haired, boyishly-dressed 'William Cather Jr'—and her adult relationships with women such as Louise Pound, Isabelle McClung, and Edith Lewis, that an increasing number of critics have been led to consider her as a 'lesbian writer.' Although no evidence exists to indicate that any of Cather's relationships with women involved an erotic dimension, many scholars agree that, at the very least, her life may be regarded as 'lesbian' in the sense of Adrienne Rich's extensive definition of the term. Briefly, Rich conceives of a broad 'lesbian continuum' which 'includes a range . . . of woman-indentified experience,' embracing any extra-sexual or emotional form of 'primary intensity between women,' and 'not simply the fact that a woman has had or [has] consciously desired genital experience with another woman' (648).

Almost invariably, however, when critics turn to Cather's novels, it is precisely the absence of any 'lesbian' sensibility which they emphasise. Thus, Jane Rule, the first writer to situate Cather specifically within a lesbian literary tradition along with Radclyffe Hall, Gertrude Stein, and others, sharply reproves readers who attempt to find a homoerotic sensibility in Cather's art, claiming that if the author's private 'sexual tastes' manifest themselves in the fiction at all, it is only in her 'capacity to transcend the conventions of what is masculine and feminine' (87, 80). More recently, Phyllis Robinson has flatly asserted that 'the loving relationships with women that were so important in [Cather's] personal life are no where reflected in her fiction' (158). In *Willa Cather: The Emerging Voice*, Sharon O'Brien concurs, noting that '[c]ertainly the most prominent absence and the most unspoken love in her work are the emotional bonds between women that were central to her life' (127). O'Brien does not insist on wholly divorcing author and text, however, and argues instead that Cather's fiction works to both disclose and conceal

† "Female Sexuality in *O Pioneers!* and the Era of Scientific Sociology" by C. Susan Wiesenthal from *Ariel* 21 (1990): 41–63. Reprinted by permission of *Ariel* and Johns Hopkins University Press.

a lesbian psyche. Nevertheless, in ' "The Thing Not Named": Willa Cather as a Lesbian Writer,' she concentrates on the latter aspect of her thesis—on those 'literary strategies' whereby Cather is able to 'disguise' or 'camouflage' the 'emotional source of her fiction.' For O'Brien, Cather's 'lesbian' sensibility represents 'the unwritten text' of the novels ('The Thing Not Named' 577, 593–94, 577).

The object of this essay is not to determine whether the authorial sensibility manifest in Cather's fiction is or is not a specifically 'lesbian' one. Rather, it is to reverse the prevailing critical preoccupation with the 'absent' and 'unwritten,' and to explore the possible ways in which an authorial attitude towards a broader concept of 'deviant' female sexuality, in general, does disclose itself in the written text. In the written text of *O Pioneers!*, in particular, this authorial attitude may be perceived to inhere implicitly in the hermaphroditic, heterosexual, and same-sex relationships Cather does portray. In this novel, for example, the heroine, Alexandra Bergson, is depicted as a character who embodies a seemingly hermaphroditic sexual nature which is viewed positively, as a potentially self-fulfilling value, while the more unambiguously heterosexual natures of other characters, on the contrary, are seen to result exclusively in unhappy and debilitating 'love' relationships. This dichotomous portrayal seems to suggest an authorial sensibility, which, while it is not specifically sympathetic to a homosexual nature, is certainly sensitive to the potential gratification which unconventional forms of sexuality may yield.

In order to grasp the full significance of Cather's portrayal of sexuality in *O Pioneers!* it is necessary to consider not only the dialectic between life and art, but the dynamic relationship between text and context as well. For in the 'golden age of scientific determinism, Social Darwinism, and eugenics' (Smith-Rosenberg 267), Cather's contemporary milieu represented, in short, a stridently heterosexual era especially obsessed with what it perceived as the 'unnatural' or 'inverted' (that is, lesbian) nature of virtually all manipulations of female sexuality or eroticism beyond heterosexual marriage (Smith-Rosenberg 53–76, 245–96; Faderman 147–277). The extent to which *O Pioneers!* courageously challenges dominant medical and cultural assumptions about female sexuality can be gauged only when the text is considered in a dialogic relation to this larger historic discourse. For indeed, Cather's positive delineation of the sexually unorthodox Alexandra, and, conversely, her negative or critical depiction of conventional heterosexuality, actually work together to controvert systematically a number of contemporary tenets about the nature of the sexually 'inverted' woman. In this way, Cather's novel of pioneer life indirectly addresses the issue of the 'New Scientific Discourse' (Smith-Rosenberg 265) being promulgated by such influential and widely popularised theorists as Richard von Krafft-Ebing and Havelock Ellis. And in so far as these late nineteenth- and early twentieth-century 'sexologists' also self-consciously beheld themselves as 'pioneers' in a hitherto unexplored psychosexual 'borderland' (Ellis 2 : 219), the subtle interplay between text and context may be regarded as a form of dialogue between two disparate sorts of frontiers.[1]

Ultimately, however, the crucial limits of the challenge implicit in Cather's treatment of sexuality in *O Pioneers!* must be also firmly acknowledged. For although she repeatedly re-inverts, as it were, contemporary convictions about the perversity of female 'inversion,' her novel also reflects an element of self-conscious restraint which expresses itself most clearly in her highly circumspect handling of close female friendship—an integral thematic and structural component of the novel, which is deftly and gingerly developed by Cather, only to be rather abruptly abandoned when she is brought to deploy a somewhat disappointing, conventional romance closure, an ending both marked and marred, as one critic suggests, by the purely 'token marriage' of the heroine (Bailey 396).[2] Whether this novelistic outcome may be ultimately ascribed, as critics such as Sharon O'Brien would contend, to 'the lesbian writer's need to conceal the socially unacceptable' ('The Thing Not Named' 592) must remain, perhaps, a moot point. A close reading of *O Pioneers!*, however, does, at least, appear to substantiate the more general claim that internalised cultural strictures governing the 'socially unacceptable' in the realm of sexuality do indeed exert a profound force upon Cather's artistic impulse, and, consequently, upon the shape of this novel as a whole.

Through a comprehensive examination of contemporary women's diaries and letters, as well as medical literature and fiction, feminist historians such as Lillian Faderman and Carroll Smith-Rosenberg have been able to trace the critical late nineteenth-century shifts in the theoretic conceptualisation and social experience of female homosexuality throughout the Western world. Unlike male homosexuality, that is, which had long been perceived as a punishable offence against scriptural and secular order, lesbianism had not only been 'generally ignored by the law' until this point, but did not even constitute a conceptual category of deviance until the 1880s and 1890s (Faderman, 'The Morbidification of Love' 77, 75; Smith-Rosenberg 266). Indeed, in the earlier decades of the Victorian

1. Ellis uses terms such as 'frontier,' 'pioneer,' and 'borderland' quite extensively throughout.
2. For a differing interpretation of the marriage of Carl and Alexandra, see O'Brien, *Willa Cather* 444–46.

century, passionate homosocial bonds between women—physically uninhibited as well as emotionally intense relationships—were 'casually accepted in American society' as forms of romantic love 'both socially acceptable and fully compatible with heterosexual marriage' (Smith-Rosenberg 53, 50).[3] Such 'legitimate' romantic friendships between women, however, came to be stigmatised by medical authorities and educators as 'morbid' and 'unnatural' during the final decades of the century, because it was at this point that such alliances first became an economically feasible alternative to heterosexual marriage for a small, but growing, group of autonomous, college-educated New Women. 'For the first time,' as Lillian Faderman remarks, 'love between women became threatening to the social structure,' posing truly portentous consequences, not only for the institutional nucleus of the social fabric, the family, but—as eugenicists and imperialists alike pointed out—for the already 'dangerously low' birth-rate of the American Republic as well (Faderman 238).[4]

As steadily increasing numbers of New Women, like Willa Cather herself, began to eschew marriage and motherhood for higher education and professional livelihoods, one form which the simultaneously escalating anti-feminist reaction took was in the widespread expression of fear and repugnance of an 'intermediate sex': an appalling type of 'semi-woman' whose behaviour and physical appearance 'violated normal gender categories' (Smith-Rosenberg 265, 271). To accommodate such freaks of nature, the leading European neurologist, Richard von Krafft-Ebing, promptly created in his *Psychopathia Sexualis* (1886) the new 'medico-sexual category' of the 'Mannish Lesbian': a nosological classification in which, as Smith-Rosenberg observes, 'women's rejection of traditional gender roles and their demands for social and economic equality' were linked directly to 'cross-dressing, sexual perversion, and borderline hermaphroditism' (272). More influential yet in Britain and America, however, were the theories of Havelock Ellis. It was his 1901 work, *Sexual Inversion*, which most powerfully contributed to the 'morbidification' of the formerly innocent 'female world of love and intimacy,' because in it, Ellis re-defined the close friendships of college-aged and adult New Women 'as both actively sexual and as actively perverted' (Smith-Rosenberg 269, 275).[5] Thus, forms of af-

3. This chapter of Smith-Rosenberg's book, entitled 'The Female World of Love and Ritual: Relations Between Women in Nineteenth Century America,' appeared originally in the first issue of *Signs* (1975).
4. Smith-Rosenberg also explores the potentially revolutionary social implications which a strong network of homosocial female bonds posed in the context of the feminist movement, and makes a similar point: see *Disorderly Conduct* 277–82.
5. The term 'morbidification,' however, is taken from Faderman.

fection between women which had long been regarded with equanimity or indifference suddenly came to be viewed with suspicion and alarm as subversive and abnormal affairs.

If the theories and beliefs of Krafft-Ebing, Ellis, and others were a matter of 'common knowledge' by the turn of the century, as Faderman contends (*Surpassing the Love of Men* 238), then by 1910–1920, the decade during which *O Pioneers!* was written, medical tropes of the 'Mannish Lesbian' or the 'unsexed' woman had been so pervasively disseminated throughout the cultural imagination—via newspaper caricatures, anti-feminist tracts, and sensational as well as 'high' literature—that they had begun to have a substantial impact upon the marital and educational standards of young women, as statistical evidence of the period clearly shows (Smith-Rosenberg 281).

That Cather herself would have been fully conscious of the contemporary medico-cultural discourse of deviant female sexuality, then, seems almost inevitable on historical bases alone. More specifically, however, biographical details further support this assumption. Cather's work as an editor for *McClure's Magazine*, for example, led her to regularly read the columns of the rival *Ladies' Home Journal*, in which articles admonishing women 'against forming exclusive romantic bonds with women' often appeared (O'Brien, *Willa Cather* 133). More importantly, despite the fact that Cather and Edith Lewis destroyed the vast majority of Cather's personal correspondence, some of the letters she wrote during her two-year obsession with Louise Pound—'the most serious romantic attachment of [her] college life'—have indeed survived. Unfortunately, testamentary restrictions prevent scholars and biographers with access to these letters from quoting them directly (Robinson 58).[6] According to Sharon O'Brien, however, Cather states in one of these epistles that 'it is so unfair that female friendships should be unnatural,' before she goes on to accede that, nevertheless, 'they are.' As O'Brien suggests, Cather's self-conscious, if grudging, awareness of the fact that female friendships are 'unnatural,' reflects the extent to which she internalised the sexual norms of her age, and recognised the nature of her intense attachment to Louise as a 'special category not sanctioned by the dominant culture' (O'Brien, *Willa Cather* 131–32).[7]

If critics' descriptions of Cather's 'turbulent' and 'passionate' 'love letters' (O'Brien, 'The Thing Not Named' 583) are accurate, her college 'crush' on Louise Pound represents precisely the sort of

6. On Cather's destruction of her letters and the legal provisions of her will, *see* Robinson 33–34 and 274; Brown xxiii, Woodress xiii–xiv.
7. See 127–37 for the most compelling and comprehensive account, to date, of Cather's complex and contradictory sense of lesbian self-identity.

'flame,' 'rave,' or 'spoon' relationship which so gravely concerned sexologists and educators of the period. Ellis, for instance, devotes a lengthy appendix in his book to documenting such unsavoury 'School-Friendships of Girls,' in which he cites the cautionary words of one 'American correspondent': 'Love of the same sex . . . though [it] is not generally known, is very common; it is not mere friendship; the love is strong, real, and passionate'—sometimes, indeed, as he has been informed, it is 'insane, intense love.'[8] Speculating on the explosive end of the Cather-Pound alliance, one biographer has even suggested that Pound's older brother may have intervened because he interpreted their relationship apprehensively in this current context:

> Perhaps he called the friendship unnatural and his sister's friend perverse. He may have even used the term 'lesbian' to describe her. We do not know. We do know, however, that losing Louise caused Willa the most intense suffering she had ever known. (Robinson 60–61)[9]

In any case, whether or not the widespread cultural anxieties of deviant female sexuality, fanned by the 'New Scientific Discourse' of the sexologists, actually affected Cather's personal life with such painful immediacy, it remains plausible to assume, at the very least, that a sharp awareness of such medico-cultural censures must have impinged uncomfortably upon her conscious mind at one time or another.

It is with such biographical and contextual background in mind that one may, perhaps, most fruitfully approach the question of sexuality in *O Pioneers!* For as Annette Kolodny has argued, whether one speaks of critics 'reading' texts or writers 'reading' the world, one 'call[s] attention to interpretive strategies that are learned, historically determined, and thereby necessarily gender-inflected' (47). In this sense, Cather's fictional portrayal of sexuality represents a cultural construct shaped largely by the lived experiences of her gender. And because she experienced and observed, or 'read,' female sexuality in an age in which traditional sexual roles and distinctions were being rapidly erased and eroded, sparking feelings of confusion, fear, and guilt, it is relatively unsurprising that her fictional treatment of the subject should embody an element of the conflict which marked both her life and her times.

Set on a wild, windswept prairie frontier, *O Pioneers!* initially appears far removed indeed from Cather's controversial modern era.

8. E.G. Lancaster, qtd. in Ellis, *Sexual Inversion* 382. The colloquial terms 'flame,' 'rave,' and 'spoon' also appear in Ellis's appendix, 368–84 *passim*.
9. It should be noted, however, that subsequent biographers have dismissed Robinson's suggestion as 'pure speculation' (Woodress 87).

And yet the profound extent to which her novel is informed by the milieu in which it was produced is apparent even in the central character of Alexandra Bergson: a heroine who incorporates many definitive features of the New Woman upon whom the contemporary debate of the 'intermediate sex' centred. In so far as the New Woman of the age 'constituted a revolutionary demographic and political phenomenon' (Smith-Rosenberg 245), of course, Alexandra eludes the historical paradigm: unlike Cather herself, she is neither part of a novel, homogeneous group of college-educated women, nor does she self-consciously resist traditional gender roles on intellectual or ideological grounds. Practical circumstances, as she angrily informs her brothers, have dicated the nature of her pioneering career: 'Maybe I would never have been very soft, anyhow; but I certainly didn't choose to be the kind of girl I was' (Cather, *O Pioneers!* 171). On the other hand, there are also strong suggestions in the text that the intellectually gifted Alexandra would have made a fine student, and that had she in fact had a choice in the matter, she would not have remained on the outside of the State University's 'long iron fence' curiously 'looking through,' and observing campus life from a distance (287).

At any rate, beyond these few fundamental differences, Cather's heroine embodies the majority of qualities typical of the late nineteenth-century New Woman: she is single, economically autonomous, and quite ready to assert her legal and social equality, defiantly maintaining her right to 'do exactly as [she] please[s] with her land' (167). Moreover, with her innovative silos and pig-breeding schemes, Alexandra is the owner of 'one of the richest farms on the Divide' (83), and as such, assumes the position of a community leader. In these respects, she corresponds closely to Smith-Rosenberg's description of the quintessential New Woman:

> Eschewing marriage, she fought for professional visibility, espoused innovative, often radical, economic and social reforms, and wielded real political power. At the same time, as a member of the affluent new bourgeoisie, most frequently a child of small-town America, she felt herself part of the grass roots of her country. (245)

It is also interesting to note that although Alexandra presents a new type of heroine in the tradition of American frontier fiction, she is by no means an anomally in a historical context; indeed, by the late nineteenth century, many women had begun to take advantage of the Homestead Act to acquire property in the West—some of them single, adventurous New Women who 'exploited their claims to earn money for other ventures' like college tuition (Myers 258–59). The conceptual distance between the modern era of the

New Woman and that of Cather's farming pioneer, then, is not so great as it may first appear to be.

The affinities between the New Woman of Cather's period and the heroine of *O Pioneers!* extend to the portrayal of Alexandra as a representative of a type of 'intermediate sex': a vaguely intimidating sort of 'mannish' woman who appears to combine certain traditional aspects of masculinity and feminity in one. This trait is immediately apparent in Cather's initial description of Alexandra as 'a tall, strong girl' who

> walked rapidly and resolutely, as if she knew exactly where she was going and what she was going to do next. She wore a man's long ulster (not as if it were an affliction, but as if it were very comfortable and belonged to her, carried it like a young soldier), and a round plush cap, tied down with a veil. She had a serious, thoughtful face, and her clear, deep blue eyes were fixed intently on the distance. (6)

Krafft-Ebing, who believed, as Smith-Rosenberg states, that 'only the abnormal woman would challenge gender distinctions—and by her dress you would know her' (272)—would have likely recognised his 'Mannish Lesbian' here, on the basis of Alexandra's manly ulster alone. Ellis, too, would have detected an element of perversity in the 'comfortable' confidence with which Alexandra 'carries' her masculine garb, since he maintained that the 'very pronounced tendency among sexually inverted women to adopt male attire when practicable' could be 'chiefly' accounted for by the fact that 'the wearer feels more at home in them' (245). Moreover, the heroine's rapid and resolute gait and the 'Amazonian fierceness' with which she cows the 'little drummer' who dares ogle her (8) also reflect the sort of 'brusque, energetic movements' and 'masculine straightforwardness and sense of honour . . . free from any suggestion of either shyness or audacity,' which, according to a 'keen observer' like Ellis, betrayed an 'underlying psychic abnormality' (250). As a heroine of epic proportions, in fact, Alexandra corresponds strikingly to one sexologist's profile of the typical female 'invert,' whom he held to be

> more full of life, of enterprise, of practical energy, more aggressive, more heroic, more apt for adventure, than either the heterosexual woman or the homosexual man.
>
> (Magnus Hirschfeld, qtd. in Ellis 251)

Endowed with a greatness of stature which dwarfs the 'little men' who surround her (181), as well as a 'direct[ness]' of manner which often makes men 'wince' (121), Alexandra is indeed the most enterprising, energetic, and heroic character in Cather's novel.

Importantly, however, this positive vision of the heroic 'manly woman' appears to constitute the exception rather than the rule in medical literature of the period. For while early nineteenth-century commentators could still gloat contemptuously that 'Amazonian' types were 'their own executioners' and presented no danger of 'perpetuating their race,' since they had 'unsexed themselves in public estimation,'[1] most of the sexologists of Cather's era were much less confident—for by then it was clear that the ranks of the 'intermediate sex' were indeed continuing to swell. Such women were thus viewed collectively with a good deal of trepidation as the 'ultimate symbol of social disorder' (Smith-Rosenberg 181).

This understandable though fallacious perception of the 'deviant' woman as an emblem of social disruption emerges as the first issue implicitly addressed and refuted by Cather in *O Pioneers!* For having once established her heroine as an 'Amazonian' or 'manly woman,' Cather proceeds to depict her not as a harbinger of chaos, but as precisely the opposite: as a preeminent symbol of order and a bedrock of stability. Under Alexandra's creative and loving will, for example, the natural world is gradually though steadily transformed from a hostile 'wild land' to a productive and geometrically neat farm, noteworthy for its 'most unusual trimness and care for detail' (83). Hence, there is an

> order and fine arrangement manifest all over [Alexandra's] great farm; in the fencing and hedging, in the windbreaks and sheds, [and] in the symmetrical pasture ponds. (84)

'Not unlike a tiny village' (83), Alexandra's farming homestead also represents a contained microcosm of fair but efficient social and domestic order. When she has no 'visitors' and dines with 'her men,' for instance, Cather's heroine sits 'at the head of the long table,' and the place to her left is routinely reserved for old Ivar, her trusted advisor (85–86). With a democratic spirit, Alexandra 'encourage[s] her men to talk' during these meals, to voice their opinions and concerns over the business affairs of the farm, but throughout the novel there is never a doubt that she retains an absolutely firm control over the hierarchical structure she has created. 'As long as there is one house there must be one head,' John Bergson declares before his death, and it is a maxim by which his 'dotter' unswervingly abides (25–26).

Cather's affirmative portrayal of the 'manly woman' also works in a similar fashion to subvert or re-invert the prevailing medical and cultural conception of the sexually inverted woman as a physiologi-

1. Anon., 'Female Orators,' *The Mother's Magazine*, VI (1838): 27, qtd. in Faderman, *Surpassing the Love of Men* 235.

cally 'morbid' or diseased, mutant being. For not only were such women of 'intermediate sex' judged to be 'unnatural' in the sense of being quirkily unconventional in dress and behaviour, but, as the 'visible symptom[s] of a diseased society,' they were also held to be innately sick—organically degenerative and neurotic as well as morally contaminating. Because contemporary authorities habitually transposed social and political evils into physiological terms, medical discourses of the sexually deviant woman abound in metaphors of morbidity and pathology (Smith-Rosenberg 245, 261–62). Krafft-Ebing, for example, believed that lesbianism was the sign of 'an inherited diseased condition of the central nervous system,' which he referred to as a form of 'taint.'[2] Similarly, Ellis, although ostensibly aware that 'the study of the abnormal is perfectly distinct from the study of the morbid,' still claimed that female sexual inversion was a type of 'germ' fostered by the feminist movement (319, 262).[3]

The Amazonian Alexandra may assume manly attire, but she is not, as the narrator notes, in any sense 'afflicted' by it; quite the contrary, in fact, she is depicted by Cather as the epitome of health and wholesomeness. Her body, so 'tall and strong' that 'no man on the Divide could have carried it very far,' is also a 'gleaming white body' (206), consistently associated with images of both vigour and purity. While Cather thus likens her heroine's sunkissed face to 'one of the big double sunflowers' in the garden, she also emphasises the contrasting 'smoothness and whiteness' of the delicate skin beneath her shirt collar and sleeves: it is skin which 'none but Swedish women ever possess; skin with the freshness of the snow itself' (88). Just as Jim Burden, in *My Ántonia*, thinks 'with pride that Ántonia, like Snow White in the fairy tale, is still the fairest of them all' (215), so in this novel does Carl Lindstrum remember admiringly how the fair Alexandra used to appear at dawn with her milking pails, 'looking as if she had walked straight out' of the 'milky light' 'of the morning itself' (126). Even as an older, successfully established farming businesswoman, the pristine aura of the dairymaid still suffuses Alexandra, who blandly admits that people find her 'clean and healthy-looking' appearance pleasant (132).

2. Krafft-Ebing, qtd. in Faderman, 'The Morbidification of Love' 77. Faderman points out that Krafft-Ebing later changed his stance on homosexuality as a disease, but that this was announced only shortly before his death in 1902 and had 'minimal' impact 'on popular notions regarding homosexuals' (77–78, n. 6).
3. In fairness, it must be noted that Ellis also uses the word 'germ' elsewhere in *Sexual Inversion* in a purely organic sense. In language very appropriate to the context of Cather's novel, in fact, he describes human sexuality in terms of a 'soil' which at conception is 'sown' with an equal amount of masculine and feminine 'seeds' or 'germs.' In bisexuals and homosexuals, he maintains, the 'normal' process whereby the 'seeds' of one sex come to 'kill off' most of those of the other sex has somehow dysfunctioned, a phenomenon, he says, that can only be attributed to an inherent abnormality 'in the soil' (309–11).

At once robust and delicate, fusing conventional attributes of male and female within herself, the heroine's healthy, hermaphroditic nature also facilitates a vital, erotically fulfilling relationship with the land—virtually the only salutary relationship offered by Cather in *O Pioneers!* Indeed, the Nebraskan prairie is charged with 'the same tonic, puissant quality' characteristic of Alexandra herself (77). Like her tanned face and white body, 'the brown earth' is yet so clean and pure that it rolls from the shear of the plow without 'even dimming the brightness of the metal' (76). And like Alexandra, too, the land is presented as a hermaphroditic entity. Thus, it both 'yield[s] itself eagerly' to her active and yearning 'human will' (76, 65), and 'stir[s]' beneath her like a giant leviathan, eliciting, in turn, a sensual responsiveness or 'yielding' in the heroine herself:

> Alexandra remembered . . . days when she was close to the flat, fallow world about her, and felt, as it were, in her own body the joyous germination in the soil. (204)

As a sexually animated presence within the text, however, the land may constitute not so much an autonomous entity in its own right as it does a specular reflection of the heroine's own hermaphroditic nature. For it is, in fact, Alexandra who sublimates her sexual energies into the land—who sets her face 'toward it with love and yearning' (65)—and it is also her perception and sense of it that are invariably conveyed to the reader, who sees only the way the land 'seem[s]' to her or the way she 'remember[s]' it (65, 204).

What Cather actually appears to present, then, is a type of autoerotic, onanistic relationship of the heroine with a part of her hermaphroditic sexual self which has been displaced onto the 'Other' of the land. In this respect, her portrayal of sexuality in *O Pioneers!* is comparable to that of Martha Ostenso's in the Canadian prairie novel *Wild Geese* (1925), in which the heroine, Judith, lies upon the 'damp ground' nude and feels that 'here was something forbiddenly beautiful;' something as 'secret as one's own body' (67). Seemingly complete in herself, Cather's heroine may be perhaps best likened, though, to the 'single wild duck' she so fondly recalls in her memory: the 'solitary bird' which 'take[s] its pleasure' quite alone, and which strikes Alexandra as more 'beautiful' than any 'living thing had ever seemed to [her]' (204–05). A subtle celebration of the hermaphroditic and perhaps even bisexual sensibility, the portrayal of Alexandra's fulfilling erotic life suggests that she may not be as lonely in her unmarried state as the narrator would sometimes have us believe.

By presenting her 'manly woman' as a fresh and vital human being whose hermaphroditic attributes constitute the source of positive erotic gratification, Cather's novel works to break down the contemporary myth of the diseased and degenerative woman of 'intermediate sex.' Significantly, however, her artistic response to the large, pseudo-scientific discourse of sexuality does not end at this point, for Cather also proceeds to challenge her culture's yet more fundamental assumption of the intrinsic desirability and 'normalcy' of heterosexuality itself. In *O Pioneers!*, indeed, it is not the seemingly 'deviant' but the socially acceptable heterosexual impulse which is portrayed as 'morbid' and unhealthy. Thus, when Alexandra does indulge in one of her rare heterosexual fantasies, she is apt to experience it as a form of profoundly sordid 'reverie': literally, an unclean impulse which she immediately attempts to wash away, via a penitential ritual of Spartan ablution, with 'buckets of cold well-water' (206). And the one and only time that Alexandra does envisage a heterosexual embrace as a positive desire to be unresisted, it is rather alarmingly associated with the booded figure of Death, 'the mightiest of all lovers' (283).

Similarly, Cather also consistently links the major heterosexual relationship within her novel—the love of Emil and Marie—to images of decay, sickness, and pain. Emil's passion, for example, is compared to a defective grain of corn which will never shoot up 'joyfully into the light' but is destined instead to rot and fester in the dark, damp earth (164). The essential morbidity of his relationship with Marie is further conveyed by the nature of the three gifts he drops into the lap of his beloved over the course of the novel: the uncut turquoises are pretty, but must, like the grain of corn, remain concealed in dark secrecy (224–25); the branch full of 'sweet, insipid fruit' is already overripe and on the verge of decay (153); and, in stark contrast to Alexandra's sportive and contented solitary duck, the birds associated with the two young lovers are dead and dripping with blood (127–28). Gone for both Emil and Marie are those 'germless days' of childhood (216), for their experience of adult heterosexuality is indeed like a type of 'affliction,' a perverse sort of malaise in the grip of which they 'cannot feel that the heart lives at all' unless 'its strings can scream to the touch of pain' (226).

Neatly reversing her society's binary equation of deviant sexuality with disease and heterosexuality with health, Cather also continues to turn contemporary medical theory upon its head by attributing to the nature of heterosexuality a number of other specific aberrations which sexologists typically ascribed to the sexual 'invert.' By the early twentieth century, for instance, the notion of 'sexual inversion' was commonly associated not only with physical disease, but with all manner of tragedy, insanity, and criminality as well. 'Inverted women,' as Ellis asserts in his work, 'present a favourable soil for the seeds of passional crime,' and to illustrate his point, he promptly proceeds to recount, in gruesome detail, several cases of lesbian homicides and suicides, deeming one particularly sensational 1892 murder of a young Memphis woman by her female lover as quite 'typical' (201). The sexual nature of the 'inverted' person, moreover, was thought to 'constitute as well a specific atavistic response, a sudden throwback to a primitive bisexuality, a tragic freak of nature' (Smith-Rosenberg 269). '[F]rom a eugenic standpoint' such as Ellis's, therefore, 'the tendency to sexual inversion' could be regarded as 'merely . . . nature's merciful method of winding up a concern which, from her point of view, has ceased to be profitable' (335).

In Cather's novel, conversely, it is heterosexuality which is presented as the direct cause of such grievous afflictions and processes. While the component of tragedy is, of course, most dramatically evident in the violent and premature deaths of Marie and Emil, almost all of the heterosexual alliances in the text are presented as unhappy or pathetic. Hence, John Bergson is 'warped' by his marriage, which is described as a mere 'infatuation' on his part: 'the despairing folly of a powerful man who [could] not bear to grow old' (23). Similarly, the snug security of Angélique's happy little family is blighted by the sudden death of Amédée; the confused young Signa is afraid of her bullish husband even before he forces her to plod home with the cows on their wedding day; and 'young farmers' like Lou betray a measure of embarrassed discomfort in their spousal relations in that they can seldom bring themselves to address their wives by name (111). And, unlike Alexandra's orderly household, the Shabata home is frequently the scene of domestic crises and violence, for Frank is a rash and volatile man whose unleashed temper has 'more than once' compelled Marie to struggle with him over a loaded gun (265–66). Uniting themselves in relationships which all too often result in animosity, violence, divorce (148), or death, the majority of heterosexual characters in this novel are to some degree culpable, like Marie, of 'spread[ing] ruin around' (304), and as such, they are viewed collectively by the author not only as a tragic lot but, indeed, as the 'ultimate symbol' of what the sexual invert was supposed to represent: utter social and domestic chaos.

It is also Frank Shabata, the most aggressively heterosexual character in the novel, who emerges from Cather's perspective as the 'most favourable soil for the seeds of passional crime,' as well as madness and degeneration. After his passionate jealousy has resulted in the murders of Emil and Marie, he regresses in prison to an atavistic creature, a grey, unshaven, and stooped figure who appears 'not altogether human.' Left to ponder his guilt in a wretched cell, the now pathetic Frank depicts a dismal future for himself; as he confesses to Alexandra when she visits him, 'I guess I go crazy sure 'nough' (294). The implicit but clear message in Cather's text, then, is that the heterosexual nature, far from embodying an unambiguously 'normal' or healthy appetite, may manifest itself as 'unnatural' and 'morbid' in precisely the same ways as those of 'inverted' or 'deviant' sexual tendencies were thought to. Or, considered from an observe angle, Cather's novel is one whose sexually unorthodox but sane, vigorous, and prosperous heroine serves as a timely reminder to those, who, like Ellis, tended to forget that what may be perceived as 'abnormal' need not necessarily be 'morbid.'

Through her own process of conceptual 'inversion,' then, Cather may be seen to respond in a creative and challenging way to dominant contemporary theories of sexuality, quietly establishing, in *O Pioneers!*, her own alternate paradigms of human sexuality. And yet it is, perhaps, an authorial consciousness of implicitly engaging—and controverting—this larger medico-cultural ethos which may also be seen to constitute the source of an inhibiting force in Cather's art. In *O Pioneers!*, this aspect of the narrative is best illustrated by Cather's treatment of the relations between women. For indeed, contrary to the pervasive critical over-generalisation that Cather 'never' deals in her fiction with the homosocial emotions and bonds which filled and fuelled her own life, a very complex and subtle relationship does unfold in this novel between Alexandra and Marie, which, to the best extent of my knowledge, has not been extensively or adequately examined. And it is important that it should be, for it suggests that within this novel of pioneer life, Cather begins to explore a second sort of 'frontier': not a historical and geographical one, but a psychic 'frontier between friendship and love' (M. Tarde, qtd. in Ellis 75). This is not to argue that Cather depicts the friendship between her heroine and Marie as one which moves toward incipient lesbianism. Rather, it is to suggest that, along with its nostalgia for the heroic cultural and geographical Nebraskan frontier of the past. Cather's text also quietly but perceptibly mourns the passing of that older world of passionate yet innocent female love, so well documented by Smith-Rosenberg, into a modern era of 'morbidified' relations.

Perhaps because of the disparity of their respective ages, the affection Alexandra feels for Marie clearly manifests itself on one level as a type of maternal love. 'Sit down like a good girl, Marie,' Alexandra says in her best matronly manner, for example, 'and I'll tell you a story' (137). Marie, that 'crazy child' who married at eighteen (119), seems in this respect to present a surrogate daughter-figure for Alexandra, just as she thinks of her younger brother, Emil, as her 'boy.' On the other hand, however, the friendship between the two women is marked by both a degree of intensity and a dimension of sensuality which makes it a far more 'romantic' relationship than, in fact, Alexandra's ostensibly 'real' romance with Carl Lindstrum. Indeed, when Cather's heroine reflects on the 'pretty lonely life' she has led, the primacy of her bond with the young Bohemian girl is indicated by the order in which she names her two closest companions: 'Besides Marie, Carl is the only friend I have ever had' (177). Unlike Carl, who drifts in and out of Alexandra's life between long intervals, Marie is woven closely into the fabric of her daily existence. 'It is not often,' therefore, that Alexandra 'let[s] three days go by without seeing Marie'—and when Carl does reappear at one point, and Alexandra postpones her regular visit, she frets guiltily that her younger friend will think she has 'forsaken her' (130). Later, of course, it is Alexandra herself who feels woefully 'forsaken' when she learns of Marie's affair with Emil:

> Could you believe that of Marie Tovesky? I would have been cut to pieces, little by little, before I would have betrayed her trust in me! (303)

Not only is it revealing that Alexandra apparently does not recognise Marie 'Tovesky' as Frank Shabata's wife, but her emphatic language and words of 'betrayal' and 'forsaken' anguish also clearly echo the 'romantic rhetoric' of 'emotional intensity' which Smith-Rosenberg notes as characteristic of close female friendships before the late nineteenth century (59).

Furthermore, while Alexandra's relationship with Carl remains a fairly dispassionate affair throughout—arrested, in fact, at the stage of hand-holding until a light kiss at the very end of the novel is offered as a prelude to a marriage of 'friends' (308–09)—her relationship with Marie allows for a great measure of uninhibited physical contact. At one point, for example, Marie runs up to her friend 'painting,'[4] throws 'her arms about Alexandra,' and then gives her arm an affectionate 'little squeeze' as they begin to walk together (134). And Alexandra similarly expresses her sentiments by 'pinch[ing] Marie's cheek playfully' when they meet (192). The two women have an acute and joyful sense of each other's physical proximity as well; hence, Alexandra confides that she is 'glad' to have Marie living 'so near' her, while Marie delights in the delicate scent of rosemary on Alexandra's dress (119, 134).

Like Cather herself, who so ardently admired female beauty that she sometimes strapped herself financially by loaning money to attractive actresses whose plays she reviewed (Woodress 105; O'Brien, *Willa Cather* 134), Alexandra responds to Marie with

4. A misprint: the word is "panting."

pleasure and admiration on an aesthetic level. Of course, almost every character in the novel does, for Marie's spectacular 'tiger eyes' (11) are irresistibly captivating. Indeed, at the risk of pressing a fine (but in this context, relevant) point too closely, Marie's striking eyes may reflect a subtle authorial allusion to Balzac's sensational lesbian novel, *The Girl With the Golden Eyes*—particularly since that novel is believed to have been inspired by the real-life relationship of George Sand (Cather's avowed role-model) and a woman named Marie Dorval.[5] At any rate, Alexandra is especially drawn by the unique blend of exoticism and innocence in Marie, comparing her to both a 'queer foreign kind of doll' and a 'little brown rabbit' (192, 133). Carl's observation of Marie's sensuously 'full' and 'parted' lips, and of the 'points of yellow light dancing in her eyes' (135) reinforces Alexandra's perception of her friend as an attractively animated yet vulnerable young woman who is 'too young and pretty for this sort of life' (121).

With Marie, Alexandra thus enjoys an emotional and physical intimacy which is a source of innocent pleasure to them both. The crucial point, however, is how others perceive their relationship. Through the perspective of Carl Lindstrum, Cather subtly but deftly probes the perverse interpretations apt to be construed from such close homosocial bonds in the new era of 'scientific' sexology. When Alexandra explains to Carl how 'nice' it has felt for her to have 'a friend' at 'the other end' of the path between the Bergson-Shabata homesteads since he has lived there, for instance, Carl responds with a rueful 'smile': 'All the same, I hope it has n't [*sic*] been *quite* the same' (130). It is an odd remark, laden with an innuendo that makes Alexandra look at Carl 'with surprise,' and respond defensively:

> Why no, of course not. Not the same. She could not very well take your place, if that's what you mean. I'm friendly with all my neighbors, I hope. But Marie is really a companion, someone I can talk to quite frankly. You would n't want me to be more lonely than I have been would you? (130)

To this, Carl laughs nervously, fusses with his hair, and replies uncertainly:

> Of course I don't. I ought to be thankful that this path has n't been worn by—well, by friends with more pressing errands than your little Bohemian is likely to have. (131)

5. On the relevance of Balzac's novel in the context of late nineteenth-century French aesthetic-decadent literature, see Faderman, *Surpassing the Love of Men* 254, 267. Cather was known to be a fan of such literature, which strengthens the possibility that she had indeed come across Balzac's book; see O'Brien, *Willa Cather* 134–35; Woodress 119; and Brown 98, 103.

Carl realises that he 'ought' to be thankful that Alexandra's female 'friend' is not 'likely' to pose a serious rival for her affections, but his hesitant manner and doubtful language suggest that his suspicions are obviously not allayed. When he does, therefore, have an opportunity to scrutinise the type of relationship the two women share, he carefully 'watch[es]' them from 'a little distance' (135). That they make a 'pretty picture' together is his first thought, but after observing Marie's intense and delighted absorption in Alexandra for a time, Carl goes on to reflect: 'What a waste . . . she ought to be doing all that for a sweetheart. How awkwardly things come about!' (136).

Significantly, it is not long after Carl's reappearance on the Divide that the pleasant state of affairs between Cather's heroine and the attractive young immigrant girl begin to alter. Indeed, the shift in Alexandra and Marie's friendship, the point at which each woman first begins to distance herself warily from the other, occurs as issues of their respective heterosexual relationships begin to impinge upon their lives. When it comes to the subject of Carl and her differences with her brothers over him, for example, Alexandra 'instinctive[ly]' feels that 'about such things she and Marie would not understand one another' (188). Suddenly, when the topic is Alexandra's relationship with a male, Marie no longer appears to represent the 'real companion' she 'can talk to quite frankly' (130). It is a blind 'instinct' which Alexandra follows without testing when she has the opportunity. For when during one of their last intimate moments together, Marie begins to speak 'frankly' about her own unhappy union with Frank, Alexandra withdraws guardedly from the conversation, abruptly recalling Marie to the 'crochet patterns' for which they have been searching: 'no good,' she rationalises, can ever come 'from talking about such things' (198).

Immediately after this incident, a reciprocal process of withdrawal takes place on Marie's part. As the narrator observes:

> After that day the younger woman seemed to shrink more and more into herself. When she was with Alexandra she was not spontaneous and frank as she used to be. She seemed to be brooding over something, and holding something back. (200–01)

The pain, confusion, or guilt which each woman experiences over her respective relationship—or relationships—with men is the one thing they cannot share with each other directly, and it is as a stave which wedges them further and further apart. Finally, when Alexandra places her hand tenderly on the arm of a pale and tired-looking Marie, just after Emil has drained the blood from her cheeks with an electrifying kiss, she can feel her young friend 'shiver': 'Marie stiffened under that kind, calm hand. Alexandra drew back, perplexed and hurt' (226).

Cather's novel thus clearly traces the steady disintegration of a formerly intimate female friendship to the point of physical recoil and abiding resentment. But what happened? Certainly, in so far that the 'pretty picture' which consists of Alexandra and Marie becomes 'awkward' only when men enter into it, it may be argued that Cather's depiction of a loving female relationship is intended as an illustration of the sad consequences of social pressures which compel women (and men) to erect psychic barriers between one another in an obsessively heterocentric culture—lest their affection, that is, be construed by the Carls of the world as suspiciously 'unnatural.' If this is what Cather attempted, however, she does not wholly accomplish her goal. For although she does begin to critique the contemporary attitude toward, and perception of, innocently romantic female friendships, she eventually abandons this daring impulse in what seems a silent submission to the established sexual prejudices and stereotypes of her day, a submission which sharply reinforces O'Brien's contention that Cather never fully 'freed herself from male constructs of femininity' ('The Thing Not Named' 596; *Willa Cather* 124–25). Because indeed, the whole tragic point of the devolution of Alexandra and Marie's relationship is undermined by Cather's ultimate reliance upon the archetypal paradigm of the fallen Eve for Marie, and by her apparently unqualified endorsement of a conventional marriage for Alexandra—an authorial enthusiasm which is nevertheless unconvincing because it purports to applaud a heterosexual alliance which has been portrayed from the beginning as tepid and watery, at best.

Ultimately, then, Cather's careful dissolution and final destruction of the poignant bond first established between her women represent an authorial retreat into literary convention and rather insipid romanticism. It is a retreat which is in itself tragic. For as the character of Carl suggests, Cather was at some point while writing her novel obviously aware of just how 'awkwardly' her portrayal of an artless and genuine female friendship might appear to her modern audience. Whether unconsciously or with a painful memory of her own past friendship with Louise Pound, Cather therefore defuses the potentially scandalous subject she has begun to probe, before it becomes too overt an issue within the text. The simple beauty of a loving friendship between women was the one central aspect of the contemporary discourse of sexuality which Cather could not fully address, because it involved not merely an indirect, artistic inversion of her culture's metaphors, myths, and theories, but entailed, rather, a direct and necessarily polemical authorial entry into the heartland of the sexologists' 'frontier' territory, that twilight and controversial no-woman's land separating socially acceptable female companionship from illicit same-sex love. And for all the dramatic adolescent rejection of frocks and frills and curls; for all the aggressively outspoken, critical target-shooting of youth; for all the steadfast, personal commitments to other women in her maturity, this was something the adult 'Billy Cather, Jr' was not rebel enough to risk.

Works Cited

Bailey, Jennifer, 'The Dangers of Femininity in Willa Cather's Fiction.' *Journal of American Studies*, 16.3, 1982: pp. 391–406.

Brown, E.K., *Willa Cather: A Critical Biography*, completed by Leon Edel, New York: Knopf, 1953.

Cather, Willa, *O Pioneers!* (1913), Boston: Houghton, 1941.

———, *My Ántonia*, (1918), Cambridge, Mass.: Riverside P, 1926.

Ellis, Havelock, *Sexual Inversion*, Vol. 2 of *Studies in the Psychology of Sex*, 6 vols., 3rd ed, Philadelphia: Davis, 1918.

Faderman, Lillian, *Surpassing the Love of Men: Romantic Friendship and Love Between Women from the Renaissance to the Present*, New York: William Morrow, 1981.

———, 'The Morbidification of Love Between Women by Nineteenth-Century Sexologists,' *Journal of Homosexuality*, 4.1, 1978: pp. 73–90.

Kolodny, Annette, 'A Map for Rereading: Gender and the Interpretation of Literary Texts,' *The New Feminist Criticism: Essays on Women, Literature, and Theory*, ed. Elaine Showalter, New York: Pantheon, 1985, pp. 46–62.

Myers, Sandra L., *Westering Women and the Frontier Experience, 1800–1915*, Albuquerque: U of New Mexico P, 1982.

O'Brien, Sharon, *Willa Cather: The Emerging Voice*, New York: OUP, 1987.

———, ' "The Thing Not Named": Willa Cather as a Lesbian Writer,' *Signs* 9.4, 1984: pp. 576–99.

Ostenso, Martha, *Wild Geese*, Toronto: McClelland & Stewart, 1925.

Rich, Adrienne, 'Compulsive Heterosexuality and Lesbian Existence,' *Signs*, 5.4, 1980: pp. 631–61.

Robinson, Phyllis, *Willa: The Life of Willa Cather*, Garden City, New York: Doubleday, 1983.

Rule, Jane, *Lesbian Images*, Garden City, New York: Doubleday, 1975.

Smith-Rosenberg, Carroll, *Disorderly Conduct: Visions of Gender in Victorian America*, New York: Knopf, 1985.

Woodress, James, *Willa Cather: A Literary Life*, Lincoln: U of Nebraska P, 1987.

MARILEE LINDEMANN

[*O Pioneers!* and the Cultural Politics of the Progressive Era]†

O Pioneers! can be read as an un-ironic reiteration of America's cherished 'heroic myth of national destiny', revisionist only in that it places a woman at the centre of 'America's story' of transplanting and resettlement.[1] However, beyond its importance as a novel of the soil or of female development, *O Pioneers!* may also be read as an aggressively managed novel of discipline—as a story which insists upon and enforces a particular vision of bodily, social, and narrative order. To consider it in these terms is to consider its place not in myth but in social history—and specifically within the context of the cultural politics of the Progressive Era, with its mania for systemization, efficiency, and both social and sexual hygiene.[2] The novel's rage for all kinds of order is evident, for example, in its images of a range of bodies and the ways in which they signify discipline or its lack, normativity or deviance, idealization or objection.[3] *O Pioneers!* is fond of putting bodies on display and interpreting their elaborate semiotics in terms which suggest the taxonimist's propensity for judgement and classification. The Norwegian hammock-maker and religious mystic called 'Crazy Ivar' by his neighbours is described as 'a queerly shaped old man' (p. 25) whose 'bandy legs' are 'completely misfitted to his broad, thick body and heavy shoulders' (p. 52). Ivar lives at war with his misshapen body, which, because it is 'strong, rebellious', threatens always to fall into disorder. He is obsessively clean yet goes barefooted to allow for 'the indulgence of the body', even allowing himself to 'trampl[e] in filth when my desires are low' (p. 154). Alexandra, on the other hand, has an idealized 'gleaming white body', but hers, too, is subject to a regime of discipline and prohibition. When she stays in bed late on Sunday mornings, indulging in erotic reveries of being lifted up and carried by a man 'yellow like the sunlight', she rises

† From *O Pioneers!*, edited by Marilee Lindemann.

1. Sharon O'Brien connects *O Pioneers!* to 'America's story' in *The Emerging Voice*, 74.
2. The period in the USA from about 1890 to 1920 is generally considered the Progressive Era, though there is a wide range of opinion on what exactly 'Progressivism' was. Suffice it to say that, in the wake of massive social transformations, wrought by industrialization and urbanization, Progressivism was a broad-based, multifaceted effort to eliminate corruption in government, restructure governmental institutions, and relieve the kinds of social and economic problems created by the growing disparity between the rich and the poor. Guy Reynolds examines Cather's relationship to Progressivism in *Willa Cather in Context: Progress, Race, Empire* (New York, 1996).
3. For a more complete discussion of the issues outlined here, see my *Willa Cather: Queering America* (New York, 1999).

hastily and angrily and goes down to the bath-house, where she 'would stand in a tin tub and prosecute her bath with vigor' (p. 112). Alexandra manages her body with the same discipline she brings to the management of her farm and is an eloquent spokesperson for Progressive Era values that linked orderly bodies with well-run businesses: 'I think myself,' she blandly explains to Carl at one point, 'it is more pleasant to do business with people who are clean and healthy-looking' (p. 74).

The disorderly body is a threat to a society conceived of as a biomedical and economic system. It must be expelled to preserve the health and efficiency of the system. In *O Pioneers!* that point is made emphatically in the subplot of Emil and Marie, the adulterous lovers who must die because their bodies, entwined 'in the shadow of the mulberry tree' (p. 145), are seriously out of order. The tableau of their dead bodies in the Shabatas' orchard is the most elaborate of the corporeal displays in the novel, and the narrative compulsively returns to the scene, presenting it first through Frank's eyes, then through Ivar's, and finally through Alexandra's. The details of Marie's slow and bloody death after 'one ball had torn through her right lung, another had shattered the carotid artery' (p. 148) suggest that the punishment for lack of bodily discipline is severe, particularly for women (Emil's death is comparatively quick and painless). Even Alexandra, despite grieving for the loss of her brother and her best friend, seems to think the punishment just. Near the end of the novel she goes to visit their killer, Frank Shabata, in prison and tells him twice that the two victims were more to blame for their deaths than he was. She also vows to get Frank pardoned for his crimes and released from prison. Upon leaving, Alexandra pronounces herself '*immune* from evil tidings' (p. 164, emphasis added), a phrase which helps to explain her otherwise puzzling actions by suggesting that the murders of Emil and Marie are a necessary expulsion of elements perceived to be alien and threatening to Alexandra's 'immune' system. Their deaths signal the end of disorder and the consolidation of Alexandra's position at the pinnacle of the novel's bodily and social hierarchy. The end of their illicit and uncontrolled passion clears the path for her companionate marriage to Carl, which is announced in the last few paragraphs of the book. 'I think we shall be very happy,' Alexandra says to Carl. 'I haven't any fears. I think when friends marry, they are safe. We don't suffer like—those young ones' (p. 170). Her emphasis on the safety of their union is in keeping with the novel's interest in policing the individual body as a means of assuring the health of the larger social body. Such an interest, linking *O Pioneers!* with the vigorous crusades against prostitution and venereal disease that were waged throughout the Progressive Era,[4] demonstrates how fully Cather's novel is enmeshed in and engaged with the period in which it was produced.

To acknowledge the pressures of history and social context upon the 'classic' is not to diminish its literary value or status but to suggest that the 'classic' acquires much of its value or status achieving a rare combination of originality and familiarity. That is precisely the case with *O Pioneers*!. Early in the twentieth century its first readers responded warmly to the novelty of its setting, its subject, and its plucky 'Amazonian' heroine, but they also found confirmation of some of their most treasured fantasies about the making of America and some of their deepest fears about threats that might lead to its unmaking. As the twentieth century draws to a close readers can still find in the pages of this book the profound pleasures of a well-told story, even as we reckon with the tensions and contradictions that make Cather's beautifully rendered prairie such an eloquent symbol, not only of the nation's pioneer past but also of the energy, discipline, and often ferocious intolerance that accompanied its emergence as a modern industrial and imperial power. *O Pioneers*! is not merely an elegy for the glories of a lost past. It is also a case study in how Americans throughout this century would design and manage their futures.

MELISSA RYAN

The Enclosure of America: Civilization and Confinement in Willa Cather's *O Pioneers!*†

Willa Cather's public persona turns on the rhetoric of wide-open space. Since the beginning of Cather's career, journalists have romanticized the wild Willa of the prairie, often obscuring the relative refinement of the Cather family. The mature Cather, too, is pictured as most at home in the open air; a 1921 piece in the *Lincoln Sunday Star* is representative: "Miss Cather had elected to take her interview out-of-doors in the autumnal sunshine, walking.

4. For a discussion of these crusades, see John D'Emilio and Estelle B. Freedman, *Intimate Matters: A History of Sexuality in America* (New York, 1988), esp. chapter 9. Through her work on *McClure's Magazine*, from 1906 to 1913, Cather would have been familiar with the arguments of the social hygienists, whose works were published there on a regular basis. When, for example, her first novel, *Alexander's Bridge*, was serialized in *McClure's* in Feb.–Apr. 1912, its first two instalments ran concurrently with the last two instalments of a five-part series on prostitution by Hull House founder Jane Addams.

† From *American Literature*, Volume 75, pp. 275–303.

The fact is characteristic. She is an outdoor person, not far different in type from the pioneers and prima donnas whom she exalts."[1] The analog to the legend of Willa Cather, hoyden and pioneer, is the language in which the evolution of her literary career is described. Her art is commonly evaluated in spatial terms. "[Cather's] talents had no real scope in the drawing-rooms of New York and London," notes Louise Bogan in a 1931 piece in the *New Yorker*.[2] Just as her protagonist Alexandra Bergson in *O Pioneers!* (1913) "expresses herself best" in the soil,[3] so Cather needed the wide-open prairie to fully flex her romantic imagination. As Bernice Slote observes of *Alexander's Bridge*, the portrait of fashionable society with which Cather began her career as a novelist, "Realism is a constriction, a drawing in."[4] For the Willa Cather who would later be mythologized as "the untutored western girl running wild on her pony," as Slote puts it,[5] there could be no such constriction of the writerly self.

Given Cather's deep roots in the prairie she describes, readers of *O Pioneers!* have found, quite rightly, a substantial authorial investment in the values of Alexandra Bergson, Cather's heroic pioneer. Ten years after *O Pioneers!*, Cather published a panegyric of Nebraska's "first cycle" that seems to cohere flawlessly with the tone of her prairie novels:

> In Nebraska, as in so many other States, we must face the fact that the splendid story of the pioneers is finished, and that no new story worthy to take its place has yet begun. The generation that subdued the wild land and broke up the virgin prairie is passing, but it is still there, a group of rugged figures in the background which inspire respect, compel admiration. With these old men and women the attainment of material prosperity was a moral victory, because it was wrung from hard conditions, was the result of a struggle that tested character.[6]

Cather's celebration of this "moral victory" appears to be consistent with the image of Cather as the "outdoor person": in both cases, identity is a function of landscape. But if the figure of Cather as

1. "Willa Cather," interview by Eleanor Hinman, *Lincoln Sunday Star*, 6 November 1921; reprinted in *Willa Cather in Person*, ed. L. Brent Bohlke (Lincoln: Univ. of Nebraska Press, 1986), 42.
2. Louise Bogan, "Profiles: American Classic," *New Yorker*, 8 August 1931; reprinted in *Willa Cather in Person*, ed. Bohlke, 115.
3. Willa Cather, *O Pioneers!* (1913; reprint, New York: Penguin, 1989), 57. Further references to this source are to this edition and will be cited parenthetically as *OP*.
4. Bernice Slote, "The Kingdom of Art," in *The Kingdom of Art: Willa Cather's First Principles and Critical Statements 1893–1896*, ed. Bernice Slote (Lincoln: Univ. of Nebraska Press, 1966), 64.
5. Bernice Slote, "Writer in Nebraska," in *The Kingdom of Art*, 3.
6. Willa Cather, "Nebraska: The End of the First Cycle," *Nation*, September 1923, 238.

constructed for public consumption is predicated on a fantasy of unboundedness, there is a fundamental conflict between that author-figure and the pioneer she memorializes. The "splendid story of the pioneers" is a story of spatial reconfiguration. The pioneers in Cather's first novel of the soil encounter an overwhelming vastness, "fierce," "savage," and "uninterrupted" (*OP*, 10); in the process of settlement and cultivation, this vastness is organized into a "checker-board, marked off in squares of wheat and corn" (*OP*, 51). In other words, settlement introduces boundaries: the demarcation and delimitation of those "outdoor" spaces by which the mythologized Cather is so often defined. This incompatibility of values is, it seems, easily overlooked. For example, Cather's longtime friend Elizabeth Sergeant reports: "Any thoroughly untamed aspect of nature refreshed her. She said that the air was totally different where fields had never been cleared and harvested nor virgin forest cut. When I thought about this, I saw that her intimacy with nature lay at the very root of her relation to *O Pioneers!*"[7] Curiously, Sergeant does not remark upon the fact that Cather's "intimacy with nature" is very much at risk in *O Pioneers!*, a novel written in homage to those very practices of clearing and harvesting and cutting that implicitly contaminate the revivifying air of nature. There may be, then, a radical ambivalence at the center of Cather's frontier hagiography.[8]

7. Elizabeth Shepley Sergeant, *Willa Cather: A Memoir* (New York: Lippincott, 1953), 120.
8. Critics have devoted substantial attention to the novel's mystification of history in service of its epic enterprise. Cather's valorization of conquest as an imaginative act and concomitant erasure of both labor and the complex issues of settlement have been well documented, described variously as generic operations of romance (that is, romanticization) or pastoral (that is, pastoralization). For excellent examples of this aproach to the novel as a romance or pastoral, see Mike Fischer, "Pastoralism and Its Discontents: Willa Cather and the Burden of Imperialism," *Mosaic* 23 (winter 1990): 31–44; Blanche Gelfant, introduction to Willa Cather, *O Pioneers!* (New York: Penguin, 1989), ix–xxxvii; Demaree C. Peck, *The Imaginative Claims of the Artist in Willa Cather's Fiction: "Possession Granted by a Different Lease"* (Selinsgrove, Penn.: Susquehanna Univ. Press, 1996); Susan J. Rosowski, *The Voyage Perilous: Willa Cather's Romanticism* (Lincoln: Univ. of Nebraska Press, 1986); David Stouck, *Willa Cather's Imagination* (Lincoln: Univ. of Nebraska Press, 1975); and Louise H. Westling, *The Green Breast of the New World: Landscape, Gender, and American Fiction* (Athens: Univ. of Georgia Press, 1996). On the other hand, some of the most interesting recent work on the novel has reversed this dominant view. Feminist critics like Judith Fryer and Sharon O'Brien don't see *O Pioneers!* as a pastoral myth, but I believe their focus on what Fryer calls an "anti-mythic" journey (246) or on the novel's regendering of the traditional pastoral landscape obscures some important justificatory maneuvers in this narrative of origins (see, respectively, *Felicitous Space: The Imaginative Structures of Edith Wharton and Willa Cather* [Chapel Hill: Univ. of North Carolina Press, 1986]; and *Willa Cather: The Emerging Voice* [New York: Oxford Univ. Press, 1987]). Some critics do find a measure of ambivalence in Cather toward the project of imperialism, but focusing chiefly on later novels, they typically attribute any ill effects of the sod-breaking spirit to character's alienation from the founding values of pioneering. I propose that this assumption of a moral decline from an imagined peak of pioneer rectitude inadequately accounts for the conflicted and conflicting implications of "subduing the wild land." Guy Reynolds, while noting the depoliticization of Cather's Nebraska and the idealization of her pioneer,

To put it another way, as I will argue in these pages, a deep anxiety about the taming of the wilderness—about the very process of civilization—makes itself in *O Pioneers!* as a crisis of space. Despite the figurative work of Cather's protagonist, whose primary labor in the novel is the symbolic resolution of ethical conflict (which requires not a plow but a vision), we can track a fundamental connection between the project of pioneering and a process of enclosure that cannot be completely dispelled by the novel's rhetoric. Significantly, Alexandra's conquest of the wilderness is represented as a process of domestication. She makes a home on and of the plains by bringing order to the landscape: "You feel that, properly, Alexandra's house is the big out-of-doors, and that it is in the soil that she expresses herself best" (*OP*, 57). But while Alexandra's house is characterized by the spatial freedom of the "out-of-doors," the same language that expands Alexandra's house inevitably shrinks the space of "the wild land." This image may provide a starting point for an analysis of what it means to tame, to cultivate, or perhaps to "discipline" the wilderness.[9]

One sign of progress on the Divide is the enclosure of Old Mrs. Lee's feet in shoes. As mother-in-law to Alexandra's conspicuously Americanized brother Lou, Mrs. Lee is obliged to exchange her "little wooden tub" for a "great white" one, to abandon her habitual nightcap, and to submit her bare feet to confinement. While Mrs. Lee is bewildered and distressed by the demands of gentility, Alexandra finds Mrs. Lee's subjection to social nicety more amusing than disturbing. As she laughingly recalls, "We can remember when half our neighbors went barefoot in summer. I expect old Mrs. Lee would love to slip her shoes off now sometimes, if she dared" (*OP*, 64). This conflict between the old world and the new is more pointed in the case of Old Ivar, the eccentric Norwegian characterized by his intolerance of firearms, intense but idiosyncratic religiosity, and deep sympathy with the natural world. Ivar is allowed to remain unshod but faces a far more threatening discipli-

finds a measure of subversion of the myth of empire in *O Pioneers!* (*Willa Cather in Context: Progress, Race, Empire* [London: Macmillan, 1996], 58–60). To Reynolds's insightful reading, I would add that the novel is in conflict with itself in ways Cather does not fully control.

9. I use *discipline* in the sense elaborated by Michel Foucault in *Discipline and Punish: The Birth of the Prison*, as a phenomenon of spatial control: "[D]iscipline proceeds from the distribution of individuals in space" and "sometimes requires enclosure" (trans. Alan Sheridan [1978; reprint, New York: Vintage, 1995], 141). According to Foucault, this deployment of power is designed "to strengthen the social forces—to increase production, to develop the economy, spread education, raise the level of public morality; to increase and multiply" (208). My point is that there is an analogous relationship between the reconfiguration of land for the purpose of productivity and the reconfiguration of social or human space for the same purpose.

nary mechanism: the Hastings mental institution. Still, despite her emotional investment in the values of the old world, Alexandra is unruffled: she jokingly proposes her own household as an "asylum for old-time people" (*OP*, 64). The threat of confinement is then fully realized in the Nebraska state penitentiary, where Frank Shabata is incarcerated for killing his wife, Marie, and her lover, Alexandra's brother Emil, at the scene of their first and last tragic embrace. The image of Frank in the penitentiary provides an emblem for the theoretical relationship between civilization and enclosure that I will delineate—but considered in the context of history, that relationship isn't merely theoretical. The discourses of discipline and Americanization that underlie Cather's treatment of Mrs. Lee, Ivar, and Frank achieved particular force in the rhetoric of Indian policy during the same decades Cather fictionalizes in *O Pioneers!* In this image of the penitentiary we may also find traces of the disciplinary enclosure of Native Americans that Cather has deliberately forgotten in weaving her pioneer narrative. My essay concludes, therefore, with the suggestion that the removal of native populations to reservations—the confinement upon which the "moral victory" of the pioneer depends—constitutes the most deeply disavowed layer of meaning embedded in Cather's complex motif of enclosure.

"Hard Molds" of Conformity

To begin uncovering the relationship between episodes of enclosure in the novel, it is useful to remember the larger context of nativism and ethnic conflict that may be read into the figure of Mrs. Lee. Cather has been notoriously critical of Americanization and its effects on the fondly remembered immigrants of her childhood in Nebraska. In a 1924 interview in the *New York Times Book Review*, she remembers the multicultural Midwest of her growing-up years: "A 'foreigner' was a person foreign to our manners or custom of living, not possible prey for reform. Nobody ever cheated a foreigner . . . . Nobody investigated them; nobody regarded them as laboratory specimens." But in twentieth-century America, Cather continues, progress manifests itself as intrusion:

> They have come here to live in the sense that they lived in the Old World, and if they were let alone their lives might turn into the beautiful ways of their homeland. But they are not let alone. Social workers, missionaries—call them what you will—go after them, hound them, pursue them and devote their days and nights toward the great task of turning them into stupid replicas of smug American citizens. This passion for American-

> izing everything and everybody is a deadly disease with us. We do it the way we build houses.[1]

This representation of the American drive toward conformity (the domestication of immigrants, whereby citizens are "built" like houses) as an assault of ethnic integrity parallels Cather's critique of "the hard molds of American provincialism."[2] A modern America shaped by what people will think and say is a confining social space—a "hard mold" of small-mindedness, routine, and scripted behavior. Moreover, as with Alexandra's house out-of-doors, domestication in every sense of the word implies the shrinking of territory. The comparison of Americanized (domesticated) immigrants to houses (domestic spaces) is apt indeed; domesticated, they are made to fit into the architecture of American identity.

The sense of confinement implicit in the language Cather uses to describe a twentieth-century phenomenon echoes a younger Cather's objection to the fashion imperatives of cultivated society. Cather biographer Mildred Bennett reports that "Mrs. Cather, who prided herself on her knowledge of high fashion, frequently objected to Willa's way of dressing and particularly her violent color combinations. Willa admitted that she loved colors like a savage," and manifested "an intense dislike of the corseted discomfort of 'civilized' apparel."[3] Apparel is similarly coded in *O Pioneers!* We can see the same discomfort in the unrefined (or "savage") Mrs. Lee's resistance to the shoes that function as a sign of civilization. And significantly, the civilization that threatens the freedom of Mrs. Lee's feet is that of Americanization; her bare feet signify not only "savagery" but ethnicity. This is made clear in the contrast between Mrs. Lee and her painfully shod daughter, Annie: "Her tight, high-heeled shoes give her an awkward walk, and she is always more or less preoccupied with her clothes . . . . Annie and Lou sometimes speak Swedish at home, but Annie is almost as much afraid of being 'caught' at it as ever her mother was of being caught barefoot" (*OP*, 67). Annie, coded American by her high heels (which give her an unnatural gait), considers her Swedishness something to hide—like naked feet. These family dynamics in the novel suggest that the pernicious force of Americanization comes not exclusively from American nativists but from within the immigrant community, if those immigrants are successful pioneers (that is, successful "civilizers") like the Bergson brothers. In other words,

1. Willa Cather, "Restlessness Such as Ours Does Not Make for Beauty," interview by Rose C. Feld, *New York Times Book Review*, 21 December 1924; reprinted in *Willa Cather in Person*, ed. Bohlke, 71–72.
2. Cather, "Nebraska," 238.
3. Mildred R. Bennett, *The World of Willa Cather* (New York: Dodd, Mead, 1951), 30–31.

civilization and Americanization are mutually constitutive processes resulting in "corseted discomfort."

On the surface, the second-generation attitude toward first-generation eccentricities may appear to be symptomatic of the pioneer spirit degraded. But the confinement of ethnic markers as represented in this episode is inherent in the founding principles of the pioneer. To be more precise, the pioneer is defined by her taming of the wilderness—of nature. Annie Lee, with the unnatural walk of civilized shoes, is thus an emblem for the successful pioneering enterprise: the reconfiguration of nature.

We should note particularly that bodies are a corollary site of reconfiguration in this novel famous for its reconfigured "checkerboard" landscape. Critics have consistently called attention to the reciprocity between land and landscaper, as Alexandra feels "in her own body the joyous germination in the soil" (*OP*, 135); accordingly, disciplined bodies both testify to and make possible the ascendancy of civilization, of somatic wilderness tamed. Marilee Lindemann's analysis of queerness in Cather's work is especially useful here. Lindemann defines *queer* as the resistance against "a system that seeks to control difference by policing the boundaries between the natural and the unnatural, male and female, white and nonwhite"—or, we might add, between the civilized and the "savage."[4] As Lindemann demonstrates, in the challenge posed by queer bodies, the disciplinary imperative fixes on bodily disorder as a disruption of the orderly community. As Lindemann claims, Alexandra's "un-queer" body stands as "an allegory of nation-building predicated on the repudiation or containment of the 'queer' and emblematized in skin so smooth and white it is said to possess 'the freshness of the snow itself.' "[5] If landscapes, bodies, and nations all stand in for each other, then the work of pioneering manifests itself in the human landscape as well.

Humor defuses this conflict in the novel, as Alexandra presents herself as a refuge—an asylum—where feet can be free: "Alexandra shook with laughter. 'Poor old Mrs. Lee! . . . Never mind; when she comes to visit me, she can do all the old things in the old way' " (*OP*, 164). But Alexandra, as the very embodiment of the pioneering spirit—of, in Lindemann's terms, the "un-queer"—cannot ultimately provide sanctuary; she is, in essence, the agent of Mrs. Lee's enclosure.

Sergeant's reflections on an incident at the market with Cather

4. Marilee Lindemann, *Willa Cather: Queering America* (New York: Columbia Univ. Press, 1999), 7–8.
5. Ibid., 46.

may help to illustrate Cather's view of American conformity as a violation of nature:

> We paused to buy from a great crony of hers, an old Italian in a blue cotton cap, with stubbled chin and obtrusive tooth. Willa compared him to a correct young man who happened to pass, wearing a hard straw hat with a black band. Surely that one sold bonds on Wall Street, and no doubt his mother had had his teeth straightened! Mouths should be left as nature made them—mouths were individual as ears, or eyes . . . but the dentists insisted on deadly conformity.[6]

Here, the American whose natural (bodily) individuality has been tamed is contrasted with the immigrant whose status is signaled by a sort of dental wilderness. Americanization, in other words, reproduces the essence of pioneering—taming the wilderness—and Mrs. Lee, then, is the target not of the pioneer spirit gone bad—contaminated by crass materialism—but of the pioneer spirit itself.

Symbolic Fences

The enclosure that results from civilization is both physical—the cramping of toes—and figurative—the symbolic constriction of an increasingly legal society. One way to characterize the state of civilization is by its increasing reliance on symbols; that is, the progress from the savage to the civil is a rejection of the natural in favor of the constructed. In an early *Nebraska State Journal* sketch, Cather evokes the idea of law to represent alienation from a natural past. In this nostalgic piece about "a little gray-haired woman with a look of sad experience" playing piano for a dance, Cather contrasts the litigious adult dancers with the emotional sincerity (or naturalness) of youth: "[The pianist] knows those of us who still carry little seared places from the old flames that died hard, she knows those of us who obtained our heart's desires and have since sought refuge from them by process of law, she knows that the friend of my youth, whom I loved better than myself and to whom I gave my sweetheart, I yesterday sued for twenty thousand dollars."[7] A simi-

6. Sergeant, *Willa Cather*, 116–17.
7. Willa Cather, "One Way of Putting It," *Nebraska State Journal*, 26 November 1893; reprinted in *The World and the Parish: Willa Cather's Articles and Reviews, 1893–1902*, ed. William M. Curtin, 2 vols. (Lincoln: Univ. of Nebraska Press, 1970), 1:10–11. In language that characterizes this increasingly civil status as a form of constriction or confinement, Cather castigated the "cramping" laws of Nebraska in a 1921 address. As reported in the *Lincoln Evening State Journal* under the headline "State Laws are Cramping," Cather charged: "Nebraska is particularly blessed with laws calculated to regulate the personal life of her citizens . . . . They are not laws that trample you underfoot and crush you but laws that just sort of cramp one" (31 October 1921; reprinted in *Willa Cather in Person*, ed. Bohlke, 147). For a much more pointed indictment of the state as a punitive entity, see also Cather's 1893 story "The Clemency of the Court."

lar pattern illustrating the ascendancy of legal constructs turns up in *O Pioneers!*: When Mrs. Hiller's hogs get into Frank Shabata's wheat, he threatens to "take dat old woman to de court" (*OP*, 94). The good fences that make good neighbors no longer hold; in civilized society, fences are provided by law instead.

This link between civilization and symbolic enclosure reflects the fundamental premise of the Lockean social contract: Law exists to regulate—to tame—the ethical wilderness of our barbaric instincts. Put another way, civil structure overwrites natural law just as dentists straighten the natural savagery of teeth. Criminality—the violation of the Lockean contract—is thus associated with nature. As Foucault confirms in *Discipline and Punish*, "[T]he criminal designated as the enemy of all, whom it is in the interest of all to track down, falls outside the pact, disqualifies himself as a citizen and emerges, bearing within him as it were, a *wild fragment of nature*; he appears as a villain, a monster, a madman, perhaps, a sick and, before long, 'abnormal' individual."[8] The penal institution that literalizes the symbolic fences of law is then equivalent to the Nebraska checkerboard that emerges from the "the wild land" of *O Pioneers!*: evidence of nature tamed, of wild land broken, the ironic sign of the pioneer's "moral victory."

We can see this dynamic in the Ivar episode, where difference is constructed as insanity, and insanity is made interchangeable with criminality. Ivar is characterized by his inability to speak English and his hyperability to communicate with animals. As Carl explains to Emil, "He came to doctor our mare when she ate green corn and swelled up most as big as the water-tank. He petted her just like you do your cats. I couldn't understand much he said, for he don't talk any English, but he kept patting her and groaning as if he had the pain himself" (*OP*, 22). While Carl sees the world in man-made terms (nature is made comprehensible by the figure of the water-tank), Ivar lives in such sympathy with animal nature that he feels the pain of the mare. Likewise, his home is indistinguishable from the wilderness: "Ivar had lived for three years in the clay bank, without defiling the face of nature any more than the coyote that had lived there before him had done" (*OP*, 24). Notably, Ivar's idiosyncrasies (especially his relation to nature) are tolerated while the prairie remains wild, but in a neat parallel, Ivar is tamed with the land—he becomes the human testament to pioneering. Having lost his land through "mismanagement," he is now installed in Alexandra's household (*OP*, 59). His refusal to work the land disqualifies him from society, but although too old to work in the fields, he has

8. Foucault, *Discipline and Punish*, 101, my emphasis.

been made to work for Alexandra. What's at stake here is labor.[9] As the task of the pioneer is to make nature productive, Ivar must be transformed from unproductive wilderness into a productive labor force.

Not satisfied by this disciplinary tactic, Alexandra's brothers lobby to have Ivar sent to the asylum. Since criminality is marked by the "wild fragment of nature," Ivar as a figure of incompletely tamed wilderness is construed by Lou and Oscar as dangerous, and the threat must be confined. As Ivar reports, "They say that your brothers are afraid—God forbid!—that I may do you some injury when my spells are on me. Mistress, how can any one think that?—that I could bite the hand that fed me!" (*OP*, 62). Ivar still views the world from the perspective of animal nature, rationalizing his harmlessness by way of natural law. In other words, he has been incompletely assimilated into the structure of civilization. Ivar makes his own status as a marginal figure quite plain:

> The way here is for all to do alike. I am despised because I do not wear shoes, because I do not cut my hair, and because I have visions. At home, in the old country, there were many like me, who had been touched by God, or who had seen things in the graveyard at night and were different afterward. We thought nothing of it, and let them alone. But here, if a man is different in his feet or in his head, they put him in the asylum. . . . That is the way; they have built the asylum for people who are different, and they will not even let us live in the holes with the badgers. (*OP*, 62)

Once again, the condition of savagery—too close a connection with the natural—is ethnically coded. As Ivar implies, the force of Americanization confines not just difference but ethnic difference (that which is tolerated in the "old country"). Ultimately, the work of the pioneer (taming the wilderness) is the work of the law (civilizing the savage) is the work of conformity (Americanizing the foreigner). And this work, as the figure of the asylum suggests, expresses itself in the delimitation of space.

As she does with Mrs. Lee, Alexandra again presents herself and her household as a refuge. But the irony here is far more meaningful than in the matter of Mrs. Lee's bare feet. When Alexandra pro-

9. As Michel Foucault makes explicit, "Confinement . . . is a 'police' matter. Police, in the precise sense that the classical epoch gave to it—that is, the totality of measures which make work possible and necessary for all those who could not live without it . . . Before having the medical meaning we give it, or that at least we like to suppose it has, confinement was required by something quite different from any concern with curing the sick. What made it necessary was an imperative of labor" (*Madness and Civilization: A History of Insanity in the Age of Reason*, trans. Richard Howard [1965; reprint, New York: Vintage, 1988], 46).

poses her household as "an asylum for old-time people," she's quite right (*OP*, 64). Lou and Oscar's talk of the Hastings institution merely mystifies the fact that Ivar is already within the confines of the asylum. As Alexandra concedes to her brothers, "In my opinion Ivar has just as much right to his own way of dressing and thinking as we have. But I'll see that he doesn't bother other people. *I'll keep him at home*" (*OP*, 69, my emphasis). Her household, presented as *an* asylum (sanctuary), is ultimately *the* asylum (the "juridical space," in Foucault's terms, of disciplinary confinement).[1]

It is worthwhile to consider in more detail this convertibility in the notion of asylum. As Leo Marx details, asylum was a key concept in the original pastoral propaganda of the new world. In early-eighteenth-century promotional documents, "many colonists described the new land as a retreat, a place to retire to away from the complexity, anxiety, and oppression of European society. A favorite epithet was *asylum*."[2] This is the sense we get of Ivar's home: it is a protective dwelling, like a burrow, in the hillside itself, which makes literal the idea that nature offers a spiritual refuge for the world-weary. But as the American civilization developing out of that asylum progresses, the notion takes an ironic turn. The institutional asylum is still the dwelling place of nature—but here, the natural is construed as dangerous. Thus, the institutional asylum is the confinement of nature for the protection of civilization; it is civilization that achieves a kind of sanctuary by cutting off and containing the wilderness. Ivar's opposition of natural asylum—badger holes—to institutional asylum in the passage quoted above points to this semantic shift, just as Alexandra's "asylum for old-time people," in simultaneously carrying both meanings of *asylum*, indicates that the institutional asylum is deeply involved with the fundamental idea of America as a natural asylum.

In Ivar's case, institutional confinement remains only a threat; he is merely semantically committed to the asylum. But that potential threat is realized in Frank Shabata's story. Frank's incarceration may be seen as the consequence of his pioneering marital spirit—his "husbandry" of Marie. The charge that "[f]or three years he had been trying to break her spirit" recalls the breaking of wild land, symbolized by "a horse that no one knows how to break to harness, that runs wild and kicks things to pieces" (*OP*, 179, 15). Murdering Marie merely literalizes the violence of taming the wilderness, of

1. Foucault, *Madness and Civilization*, 269. See also Lindemann, *Willa Cather*: "Ivar has in effect been to the asylum without ever actually going there, having internalized the disciplinary mechanisms Foucault associates with asylums" (38). I would add that this figurative asylum also, if redundantly, finds material walls in Alexandra's house, and that she is deeply implicated in this process of internalization.
2. Leo Marx, *The Machine in the Garden: Technology and the Pastoral Ideal in America* (1964; reprint, New York: Oxford Univ. Press, 2000), 87.

breaking her spirit; and if the activity of the pioneer necessarily implies containment, it is then ironically appropriate that Frank is effectively incarcerated by his own attempt to "cultivate."

The temporary insanity that drives Frank to commit double murder is linked, like Ivar's criminal madness, to nature. Just after the fatal shots, "[h]e dropped on his knees beside the hedge and crouched like a rabbit"; he then "stood like the hare when the dogs are approaching from all sides. And he ran like a hare, back and forth about that moonlit space" (*OP*, 177, 178). Moreover, Frank's crime is associated not just with animal nature but with his own nature, with the human nature that is purposefully set aside in legal, civil society: "Being what he was, [Alexandra] felt, Frank could not have acted otherwise" (*OP*, 193). When we see Frank in prison, the essential purpose of the civil institution becomes manifest. Human nature is stripped away by a penal system that deprives him of a meaningful name, the marker of personhood: "You the lady that wanted to talk to 1037? Here he is" (*OP*, 198). Indeed, Frank Shabata has been transformed from a person into a number: a pure sign. He is bereft of his reason, that which would separate him from an animal—"I no can t'ink without my hair"—and, echoing Ivar's ethnic otherness, "I forget English." He seemed to Alexandra "somehow, not altogether human" (*OP*, 199, 200). He is, therefore, wholly under the control of the state; in this sense, he is associated with the wilderness tamed, like a wild horse broken to harness.

Again, Alexandra presents herself as the solution to the crisis of enclosure. Her pledge to have Frank released echoes her promises to keep Ivar out of the asylum and Mrs. Lee out of her shoes. In this case, she proposes the land itself as the redemptive source of freedom; by promising to liberate Frank from the institution, she is promising him the original "asylum" of America. Safely back on the Divide, Alexandra tells Carl: " 'I thought when I came out of that prison, where poor Frank is, that I should never feel free again. But I do, here.' Alexandra took a deep breath and looked off into the red west" (*OP*, 208). But here we see the novel divided against itself: Cather's pioneer epic is undermined by this invocation of the West as mere pastoral nostalgia, because this longing for breathing room inevitably appears precisely when that open space is unrecoverable. Ironically, Alexandra's pledge to liberate Frank rests on a paradigm of literal space—as if there is territory outside the prison walls. But the checkerboard prairie is caught up in the figurative legal fences of civil society whose boundaries are less easily crossed.

Nearly twenty years after Frederick Jackson Turner's famous 1893 thesis, a mere decade before the landmark census of 1920 that would quantify the transformation of the United States into an urban population, Alexandra's westward gaze can only be nostalgic: a yearning for asylum when the irrevocable semantic shift from refuge in nature to refuge from nature has already occurred. Alexandra "refused with horror the warden's cordial invitation to 'go through the institution' " (*OP*, 202)—to revel, that is, in the proud testament to a civilization that has produced so efficient a machine for breaking wild horses to harness. And refuse with horror she well might, for her assertion of opposition between the prison and her own tamed wilderness is ultimately a false claim.

Cather's Indian Removal

I have attempted to show the interconnected levels of significance associated with confinement as a manifestation of Cather's latent ambivalence toward the pioneering enterprise. There is, in addition, a silenced historical narrative that may be read out of this connection between civilization and confinement. Finally, therefore, I would like to propose that confinement in the novel also evokes the historical act of enclosure most intimately connected to the establishment of white civilization and most notably absent from Cather's narrative of those origins: the removal of Native Americans to reservations. Cather has tried to erase the Indian from her Nebraska landscape, but we may find that the vanished Indian returns as an unconscious element of her text.[3]

In discussing Cather's aversion to Americanization, it is useful to remember that the discourse of assimilation was not limited to immigrants—it was also a key theme of the Indian debate. Given Cather's sympathetic concern for foreigners within the state, then, we might wonder what she thought about the literal enclosure of "person[s] foreign to our manners or custom of living" on reservations or in Indian schools. Many of Cather's statements on the ethnic integrity of immigrants could be read out of context as an eloquent defense of tribal rights. However, it is highly unlikely that she made any conscious connection between white Northern European immigrants and the Indians those newcomers helped displace. As Slote points out, "[Cather] lived in Nebraska in the 1880s and 1890s, when Indians were noticed in the newspapers chiefly as warring tribes with dirty living habits. In any case, they were far from Red Cloud, and Wounded Knee was only a column or so of

3. Lucy Maddox has persuasively argued that all nineteenth-century writing in one way or another addresses the "Indian question" (*Removals: Nineteenth-Century American Literature and the Politics of Indian Affairs* [New York: Oxford Univ. Press, 1991], 10–11). I would add that the production or rehearsal of national origin mythologies in any period cannot avoid engaging these questions on some level.

print. Literary views in Nebraska were composed in highly romanticized legends."[4] Of course, Cather couldn't consciously establish a sympathetic bond with the Native Americans whose dispossession was the prerequisite for her pioneer epic. Cather said in an August 1913 *Philadelphia Record* interview: "It is always hard to write about the things that are near to your heart, from a kind of instinct of self-protection you distort them and disguise them."[5] She's not thinking of Indians at all in this statement, but the point is well taken; she has to protect her own narrative of origins by mystifying history. We can see the rhetorical process of self-protection in the very same conversation. Cather tells her interviewer:

> My grandfather's homestead was about eighteen miles from Red Cloud—a little town on the Burlington, named after the old Indian chief who used to come hunting in that country, and who buried his daughter on the top of one of the river bluffs south of the town. Her grave had been looted for her rich furs and beadwork long before my family went West, but we children used to find arrowheads there and some of the bones of her pony that had been strangled above her grave.[6]

In this one passage, we find both the history she needs to "distort and disguise" (the Anglo-Indian relationship characterized by "looting" of various sorts) and her disavowal of participation or responsibility (it happened "long before" her particular pioneers arrived).

We find similar maneuvers in her brief history of Nebraska written for the *Nation* in 1923. Cather acknowledges that "[b]efore 1860 civilization did no more than nibble at the eastern edge of the State, along the river bluffs. Lincoln, the present capital, was open prairie; and the whole of the great plain to the westward was still a sunny wilderness, where the tall red grass and the buffalo and the

4. Bernice Slote, "Willa Cather and Plains Culture," in *Vision and Refuge: Essays on the Literature of the Great Plains*, ed. Virginia Faulkner with Frederick C. Luebke (Lincoln: Univ. of Nebraska Press, 1982), 98–99. But Slote's explanation doesn't put an end to the question. Fischer emphasizes that " 'columns of print' describing the Indians did in fact exist. On one level, some late-nineteenth-century Nebraskans were still aware of the Indians, as they could not help being, given how recently—as late as the 1870s—much of western Nebraska had still been under Sioux control" ("Pastoralism," 33). Furthermore, it may not be wholly accurate to assume that the entirety of Nebraska press coverage would preclude awareness of or even sympathy with the increasing enclosure of native peoples. For example, James C. Olson details the case of the arbitrarily relocated Ponca Indians in his *History of Nebraska*: "The plight of the Poncas attracted wide attention, and a commission appointed by President Hayes in 1880 to inquire into the matter worked out an arrangement whereby those who wanted to return to Nebraska . . . were allowed to do so" ([Lincoln: Univ. of Nebraska Press, 1955], 137). While Cather would have been too young to take notice of this particular case, the "wide attention" attracted by the Poncas suggests that the plight of dispossessed Native Americans may not have been entirely obscured by romanticized legends.
5. Willa Cather, "Willa Cather Talks of Work," interview by F. H., *Philadelphia Record*, 9 August 1913; reprinted in *Kingdom of Art*, ed. Slote, 449.
6. Ibid., 448.

Indian hunter were undisturbed." Yet she can simultaneously claim that "[i]t was a State before there were people in it."[7] While this claim refers literally to the legal status of Nebraska and its inhabitants, her reference to "people" when what she means is citizens also implies that the non-white inhabitants of the region at the time it achieved statehood were not people. If she can unselfconsciously deprive the plains Indians of their humanity with the stroke of a pen, we certainly wouldn't look to Cather for a sympathetic view of Native American dispossession; indeed, we may see this as the linguistic repetition of what the penitentiary does to Frank Shabata. Ultimately, Cather's position is made most clear in her telling statement about her later novel *Shadows on the Rock*: "An orderly little French household that went on trying to live decently, just as ants begin to rebuild when you kick their house down, interests me more than Indian raids or the wild life in the forests . . . . And really, a new society begins with the salad dressing more than with the destruction of Indian villages."[8] Society for Cather is a function of quotidian concerns and intimate domestic affairs; her imaginative world is centered on the details of the Euro-American dinner table. And if history begins with the salad dressing, then Native American dispossession is relegated to prehistory, and it is therefore irrelevant to Cather's myth of origins. But despite this rhetorical sleight-of-hand, Cather's inescapable awareness of the profound "disturbance" visited upon "the tall red grass and the buffalo and the Indian hunter" may provide an entry into the repressed content of her narrative.[9]

We must first pause to clarify what, indeed, Indians might have meant for Cather. Careful delineations must be made. To begin with, Cather's Nebraska is a site for universals—the "old story" that "writ[es] itself over" (*OP*, 208). Cather's encounter with Indian civilizations of the Southwest during the spring before she finished *O Pioneers!* is characterized more by admiration than dehumanization, but she is drawn to those cultures as manifestations of a uni-

7. Cather, "Nebraska," 236.
8. Willa Cather, "On *Shadows on the Rock*," in *On Writing: Critical Studies on Writing as an Art* (New York: Knopf, 1949), 16. In reading this statement, however, it is important to recognize not just its disavowal of Indian history but also its celebration of a female frontier; certainly, the contrast of domestic detail with military aggression is gender-coded, and thus has crucial significance for the critic attempting to delineate Cather's relationship to the American literary tradition that Nina Baym famously terms "melodramas of beset manhood."
9. Fischer investigates this repressed content in his article on *My Ántonia*. Pointing out that "[the Indians] were not so far away . . . either temporally or geographically, as Cather might have wanted—and successfully managed—to believe" ("Pastoralism," 33), he argues that *My Ántonia* bears traces of this deliberately forgotten history. I am indebted to Fisher's argument; in attempting to read *O Pioneers!* with an analogous attention to erasures and disruptions, I hope to further the groundbreaking contribution he has made to Cather studies.

versal human history; moreover, the agrarian culture of Southwest Indians would cohere with Cather's sense of universals in a way the nomadic plains tribes would not. According to Cather biographer E. K. Brown:

> In Nebraska there was no past unless one was geologically minded; everything that had not happened yesterday had happened the day before. In the villages of the Cliff-Dwellers Willa Cather found something that was not only extremely simple and extremely beautiful, but extremely old. The discovery was a lengthening of one's past as an American, especially if one were a Western American, an enlarging of one's frame of reference.[1]

He is, of course, patently wrong about Nebraska—it wasn't invented yesterday or the day before, and only a willful forgetting can obscure the history encoded in the name of Cather's childhood home of Red Cloud. The "old Indian chief" Cather refers to in the 1913 *Philadelphia Record* interview figured prominently in an era of plains history that Cather might well have preferred to overlook. Red Cloud, who died in 1909 "a captive and a pensioner,"[2] was an Oglala Sioux whose people were dispossessed, exiled, and ultimately confined to the reservation through a series of treaties with the United States that were consistently violated by government officials. But Brown is presumably giving an accurate reflection of the position Cather assumes: Plains Indian history was so long ago as to be geologic, not human history at all. The incommensurability of these histories enables the necessary erasure of more recent Indian matters. As Mike Fischer notes, "[I]n *O Pioneers!*, [Cather] conceives of 'the feeble scratches on stone left by prehistoric races [as] so indeterminate that they may, after all, be only the markings of glaciers, and not a record of human strivings.' In a powerful demonstration of circular logic, Cather's reading of such 'feeble scratches' as 'indeterminate' allows her to relegate the people who made them to a time before writing—to prehistory."[3] We can go even further: If these "scratches" might not reflect human activity at all, then the very existence of those "prehistoric" peoples is reduced to shadowy possibility. For Cather, Southwest Indians may provide the link between an ancient universal human past and the universal human present, but for her to address the plains Indians in the same way would be to encounter the perils of historical specificity. In other words, while Brown finds continuity in Cather's experience of Southwest Indian culture, there is a necessary rup-

1. E. K. Brown, *Willa Cather: A Critical Biography* (New York: Knopf, 1953), 171.
2. "The Era of Red Cloud," *New York Times*, 14 December 1909.
3. Fischer, "Pastoralism," 32.

ture of that continuity on the plains: these Indians can only be part of ancient and irrelevant history for Cather.[4]

As managing editor for *McClure's*, the foremost muckraking periodical of its day, Cather was—however unwillingly—breathing the air of progressivism even as she disclaimed all interest in or connection to the concerns in circulation. One of the topics in the atmosphere would doubtless have been the Indian question.[5] Regardless of her own position on the issues—and, as she repeatedly told Sergeant in later years, she emphatically had no position—Cather spent these early years of the century beyond the borders of Nebraska in contexts where the ideological hold of her growing-up environs might well have been, on some level, vulnerable to contradiction.

4. Reading the absence of Indians in *O Pioneers!* in the context of Cather's earlier writing leads to an important conclusion. In texts whose key theme is nostalgic longing or lament for the unrecoverable past, Indians are part of the landscape. For example, she links vanished Indians with the vanished glory of an old steamboat town (see "Brownville," *Nebraska State Journal*, 12 August 1894; reprinted in *The World and the Parish*, 1:110); likewise, old Indians, buried Indians, and mythic Indians treated in such Cather tales as "The Enchanted Bluff" and "A Resurrection" parallel the old, buried, mythic kingdom of childhood imagination. *O Pioneers!*, however, has a different agenda. The purpose of the novel is to reestablish the heroism of origins—not of childhood but of history. Cather must then mystify the conquest of native peoples in order to obscure the loss in which the pioneering enterprise is implicated. In other words, there's no room for Indians in *O Pioneers!*, because Cather is trying to rhetorically recover the past, not lament its passing. However, given her ambivalence toward "progress," this recovery is not wholly innocent of lament. Accordingly, I would argue that her vanished Indian is not wholly vanished.
5. A brief survey of the *New York Times* in the few years leading up to *O Pioneers!* suggests some of the forms this debate assumed. While a consistently or overwhelmingly sympathetic attitude toward Native Americans doesn't emerge in the *Times*, there was certainly ample coverage of official misdealings and some particular emphasis on issues of space and enclosure. For example: "The red men will never endure civilization. Of the millions who formerly overran the National domain, some 300,000 survive on reservations. Rum is slaying its thousands, tuberculosis its ten thousands . . . . But it is their domesticated state, not primarily disease, that ails them" (24 March 1909); "[Red Cloud] returned westward to go into peaceful retirement, a captive and a pensioner" ("The Era of Red Cloud," 14 December 1909; this item might have had particular interest for Cather, given the name of her home town); and "an investigation . . . has disclosed 'a disgraceful condition' affecting the material and moral welfare of the [Indian] schools" ("Balinger Suspends Indian Officials," 10 January 1910). A similar concern about the destructive effects of confinement is expressed by former Indian affairs commissioner Francis E. Leupp, whose *The Indian and His Problem* was quoted extensively in a *Times* review ("Francis E. Leupp Writes of The Indian and His Problem," 27 March 1910, pt. 5, 8). The *Times* reported at some length on "Grafting on the Indians and How It Is Done—How Our 'Century of Dishonor' Has Been Replaced by an Era of Plain Swindling," including coverage of the scandal of the McMurray law firm, under investigation for exploitation of the allotment system (7 August 1910, pt. 5, 6), and of Oklahoma Senator Thomas P. Gore's investigation into the "dark and devious ways by which the native wards of the Government have been despoiled of their heritage" ("Yankee Tricks Played on the Indians," 13 August 1910). The series concludes pointedly: "[A]lready, as the record shows, the Indians had been cheated out of millions upon millions of their rightful inheritance" (" 'Grafting' on the Indians," 14 August 1910). My summary of the *Times*'s coverage of the "Indian question" illustrates a perspective to which Cather would have been exposed. Comparable pieces in *McClure's* would be more conclusive, but I have found no articles or editorials on Native American issues during Cather's tenure there.

In order to identify how the discourse of the Indian question haunts Cather's narrative, it may be useful to briefly review the history of Indian enclosure, noting the parallels between reservation policy and the forms of confinement treated in the novel. As Lucy Maddox demonstrates, the rhetoric of Indian policy has consistently been organized into a series of false dichotomies: "The fundamental question of the Indians' capacity for assimilation into white American society was usually contextualized by the almost universally shared assumption that there were only two options for Indians: to become *civilized*, or to become *extinct*." Put this way, a policy of dispossession can thus be easily reimagined as a humanitarian alternative to outright destruction. This explains the marked paternalism we find again and again in the documentary history of Indian affairs. The underlying agenda of discipline—building a labor force—is couched in language that opposes the degradation of government "handouts" to the true "charity" of enforced industry. As Indian Commissioner Hiram Price maintained, in language echoed repeatedly by Indian policy-makers of the late nineteenth and early twentieth centuries, "Labor is an essential element in producing civilization . . . The greatest kindness the government can bestow upon the Indian is to teach him to labor for his own support, thus developing his true manhood, and, as a consequence, making him self-relying and self-supporting."[6] Similarly, Indian Commissioner Francis Amasa Walker conceived of the reservation system as a disciplinary enclosure, where assimilation takes the form of taming the moral wilderness of "strong animal appetites" and making that wilderness productive—in some cases, having the Indians both experience and dramatize the process by farming the land (cultivating as a means of being themselves cultivated). As Ronald Takaki describes Walker's plan for the assimilation of Indians, "the government would subject them to 'a rigid reformatory discipline' . . . [because t]hey were unable to control their 'strong animal appetites.' . . . Grateful for the 'whipping' he had received as a child and the self-discipline he had developed, Walker was certain 'wild Indians' would become 'industrious' and 'frugal' through 'a severe course of industrial instruction and exercise under restraint.' "[7] This emphasis on overcoming nature by restraint and making

6. Hiram Price, extract from the *Annual Report of the Commissioner of Indian Affairs*, 24 October 1881, in *Documents of United States Indian Policy*, 2d ed., ed. Francis Paul Prucha (Lincoln: Univ. of Nebraska Press, 1990), 155. Price continues: "To domesticate and civilize wild Indians is a noble work, the accomplishment of which should be a crown of glory to any nation" (156), a flourish which may remind us of Cather's celebration of the pioneer's "moral victory."
7. Ronald Takaki, *A Different Mirror: A History of Multicultural America* (Boston: Little, Brown, 1993), 233–34. Further references to this source will be cited parenthetically as *DM*.

"wilderness" productive allows us to see a fundamental link between the civilization of savages and the cultivation of land—an exercise of power that extends in *O Pioneers!*, as we have seen, to the "savage" in Mrs. Lee, Ivar, and Frank.

A closer look at rhetorical patterns in documentary history illustrates the degree of this link. To begin with, we should note that the emphasis on labor is in part an attempt at bodily control: at turning ostensibly idle bodies into productive bodies. Recalling Lindemann's analysis of the "queer body" as a subversive site of indiscipline, it is particularly interesting to note to what extent bodily activity—interpreted, when those bodies are Indian, as bodily disorder—becomes a primary focus of Indian policy. For example, Secretary of the Interior Henry M. Teller, in listing the misdeeds to come under the jurisdiction of the Courts of Indian Offenses (tribunals for censuring misbehavior on the reservations), focuses especially on bodily matters: erotic relations, medical practices, and dancing.[8] A reissue of these rules in 1892 reiterates these same concerns, adding a proscription against prostitution and a set of criteria for selecting Indians to sit on the courts. In order to participate in this self-policing—a Foucauldian internalization of disciplinary power—Indians must, among other things, "wear citizens' dress"[9]—testifying to their orderly bodies like Cather's Mrs. Lee.[1]

The Indian body in American cultural history has been a deep and enduring source of fascination. Indian Commissioner Francis E. Leupp, in his 1905 report, includes the provocative claim, "I like the Indian for what is Indian in him. I want to see his splendid inherited physique kept up, because he glories, like his ancestors, in fresh air, in freedom, in activity, in feats of strength."[2] It is tempting to read this celebration of the Indian physique as a nostalgic lament for lost wilderness itself: a romanticizing gesture akin to Alexandra's westward gaze prompted by Frank's incarceration. Indeed, it wouldn't be quite safe for Leupp to make such a remark until the confinement of that splendid body is secure, because the Indian body is also threatening in its mobility. One of the clearest disciplinary imperatives satisfied by reservation policy is immobi-

8. Henry M. Teller, extract from the *Annual Report of the Secretary of the Interior*, 1 November 1883, in *Documents of United States Indian Policy*, ed. Prucha, 160–61.
9. Thomas J. Morgan, "Rules for Indian Courts," 27 August 1892, in *Documents of United States Indian Policy*, ed. Prucha, 187.
1. In the twentieth century especially, the diseased Indian body became the object of particular attention. In his 1910 report, Indian Commissioner Robert Valentine outlined a plan of inspection and education that implicitly identifies the unsanitary or unhygienic Indian body as another manifestation of its indiscipline (extract from the *Annual Report of the Commissioner of Indian Affairs*, 1 November 1910, in *Documents of United States Indian Policy*, ed. Prucha, 212–13).
2. Francis E. Leupp, extract from the *Annual Report of the Commissioner of Indian Affairs*, 30 September 1905, in *Documents of United States Indian Policy*, ed. Prucha, 206.

lization; as Foucault claims, "One of the primary objects of discipline is to fix . . . [I]t arrests or regulates movements; it clears up confusion; it dissipates compact groupings of individuals wandering about the country in unpredictable ways."[3] Indians in these documents are always "wild roving" and "roaming wild";[4] clearly, wildness (or wilderness) is a spatial phenomenon, posited in opposition to the orderly space of, for example, Cather's checkerboard.

But as land greed intensified through the nineteenth century, the reservation ceased to provide a satisfactory solution to the Indian problem. The reservation system then evolved into a new policy intensifying the series of dispossessions that began with initial contact. The later years of the nineteenth century and the early years of the twentieth witnessed an assault on tribalism through the policy of allotment, whereby the lands of the initial enclosure—reservations—were cut up into family parcels in an attempt to indoctrinate Indians into the dominant value system. Ironically, Leupp employs this "fresh-air" Indian body as the rhetorical foundation for the allotment policy he champions. His strategy for "improvement" of the Indian, a word with suggestive links to the improvement of land upon which ownership rights are predicated, is to "keep him moving steadily down the path which leads from his *close domain* of artificial restraints and artificial protection toward the *broad area* of individual liberty enjoyed by the ordinary citizen."[5] Figuring the reservation as a "close domain," he transforms the even closer allotment perimeter into an area made "broad" by an Anglo-American definition of "liberty."[6]

In order to educate Indians in the virtues of private property ownership, the 1887 Dawes Act granted the president "the power, at his

3. Foucault, *Discipline and Punish*, 218–19.
4. Hiram Price, extract from the *Annual Report of the Commissioner of Indian Affairs*, 10 October 1882, in *Documents of United States Indian Policy*, ed. Prucha, 158.
5. Leupp, extract from the *Annual Report*, 30 September 1905, 205–6, my emphasis.
6. What's ultimately at stake, in other words, is a fundamental conflict over land use, property, and definitions of identity. As Priscilla Wald demonstrates, this conflict formed the legal basis for the nineteenth-century Indian policy of exclusion. According to America's Lockean understanding of itself, the commodification of nature—the idea of land as privately ownable—is the foundation of civil personhood itself. As Wald argues, "Where citizenship is defined through the natural right to own property, and following Locke, the most basic expression of this concept rests in the citizen's *self*-ownership," Indians are dispossessed of personhood "in the tribal absence of an 'American' concept of private property" ("Terms of Assimilation: Legislating Subjectivity in the Emerging Nation," in *Cultures of United States Imperialism*, ed. Amy Kaplan and Donald E. Pease [Durham, N.C.: Duke Univ. Press, 1993], 65). By the late nineteenth century, assimilation—civilization or extinction—had also become for the Indians a matter of *civil* life and death. Civil life could only be produced by private property—by tribal dispossession and spatial reduction. The state thus grants that life only on condition of enclosure. On the notion of property and property law in Indian policy and how the law "demanded that these cultures accept the terms of property/individualism/representation or die fighting for another set of terms" (112), see also Eric Cheyfitz, "Savage Law: The Plot against American Indians in *Johnson and Graham's Lessee* v. *M'Intosh* and *The Pioneers*," in *Cultures of United States Imperialism*, ed. Kaplan and Pease, 109–28.

discretion and without the Indians' consent, to allot reservation lands to individual heads of families in the amount of 160 acres," while "[t]he federal government was authorized to sell 'surplus' reservation land—land that remained after allotment—to white settlers in 160-acre tracts" (*DM*, 234). An "inalienability" clause prohibiting the sale of alloted lands for 25 years proved ineffectual; legislation in 1902 (the Dead Indian Land Act), 1906 (the Burke Act), and 1908 (a congressional statute known to reformers as the "Crime of 1908"), as well as rampant corruption among those controlling implementation of the legislation, made allotments vulnerable to white buyers, such that, as a government official told President Roosevelt in 1902, "[I]t will be but a few years at most before all the Indians' land will have passed into the possession of the settlers" (*DM*, 237). Indian lands, in other words, were shrinking; not only were "surplus" reservation lands taken out of Indian hands, but many Native Americans were obliged to participate in their own dispossession by selling allotments in order to survive. The displacement of native peoples was not, therefore, a single irrevocable gesture so far in the past as to be beyond redress; the confinement of the Indians was in fact an ongoing series of enclosures and spatial reductions, enacted and debated while Cather was situated in one of the major centers of debate in the country. In other words, the consequences for Native Americans of the "moral victory" of Cather's pioneers were not obscured by the mists of time but repeatedly reenacted even as she spun her epic of American heroism.

Relatively few critics have seriously addressed the erasure of the Indian in *O Pioneers!*, although the important work of analyzing the rhetorical strategies by which this mystification of history is accomplished has begun.[7] For example, Louise Westling reads Ivar as a replacement for and displacement of the Indian, an overwriting of the Native American story with the immigrant story Cather prefers: "Through him, Cather erases the original inhabitants of the Plains whom the white man had evicted not long before the time of the novel. She replaces the Pawnee, Crow, Cheyenne, and Arapaho with a European immigrant literally dug into the American earth to establish his legitimacy and supplant Indian ways of living on the land."[8] But despite this attempt to legitimate the authority of immigrant over native claims to the land, we might say that Ivar's story,

7. Stouck merely observes: "In her Nebraska novels Willa Cather does not describe the Indians who inhabited the plains before the white settlers. . . . Curiously, the drama of the Plains Indians did not play a part in Willa Cather's imagination" ("Willa Cather and the Indian Heritage," *Twentieth Century Literature* 22 [December 1976]: 434). Both Fischer and Westling do take up this question—Fischer in a detailed analysis of *My Ántonia* ("Pastoralism"), and Westling in brief in her larger study of the novel (*Green Breast of the New World*).

8. Westling, *Green Breast*, 66–67.

in overwriting the Indian history, also retains its shadow. Ivar loses his land due to mismanagement and is given a "comfortable" but not especially desired space in Alexandra's household (*OP*, 59). Only agriculture is proper "management" of the land; alternative relations to the physical world like Ivar's—or like those of the plains Indian cultures—are deemed to nullify the claim to rightful possession and leave the dispossessed vulnerable to social engineering—proper "management"—for their own good.

Cather's text endorses Alexandra's proper management of Ivar—his assimilation into her household—as a way to avoid confinement in the asylum, at least on the literal level. Like Alexandra's household, Indian policies of progressive shrinkage as a means of social integration ostensibly provide asylum from the threatened alternative of extermination (and the historical fact that an asylum, like the reservation, proved the most effective means of obliterating Indian peoples and cultures reminds us of this word's dangerous duality). But the threat of confinement is not abolished from the text; it returns in Frank's incarceration. And once again, we may find in this prison image an echo of history. The rhetoric of disciplinary enclosure discussed above offers suggestive parallels to Frank's condition as a ward of the state; but there is another figure we should consider at this moment in the narrative. In his analysis of the corn god fantasy-figure who appears to Alexandra in moments of repose or exhaustion, J. Russell Reaver points out that "[s]ignificantly, just before she resolves to visit Frank Shabata, who is now in prison for his double murder, [Alexandra] has a vision more vivid than it had been for many years."[9] For Reaver, this significance is unrelated to the history of Native American dispossession, but this narrative juxtaposition of Alexandra's recurring vision and the penitentiary may direct us to look more closely at the fantasy image.

We first encounter Alexandra's fantasy at the close of "Winter Memories":

> Sometimes, as she lay thus luxuriously idle, her eyes closed, she used to have an illusion of being lifted up bodily and carried lightly by some one very strong. It was a man, certainly, who carried her, but he was like no man she knew; he was much larger and stronger and swifter, and he carried her as easily as if she were a sheaf of wheat. She never saw him, but, with eyes closed, she could feel that he was yellow like the sunlight, and there was the smell of ripe cornfields about him. (*OP*, 137)

9. J. Russell Reaver, "Mythic Motivation in Willa Cather's *O Pioneers!*" *Western Folklore* 27 (January 1968): 22.

This image of sun-kissed eroticism quickly becomes threatening. When he then "bend[s] over her," we see not the Genius of the Divide entering into reciprocal desire but an erotic kidnapping—"she could feel herself being carried swiftly off across the fields." If, as Sharon O'Brien claims, "on some level she wants to be harvested,"[1] Alexandra experiences this desire as traumatic: "After such a reverie she would rise hastily, angry with herself, and go down to the bath-house that was partitioned off the kitchen shed. There she would stand in a tin tub and prosecute her bath with vigor, finishing it by pouring buckets of cold well-water over her gleaming white body which no man on the Divide could have carried very far" (*OP*, 137). As several critics have pointed out, the threat of this figure is linked to his emphatic heterosexuality (in contrast to the lesbian eroticism of Alexandra's relation to the land). Indeed, he is the land bodied forth in masculine sexual aggression—a reminder of the sexual threat associated with Frank's attempt to tame Marie.[2]

But considered in its entirety, this image may also suggest another kind of threat. Reaver, in providing mythological contexts for Alexandra's fantasy figure, suggests that this corn god embodies certain Native American beliefs. When Alexandra does finally see him clearly, his arm is "dark and gleaming, like bronze," and he wears a white cloak (*OP*, 192). According to Reaver,

> the hero's shining cloak in this version has analogs closer to home . . . The Pawnee have a sacred rite in the form of a dramatic prayer for life and children, health and prosperity, addressed to the universal powers: Father Heaven and celestial forces and Mother Earth and terrestrial forces. The central symbol in the bird imagery serving as intermediaries between heaven and earth is the 'plume of white featherdown, typifying the fleecy clouds of heaven, and hence the winds and breath of life.' In Navaho lore also, it is interesting to note, Atse Hastin or 'First Man' was created from white maize, and in the cult-symbols of the Navaho *white* is the mantel of dawn.[3]

While he doesn't address whether Cather would have been familiar with these native beliefs, Reaver does offer potential validation for the intuitive sense that this fantasy figure has a certain Native American resonance. We might add that, as Nebraska historian James C. Olson details, Pawnee culture was profoundly connected

1. Sharon O'Brien, "The Unity of Willa Cather's 'Two-Part Pastoral': Passion in *O Pioneers!*" *Studies in American Fiction* 6 (autumn 1978): 163.
2. For the argument that heterosexuality is consistently associated with violence throughout the novel, see especially O'Brien, "Unity"; and C. Susan Wiesenthal, "Female Sexuality in Willa Cather's *O Pioneers!* and the Era of Scientific Sexology: A Dialogue between Frontiers," *Ariel* 21 (January 1990): 41–63.
3. Reaver, "Mythic Motivation," 23.

to the image of corn: "Corn was their mother, figuring in their rituals and in their mythology even more prominently than did the buffalo."[4] A "larger, stronger, swifter" mythological being with a deeply symbolic relationship to corn may not be inconsistent with the romanticized view of Indians to which Cather would have been exposed; this figure does boast the "splendid inherited physique" that, for Indian Commissioner Leupp, made the Indian an Indian. Moreover, the profound otherness of this figure suggests an eruption, perhaps both of time and of culture: a return of repressed history.[5] The fantasy is then doubly threatening, as both heterosexual aggression and as the symbolic Indian whose literal presence would disrupt Cather's epic narrative.[6]

If we follow through on Reaver's observations and identify the corn god as a representation of the vanished Indian, Alexandra's decision to visit the penitentiary just after this fantasy may likewise take on further meaning. Alexandra has been "haunted" by Frank's "haggard face and wild eyes," as the heroic myth of the pioneer is haunted by its untold history (*OP*, 192). If what we see here is the disturbing recollection of the "disturbance" of the plains Indian in the "first cycle" of Nebraska history, then it is significant indeed that the fantasy is linked to the site of confinement. Alexandra's attempted resolution of the problem of civilization—her promise to get Frank released—may then point to another historically troublesome problem of civilization: the shrinking space of Indian culture. In this moment of rupture, we might say that the novel tells the story of its own production: pastoral nostalgia (Alexandra's fantasized restoration of wide-open space to an irrevocably "tamed" Frank) both springs from and compensates for its own primal crime of civilizing the wilderness—both the land and the bodies, white and red, that inhabit it.

According to Fischer, "Any story of the (white) settlement of Nebraska—or 'America'—will inevitably find itself referring to those peoples whose 'removal' preceded that settlement. The function of

4. Olson, *History of Nebraska*, 23.

5. The queer or unassimilable body, to use Lindemann's terms, may at the same time function as a kind of legal uncanny. As Wald notes in her analysis of *Cherokee Nation v. Georgia* (1831), "The Courts' decisions turn the Cherokee . . . into uncanny figures who mirror the legal contingency—and the potential fate—of all subjects in the Union, a fate made all the more plausible by the instability of the Union and the tenuousness of national unity" ("Terms of Assimilation," 59).

6. We may then find more than passing interest in one of Cather's repeated disavowals of interest in Indians: "[U]nless [the poet] is more interested in his own little story and his foolish little people than in the Preservation of the Indian or Sex or Tuberculosis, then he ought to be working in a laboratory or bureau" ("Light on Adobe Walls," in *On Writing*, 125). In this statement, Cather links Indians, the disease that was decimating Indian populations, and sexuality. This indirect association of Native Americans with sexuality may allow us to identify a familiar pattern in Alexandra's corn-god fantasy: the eroticization of the other, where a racial threat is coded as a sexual threat.

criticism, accordingly, is to uncover these traces."[7] I have argued that civilization is fundamentally linked to disciplinary enclosure, an attempt to tame wilderness in its many manifestations. The Indian is perhaps the most culturally potent figure for untamed landscape, and the removal of native populations was the historical act of enclosure most fundamentally linked to the spirit of the pioneer. We may then see a deep anxiety about that untold history as one among several interrelated historical and theoretical phenomena that are condensed in *O Pioneers!* in the motif of confinement.

In one of Cather's many statements about the process of composition—which, read in this context of Indian erasure, is especially telling—she endorses an art of deletion:

> Art, it seems to me, should simplify. That, indeed, is very nearly the whole of the higher artistic process; finding what conventions in form and what detail one can do without and yet preserve the spirit of the whole—so that all that one has suppressed and cut away is there to the reader's consciousness as much as if it were type on the page.[8]

In *O Pioneers!*, Cather has "suppressed and cut away" the historical record of Native American removal, but her narrative of Nebraska origins is nonetheless haunted by a shadow text, available to the reader "as if it were type on the page." The text's preoccupation with enclosure may lead us to one of those "traces" Fischer challenges us to uncover—and to the unacknowledged history we continue to restore.

GUY REYNOLDS

[Willa Cather and the Pioneer Myth in *O Pioneers!*]†

Cather has been read as a novelist who straightforwardly depicted the pioneer settlement of the West and the triumphant imposition of civilisation on the wilderness.[1] The very title, *O Pioneers!*, quotes Whitman's exhortation to the frontiersman, placing the text within a

7. Fischer, "Pastoralism," 32.
8. Willa Cather, "On the Art of Fiction," in *On Writing*, 102.
† From *Willa Cather in Context: Progress, Race, Empire* by Guy Reynolds (1996). Reprinted by permission of Palgrave MacMillan.
1. For Susan Rosowski *O Pioneers!* confronts 'centrally the problem of establishing spatial order': 'from chaos has come order, from a wasteland a great, rich farm'. Rosowski, 'Willa Cather and the Fatality of Place: *O Pioneers!*, *My Ántonia*, and *A Lost Lady*' in *Geography and Literature: A Meeting of the Disciplines* ed. William E. Mallory and Paul Simpson-Housley (Syracuse, 1987), pp. 86, 88.

tradition of pioneer eulogies. The text itself tracks the movement from wilderness to settlement, bare earth to tilled land. Nebraska evolves from a place where 'the germs of life and fruitfulness were extinct forever' to one where Alexandra felt 'the joyous germination in the soil'; from the wilderness of Part I ('The Wild Land') to settlement in Part II ('Neighbouring Fields') and on to wholehearted concentration on the human story (Part V, 'Alexandra'). Cather's characters, especially Alexandra, seem to embody the ideology that underpinned the movement west: self-reliance, hard work, faith in technology.

At times, however, the novel plays out various conflicts within that ideology, as when Alexandra and her brothers argue about their farm's future. Cather presents this debate as a clash between conservative, retrogressive pioneering and the more daring, experimental and ultimately successful pioneering of Alexandra. She borrows money to speculate in land:

> 'We borrow the money for six years. Well, with the money we buy a half-section from Linstrum and a half from Crow, and a quarter from Struble, maybe. That will give us upwards of fourteen hundred acres, won't it? You won't have to pay off your mortgages for six years. By that time, any of this land will be worth thirty dollars an acre—it will be worth fifty, but we'll say thirty; then you can sell a garden patch anywhere, and pay off a debt of sixteen hundred dollars. It's not the principal I'm worried about, it's the interest and taxes. We'll have to strain to meet the payments.' (66–7)

If we compare Cather's version of pioneering to historical accounts of Midwestern settlement, then her account emerges as broadly accurate. *** Alexandra expands her farm by borrowing money and hoping that the revenue from the new land will be sufficient to pay off the interest. This speculation in land is in keeping with historical evidence about the development of Midwestern farms. Frontier expansion was carried forward less by the mythic homesteader staking his claim than by entrepreneurial landowners who bought up larger and larger estates. Some historical accounts envisage the land speculator as a ravenous capitalist; many small farmers, bought out by larger landowners, ended up as indigent tenants on land they formerly owned. But Alexandra represents a purified or honourable speculator whose deals cause no harm.[2]

2. Robert P. Swierenga, 'The Land Speculation Tradition' in *Pioneers and Profits: Land Speculation on the Iowa Frontier* (Ames, Iowa, 1968). Allan G. Bogue, 'Farm Tenants in the Nineteenth-Century Middle West' in *Farmers, Bureaucrats and Middlemen—Historical Perspectives on American Agriculture* (Washington, DC, 1980), pp. 103–19. Two important works on the development of the West which have generally informed my discussion are *The Frontier in American Development*, ed. David M. Ellis (Ithaca, 1969) and Ray Allen Billington, *Westward Expansion*, fourth edition (New York, 1974).

She is a good pioneer, tending the land and making it fruitful; has a personal stake in the land; becomes a kind of mythic earth mother. Although Alexandra brings civilisation to the wilderness, she is insistently identified with nature: 'Her mind was a white book, with clear writing about weather and beasts and growing things' (205). This identification culminates in the last sentence of the novel, where Alexandra is absorbed into the land ('Fortunate country, that is one day to receive hearts like Alexandra's into its bosom'); but this mythic characterisation also transforms the historical detail of land speculation. Cather grafts an idealised mythic discourse onto her historical subject-matter. The land speculator was resented for his mercenary relationship to the land. The Jeffersonian ideal of a farmer working with the soil was supplanted by a commercial model where tenant farmers did the work. But Alexandra, a speculator, preserves the farmer's closeness to the land; the 'mother earth' idealisation, a mythic discourse, ties her to the land. It is almost as if Cather believed that mythic characterisation could offset the entrepreneurial basis of pioneering, where farming is simply a matter of cents and dollars. But, of course, *O Pioneers!* also illustrates that very entrepreneurial endeavour (the arguments with her brothers about borrowing money). Alexandra then becomes a conflation of two types of settler: the canny speculator and the idealised pioneer farmer.

The conflation is not easily achieved; the prose sometimes shows the tension between the two types rather than their marriage. Presenting Alexandra as a speculator and an idealised pioneer led Cather into convoluted, if not illogical, characterisation. Alexandra is depicted as a successful settler; but the obvious index of success, material wealth, suggests the speculator's greed. Cather's solution is to portray Alexandra as a woman whose life has the *potential* for material ease, even though she is pointedly unconcerned by materialism. Alexandra's house, therefore, is conspicuously grand, but Cather cannot allow her to furnish it—it then simultaneously represents the speculator's commercial success and the pioneer's dogged austerity. Approaching the estate the visitor sees 'a big white house', which with its outbuildings suggests 'a tiny village' (83). The impression of grandeur is undermined when one arrives at Alexandra's bizarrely furnished home:

> If you go up the hill and enter Alexandra's big house, you will find that it is curiously unfinished and uneven in comfort. One room is papered, carpeted, over-furnished; the next is almost bare. The pleasantest rooms in the house are the kitchen—where Alexandra's three young Swedish girls chatter and cook and pickle and preserve all summer long—and the sitting-

> room, in which Alexandra has brought together the old homely furniture that the Bergsons used in their first log house, the family portraits, and the few things her mother brought from Sweden. (84)

Alexandra *has* to be made uncomfortable with her own material success. Her domestic comfort is retrospective, resting in the continuity of tradition (European cooking, furniture from the old house) rather than new moneyed ways. Then, as if confirming the difficulty of imagining the amalgamation of pioneer and speculator, Cather's focus drifts outside:

> When you go out of the house into the flower garden, there you feel again the order and fine arrangement manifest all over the great farm; in the fencing and hedging, in the windbreaks and shed, in the symmetrical pasture ponds, planted with scrub willows to give shade to the cattle in fly-time. There is even a white row of beehives in the orchard, under the walnut trees. You feel that, properly, Alexandra's house is the big out-of-doors, and that it is in the soil that she expresses herself best. (84)

In the garden Cather projects an idealised conflation of pioneering and speculation, traditional agrarianism and innovative farming. The garden itself is a middle ground, positioned between home and prairie, civilisation and wilderness. Alexandra here achieves a self-expression harmonised with the natural world, a human order finely adjusted to the exigencies of animal life (the willows planted to shade the cattle). The development of the land is presented as a formalism that is an end in itself ('order', 'arrangement', 'symmetrical', 'row') or as a process dedicated to animals and plants. The financial rewards of farming are carefully excised or excluded. Alexandra's wealth becomes a happy accident, the fortuitous spin-off from sound pioneering.

Cather's family moved to Nebraska in the mid-1880s, a time when the notorious landowner William Scully was arousing animosity in that State and others for his aggressive acquisition of prairie lands. Scully, an Irishman who belatedly took out American citizenship, provoked enormous opposition to 'alien' landowners. The agitation was long-standing, spilling into the local press and politics (populism was in part a reaction against alien encroachments). Nebraska, along with other States, passed legislation during 1887 to prohibit 'aliens' from acquiring real estate. There is, of course, no reason why a novel written in 1913 should demonstrate absolute fidelity to life several decades earlier. But *O Pioneers!* never hints that Europeans might find it difficult to own American soil; the controversy about land dealing and 'aliens' is erased from

Cather's account. She opts instead for a familial row about the tactics of development.[3]

This is undoubtedly a depoliticised representation of settlement, and one can easily imagine a critique that would attack Cather for erasing or displacing historical actuality. But we have to look at *O Pioneers!* from the point of view of 1913. Inaccurate as the novel might have been, the multicultural frontier of *O Pioneers!* is an example of 'innovative nostalgia', the projection onto a past decade of a historical reading whose real relevance is to the period when the novelist was writing. The novel's refutation of nativism, of narrow or xenophobic provincialism is pertinent to the context in which Cather wrote. Cather created an American frontier which diverges from the actualities of the late nineteenth-century Midwest; but her fictionalised frontier tells us a great deal about her fascination with an open, pluralist, cosmopolitan culture of the American plains. The frontier of *O Pioneers!* is at ease with itself, and thus becomes a progressive 'good community' that rebuffs the xenophobia implicit in the actual history of the Midwest. *O Pioneers!* projects a wilfully distorted frontier not, as many critics have suggested, because of an instinctive nostalgia in Cather's creative temperament, but because Cather is setting up fictionalised communities of immediate relevance to an America that was becoming ever more marked by racial diversity.

Cather's unsettling and unconventional representations of landscape form part of a larger revisionary strategy in *O Pioneers!* The novel is best understood, I believe, as a transformation of the conventions underpinning the pioneer myth. First, Cather recast the gender of pioneering. *O Pioneers!*, as many commentators have emphasised, is a novel about female pioneering: Alexandra Bergson explores, settles and develops the land, just as the archetypal male pioneer had done.[4] The idiosyncrasy of deploying a female protagonist becomes evident when we look back over written accounts of the pioneer effort. Annette Kolodny's survey of pioneering literature from the colonial period through to the nineteenth century demonstrates the highly *sexualised* language of these letters, diaries and journals. The language of the pioneers encoded their experiences in very gender-specific ways. Pioneers, usually men, insistently imagined a male pioneer moving across a feminised landscape. That landscape, Kolodny argues, is symbolised as either the virgin earth

3. Paul W. Gates, *Landlords and Tenants on the Prairie Frontier* (Ithaca and London, 1973), pp. 48–71 and 238–302, writes on 'The Role of the Land Speculator in Western Development' and 'Frontier Landlords and Pioneer Tenants'. The latter supplies an account of William Scully and the anti-alien land agitation in the Midwest.
4. Ellen Moers, *Literary Women* (London, 1978), p. 231. Susie Thomas, *Willa Cather* (London, 1990), pp. 54–76.

which the pioneer ravishes, or as a mother, 'the total female principle of gratification' promising 'a return to the primal warmth of womb or breast in a feminine landscape'.[5] Kolodny's argument sometimes becomes dangerously ahistorical—she posits a synchronic model which appears to lie outside historical change. But the suggestiveness of her pattern is undeniable, enabling us to identify motifs and symbols across a range of American texts. Using Kolodny's model as a basis for exploring Cather's novels, we can discover how the individual artist transforms and revises a cultural inheritance of established metaphorical patterns.

A nice illustration of Cather's self-conscious use of motifs from the history of pioneering is her reference to *Robinson Crusoe*. Early in the novel Carl Linstrum carries a magic lantern whose wide range of pictures from the New and Old Worlds represents a masculine world of adventure: 'hunting pictures in Germany, and Robinson Crusoe and funny pictures about cannibals' (17). But several pages later we read this sentence: 'Alexandra often said that if her mother were cast upon a desert island, she would thank God for her deliverance, make a garden, and find something to preserve' (29). Mrs. Bergson here becomes a female Robinson Crusoe who brings to her catastrophe the practical domestic arts. The sentence demonstrates how in Cather's fiction the 'pots and pans' derided by Trilling are used to tease, if not subvert, the stereotyped image of the feminine sphere. Later in the book Alexandra reads 'The Swiss Family Robinson' aloud to an appreciative audience. This is another moment where Cather's pioneers take a self-referential pleasure in stories which reflect back their own experiences. Again Cather shifts the focus from masculine pioneering (so often imagined as the activity of the single male, the male duo, or the small posse of men) to a feminised pioneering. It is a family which settles the wilderness—and a family responds to the story: 'They were all big children together, and they found the adventures of the family in the tree house so absorbing that they gave them their undivided attention' (63).

Similar reversals occur in Cather's descriptions of the western land. Reading Kolodny's study, it becomes clear that the American land was symbolically fecund, a land of plenitude not only for its profusion of material goods but also in its supply of feminine imagery. The land could be imagined again and again as a configuration of the mother or the virgin. As Ellen Moers has brilliantly

5. Annette Kolodny, *The Lay of the Land: Metaphor as Experience and History in American Life and Letters* (Chapel Hill, 1975), pp. 4, 6. Kolodny's later work surveys the largely overlooked female response to the frontier: *The Land Before Her: Fantasy and Experience of the American Frontiers, 1630–1860* (Chapel Hill, 1984).

demonstrated, scattered throughout Cather's fiction are landscapes which appropriate the feminised landscape and renew its coded womanliness with a powerfully sexual symbolism. Moers draws attention to the South-western landscapes in *The Song of the Lark.* Discussing the feminine topography of the Panther Canyon, its grooves and recesses and exhilarating open spaces, Moers argues that the descriptive passages are 'concerned with female self-assertion in terms of landscape'.[6] *O Pioneers!* eventually forges such a self-assertion. The last passages of the book witness a fulfilled Alexandra received into the 'bosom' of the land (309). This reciprocity with the land has to be earned. At first Cather's native soil is stark and denuded, proffering little literally or symbolically. This bareness (the emptiness, as we have seen, of prehistoric ages) resists symbolising acquisitiveness. Whereas the pioneer appropriated the land by imaginatively converting it into a female body, in the opening chapters of *O Pioneers!* the emptiness of the land prevents this—there is nothing to symbolise. The pioneer is rebuffed by the land, but slowly becomes intimate with it and finds an austere consolation in nature's workings:

> It fortified her to reflect upon the great operations of nature, and when she thought of the law that lay behind them, she felt a sense of personal security. That night she had a new consciousness of the country, felt almost a new relation to it . . . She had never known before how much the country meant to her. The chirping of the insects down in the long grass had been like the sweetest music. She had felt as if her heart were hiding down there, somewhere, with the quail and the plover and all the little wild things that crooned or buzzed in the sun. Under the long shaggy ridges, she felt the future stirring. (70–1)

If this passage is not entirely successful ('The chirping of the insects . . . like the sweetest music'!), then this is because, first of all, Cather writes from the perspective of an imaginatively limited character (Alexandra is not given to reflection). Second, Cather awkwardly straddles several linguistic registers in this passage. Her writing turns from symbolism to a factual language, but she preserves the heightened rhetoric associated with the westerner's first energising encounter with the land. She grafts together a heightened, almost mystical language of pastoral bliss with microscopic observation of 'the little wild things'—the latter discourse reminding us of the prose of natural history.

6. Moers, *Literary Women*, p. 258.

Cather's second major revision of the pioneer myth stems from her doubts about American claims to represent the culmination of historical progress.

* * *

Three years before *O Pioneers!* was published Roosevelt, who by now had served a term as President, delivered his speech, 'The World Movement' (1910). Talking in Berlin, Roosevelt envisaged America as the highpoint of 'Civilization'; his unabashedly progressive thesis saw history as a steady ascent towards the zenith of the modern United States. 'Civilization' began 'with that series of bold sea ventures which culminated in the discovery of America'. America was then 'changing and developing every inheritance and acquisition into something new and strange'—having emerged out of Europe, America had radically transformed its inheritance. Comparisons with earlier cultures were now redundant. Roosevelt adduces a comparison with the Roman empire, only to prove the large-scale differences between America and Rome: 'it is well to emphasize in the most emphatic fashion (*sic*) the fact that in many respects there is a complete lack of analogy between the civilization of to-day and the only other civilization in any way comparable to it'. He concludes that 'the present civilization can be compared to nothing that has ever gone before'.[7]

The convergence of economic success, imperial expansion and a rhetoric of 'natural' supremacy derived from Darwin led to a renewed sense of American triumphalism and exceptionalism. There was an intensified sense of the nation's singularity; Roosevelt can find nothing to compare with his country. His argument is hardly a worked-out thesis, but this is partly because he felt it sufficient to allude to the academic historiography of the period, which similarly stressed the strength and the uniqueness of the United States. Roosevelt was indebted to the 'Frontier thesis' formulated by the historian, Frederick Jackson Turner, in the 1890s. Turner, whose work was enormously influential, directed historians away from the search for European sources of American culture, politics and society—earlier commentators had located these roots either in English institutions or even further back, in medieval Germany. Turner believed that America was societally and politically divorced from Europe. His seminal essay, 'The Significance of the Frontier in American History' (1893), emphasised the centrality of the westward movement and the frontier to the formation of a national culture that was unique. American exceptionalism arose from the

7. Theodore Roosevelt, 'The World Movement' in *History as Literature and Other Essays* (London, 1914), pp. 109, 99, 125. This is a progressive thesis in both the broader and the narrower senses of the word: Roosevelt stood and lost as a Progressive candidate in the Presidential election of 1912.

unique geographical attribute of the frontier; analogies with Europe were irrelevant: 'Whatever be the truth regarding European history, American history is chiefly concerned with social forces, shaping and reshaping under the conditions of a nation changing as it adjusts to its environment'. For Turner, separation from Europe fosters cultural homogeneity. The frontier, the movement of the people, the drive to colonise the wilderness—in the very act of settlement the American people become one.

* * *

Not surprisingly, Turner disliked Cather's fiction. His criticism of *O Pioneers!* is an important but neglected moment in the reception of Cather's novels. It illustrates the gulf between her vision of a pluralist America still linked to Europe and the increasingly dominant historiographical views of Turner and Roosevelt, where America is exceptional, unique and culturally homogeneous. After reading *O Pioneers!* and *A Lost Lady* Turner expressed his dissatisfaction to Alice Hooper, claiming that Cather represented too sympathetically what he called 'non-English stocks' (that is, immigrants from Scandinavia and central Europe). Fascinated as he was by social mobility, this comment suggests that he was less enamoured of racial mixing and interfusion. The frontier thesis dealt with the trends of modern America—immigration, settlement, movement—and enlisted them to establish a historical theory of powerful simplicity. Turner's America was in essence a proleptic idealisation of a nation that he thought was coming into being; and the hallmark of that society was its homogeneity. Despite his interest in the culturally varied West it is clear that Turner's America was a nativist Utopia filled with immigrants of English and north European descent. Although Turner was anything but a racist, there is no doubt that he was happiest in envisaging an America made up of migrants from a relatively confined and traditional stock of origins.[8]

* * *

Cather famously declared that in order to know the parish one must know the world first. Although the statement implies a return to the locality, it places the 'world' first syntactically, establishing synoptic knowledge as the basis of the novelist's art. This wider, comparative perspective is more important in her novels than the regionalism, provincialism and 'local color' denoted by the 'parish'. When Cather portrays the parish, as in *O Pioneers!*, her native soil is variegated and cosmopolitan. The title *O Pioneers!* proffers nationalist triumphalism, Whitman's visionary future of westward colonisation; but this is offset by the novel's epigraph, drawn from a

8. Letters of July 16 1913 and March 7 1925 in *'Dear Lady': The Letters of Frederick Jackson Turner and Alice Forbes Perkins Hooper, 1910–1932*, ed. R. A. Billington (San Marino, 1970), pp. 149, 365.

foreigner, the Polish poet Mickiewicz: 'Those fields, colored by *various* grain!' (my emphasis). The epigraph replaces the unitary native soil (an American land for a single American people) with a diverse, patchwork country. Turner hypothesised that the hegemonic power of the land would weld the diverse races together and create national coherence. For Cather, on the other hand, the soil is either polymorphous ('various grain') or tantalisingly bare ('an iron country'); her landscapes stand empty or swarm with a multitude of peoples. In both ways the pressure of nativism, of the *native* soil, of a land for one people, is resisted.

The narrator's timbre in *O Pioneers!* shifts from the intimate informalities of the 'parish' to the more impersonal tones in which Cather accounts for, and talks to, the 'world'. The narrating voice is pitched between easy familiarity and careful distance—she mimes amused intimacy and anthropological curiosity:

> The country children thereabouts wore their dresses to their shoe-tops, but this city child was dressed in what was then called the 'Kate Greenaway' manner, and her red cashmere frock, gathered full from the yoke, came almost to the floor. This, with her poke bonnet, gave her the look of a quaint little woman. (11–12)

Cather's tone (that of the local historian) and her fastidious specificity (noting the length of dresses) create an enquiring, annotating authorial voice. Yet there is also an ironic, amused knowingness to the writing; the distance never hardens into sneering at the foibles of provincial dress. The doubleness of the prose, the sense of being both within and without the scene, might remind the reader of Thomas Hardy, another provincial writer who maintained an ironic familiarity towards his rural material.

Throughout *O Pioneers!*, where the focus seems to be so narrowly upon the Midwest, she habitually mentions other cultures. There are passing references to Lombardy, France, Mexico. A typical sentence describes the French church, which 'reminded one of some of the churches built long ago in the wheat-lands of middle France' (211). The reader of Cather's novels becomes attuned to these windows into other times and places (often medieval and European). Memories or similes, the sentences broaden our perspective, displacing the reader, if only temporarily, away from regional America into another context. Cather turned an apprentice writer's tic—the need to seem *au fait*, conversant with culture (resulting in a gauche display of cultural reference)—into a strength. Her edgy desire to show herself knowledgeable led to a healthy interest in the outside world; to rebuff accusations of provincial ignorance she developed a style which, while concentrating on the parish, never forgot the world. Cather is one of the few modern Midwestern writers unaffected by that cult of insularity which seems to have stamped writers from Hamlin Garland and Sherwood Anderson through to Garrison Keillor. In their works the small town is everything; in Cather's fiction everything comes to the small town, filtered through memory, migration and cultural inheritance.

* * *

Willa Cather: A Chronology

1873 Born December 7 in Back Creek Valley, near Winchester, Virginia.

1883 Family moves to the Nebraska Divide to join relatives farming there: Cather's uncle and aunt, George Cather and Franc Smith Cather, and Cather's grandparents, William and Caroline Cather.

1884 Family moves into small prairie town of Red Cloud.

1890 Graduates from high school; in September moves to Lincoln, where she enrolls as a second-year student in the Latin School, a two-year preparatory school of the University of Nebraska.

1892 First short story, "Peter," published in Boston literary weekly.

1895 Graduates from the University of Nebraska.

1896 Leaves for Pittsburgh to take up job as editor of women's magazine, the *Home Monthly*.

1897 Resigns from *Home Monthly* and begins working at the Pittsburgh *Leader*, where she writes drama criticism and a "Books and Magazines" column.

1899 Meets Isabelle McClung, daughter of prominent Pittsburgh judge; the two begin a lifelong intimacy.

1901 Moves into the McClung household, where she will remain until 1906. Teaches Latin, and then English, at Central High School.

1903 *April Twilights*, a collection of poems, published in April. Sends several short stories to S. S. McClure, publisher of *McClure's Magazine*. He invites her to New York and praises her fiction. Returns to Nebraska for the summer and meets Edith Lewis. In September begins teaching English at Allegheny High School.

1904 "A Wagner Matinee" published in *Everyman's Magazine*; she is criticized by some Nebraska readers for her bleak portrayal of farm life.

1905 *The Troll Garden*, a collection of seven stories that includes "A Wagner Matinee" and "Paul's Case" is published by McClure, Phillips & Co.

1906 Accepts offer from S. S. McClure of job at *McClure's Magazine*. Moves to New York in late spring and lives in same Greenwich Village apartment building as Edith Lewis, 60 Washington Square South.

1907–08 In Boston on assignment for *McClure's*, meets Annie Fields, widow of Boston publisher James T. Fields, and Sarah Orne Jewett, author of *The Country of the Pointed Firs*. Develops close friendships with both women. Returns to New York in fall and moves into apartment at 82 Washington Place with Edith Lewis. Becomes managing editor of *McClure's*.

1909 Sarah Orne Jewett dies. Cather writes Fields that life is dark and purposeless without her.

1910 Meets Elizabeth Sergeant, who had submitted an article to *McClure's*. The two women become close friends and literary confidantes.

1911 Writes *Alexander's Bridge* and *The Bohemian Girl* and finishes "Alexandra."

1912 Houghton Mifflin publishes *Alexander's Bridge*, and "The Bohemian Girl" appears in *McClure's*. Travels to the Southwest in the spring, and stays with the McClungs in Pittsburgh in the fall, writing short story "The White Mulberry Tree," then combining it with "Alexandra" to form basis of *O Pioneers!*

1913 *O Pioneers!*, dedicated to Sarah Orne Jewett, published by Houghton Mifflin. Moves with Edith Lewis to seven-room apartment at 5 Bank Street, in Greenwich Village.

1915 *The Song of the Lark* published by Houghton Mifflin.

1916 Isabelle McClung marries violinist Jan Hambourg; Cather is surprised and devasted. Signs with literary agent Paul Reynolds.

1917 Works on *My Ántonia* at the Shattuck Inn in Jaffrey, New Hampshire, which will become a beloved writing retreat.

1918 *My Ántonia* published by Houghton Mifflin; receives glowing reviews.

1920 Signs contract with recently established publisher Alfred A. Knopf for collection of stories *Youth and the Bright Medusa*. He becomes her publisher for the rest of her writing life.

1922 *One of Ours* published.

1923 *A Lost Lady* published. Cather awarded Pulitzer Prize for *One of Ours*.

1924 Selects stories and writes an introduction for *The Collected Stories of Sarah Orne Jewett*, published by Houghton Mifflin in 1925.

1925 *The Professor's House* published. Travels to the Southwest with Edith Lewis for the summer and finds inspiration for *Death Comes for the Archbishop*. Has cottage built for her on Grand Manan Island.

1926 *My Mortal Enemy* published.

1927 *Death Comes for the Archbishop* published. Moves with Edith Lewis to Grosvenor Hotel when Bank Street apartment building is torn down.

1929 Elected to the National Academy of Arts and Letters. Summers on Grand Manan.

1930 Awarded Howells Medal for Fiction by the American Academy of Arts and Letters for *Death Comes for the Archbishop*.

1931 *Shadows on the Rock* published. Sends money to Nebraska families hit hard by the Depression.

1932 *Obscure Destinies*, grouping of three short stories set in Nebraska, published. Moves, with Lewis, to new apartment on Park Avenue.

1933 Sprains tendon in right wrist, which becomes chronically inflamed. Condition, which persists through her life, often requires her to wear an immobilizing brace and interferes with her writing.

1935 *Lucy Gayheart* published.

1936 *Not Under Forty*, collection of essays on literature, published.

1937 Spends year helping Houghton Mifflin prepare the Library Edition of her work. Decides that *O Pioneers!* should be Volume I, and groups *Alexander's Bridge* with *April Twilights* in Volume III.

1940 *Sapphira and the Slave Girl* published.

1941 Begins novel set in Avignon, but is unable to make progress because of recurring hand pain and other health problems.

1943 Unable to travel to Grand Manan due to war. Spends summer (and three succeeding) at Asticou Inn in Maine. Receives hundreds of letters from servicemen who have read her books in armed services editions.

1944 Receives Gold Medal of the National Institute of Arts and Letters. Embraces S. S. McClure, now 87, at the ceremony.

1947 Dies at home in New York City of cerebral hemorrhage

on April 24. Buried in Jaffrey, New Hampshire, on April 28. Inscribed on her tombstone will be a quotation from *My Ántonia*: "That is happiness, to be dissolved into something complete and great, to become part of something entire."

Selected Bibliography

• indicates works included or excerpted in this Norton Critical Edition.

WILLA CATHER

Arnold, Marilyn. *Willa Cather: A Reference Guide*. Boston: G. K. Hall, 1986.

Bennett, Mildred R. *The World of Willa Cather*. Lincoln: U of Nebraska P, 1961.

Bloom, Harold., ed. *Modern Critical Views: Willa Cather*. New York: Chelsea House Publishers, 1985

Bohlke, L. Brent. *Willa Cather in Person: Interviews, Speeches, and Letters*. Lincoln: U of Nebraska P, 1986.

Brown, E. K. *Willa Cather: A Critical Biography* (completed by Leon Edel). New York: Knopf, 1953.

Carlin, Deborah. *Cather, Canon, and the Politics of Reading*. Amherst: U of Massachusetts P, 1992.

Crane, Joan. *Willa Cather: A Bibliography*. Lincoln: U of Nebraska P, 1982.

Curtin, William, ed. *The World and the Parish: Willa Cather's Articles and Reviews, 1893–1902*, 2 vols. Lincoln: U of Nebraska P, 1970.

• Fischer, Mike. "Pastoralism and Its Discontents: Willa Cather and the Burden of Imperialism." *Mosaic* 23 (1990): 31–44.

Fryer, Judith. *Felicitous Space: The Imaginative Structures of Willa Cather and Edith Wharton*. Chapel Hill: U of North Carolina P, 1986.

Harvey, Sally Peltier. *Redefining the American Dream: The Novels of Willa Cather*. Rutherford, NJ: Fairleigh Dickinson UP, 1995.

Hoover, Sharon, ed. *Willa Cather Remembered*. Lincoln: U of Nebraska P, 2002.

Lee, Hermione. *Willa Cather: Double Lives*. New York: Pantheon, 1990.

Lewis, Edith. *Willa Cather Living: A Personal Record*. New York: Knopf, 1953.

Lindemann, Marilee, ed. *The Cambridge Companion to Willa Cather*. New York: Cambridge UP, 2005.

———. *Willa Cather: Queering America*. New York: Columbia UP, 1999.

March, John. *A Reader's Companion to the Fiction of Willa Cather*. Westport, CT: Greenwood Press, 1993.

• Murphy, John, ed. *Critical Essays on Willa Cather*. Boston: G. K. Hall, 1983.

• O'Brien, Sharon. *Willa Cather: The Emerging Voice*. New York: Oxford UP, 1987.

———. " 'The Thing Not Named': Willa Cather as a Lesbian Writer." *Signs: Journal of Women in Culture and Society* 9 (1984): 576–99.

• Reynolds, Guy. *Willa Cather in Context: Progress, Race, Empire*. New York: St. Martin's Press, 1996.

———, ed. *Willa Cather: Critical Assessments*. Mountfield, East Sussex: Helm Information, 2003.

Rosowski, Susan J. *The Voyage Perilous: Willa Cather's Romanticism*. Lincoln: U of Nebraska P, 1986.

• Sergeant, Elizabeth Shepley. *Willa Cather: A Memoir*. Philadelphia: Lippincott, 1953.

Shively, James R., ed. *Writings from Willa Cather's College Years*. Lincoln: U of Nebraska P, 1950.

Schroeter, James. *Willa Cather and Her Critics*. Ithaca: Cornell UP, 1967.

Slote, Bernice. *The Kingdom of Art: Willa Cather's First Principles and Critical Statements, 1893–1896*. Lincoln: U of Nebraska P, 1967.

• Stouck, David. *Willa Cather's Imagination*. Lincoln: U of Nebraska P, 1975.

Stout, Janis, ed. *A Calendar of the Letters of Willa Cather*. Lincoln: U of Nebraska P, 2002.

Stout, Janis. *Willa Cather: The Writer and Her World*. Charlottesville: UP of Virginia, 2000.

Urgo, Joseph. *Willa Cather and the Myth of American Migration*. Urbana: U of Illinois P, 1995.

Williams, Deborah Lindsay. *Not in Sisterhood: Edith Wharton, Willa Cather, Zona Gale, and the Politics of Female Authorship*. New York: Palgrave, 2001.

Woodress, James. *Willa Cather: A Literary Life*. Lincoln: U of Nebraska P, 1987.

O PIONEERS!

Carden, Mary Paniccia. "Creativity and the National Romance in Willa Cather's *O Pioneers!* and *My Ántonia." Modern Fiction Studies* 45.2 (1999): 275–302.

Frus, Phyllis, and Corkin, Stanley. "Willa Cather's 'Pioneer' Novels and (Not New, Not Old) Historical Reading." *College Literature* 26.2 (Spring 1999): 36–58.

Gustafson, Neil. "Getting Back to Cather's Text: The Shared Dream in O *Pioneers!." Western American Literature* 30.2 (1995): 151–62.

Horwitz, Howard. "*O Pioneers!* and the Paradox of Property: Cather's Aesthetics of Divestment." *Prospects: An Annual Journal of American Cultural Studies* 13 (1998): 61–93.

• Lindemann, Marilee. Introduction. *O Pioneers!* Oxford: Oxford UP, 1999. vii–xxii.

Meyering, Sheryl L. *Understanding* O Pioneers! *and* My Ántonia: *A Student Casebook to Issues, Sources, and Historical Documents*. Westport, CT: Greenwood Press, 2002.

Mullins, Marie. " 'I Bequeath Myself to the Dirt to Grow from the Grass I Love': The Whitman-Cather connection in *O Pioneers!*" *Tulsa Studies in Women's Literature* 20 (2001): 123–36.

O'Brien, Sharon. "The Unity of Willa Cather's 'Two-Part Pastoral': Passion in *O Pioneers!*" *Studies in American Fiction* 6 (1978): 157–71.

Peck, Demaree. " 'Possession Granted by a Different Lease': Alexandra Bergson's Imaginative Conquest of Cather's Nebraska." *Modern Fiction Studies* 36.1 (Spring 1990): 5–22.

• Ryan, Melissa. "The Enclosure of America: Civilization and Confinement in Willa Cather's *O Pioneers!*" *American Literature* 75.2 (June 2003): 275–303

• Wiesenthal, C. Susan. "Female Sexuality in Willa Cather's *O Pioneers!* and the Era of Scientific Sexology: A Dialogue between Frontiers." *Ariel* 21 (1990): 41–63.

BACKGROUNDS AND CONTEXTS

Ammons, Elizabeth. *Conflicting Stories: American Women Writers at the Turn into the Twentieth Century*. New York: Oxford UP, 1991.

Bartley, Paula, and Loxton, Cathy. *Plains Women: Women in the American West*. New York: Cambridge UP, 1991.

Baym, Nina. "Melodramas of Beset Manhood: How Theories of American Literature Exclude Women Authors." In *Locating American Studies: The Evolution of a Discipline*, ed. Lucy Maddox. Baltimore: Johns Hopkins UP, 1999: 215–31.

Deverall, William, ed. *A Companion to the American West*. Malden, MA: Blackwell, 2004.

DuPlessis, Rachel Blau. *Writing Beyond the Ending: Narrative Strategies of Twentieth-Century Women Writers*. Bloomington: Indiana UP, 1985.

Grossman, James R., ed. *The Frontier in American Culture: An Exhibition at the Newberry Library, August 26, 1994–January 7, 1995*. Berkeley: U of California P, 1994.

Kolodny, Annette. *The Land Before Her: Fantasy and Experience of the American Frontiers, 1630–1860*. Chapel Hill: U of North Carolina P, 1984.

———. *The Lay of the Land: Metaphor as Experience and History in American Life and Letters*. Chapel Hill: U of North Carolina P, 1975.

Lewis, R. W. B. *The American Adam: Innocence, Tragedy, and Tradition in the Nineteenth Century*. Chicago: U of Chicago P, 1955.

Limerick, Patricia Nelson. *The Legacy of Conquest: The Unbroken Past of the American West*. New York: Norton, 1987.

Marx, Leo. *The Machine in the Garden: Technology and the Pastoral Ideal in America*. New York: Oxford UP, 1964.

Myres, Sandra L. *Westering Women and the Frontier Experience, 1800–1915*. Albuquerque: U of New Mexico P, 1982.

Olson, James. *History of Nebraska*. Lincoln: U of Nebraska P, 1955.

Overland, Orm. *Immigrant Minds: Making the United States Home, 1870–1930*. Urbana: U of Illinois P, 2001.

Peavy, Linda S. *Pioneer Women: The Lives of Women on the Frontier*. Norman: U of Oklahoma P, 1998.

"Prairie Settlement: Nebraska Photographs and Family Letters, 1862–1912." *American Memory* (memory.loc.gov).

Riley, Glenda. *Women on the American Frontier*. St. Louis: Forum P, 1977.

Romines, Ann. *The Home Plot: Women, Writing, and Domestic Ritual*. Amherst: U of Massachusetts P, 1992.

Rosowski, Susan J. *Birthing a Nation: Gender, Creativity, and the West in American Literature*. Lincoln: U of Nebraska P, 1999.

Slotkin, Richard. *Regeneration Through Violence: The Mythology of the American Frontier, 1600–1860*. Middletown, CT: Wesleyan UP, 1973.

Smith, Henry Nash. *Virgin Land: The American West as Symbol and Myth*. Cambridge: Harvard UP, 1950.

Stephan Thernstrom, ed. *Harvard Encyclopedia of Ethnic Groups*. Cambridge: Harvard UP, 1980.

Stratton, Joanna L. *Pioneer Women: Voices from the Kansas Frontier*. New York: Simon and Schuster, 1981.

Turner, Frederick Jackson. *The Frontier in American History*. New York: Holt, Rinehart, 1962.

Westling, Louise H. *The Green Breast of the New World: Landscape, Gender, and American Fiction*. Athens: U of Georgia P, 1996.